Lecture Notes in Computer Science 768

Edited by G. Goos and J. Hartmanis

Advisory Board: W. Brauer D. Gries J. Stoer

Lecture Notes in Computer Science   768
Edited by G. Goos and J. Hartmanis

Advisory Board: W. Brauer D. Gries J. Stoer

Utpal Banerjee   David Gelernter
Alex Nicolau   David Padua (Eds.)

Languages and Compilers for Parallel Computing

6th International Workshop
Portland, Oregon, USA, August 12-14, 1993
Proceedings

Springer-Verlag

Berlin Heidelberg New York
London Paris Tokyo
Hong Kong Barcelona
Budapest

Series Editors

Gerhard Goos
Universität Karlsruhe
Postfach 69 80
Vincenz-Priessnitz-Straße 1
D-76131 Karlsruhe, Germany

Juris Hartmanis
Cornell University
Department of Computer Science
4130 Upson Hall
Ithaca, NY 14853, USA

Volume Editors

Utpal Banerjee
Intel Corporation
2200 Mission College Blvd., P. O. Box 58119, RN6-18
Santa Clara, CA 95052, USA

David Gelernter
Dept. of Computer Science, Yale University
51 Prospect St., New Haven, CT 06520, USA

Alex Nicolau
Dept. of Information & Computer Science, University of California
444 Computer Science Bldg., Irvine, CA 92717, USA

David Padua
Center for Supercomputing Research and Development
465 Computer and Systems Research Laboratory
1308 West Main St., Urbana, IL 61801, USA

CR Subject Classification (1991): F.1.2, D.1.3, D.3.1, B.2.1, I.3.1

ISBN 3-540-57659-2 Springer-Verlag Berlin Heidelberg New York
ISBN 0-387-57659-2 Springer-Verlag New York Berlin Heidelberg

Typesetting: Camera-ready by author
45/3140-543210 - Printed on acid-free paper

Foreword

This book contains papers which were presented at the Sixth Annual Workshop on Languages and Compilers for Parallel Computing. This workshop was hosted by the Oregon Graduate Institute of Science and Technology, and sponsored by Intel Supercomputer Systems Division (SSD), and by the Portland Group, Inc. (PGI), to whom we offer our gratitude.

This workshop was organized by inviting the leading research groups in languages and compilers for parallel systems to submit papers for consideration. The editors reviewed the submissions and selected papers for presentation and publication in this volume. All the major research efforts in parallel languages and compilers are represented in this workshop series.

This book comprises nine sections. Several of these sections show new advances in traditional areas, such as parallelizing compilers, loop transformations and fine grain parallelism. Other sections are devoted to more recent topics, such as analyzing and optimizing dynamic data structures, and compiling the High Performance Fortran language.

We, the editors, are pleased to be associated with the papers presented in this volume. The work discussed herein represents a valuable snapshot of the state of research in languages and compilers for parallelism in 1993. This should prove useful for anyone working or interested in this field. We thank Springer-Verlag for publishing the workshop papers for the third year; most of the authors used the LaTeX style files provided by Springer-Verlag, simplifying manuscript preparation. We also thank the authors and participants for a dynamic workshop, and again express our gratitude to our sponsors, Intel SSD and PGI, whose contributions helped to keep the registration costs down.

November, 1993

Utpal Banerjee
David Gelernter
Alexandru Nicolau
David A. Padua

Dynamic Data Structures

Early Experiences with Olden 1
Martin C. Carlisle and Anne Rogers
Princeton University, New Jersey
John H. Reppy, *AT&T Bell Laboratories, Murray Hill, New Jersey*
Laurie J. Hendren, *McGill University, Montréal, Quebec, Canada*

Arbitrary Order Operations on Trees 21
Jon A. Solworth and Bryan B. Reagan
University of Illinois at Chicago

Analysis of Dynamic Structures for Efficient Parallel Execution ... 37
John Plevyak, Andrew A. Chien and Vijay Karamcheti
University of Illinois at Urbana-Champaign

**On Automatic Data Structure Selection and Code Generation
for Sparse Computations** 57
Aart J. C. Bik and Harry A. G. Wijshoff
Leiden University, The Netherlands

Parallel Languages

Synchronization Issues in Data-Parallel Languages 76
Sundeep Prakash, Maneesh Dhagat and Rajive Bagrodia
University of California, Los Angeles

ZPL: An Array Sublanguage 96
Calvin Lin and Lawrence Snyder, *University of Washington, Seattle*

Event-Based Composition of Concurrent Programs 115
Raju Pandey and James C. Browne, *University of Texas at Austin*

**Adaptive Parallelism on Multiprocessors: Preliminary
Experience with Piranha on the CM-5** 139
Nicholas Carriero, Eric Freeman and David Gelernter
Yale University, New Haven, Connecticut

High Performance Fortran

Slicing Analysis and Indirect Accesses to Distributed Arrays 152
Raja Das and Joel Saltz, *University of Maryland, College Park*
Reinhard von Hanxleden, *Rice University, Houston, Texas*

Do&Merge: Integrating Parallel Loops and Reductions 169
Bwolen Yang, Jon Webb, James M. Stichnoth, David R. O'Hallaron
and Thomas Gross
Carnegie Mellon University, Pittsburgh, Pennsylvania

Automatic Support for Data Distribution on Distributed
Memory Multiprocessor Systems 184
Barbara M. Chapman, Thomas Fahringer and Hans P. Zima
University of Vienna, Austria

A Compilation Approach for Fortran 90D/HPF Compilers 200
Zeki Bozkus, Alok Choudhary, Geoffrey Fox, Tomasz Haupt and
Sanjay Ranka, *Syracuse University, New York*

A Framework for Exploiting Data Availability to Optimize
Communication 216
Manish Gupta and Edith Schonberg
IBM T. J. Watson Research Center, Yorktown Heights, New York

The Alignment-Distribution Graph 234
Siddhartha Chatterjee and Robert Schreiber
Research Institute for Advanced Computer Science, California
John R. Gilbert
Xerox Palo Alto Research Center, California

An Overview of a Compiler for Scalable Parallel Machines 253
Saman P. Amarasinghe, Jennifer M. Anderson, Monica S. Lam and
Amy W. Lim, *Stanford University, California*

Loop Transformations

Toward a Compile-Time Methodology for Reducing False
Sharing and Communication Traffic in Shared Virtual
Memory Systems 273
Elana D. Granston, *Leiden University, The Netherlands*

Program Transformation for Locality Using Affinity Regions 290
Bill Appelbe, Charles Hardnett and Sri Doddapaneni
Georgia Institute of Technology, Atlanta

Maximizing Loop Parallelism and Improving Data Locality via
Loop Fusion and Distribution 301
Ken Kennedy, *Rice University, Houston, Texas*
Kathryn S. McKinley, *University of Massachusetts, Amherst*

Align and Distribute-based Linear Loop Transformations 321
Jordi Torres, Eduard Ayguadé, Jesús Labarta and Mateo Valero
Universitat Politècnica de Catalunya, Barcelona, Spain

Extending Software Pipelining Techniques for Scheduling Nested Loops 340
Guang R. Gao
McGill University, Montréal, Quebec, Canada
Qi Ning and Vincent Van Dongen
Centre de recherche informatique de Montréal, Quebec, Canada

A Methodology for Generating Efficient Disk-Based Algorithms from Tensor Product Formulas 358
S. D. Kaushik, C.-H. Huang and P. Sadayappan
Ohio State University, Columbus
R. W. Johnson, *St. Cloud State University, Minnesota*

Logic and Dataflow Language Implementations

Loop Transformations for Prolog Programs 374
David C. Sehr, *Intel Corporation, Santa Clara, California*
Laxmikant V. Kale and David A. Padua
University of Illinois at Urbana-Champaign

A Multithreaded Implementation of Id using P-RISC Graphs 390
Rishiyur S. Nikhil
Digital Equipment Corporation, Cambridge, Massachusetts

Fine Grain Parallelism

Acceleration of First and Higher Order Recurrences on Processors with Instruction Level Parallelism 406
Michael Schlansker and Vinod Kathail
Hewlett-Packard Laboratories, Palo Alto, California

Efficient Compile-Time/Run-Time Contraction of Fine Grain Data Parallel Codes 430
Richard Neves and Robert B. Schnabel
University of Colorado, Boulder

VISTA: The Visual Interface for Scheduling Transformations and Analysis 449
Steven Novack and Alexandru Nicolau
University of California, Irvine

Scalar Analysis

Efficiently Computing ϕ-Nodes On-The-Fly 461
Ron K. Cytron, *Washington University, St. Louis, Missouri*
Jeanne Ferrante
IBM T. J. Watson Research Center, Yorktown Heights, New York

Construction of Thinned Gated Single-Assignment Form 477
Paul Havlak, *Rice University, Houston, Texas*

Parallelizing Compilers

Automatic Array Privatization 500
Peng Tu and David Padua
University of Illinois at Urbana-Champaign

**FIAT: A Framework for Interprocedural Analysis and
Transformations** 522
Mary W. Hall
Stanford University, California
John M. Mellor-Crummey, Alan Carle and René G. Rodríguez
Rice University, Houston, Texas

**An Exact Method for Analysis of Value-based Array Data
Dependences** 546
William Pugh and David Wonnacott, *University of Maryland*

**Symbolic Analysis: A Basis for Parallelization, Optimization,
and Scheduling of Programs** 567
Mohammad R. Haghighat and Constantine D. Polychronopoulos
University of Illinois at Urbana-Champaign

Analysis of Parallel Programs

**Towards a Non-intrusive Approach for Monitoring Distributed
Computations through Perturbation Analysis** 586
Rajiv Gupta, *University of Pittsburgh, Pennsylvania*
Madalene Spezialetti, *Lehigh University, Bethlehem, Pennsylvania*

**Efficient Computation of Precedence Information in Parallel
Programs** 502
Dirk Grunwald and Harini Srinivasan
University of Colorado, Boulder

Trace Size vs. Parallelism in Trace-and-Replay Debugging of Shared-Memory Programs 617
Robert H. B. Netzer, *Brown University, Providence, Rhode Island*

Parallel Program Graphs and Their Classification 633
Vivek Sarkar and Barbara Simons
IBM Santa Teresa Laboratory, San Jose, California

Springer-Verlag
and the Environment

We at Springer-Verlag firmly believe that an international science publisher has a special obligation to the environment, and our corporate policies consistently reflect this conviction.

We also expect our business partners – paper mills, printers, packaging manufacturers, etc. – to commit themselves to using environmentally friendly materials and production processes.

The paper in this book is made from low- or no-chlorine pulp and is acid free, in conformance with international standards for paper permanency.

Early Experiences with Olden

Martin C. Carlisle,[1*]
Anne Rogers,[1**]
John H. Reppy,[2] and
Laurie J. Hendren[3***]

[1] Princeton University, Princeton NJ 08544, USA
[2] AT&T Bell Laboratories, Murray Hill NJ 07974, USA
[3] McGill University, Montreal, Quebec, Canada H3A 2A7

Abstract. In an earlier paper[RRH92], we presented a new technique for the SPMD parallelization of programs that use dynamic data structures. Our approach is based on migrating the thread of computation to the processor that owns the data, and annotating the program with *futures* to introduce parallelism. We have implemented this approach for the Intel iPSC/860. This paper reports on our implementation, called *Olden*, and presents some early performance results from a series of non-trivial benchmarks.

1 Introduction

Compiling for distributed memory machines has been a very active area of research in recent years; particularly in the area of programs that use arrays as their primary data structure and loops as their primary control structure. Such programs tend to have the property that the arrays can be partitioned into relatively independent pieces and therefore operations performed on these pieces can proceed in parallel. This property of scientific programs has been exploited in vectorizing compilers [ABC+88, AK87, PW86, Wol89]. More recently, this property has been used by researchers investigating methods for automatically generating parallel programs for SPMD (Single-Program, Multiple-Data) execution on distributed memory machines.[4] To date, this research has largely ignored the question of how to compile programs that use trees as their primary data structures and recursion as their primary control structure. In part, this is because there are fundamental problems with trying to apply the techniques, such

---

[*] Supported, in part, by a National Science Foundation Graduate Fellowship and the Fannie and John Hertz Foundation.
[**] This work was supported, in part, by NSF Grant ASC-9110766, by DARPA and ONR under contracts N00014-91-J-4039, and by the Intel Supercomputer Systems Division.
[***] The research supported, in part, by FCAR, NSERC, and the McGill Faculty of Graduate Studies and Research.
[4] For examples, see [CK88, ZBG88, RP89, Ger90, KMvR90, Koe90, Rog90, RSW90, HKT91, AL93, AM93].

as runtime resolution, currently used to produce SPMD programs for scientific programs, to programs that use dynamic data structures. In the case of scientific programs, the array data structures are statically allocated, statically mapped, and directly addressable. Dynamic data structures, on the other hand, are dynamically allocated, dynamically mapped, and must be recursively traversed to be addressable. These properties of dynamic data structures preclude the use of simple local tests for ownership, and therefore make the runtime resolution model ineffective.

One exception is a recent paper by Gupta [Gup92] that suggests a mechanism for introducing global names for each element of a data structure at runtime to allow an approach similar to runtime resolution. In his approach, a name, which is determined by the node's position in the structure, is assigned to each node as it is added to a data structure. This name is then registered with the other processors. Once a processor has a name for the nodes in a data structure, it can traverse the structure without further communication. A problem is that this new way of naming dynamic data structures leads to restrictions on how they may be used. For example, because the name of a node is determined by its position, only one node can be added to a structure at a time. Another problem is that node names may have to be reassigned when a new node is introduced. For example, consider a list in which a node's name is simply its position in the list. If a node is added to the front of the list, the rest of the list's nodes will have to be renamed to reflect their change in position. These problem arise from trying to retrofit runtime resolution, a method designed for statically allocated, directly addressable structures, to handle dynamic data structures, which are neither directly addressable nor statically allocated.

In a previous paper [RRH92], we presented an execution model with associated compiler techniques for parallelizing programs that use dynamic data structures using an SPMD approach. We have since implemented our execution model on the Intel iPSC/860. This paper starts with a review of our proposed execution model and compiler techniques. This review is followed by a description of our implementation, which we call *Olden*, and a discussion of our early experiences with using Olden on a series of non-trivial benchmarks.

2 Data-driven Execution

In this section, we review our technique for executing SPMD programs on hierarchical data structures.[5] This technique consists of two mechanisms: thread migration and thread splitting.

In our SPMD model, each processor has an identical copy of the program, as well as a local stack that is used to store procedure arguments, local variables, and return addresses. In addition to these local stacks, there is a distributed heap. We view a heap address as consisting of a pair of a processor name and a local address. This information is encoded as a single address. For simplicity

---

[5] We suggest that readers unfamiliar with our proposed execution model consult our original paper[RRH92], which contains an in-depth discussion of the model.

we assume that there is no global data. We also require that programs do not take the address of stack-allocated objects; thus there are no pointers into the processor stacks.

The basic programming model may be summarized as follows. The programmer writes a normal sequential program except for a slight difference in how dynamic data structures are allocated. In our programming model, the programmer explicitly chooses a particular strategy to map the dynamic data structures over the distributed heap. This mapping is achieved by including a processor number in each allocation request. A typical choice of mapping is to build a tree such that the sub-trees at some fixed depth are equally distributed over all processors. Appendix A contains a sample allocation routine.

2.1 Thread Migration — Exploiting Locality

This section briefly describes our mechanism for migrating a single thread of control through a set of processors based on the placement of heap-allocated data. When a thread executing on Processor P attempts to access a word residing on Processor Q, the thread is migrated from P to Q. Full thread migration entails sending the current program counter, the thread's stack, and the current contents of the registers to Q. Processor Q then sets up its stack, loads the registers, and resumes execution of the thread at the access that caused the migration. Notice that because the stack is sent with the thread, stack references are always local and cannot cause a migration.

Full thread migration is potentially quite expensive, since the thread's entire stack is included in the message. To make thread migration affordable, we send only the portion of the thread's state that is necessary for the current procedure to complete execution: namely, the registers, program counter, and current stack frame. When it is time to return from the procedure, it is necessary to return control to Processor P, since it has the stack frame of the caller. To accomplish this, Q sets up a stack frame for a special return stub to be used in place of the return to the caller. This frame holds the return address and the return frame pointer for the currently executing function. The stub code migrates the thread of computation back to P by sending a message that contains the return address, the return frame pointer, and the contents of the registers. Processor P then completes the procedure return by restarting the thread at the return address. Note that the stack frame is not returned because it is no longer needed.

2.2 Thread Splitting — Introducing Parallelism

While the migration scheme provides a mechanism for operating on distributed data, it does not provide a mechanism for extracting parallelism from the computation. When a thread migrates from Processor P to Q, P is left idle. In this section, we describe a mechanism for introducing parallelism. Our approach is to use compiler transformations to introduce *continuation capturing* operations at key points in the program. When a thread migrates from P to Q, Processor P can start executing one of the captured continuations. The natural place to capture continuations is at procedure calls, since the return linkage is effectively a continuation; this provides a fairly inexpensive mechanism for labeling work that can be done in parallel. This capturing technique effectively splits the thread of execution into many pieces that can be executed out of order, thus the introduction of continuation capturing must be based on an analysis of the program (see Section 3).

Our continuation capturing mechanism is essentially a variant of the *future* mechanism found in many parallel Lisps [Hal85]. In the traditional Lisp context, the expression (future *e*) is an annotation to the system that says that *e* can be evaluated in parallel with its context. The result of this evaluation is a *future cell* that serves as a synchronization point between the child thread that is evaluating *e* and the parent thread. If the parent attempts to read the value of the future cell, called a *touch*, before the child is finished, then the parent blocks. When the child thread finishes evaluating *e*, it puts the result in the cell and restarts any blocked threads.

Our view of futures, which is influenced by the *lazy task creation* scheme of Mohr, Krantz, and Halstead [MKH91], is to save the future call's context (return continuation) on a work list and to evaluate the future's body directly.[6] If a migration occurs in the execution of the body, then we grab a continuation from the work list and start executing it; this is called *future stealing*.

3   Compiler Issues

In order to generate a data-driven SPMD program automatically, one needs compiler analysis to determine which sub-computations may be executed in parallel safely, and where it is best to place the futurecall and touch operations.

To support this analysis, we can build upon the techniques previously proposed in the context of parallelizing imperative programs with recursive data structures [Hen90, HN90, HHN92], and the CURARE restructuring compiler for Lisp [LH88a, LH88b, Lar89]. In both these cases, the objective is to analyze the program to determine which computations refer to disjoint pieces of the hierarchical data structure, and then to use this information to insert parallel function calls or futures automatically.

For our purposes, we plan to build on the *path matrix* analysis [Hen90, HN90], an interprocedural analysis designed to determine statically if the data structures are indeed tree-like, and to approximate the relationships between different parts of the data structure. A typical analysis provides information about the disjointness of sub-trees, or the non-circularity of lists. Based on information available from this analysis, we have defined the appropriate tests to determine when it is safe to introduce futures. For a typical divide-and-conquer type recursive procedure, we say that the procedure consists of *pre-computation*, followed by the recursive calls implementing the *conquer part*, followed by *post-computation*.

---

[6] This is also similar to the workcrews paradigm proposed by Roberts and Vandecoorde [RV89].

Our analysis must be used to: (1) determine if it is safe to execute the various sub-computations for the conquer step in parallel, (2) determine if the pre-computation can be overlapped with the conquer step, and (3) place the touches in the latest possible position to ensure maximum concurrency. Our previous paper describes this in more detail [RRH92].

4 A Simple Example

To make the ideas of the previous two sections more concrete, we present a simple example. Figure 1(a) gives the C code for a prototypical divide-and-conquer program. Using the analyses outlined in Section 3, a compiler would generate the semantically equivalent program annotated with futures give in Figure 1(b). In the annotated version, the left recursive call to **TreeAdd** has been replaced by a **futurecall**,[7] and the result is not demanded until after the right recursive call.

To understand what this means in terms of the program's execution, consider the case where a tree node t_P (on processor P) has a left child t_Q (on processor Q). When **TreeAdd**, executing on P, is recursively called on t_Q, it attempts to fetch the left child of t_Q, which causes a trap to the runtime system. This will cause the thread of control to migrate to processor Q, where it can continue executing. Meanwhile, execution resumes on processor P at the return point of the **futurecall**. Assuming that the right subtree of t_P is on processor P, execution of the stolen future continues until it attempts to touch the future cell associated with the call on t_Q. At this point, execution must wait for the thread of control to return from processor Q.

5 Implementation

We have implemented a prototype of our execution model at Princeton on a 16 node Intel iPSC/860 hypercube. The input to the system is a C program annotated with **futurecalls** and **touches**. Our system consists of a runtime system and a compiler for the annotated C code; the compiler also generates tests for pointer locality.

5.1 The Runtime System

Figure 2 provides an overview of the control structure of the runtime system. The main procedure is **MsgDispatch**, which is responsible for assigning work to a processor when it becomes idle. Captured futures are given first priority, then messages from other processors in the order received. The runtime system processes four different events: migrate on reference, migrate on return, steal future, and suspend touch. We discuss futures in the next section, so we focus on migration in this section.

---

[7] Note that using a **futurecall** on the right subtree is not cost effective, since there is very little computation between the return from **TreeAdd** and where the result is needed. Also note that the fetching of t's **right** field cannot cause a migration.

```
typedef struct tree {
    int       val;
    struct tree *left, *right;
} tree;

int TreeAdd (tree *t)
{
    if (t == NULL)
        return 0;
    else
        return (TreeAdd(t->left) + TreeAdd(t->right) + t->val);
}
```

(a) Original code

```
int TreeAdd (tree *t)
{
    if (t == NULL)
        return 0;
    else {
        tree        *t_left;
        future_cell f_left;
        int         sum_right;

        t_left = t->left;               /* this can cause a migration */
        f_left = futurecall (TreeAdd, t_left);

        sum_right = TreeAdd (t->right);

        return (touch(f_left) + sum_right + t->val);
    }
}
```

(b) Annotated code

Fig. 1. TreeAdd code

Migrate on Reference As previously mentioned, a thread will migrate if it attempts to dereference a non-local pointer. The code to test the pointer and call **Migrate**, if necessary, is inserted by the compiler. **Migrate** packages the necessary data and sends it to the appropriate processor. A migration message contains the current stack frame, the argument build area of the caller, the contents of callee save registers, and some bookkeeping information: the name of the processor that originated the current function, an address to continue

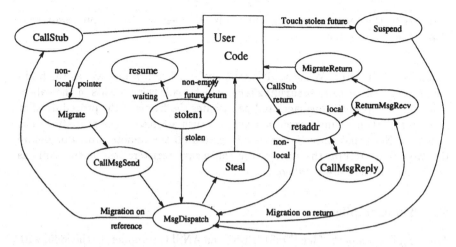

Fig. 2. The Runtime System

execution, the frame pointer, the pointer causing the migration, the return value size, the framesize, and the argument build area size. We allocate extra space in stack frame for the callee save registers and bookkeeping information, which allows us to construct messages *in situ*, reducing the cost of migrations. Once the migration is complete, the sending processor calls MsgDispatch to assign a new task.

A simple optimization is added to avoid a chain of trivial returns in the case that a thread migrates several times during the course of executing a single function. **Migrate** examines the current return address of the function to determine whether it points to the return stub. If so, the original return address, frame pointer, and node id are pulled from the stub's frame and passed as part of the migration message. This is analogous to a tail-call optimization and is similar to the *tail forwarding* optimization used in the Concurrent Smalltalk compiler[HCD89]. A similar optimization is that if a migrated procedure exits on the same processor as it began (for example, it migrated from P to Q then back to P), the return message is not sent, rather **ReturnMsgRecv** is called directly.

When **MsgDispatch** selects an incoming migration message as the next task, it transfers control to CallStub to process the message. CallStub allocates space for a return message, in which it stores the framesize, return value size, and frame pointer from the migration message. Then space on the stack is allocated for the frame, the argument build area and a stub frame. The callee-save register values from the message are loaded, and the pointers to the return area and the argument build area are adjusted (if they exist). The return address stored in the frame is changed to **retaddr**, the stub return procedure. Finally, the pointer causing the migration, the frame pointer and the program counter are loaded, and execution resumes on the new processor. When this procedure exits, it will go to the procedure **retaddr**. This code stores the values of the callee-save registers in the return message, and sends the message to the processor that began execution of the procedure.

Migrate on Return When **MsgDispatch** selects a return message as the highest priority task, it calls **ReturnMsgRecv**, which loads the contents of the callee-save registers from the message, and deactivates the frame of the procedure that migrated. It then resumes execution at the return address of the procedure that migrated. Note that since the procedure exited on the remote processor before the migrate on return, the state of the callee-save registers will be the same as before the procedure was called.

5.2 The Compiler

The compiler is a port of lcc [Fra91, FH91], an ANSI C compiler, to the i860, with modifications to handle our execution model. lcc does not have an optimizer.

Testing Memory References As previously mentioned, a process will migrate on a reference if it attempts to dereference a non-local heap pointer. In our implementation, heap pointers consist of a tag indicating the processor where the data resides and a local address, so it is necessary to check the tag on each heap pointer dereference.[8] lcc has a command-line option for generating null pointer checks on all pointer dereferences. We modified this mechanism to generate code that examines the tag to see if the pointer is local, conditionally calls **Migrate**, and removes the tag to reveal the local address.

The additional overhead of testing each pointer dereference is three integer instructions and a conditional branch on the i860. This overhead can be reduced by observing that only the first reference in a string of references to the same pointer can cause a migration. In the **TreeAdd** example, only the reference **t->left** can cause a migration. All subsequent references are guaranteed to be local.[9] The Olden compiler provides an annotation, **local**, which allows allows us to take advantage of this observation. The expression **local**(t) removes the pointer tag and forces a migration if t is non-local. Subsequent references use the resulting local pointer.

A simple compiler optimization can take advantage of this construct. A pointer dereference is *aligned* with another pointer dereference if it is *dominated* by that reference and if there are no intervening references to other pointers. A dominating reference, that is the first reference in the string, can be tested using local. The local address that results can be used by the aligned references. The code in Figure 3 shows the result of applying this optimization to the **TreeAdd** example. Note that the deferences of **local_t** require no special handling.

---

[8] Note that the address translation hardware could be used to detect non-local references [AL91].

[9] Note that this observation relies on the fact that function calls always return to the original processor on return.

```
int TreeAdd (tree *t)
{
    if (t == NULL)
        return 0;
    else {
        tree        *t_left, *local_t;
        future_cell f_left;
        int         sum_right;

        local_t = local(t);         /* this can cause a migration */
        t_left = local_t->left;
        f_left = futurecall (TreeAdd, t_left);

        sum_right = TreeAdd (local_t->right);

        return (touch(f_left) + sum_right + local_t->val);
    }
}
```

Fig. 3. TreeAdd code using local

Compiling futurecall As noted previously, future calls allow the introduction of parallelism. We use two data structures to support future calls: future cells and the future stack, which serves as work list. A future cell can be in one of four states:

Empty This is the initial state and contains the information necessary to restart the parent.

Stolen This is the state when the parent continuation has been stolen.

Waiting This is the state when the parent continuation has been stolen and subsequently touched the future. It contains the continuation of the blocked thread (Note: when inserting futures, the compiler insures that no future can be touched by more than one thread).

Full This is the final state of a future cell, and contains the result of the computation.

Figure 4 gives the allowable state transitions for a future cell. The future stack is allocated as part of the processor's stack. In particular, this means that no migrations may occur between a future call and its corresponding touch.

When the backend (unoptimized) encounters a futurecall annotation, it generates in-line code to store the continuation, which consists of the callee-save registers, the frame pointer, the state of the future cell (**Empty**), and the program counter. This information is stored in the future cell. Then the call is generated. After the call, code is generated in-line to store the return value in the future cell, and check the state of the future. If it is **Empty**, the cell is popped from the stack, and execution continues.

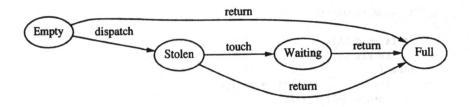

Fig. 4. Future cell state transitions

In the case that the cell is not **Empty**, (that is, the function or one of its descendants migrated), we test to see whether the future is **Stolen** or **Waiting**. If it is **Stolen**, then **MsgDispatch** is called to assign work to the processor. If it is **Waiting**, there must have been a touch on this future cell. In Section 5.3, we describe how to resume this thread of computation.

As described, the overhead of future calls is quite large. Ideally, we would like to avoid having to save all of the callee-save registers, and instead just save those that are live using an interprocedural analysis to determine the subset of live registers. But, even this would be a duplication, since the callee-save registers that are used by the **futurecall** will be stored upon entry to the function. We can do better by exploiting the fact that MsgDispatch gives stealing futures the highest priority. As a result, a descendant of the future call must have been executing immediately before the steal. Therefore, the state of the callee-save registers may be restored by a process called *register unwinding*, which involves executing the restores of callee save registers for each procedure in the call chain from the user code function last executing to the function called in the future call.

To implement register unwinding, we generate a callee-save restore sequence for each procedure, and store its address at each call site in the procedure. Then, when stealing a future, we traverse the list of frame pointers to the frame that contains the future cell, executing each callee-save restore sequence as we go. Since the address of a restore sequence is stored at the appropriate call site, it can be obtained by reading a word at a constant offset from the return address stored in the frame.

A second optimization is to eliminate the necessity of storing the state **Empty** in the future cell. The return address for a future call is initially set to the sequence of instructions for an **Empty** future cell. When a future cell is stolen, the return address of the body of the future is modified to point to code which will test for **Stolen** or **Waiting**, and perform the appropriate function.

Given these optimizations, the overhead of a future call on the i860 is only seven instructions (four stores, two integer instructions and one load) in the expected case where the future cell is not stolen.

5.3 Compiling touch

The touch annotation generates in-line code to synchronize on the state of the future cell. If the state is Full, then the procedure continues, otherwise the library routine Suspend is called. Suspend stores the values of the callee-save registers and the program counter in the future cell, marks the cell as Waiting, and calls MsgDispatch to assign work to the processor. When the future call returns and finds the cell marked Waiting, it loads the registers and program counter from the suspended cell, and resumes execution of the procedure.

5.4 Stack Management

In the discussion thus far, we have glossed over certain details related to stack management. When a future is stolen, the portion of the stack between the frame belonging to the stolen continuation and the frame that migrated must be preserved for when the migrated thread returns. The stolen continuation may allocate new stack frames, overwriting the frames of the migrated thread. To avoid this problem, we adopt a simplification of a single stack technique for multiple environments by Bobrow and Wegbreit [BW73].

Their method maintains counters for the number of uses and frame extensions, which arise from the use of backtracking, for each frame. On entry, a basic frame and extension are allocated contiguously at the end of the stack, with the counters set to 1. The use of a coroutine, for example, would cause a copy of the frame extension to be made so the returns may go to different continuation points. On exit from an access module, the appropriate extension is deleted, and the basic frame is freed if no other extension references it (that is, the extension count is 1). The end of stack pointer is then adjusted appropriately. When control returns to an extension, if active frames exist between this extension and the end of the stack, it is moved to the end to allow it to allocate new frames. Thus, the stack is split into various segments. Compaction is performed as necessary to prevent stack overflow, as the stack will have a tendency to be ever increasing.

Since our model does not require more than one extension per frame, we can simplify the method and reduce the overhead on function calls and returns. We maintain a single stack, called a *simplified spaghetti stack*, that contains frames from the continuations interleaved.[10] In a simplified spaghetti stack, new stack frames are allocated off the global stack pointer. We maintain the invariant that *the global stack pointer always marks the end of a live frame*. The exit routine for a frame is split into two parts: deactivation and deallocation. If a procedure whose frame is in the middle of the stack exits, it is deactivated by marking it as garbage. If the frame is at the end of the stack, the global stack pointer is adjusted, thus deactivating and deallocating the frame simultaneously. Additionally, the stack pointer is adjusted to the end of the live frame nearest the end of the stack, which deallocates garbage frames.

---

[10] A similar method, called a meshed stack, was developed by Hogen and Loogen in the context of parallel implementations of functional or logic languages [HL93].

To implement deactivation, one word of memory in each frame, *splink*, is reserved for stack management information. If the frame is live, then a null pointer is stored at splink. Otherwise, splink contains a pointer to the beginning of the frame. By placing this word at the end of each frame, these pointers form linked lists of garbage frames. To maintain the invariant, after deallocating a live frame at the end of the stack, it is merely necessary to traverse the list until reaching a null pointer, and then set the global stack pointer to the location containing the null pointer.

Figure 5 provides an example of this process. Assume that initially the pro-

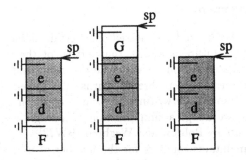

Fig. 5. Simplified Spaghetti Stack — simple case

cedure F is executing. F calls G, a new frame is allocated at the end of the stack. Notice that there are live frames between F and the end of the stack that belong to another thread of execution. When G exits, since the preceding frame (e) is live, the stack returns to the initial state. Figure 6 provides a more complex example. Again, F calls G. G migrates, and the runtime system gives control to

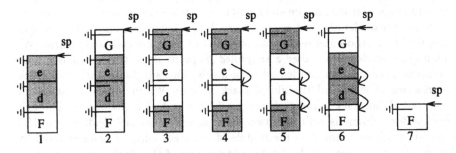

Fig. 6. Simplified Spaghetti Stack — complex case

e. The frame e is not at the end of the stack; hence, when it exits, a pointer is placed at the end of its frame marking it as garbage. The exit for d is similar. When G resumes execution and exits, its frame is deactivated. Since it is at the end of the stack, the list of garbage frames will be followed until a null pointer is reached (in the frame labelled F), thus deallocating all of the garbage frames.

The overhead resulting from our simplified spaghetti stacks is minimal. One extra instruction is required on entry to store zero at splink. The expected exit path (topmost frame, with live frame underneath), requires four additional instructions (an add, load, and two conditional branch instructions) over the basic stack exit code for the i860.

There is one problem with the scheme that we have proposed. Since the simplified spaghetti stack scheme does not deallocate dead frames immediately, we cannot give a bound for how the size of the simplified spaghetti stack in terms of the number of live frames. In certain degenerate communication patterns, there is no bound. For example, in the case where p threads numbered $[1..p]$ alternately migrate between Processor 0 and Processor p, the stack size on Processor 0 is bounded only by the number of migrations. In our experience, it has not been necessary or desirable for programs to have this property. However, we must be able to detect and correct this problem should it arise. It suffices to check the stack explicitly in the runtime system because dead frames that are not deallocated can only be generated by calls to the runtime system. A metric based on fragmentation of the stack or one based on the remaining capacity of the stack can be used to determine when the stack needs to be compacted. The cost of the checks is minimal. Our prototype implementation does not check for stack overflow.

6   Results

This section describes out early experiments with our prototype implementation of Olden. We report results for four benchmarks: TreeAdd, Bitonic Sort, Barnes-Hut, and Voronoi Diagram. For each benchmark, the speedups are reported with respect to an implementation that was compiled using our compiler, but without the overhead of futures, pointer testing, or the spaghetti stack. We refer to this as the *plain* implementation. The speedup curves include a data point for one processor. This implementation, which we refer to as *one*, includes the cost of futures, pointer testing, and spaghetti stacks.

The benchmarks were hand-annotated to include future calls and touches. The programs were annotated aggressively. Our goal is to show that the execution model is not a barrier to efficient parallelization. We do not claim that all of the annotations can be generated automatically using existing compiler technology.

6.1   TreeAdd

Figure 7 shows the speedup for running `TreeAdd` on a 1,048,575 node tree. The speedup is not as large as one might hope because there is very little work over which to amortize the overhead of futures, pointer tests, and the spaghetti stack. The second curve represents the speedup using one rather than plain

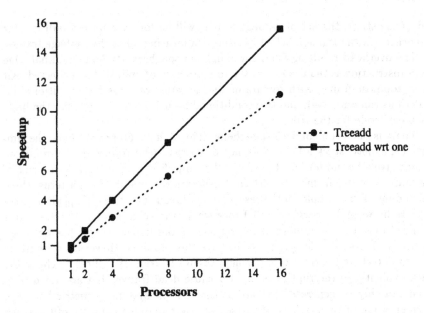

Fig. 7. TreeAdd speedup

as the baseline. This curve demonstrates that the execution model can exploit parallelism. The problem for this benchmark is that there is not enough real work to amortize the overhead of the system. The difference between plain and one is mostly attributable to the overhead of futurecalls. This is the only benchmark in which futurecalls represent the dominant factor in the overhead.

6.2 Bitonic Sort

The bitonic sort benchmark[BN89] allocates a random tree and performs two bitonic sorts: one forward and one backward. The benchmark has been modified to maintain data locality across the processors. We report speedup only for the sorting phases to avoid having the easily parallelizable build phase skew the results. Figure 8 contains four curves: two runs of the original implementation and two runs of an improved implementation. The original implementation, which does quite respectably on a medium sized problem (128K numbers), performs an unnecessary malloc for each recursive sort, thereby artificially increasing the amount of work per call. The improved Bitonic Sort, which removed this extra call, still displays parallelism but not nearly as much as the original version.

The difference between plain and one is substantial for this benchmark. The overhead from futures, pointer tests, and the spaghetti stack causes a .75 slow-down. Seventy-five percent of this overhead is attributable to pointer tests.

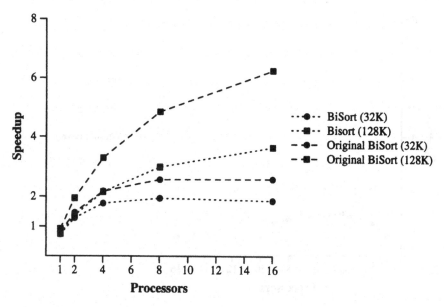

Fig. 8. Bitonic Sort speedup

6.3 Building Voronoi Diagrams

The Voronoi Diagram benchmark[GS85, LS80] generates a random set of points and computes a Voronoi Diagram for these points. To compute a Voronoi diagram, the algorithm splits the point set into two sets using the median point as the dividing line, it recursively computes the Voronoi Diagrams of the smaller sets, and merges them to form the final result. The merge phase is sequential and may require a linear number of migrations when the subsets are on different processors. In Figure 9, we report the speedup obtained for building the Voronoi Diagram for 64K points. The reported speedup does not include the cost of generating the points or building the tree used to represent the sets of points. This example displays almost no parallelism for two reasons. First, the merge phase is sequential and represents a substantial fraction of the computation. But more importantly, migrations are expensive in our current implementation because the speed of message passing is not well matched to the speed of the processor.

As in Bitonic Sort, we suffer from a significant slowdown in going from plain to one (.68), which is attributable to the cost of testing for non-local pointers.

6.4 Barnes Hut

The Barnes Hut benchmark[BH86] simulates the motion of particles in space using an $O(n \log n)$ algorithm for computing the accelerations of the particles. This is a classic n-body problem. We report the cost of generating the points using a uniform distribution and computing the new acceleration and position for each particle for ten time steps. The results for this benchmark, shown in

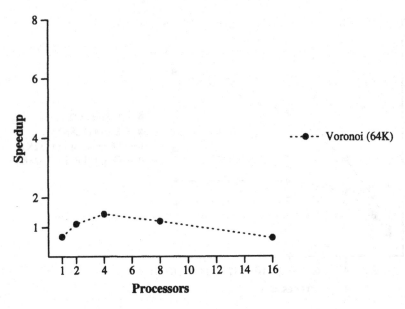

Fig. 9. Voronoi Diagram speedup

Figure 10, are encouraging. For a relatively small problem (4K particles), we achieve a speedup of almost eight for 16 processors. This computation is broken into three pieces: building the tree used to represent the particles, the acceleration calculation, and computing the new positions of the particles. The second two pieces perform quite well, in part, because we build a copy of the tree of every processor. This will not work for larger problem sizes. The tree building is sequential and starts to represent a substantial amount of the computation as the number of processors increases. Another factor is the cost of transmitting the particle and acceleration information to the processors. This cost increases as the number of processors increases.

6.5 Discussion

In our current implementations, migrations are expensive. Sending the data accounts for roughly ninety percent of the cost of a migration. We believe that by switching a machine with a better communication system, we will see a substantial improvement in the results for the Bitonic Sort and Voronoi Diagram benchmarks. We expect to see a less dramatic improvement in Barnes-Hut.

In early experiments, we observed super-linear speedup for several of these benchmarks. We traced this to the quadratic behavior of the i860's memory allocation routines. We reduced the effect of this problem by calling malloc only a few times and managing the acquired storage explicitly.

Both the Voronoi Diagram and Bitonic Sort benchmarks suffer from substantial overhead due to pointer testing. It may be possible to reduce this overhead

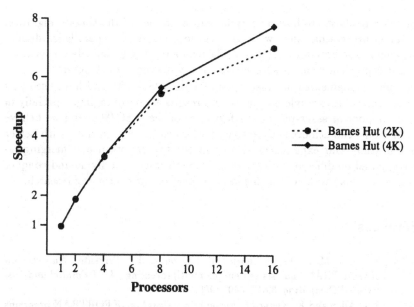

Fig. 10. Barnes-Hut speedup

pointers by using the address translation hardware and a user-level trap handler to detect and manage non-local references. The effectiveness of such a scheme will depend heavily on the cost of servicing a user-level trap[AL91].

7 Conclusions

We have presented a new approach for generating SPMD parallel programs automatically from sequential programs that use hierarchical data structures. In developing our new approach, we have noted fundamental problems with trying to apply runtime resolution techniques, currently used to produce SPMD programs for scientific programs, to programs that use dynamic data structures. In the case of scientific programs, the array data structures are statically allocated, statically mapped, and directly addressable. Dynamic data structures, on the other hand, are dynamically allocated, dynamically mapped, and must be recursively traversed to be addressable. These properties of dynamic data structures preclude the use of simple local tests for ownership, and therefore make the runtime resolution model ineffective.

Our mechanism avoids these fundamental problems, by more closely matching the dynamic nature of the data structures. Rather than making each processor decide if it should execute a statement by determining if it owns the relevant piece of the data structure, we use a thread migration strategy that migrates the computation to the processor that owns the data automatically. Coupled with the thread migration technique is our futurecall mechanism, which introduces parallelism by allowing processors to split the thread of computation.

In order to illustrate how a compiler can make use of the thread migration and lazy future mechanisms, we also outlined a strategy to parallelize divide-and-conquer type programs. This compilation method relies heavily on accurate alias and dependency analysis for hierarchical dynamic data structures.

We have implemented our mechanism for the iPSC/860, and have used this system to run some example programs. Our results are encouraging, especially in light of the poor message-passing performance of the iPSC/860, and we believe that our model can achieve substantially better results on a machine with better communication. Our experiences also point out the importance of merging results computed on different processors to the performance of divide-and-conquer programs. We plan to focus on this issue as part of our continuing research.

References

[ABC+88] F. Allen, M. Burke, P. Charles, R. Cytron, and J. Ferrante. An overview of the PTRAN analysis system for multiprocessing. *J. of Parallel and Distributed Computing*, 5:617–640, 1988.

[AK87] J.R. Allen and K. Kennedy. Automatic translation of FORTRAN programs to vector form. *ACM Transactions on Programming Languages and Systems*, 9(4):491–542, October 1987.

[AL91] A. W. Appel and K. Li. Virtual memory primitives for user programs. In *Proceedings of the Fourth International Conference on Architectural Support for Programming Languages and Operating Systems*, pages 96–107, April 1991.

[AL93] J.M. Anderson and M.S. Lam. Global optimizations for parallelism and locality on scalable parallel machines. In *Proceedings of the SIGPLAN '93 Conference on Programming Language Design and Implementation*, June 1993.

[AM93] S.P. Amarasinghe and M.S.Lam. Communication optimization and code generation for distributed memory machines. In *Proceedings of the SIGPLAN '93 Conference on Programming Language Design and Implementation*, June 1993.

[BH86] Josh Barnes and Piet Hut. A hierarchical $O(N \log N)$ force-calculation algorithm. *Nature*, 324:446–449, December 1986.

[BN89] G. Bilardi and A. Nicolau. Adaptive bitonic sorting: An optimal parallel algorithm for shared-memory machines. *SIAM Journal of Computing*, 18(2):216–228, 1989.

[BW73] D. Bobrow and B. Wegbreit. A model and stack implementation of multiple environments. *Communications of the ACM*, 16(10):591–603, 1973.

[CK88] D. Callahan and K. Kennedy. Compiling programs for distributed memory multiprocessors. *The Journal of Supercomputing*, 2(2), October 1988.

[FH91] C. Fraser and D. Hanson. A retargetable compiler for ANSI C. *SIGPLAN Notices*, 26(10):29–43, 1991.

[Fra91] C. Fraser. A code generation interface for ANSI C. *Software–Practice & Experience*, 21(9):963–988, 1991.

[Ger90] M. Gerndt. *Automatic Parallelization for Distributed-Memory Multiprocessing Systems*. PhD thesis, University of Bonn, 1990.

[GS85]   L. Guibas and J. Stolfi. General subdivisions and voronoi diagrams. *ACM Transactions on Graphics*, 4(2):74–123, 1985.

[Gup92]   R. Gupta. SPMD execution of programs with dynamic data structures on distributed memory machines. In *Proceedings of the 1992 International Conference on Computer Languages*, pages 232–241, April 1992.

[Hal85]   R H. Halstead, Jr. Multilisp: A language for concurrent symbolic computation. *ACM Transactions on Programming Languages and Systems*, 7(4):501–538, October 1985.

[HCD89]   W. Horwat, A.A. Chien, and W.J. Dally. Experience with CST: Programming and implementation. In *Proceedings of the SIGPLAN '89 Conference on Programming Language Design and Implementation*, pages 101–108, June 1989.

[Hen90]   L. J. Hendren. *Parallelizing Programs with Recursive Data Structures*. PhD thesis, Cornell University, January 1990.

[HHN92]   L. J. Hendren, J. Hummel, and A. Nicolau. Abstractions for recursive pointer data structures: Improving the analysis and transformation of imperative programs. In *Proceedings of the SIGPLAN '92 Conference on Programming Language Design and Implementation*, June 1992.

[HKT91]   S. Hiranandani, K. Kennedy, and C. Tseng. Compiler optimizations for FORTRAN D on MIMD distributed memory machines. In *Proceedings of Supercomputing 91*, pages 86–100, November 1991.

[HL93]   Guido Hogen and Rita Loogen. A new stack technique for the management of runtime structures in distributed implementations. Technical Report 3, RWTH Aachen, {ghogen,rita}@zeus.informatik.rwth-aachen.de, 1993.

[HN90]   L. J. Hendren and A. Nicolau. Parallelizing programs with recursive data structures. *IEEE Transactions on Parallel and Distributed Systems*, 1(1), 1990.

[KMvR90]   C. Koelbel, P. Mehrotra, and J. van Rosendale. Supporting shared data structures on distributed memory architectures. In *Proceedings of the Second ACM SIGPLAN Symposium on the Principles and Practice of Parallel Programming*, 1990.

[Koe90]   C. Koelbel. *Compiling Programs for Nonshared Memory Machines*. PhD thesis, Purdue University, West Lafayette, IN, August 1990.

[Lar89]   James R. Larus. *Restructuring Symbolic Programs for Concurrent Execution on Multiprocessors*. PhD thesis, University of California, Berkeley, 1989.

[LH88a]   J. R. Larus and P. N. Hilfinger. Detecting conflicts between structure accesses. In *Proceedings of the SIGPLAN '88 Conference on Programming Language Design and Implementation*, pages 21–34, June 1988.

[LH88b]   James R. Larus and Paul N. Hilfinger. Restructuring Lisp programs for concurrent execution. In *Proceedings of the ACM/SIGPLAN PPEALS 1988 - Parallel Programming: Experience with Applications, Languages and Systems*, pages 100–110, July 1988.

[LS80]   D. T. Lee and B. J. Schachter. Two algorithms for constructing a delaunay triangulation. *International Journal of Computer and Information Sciences*, 9(3):219–242, 1980.

[MKH91]   E. Mohr, D. A. Kranz, and R. H. Halstead, Jr. Lazy task creation: A technique for increasing the granularity of parallel programs. *IEEE Transactions on Parallel and Distributed Systems*, 2(3):264–280, July 1991.

[PW86]   D. Padua and M. Wolfe. Advanced compiler optimizations for supercom-
          puters. *Communications of the ACM*, 29(12), December 1986.

[Rog90]   A. Rogers. *Compiling for Locality of Reference*. PhD thesis, Cornell Uni-
          versity, August 1990.

[RP89]   A. Rogers and K. Pingali. Process decomposition through locality of ref-
          erence. In *Proceedings of the SIGPLAN '89 Conference on Programming
          Language Design and Implementation*, June 1989.

[RRH92]   A. Rogers, J. H. Reppy, and L. J. Hendren. Supporting SPMD execution
          for dynamic data structures. In *Conference Record of the Fifth Workshop on
          Languages and Compilers for Parallel Computing*, August 1992. To appear
          as volume of Springer's Lecture Notes in Computer Science series.

[RSW90]   M. Rosing, R. Schnabel, and R. Weaver. The DINO parallel programming
          language. Technical Report CU-CS-457-90, University of Colorado at Boul-
          der, April 1990.

[RV89]   E. S. Roberts and M. T. Vandevoorde. WorkCrews: An abstraction for con-
          trolling parallelism. Technical Report 42, DEC Systems Research Center,
          April 1989.

[Wol89]   M. Wolfe. *Optimizing Supercompilers for Supercomputers*. Pitman Publish-
          ing, London, 1989.

[ZBG88]   H. Zima, H. Bast, and M. Gerndt. SUPERB: A tool for semi-automatic
          MIMD/SIMD parallelization. *Parallel Computing*, 6(1):1–18, 1988.

A   Allocation Example

```
/* Allocate a tree with level levels on processors
   lo..lo+num_proc-1 */

tree_t *TreeAlloc (int level, int lo, int num_proc)
{
  if (level == 0)
    return NULL;
  else {
    struct tree *new, *right;
    int mid, lo_tmp;
    future_cell fleft;

    new = (struct tree *) ALLOC(lo, sizeof(tree_t));
    fleft = futurecall(TreeAlloc, level-1, lo+num_proc/2, num_proc/2);
    right=TreeAlloc(level-1,lo,num_proc/2);
    new->val = 1;
    new->right = (struct tree *) right;
    new->left = (struct tree *) touch(fleft);
    return new;
  }
}
```

Arbitrary Order Operations on Trees

Jon A. Solworth and Bryan B. Reagan

Dept. of EECS (m/c 154)
University of Illinois at Chicago
851 S. Morgan, Rm 1120 SEO
Chicago, IL, 60607-7053
{solworth,reagan}@parsys.eecs.uic.edu

Abstract. We consider techniques for the large scale parallel execution of algorithms on trees. We show that there is much parallelism in these algorithms, and introduce efficient means to exploit this parallelism. In particular, arbitrary order operations on trees are considered. An execution of a set arbitrary order operations must be equivalent to some sequential execution of a permutation of these operations.

A new algorithm is introduced for efficiently performing these operations under the condition that an operation consists of a sequence of reads starting at the root of a tree down a path towards some leaf, followed by a partial retrace of that path in reverse during which writes can occur — this is the standard form for performing inserts, searches, and deletes on most forms of balanced and unbalanced binary trees. We show that this new algorithm, *tree interference* is correct and produces execution schedules which are at least as parallel as other techniques including locking and graph coloring based interference. We also show some estimate of the performance on a sample computation, AVL trees.

1 Introduction

In this paper, the problem of parallelizing operations of tree-based algorithms is considered. On first glance, it may appear that tree-based algorithms have little inherent parallelism, since operations such as delete, insert, and find are very short lived, usually only requiring logarithmic time in the size of the tree. Hence, any parallelism which is found will be fine-grained (even for large trees) and hence the overheads must be made quite small.

A second problem is that the most straightforward approaches require some form of locking of the root. This technique allows some types of tree algorithms to be pipelined, but the pipeline is proportional to the average path length in the tree, allowing only logarithmic parallelism. Hence, a tree with 1 million nodes would be able to use only on the order of 20 fold parallelism. Clearly, such techniques are insufficient for large scale parallelism.

A third problem is that trees are very often used for on-line algorithms in which successive operations depend on each other. Such applications have very little parallelism, and hence are not amenable to large scale parallelism. Therefore, we shall consider tree operations which consists of sequences of operations which can be performed in any order. For example, one such sequence is a homogeneous set of operations such as inserts (or deletes, or finds).

The algorithm presented here, *tree interference*, has the following properties:

- It exhibits greater parallelism than other techniques,
- It has lower overhead than competitive techniques, and
- It is applicable to more types of tree algorithms, including self adjusting trees such as AVL trees and B-trees.

The tree interference algorithm takes advantage of the fact that while there is little parallelism at the root, there is much parallelism at the leaves. Since most of the updates, even on balanced tree structures, take place near the leaves and since the number of leaves are linear in the size of the tree there is close to linear parallelism to exploit.

The rest of the paper is organized as follows. Section 2 describes in more detail the semantics of our iterations. Section 3 describes the various approaches to tree-based algorithms, while section 4 describes how the various algorithms can be implemented and their effect on performance, as well as a proof of correctness for tree interference. Performance results are presented in Section 5, followed by related work in Section 6 and Conclusions.

2 Arbitrary order

In this paper, arbitrary order operations on tree data structures are considered. The execution of a collection of *arbitrary ordered* operations must be equivalent to the execution of those operations *in some sequential order*. For example, an arbitrary order loop with five iterations labeled $i_0...i_4$ could be executed in the order i_0, i_1, i_2, i_3, i_4 or i_1, i_4, i_3, i_2, i_0 or any other permutation of those elements. Arbitrary ordered operations are *not* explicitly parallel — they are sequential operations whose order is unspecified.

Arbitrary order operations were first introduced in SETL [SDDS86], a purely sequential programming language. They are often used in algorithm books as a natural way of specifying computations using such notation as $\forall x \in set$ or $\exists x \in set | P(x)$ [AHU75]. Arbitrary order iterations reduce over specification while enabling independent choice of data structures and algorithm.

They have also been proposed for specifying implicitly parallel algorithms, both pointer-based [Sol90] and numeric [Wol92]. Arbitrary order operations enable the programmer to specify to the programming system when the order of operations is important and when it is not. When the order is not important, the compiler and the runtime system can often provide more parallel and lower overhead executions. They are the sequential analog of such parallel techniques as Linda's bags (in which an arbitrary element is selected from tuple space) [ACG86], Ultracomputer's Fetch&Add which is often used to remove an arbitrary element from a queue [GLR83], and many other lock based approaches.

In Figure 1, a set of 4 operations are to be performed, each operation consists of two assignments. We shall say that two operations **conflict** iff one operation

$$op_0 \qquad op_1 \qquad op_2 \qquad op_3$$
$$x \Leftarrow 1 \qquad y \Leftarrow z \qquad w \Leftarrow p+q \quad q \Leftarrow r^*s$$
$$y \Leftarrow v - z \quad m \Leftarrow w\text{-}x \quad q \Leftarrow r\&p \quad p \Leftarrow v$$

Fig. 1. Arbitrary order operations

writes a location that the other operations accesses (either reads or writes). Note that op_0 conflicts with op_1 on x and y; op_1 conflicts with op_2 on w; op_2 conflicts with op_3 on p and q. The conflicts relation is symmetric so if op_i conflicts with op_j then op_j also conflicts with op_i. The conflicts can be represented with an undirected graph called the conflict graph whose nodes are operations and edges correspond to conflicts relations. The conflict graph for the operations in Figure 1 is shown in Figure 2.

To perform these operations in parallel, it is sufficient that each of these operations be performed atomically. As we shall see, we can either use synchronization (locks) to atomically execute the operations, or we can execute subsets of operations which do not conflict; for such subsets, no synchronization is needed among the operations in the subset. Since op_1 and op_3 do not conflict, they can be executed in parallel. Similarly, op_0 and op_2 do not conflict, and can be run in parallel. Hence, the four operations could be performed in two phases, with odd numbered operations in one phase and even numbered operations in the other. We shall call a set of operations whose elements pairwise don't conflict to be a *conflict free set (cfs)*. The concurrent execution of a *cfs* is equivalent to the result of executing the *cfs* in any sequential permutation. Note that without arbitrary order semantics, each operation in the above example would need to be executed sequentially, since op_i conflicts with op_{i+1}.

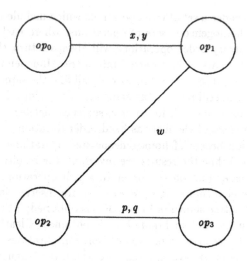

Fig. 2. A conflict graph

The conflict graph in the above example could be computed statically, since the only locations specified were simple variables. However, in the more general case of arrays, pointers, and other memory aliasing techniques the conflict sets cannot, in general, be statically determined. Furthermore, if the locations written include indicies for arrays or pointers, the conflict set changes after each phase and needs to be recomputed.

Arbitrary order operations lead to interesting compile-time and run-time optimizations to enable efficient executions. In previous papers we have considered the effect of these operations over list [Sol88, Sol91] and graph based data structures [Sol92]; in this paper we consider the operations performed over tree-based data structures, and in particular a new algorithm for performing arbitrary order tree updates called the tree interference algorithm.

The tree interference algorithm we shall introduce:

- Has a more parallel execution, and
- Less overhead

than alternative techniques. We shall prove each of the above assertions.

3 Tree-based Algorithms

There has been wide interest in detecting and optimizing tree based algorithms for both sequential and parallel executions [HHN92, CWZ90, Har92]. Most of the optimization have been in the area of pointer disambiguation; by refining alias information it becomes possible to map nodal data to registers, improving locality. There has been relatively little work in the area of parallelizing tree operations. In this paper, we consider the parallelization of arbitrary order operations on trees.

For example, consider a set of tree operations which include inserts, searches, and deletes. With homogeneous sets of operations, where each operation is of the same type, arbitrary order operations will always return the same results. Consider a set of elements to be inserted into a tree. Independent of the order inserted into the tree, subsequent searches will still find the same set of elements; subsequent deletes will still remove the same set of elements. Hence, three arbitrary order iterations – one each for inserts, searches, deletes – will insert, find, and remove the same set of elements as fixed order iterations.

Different iteration orders of homogeneous tree operations do not result in the same execution. While the results are invariant, the resulting tree will have a different shape depending on the order in which operations are performed. For example, if the elements $e_1 < e_2 < e_3 < e_4$ are inserted into a tree in the order e_2, e_1, e_3, e_4 the tree shown in Figure 3(a) is obtained; if the insertion order is e_3, e_1, e_2, e_4, then the tree in Figure 3(b) is obtained. Clearly, these are two different trees, and hence arise from two different computations. To indicate that the shape of the tree is irrelevant, either programming language constructs or compile-time analysis can be used. We believe it is an interesting problem in

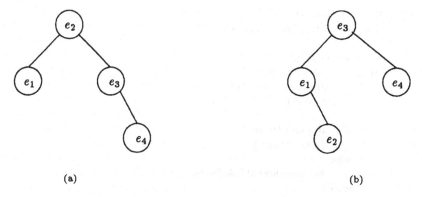

Fig. 3. Result of inserting for elements in two different orders

compile-time analysis to determine under what conditions it is safe to replace fixed iteration order loops with arbitrary order loops.

The techniques discussed in this paper make use not only of the tree structure, but of the typical way in which the tree is traversed and updated. Consider the AVL tree insertions shown in Figure 4. All operations start at the root and traverse down to the bottom fringe of the tree, at which the update is performed. Then a rebalancing step is performed as the path down to the insert path is traced in reverse. This is a general paradigm for trees in which the path down uses only reads starting at the root, and the path up update the tree for one or more levels. It is characteristic for AVL trees, B-trees, Binary Search trees, [AHU75] Red-Black trees, and many other tree structures. In fact, Splay trees [ST85] are the only tree-structure which the authors are aware which does not fit into this paradigm; however, the large, tree-global data structure changes of splay trees makes it unlikely to perform well in parallel.

This paradigm is illustrated with the tree interference diagram shown in Figure 5. Five operations, labeled $x_1...x_5$, are to be performed in arbitrary order. These operations are shown in the figure as dotted lines. An operation reads the nodes from the root to the fringe on the way down, and then modify nodes coming up to some level. For example, x_1 read nodes n_0, n_1, n_3, n_7 on the way down, and then modifies nodes n_7, n_3 on the way up. We shall use Figure 5 as a running example to show how the various strategies for implementing arbitrary order operations on trees work[1].

When pointers are present, the problem of finding conflict-free sets (*cfs*) of operations becomes more expensive since the set of locations accessed depend on the order in which the iterations are performed. For example, after an insertion is performed the tree is changed, and so is the path (and conflicts) for future operations. Hence, the size of the *cfs* has two impacts on performance: with

---

[1] We assume in the example that the conflict set is invariant with respect to the order of execution. This is not the case in general but serves as an adequate first order approximation

```
forall x ∈ elements do
    root ⇐ avl_tree_insert(root, x);

avl_tree_insert(node, x)
    if node = NULL then
        - empty tree, create root
        return Node(x);
    else
        if Leaf(node) then
            Insert(node,x);
        else
            avl_tree_insert(Child(node,x), x);
        endif;
        if Unbalanced(node) then
            rebalance(node)
        endif;
    endif;
endproc;
```

Fig. 4. A program to insert elements into an AVL tree data

larger *cfss*, there is both more parallelism and less overhead for determining the other *cfs*. The tree-based interference produces a partitioning which is not a *cfs* but which is guaranteed to be equivalent to some sequential execution.

4 Implementing Arbitrary Order Operations

In this section we consider several methods for implementing arbitrary order operations on trees. These mechanisms fall into three categories:

Locking Tree nodes are locked to ensure exclusive use before making any updates.

Graph coloring interference A trial execution of the loop is performed, computing which iterations conflict with other iterations. Pairs of iterations which do not conflict can be executed simultaneously.

Tree-based interference This is a new method introduced in this paper which enables more parallel executions than the (more general) graph coloring techniques.

4.1 Locking

There are many ways of performing tree operations using locking. Any locking protocol must place read locks (shared locks) on locations read which can be written by other operations, and must place write locks (exclusive locks) on

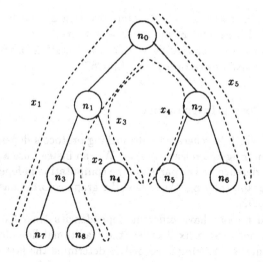

Fig. 5. Tree inserts of arbitrary order operations

locations written which might be accessed by other operations. We will review the major techniques here and discuss their strengths and weaknesses.

Using *pessimistic read and write locking*, each node which could be written (read) would require a write (read) lock. Write locks would need to have priority over read locks, enabling writes to force the reads to release its locks and retry later to prevent deadlock. Similarly, write-write lock conflicts would cause one of the two operations to abort. By prioritizing write-write conflict resolution, these schemes can be made free of starvation.

An alternative to aborting operations is to lock all nodes which might be written, called *pessimistic write locking*. This leads to an algorithm which is at best linear in the case when writes can occur arbitrarily high in the tree, since the root becomes a sequential bottleneck, yielding a speedup of at most $\log(N)^2$. Futures, for example, can be used to create these kinds of locks with each operation creating a newly rooted tree [Hal85].

Another way is to performing *optimistic locking*, locking the nodes it actually writes on the way up. It then needs to check that the values read for that operation have not changed. If any of the unlocked values have changed, the operation must release its locks and try again.

The choice is either to lose parallelism (using pessimistic write locking) or to abort operations (otherwise). The effectiveness of locking depends on the degree of interference and the amount of overlap in processing. For example, if x_1 reached n_3 on the return path after x_2 reached n_3 on the forward path, a conflict would exist, and either x_1 or x_2 would need to abort. On the other hand, if x_2 reached n_3 after x_1 had updated it, then no lock conflict would exist. In the

---

[2] In the less general case when writes can occur only at the root (for example, on inserts in a search tree), this is an efficient protocol.

example, x_1 interferes with x_2, x_5; x_2 interferes with x_1, x_5; x_3 interferes with x_5; x_4 interferes with x_5; and x_5 interferes with everything.

Another disadvantage of locking is that the iteration order is not known unless extra information is recorded, see [LMC87].

4.2 Graph Coloring Interference

The interference which is generated with locking protocols depends on the relative timing of acquiring and releasing locks. We can instead use a global protocol to determine interference and to partition the computation independently of timing issues using graph coloring. We review the graph coloring based interference introduced in [Sol92].

Arbitrary order loops have different dependencies than fixed order loops. Since there does not exist a fixed order, the traditional flow dependencies are not applicable since an ordering is needed to determine the flow of information. One way of creating a parallel execution at runtime is with an optimistic scheme which first executes each iteration in isolation. An isolated execution of iteration performs a read of location by first looking for that location in a local cache. If the value is in the cache, it is retrieved from there, otherwise a read is performed to the global store. A write is always performed only to the cache. Then, any subset of iterations, I, whose only shared locations (if any) are read only can be executed in parallel by committing its written cache location to the global store[3]. The process of optimistic execution is then repeated on the remaining unexecuted iterations. The sequential semantics are preserved since a concurrent execution of I is equivalent to a sequential execution of any permutation of I.

Graph coloring explicitly builds an interference graph which can then be colored, each color corresponding to a phase in the parallel execution — nodes which have the same color can be executed in parallel. This has been shown to be efficiently implementable in the case of a graph [Sol92].

For example, in the tree updates shown in Figure 5, has a conflict graph as shown in Figure 6. This conflict has a clique of size 3 (x_1, x_2, x_5), and requires three colors. Hence, these updates could be performed in three phases.

4.3 Tree interference

We now introduce the tree interference algorithm which works as follows.

1. Perform a preliminary execution of the operations on a tree.
2. Let $Lev(op)$ be the level, or distance from the root, at which the write closest to the root occurs for operation op.

---

[3] The execution of any two iterations (in an arbitrary order loop) is pairwise *raceless* if no location which is used in both iterations can be written by either one. Two raceless iterations $i_0 \ldots i_1$ can be executed concurrently or in either i_0, i_1 or i_1, i_0 order with exactly the same result.

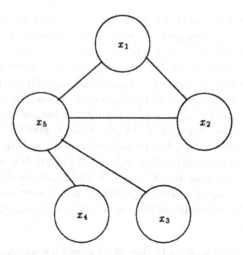

Fig. 6. Conflict graph for tree insertions shown in Tree interference

3. Two operations which do not have a write-write conflict can be scheduled to the same partition. Priority is given to the operations with the maximum *Lev*.
4. Repeat recursively on the remaining unexecuted operations.

Using tree interference the entire set of operations shown in Figure 5 can be performed in parallel, in a single phase. Although all of the operations in this example execute in a single phase, there is a conflict between the reads performed in part 1 and the writes performed in part 3. Hence it is necessary to perform all of the reads for every operation during part 1 before any of the writes during part 3 — part 3 may not repeat any read but must use the values read in part 1. However, while each part is executed in sequence, operations are operated on in parallel during each part.

Lemma 1. *The tree interference algorithm produces partitions, each of which is equivalent to some sequential ordering of the operations it contains.*

proof: by induction on the levels in a partition

base case: Consider a set S of operations in the partition P for which $l = Lev(op)$ is a maximum. We shall show that this set of operations consitutes a *cfs*. By the formation of P, the operations pairwise have no write-write conflict. It remains to show only that there are no read-write conflict (and hence by symmetry no write-read conflicts). Clearly there are no write-read conflicts for any level less than l, since by the formation of the set there are no writes at any level less than l. It remains to be shown that there are no read-write conflicts at or below l. However, by the definition of $Lev(op)$, there are only writes at levels greater than or equal to l, and hence any conflicts would be write-write conflicts, of which there are none.

induction case: Assume that the inductive hypothesis holds for some set of operations S in the partition P, we will show how to maintain the criteria while increasing the size of this set by one. The operation added, op is $min_{op \in P-S} Lev(op)$. Clearly, by the definition of P there is no write-write conflict. We shall show that executing S concurrently with op is semantically equivalent to executing S, in some order, followed by op. Clearly there cannot be any conflict at any level less than l because by definition only reads occur at these levels on $S \cup \{op\}$. At level greater than l, there can be read-write conflicts but, by the formation of P, no write-write conflicts. Moreover, op performs only writes at levels of l or greater, so any read-write conflicts must occur from operations in S reading nodes that op writes. But since these nodes execute before op and do not change the set of the tree, op sees the same values in its sequential order as it did in its preliminary execution.

We have in fact shown not only that there exists a sequential order, we have shown what that order is, that is:

Lemma 2. *The execution in parallel of P is equivalent to the sequential execution of the operations in P performed in sorted descending order by Lev.*

Hence, given the tree in Figure 5, we have the sequential order

$$x_2, \{x_1, x_3, x_4\}, x_5$$

Meaning that x_2 is logically executed first, followed by the conflict free set $\{x_1, x_3, x_4\}$ logically executed in any order, followed by x_5. Note that this is the semantically equivalent sequential execution order; in fact, the execution of these operation is completely in parallel.

5 Performance

Having described tree interference, and prove its correct, the next issue is to prove that there is sufficient parallelism to be exploited. In this section we shall show that tree-based interference is strictly more parallel, that is yields larger partitions, than coloring based interference. Furthermore, we shall show how much parallelism exists on AVL balanced trees of various sizes and using various number of inserts.

5.1 Performance bounds

In this section we shall show that tree intereference is at least as good as locking and graph coloring based algorithms.

Lemma 3. *Locking produces executions which are no more parallel than graph coloring.*

proof:

Two operations can attain all their locks at the same time iff there is no conflict between them. Hence, locking produces no more parallelism than graph coloring (in fact, pessimistic write locking produces less).

Lemma 4. *Tree based interference produces partitions which are at least as large as coloring based interference.*

proof:

The proof follows trivially, since tree-based partitioning prevents only operations with write-write conflicts from occurring in the same partition, while coloring based conflict prevents operations with either write-write conflicts or read-write conflicts from occurring in the same partition.

Lemma 5. *Tree based interference requires less overhead than graph based interference*

proof:

The proof follows trivially, since tree-based interference is a subset of graph based interference. (Tree based interference differs from graph based interference in that it ignores reads).

Hence, we have shown that tree-based interference is capable of producing at least as much parallelism as dynamic locking or coloring based interference.

5.2 Parallelism in AVL tree inserts

We wish to at least show the amount of parallelism that such an algorithm would have for example on an AVL tree. We consider a tree of size S, having either $8S$, $4S$, $2S$, S, $S/2$, $S/4$ or $S/8$ inserts. For example consider an AVL tree with $S = 2048$ nodes, we consider the cases of inserting $16K, 8K, 4K, 2K, 1K, 512$, and 256 additional nodes. Both the AVL tree and the additional nodes are randomly generated.

Obviously, the more nodes that are inserted, the more the potential for parallelism since there are more inserts which can be done in parallel. However, the more nodes to be inserted, the greater the conflict. For example, Figure 7 shows that a graph coloring on a tree with 2048 nodes, would take on average 10.1 phases to insert 256 elements, 12.4 phases to insert 512, 23.3 phases to insert 1K, 38.7 phases to insert 2K, 56.1 phases to insert 4K, 83.1 phases to insert 8K, and 115.8 phases to insert 16K nodes. In the above example, each phase on average inserts 25.3, 41.3, 43.9, 52.9, 73.0, 98.6, 141.5. These numbers were collected by averaging the result of 10 different runs per data point.

In Figure 8, we show the parallelism that results from performing graph coloring on different size trees with the number of inserts proportional to the size of the tree (this is from the data in Figure 7). Clearly this graph shows that as the tree and number of inserts increases so does the parallelism.

Several patterns emerge.

Tree Size	Number of Phases							Operations per Phase						
S	S/8	S/4	S/2	S	2S	4S	8S	S/8	S/4	S/2	S	2S	4S	8S
32	1.4	4.5	6.7	13.8	20.3	33.9	51.2	2.9	1.8	2.4	2.3	3.2	3.7	5.0
64	3.0	5.8	11.1	17.2	28.1	42.7	63.1	2.7	2.8	2.9	3.7	4.6	6.0	8.1
128	5.0	6.2	12.9	21.2	37.0	49.3	71.7	3.2	5.1	5.0	6.0	6.9	10.4	14.3
256	5.1	8.5	15.2	25.9	41.0	58.7	83.5	6.3	7.5	8.4	9.9	12.5	17.4	24.5
512	7.4	11.7	18.0	29.0	45.6	65.7	94.9	8.6	10.9	14.2	17.7	22.5	31.2	43.2
1024	7.5	11.6	20.2	35.3	52.6	77.0	102.0	17.1	22.1	25.3	29.0	38.9	53.2	80.3
2048	10.1	12.4	23.3	38.7	56.1	83.1	115.8	25.3	41.3	43.9	52.9	73.0	98.6	141.5
4096	10.1	16.1	27.4	40.3	66.5	99.4	NA	50.7	63.6	74.7	101.6	123.2	164.8	NA

Fig. 7. Graph Coloring: Number of Phases and Operations per Phase

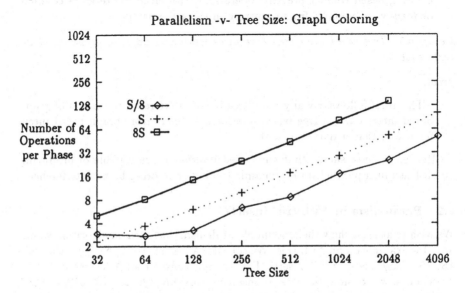

Fig. 8. Graph coloring parallelism for $8S$, S, and $S/8$ inserts

1. For a given size tree each time the number of inserts doubles the number of phases increases by a smaller factor. Part of this is due to the larger size decreasing the variance, ensuring that the inserts are better distributed, but the larger factor is that most of the writes are performed close to the leaves. Hence, although rebalancing can go all the way from leaf to root, this is in practice quite rare.
2. The growth in the number of phases with tree size is also definitely less than linear (it seems to be logarithmic).
3. Significantly more parallelism is available than path length would indicate.

Graph coloring is a good approach to performing tree operations.

Tree interference is a much better algorithm. For example, in Figure 9, 2048

Tree Size	Number of Phases							Operations per Phase						
S	S/8	S/4	S/2	S	2S	4S	8S	S/8	S/4	S/2	S	2S	4S	8S
32	1.4	2.7	3.6	3.6	11.3	17.7	22.9	2.9	3.0	4.4	8.9	5.7	7.2	11.2
64	1.6	3.7	6.3	9.0	11.9	16.7	24.7	5.0	4.3	5.1	7.1	10.8	15.3	20.7
128	3.1	3.9	6.4	9.4	15.1	19.1	30.8	5.2	8.2	10.0	13.6	17.0	26.8	33.2
256	3.6	4.4	6.8	10.6	17.7	21.4	28.1	8.9	14.5	18.9	24.2	28.9	47.9	72.9
512	4.4	5.6	7.9	11.7	15.9	22.1	30.0	14.5	22.9	32.4	43.8	64.4	92.7	136.5
1024	4.0	6.5	10.2	12.8	18.3	26.1	30.7	32.0	39.4	50.2	80.0	112.0	156.9	266.8
2048	5.0	5.7	9.0	12.8	17.6	25.6	34.0	51.2	89.8	113.8	160.0	232.7	320.0	481.8
4096	6.9	6.7	9.7	15.0	20.2	27.7	34.4	74.2	152.8	211.1	273.1	405.5	591.5	952.6

Fig. 9. Tree Interference: Number of Phases and Operations per Phase

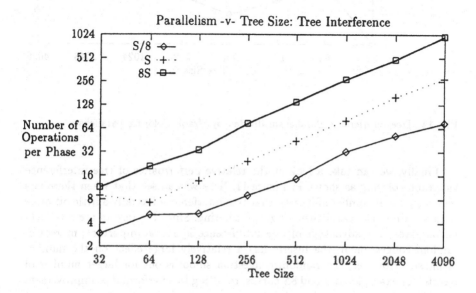

Fig. 10. Tree interference parallelism for $8S$, S, and $S/8$ inserts

inserts can be performed on a 2048 node tree in only 12.8 phases which is approximately 1/3 of that needed by graph coloring (and hence tripling the parallelism). When inserting 32K elements into a 4K node tree, thousand fold parallelism is achievable. Moreover, it requires less overhead since it need only use the write-write conflicts vs. Graph coloring's read-write and write-write conflicts. Even for quite small trees, Tree Interference gets the job done in less phases and in all cases is at least as good as graph coloring and almost always better. Tree Interference's growth rate is smaller than Graph Coloring, so that the larger the tree the greater the advantage.

Comparing the parallelism of graph coloring (Figure 8) to that of tree interference (Figure 10), we see that the graph for tree interference is both larger in magnitude and steeper in grow, resulting in ever widening parallelism.

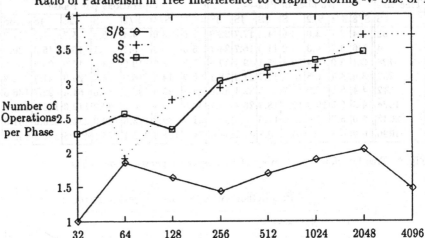

Fig. 11. Tree Interference Parallelism divided by Graph Coloring Parallelism

Finally, we can take a look at the relative performance of tree interference vs. graph coloring as shown in Figure 11. Here we can see that when there is a relatively small number of inserts, that tree interference has only a little bit more than 1.5 times the parallelism of graph coloring. Since the inserts are relatively uncongested, the advantage of tree interference is not as important; moreover, random congestion in the inserts has a relatively large effect on the number of phases. However, the random congestion smooths out for larger number of inserts: for example, at S and $8S$ curves, resulting in a performance improvement up to 3.5 times at higher insert rates.

The one remaining issue is the number of phases required. Consider an execution which requires p phases, then ever insert must be done almost p times, loosing a factor of p in efficiency. There are several approaches we are investigating to remove or reduce this factor, including:

1. N inserts can be performed k at a time in N/k rounds. While this reduces parallelism, it also reduces the number of phases needed. For example, by reducing the number of elements being inserted at a time by a factor of 64, we can save about a factor of 7 in overhead.

2. We can use the results from the first partitioning step to tune the later partitioning steps. For example, assume that when we initially insert N elements we get k writes for a given node. Then we can form a queue for

each node, placing an insert at the highest level in the tree at which it writes. Then during any phase we just schedule the head of each queue. This should result in looking at each node twice; once in the fist phase and once when it is actually scheduled.

Reducing the number of phases, and its effect on parallelism, is the subject of future research.

6 Related Work

There are many example of programs which use runtime algorithms, either performing optimistic execution with rollback [Kat86] or by performing runtime analysis to create program schedules. Examples of the later, besides the authors work previously cited, include Salz et. al's work [SMC91] on runtime parallelization of fixed ordered loops on graph computations.

Corresponding static non-numeric scheduling has been studied by Larus and Hillfinger [LH88], in addition to previously cited work on linked lists and tree analysis.

7 Conclusions

We have shown a promising technique for parallelizing a set of arbitrary ordered tree updates, under the very general condition that those tree updates are of a generic and widely applicable form. This technique produces schedules which are more parallel than either runtime locking or graph coloring and in addition has lower overhead than graph coloring based interference. We have also shown that there is much parallelism that can be exploited by this algorithm.

Acknowledgements

The authors gratefully acknowledge the support of ONR, grant number ONR 93-1-0655. And the comments of the referees and Jerry Stamatopoulos.

References

[ACG86] S. Ahuja, N. Carriero, and David Gelertner. Linda and friends. *Computer*, 19(8):26–34, August, 1986.

[AHU75] A. V. Aho, J. E. Hopcroft, and J. D. Ullman. *The design and analysis of computer algorithms*. Addison-Wesley, Reading, Mass., 1975.

[CWZ90] David R. Chase, Mark Wegman, and F. K. Zadek. Analysis of pointers and structures. In *Programming Language Design and Implementation*, pages 296–310. ACM, June 1990.

[GLR83] Allan Gottlieb, B. D. Lubachevsky, and Larry Rudolph. Basic techniques for the efficient coordination of very large numbers of cooperating sequential processes. *ACM Transactions of Programming Languages*, 5(2):164–189, April, 1983.

[Hal85]   Robert H. Halstead. Multilisp: a language for concurrent symbolic computation. *TOPLAS*, 7(4):501–538, October 1985.

[Har92]   W. Ludwell Harrison. Generalized iteration space and the parallelization of symbolic languages. In Ian Foster and Evan Tick, editors, *Workshop on Computation of Symbolic Languages for Parallel Computers*. Argonne National Labs, October 1992.

[HHN92] Laurie J. Hendren, Joseph Hummel, and Alexandru Nicolau. Abstraction for recursive pointer data structures: Improving the analysis and transformation of imperative languages. In *Programming Language Design and Implementation*, pages 249–260. ACM, June 1992.

[Kat86]   Morris J. Katz. Paratran: A transparent, transaction based runtime mechanism for the parallel execution of scheme. Master's thesis, MIT, June 1986. Masters Thesis.

[LH88]   James R. Larus and Paul N. Hilfinger. Detecting conflicts between structure accesses. In *SIGPLAN'88 Conference on Programming Language Design and Implementation*, June 1988.

[LMC87]   Thomas J. LeBlanc and John M. Mellor-Crummey. Debugging parallel programs with instant replay. *TOC*, C-36(4):471–482, April 1987.

[SDDS86] Jacob T. Schwartz, R. B. K. Dewar, E. Dubinsky, and E. Schonberg. *Programming with sets: an introduction to SETL*. Springer-Verlag, New York, New York, 1986. setl book.

[SMC91]   Joel H. Saltz, Ravi Mirchandaney, and Kay Crowley. Run-time parallelization and scheduling of loops. *IEEE Trans. on Computer*, 40(5):603–612, May 1991.

[Sol88]   Jon A. Solworth. Programming language constructs for highly parallel operations on lists. *The Journal of Supercomputing*, 2:331–347, 1988.

[Sol90]   Jon A. Solworth. The PARSEQ project: An interim report. In *Languages and Compilers for Parallel Computing*, pages 490—510. Pittman/MIT, 1990.

[Sol91]   Jon A. Solworth. On the performance of parallel lists. In *Advances in Languages and Compilers for Parallel Computing*, pages 152—171. Pittman/MIT, 1991.

[Sol92]   Jon A. Solworth. Arbitrary order iterations over pointer-based data structures. In *5th Workshop on Programming Languages and Compilers*, August 1992. to appear.

[ST85]   Daniel Dominic Sleator and Robert Endre Tarjan. Self-adjusting binary search trees. *JACM*, pages 652–686, July 1985.

[Wol92]   Michael Wolfe. Doany: Not just another parallel loop. In *5th Workshop on Programming Languages and Compilers*, August 1992. to appear.

Analysis of Dynamic Structures for Efficient Parallel Execution*

John Plevyak, Andrew A. Chien, Vijay Karamcheti

Department of Computer Science***
University of Illinois at Urbana-Champaign
Urbana, IL 61801

Abstract. This paper presents a new structure analysis technique handling references and dynamic structures which enables precise analysis of infinite recursive data structures. The precise analysis depends on an enhancement of Chase et al.'s Storage Shape Graph (SSG) called the Abstract Storage Graph (ASG) which extends SSG's with choice nodes, identity paths, and specialized storage nodes and references. These extensions allow ASG's to precisely describe singly- and multiply-linked lists as well as a number of other pointer structures such as octrees, and to analyze programs which manipulate them.
We describe program analysis to produce the ASG, and focus on the key operations: the transfer functions, summarization and deconstruction. Summarization compresses the ASG in such a way as to capture critical interdependencies between references. Deconstruction uses this information, stored by identity paths and refined references and nodes, to retrieve individual nodes for strong updates.

1 Introduction

An essential element in optimizing compilers is accurate program analysis which provides the compiler with information as to which program transformations may be safely applied without changing the program's functional behavior. Thus, good program analysis is necessary for effective optimization and efficient implementations.

Recent developments in programming languages and the widespread use of computing in non-numeric applications have produced a broad class of computer applications and algorithms. These applications and algorithms make use of sophisticated data structures which rely on dynamic storage allocation and the use of references as basic tools for efficiency and expressibility. Though their use is ubiquitous, references and dynamic storage allocation raise difficult problems in program analysis. In this paper we focus on structure analysis, the problem of building a safe approximation of the program's run time data structures.

*** {jplevyak,achien,vijayk}@cs.uiuc.edu
* The research described in this paper was supported in part by National Science Foundation grant CCR-9209336, Office of Naval Research grant N00014-92-J-1961, and National Aeronautics and Space Administration grant NAG 1-613.

Structure analysis is used to direct program optimization at compile time, consequently its accuracy is critical to improving code efficiency.

Structure analysis estimates at compile time the shape of the runtime store. Alias analysis is a related problem, but is subsumed by structure analysis since alias relations are described by the abstract store. However, the shape of unaliased dynamic structures cannot in general be inferred from alias information alone. While the alias information produced by structure analysis suffices for traditional serial optimizations and for dependence analysis based parallelization, the unique structure information is required for other important optimizations. Since determining precise alias information even in a single function is NP-complete [LH88, Mye81] practical structure analysis algorithms approximate the program store.

2 Background

2.1 Related Work

Most of the work on structure and alias analysis has been based on a data flow analysis framework. Such a framework defines a lattice of possible structure or alias situations, a function for each part of a program which models the effect of that part on an element of the lattice, and a meet operator which combines two elements into one.

Three basic approaches to both structure analysis and the alias problem have been explored. These basic approaches are (1) explicit annotation [Lar89] (2) access paths [HN90] and (3) graph based approaches [CWZ90]. Explicit annotations allow the user to supply the compiler with information which either cannot be derived, or is more easily verified than derived. In access path approaches, the aliases at each program point are described by pairs of access paths. In the graph based approaches, an approximation of the entire heap is computed for each program point and the graph nodes and edges express the possible sets of aliases and structure relations at execution time.

Many algorithms also use a combination of these approaches. For instance, the Abstract Dynamic Data Structure description (ADDS) approach [HNH92] combines annotation with access paths and seeks to verify programmer assertions. Larus [LH88] uses graphs to represent the structures reachable from each program variable, but labels the nodes with access paths and uses the labels to identify aliases. In contrast, Chase [CWZ90] uses graphs alone in which each node in the graph corresponds to one or more nodes in the runtime heap and the edges correspond to references. In this paper we do not consider annotations. The addition of program annotations is orthogonal to the problem of analyzing an unannotated program since for any imprecise algorithm, annotations could be added which guide and assist analysis at the cost of programmer effort.

In recent work, access path and graph based approaches have been drawn together [CBC93]. With access paths, the aliases at a program point are described by alias relations (pairs of access paths). An access path is a tuple consisting of a cell and a sequence of fields. The cell is either a program variable or a storage location name and the set of alias relations determines the edges of a directed graph. If the alias relations are stored with only one level of dereferencing, the aliases are precisely the edges of a graph whose vertices are the starting cells of the access paths [CBC93]. As a result, access paths are used to implement an essentially graph based algorithm.

Current alias and structure analysis algorithms are unable to accurately analyze many common data structures. Structure analysis approaches based on k-limited graphs [JM81, LH88, HPR89] or on k-limited naming schemes [CBC93] are unable to adequately describe recursive structures such as lists; in general, structures extend beyond the k-limit and the summary process destroys all structure beyond k nodes. If the list is traversed beyond k elements, the analysis cannot preserve the list structure, losing precision in analysis which leads to missed opportunities for optimization.

Chase et al.'s SSG algorithm [CWZ90] circumvents the k-limitation by augmenting the basic reference graph with heap reference counts. Thus, for singly-linked structures, SSGs can sometimes obtain a precise analysis of the program. However, the SSG algorithm suffers from two major limitations: it cannot analyze singly-linked lists in the face of mutation nor can it precisely analyze multiply linked structures.[4]. To remedy these limitations, the ASG incorporates extensions to the SSG (not based on heap reference counts). These extensions are described in detail in Section 3.

2.2 Project Context

This work has been done as part of the *Concert* Project [CKP93]. The objective of the *Concert* system is to achieve efficient, portable implementations of fine-grained concurrent object-oriented languages on parallel machines. Current commercial multicomputers are the primary target and present a variety of difficult problems since the cost of fine grained synchronization, consistency, communication and context switching in these machines can easily overwhelm that of computation. Controlling these costs requires determining the runtime shape of program structures and transforming both them and the program to increase the computation grain size.

These transformations fall in the general category of optimizations addressed via *grain size tuning* [CFKP92] which seeks to match the amount of serial processing between communication or synchronization points in the program to that efficiently supported by hardware. In parallel programs, merging computational grains requires enhancing data locality. For programs with complex data structures, accurate structure information at compile time allows identification of collections of data which are transformable for enhanced locality. For example when an object (dynamic structure) has an invariant reference to an unaliased

---

[4] An extension to heap reference counts is mentioned to handle the construction of multiply-linked structures, but is not developed.

object, the second object may be fused with (allocated as part of) the first object. A special case of object fusion is *tiling* in which recursive data structures consisting of unaliased objects can be blocked along dimensions and treated as a unit. Operations on the resultant object are scheduled as a single computation grain.

Such data transformations not only increase the execution grain size, they also increase the effectiveness of traditional optimizations such as instruction scheduling and register allocation which are more effective on the resulting larger schedulable units of instructions.

2.3 Overview of the Paper

The general mechanism of the reference graph based approach to structure analysis follows a standard dataflow analysis framework consisting of an abstract store as the lattice, abstract interpretation as transfer functions, and a safe merge as the meet operator. The approach combines an approximation[5] of the runtime store with an approximation of the effect of the program.

In this paper, we describe an extension of the generic reference graph (called the Abstract Storage Graph) which can model multiply-linked infinite structures precisely in a finite representation. Our structure analysis algorithm interprets the effects of the program on the abstract store while preserving the information which it contains. The algorithm deconstructs the finite representation to reveal portions of the infinite structure enabling precise updates.

In Section 3, we discuss the Abstract Storage Graph (ASG). Section 4 describes the construction of the ASG through abstract interpretation of program statements. Section 5 presents the finite summarization and iteration mechanisms. The safety and complexity of the intraprocedural algorithm are discussed in Sections 6 and 7. Finally, we conclude with current status and future work in Sections 8 and 9.

3 Abstract Storage Graphs

A store representation finitely approximates the reference pattern of a program at an execution point. It must safely approximate the pattern so that transformations which use the reference information will preserve program semantics. In this section, we describe our store representation, the Abstract Storage Graph (ASG).

3.1 Definition

A generic reference graph is a store representation containing nodes which model dynamic program structures, and edges which model references. In order to

---

[5] In this paper *approximation* should be taken to mean *safe approximation* in the sense of describing or creating at least as many aliases as that which it approximates.

produce a precise approximation, the reference graph must preserve as much deterministic reference information as possible. Determinism in the graph refers to the knowledge that a particular reference *does* exist as opposed to *may* exist.

The ASG is a variant of the generic reference graph with the following extensions which enable it to preserve deterministic reference information:

- **single nodes** and **summary nodes** refine generic storage nodes.
- **deterministic references** and **nondeterministic references** refine generic references.
- **choice nodes** encode unique alternatives between references.
- **identity paths** are used to annotate summary nodes preserving their internal structure.

The nodes of the ASG are *variables*, *single nodes*, *summary nodes* and *choice nodes*. The edges represent different types of references between nodes and include *deterministic* (d-references) and *non-deterministic* (n-references) references[6]. The different components of the ASG are described below (Figure 1 shows the symbols used in the rest of the paper).

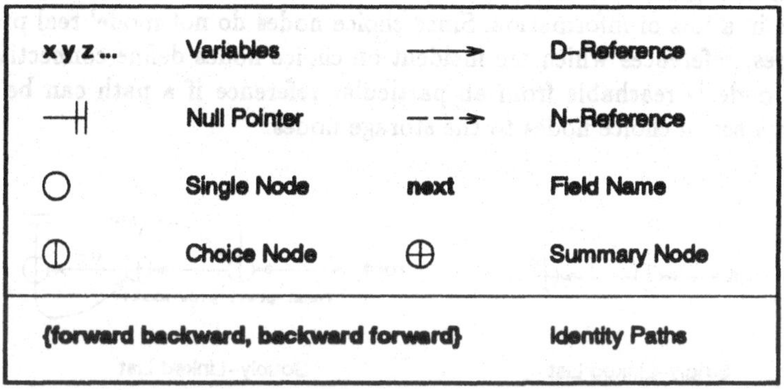

x y z ...	Variables	⟶	D–Reference
⊣⊦	Null Pointer	– – ⤏	N–Reference
◯	Single Node	next	Field Name
⦶	Choice Node	⊕	Summary Node
{forward backward, backward forward}			Identity Paths

Fig. 1. Abstract Storage Graph Elements

References can have two orthogonal attributes. All references incident on storage nodes have an attribute indicating whether or not they are deterministic, and all references leaving storage nodes have a field name attribute. Deterministic references indicate that a reference emanating from exactly one node enters exactly one instance of the target node[7]. Nondeterministic references indicate that a node may be referenced zero or more times. N-references arise from control flow confluence, summarization and other sources of imprecision. They correspond to the traditional definition of a reference in a generic reference graph where nodes represent multiple pieces of storage.

---

[6] One restriction is that variables may not be the target of references.

[7] Contingent on the existence of both the source and destination nodes

The nodes of a generic reference graph (here called **storage nodes**) are refined into summary nodes and single nodes which correspond to single pieces of storage. A single node of a particular type can have only one field reference for each field in its type, and this reference refers to only one node (choice or storage). Summary nodes correspond to an indeterminate number of pieces of storage of the same type. Summary nodes arise when storage nodes are combined, and may be deconstructed (uncombined) while preserving deterministic reference information. A d-reference to a summary node indicates that each summarized node is referenced exactly once along that arc.

Choice nodes describe a set of disjoint possibilities and along with identity paths are used to avoid unnecessary introduction of non-determinism into the ASG. Choice nodes are introduced during the combining phase of the algorithm, preserving the two sets of disjoint alternatives represented by the nodes being combined. For instance, if two nodes each of which have a single deterministic reference are combined, a choice node is inserted between the two incoming references and the combined node. The choice node preserves the information that the combined node can have only a single incoming deterministic reference; thus, the two references which come into the choice node are unaliased. Note that converting the two references into a non-deterministic reference would have resulted in a loss of information. Since choice nodes do not model real program structures, references which are incident on choice nodes define connectivity. A storage node is reachable from an particular reference if a path can be found through a set of choice nodes to the storage nodes.

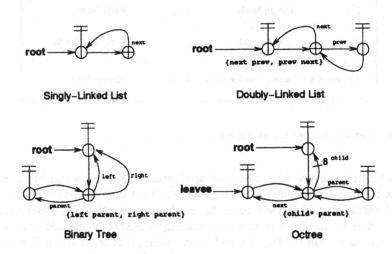

Fig. 2. ASG Examples

Identity paths are pairs of labels which describe cycles in the reference graph. Identity paths preserve the internal structure of summary nodes enabling storage nodes to be summarized and deconstructed while preserving d-references between them. This allows, a precise, finite representation of some infinite data structures. For instance, in a doubly-linked list, the identity path (**next prev**) describes the relationship that the previous node of any next node is the node itself. Reversing labels in an identity path does not always produce a valid identity path. For example, in a binary tree, (**left parent, right parent**) is a valid identity path, but (**parent left**) is not (see Figure 2. Section 5.2 shows how identity paths can be used to extract a list of storage nodes from a single summary node without introducing non-determinism.

3.2 Examples

ASGs can model many common recursive data structures precisely in a small amount of space. Some examples of different structures and how they are modeled using an ASG are shown in in Figure 2. A singly-linked list is modeled with a choice node and a summary node. The key piece of information is that each node has only one incoming reference (a reference count of one); this describes the structure as acyclic. For a doubly-linked list the ASG consists of two choice nodes and a summary node annotated with the identity paths (**next prev, prev next**). The key information is that (*i*) the reference from *root* shares the d-reference incident on the summary node with the summary node's own **next** reference. This means that the one of the summarized nodes is pointed to directly by *root*, and the list which follows is unaliased along **next**. And (*ii*) the identity paths preserve the information that the references in the **next** and **prev** fields are inverses of each other. As a result, we can conclude that the graph accessible from *root* is indeed that of a doubly-linked list.

4 Building ASGs

Structure analysis begins with an initial store, built from initial values of program variables (global and static data declarations). The program is then interpreted against this store, statement by statement. For our purposes, the program consists of storage allocation, assignment, conditional and loop statements. Assignments are to and from a variable or a field of an object referenced from a variable. The program is considered to be in Static Single Assignment form [CFR+91].

4.1 Driver

The overall structure of the analysis algorithm follows that of conventional iterative dataflow analysis. The solution at every program point is related to the solution at other points. Program points are program statements and the relations are defined on control flow arcs. The driver procedure appears in Figure 3.

```
COMPUTE-PROCEDURE-ASG(procedure)
  work.Enqueue(procedure.entry)
  while work.Not-Empty() do
    s ← work.Dequeue()
    s.COMPUTE-STATEMENT-ASG()
    if (s.outASG ≠ s.old-outASG)
      work.Enqueue(s.Successors())
    end if
  end while
end
```

Fig. 3. Driver Function

Each statement affects the ASG as shown in Figure 4 and described below. Most of the functions in italics have the obvious definitions. The others are described with the code.

4.2 Allocation

When a new node is allocated and assigned to a variable, a new single node of the appropriate type is created, and the variable is set to d-reference that node.

4.3 Assignment

In order to analyze programs which manipulate structures (as opposed to simply building them), we must remove as many references as we create. This follows from the observation that the graph before the manipulation must match the resulting graph. We therefore differentiate between two types of updates — *strong* and *weak*. When one reference replaces another it is called a *strong* update [CWZ90] and corresponds to the killing rules of standard dataflow techniques. Strong updates can only occur when a location is definitely updated. When a location may or may not be changed this results in a *weak* update. Not only is the new reference nondeterministic, but any existing references must be weakened (made nondeterministic) as well.

Manipulating summary nodes directly results in weak updates introducing nondeterminism into the graph. We present a technique called *deconstruction* in Section 5.2 which separates out a single node from a summary node making strong updates possible. With this facility, we discuss the steps to interpret a general assignment of and through a field $(a \rightarrow b = c \rightarrow d)$.

First, any summary nodes pointed to by a, c and $c \rightarrow d$ are deconstructed. This step is not necessary to preserve a safe approximation, but it improves precision by enabling strong updates of nodes which have been summarized. Deconstructing the nodes in which the update will occur allows single locations to be updated and deconstructing the right hand side make it possible to assign a pointer to a particular node.

Second, for each node on the left hand side (pointed to by a) we decide if we can make a strong update. If the node is reached from a by only d-references

```
allocation::COMPUTE-STATEMENT-ASG()
  n ← new-single-node(struct-type(rhs))
  outASG.make-ref(d-ref,lhs,n)
end

cfg-diverge::COMPUTE-STATEMENT-ASG()
  outASG-1 ← inASG
  outASG-2 ← inASG
end

cfg-converge::COMPUTE-STATEMENT-ASG()
  s-vars ← inASG-1.vars()∩inASG-2.vars()
  ∀v ∈ s-vars
    c ← new-choice-node()
    outASG.make-ref(ref,v,c)
    outASG.make-ref(inASG-1.ref-type(v),c,
            inASG-1.dest(v))
    outASG.make-ref(inASG-2.ref-type(v),c,
            inASG-2.dest(v))
  outASG.COMPRESS()
end
```

```
assignment::COMPUTE-STATEMENT-ASG()
  lvals ← reachable-along(lhs)
  rvals ← reachable-from(rhs)
  ∀v ∈ node(lvals),type(v) = summary,
      type(ref-from-to(lhs,v)) = d-ref
    inASG.DECONSTRUCT(lhs,v)
  ∀v ∈ rvals,type(v) = summary,
      type(ref-from-to(rhs,v)) = d-ref
    inASG.DECONSTRUCT(rhs,v)
  ∀r ∈ lvals
    c ← new-choice-node()
    if (type(node(r)) ≠ summary and
        ∀v ∈ refs(lhs,node(r)),type(v) = d-ref)
      ∀m ∈ rvals
        outASG.strong-update(c,m,rhs)
    else
      ∀k reachable from node(r) along r
        outASG.make-ref(n-ref,c,k)
      ∀m ∈ rvals
        outASG.make-ref(n-ref,c,m)
    end if
    outASG.make-label-ref(label(r),ref,node(r),c)
  end
```

reachable-along Given an access path a → b, the locations labeled b in the nodes which are pointed to by a.
reachable-from Given an access path a → b, the nodes which are pointed to with label b from all nodes pointed to by a.
node Given a location, return the node which contains it.
type For nodes, return single or summary. For references, return d-ref or n-ref.
refs Given an access path and a node, returns all the incoming references along the path to the node.
strong-update Given a location to update, a node and its access path, if the node is a single node and all references along the access path to the node are d-references then make a d-reference from the location to the node, otherwise make an n-reference.

Fig. 4. Basic Functions

then, if the node exists, a definitely points to it. If that node is also a single node, then we have a single location to update and can do a strong update, otherwise we do a weak update. The pseudocode for assignment appears on the right side of Figure 4.

4.4 Conditionals and Loops

The effect of the conditional can be safely approximated by applying the effects of each branch separately, and then taking a safe merger of the results. This is accomplished by starting each branch of the conditional with the ASG at the conditional.

At any point where control flow converges, for instance at the back-edge of a loop, a merge is taken (see Section 4.5). Loops are automatically handled by the worklist approach where transfer functions for statement successors are evaluated if the incoming ASG changes. However, for the data flow algorithm to terminate the fixed-point of the iteration must be detected.

Detection of the fixed point requires a node labeling which allows nodes in different ASGs to be matched. The nodes are labeled on the basis of their creation points as represented by (i) the program statement which caused their creation, and (ii) a timestamp based on the flow of ASGs through the program (the order in which program statements are required to be evaluated). When two summary nodes are combined, a total order over creation points determines the label of the resulting node. Nodes match when they either have identical labels, or the same label relative to the current timestamp. The fixed-point is detected if all the edges match for the matched nodes. Since matching is deterministic, the size of the graph is bounded and the references increase monotonically, all nodes will be matched at the fixed point.

4.5 A Safe Merge

At points of control confluence, such as the exits of loops or the point below a conditional, the ASGs from each path must be combined. Merging combines two ASGs, producing a safe approximation to the reference patterns of both. Any number of paths may merge at a program point, but such cases can be handled as a sequence of pairwise merges.

A safe merge is achieved by inserting choice nodes in front of each program variable pointing to the alternatives from each graph. Such a merge is safe because each variable points to everything it pointed to in either graph. The result, however, is large since it includes all the nodes of both graphs. Consequently, while merging ASGs is logically the result of compressing the result of the safe merge above, a more efficient mechanism should be used in practice. In Figure 4, a safe merge occurs in the function cfg-converge::COMPUTE-STATEMENT-ASG.

5 Bounding the Size of ASGs

While the preceding description yields an algorithm which is safe, it is not efficient. Since we have presented no mechanism for summarization, the ASG will continue to expand (in most programs) forever. In order to prevent this, the ASG at a program point is compressed to a size proportional to the number of program variables. This is done by combining storage nodes into summary nodes. Unfortunately, summarization can result in the loss of critical information. ASGs provide two additional mechanisms for dealing with this problem:

- **Identity paths** to preserve the internal structure of summary nodes.
- **Deconstruction** to enable the extraction of a single node from a summary node.

The pseudocode for these functions is given in Figure 5 with the subfunctions.

5.1 Identity Paths

Identity paths are pairs of labels which define circular relationships following d-references between pairs of storage nodes. They preserve the reference pattern internal to summary nodes. This information is used during deconstruction to retrieve the infinite structure of the data structure. If this information were not stored, self references would always imply a potential cycle.

Identity paths are initially created and attached to single nodes where the circular relationship is explicit in the d-references. They are preserved when storage nodes are combined, resulting in a summary node which inherits the intersection of the identity paths *compatible* with both its constituents. An identity path (a b) is compatible if it either holds for the node or if the outgoing reference labeled a is NIL.

After adding or deleting a reference, storage nodes may fall into or out of identity relationships. The pseudocode for updating identity paths appears in Figure 5. Identity paths are determined locally by examining the nodes which are either sources or targets of the changed reference. All identity paths which are effected by the change are checked for validity (using function CHECK-VALIDITY), and if the nodes are both single nodes, any new valid identity paths are created.

An identity path (a b) is valid for a storage node if all nodes reachable along the reference a are d-referenced, and the node itself is d-referenced with label b starting from these nodes. If the node in question is a summary node, we assume that the current identity paths attached to the summary node are valid. This assumption is safe since the only d-references incident on summary nodes were created between single nodes.

5.2 Deconstruction

To preserve as much information as possible, variables used in updates must refer to storage nodes not summary nodes. As necessary, summary nodes are *deconstructed* into a storage node and a summary node, isolating the node to be assigned to or from. An example of deconstruction is shown in Figure 6.

Deconstruction is done on all summary nodes which are d-referenced from a location. A new storage node is created with all the references of the summary node, except those that can be eliminated by exploiting disjunction information or by considering identity paths. In addition, since the new single node is defined to be the one which is reached along the d-reference, other references which refer to the new node along the d-reference are removed. The pseudocode for deconstruction appears in Figure 5.

Consider the graphs in Figure 6. We have eliminated the f reference to the new storage node because the reference from x and an f reference are disjoint alternatives. Identity paths also constrain the new node's references. In the example, the b reference for the new storage node must be NIL since the identity path would require it to point to the source of an f reference which does not exist. Lastly, the NIL reference from the b field of the summary node is also removed since some incoming d-reference must have been generated only by an

48

```
DECONSTRUCT(src, n)                          UPDATE-IDENTITY-PATHS(r)
  m ← new-single-node(struct-type(n))          ∀n ∈ back-reachable-from(r)
  ∀r ∈ in-refs(n)                                ∀p ∈ id-paths(n),∃s ∈ out-refs-to(n,r),
    make-ref(type(r),src(r),m)                      p.out-label = label(s)
  ∀r ∈ out-refs(n)                               if (CHECK-VALIDITY(n,p) = FALSE)
    make-ref(type(r),m,dest(r))                     remove-path(n,p)
  ∀s ∈ locations(src)                          ∀n ∈ reachable-from(r)
    c ← new-choice-node()                        ∀p ∈ id-paths(n),∃s ∈ in-refs-from(n,r),
    make-ref(ref,s,c)                               p.in-label = label(s)
    ∀x ∈ reachable-from(s), x ≠ n                 if (CHECK-VALIDITY(n,p) = FALSE)
      make-ref(type(ref-from-to(s,x)),c,x)          remove-path(n,p)
    end for                                    ∀n ∈ back-reachable-from(r)
  end for                                        ∀m ∈ reachable-from(r)
  ∀k ∈ {n,m}                                     ∀p ∈ paths(label(out-refs-to(n,r)),
    ∀p ∈ id-paths(k),p = a.b                                 label(out-refs(m)))
      if (∀s ∈ reachable-from-label(k,a),         if (CHECK-VALIDITY(n,p) = TRUE)
          k ∉ reachable-from-label(s,b)             add-path(n,p)
        remove-ref(ref-along(k,a))               ∀p ∈ paths(label(out-refs(n)),
      end if                                                label(out-refs-to(m,r)))
end                                              if (CHECK-VALIDITY(n,p) = TRUE)
                                                   add-path(n,p)
CHECK-VALIDITY(n,p)                          end
  if ∀m ∈ reachable-from-label(n,p.out-label)
    (type(ref-along-label(n,m,p.out-label))
      = d-ref and
    type(m) = single or p⁻¹ ∈ id-paths(m)
      and
    type(ref-along-label(m,n,p.in-label))
      = d-ref and
    type(n) = single or p ∈ id-paths(n))
    return TRUE
  else
    return FALSE
end
```

ref-along-label Given two nodes and a label, return *d-ref* if all the references from the first node with the label to the second node are d-references, otherwise if a reference exists return *n-ref* otherwise return *no-ref*.

ref-from-to Given a location and a target node, returns the *ref-along-label* of the node of the location, target node, and the label of the location.

ref-along Given a node and a label, return the reference from the node along the label.

locations Given an access path, return all the locations which store the terminal reference.

Fig. 5. Identity Path and Deconstruction Functions

f field reference. Figure 9, Step 4 shows how the deconstructed storage nodes form a doubly-linked list as required by the identity path.

5.3 Compression

Approximating the store in finite space and detecting termination requires an upper bound on the size of the ASG along with a deterministic compression function. The compression function is composed of the following subroutines:

1. Remove redundant choice nodes, references and storage nodes.
2. Select storage nodes to be combined.
3. Combine storage nodes.

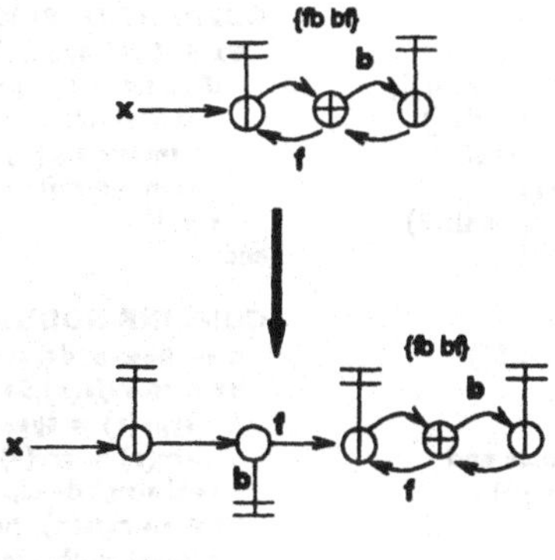

Fig. 6. Deconstruction

The pseudocode for the compress function appears in Figure 7 with the subfunctions.

Redundancies Redundancies in the ASG arise from merge points. An edge is redundant if removing it does not change the alias pattern between variables. Any two edges from a choice node to a storage node (one of which must be an n-reference by definition) can be combined into a single n-reference since the reference pattern through the choice node to the storage node is already nondeterministic.

Choice nodes are redundant when merging them would not change the ASG's connectivity. Connectivity must be determined independently for the d- and n-references emanating from a group of choice nodes. Any pair of choice nodes which reach the same outputs may be merged without changing the connectivity. Connectivity is determined by a transitive closure algorithm followed by pairwise comparison of directly connected nodes.

A storage node is redundant if combining it with a summary node does not change the connectivity of the summarized nodes (deconstruction would result in recovery of the original graph).

For example, in Figure 8, Step 6, the storage node to the far right is redundant, and combining it with the summary node in the center results in the addition of a reference to NIL to the choice node referenced by the f field in Step 8. In Step 7, a set of choice nodes are all connected to the summary node and the storage node pointed to by x, so they are merged. In Step 9, the last storage node with a compatible identity path is combined because no variable directly references the storage node. The resulting graph matches that for the doubly-linked list in Figure 2.

Combine Criteria The combine criteria determines which nodes to combine such that the size of the ASG is within a constant factor of the number of program variables and as much deterministic reference information is preserved

```
COMPRESS()
  pair-nodes-by-combine-criteria()
  while (|ASG.nodes()| > c*|ASG.vars()|)
    REMOVE-REDUNDANT-NODES()
    COMBINE-DUPLICATE-EDGES()
    n-pair ← remove-first-pair()
    COMBINE-NODES(n-pair.1,n-pair.2)
  end while
end


REMOVE-REDUNDANT-NODES()
  compute-connectivity()
  ∀x,y ∈ ASG.nodes()
    if (type(x) = type(y) = choice and
        connects(x) = connects(y))
      fuse(x,y)
    end if
    if (type(x) = type(y) = storage and
        struct-type(x) = struct-type(y) and
        connects(x)/y = connects(y)/x)
      fuse(x,y)
    end if
end
```

```
COMBINE-DUPLICATE-EDGES()
  ∀x ∈ ASG.nodes(),type(x) = choice
    if (∃u,v ∈ x.edges(),dest(u) = dest(v))
      make-ref(n-ref,x,dest(u))
      remove-ref(u)
      remove-ref(v)
    end if
end


COMBINE-NODES(x,y)
  n ← new-node(comb-type(x,y),struct-type(x))
  ∀r ∈ in-refs(x),∃s ∈ in-refs(y),
      type(r) = type(s) = d-ref and
      src(r) = src(s)
    make-ref(d-ref,src(s),n)
  ∀r ∈ in-refs(x),choose unadded s ∈ in-refs(y)
    c ← new-choice-node()
    make-ref(ref,src(s),c)
    make-ref(ref,src(r),c)
    make-ref(d-ref,c,n)
  ∀r ∈ in-refs(x) ∪ in-refs(y),
      r has not been added yet
    make-ref(n-ref,src(r),n)
  ∀r ∈ out-refs(x)
    c ← new-choice-node()
    make-label-ref(label(r),ref,src(r),c)
    make-ref(type(r),c,dest(r))
    s ← ref-along(y,label(r))
    make-ref(type(s),c,dest(s))
  id-paths(n) = valid-path-union(x,y)
end
```

pair-nodes-by-combine-criteria This is defined as part of the **Combine** operation later in this section.

compute-connectivity Compute for each choice node, the set of incoming references which are reachable from the choice node. This is a transitive closure calculation.

connects Given a choice node, the set of incoming references reachable from that choice node.

in-refs Given a node, all the incoming references.

out-refs Given a node, all the outgoing references.

valid-path-union Given two nodes, all the identity paths attached to either of them that are valid for both of them.

fuse Given two nodes with identical connectivity and identity paths, combine them into a summary node.

comb-type Given two nodes, returns *single* if the two nodes can be combined into a single node, otherwise returns *summary*.

Fig. 7. Compression Functions

as possible. The following heuristics are used to identify nodes to be combined and are used to implement the subfunction *pair-nodes-by-combine-criteria*.

1. *Similar Nodes*: two nodes which were the same node before a control flow divergence and are now in the graph being compressed.
2. *Directly-referenced Nodes*: two nodes which are d-referenced from the same variable.
3. *Distant Nodes*: nodes which are "farthest" from variables using the number of intermediate storage nodes as a measure of distance.

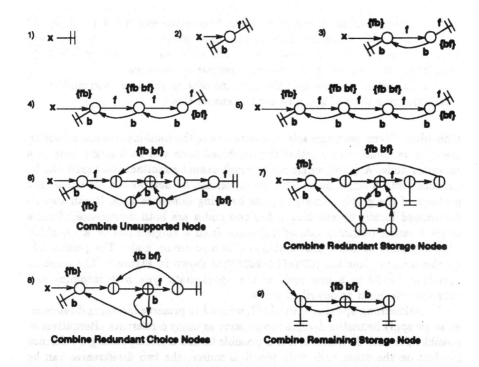

Fig. 8. Doubly-linked List Loop ASG

The first heuristic pairs up natural combinations, such as nodes which have not changed. This can be accomplished logically as follows: starting from the set of variables which are not listed in the ϕ-functions at the merge point [CWZ90] (those that were not assigned in the region of the program for which the merge point is on the post-dominator front), select all nodes referenced only by these variables whose outgoing references have not changed. Applying this criteria recursively will result in the combining of untouched portions of the graph. In practice, storing the graph as edge difference lists attached to variables and nodes allows the untouched portion of the graph to be determined quickly.

The second heuristic chooses to pair nodes which have similar reference patterns. The rationale for this is that fewer n-references are created as a result of combining two such nodes.

The third heuristic chooses nodes which are distant from variables since updates occur in the vicinity of variables. Such nodes are less likely to contain information which will be needed by the algorithm in succeeding steps; consequently, these nodes can be summarized. One way of identifying such nodes is by distributing a unit weight among nodes within a neighborhood of all variables, such that distant storage nodes get a lower weight.

Nodes selected through the latter two heuristics are matched with a node of the same type selected through a limited breath first search since neighboring nodes are likely to share reference patterns. Should the search fail, the node will be combined with a random node of the same type, but it will be combined after all those for whom the search succeeded since, as was noted in [CWZ90], combining two unrelated nodes will not decrease space usage.

It is important to note that the combine criteria must be deterministic. A total order over the nodes can be used to ensure this.

Combine Given two nodes selected according to the combine criteria, a decision needs to be made as to whether the combined node will be a single node or a summary node. Any two single nodes which cannot simultaneously exist can be combined into a single node. This condition can be determined for unchanged portions of the graph at merge points by using difference lists. It can also be determined locally by checking if the two nodes are both d-referenced from a single location (either a labeled reference from a single node or a variable). All other pairs of nodes are combined into a summary node. The pseudocode for the combine function (COMBINE-NODES) is shown in Figure 7. The combine operation results in a new node of the appropriate type with incoming and outgoing references as described below.

To make strong updates to the ASG, we need to preserve incoming d-references, so we apply heuristics designed to preserve as many d-reference alternatives as possible. For each d-reference, if it is possible to find a corresponding d-reference incident on the other node with identical source, the two d-references can be combined into one. If it is not possible to find a corresponding d-reference with identical source, the d-reference is paired heuristically with a d-reference incident on the other node giving priority to references originating at variables, and to references sharing the same field name. For each pair of d-references a choice node is created to join the d-references from the two sources into one d-reference. All other incoming references become n-references. For outgoing references choice nodes are simply inserted which point to the two alternatives for the different nodes. These heuristics attempt to prevent the introduction of n-references since their introduction results in a loss of deterministic reference information.

In Figure 8, Steps 5 and 6 show the combination of two nodes in a doubly-linked list. First, the two central nodes in Step 5 are selected for combining since they are (*i*) not pointed to directly by a variable and (*ii*) have the same number of incoming d-references. Then new choice nodes are inserted with edges attached according to the rules above (see Step 6).

6 Safety

The ASG's approximation of the structure of the program store is contingent on the safety of the initial approximation and the safety of the functions which manipulate it. The abstract interpretation of program statements and the safe merge have been shown to be safe in their respective sections.

The identity path operations are safe since (*i*) identity paths are only created when the identity relation is explicit in the graph and (*ii*) combining of nodes

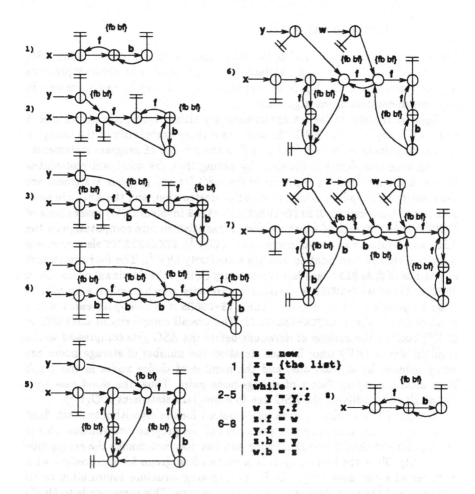

Fig. 9. Insertion in a Doubly-linked List

results in the combined node getting identity paths which are compatible with both the constituent nodes.

Compress is safe since the resulting nodes have at least the connectivity of the constituent nodes and at least as many potentially incoming edges from any source. It follows that the resulting graph has at least the connectivity of the source graph.

Deconstruction is safe since the newly created node has the same connectivity as the parent summary node which is logically an infinite set of single nodes of like connectivity. The references which are removed are the result of the definition of the deconstructed node as the node which is reached along the incoming d-reference. Since such a node must exist, and since the identity path operations are safe, removing these edges is safe as well.

7 Complexity Analysis

The analysis below assumes that the maximum number of nodes in the ASG is bounded from above by a constant times the number of distinct program objects (variables, etc.) (V). Note that this condition can be easily ensured in any implementation of the algorithm.

Since at the end of the intraprocedural algorithm, each program statement stores $O(1)$ copies of the ASG, the worst-case space complexity of the intraprocedural algorithm is $O(S * V^2)$, where S is the number of program statements.

The time complexity is obtained by noting that the dominant cost-contributors in the construction (update) of the ASG for any program statement are the identity-path update, summary-node deconstruction, and the ASG compression steps. Each call to UPDATE-IDENTITY-PATHS involves $O(V)$ invocations of CHECK-VALIDITY, each of which requires a transitive-closure computation on the ASG, and results in an overall complexity of $O(V^4)$. DECONSTRUCT also requires a transitive-closure computation and has complexity $O(V^3)$. The four constituent operations of COMPRESS each have complexity $O(V^3)$: the dominant operation in REMOVE-REDUNDANT-NODES is *compute-connectivity* which involves a transitive-closure operation, while in case of COMBINE-NODES it is *valid-path-union* which requires $O(1)$ calls to CHECK-VALIDITY. The overall complexity of COMPRESS is $O(V^4)$ because the number of iterations before the ASG gets compressed to the required size is $O(V)$ since in each iteration the number of storage nodes are being reduced by at least one, and the number of choice nodes in the graph is at most a constant factor of storage-node pairs. Thus, the worst-case time complexity of modifying the ASG due to a program statement is $O(V^4)$.

To bound the number of iterations required for the algorithm to reach fixed point, we consider a round-robin evaluation of the program statements. This is more inefficient than the worklist approach but does not change the asymptotic complexity. Since the longest cycle in a control-flow graph for a procedure with S statements can have length $O(S)$, propagating structure information to all statements of the procedure requires $O(S)$ iterations. This corresponds to $O(S^2)$ statement evaluations; consequently, the overall complexity of the iterative algorithm is $O(S^2 V^4)$. This is a pessimistic measure of the algorithm complexity; in practice, we expect the asymptotic complexity to be considerably less since the improved precision of the algorithm should result in sparse connectivity.

8 Current Status

We are implementing this algorithm as part of the *Concert* compiler. The resulting information will be used to enable transformations of runtime data structures such as fusion, clustering and tiling as well as a host of other traditional and novel optimizations. Structure analysis is so critical to attaining efficient use of distributed memory parallel machines that we believe the cost of such analysis is justified. Uninformed compilation of such languages can result in programs which are several orders of magnitude slower than corresponding fast serial implementations.

The *Concert* system includes a compiler for an extended version of Concurrent Aggregates [CD90] and a runtime which exposes the cost hierarchy among the basic operations required for fine grained reactive computation [KC93].

9 Summary and Future Work

Efficient execution of irregular computations containing dynamic structures on parallel architectures requires that the compiler know the shape of the runtime store. The ease of general purpose parallel programming depends on future compilers being able to determine this information without programmer assistance. We present an algorithm for determining structure information.

We have described a new structure graph, the ASG, which can model multiply-linked infinite structures in a finite representation without loss of information. We have also described an algorithm for computing the ASG which can analyze programs with such structures, even in the presence of mutation. The key to this analysis is to preserve deterministic reference information. This is accomplished through the novel features of the ASG — deterministic references, choice nodes and identity paths, and the novel features of the algorithm including deconstruction of summarized nodes.

Successful structure analysis results when the functions which manipulate the real data structures can be be shown to preserve the ASG which models the data structures. The key issues are:

1. The ability to precisely model recursive structures in finite space.
2. The ability to *deconstruct* the finite model revealing part of the infinite structure.
3. The ability to make strong updates to the revealed portion.

While we are pursuing a much needed implementation and empirical verification of the algorithm, manual application on small examples has encouraged us to believe that our algorithm meets these criteria. In Figure 9, we show the analysis of a code segment which inserts a node into a doubly linked list. A variable y traverses the list starting in step 2. Values of the graph within the loop are given in steps 3 and 4 with the fixed point being reached in 5. In steps 6 and 7, strong updates are done to the graph to insert the new node. The temporary variables fall out of scope, and the graph is compressed in step 8, resulting in the same graph that we started with.

In the future, we plan to enhance the algorithm for incremental flow-sensitive analysis by storing information about distinct call paths and their entry ASGs. If the ASGs entering a procedure are sufficiently distinct, the path through the procedure can be split incrementally resulting in flow-sensitive analysis.

References

[ASU87] A. V. Aho, R. Sethi, and J. D. Ullman. *Compilers: Principles, Techniques and Tools*. Computer Science. Addison-Wesley, Reading, Massachusetts, 1987.

[CBC93] Jong-Deok Choi, Michael Burke, and Paul Carini. Efficient flow-sensative interprocedural computation of pointer-induced aliases and side effects. In *Twentieth Symposium on Principles of Programming Languages*, pages 232–245. ACM SIGPLAN, 1993.

[CD90] A. A. Chien and W. J. Dally. Concurrent Aggregates (CA). In *Proceedings of Second Symposium on Principles and Practice of Parallel Programming.* ACM, March 1990.

[CFKP92] A. A. Chien, W. Feng, V. Karamcheti, and J. Plevyak. Techniques for efficient execution of fine-grained concurrent programs. In *Proceedings of the Fifth Workshop on Compilers and Languages for Parallel Computing*, pages 103–13, New Haven, Connecticut, 1992. YALEU/DCS/RR-915, Springer-Verlag Lecture Notes in Computer Science, 1993.

[CFR+91] R. Cytron, J. Ferrante, B. Rosen, M. Wegman, and F. Zadeck. An efficient method of computing static single assignment form and the control dependence graph. *ACM Transactions on Programming Languages and Systems*, 13(4):451–490, October 1991.

[CKP93] Andrew Chien, Vijay Karamcheti, and John Plevyak. The concert system – compiler and runtime support for efficient fine-grained concurrent object-oriented programs. Technical Report UIUCDCS-R-93-1815, Department of Computer Science, University of Illinois, Urbana, Illinois, June 1993.

[CWZ90] D. Chase, M. Wegman, and F. Zadeck. Analysis of pointers and structures. In *Proceedings of SIGPLAN Conference on Programming Language Design and Implementation*, pages 296–310, June 1990.

[HN90] L. Hendren and A. Nicolau. Parallelizing programs with recursive data structures. *IEEE Transactions on Parallel and Distributed Systems*, 1(1):35–47, January 1990.

[HNH92] L. Hendren, A. Nicolau, and J. Hummel. Abstractions for recursive pointer data structures: Improving the analysis and transformation of imperative programs. In *Proceedings of the SIGPLAN Conference on Programming Language Design and Implementation*, pages 249–260. ACM SIGPLAN, ACM Press, June 1992.

[HPR89] S. Horwitz, P. Pfeiffer, and T. Reps. Dependence analysis for pointer variables. In *Proceedings of the SIGPLAN Conference on Programming Language Design and Implementation*, pages 28–40. ACM SIGPLAN, ACM Press, 1989.

[JM81] N. Jones and S. Muchnick. Flow analysis and optimization of lisp-like structures. In S. Muchnick and N. Jones, editors, *Program Flow Analysis: Theory and Applications*, pages 102–131. Prentice-Hall, 1981.

[KC93] Vijay Karamcheti and Andrew Chien. Concert – efficient runtime support for concurrent object-oriented programming languages on stock hardware. In *Proceedings of Supercomputing'93*, 1993.

[Lar89] James Richard Larus. Restructuring symbolic programs for concurrent execution on multiprocessors. Technical Report UCB/CSD 89/502, University of California at Berkeley, 1989.

[LH88] J. R. Larus and P. N. Hilfinger. Detecting conflicts between structure accesses. In *SIGPLAN Conference on Programming Language Design and Implementation*, pages 21–33. ACM, June 1988.

[Mye81] E. Myers. A precise interprocedural data flow algorithm. In *Eighth Symposium on Principles of Programming Languages*, pages 219–30, 1981.

On Automatic Data Structure Selection and Code Generation for Sparse Computations*

Aart J.C. Bik and Harry A.G. Wijshoff

High Performance Computing Division, Department of Computer Science, Leiden University

P.O. Box 9512, 2300 RA Leiden, the Netherlands

ajcbik@cs.leidenuniv.nl and harryw@cs.leidenuniv.nl

Abstract

Traditionally restructuring compilers were only able to apply program transformations in order to exploit certain characteristics of the target architecture. Adaptation of data structures was limited to e.g. linearization or transposing of arrays. However, as more complex data structures are required to exploit *characteristics of the data* operated on, current compiler support appears to be inappropriate. In this paper we present the implementation issues of a restructuring compiler that automatically converts programs operating on dense matrices into sparse code, i.e. after a suited data structure has been selected for every dense matrix that in fact is sparse, the original code is adapted to operate on these data structures. This simplifies the task of the programmer and, in general, enables the compiler to apply more optimizations.

Index Terms: Restructuring Compilers, Sparse Computations, Sparse Matrices.

1 Introduction

Development and maintenance of sparse codes is a complex task. The user has to deal with complicated data structures to exploit sparsity of matrices with respect to *storage requirements* and *computational time.* Additionally, the application of conventional transformations to sparse programs becomes more complex because the functionality of the

---

*Support was provided by the Foundation for Computer Science (SION) of the Netherlands Organization for the Advancement of Pure Research (NWO) and the EC Esprit Agency DG XIII under Grant No. APPARC 6634 BRA III. This paper is an extended abstract of technical report 93-04 [9].

code is obscured. Therefore, in [7, 8] we have examined if it is possible to let the compiler handle sparsity, i.e. the program is written in a dense format, while the compiler performs program and data structure transformations to deal with the fact that some of the matrices operated on are sparse. We have proposed a data structure selection and transformation method that enables the compiler to select appropriate data structures. Since run-time behavior of sparse codes is heavily dependent on the input data, efficient code is only achieved if certain peculiarities of sparse matrices are accounted for in this selection.

In this paper we generalize this method and present implementation issues. In section 2, a brief description of the data structure selection and transformation method is given, in combination with the notation used throughout this paper. Since reduction of sparse overhead is only obtained if certain constraints on the data structure are satisfied, we present a mechanism to select a data structure according to these constraints in section 3. In section 4, the generation of code is discussed, illustrated with examples in section 5. Finally, we state issues for future research.

2 Background

Exploitation of sparsity requires identification of statements of which some instances are nullified, and selection of an appropriate *compact* data structure.

2.1 Sparsity Exploitation

A **sparse matrix** A is defined by its nonzero structure: $Nonz_A = \{(i,j) \in I_A \times J_A | a_{ij} \neq 0\}$, where $I_A = \{1,..,m\}$ and $J_A = \{1,..,n\}$

determine the **index set** $I_A \times J_A$ of the enveloping dense matrix. Reduction of *storage requirements* is achieved by only storing the nonzero elements in **primary storage**, although some storage is necessary to reconstruct the underlying matrix, referred to as **overhead storage**. Elements that are stored explicitly are called **entries**. Set E_A with $Nonz_A \subseteq E_A \subseteq I_A \times J_A$ is used to indicate the indices of all entries. If E_A changes during program execution, a *dynamic* data structure is required to handle the insertion of a new entry (**creation**) and the deletion of an entry that becomes a zero element (**cancellation**), while a *static* data structure might be used otherwise.

Because the original code operates on dense matrices, every occurrence of a sparse matrix A appears as a two-dimensional array in an **indexed statement** S of degree l, where the strides of all surrounding loops have been normalized to 1:

$$\begin{aligned}
&\texttt{DO } \texttt{I}_1 \in V_1 \\
&\quad \cdots \\
&\qquad \texttt{DO } \texttt{I}_l \in V_l \\
&S: \quad \cdots \texttt{A}(f_1(\vec{\texttt{I}}), f_2(\vec{\texttt{I}})) \cdots \\
&\qquad \texttt{ENDDO} \\
&\quad \cdots \\
&\texttt{ENDDO}
\end{aligned}$$

The bounds of **execution set** V_i might depend on indices $\texttt{I}_1, \ldots, \texttt{I}_{i-1}$. Only linear subscript functions with integer coefficients are considered. Consequently, both functions can be represented by a single mapping $F_A : \mathbf{Z}^l \to \mathbf{Z}^2$ of the form $F_A(\vec{\texttt{I}}) = \vec{m}_A + M_A \cdot \vec{\texttt{I}}$:

$$\begin{pmatrix} m_{10} \\ m_{20} \end{pmatrix} + \begin{pmatrix} m_{11} & \cdots & m_{1l} \\ m_{21} & \cdots & m_{2l} \end{pmatrix} \cdot \vec{\texttt{I}}$$

Subscript bounds are not violated, i.e. $F_A(\vec{\texttt{I}}) \in I_A \times J_A$ for all valid $\vec{\texttt{I}}$. A loop at nesting depth i is called **controlling** if $(m_{1i} \neq 0) \vee (m_{2i} \neq 0)$, or **non-controlling** otherwise. The indices of all elements operated on by different **instances** of statement S in one execution of the innermost controlling loop at nesting depth c, i.e. $(m_{1i} = 0) \wedge (m_{2i} = 0)$ for $c < i \leq l$, is referred to as an **access pattern** of the corresponding occurrence of matrix A:

$$P_A^{\texttt{I}_1, \ldots, \texttt{I}_{c-1}} = \{F_A(\vec{\texttt{I}}) | \texttt{I}_c \in V_c\}$$

Access patterns are called **row-wise** if $(m_{1c} = 0) \wedge (m_{2c} \neq 0)$, **column-wise** if $(m_{1c} \neq 0) \wedge (m_{2c} = 0)$, while all remaining access patterns are referred to as **diagonal-wise**.[1] The **direction** of an access pattern is $\vec{d}_A = (m_{1c}, m_{2c})$.

The notion of an **abstract data structure** $\texttt{A}'$ is introduced to reason about a compact data structure as long as no actual implementation has been selected. For an occurrence $\texttt{A}(F_A(\vec{\texttt{I}}))$ a guard '$F_A(\vec{\texttt{I}}) \in E_A$' is used in a multiway IF-statement to differentiate between operations on an entry or a non-entry. Function $\sigma_A : E_A \to AD_A$ maps indices of an entry to its address in $\texttt{A}'$. Consequently, the following notation is used for an assignment of an arbitrary expression to an element, where function new_A returns a new address in $\texttt{A}'$ and adapts σ_A, E_A and AD_A accordingly as side-effect to account for creation:

$$\begin{aligned}
&\texttt{IF } F_A(\vec{\texttt{I}}) \in E_A \texttt{ THEN} \\
&\quad \texttt{A}'[\sigma_A(F_A(\vec{\texttt{I}}))] = \ldots \\
&\texttt{ELSEIF } F_A(\vec{\texttt{I}}) \notin E_A \texttt{ THEN} \\
&\quad \texttt{A}'[new_A(F_A(\vec{\texttt{I}}))] = \ldots \\
&\texttt{ENDIF}
\end{aligned}$$

This kind of notation offers the possibility to eliminate the branches in which sparsity can be exploited to save *computational time*, because statement instances where a zero is assigned to a non-entry or where an arbitrary variable is updated with a zero do not have to be executed. For example, one branch remains for statement '$\texttt{ACC} = \texttt{ACC} + \texttt{A}(F_A(\vec{\texttt{I}}))$':

$$\begin{aligned}
&\texttt{IF } F_A(\vec{\texttt{I}}) \in E_A \texttt{ THEN} \\
&\quad \texttt{ACC} = \texttt{ACC} + \texttt{A}'[\sigma_A(F_A(\vec{\texttt{I}}))] \\
&\texttt{ENDIF}
\end{aligned}$$

The identification of statements that can exploit sparsity is done by means of an attribute grammar [1, 17], based on a context free grammar for assignment statements.[2] The following semantic rules are used to associate the strongest **condition** ψ, constructed from guards, with each expression in a synthesized attribute nz, to indicate when the value of this expression is nonzero, under the assumption that the value of dense variables and entries is always nonzero:

---

[1] Occurrences without controlling loops give rise to **scalar-wise** singleton access patterns.

[2] The ambiguity of this grammar is resolved by assignment of the usual precedence and associativity to all operators.

Production	Semantic Rule
$E \rightarrow E_1 + E_2$	$E.nz = dis(E_1.nz, E_2.nz);$
$E \rightarrow E_1 - E_2$	$E.nz = dis(E_1.nz, E_2.nz);$
$E \rightarrow E_1 * E_2$	$E.nz = con(E_1.nz, E_2.nz);$
$E \rightarrow E_1 / E_2$	$E.nz = E_1.nz;$
$E \rightarrow E_1 ** E_2$	$E.nz = E_1.nz;$
$E \rightarrow - E_1$	$E.nz = E_1.nz;$
$E \rightarrow (E_1)$	$E.nz = E_1.nz;$
$E \rightarrow var$	$E.nz = var.grd;$
$E \rightarrow const$	$E.nz = is\_zero(const.val)$? 'false':'true';

The guard of each variable is supplied as synthesized attributed grd, and is 'true' for dense variables. The value of constants is supplied in attribute val. Functions dis and con construct a disjunction and conjunction respectively of the arguments. The result is simplified according to logical equivalences that are based on e.g. absorption laws or the fact that 'true' is the identity of the '$\wedge$'-operator. The subtlety of a zero right operand for '$/$'- and '$**$'-operators is ignored. For example, (simplified) condition ψ is shown below for some expressions, if A and B are sparse matrices:

Expression	ψ
$A(I,J)+A(I,J)*B(I,J)$	$(I, J) \in E_A$
$A(I+1,J)*(X+B(I,J))$	$(I + 1, J) \in E_A$
$A(I,J)+B(I,J)/5.0$	$(I, J) \in E_A \vee$ $(I, J) \in E_B$
$X+A(I,J)$	'true'
$-0.0*(X+A(I,J))$	'false'

From these conditions, the strongest condition χ is associated with each statement in attribute cnd, that indicates the instances that must be executed. A pointer to the left-hand side variable in an assignment statement, supplied as synthesized attribute nm, is copied in an inherited attribute lhs of the right-hand side expression, and is passed down the parse tree:

Production	Semantic Rule
$stmt \rightarrow var = E;$	$E.lhs = var.nm;$
$E \rightarrow E_1 + E_2$	$E_1.lhs = E_2.lhs = E.lhs;$
$E \rightarrow E_1 - E_2$	$E_1.lhs = E_2.lhs = E.lhs;$
$E \rightarrow E_1 * E_2$	$E_1.lhs = E_2.lhs = E.lhs;$
$E \rightarrow E_1 / E_2$	$E_1.lhs = E_2.lhs = E.lhs;$
$E \rightarrow E_1 ** E_2$	$E_1.lhs = E_2.lhs = E.lhs;$
$E \rightarrow - E_1$	$E_1.lhs = E.lhs;$
$E \rightarrow (E_1)$	$E_1.lhs = E.lhs;$

From attributes nz and lhs, another synthesized attribute ne associated with expressions is constructed that records when the right-hand side expression is not equal to the left-hand side variable:

Production	Semantic Rule
$E \rightarrow E_1 + E_2$	$E.ne = con(dis(E_1.ne,$ $E_2.nz), dis(E_1.nz, E_2.ne));$
$E \rightarrow E_1 - E_2$	$E.ne = dis(E_1.ne, E_2.nz);$
$E \rightarrow (E_1)$	$E.ne = E_1.ne;$
$E \rightarrow var$	$E.ne = equal(var.nm.E.lhs)$? 'false':'true';
/* others */	$E.ne = $ 'true';

For example, the value of attribute ne associated with the right-hand side expression in assignment statement '$ACC=ACC+A(I,J)*X$' is '$(I,J) \in E_A$'. Evaluation dependences are depicted in figure 1:

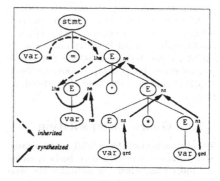

Figure 1: Parse Tree

Finally, the condition of each statement is determined. An instance of an assignment statement must be executed if the left- and right-hand sides are not equal, and at least one of these expressions is nonzero: for production 'stmt $\rightarrow$ var = E;', the semantic rule is 'stmt.cnd = con(E.ne,dis(var.grd,E.nz));'. The condition χ associated with some statements is shown below. If $\chi =$'false', the statement can be eliminated since none of its instances have to be executed.

Statement	χ
$B(I,J)=B(I,J)+A(I,J)$	$(I, J) \in E_A$
$A(2*I,J)=X*A(2*I,J)$	$(2I, J) \in E_A$
$A(I,J)=X$	'true'
$A(I,J)=A(I,J)$	'false'
$A(I,J)=A(I,J)*B(I,J)$ $+C(I,J)$	$(I, J) \in E_A$ $\vee (I, J) \in E_C$

Effectively, condition χ consists of the disjunction of all conditions in the branches that remain in the corresponding IF-statement, as is illustrated below for statement 'A(I,J)=B(I,J)' with condition '(I,J) ∈ E_A ∨ (I,J) ∈ E_B', where subroutine del_A is used to indicate cancellation:

```
IF (I,J) ∈ E_A ∧ (I,J) ∈ E_B THEN
    A'[σ_A(I,J)] = B'[σ_B(I,J)]
ELSEIF (I,J) ∈ E_A ∧ (I,J) ∉ E_B THEN
    CALL del_A(I,J)
ELSEIF (I,J) ∉ E_A ∧ (I,J) ∈ E_B THEN
    A'[new_A(I,J)] = B'[σ_B(I,J)]
ENDIF
```

2.2 Overhead Elimination

The presence of guards and σ_A-lookups reflects overhead that is due to the fact that a compact data structure must be scanned to determine *if* and *where* an entry is stored. Additionally, skipping operations by means of conditionals does not result in much gain in execution time, because usually such tests are equally expensive [14, 24]. Therefore, techniques to eliminate this kind of overhead are required.

2.2.1 Guard Encapsulation

The disjunction of the conditions associated with all statements in a loop body is called the **loop condition**. It indicates the iterations in which at least one statement instance has to be executed. A *guard* ψ **dominates** a *condition* χ, iff. $\chi \rightarrow \psi$ is a tautology. So, if a guard ψ dominates a loop condition χ, iterations in which ψ does not hold do not have to be executed. This can be achieved by **encapsulation** of a dominating guard '$F_A(\vec{I}) \in E_A$' in the execution set of a directly surrounding *controlling* loop. Because the resulting execution set $\{I_c \in V_c | F_A(\vec{I}) \in E_A\}$ cannot be generated directly in general, the following conversion is performed:

```
DO I_c ∈ V_c
    IF F_A(Ī) ∈ E_A THEN
        ACC = ACC + A'[σ_A(F_A(Ī))]
    ENDIF
ENDDO          ↓
        DO AD ∈ PAD_A^{I_1,...,I_{c-1}}
            ACC = ACC + A'[AD]
        ENDDO
```

If we can easily obtain $PAD_A^{I_1,...,I_{c-1}} = \{\sigma_A(t) | t \in (P_A^{I_1,...,I_{c-1}} \cap E_A)\} \subseteq AD_A$, only iterations in which an entry (an element for

which the dominating guard holds) is operated on, are executed. Fewer iterations result since the size of the execution set decreases, while test overhead is eliminated completely. Because $AD = \sigma_A(F_A(\vec{I}))$ holds and σ_A is invertible, the value of I_c can be restored by using the following equations, where $\pi_i \cdot \vec{x} = x_i$:

$$\begin{cases} \pi_1 \cdot \sigma_A^{-1}(AD) = m_{10} + m_{11}I_1 \ldots + m_{1c}I_c \\ \pi_2 \cdot \sigma_A^{-1}(AD) = m_{20} + m_{21}I_1 \ldots + m_{2c}I_c \end{cases}$$

Guard encapsulation is feasible if the following constraints on the data structure are satisfied: (1) fast generation of addresses in $PAD_A^{I_1,...,I_{c-1}}$ is supported for all valid $I_1, \ldots, I_{c-1}$, (2) if a dependence is carried by the I_c-loop, address-generation corresponds to the original execution order of this loop,[3] and (3) to restore the value of I_c, $\pi_1 \cdot \sigma_A^{-1}$ values are available if $m_{1c} \neq 0$ or $\pi_2 \cdot \sigma_A^{-1}$ values if $m_{2c} \neq 0$ (i.e. row or column index of each entry). For example, in the following fragment encapsulation of guard '(I,I + J) ∈ E_A', that dominates the (identical) loop condition, in the execution set of the J-loop is possible and requires $\pi_2 \cdot \sigma_A^{-1}(AD)$ to reconstruct the value of J. Addresses in PAD_A^I belong to entries along $P_A^I = \{(I,I+J)|1 \leq J \leq 3\}$:

```
DO I = 1, M
    DO J = 1, 3
        IF (I,I+J) ∈ E_A THEN
            ACC = ACC + A(I,I+J) * J
        ENDIF
    ENDDO
ENDDO          ↓
        DO I = 1, M
            DO AD ∈ PAD_A^I
                J = π_2 · σ_A^{-I}(AD) - I
                ACC = ACC + A'[AD] * J
            ENDDO
        ENDDO
```

Constraint (1) can be relaxed at the expense of run-time overhead, if fast generation of addresses in $\overline{PAD}_A^{I_1,...,I_{c-1}}$ that corresponds to entries along an **enveloping** access pattern $\overline{P}_A^{I_1,...,I_{c-1}} \supseteq P_A^{I_1,...,I_{c-1}}$ is required, under the condition that it can be determined at run-time whether an entry corresponds to the actual access pattern. If only

---

[3] Usually, dependences caused by accumulations are ignored.

longitudinal enveloping access patterns are considered this can be done for each entry by testing inclusion '$I_c \in V_c$' on the restored loop index (see section 4.2). A longitudinal enveloping access pattern $\overline{P}_A^{I_1,\ldots,I_{c-1}}$ has the following form, where $g = \gcd(m_{1c}, m_{2c})$, $T_1 \leq g \cdot \min(V_c)$, and $T_2 \geq g \cdot \max(V_c)$:

$$\{(\ldots + \tfrac{m_{1c} \cdot t}{g}, \ldots + \tfrac{m_{2c} \cdot t}{g})|T_1 \leq t \leq T_2\}$$

Examples are $P_A^I = \{(100 - 3J, I)|1 \leq J \leq 33\}$ with $\overline{P}_A^I = \{(100 - t, I)|3 \leq t \leq 99\}$ and $P_A = \{(4J, 2J)|1 \leq J \leq 25\}$ with $\overline{P}_A = \{(2t, t)|2 \leq t \leq 50\}$.

Complications occur for guard encapsulation if creation or cancellation along the (enveloping) access pattern affects the corresponding address set. We distinguish **forward** and **backward** creation, corresponding to insertions that affect the value of an encapsulated guard in following or preceding iterations respectively. For some data structures, creation along *arbitrary* access patterns might affect other address sets if garbage collection is occasionally required. Deletion of an entry that corresponds to the encapsulated guard is referred to as **inward** cancellation. If inward cancellation cannot occur, the corresponding dominating guard in a loop body for which $c < l$ holds can be **hoisted** out the innermost non-controlling loops.

Note that if entries are sorted on column or row index, encapsulation of more general conditions, like conjunctions and disjunctions of guards, becomes possible by generating code that performs an in-phase scan of the associated data structures [14].

2.2.2 Access Pattern Expansion

Another way to reduce overhead is based on the idea to avoid binary operations that involve two sparse vectors and to reduce test overhead of certain occurrences that cannot exploit sparsity, with work dependent on the number of entries only [11, 14, 24]. The compiler can decide to **expand** a sparse access pattern before it is operated on with a **scatter**-operation, so that operations on this dense representation do not suffer from sparse lookup overhead. If assignments occur, storage is obtained or released directly to account for creation or cancellation if necessary. This can be done with a variant on the switch technique [24], where a bit array

records which elements are entries. The actual values are stored back afterwards with a **gather**-operation. These operations are feasible under constraints that are similar to the requirements for guard encapsulation: (1) the address set of the (enveloping) access pattern is available, and (2) appropriate index information is available per entry.

2.2.3 Nonzero Structures

If with information about the nonzero structure, that is either user-supplied or obtained by on-file analysis, it can be determined that certain (enveloping) access patterns are rather dense, or become dense by frequently occurring creation, the compiler can decide to use the dense representation as *only* storage during the whole program. This eliminates the lookup and creation overhead that is inherent to sparse data structures, while the number of redundant operations performed is probably small.

Information about the nonzero structure can also be used to apply **iteration space reduction**. Consider for example the code for $\vec{y} \leftarrow A \cdot \vec{x}$ for a band matrix A, i.e. $(a_{ij} \neq 0) \rightarrow (-b_1 \leq j - i \leq b_2)$. After application of the unimodular transformation $U = \begin{pmatrix} -1 & 1 \\ 1 & 0 \end{pmatrix}$ [6, 27], all elements a_{ij} with $j - i = J$ are accessed in one execution of the I-loop:

```
DO I = 1, M
  DO J = 1, N
    Y(I) = Y(I) + A(I,J) * X(J)
  ENDDO
ENDDO                    ↓
DO J = 1 - M, N - 1
  DO I = MAX(1,1-J), MIN(M,N-J)
    Y(I) = Y(I) + A(I,J+I) * X(J+I)
  ENDDO
ENDDO
```

Compile-time encapsulation in the execution set of the *outermost* controlling loop results in a reduced execution set $\{-b_1, \ldots, b_2\}$ for the J-loop, and dense storage of the remaining diagonals becomes desirable.

2.3 Storage

Access patterns that are dense are stored in full-sized arrays. Sparse access patterns are stored as sparse vectors in data structures (D1) or (L1), illustrated in figure 2 (inspired on existing data structures [14, 24, 26, 30]). In these implementations, the numerical values of entries are stored in an array AVAL, while corresponding column or row indices are stored in a parallel integer array AIND. The implementations differ in the way each access pattern is stored: consecutively (D1), or as a linked list (L1), and the information required per access pattern: first and last index (D1), or a pointer to the first entry (L1). Enough **working space** must be available to account for creation in case of dynamic data structures. An ordering (determined by links for (L1)) between entries on the associated index within one access pattern can be maintained at the penalty of more expensive insertions and deletions.

An insertion or deletion in (L1) only affects the values of a few links. For (D1) the addresses of other entries in the same access pattern might alter as a result of data movement, while *extra* data movement results if an insertion is performed in an access pattern with no directly surrounding space.[4]

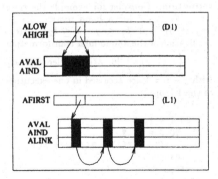

Figure 2: Sparse Data Structure

3 Storage Selection

Most overhead reduction would be obtained if all imposed constraints on the actual data structure of sparse matrices were satisfied. However, because usually elements are involved in differently shaped access patterns,

---

[4]The access pattern is moved to the end of the array where most working space is kept. If insufficient space remains, garbage collection is required to compress all data, which might affect the addresses of *all* entries.

this would demand for storage schemes with much overhead storage that are expensive to maintain in order to support fast generation of addresses in all address sets. For example, storing entries according to row- *and* column-wise access patterns requires a linked-lists implementation, where four integers are associated with each entry (row and column index, and two links). The overhead storage requirements of this scheme can be reduced, but at the expense of more expensive lookups [10]. Additionally, to simplify data structure construction and code generation, a simple correspondence between address sets and loop indices must hold.

Overhead storage can be kept reasonably small if only the constraints of **consistent** access patterns, i.e. that are either *disjoint* or *identical*, are satisfied. Data structure selection for each sparse matrix in a program is, therefore, controlled by an **inconsistency table**, which initially has the following form:

A	d	c	r
r	0	0	0
c	0	0	
d	0		

Every table-entry contains the number of static inconsistencies between row-, column- or diagonal-wise access patterns of occurrences of a sparse matrix A. Since an implementation is straightforward to select in case of an empty table, reducing the number of nonzero entries in this table is the most important goal during data structure selection. Clearly, compromises have to be made in some cases.

3.1 Self-Inconsistencies

Although all elements along one access pattern are distinct, it is possible that access patterns $P_A^{I_1,\ldots,I_{c-1}}$ of one occurrence overlap for different $I_1,\ldots,I_{c-1}$. If such access patterns are not identical, a static self-inconsistency arises, as is illustrated for row-wise access patterns in the following example:

```
DO J = 1, N / 2
  DO K = 1, J
    ACC = ACC + A(2,2*K)
  ENDDO
ENDDO
```

A	d	c	r
r	0	0	1
c	0	0	
d	0		

Encapsulation of '$(2, 2\mathbb{K}) \in E_A$' in the execution set of the $\mathbb{K}$-loop, for instance, is feasible if fast generation of the addresses of entries at even positions in *every prefix* of the second row is supported. This abundance of constraints is reflected in the inconsistency between $P_A^J = \{(2, \mathbb{K}) | 1 \leq \mathbb{K} \leq J\}$ for different values of J. Consideration of e.g. $\overline{P}_A^J = \{(2, t) | 1 \leq t \leq \mathbb{I}\}$ achieves self-consistency, and requires fast generation of addresses of entries in only one access pattern, justifying the simplification made in the next section.

3.2 Collection

In order to get a better grip on all access patterns of *one* occurrence, these are characterized by an **access pattern collection** C_A^i. This is a possibly enveloping, but also consistent and simple description of all access patterns. First, a conservative approximation of the index set of all used elements a_{xy} is constructed in terms of a variant on the **simple section** [3, 4]:

$$
\left\{
\begin{array}{c}
l_1 \leq x \leq u_1 \\
l_2 \leq y \leq u_2 \\
l_3 \leq r_1 \cdot x + r_2 \cdot y \leq u_3 \\
l_4 \leq r_2 \cdot x - r_1 \cdot y \leq u_4
\end{array}
\right. \quad (3.2)
$$

We use $\vec{r} = (\frac{s \cdot |m_{1c}|}{\gcd(m_{1c}, m_{2c})}, \frac{|m_{2c}|}{\gcd(m_{1c}, m_{2c})})$, where $s = (m_{1c} \cdot m_{2c} \geq 0)$? 1:-1, in case of diagonal-wise access patterns, or $\vec{r} = (1, 1)$ otherwise. Consequently, two **section bounds** are parallel to the access patterns, and fairly complex shaped sections can be dealt with. Since the correspondences $x = f_1(\vec{I})$ and $y = f_2(\vec{I})$ hold, the values of $\vec{l}$ and $\vec{u}$ in a section of form (3.2) are easily obtained by successive consideration of worst-case values for I_i in decreasing order, since execution set V^i might depend on I_j, for all $j < i$. Consider, for example, $P_A^{I,J} = \{(I + \mathbb{K}, J + 2\mathbb{K}) | 1 \leq \mathbb{K} \leq 3\}$ for $1 \leq I \leq 3$ and $1 \leq J \leq 3$. The following section results, where the value of e.g. u_4 is determined as $2x - y = 2I - J \leq 2I - 1 \leq 5$:

$$
\left\{
\begin{array}{c}
2 \leq x \leq 6 \\
3 \leq y \leq 9 \\
8 \leq x + 2y \leq 24 \\
-1 \leq 2x - y \leq 5
\end{array}
\right.
$$

The access pattern collection consists of an enumeration of *all* access patterns within this section: $C_A^i = \{(R^i + \frac{s \cdot |m_{1c}| \cdot t}{\gcd(m_{1c}, m_{2c})}, C^i + \frac{|m_{2c}| \cdot t}{\gcd(m_{1c}, m_{2c})}) | T_1^i \leq t \leq T_2^i\}$, for $I_1 \leq i \leq I_2$.

In this way, distinctions between partially overlapping or multiple traversed access patterns are eliminated, while the direction is normalized such that the y-component is non-negative.

Offsets and bounds for row-, column- and diagonal-wise access patterns are given in the following tables, where $l^* = l_1$ and $u^* = u_1$ if $s = 1$, or $l^* = u_1$ and $u^* = l_1$ otherwise:

	R^i	C^i	I_1	I_2
row	i	0	l_1	u_1
col.	0	i	l_2	u_2
diag.	$v_2 \cdot i$	$-v_1 \cdot i$	l_4	u_4

T_1^i
$\max(l_2, l_3 - i, i - u_4)$
$\max(l_1, l_3 - i, i + l_4)$
$\lceil \max(\frac{l^* - v_2 \cdot i}{r_1}, \frac{l_2 + v_1 \cdot i}{r_2}, \frac{l_3 + (r_2 v_1 - r_1 v_2) \cdot i}{r_1^2 + r_2^2}) \rceil$

T_2^i
$\min(u_2, u_3 - i, i - l_4)$
$\min(u_1, u_3 - i, i + u_4)$
$\lfloor \min(\frac{u^* - v_2 \cdot i}{r_1}, \frac{u_2 + v_1 \cdot i}{r_2}, \frac{u_3 + (r_2 v_1 - r_1 v_2) \cdot i}{r_1^2 + r_2^2}) \rfloor$

Diagonal-wise enumeration along $r_2 \cdot x - r_1 \cdot y = i$ for successive i is obtained by application of unimodular transformation $U = \begin{pmatrix} r_2 & v_1 \\ -r_1 & v_2 \end{pmatrix}$ on the row-wise enumeration, where $\vec{v}$ is taken such that $\det(U) = r_2 \cdot v_2 + r_1 \cdot v_1 = 1$. Such integers can be found during computation of $\gcd(m_{1c}, m_{2c})$ as shown in [6]. Consequently, the access pattern collection of the previous example is $C_A^i = \{(t, 2t - i) | \lceil \max(2, \frac{3+i}{2}) \rceil \leq t \leq \lfloor \min(6, \frac{9+i}{2}) \rfloor\}$ for $-1 \leq i \leq 5$:

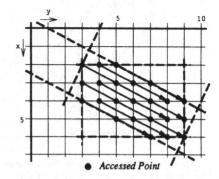

● *Accessed Point*

The collection of $P_A^{I,J} = \{(I + J, \mathbb{K}) | 1 \leq \mathbb{K} \leq I + J\}$ for $1 \leq I \leq 3$ and $1 \leq J \leq 2$ is

$C_A^i = \{(i,t)|1 \leq t \leq i\}$ for $2 \leq i \leq 5$, as depicted in the following figure. Section bound $0 \leq x - y$ results, because the minimum value of $-K$ is $-I-J$:

$$\begin{cases} 2 \leq x \leq 5 \\ 1 \leq y \leq 5 \\ 3 \leq x + y \leq 10 \\ 0 \leq x - y \leq 4 \end{cases}$$

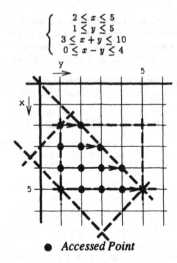

● *Accessed Point*

The collection of column-wise access patterns $P_A^I = \{(2I + J - 2, I)|1 \leq J \leq 2\}$ for $1 \leq I \leq 4$, is $C_A^i = \{(t,i)|i \leq t \leq i + 4\}$ for $1 \leq i \leq 4$:

$$\begin{cases} 1 \leq x \leq 8 \\ 1 \leq y \leq 4 \\ 2 \leq x + y \leq 12 \\ 0 \leq x - y \leq 4 \end{cases}$$

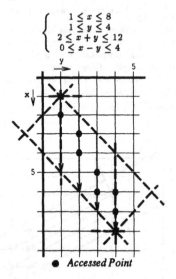

● *Accessed Point*

Approximation of actual access patterns by the access pattern collection, which is uniquely determined by the values of $\vec{d}_A$, $\vec{l}$, and $\vec{u}$, yields a uniform and self-consistent description. However, some accuracy might

be lost as shown in the previous example where longitudinal enveloping access patterns result. The collection of $P_A^I = \{(4J - 3, 2I - 2J + 5)|1 \leq J \leq 3\}$ for $1 \leq I \leq 3$ with normalized direction, which is $C_A^i = \{(i - 2t, t)|\lceil\frac{i-9}{2}\rceil \leq t \leq \lfloor\frac{i-1}{2}\rfloor\}$ for $11 \leq i \leq 19$, consists of too many points because not only longitudinal enveloping access patterns are considered, but also because **transversal** enveloping access patterns are included, e.g. for $i = 12$:

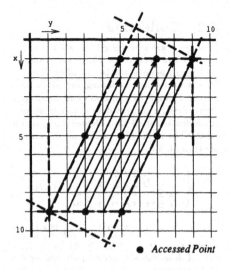

● *Accessed Point*

Clearly, there are $I_2 - I_1 + 1$ access patterns in C_A^i, with a total number of $\sum_{i=I_1}^{I_2}(T_2^i - T_1^i + 1)$ elements. For an arbitrary element a_{xy} in collection C_A^i, the value of i is determined as x, y, or $r_2 \cdot x - r_1 \cdot y$ for row-, column- and diagonal-wise access patterns respectively, so that it is stored in the kth access pattern, where k is $i - l_1 + 1$, $i - l_2 + 1$, or $i - l_4 + 1$. Element a_{74}, for example, belongs to the 5th access pattern in the previous example, since $i = 15$ and $l_4 = 11$. The value of t is determined as y, x, or $v_1 \cdot x + v_2 \cdot y$ for row- column- and diagonal-wise access patterns.

3.3 Complications

Although most occurrences of matrices in numerical programs fit the framework of section 2.1, the compiler must occasionally deal with complex subscripts (e.g. subscripted subscripts), or unknown loop bounds, as in the following fragments for an 100 × 100 matrix A:

```
DO I = 1, 10
   Z = ...
   ... A(Z,I)
ENDDO
```

```
DO I = 1, 50
   DO J = 1, 90
      ... A(PV(I),J)
   ENDDO
ENDDO
Z = ...
DO I = 10, Z
   DO J = 1, I
      ... A(5+I,J)
   ENDDO
ENDDO
```

If a complex subscript occurs, direction $\vec{d}_A$, and thus the access pattern collection, can only be determined if this subscript is *invariant* in one execution of the innermost controlling loop. Otherwise, only the *section* with e.g. $\vec{r} = (1,1)$ can be determined, which is used in the computation of static inconsistences. Clearly, the direction is unknown for the first fragment, while $\vec{d}_A = (0,1)$ holds in the second.

An approximation of the section can still be obtained, if constraints $1 \leq x \leq m$ and $1 \leq y \leq n$, that hold if subscript bounds are not violated, are used in those cases where compile-time analysis fails (cf. [3]). For complex subscripts, the new constraints are used directly for the *whole* subscript, so that, for instance, $u_3 = 190$ results for the second fragment since $x + y = \text{'PV(I)'} + J \leq \text{'PV(I)'} + 90$. This yields collection $C^i_A = \{(i,t) | 1 \leq t \leq 90\}$ for $1 \leq i \leq 100$. Taking this simple approach for subscripts in which at least one loop index has (indirectly) unknown bounds yields, for example, $u_3 = 200$ and $l_4 = -99$ for the third fragment because both x and y contain such indices. However, in this case more accurate results are obtained if constraint $5 + I \leq 100$ is used to derive an upper bound for I.[5] For example, $u_3 = 195$ is obtained by $x + y = 5 + I + J \leq 5 + 2I$, while computation of $l_4 = 5$ does not require any bounds, because $x - y = 5 + I - J \geq 5 + I - I$. Collection $C^i_A = \{(i,t) | 1 \leq t \leq i - 5\}$ for $15 \leq i \leq 100$ results.

More accuracy is achieved by incorporation of advanced techniques. Induction variable recognition [1] can be used to replace

some complex subscripts by linear functions of loop indices, while symbolic manipulations (cf. symbolic dependence testing [23]) improve computations on remaining complex subscripts.

3.4 Table Computation

Computation of the inconsistency table is closely related to the data dependence analysis problem, where static dependence between the statements of occurrences A_k and $A_{k'}$ is assumed if the sections of $C^i_{A_k}$ and $C^i_{A_{k'}}$ overlap. However, a static inconsistency between the access patterns of these occurrences is only recorded if also the sections *or* normalized directions differ. As a result of normalization, identical access patterns that are traversed in opposite directions are also considered consistent.

The intersection of two sections of form (3.2) with identical $\vec{r}$ is again a section of form (3.2), and is constructed by taking the most interior values for all section bounds (cf. [3]). Consequently, two sections described by $\vec{l}, \vec{u}$ and $\vec{l}', \vec{u}'$ respectively overlap, if this intersection is non-empty:

$$\bigwedge_{1 \leq i \leq 4} \max(\pi_i \cdot \vec{l}, \pi_i \cdot \vec{l}') \leq \min(\pi_i \cdot \vec{u}, \pi_i \cdot \vec{u}')$$

The sections are identical if $\vec{l} = \vec{l}'$, $\vec{u} = \vec{u}'$. The intersection of two sections with different $\vec{r}$ is not necessarily of form (3.2), and more computations are required to detect overlap. It should be noted that, since sections are a conservative approximation, overlap does not necessarily imply that the underlying diophantine equations ($F_{A_k}(\vec{I}) = F_{A_{k'}}(\vec{I}')$ for valid $\vec{I}$ and $\vec{I}'$) actually have a solution [4, 5, 16, 22, 28]. Consider, for example, code that computes the sum of the diagonal and off-diagonal parts of a square sparse matrix A:

```
DO I = 1, N
   DG = DG + A1(I,I)
   DO J = 1, I - 1
      LW = LW + A2(I,J)
      UP = UP + A3(J,I)
   ENDDO
ENDDO
```

A	d	c	r
r	0	0	0
c	0	0	
d	0		

---

[5] The compiler must also deal with a system of inequalities if maximum and minimum functions are used in lower and upper bounds, which increases the complexity of section computation.

Clearly, the sections of $C^i_{A_1}$, $C^i_{A_2}$ and $C^i_{A_3}$ are disjoint. For example, the sections of $C^i_{A_1}$ and $C^i_{A_2}$ do not overlap because $\max(0,1) > \min(0, \blacksquare - 1)$:[6]

$$\left\{ \begin{array}{ll} 1 \leq x \leq N & 1 \leq x \leq N \\ 1 \leq y \leq N & 1 \leq y \leq N-1 \\ 2 \leq x+y \leq 2N & 2 \leq x+y \leq 2N-1 \\ 0 \leq x-y \leq 0 & 1 \leq x-y \leq N-1 \end{array} \right. $$

If the following fragment also appears in the program, the inconsistency table changes because the section of $C^i_{A_4}$, that consists of the whole index set, overlaps with parts of all other sections:

```
DO I = 1, ∎
  DO J = 1, ∎
    A₄(I,J) = A₄(I,J) * 10.0
  ENDDO
ENDDO
```

A	d	c	r
r	1	1	1
c	0	0	
d	0		

Inconsistences between access patterns of two collections with *identical* normalized directions can be solved, if the collections are combined by minimal expansion of the sections into one section of form (3.2), i.e. the section described by bounds $\min(\pi_i \cdot \vec{l}, \pi_i \cdot \vec{l'})$ and $\max(\pi_i \cdot \vec{u}, \pi_i \cdot \vec{u'})$ for $1 \leq i \leq 4$ (cf. [3]) is considered. For example, combining $C^i_{A_2}$ and $C^i_{A_4}$ yields collection $C^i_{A_4}$ for *both* occurrences and eliminates the 'r-r' entry. However, since the section of A_2 is expanded, two new static inconsistencies arise:

A	d	c	r
r	2	2	0
c	0	0	
d	0		

Reshaping access pattern by application of conventional loop transformations, such as distribution, index set splitting, unrolling, and unimodular transformation [2, 6, 20, 23, 25, 27, 28, 29], can assist in eliminating inconsistencies between arbitrary access patterns. For example, the previous code is consistent after fragmentation of collection $C^i_{A_4}$ by a sequence of such transformations on the loop-nesting of A_4:

---

[6]The peculiarity of section bounds $1 \leq x$ and $2 \leq x+y$ for $C^i_{A_2}$ arises because the execution of J is empty for I=1. Making these bounds more tight is desirable for comparisons.

```
DO I = 1, ∎
  DO J = 1, I - 1
    A₄ₐ(I,J) = A₄ₐ(I,J) * 10.0
  ENDDO
  A₄♭(I,I) = A₄♭(I,I) * 10.0
ENDDO
DO J = 1, ∎
  DO I = 1, J - 1
    A₄c(I,J) = A₄c(I,J) * 10.0
  ENDDO
ENDDO
```

$$C^i_{A_{4a}} = C^i_{A_2}$$
$$C^i_{A_{4b}} = C^i_{A_1}$$
$$C^i_{A_{4c}} = C^i_{A_3}$$

A	d	c	r
r	0	0	0
c	0	0	
d	0		

If the compiler cannot eliminate all inconsistencies, constraints imposed by certain occurrences are favored over those of less relevant occurrences. This is done by combining the collections of inconsistent access patterns by minimal expansion of both sections into a new section of form (3.2) for *one* direction. This requires partial recomputation of the sections for occurrences with **ignored** direction, to account for another value of $\vec{r}$. Since encapsulation or expansion is disabled if storage is not done according to the normalized direction, the direction that belongs to occurrences with the potential of encapsulation or expansion in frequently executed statements is taken. This approach has as advantage that only *one* collection is associated with every occurrence, avoiding the need for run-time tests to determine in which of the data structures of overlapping collections an element might be stored. The major disadvantage, however, is that the presence of collections with large associated sections that cannot be fragmented, diminish the potential to account for peculiarities of the sparse matrix.

3.5 Storage Construction

Because some collections are combined or fragmented, a number of non-overlapping access pattern collections remains per sparse matrix A that belong to representative occurrences $A_{k_1} \cdots A_{k_r}$. The sections of these $C^i_{A_{k_j}}$ usually form a partition of the index set of the matrix, as illustrated in figure 3. Per collection it is recorded whether dense or sparse storage of the access patterns is appropriate. All sparse collections are stored in one data structure (D1) or (L1), where per collection $\pi_1 \cdot \sigma_A^{-1}$ or $\pi_2 \cdot \sigma_A^{-1}$ values are stored for column-wise, or row- or diagonal-wise access pattern respectively. If *at least* one loop for which guard encapsulation will be applied requires an ordering as explained in section 2.2, this is also recorded for the corresponding collection. This requires insertion and deletion routines that keep the entries stored in monotonic *increasing* order on stored values, as a result of direction normalization. Because the access patterns in one collection will be stored in one format, application of transformations is also useful to isolate access patterns with different properties.

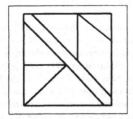

Figure 3: Partition

One of the following declarations results for sparse storage of a matrix A. Sufficient working space is supplied for dynamic data structures. Parameter ρ is the density, u is the total number of access patterns (sum of $I_2 - I_1 + 1$ over all collections), v is the total number of *elements* along all access patterns (sum of $\sum_{i=I_1}^{I_2} (T_2^i - T_1^i + 1)$ over all collections), w is the maximum number of elements along one access pattern (maximum of $1 + \max_{I_1 \le i \le I_2} (T_2^i - T_1^i)$ over all collections), and x is some tunable constant:

```
INTEGER   ANP, ASZ

(D1):PARAMETER (ANP = u,ASZ =
+              ρ·v + 2·w + x)⁷
      REAL     AVAL(ASZ)
      INTEGER  AIND(ASZ), AHIGH(ANP),
+              ALOW(ANP), ALAST
```

---

[7]The size of *extra* working space in (D1) to prevent the need for frequent garbage collection is inspired on [13, 15].

```
(L1):PARAMETER (ANP = u,ASZ =
+              ρ·v + x)
      REAL     AVAL(ASZ)
      INTEGER  AIND(ASZ), ALINK(ASZ),
+              AFIRST(ANP), AFREE
```

Scalar ALAST points to the last used element in (D1) to support extra data movement, while AFREE is a pointer to a linked list in (L1) that contains all free elements. Per collection $C^i_{A_{k_j}}$, an initially zero offset is recorded, and increased with $I_2 + I_1 + 1$ after consideration of each collection, such that the kth access pattern in a collection starts at location ALOW(D) or AFIRST(D) in the data structure, where $D = offset_{A_{k_j}} + k$. For every access pattern collection $C^i_{A_{k_j}}$ that requires dense storage, the following declaration is generated, where a unique label $lab_{A_{k_j}}$ is used per collection and $m = \max_{I_1 \le i \le I_2} (T_2^i - T_1^i)$. Because the maximum length is taken, this format is not very well suited for e.g. triangular shaped dense access patterns. If $I_2 - I_1 = 0$ holds, a one-dimensional array is used.

$$\texttt{REAL ADNS}lab_{A_{k_j}} (1 + m, I_2 - I_1 + 1)$$

4 Code Generation

First, compiler-supplied primitives are presented, followed by a discussion of code generation for specific program constructs and sparse occurrences.

4.1 Primitive Operations

The definition of certain primitive operations for data structures (D1) and (L1) is supplied by the compiler, so that these primitives can be used in the generated code. The following table lists some basic operations with a short description, where '_' can be D1 or L1:

INT_()	Initialization of data structure
LKP_()	Lookup of location of an entry ($\perp$ otherwise)
INS_()	Insertion of an entry
DEL_()	Deletion of entry at a location

Location $\perp$ cannot be used as storage in a data structure for A, but it has the property that AVAL($\perp$)=0.0. Insertions and deletions are fast, provided that data movement is not required in (D1). However, no ordering is maintained on the entries. Therefore, the following primitives are also supported, where ODELL1 is equal to DELL1 since data movement does not occur for data structure (L1):

OINS_()	Ordered insertion of an entry
ODEL_()	Ordered deletion of an entry

Two operations are supplied to support expansion of an access pattern:

SCAT_()	Expansion into dense
GATH_()	Compression into sparse

A detailed description and definitions of these primitives are given in [9].

4.2   Encapsulated Guards

If guard encapsulation in the execution set of a surrounding I_c-loop is feasible and cancellation or creation along the (enveloping) access pattern cannot occur, code for the following conversion is generated:

```
DO Ic ∈ Vc
    IF (FA(I) ∈ EA) THEN
        ...A(FA(I))...
    ENDIF
ENDDO       ↓
    DO AD ∈ PAD_A^{I1,...,Ic-1}
        ...A'[AD]...
    ENDDO
```

Addresses in $\overline{PAD}_A^{I_1,...,I_{c-1}}$ that correspond to an access pattern in a sparse collection $C_{A_{k_j}}^i$ are found through $D = offset_{A_{k_j}} + k$ in the data structure, where the value of k is determined *independently* of the value of I_c before the resulting loop as shown below, where $R = m_{10} + m_{11}I_1 + ... + m_{1c-1}I_{c-1}$ and $C = m_{20} + m_{21}I_1 + ..., + m_{2c-1}I_{c-1}$ (see section 3.2):

	k	i
r	$i - l_1 + 1$	R
c	$i - l_2 + 1$	C
d	$i - l_4 + 1$	$r_2 \cdot R - r_1 \cdot C$

One of the following frameworks is generated:

```
(D1): DO AD = ALOW(D), AHIGH(D)
          ...
      ENDDO
(L1): AD = AFIRST(D)
      DO WHILE (AD ≠ ⊥)
          ...
          AD = ALINK(AD)
      ENDDO
```

Within the loop body, the value of I_c is restored and inclusion in V_c is tested. The resulting code for column-wise access patterns in shown below, where execution set $V_c = \{L^{I_1,...,I_{c-1}}, ..., U^{I_1,...,I_{c-1}}\}$:

```
Ic = AIND(AD)−m10 − m11 * I1
+ ... − m1c-1 * Ic-1
IF (MOD(Ic,m1c) = 0) THEN
    Ic = Ic / m1c
    IF (L^{I1,...,Ic-1} ≤ Ic)
+   AND (Ic ≤ U^{I1,...,Ic-1}) THEN
        ...
    ENDIF
ENDIF
```

In this construct, the original loop body is generated in which most occurrences $A(F_A(I))$ that correspond to the encapsulated guard are replaced by AVAL(AD) (details are given in section 4.5). If $m_{1c} = 1$, the MOD and integer division operations are not required, while a compare is eliminated if the compare value corresponds to the value of the index bound of the stored access patterns. If I_c is not used in the tests or loop body, this computation is omitted.

If the execution order must be preserved, an ordering on the entries will be maintained, and the same constructs can be used, with a negative stride for (D1) or preceding list reversal for (L1) if the direction in storage is reversed by normalization.[8] If forward or backward creation, or inward cancellation might occur, the same construct is used for (L1), in which computation AD=ALINK(AD) is performed *before* inward cancellation. For (D1) the following framework accounts for changes in the address set:

```
AD = ALOW(D)
DO WHILE (AD ≤ AHIGH(D))
    ...
    AD = AD + 1
ENDDO
```

Since in a WHILE-loop the condition is evaluated in every iteration, it might be useful to hoist an expensive computation of D out this loop. Additionally, adjustments to AD are

---

[8]For both data structures, we can also use a WHILE-loop that scans entries until the bounds are exceeded in order to limit the number of entries examined. Storing access patterns according to most frequent occurring directions reduces overhead for (L1), but might require routines that maintain a monotonic *decreasing* ordering on $\pi_i \cdot \sigma_A^{-1}$ values.

made for one of the following events, while AD is decremented after inward cancellation:

forward creation	backward creation
AD=AD-ALOW(D)	AD=AD-ALOW(D)
...	...
AD=AD+ALOW(D)	AD=AD+ALOW(D)+1

After backward creation, the offset to the base address has to be incremented, as is illustrated in figure 4 for insertion of a_{32} in row-wise storage during operation on a_{33}, where extra data movement occurs.

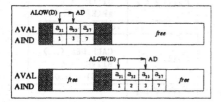

Figure 4: Extra Data Movement

Insertions in *other* access patterns of this collection that might cause garbage collection are correctly handled if the construct for forward creation is used, because this preserves the offset to the possibly changed base address. If several guards are encapsulated in the execution sets of loops in one nesting, different variables $ADlab$, declared as INTEGER, are used in the resulting nested constructs.

4.3   Dense Storage

An occurrence $A(F_A(\vec{I}))$ in the program that is contained in the section of a dense and consistent collection $C^i_{A_{k_j}}$ is replaced by the corresponding dense data structure '$ADSlab_{A_{k_j}}$ (E,D)', where D is determined as shown in the previous section for a zero offset. For index E, the normalized value of t is taken, i.e. $v_1 \cdot f_1(\vec{I}) + v_2 \cdot f_2(\vec{I}) - T^i_1 + 1$, where i is determined as for D. For example, if dense storage is selected for collection $C^i_A = \{(t,i)|i \leq t \leq i+4\}$ for $1 \leq i \leq 4$ (cf. section 3.2), the following conversion is applied on the next loop, since $i = I$:

```
DO I = 1, 4
  DO J = 1, 2
    B(I,J) = A(2*I+J-2,I)
  ENDDO              ↓
ENDDO      ADS(I+J-1,I)
```

The trapezoidal part of the matrix is stored in rectangular storage, i.e. access patterns are skewed in storage. This also occurs for the dense storage of collection $C^i_A = \{(t,t-i)|\max(1,1+i) \leq t \leq \min(M,M+i)\}$ for $-b_2 \leq i \leq b_1$ in the following fragment on a band matrix A (cf. section 2.2.3), since $i = -J$:

```
DO J = -b1 , b2
  DO I = MAX(1,1-J), MIN(M,M-J)
    Y(I) = Y(I) + A(I,J+I) * X(J+I)
  ENDDO              ↓
ENDDO      ADS(I-MAX(1,1-J)+1,b2+1-J)
```

Loop invariant computations in D and E can be hoisted out the loop. In the resulting storage scheme, all access patterns are up-justified, as is illustrated below for a 4×4 band matrix A with $b_1 = b_2 = 1$:

$$A = \begin{pmatrix} a_{11} & a_{12} & 0 & 0 \\ a_{21} & a_{22} & a_{23} & 0 \\ 0 & a_{32} & a_{33} & a_{34} \\ 0 & 0 & a_{43} & a_{44} \end{pmatrix}$$

a_{12}	a_{11}	a_{21}
a_{23}	a_{22}	a_{32}
a_{34}	a_{33}	a_{43}
-	a_{44}	-

However, in this case it is also valid to use just *one* of the bounds that is derived from the section bounds without increasing storage requirements, i.e. only $1 + i \leq t$ or $1 \leq t$ is considered. This automatically yields more sophisticated storage schemes with regular properties [14, 24], since E=I+J or E=I:

-	a_{11}	a_{21}	a_{12}	a_{11}	-
a_{12}	a_{22}	a_{32}	a_{23}	a_{22}	a_{21}
a_{23}	a_{33}	a_{43}	a_{34}	a_{33}	a_{32}
a_{34}	a_{44}	-	-	a_{44}	a_{43}
$1 + i \leq t$			$1 \leq t$		

If transversal enveloping access patterns occur in the collection, or directions have been normalized, this is correctly accounted for in D and E, as is illustrated with the following conversion for dense storage of $C^i_A = \{(i - 2t, t)|\lceil \frac{i-9}{2} \rceil \leq t \leq \lfloor \frac{i-1}{2} \rfloor\}$ for $11 \leq i \leq 19$, since $i = 4I + 7$ (cf. section 3.2):

```
DO I = 1, 3
  DO J = 1, 3
    B(I,J) = A(4*J-3,2*I-2*J+5)
  ENDDO              ↓
ENDDO      ADS(7-2*J,4*I-3)
```

If the direction belonging to an occurrence that is contained in the section of a dense collection $C^i_{A_{k_j}}$ has been ignored, the value of D and E are both variant in the innermost loop because i is determined as $f_1(\vec{I})$, $f_2(\vec{I})$, or $r_1 \cdot f_1(\vec{I}) - r_2 \cdot f_2(\vec{I})$ for row-, column- and diagonal-wise *stored* access patterns respectively. For instance, if the previous up-justified diagonal-wise storage is used, the following conversion is applied on a fragment with row-wise access of this band, since $i = I - J$:

```
DO I = 1, 4
  DO J = MAX(I-1,1), MIN(I+1,4)
    Y(I) = Y(I) + A(I,J) * X(J)
  ENDDO                    ↓
ENDDO              ADNS(I-MAX(1,1+I-J)+1,I-J+2)
```

4.4   Expansion

Expansion of an access pattern in a sparse collection $C^i_{A_{k_j}}$, found through D, into a dense vector AP of appropriate length in which all elements are initialized to zero, is performed with a scatter-operation. The value of each entry in the sparse data structure is assigned to the corresponding element in AP at index E. During the scatter, each Eth bit in an initially reset bit-vector BIT is also set to support a so-called switch [24], which provides information about the nonzero structure. Index E is computed as $\frac{val+o}{f}$ for integers f and o:

	val	f	o
r	y	1	$1 - T^i_1$
c	x	1	$1 - T^i_1$
d	y	r_2	$v_1 \cdot i - r_2(1 - T^i_1)$

These integers are passed as parameters to the scatter and gather subroutines, to construct index E from the stored row or column indices. Expansion of access pattern $P^{I,J}_A = \{(I + K, J + 2K) | 1 \leq K \leq 3\}$ for I=1 and J=1, for example, where storage is done according to the first collection in section 3.2, is performed as shown below, since D=3, $o = -1$ and $f = 2$:

ALOW(3)..AHIGH(3)

| AVAL | ... | a_{23} | a_{59} | a_{47} | ... |
| AIND | ... | 3 | 9 | 7 | ... |

| AP | a_{23} | 0.0 | a_{47} | a_{59} |

Within the scope of this expansion, all operations are performed on the dense representation AP. A right-hand side occurrence $A(F_A(\vec{I}))$ along the expanded access pattern is replaced by AP(E), while the following constructs are used for a left-hand side occurrence, depending on the value of the associated guard and right-hand side expression:

	nonzero r.h.s.
$F_A(\vec{I}) \in E_A$	AP(E) = ...
$F_A(\vec{I}) \notin E_A$	CALL INS_(...) BIT(E) = 1 AP(E) = ...
	zero r.h.s
$F_A(\vec{I}) \in E_A$	AD = LKP_(...) CALL DEL_(...) BIT(E) = 0 AP(E) = 0.0
$F_A(\vec{I}) \notin E_A$	–

Guard '$F_A(\vec{I}) \in E_A$' is evaluated without lookup overhead by bit-vector test 'BIT(E)=1' (details of code generation are given in the next section). Creation or cancellation are directly accounted if required. Because each deletion (or *ordered* insertion) requires a preceding lookup, expansions become more useful if this does not occur frequently. After all operations have been performed on this access pattern, the actual values are stored back with a gather operation. Used elements of AP and BIT are reset during the gather operation to support next expansions.[9]

For example, expansion of each access pattern of A results in the following conversion if sparse matrices A and B are stored in row-wise (D1) data structures, so that D=I, $f = 1$ and $o = 0$. Since guard '(I, J) $\in E_B$' has been encapsulated, the right-hand side expression is nonzero in every iteration, and the appropriate constructs are used:

```
DO I = 1, M
  DO J = 1, N
    A(I,J) = A(I,J) + B(I,J)
  ENDDO
ENDDO
                    ↓
```

---

[9]Resetting BIT is not necessary if the multiple switch technique [19, 24] is used with the value of D, but increases the storage requirements of vector BIT.

```
DO I = 1, M
  CALL SCATD1(AVAL,AIND,ALOW(I),
+   AHIGH(I),AP,BIT,1,0)
  DO AD = BLOW(I), BHIGH(I)
    IF (BIT(J) = 0) THEN
      CALL INSD1(AVAL,AIND,ALOW,
+       AHIGH,I,ANP,ASZ,ALST,J,.0)
      BIT(J) = 1
    ENDIF
    AP(J) = AP(J) + BVAL(AD)
  ENDDO
  CALL GATHD1(AVAL,AIND,ALOW(I),
+   AHIGH(I),AP,BIT,1,0)
ENDDO
```

The more operations are performed on an expanded access pattern, the less scatter and gather overhead dominates. Insertions are performed to obtain storage only and, therefore, do not require actual values. If assignments to AP occur, all operations along the expanded access pattern must be done on AP, since it contains the most recent value. To avoid run-time tests for inclusion in an expanded access pattern, expansion of an access pattern in a sparse collection is only performed if there are no occurrences in the loop-body with ignored direction and the same collection.

Expansions for which E equals the stored column or row indices because $f = 1$ and $o = 0$, can be done with sparse BLAS subroutines [11] if available, although the switch has to be handled separately in that case. For example, a scatter and gather that resets used elements of AP in sparse BLAS for (D1) are shown below:

```
CALL SSCTR(AHIGH(D)-ALOW(D)+1,
+   AVAL(ALOW(D)),AIND(ALOW(D)),AP)
   ...
CALL SGTHRZ(AHIGH(D)-ALOW(D)+1,AP,
+   AVAL(ALOW(D)),AIND(ALOW(D)))
```

4.5 Sparse Occurrences

In this section we present a 'condition-driven' code generation method for the occurrences of sparse matrices in a statement. Most explanation is done for (D1) because conversion into (L1) is straightforward. The approach is based on the fact that guard '$F_A(\vec{I}) \in E_A$' is 'true' for an occurrence with encapsulated guard or in dense storage, is evaluated with test 'BIT(E)=1' for an occurrence along an expanded access pattern, or is evaluated as follows otherwise:

```
AD = LKPD1(AIND,ALOW(D),AHIGH(D),E)
IF (AD ≠ ⊥) ...
```

Index E and D are determined as explained earlier. The σ_A-lookup is obtained as 'side-effect' of guard evaluation if the test succeeds. An occurrence at the right-hand side is replaced by AVAL(AD). For a left-hand side occurrence, the following constructs are required, depending on the value of its guard and right-hand side expression:[10]

	nonzero r.h.s.
$F_A(\vec{I}) \in E_A$	AVAL(AD) = ...
$F_A(\vec{I}) \notin E_A$	CALL INS_(...)
	zero r.h.s.
$F_A(\vec{I}) \in E_A$	CALL DEL_(...)
$F_A(\vec{I}) \notin E_A$	-

First, two variables χ and ψ are set to the conditions associated with the statement under consideration and right-hand side expression respectively (cf. section 2.1). All occurrences that are contained in the section of a dense collection are replaced as explained in section 4.3. Right-hand side occurrences with encapsulated guards are replaced by AVAL(AD), while code generation for left-hand side occurrences is deferred. Corresponding guards in χ and ψ changed into 'true'.

Subsequently, evaluation code is generated for each occurrence $A(F_A(\vec{I}))$ where guard '$F_A(\vec{I}) \in E_A$' dominates χ. If guard hoisting is valid (see section 2.2.1) this evaluation is generated at higher level, so that the test becomes more useful. A right-hand side occurrence is replaced by AVAL(AD) or AP(E), while code generation is deferred again otherwise. Conditions χ and ψ are adapted accordingly.

Evaluation code for all disjunctions in χ is generated next, while ψ is adapted accordingly. Right-hand side occurrences are replaced by AP(E) or AVAL(AD), which is valid since AVAL(⊥) = 0.0 holds. For example, the following code results for 'X=X+A(I,J)+B(J,K)', if occurrence B is along an expanded access pattern, because $\chi =$'$(I,J) \in E_A \lor (J,K) \in E_B$' holds:

---

[10] To support fast deletion in DELL1, function LKPL1 also supplies a pointer to an eventual *previous* entry. For an encapsulated guard, this pointer is maintained during the WHILE-loop.

```
AD = LKPD1(AIND,ALOW(D1),AHIGH(D1),E1)
IF (AD ≠ ⊥ ∨ BIT(E2)=1) THEN
  X = X + AVAL(AD) + AP(E2)
ENDIF
```

If there is a left-hand side sparse occurrence, further evaluation code on remaining guards in ψ is generated to differentiate between the cases ψ='true' and ψ='false' respectively. All remaining right-hand side occurrences are replaced by AP(E) or by:

$$AVAL(LKPD1(AIND,ALOW(D),AHIGH(D),E)) \qquad (4.5)$$

Finally, code for a possible left-hand side occurrence $A(F_A(\vec{I}))$ is generated. If the value of guard '$F_A(\vec{I}) \in E_A$' is not known in the current scope, differentiating evaluation code is generated. The value of the right-hand side expression is determined from the value of ψ in the current scope. Corresponding constructs are taken from the previous tables.

For example, the following code results for statement 'A(I,J)=X+A(I,J)*B(J,I)', because conditions χ and ψ are both 'true':

```
AD = LKPD1(AIND,ALOW(D),AHIGH(D),E)
EXPR = X + AVAL(AD) * BVAL(
+      LKPD1(BIND,BLOW(D1),BHIGH(D1),E1))
IF (AD ≠ ⊥) THEN
  AVAL(AD) = EXPR
ELSE
  CALL INSD1(AIND,ALOW,AHIGH,D,
+            ANP,ASZ,ALST,E,EXPR)
ENDIF
```

The address of construct (4.5) is saved, since it can be used by the following evaluation code. Identical parts in both branches are computed in variable EXPR before the IF-statement to prevent code duplication. Similarly, identical parts in the constructs for an expanded access pattern can be placed after the IF-statement, as was done in section 4.4.

Statement 'A(I,J)=0.0' is converted as shown below, since χ='(I,J) $\in E_A$' and ψ='false':

```
AD = LKPD1(AIND,ALOW(D),AHIGH(D),E)
IF (AD ≠ ⊥) THEN
  CALL DELD1(AIND,ALOW(D),
             AHIGH(D),ALST,AD)
ENDIF
```

For statement 'A(I,J)=A(I,J)*B(I,K)', code generation proceeds as follows, since χ='(I,J) $\in E_A$' and ψ='(I,J) $\in E_A \wedge$(I,K) $\in E_B$' hold. First, evaluation code for the dominating guard is generated. Since ψ='(I,K) $\in E_B$' holds afterwards, and a sparse occurrence appears at the left-hand side, further distinction on B is made. Finally, the constructs for a nonzero and zero right-hand side expression that correspond to '(I,J) $\in E_A$' are generated:

```
AD1 = LKPD1(AIND,ALOW(D1),
+            AHIGH(D1),E1)
IF (AD1 ≠ ⊥) THEN
  AD2 = LKPD1(BIND,BLOW(D2),
+              BHIGH(D2),E2)
  IF (AD2 ≠ ⊥) THEN
    AVAL(AD1) = AVAL(AD1) * BVAL(AD2)
  ELSE
    CALL DELD1(AIND,ALOW(D1),
+               AHIGH(D1),ALST,AD1)
  ENDIF
ENDIF
```

A complication arises if the guard of the left-hand side occurrence is involved in a disjunction in condition χ, since the exact value of this guard must be known to generate appropriate constructs. Therefore, evaluation code for that guard is generated first. In statement 'A(I,J)=A(I,J)*2.0+B(K,J)', for example, χ='(I,J) $\in E_A \vee$ (K,J) $\in E_B$' holds. Consequently, the following IF-statement results, differentiating between the cases χ ='true' and χ ='(K,J) $\in E_B$'. Further evaluation of χ results in the ELSE-branch, followed by an insertion because ψ ='true' holds:

```
AD1 = LKPD1(AIND,ALOW(D1),
+            AHIGH(D1),E1)
IF (AD1 ≠ ⊥) THEN
  AVAL(AD1) = AVAL(AD1) * 2.0 +
+   BVAL(LKPD1(BIND,BLOW(D2),
+              BHIGH(D2),E2))
ELSE
  AD2 = LKPD1(BIND,BLOW(D2),
+              BHIGH(D2),E2)
  IF (AD2 ≠ ⊥) THEN
    CALL INSD1(AIND,ALOW,AHIGH,D1,
+     ANP,ASZ,ALST,E1,BVAL(AD2))
  ENDIF
ENDIF
```

4.6 Storage Initialization

The most general and flexible initialization method is from-file construction, since it can be used for arbitrary sparse matrices. In order to keep the input storage scheme simple, coordinate scheme storage is used, where each file consists of an integer nz, followed by nz triples (i, j, a_{ij}) [14, 12, 15, 18, 30]. In [9], it is discussed how the compiler can generate appropriate initializing routines.

5 Examples

Consider code generation for the first fragment of section 3.4, where the diagonal of a sparse matrix A is dense. For $C_{A_1}^i$, data structure ADNS(N) is used (note that $I_2 - I_1 = 0$ holds for this collection), while the row- and column-wise access patterns of $C_{A_2}^i$ and $C_{A_3}^i$ are stored in AVAL. After distribution of the J-loop, guard encapsulation of '$(I,J) \in E_A$' and '$(J,I) \in E_A$' becomes feasible, and the following code results for (D1):

```
DO I = 1, N
  DG = DG + ADNS(I)
  DO AD = ALOW(I), AHIGH(I)
    LW = LW + AVAL(AD)
  ENDDO
  DO AD = ALOW(N+I), AHIGH(N+I)
    UP = UP + AVAL(AD)
  ENDDO
ENDDO
```

Consider a 4 × 4 matrix, with zero elements a_{31}, a_{42}, a_{24}, and $a_{34} = 0$. Possibly resulting contents of data structure (D1) and ADNS for this matrix are shown in figure 5, where array AHIGH has been omitted for clarity. Row or column indices are stored for column- and row-wise access patterns respectively. No ordering is required on the entries.

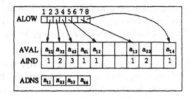

Figure 5: Data Structure (D1)

However, if many other occurrences in the program have row-wise access patterns, row-wise storage is selected for the whole matrix. If all attempts to reshape access patterns fail, the following code results. Usage of preceding tests for the first and last statement probably does not gain much execution time:

```
DO I = 1, N
  AD = LKPD1(AIND,ALOW(I),AHIGH(I),I)
  IF (AD ≠ ⊥) DG = DG + AVAL(AD)
  DO AD = ALOW(I), AHIGH(I)
    J = AIND(AD)
    IF (J ≤ I-1) LW = LW + AVAL(AD)
  ENDDO
  DO J = 1, I - 1
    AD = LKPD1(AIND,ALOW(J),AHIGH(J),I)
    IF (AD ≠ ⊥) UP = UP + AVAL(AD)
  ENDDO
ENDDO
```

Consider outer product code for matrix multiplication $C \leftarrow C + A \cdot B$, where matrices A, B and C are in fact sparse [14, 19, 21, 24]:

```
DO K = 1, N
  DO I = 1, M
    DO J = 1, L
      C(I,J) = C(I,J) + A(I,K) * B(K,J)
    ENDDO
  ENDDO
ENDDO
```

Condition. '$(I,K) \in E_A \land (K,J) \in E_B$' is associated with the assignment statement. Clearly, guard '$(K,J) \in E_B$' can be encapsulated in the execution set of the J-loop. However, because inward cancellation does not occur for A, the guard '$(I,K) \in E_A$' can be hoisted and encapsulated in the execution set of the I-loop. Additionally, to avoid expensive lookups for matrix C, each row of this matrix is expanded before operated on. Selecting column-wise storage for A and row-wise storage for B and C results in the following code for (D1):

```
  DO K = 1, N
    DO AD1 = ALOW(K), AHIGH(K)
    I = AIND(AD1)
    CALL SCATD1(CVAL,CIND,CLOW(I),
+               CHIGH(I),AP,BIT,1,0)
    DO AD2 = BLOW(K), BHIGH(K)
      J = BIND(AD2)
      IF (BIT(J) = 0) THEN
        CALL INSD1(CVAL,CIND,CLOW,
+             CHIGH,I,CNP,CSZ,CLST,J,0.0)
```

```
        BIT(J) = 1
      ENDIF
      AP(J) = AP(J) + AVAL(AD1)
+                  * BVAL(AD2)
    ENDDO
    CALL GATHD1(CVAL,CIND,CLOW(I),
+                  CHIGH(I),AP,BIT,1,0)
  ENDDO
ENDDO
```

Similarly, two guard encapsulations are feasible for the middle product JKI and inner product IKJ if both matrices are stored column- or row-wise respectively, and for middle product JIK if A and B are stored row- and column-wise. However, in inner product IJK operations on zeros are likely to occur, since a conjunction cannot be encapsulated.

In [8] several version for LU-factorization for (D1) were presented under the assumption that garbage collection did not occur. Here, we present a version for row-wise storage that correctly accounts for garbage collection, possibly caused by insertions in the Jth row.

```
DO J = 2, N
  DO I = 1, J - 1
S1 : A(J,I) = A(J,I) / A(I,I)
    DO K = I + 1, N
S2 :    A(J,K) = A(J,K) - A(J,I) * A(I,K)
    ENDDO
  ENDDO
ENDDO      ↓
  DO J = 2, N
  CALL SCATD1(AVAL,AIND,ALOW(J),
+              AHIGH(J),AP,BIT)
    DO I = 1, J - 1
    IF (BIT(I) ≠ 0) THEN
    AP(I) = AP(I) / AVAL(
+      LKPD1(AIND,ALOW(I),AHIGH(I),I))
    KA = ALOW(I)
    DO WHILE (KA ≤ AHIGH(I))
      K = AIND(KA)
      IF (I+1 ≤ K) THEN
        IF (BIT(K) = 0) THEN
        KA = KA - ALOW(I)
        CALL INSD1(AVAL,AIND,ALOW,
+        AHIGH,J,ANP,ASZ,ALST,K,0.0)
        KA = KA + ALOW(I)
        BIT(K) = 1
        ENDIF
      AP(K) = AP(K)-AP(I)*AVAL(KA)
      ENDIF
    KA = KA + 1
```

```
    ENDDO
  ENDIF
  ENDDO
  CALL GATHD1(AVAL,AIND,ALOW(J),
+              AHIGH(J),AP,BIT)
  ENDDO
```

Because $\psi=$'true' holds after code generation for condition $\chi=$'$(J,I) \in E_A \wedge (I,K) \in E_A$' of S_2, only a nonzero right-hand side construct is generated.

6 Future Research

More research is necessary into strategies for solving inconsistencies, automatic analysis of nonzero structures, and problems that are transparent in the original dense code, such as the reduction of creation (fill-in). Since in practical implementations user-defined subroutines appear, problems that arise if sparse matrices are passed as parameter in the original code must also be dealt with.

Acknowledgements The authors would like to thank Arnold Niessen for his comments.

References

[1] A.V. Aho, R. Sethi, and J.D. Ullman. *Compilers Principles, Techniques and Tools.* Addison-Wesley publishing company, 1986.

[2] Randy Allen and Ken Kennedy. Automatic translation of fortran programs to vector form. *ACM Transactions on Programming Languages and Systems*, Volume 9:491–542, 1987.

[3] Vasanth Balasundaram. *Interactive Parallelization of Numerical Scientific Programs.* PhD thesis, Department of Computer Science, Rice University, 1989.

[4] Vasanth Balasundaram. A mechanism for keeping useful internal information in parallel programming tools: The data access descriptor. *Journal of Parallel and Distributed Computing*, Volume 9:154–170, 1990.

[5] U. Banerjee. *Dependence Analysis for Supercomputing.* Kluwer Academic Publishers, Boston, 1988.

[6] U. Banerjee. Unimodular transformations of double loops. In *Proceedings of Third Workshop on Languages*

and *Compilers for Parallel Computing*, 1990.

[7] Aart J.C. Bik and Harry A.G. Wijshoff. Advanced compiler optimizations for sparse computations. In *Proceedings of Supercomputing 93*, 1993. To appear.

[8] Aart J.C. Bik and Harry A.G. Wijshoff. Compilation techniques for sparse matrix computations. In *Proceedings of the International Conference on Supercomputing*, pages 416–424, 1993.

[9] Aart J.C. Bik and Harry A.G. Wijshoff. A sparse compiler. Technical Report no. 93-04, Dept. of Computer Science, Leiden University, 1993.

[10] A.R. Curtis and J.K. Reid. The solution of large sparse unsymmetric systems of linear equations. *Journal Inst. Maths. Applics.*, Volume 8:344–353, 1971.

[11] David S. Dodson, Roger G. Grimes, and John G. Lewis. Sparse extensions to the fortran basic linear algebra subprograms. *ACM Transactions on Mathematical Software*, Volume 17:253–263, 1991.

[12] I. S. Duff, Roger G. Grimes, and John G. Lewis. Sparse matrix test problems. *ACM Transactions on Mathematical Software*, Volume 15:1–14, 1989.

[13] I.S. Duff. Data structures, algorithms and software for sparse matrices. In David J. Evans, editor, *Sparsity and Its Applications*, pages 1–29. Cambridge University Press, 1985.

[14] I.S. Duff, A.M. Erisman, and J.K. Reid. *Direct Methods for Sparse Matrices*. Oxford Science Publications, 1990.

[15] I.S. Duff and J.K. Reid. Some design features of a sparse matrix code. *ACM Transactions on Mathematical Software*, pages 18–35, 1979.

[16] C. Eisenbeis, O. Temam, and H. Wijshoff. On efficiently characterizing solutions of linear diophantine equations and its application to data dependence analysis. In *Proceedings of the Seventh International Symposium on Computer and Information Sciences*, 1992.

[17] J. Engelfriet. Attribute grammars: Attribute evaluation methods. In B. Lorho, editor, *Methods and Tools for Compiler Construction*, pages 103–138. Cambridge University Press, 1984.

[18] Alan George and Joseph W. Liu. The design of a user interface for a sparse matrix package. *ACM Transactions on Mathematical Software*, Volume 5:139–162, 1979.

[19] Fred G. Gustavson. Two fast algorithms for sparse matrices: Multiplication and permuted transposition. *ACM Transactions on Mathematical Software*, Volume 4:250–269, 1978.

[20] David J. Kuck. *The Structure of Computers and Computations*. John Wiley and Sons, New York, 1978. Volume 1.

[21] John Michael McNamee. Algorithm 408: A sparse matrix package. *Communications of the ACM*, pages 265–273, 1971.

[22] Samuel P. Midkiff. *The Dependence Analysis and Synchronization of Parallel Programs*. PhD thesis, C.S.R.D., 1993.

[23] David A. Padua and Michael J. Wolfe. Advanced compiler optimizations for supercomputers. *Communications of the ACM*, pages 1184–1201, 1986.

[24] Sergio Pissanetsky. *Sparse Matrix Technology*. Academic Press, London, 1984.

[25] C.D. Polychronoupolos. *Parallel Programming and Compilers*. Kluwer Academic Publishers, Boston, 1988.

[26] Harry A.G. Wijshoff. Implementing sparse blas primitives on concurrent/vector processors: a case study. Technical Report no. 843, Center for Supercomputing Research and Development, University of Illinios, 1989.

[27] Michael E. Wolf and Monica S. Lam. A loop transformation theory and an algorithm to maximize parallelism. *IEEE Transactions on Parallel and Distributed Algorithms*, pages 452–471, 1991.

[28] Michael J. Wolfe. *Optimizing Supercompilers for Supercomputers*. Pitman, London, 1989.

[29] H. Zima. *Supercompilers for Parallel and Vector Computers*. ACM Press, New York, 1990.

[30] Zahari Zlatev. *Computational Methods for General Sparse Matrices*. Kluwer Academic Publishers, 1991.

Synchronization Issues in Data-Parallel Languages*

Sundeep Prakash and Maneesh Dhagat and Rajive Bagrodia

Computer Science Department, University of California, Los Angeles, CA 90024

Abstract. Data-parallel programming has established itself as the preferred way of programming a large class of scientific applications. In this paper, we address the issue of reducing synchronization costs when implementing a data-parallel language on an asynchronous architecture. The synchronization issue is addressed from two perspectives: first, we describe language constructs that allow the programmer to specify that different parts of a data-parallel program be synchronized at different levels of granularity. Secondly, we show how existing tools and algorithms for data dependency analysis can be used by the compiler to both reduce the number of barriers and to replace global barriers by cheaper clustered synchronizations. Although the techniques presented in the paper are general purpose, we describe them in the context of a data-parallel language called UC developed at UCLA. Reducing the number of barriers improves program execution time by reducing synchronization time and also processor stall times.

1 Introduction

Data-parallel programming has established itself as the preferred way of programming a large class of scientific applications. The primary distinction between a data-parallel program and a control (or task) parallel program is that the former has a single locus of control whereas the latter typically has multiple locii of control. This feature makes it considerably easier to design and debug data parallel programs.

A number of data-parallel languages have been designed and implemented. In most exisiting language proposals, the granularity of synchronization is determined by the specific constructs provided by the language. For instance, at one extreme we have essentially SIMD languages like C* [RS87] and Dataparallel C [HQL+91] where synchronization is defined at the level of individual operations: all parallel threads are either executing the same operation or are idle. On the other hand, languages like Kali [MR90] restrict access to remote data only at selected points in a program, like at the beginning of successive iterations of a *forall* loop. This ensures that a Kali program needs to be synchronized only at precisely those points where communication is possible; the multiple threads can execute asynchronously between two successive synchronization points. Other

* This research was partially supported under NSF PYI Award No. ASC-9157610, ONR Grant No. N00014-91-J-1605, and Rockwell International Award No. L911014.

languages like UC [ABCD93] and DINO [RSW91] permit synchronization with multiple grain size: for instance parallel functions use copy in/copy out semantics so that they need to be synchronized only at the point of call and return; other statements are synchronized at a finer level of granularity.

The synchronization granularity of a language impacts both its semantics and the efficiency of its implementations on asynchronous architectures. Thus, languages that are synchronized at the operation level have simple semantics, as the programmer has access to the correct global state of the program before executing any operation. However, implementing such a strict notation on an asynchronous distributed memory architecture is expensive as a barrier may potentially be required before the execution of every operation[2]. This is particularly the case if the language uses a universal shared memory model where no syntactic distinction is made between local and remote data. In contrast, a language with a weaker synchronization model forces the programmer to restrict remote data access to specific points in their code. This places the burden of maintaining a coherent view of the shared data explicitly on the programmer. However, an implementation of this model on an asynchronous architecture requires a smaller number of barrier synchronizations as compared with the previous model. Reducing barrier synchronizations improves execution efficiency by reducing both the blocking and communication times.

In this paper, we address the issue of reducing synchronization costs when implementing a data-parallel language on an asynchronous architecture. The synchronization issue is addressed from two perspectives: first, we describe language constructs that allow the programmer to specify that different parts of a data-parallel program be synchronized at different levels of granularity. This allows the programmer to take on the burden of explicit data management to reduce synchronization costs. It also supports an iterative approach to program design where programs are initially designed assuming operation level synchronization and may be later refined to use a weaker synchronization granularity. Secondly, we show how existing tools and algorithms for data dependency analysis can be used by the compiler to both reduce the number of barriers and to replace global barriers by cheaper clustered synchronizations. The next section is a brief description of the language constructs. Particular emphasis has been placed on the constructs that are used to alter the synchronization granularity of the programs. Section 3 describes the code transformations used by the compiler to either remove unnecessary barriers or replace them by less expensive operations. Section 4 presents a preliminary performance analysis of the compiler transformations. Section 5 is the conclusion.

2 The UC Programming Language

UC [ABCD93] is a data-parallel extension of C. This section gives a brief description of the language. For a complete description, the reader is referred to [BA92].

---

[2] The issue of compiler optimizations and data distributions that reduce the number of synchronizations is addressed subsequently.

UC enhances C with a data-type called *index-set* and some new operators to specify parallel execution of statements. An index-set represents an ordered set of integers. The most commonly used UC operators are *reduction* and *parallel assignment*. Reduction is used to perform an associative, commutative binary operation on a set of elements; a parallel assignment is used to simultaneously modify a set of elements. The set of elements used by these parallel operators is specified by an *index-set*. In addition, an optional predicate allows the operation to be performed on a subset of elements.

Consider the UC program in Figure 1. The program computes matrix c as the product of two $N \times N$ matrices a and b. The program declarations include the standard C declarations for matrices a, b and c (line 1). In addition, three index-sets I, J and K are declared (line 2). The declaration of an index-set uses two identifiers, the first one (for example I) refers to the index-set itself and the second (for example i) refers to an arbitrary element of the set. Each index-set in the example consists of N integers from 0 to N-1.

```
1  int a[N][N], b[N][N], c[N][N];
2  index_set I:i = {0..N-1}, J:j=I, K:k=I;
3  par(I,J)
4      c[i][j] = $+(K; a[i][k]*b[k][j]);
```

Fig. 1. Matrix multiplication in UC

The UC keyword **par** (line 3) specifies parallel execution of the assignment statement in line 4. The index-set(s) contained in the par statement determine the number of instances of the assignment statement that are executed in parallel. In this case, N^2 instances of the assignment will be executed, one for each of the N^2 elements in the product set $I*J$. Now consider the assignment statement itself. For a given (i, j), the value of *c[i][j]* is computed as the dot product of two vectors: the ith row of a and the jth column of b. The dot product is programmed in UC as a reduction (line 4). The reduction (denoted by '$+') specifies the addition of N expressions, one for each value of index-element k, where the k^{th} expression is *a[i][k]*b[k][j]*. Besides addition, other associative, symmetric operators may also be used in a reduction. These include '$&&' for logical AND, '$||' for logical OR, '$>' for maximum, '$<' for minimum, '$*' for multiplication and '$,' to return the value of an arbitrary operand.

The next example illustrates the use of a mask to select a subset of the elements from an index-set. The program in Figure 2 computes the trace of array a (the sum of elements on its main diagonal). The declarations are similar to the previous example and are omitted. The body is a single reduction which computes the sum of the diagonal elements. The predicate *(i == j)* selects the diagonal elements of array a. The keyword **st** (such that) in the reduction separates the index-sets from the boolean expression. (Note that this reduction may be expressed more concisely as: $+ *(I; a[i][i])*. If the operand list of a reduction is empty, the reduction returns the identity value for the corresponding reduction operator. A boolean expression may also be used in a par statement to restrict the assignment operation to a subset of the array elements. The par statement may also contain a sequence of statements. In this case, successive statements are executed synchronously for each element in the index-set(s) named in the enclosing par statement. If a par statement includes (parallel) function calls, multiple instances of the called function are executed asynchronously. Function parameters are passed by value result and output parameters of the parallel function are required to be non-interfering, i.e. an actual parameter may be modified by at most one instance of the parallel function. Global access in a parallel function is restricted to read only data. The mask in a par statement can be an arbitrary predicate and the par statement may contain any UC or C statements including conditionals, iterative construct or nested par statements.

$$\text{trace} = \$+(I,J \text{ st } (i == j) \text{ a}[i][j]);$$

Fig. 2. Trace computation in UC

A par statement specifies synchronous execution of a a set of statements, where the multiple instances are synchronized at the operation level. The keyword **par** may be thought of as a composition operator that specifies synchronous execution of its statement operands. A number of other composition operators are also supported by UC. These include **seq** for sequential execution, **arb** for asynchronous execution, and ***solve** for fixed-point computations. We describe the **seq** and **arb** composition operators.

If the keyword **par** of a UC statement is replaced by **seq**, the corresponding statement (or statement block) is executed sequentially for each element in the index-set. The elements are selected in the order specified in the declaration of the corresponding index-set. If a seq statement includes multiple index-sets then the order of the elements in the product set is determined by the order in which the index-sets are specified in the statement. For example, consider the UC program of Figure 1 with keyword par in line 3 replaced by seq. This modification will cause elements in matrix c to be computed sequentially in row major order.

If the keyword **par** of a UC statement is replaced by **arb**, the multiple instances of the corresponding statement are assumed to be independent and may hence be executed asynchronously. The arb statement may be implemented more efficiently than the par statement on asynchronous architectures. To preserve the synchronous semantics of a par statement on an asynchronous architecture, a barrier synchronization is needed prior to the evaluation of each operation in the statement. Of course, a smart compiler may be able to analyze the dependencies in the statement and remove unnecessary barriers. However, for many statements, particularly those where array subscript expressions include variables or array references, the analysis is hard and the compiler may be forced to insert barriers in a conservative manner. The arb statement may be used by a programmer to specify a weaker granularity of synchronization for the program. Consider the following code fragments:

```
par (I) {                          arb (I) {
    a[f(i)] = b[i];                    a[f(i)] = b[i];
    c[i] = a[g(i)];                    c[i] = a[g(i)];
}                                  }
```

When compiling the fragment on the left, the compiler must place a barrier between the two statements for consistency with the semantics of a par statement. However, if the programmer can infer that the two statements access non-overlapping sets of elements from array a, the par statement may be replaced by the arb statement on the right, rendering the barrier unnecessary. Arb and par statements may be nested within each other to modify the synchronization as needed. In the following example, the arb statement is used to specify that functions f and g reference non-overlapping elements of a, which allows the statement to be executed asynchronously – thus reducing the number of barrier synchronization. Note that an optimizing compiler could easily deduce that the first assignment to array a may also be moved within the arb statement, although making this determination for the third assignment statement is harder. Compiler optimizations are discussed in the next section.

```
par (I) {
    a[i] = h(i);
    arb
        a[f(i)] = b[i] + a[g(i)];
    c[i] = a[h(i)];
}
```

3 Multicomputer Implementation

The main issues in implementing a dataparallel language on a multicomputer are (1) Data mapping and (2) Synchronization detection. In this paper, we concentrate on the second issue. We use standard data dependency analysis to reveal and efficiently implement the minimum number of synchronization points needed to correctly implement the statements of a dataparallel language. We use the par statement of UC as an example.

The synchronous semantics of a par statement may be obtained by a straightforward implementation that introduces a barrier before evaluating every parallel operand. However, for almost any program, the number of barriers can be dramatically reduced by examining the data dependencies among variables referenced and updated in the statement.

We first show how well-known data dependence analysis techniques can be used to construct a *synchronization graph* for a par statement. This graph can be used to deduce the minimal number of barriers needed to preserve program dependencies. We then show how additional information from the synchronization graph can be used to replace some barriers with less expensive pair-wise synchronization operations. There are obvious similarities between our goals and the use of dependency graphs for concurrentization of sequential programs[PW86]. However, there are some important differences: whereas concurrentization requires that all analysis be completed at compile-time, we are able to do some run-time analysis to further refine dependency information. Secondly, we use dependency information to replace barriers by fuzzy barriers[Gup89] which allow a thread to conditionally continue execution beyond the global barrier, before the other threads have reached the barrier. Although analysis is presented here in the context of a UC program, the results and techniques are equally applicable for other data parallel languages including HPF[For92].

In the remainder of this section, we assume that each array has been folded into a number of uniform segments, where each segment is mapped to a unique processor.

3.1 Synchronization Graphs

Here we briefly describe the three types of data dependencies that occur in UC programs. The description is adapted from [BENP93] where the dependencies were introduced in the context of for loops in sequential programs. In this section, these dependencies are defined in the context of par statements and it is shown how they can be easily extracted and used to construct synchronization graphs for UC programs. The following small example illustrates the three types of data dependencies:

```
par (I)
{
    a[i] = c[i];                /* s1 */
    b[i] = a[i+1] + c[i];       /* s2 */
    b[i] += d[f(i)];            /* s3 */
    d[i] = c[i];               /* s4 */
}
```

The notation s_j denotes the instance of statement s for an element j of the index-set I.

- **Flow** dependence: the value computed by the instance $s1_j$ is used by the instance $s2_{j-1}$. $s2$ is said to be flow dependent on $s1$, or $s1\ \delta^f\ s2$.
- **Anti**-dependence: a value for variable $d[f(j)]$ is used by the instance $s3_j$, and another value for this variable is later computed by instance $s4_{f(j)}$. $s4$ is anti-dependent on $s3$, or $s3\ \delta^a\ s4$.
- **Output** dependence: the instance $s2_j$ and the instance $s3_j$ both compute a value for the variable $b[j]$, such that the value computed by $s3_j$ is stored after the value computed by $s2_j$. $s3$ is output dependent on $s2$ or $s2\ \delta^o\ s3$.

Note that, in using par, we are working with an explicitly parallel notation. If the body of the above par statement existed instead in a *do-loop* (or, equivalently, a UC seq loop), the dependencies would become the following (where the notation s_j denotes that the instance of statement s for an iteration j): (1) $s2_j$ $\delta^o\ s3_j$, (2) $s2_j\ \delta^a\ s1_{j+1}$, and (3) $s3_j\ \delta\ s4_{f(j)}{}^3$.

---

[3] May be a flow or anti-dependence, depending on the nature of the expression $f(j)$

A synchronization graph for a par statement may be obtained by simple transformations on a data dependency graph derived for a corresponding *do loop*. The do loop is derived as follows: the body of the loop is the same as the body of the par statement and the iteration range is defined by the bounds of the index-set. The dependency graph for the loop can be derived using well-known techniques presented in standard references on dependency analysis [AK87, Wol89, FOW87, BENP93]. The transformation rules for deriving a synchronization flow graph from a dependency graph are summarized below:

- Flow and anti-dependencies within the same statement both translate to anti-dependencies. Consider the following statement:

  a[e(i)] = ... a[f(i)] ...;

  If $e(i)$ were i and $f(i)$ were i-1 this would be flow dependency in a do loop. If $f(i)$ were i+1 this would be an anti-dependency. In a par statement both are anti-dependencies.

- All flow and anti-dependencies in which the statement using a variable occurs before the statement defining it translate to antidependencies. Consider the following statements:

... = ... a[f(i)] ...;	/* s1 */
a[g(i)] = ...;	/* s2 */

  If $f(i)$ were i-1 and $g(i)$ were i there would be a flow dependency from s2 to s1 in a do loop. If $f(i)$ were i+1 there would be an anti-dependency from s1 to s2. In a par statement both are anti-dependencies from s1 to s2.

- All flow and anti-dependencies in which the statement defining a variable occurs before the statement using it, translate to flow dependencies. Consider the following statements:

a[g(i)] = ...;	/* s1 */
... = ...a[f(i)]...;	/* s2 */

  There could either be a flow dependency from s2 to s1 or an anti-dependency from s1 to s2 in a do loop. In a par statement there will be a flow dependency from s1 to s2.

- Output dependencies remain output dependencies in all cases.

In concurrentizing a do-loop, we distinguish between inter-iteration and intra-iteration dependencies. In the context of par statements, we similarly distinguish between *inter-thread* and *intra-thread* dependencies. Intra-thread dependencies can be deleted from the synchronization graph, since a thread executes sequentially, such dependencies are automatically obeyed.

The synchronization graph for the par statement shown in the beginning of the section appears in figure 3(a). We now show how some simple program transformations can eliminate some of the dependencies in the synchronization graph.

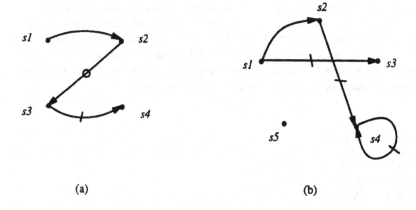

Fig. 3. Synchronization Graphs

3.2 Program transformations

As shown in [PW86], simple program transformations can eliminate some dependencies in do loops. Many of the same transformations can be applied on par statements to eliminate dependencies in the synchronization graph. In particular, we show how *renaming* and *alignment* can be used to remove some dependencies.

The program fragment in figure 4 (on left) exhibits the inter-thread dependencies: (1) $s1\ \delta^{a}\ s1$, (2) $s1\ \delta^{o}\ s3$, and (3) $s1\ \delta^{f}\ s2$. The first two dependencies can be eliminated by renaming the array a as shown in the transformed program on the right.

```
par (I) {
    a[i+1] = a[i] + 1;      /* s1 */
    b[i] = a[i] + c[i];     /* s2 */
    a[i] = d[i] + e[i];     /* s3 */
}
par (I) {
    tmp[i+1] = a[i] + 1;    /* s1 */
    b[i] = tmp[i] + c[i];   /* s2 */
    a[i] = d[i] + e[i];     /* s3 */
}
```

Fig. 4. Using Renaming to remove Output and Anti-Dependencies

Alignment or loop skewing [MA87] is another technique to remove inter-thread dependencies. By selectively shifting the access pattern of some statements in the par statement body it is possible to reduce the number of dependencies. Consider the code fragment in figure 5 (on left) which exhibits the dependencies: (1)$s1\ \delta^f\ s2$, (2) $s2\ \delta^a\ s3$ and (3) $s1\ \delta^o\ s3$. Shifting the access patterns of $s1$ and $s3$ results in the transformed code on the right where no inter-thread dependencies exist. This transformed par statement can now be re-written as an arb statement, which does not require any synchronization.

```
index_set I:i = {0..N};
par (I) {
    a[i+1] = 2 * c[i];        /* s1 */
    b[i] = a[i] + c[i];       /* s2 */
    a[i+2] = d[i] + e[i];     /* s3 */
}
index_set I:i = {0..N+2};
par (I) {
    if ((i >= 1) && (i <= N+1))
        a[i] = 2 * c[i-1];              /* s1 */
    if ((i >= 0) && (i <= N))
        b[i] = a[i] + c[i];            /* s2 */
    if ((i >= 2) && (i <= N+2))
        a[i] = d[i-2] + e[i-2];        /* s3 */
}
```

Fig. 5. Using Alignment to remove Dependencies

3.3 Minimizing Number of Barrier Synchronizations

The operation-by-operation synchronization model persented thus far is overly restrictive. Given a synchronization graph, it is possible to deduce the minimal number of barriers required such that each dependency is enforced. More precisely, given a set of intervals spanned by flow, anti, and output dependencies, the minimal number of barrier sychronizations must be determined such that each interval spans at least one barrier. This problem can be solved in polynomial time[Gav72]; a simple greedy algorithm devised by Quinn and Hatcher[QHS91] extracts a minimal set of synchronizations from a set of dependencies arcs represented as a sychronization graph. At each step the algorithm selects, of all arcs, the dependency arc whose head points to the earliest point in the program. A barrier is inserted before this point and the arc is removed from the synchronization graph. Additionally, all arcs whose tail is at a point before and the head at a point after the barrier are removed from the synchronization graph. The algorithm terminates when the synchronization graph contains no more arcs.

The example in figure 6 (on left) illustrates the use of this algorithm. The dependency arcs are shown in the synchronization graph of figure 3(b). The algorithm determines that two barriers are needed: before statement *s2*, and before the assignment in *s4*. Finally, the equivalent code with minimum number of barriers implemented with UC arb statements is shown in figure 6 (on right).

```
par (I)
{
    a[i] = b[i] + c[i];          /* s1 */
    d[i] = a[i+1] + e[i];        /* s2 */
    b[i+1] = m[i] + g[i];        /* s3 */
    e[i-1] = e[i+1] + d[i];      /* s4 */
    m[i] = h[i] + j[i];          /* s5 */
}
arb (I) {
    a[i] = b[i] + c[i];
}
arb (I) {
    d[i] = a[i+1] + e[i];
    b[i+1] = m[i] + g[i];
    tmp[i] = e[i+1] + d[i];
}
arb (I) {
    e[i-1] = tmp[i];
    m[i] = h[i] + j[i];
}
```

Fig. 6. Deducing Minimal Number of Barriers

3.4 Conditions for Weakening Barriers

On an asynchronous distributed memory machine, implementation of an inter-thread dependency requires a set of communication operations between pairs (or clusters) of processors. Barriers perform only a part of this function by synchronizing all processors. Processors must, at run-time, request and obtain data from each other to complete the communication operation. This implies that processors must block at two points (1) at the barrier (2) while waiting for the requested data. In many cases, it is possible to identify the communication pattern at compile time, which enables processors to send data to other processors without having to wait for a request. This not only eliminates barriers, but reduces the time a processor waits for a data item to arrive.

Consider the following code fragment which shows how a flow dependency may be implemented by a communication operation. We assume that all the statements are aligned, hence every flow dependency must be of the form shown:

```
par (I) {
    a[i] = ... ;                    /* s1 */
    ...
    b[i] = a[g(i)];                 /* s2 */
}
```

Here, $a[i]$ is written by processor i and later used by processor $g^{-1}(i)$. If $g^{-1}(i)$ can be calculated at compile time, the par statement may be rewritten as shown below. We use the notation **send**(a, {i}) to mean "send a message containing the value of the locally stored variable a to the set of processors i." Similarly, the notation **blx_recv**(b, i) means "block until a message is received from processor i, and assign the value contained in the message to the locally stored variable b." For simplicity, we assume that the order of messages is preserved.

```
par (I) {
    a[i] = ... ;                    /* s1 */
    send(a, {g⁻¹(i))});

    ...
    blx_recv(tmp, g(i));
    b[i] = tmp;                     /* s2 */
}
```

The code for sending $a[i]$ to processor $g^{-1}(i)$ should be moved up as much as possible in order to hide the communication latency.

Anti-dependencies can be handled in much the same way. Consider the above code fragment with the statements *s1* and *s2* interchanged. The antidependency requires processor i to transmit the value of $a[i]$ to processor $g^{-1}(i)$ before it writes it at statement *s1*. In fact, for every anti-dependency, there must exist a flow dependency before it. Implementing the flow dependency by a communication operation automatically eliminates the need for the implementation of the anti-dependency.

An example clearly shows the working of this method: The following **par** statement

```
par (I) {
    a[i] = b[i+1] + c[i];          /* s1 */
    f(c[i]);
    b[i] = a[i+1] / 2;             /* s2 */
}
```

contains the dependencies *s1* δ^f *s2* and *s1* δ^a *s2*. The following is the transformed program:

```
arb (I) {
    if (i > 0) send(b, i-1);
    if (i < N-1) blx_recv(a, i+1);
    a[i] += c[i];                  /* s1 */
    if (i < N-1) send(a, i+1);
    f(c[i]);
    if (i > 0) blx_recv(b, i-1);
    b[i] /= 2;                     /* s2 */
}
```

As stated earlier, we have assumed that all statements are aligned. This automatically eliminates output dependencies. However, not all statements can be aligned. A statement of the following form may only be aligned if $g^{-1}(i)$ can be calculated at compile time:

```
par (I)
    a[g(i)] = ... ;
```

In general, whenever $g^{-1}(i)$ can be calculated (for all dependencies), a barrier can be replaced by significantly cheaper communication operations. In other cases, a barrier may be used. However, some run-time methods may be used to eliminate a barrier in some of these cases. Such cases are explored in subsequent sections.

3.5 Run Time Methods

Fuzzy Barriers and Non-blocking Requests If communicating pairs (or clusters) between two dependent statements cannot be identified at compile-time, the compiler is forced to insert a barrier to maintain the semantics of the par statement. However, the total blocking time may be reduced by time taken for the computation in between the two statements, either by using fuzzy barriers or issuing early requests for data. Consider the following code segment:

```
par (I) {
    a[i] = ... ;              /* s1 */
    ...
    b[i] = a[g(i)];           /* s2 */
    ...
    a[i] = ... ;              /* s3 */
}
```

If the function $g^{-1}(i)$ is unkown at compile-time, a barrier must be inserted between s1 and s2; and between s2 and s3. Also, a request must be generated at s2 for data element a[g(i)]. The two blocking points are (1) at the barrier and (2) at the data request point. The time at the blocking points may be reduced by two methods: *fuzzy barriers* and *non-blocking requests*.

The blocking time at the barrier can be reduced by replacing it with a fuzzy barrier[Gup89] extending from just after s1 to just before s2. No thread may proceed to s2 till all thread have finished executing s1. This reduces blocking time at the barrier by overlapping it with the computation performed between s1 and s2. Fuzzy barriers can be implemented in hardware[Gup89], or in software in much the same way as a barrier. Each processor broadcasts to all other processors on reaching the beginning of the fuzzy barrier, continues computation until the end, and then waits until it has collected the broadcast messages of all other processors.

The blocking time at request for remote data can be reduced by inserting a barrier just after s1 and making a non-blocking request for a[g(i)]; the value is later received by a blocking receive operation at s2. This reduces the communication latency by overlapping with the computation performed between s1 and s2.

Both methods, however, cannot be applied simultaneously. In case where processors are synchronized to a greater degree, the second method may be preferable, and in cases where processors are loosely synchronized (and waiting time at the barrier is high) the first method may perform better.

The symmetrical case to the above is the following:

```
par (I) {
    a[g(i)] = ... ;                 /* s1 */
    ...
    b[i] = a[i];                    /* s2 */
}
```

In this case, it is not known (and cannot be locally calculated) which thread will write the value of $a[i]$ at $s1$, which is then to be used at $s2$. However, a fuzzy barrier between statements $s1$ and $s2$ guarantees that when thread i reaches $s2$ all threads have completed $s1$, hence ensuring that the value of $a[i]$ read is the most recent one.

Definition Variables In the first case considered in the previous section, the reason a barrier is needed is to guarantee that all requests for data have been serviced before the data is changed. The requests cannot be anticipated at compile time. An obvious solution is to make a copy of the data at the point its value is initialized. This is the function performed by a definition variable. Requests for the value of a definition variable wait for service until the variable gets initialized. The blocking time of the barrier is thus eliminated, leaving only the blocking time waiting for the request to be serviced. There is also the run-time overhead of implementing the definition variable, which is as yet unmeasured.

Consider the first code fragment of the previous section. If implemented without any barriers, the data request for $a[g(i)]$ is made as early as possible before statement $s2$. However, if this request arrives at processor $g(i)$ (1) before it has executed statement s1 or (2) after it has executed statement $s3$, a race condition is generated. To prevent this we use a *definition variable* which is assigned the value of $a[i]$ at statement $s1$. Consider the following transformed code fragment (where **request** is defined similarly as send):

```
par (I) {
    a[i] = ...;                     /* s1 */
    def_a[i] = a[i];                /* s1' */
    request(def_a, g(i));           /* s1" */
    ...
    blx_recv(tmp, g(i));            /* s2' */
    b[i] = tmp[i];                  /* s2 */
    ...
    a[i] = ...;                     /* s3 */
}
```

In the above code, $def_a[i]$ is assigned at statement $s1'$. Any requests received before that are queued at the variable. The moment it is assigned, all waiting requests are serviced. The definition variable can be freed after all processors get past statement $s2$ as no more requests for the value of $def_a[i]$ will be received.

The life of the definition variable extends from $s1'$ to a barrier after $s2$ referred to as the *garbage collection barrier*. No processor actually needs to wait at a garbage collection barrier; it is merely used to detect the point at which we may free the memory used for the definition variable. Using this method, the processor only wait which its data request is being serviced.

The same method of definition variables cannot be used for the second code fragment of the previous section. If we make $a[i]$ a definition variable at $s1$, then thread i would wait at statement $s2$ for some other thread to define the value of $a[i]$. This may never happen as $g(j) = i$ may not have a solution for $j \in I$. A fuzzy barrier is the only solution to such a case.

3.6 Parallel Assignment with Conditionals

If only barrier synchronization is used, it is sufficient to perform a data dependency analysis on a par statement ignoring conditionals (and conservatively put barriers). However, when substituting these barriers with pairwise or clustered synchronizations, we must additionally take into consideration that only a subset of the processors may actually need to transmit values, since only a subset of processors may be executing matching receives. Consider the example:

```
par (I) st (e[i] < f[i]) {
    a[i] = b[i+1] + c[i];           /* s1 */
    b[i] = (a[i] + a[i+1])/2;       /* s2 */
}
```

Consider the following transformed code where the guard in the par statement is evaluated and saved in a temporary array called *guard*:

```
par (I) {
    if (guard[i-1])    send (b, i-1);
    if (guard[i]) {    blx_recv(tmp, i+1);
                       a[i] = tmp[i] + c[i];   }
    if (guard[i-1])    send(a, i-1);
    if (guard[i]) {    blx_recv(tmp, i+1);
                       b[i] = (a[i] + tmp[i])/2;   }
}
```

This assumes that the guard for the $(i-1)^{th}$ processor is available to the ith processor. In general, whenever send-receive pairs are used, the guards can also be communicated using send-receive pairs. The code to communicate the guards can be inserted immediately after the point the guards are evaluated.

A par statement that contains a nested if statement is handled similarly.

3.7 Loops inside par statements

In general, data dependency analysis for statements within a loop tends to be more complex. To isolate the loop from the enclosing code, we put a barrier before and after the loop body. A synchronization graph is then built for the statements within the loop. Standard data dependency analysis for sequential do loops can be used to determine the flow, output and anti-dependencies. In following code fragment,

```
par (I)
  seq (J) {
      ...
      a[i][j] = ...;
      ...
      ... = a[f(i,j)][g(i,j)];
  }
```

dependencies that occur across index-set J are intra-thread dependencies and can be ignored for the purposes of synchronization. Only dependencies that occur only across index-set I are significant and can be renamed according to the rules mentioned before. The dependencies that occur across both the index-sets (I and J) remain unchanged.

In this manner, a synchronization graph can be obtained for the statements within a loop in a par statement. The dependencies can now be handled in the same way as before, except the arcs in the synchronization graph now represent J communication operations per thread rather than a single operation. In the case where we need definition variables, J separate definition variables must be used, one per communication operation.

4 Performance Estimation

This section presents a preliminary performance study of the effectiveness of the optimizations. We estimate the blocking time due to barriers and send-receive pairs and use the formula to estimate the improvements for a UC program fragment from a fluid dynamics application. The implementation of the compiler is in progress.

We use the term *block time* to refer to the stall time of a processor (we assume that a thread is assigned to each processor). A barrier synchronization involves all processors. Assume t_i is the time thread i arrives at the barrier, and t_{last} is the time the final thread arrives at barrier. Assuming N processors are involved in a synchronization, the average block time at the barrier is given by

$$T_{bar} = \frac{\sum_i (t_{last} - t_i)}{N}$$

A send-receive pair (or binary synchronization) involves two processors. To estimate average block time we use the average over the time any processor waits for any other processor. This is represented as a difference in arrival times as follows:

$$T_{sr} = \frac{\sum_j \frac{\sum_i |t_j - t_i|}{N-1}}{N}$$

Note that we have assumed that any pair of processors are equally likely to communicate[4]. A number of synthetic benchmarks were executed assuming various distributions for the process arrival time at the barrier. In particular, T_{bar}

---

[4] However, in reality, communication may display locality, with processors communicating more often with neighbors.

and T_{sr} were computed for 3 different distributions. For N = 100 ($\lambda = 0.5$, mean = 50), these values are shown in Figure 7. In addition to the higher average block time, the overhead for barrier implementations are generally higher than for point-to-point communication.

distribution	T_{bar}	T_{sr}
uniform	50.016	32.881
normal	64.997	16.751
exponential	64.767	16.736

Fig. 7. Average block times under various distributions

In implementing UC programs, we distinguish between the following types of operations (and the cost associated with them) (1) local computation (C_l) (2) communication with a neighbor (C_n), and (3) communication with a arbitrary processor (C_a). In addition we distinguish between the costs of blocking caused by the use of barrier synchronizations (T_{bar}) and point-to-point communications (T_{sr}). O_{bar} is the overhead to implement barrier synchronization. The cost of communication operations immediately preceded by a barrier is C_n (or C_a), whereas when such an operation is not preceded by a barrier the cost is $C_n + T_{sr}$ (or $C_a + T_{sr}$). Note that the latter case is strictly an upper bound; as it represents the case of a thread arriving at the blocking receive T_{sr} units before a corresponding thread executes a send. We will show that even with this conservative estimate, our optimizations show an improvement.

The total time is computed by including the cost of each of these components as follows:

$$T_{ex} = n_l C_l + n_{bar}(T_{bar} + O_{bar}) + n_{bn}C_n + n_n(C_n + T_{sr}) + n_{ba}C_a + n_a(C_a + T_{sr})$$

where n_l is the number of local operations, n_{bar} the number of barriers, n_{bn} the number of neighbor communications immediately preceded by a barrier, n_n the number of neighbor communications not preceded by a barrier, n_{ba} the number of arbitary communications immediately preceded by a barrier, n_a are the number of arbitary communications not preceded by a barrier. We assume that O_{bar} is algorithmically dependent on the number of processors, p. Specifically, $O_{bar} = c * \log p$.

An Example

The following program fragment is from an application modelling diffusion aggregation in fluid flow (further details can be found in [ABCD93]). It contains a guarded par statement block, where the guard can be evaluated locally.

```
index_set I:i = {0..N-1};
index_set J:j = {0..M-1};
int particle[N][M], s[N][M], swapped[N][M], count[N][M], tmp[N][M];
int A, P, D;
...
par (I,J) st (particle[i][j] == A)
{
    s[i][j] = P;                        /* s1 */
    s[i-1][j] = D;                      /* s2 */
    swapped[i-1][j] = 1;                /* s3 */

    tmp[i][j] = count[i][j];            /* s4 */
    count[i][j] = count[i-1][j];        /* s5 */
    count[i-1][j] = tmp[i][j];          /* s6 */
}
```

In the absence of optimizations that reduce the number of barriers, an upper bound on the cost of implementing this fragment is given by:

$$T_{ex} = 3C_l + 4C_n + 14(T_{bar} + O_{bar})$$

By analyzing the code fragment for dependency relationships, it is possible to reduce the barrier synchronizations. The following is the transformed code fragment with the looser synchronization specified using *arb* statements:

```
arb (I,J) {
    guard[i][j] = (particle[i][j] == A);
    if (guard[i][j]) s[i][j] = P;       /* s1 */
}
arb (I,J) st (guard[i][j])
{
    s[i-1][j] = D;                      /* s2 */
    swapped[i-1][j] = 1;                /* s3 */
    tmp[i][j] = count[i][j];            /* s4 */
    count_copy[i][j] = count[i-1][j];   /* s5 - part 1 */
}
    count[i][j] = count_copy[i][j];     /* s5 - part 2 */
arb (I,J) st (guard[i][j])
    count[i-1][j] = tmp[i][j];          /* s6 */
```

The execution time of the fragment after implementing these optimizations is given by the following equation:

$$T_{ex} = 4C_l + 3(T_{bar} + O_{bar}) + 2C_n + 2(C_n + T_{sr})$$

All subscript expressions in the program fragment can be evaluated at compile time. This allows us to replace each barrier by a *send–blocking receive* pair using the optimizations discussed in the previous secton. The final code fragment that results from this transformation is as follows:

```
arb (I,J) {
    guard[i][j] = (particle[i][j] == A);
    send(guard, (i-1,j));
    blx_recv(n_guard, (i+1,1));
    send(guard, (i+1,j));
    blx_recv(p_guard, (i-1,1));

    if (guard[i][j])      s[i][j] = P;                  /* s1 */
    if (guard[i][j])      send (D, (i-1,j));
    if (n_guard[i][j])    blx_recv (s, (i+1,j));        /* s2 */
    if (guard[i][j])      swapped[i-1][j] = 1;          /* s3 */
    if (guard[i][j])      tmp[i][j] = count[i][j];      /* s4 */
    if (p_guard[i][j])    send (count, (i+1, j));
    if (guard[i][j])      blx_recv (count, (i-1,j));    /* s5 */
    if (guard[i][j])      send (tmp, (i-1, j));
    if (n_guard[i][j])    blx_recv (count, (i+1,j));    /* s6 */
}
```

With this optimization, our estimated execution time becomes:

$$T_{ex} = 3C_l + 6(C_n + T_{sr})$$

The execution time for the three programs may be compared using representative costs for the different operations We assume $C_l = 1$ unit, $C_n = 200$ units. [5] A normal distribution of arrival times gives $T_{sr}:T_{bar} = 1:4$. Hence, we assume $T_{sr} = k$ units and $T_{bar} = 4k$ units. Figure 8 shows two graphs. The first graph shows execution times for each of the three programs for increasing values of O_{bar} (while maintaining blocking times constant for $k = 2$). We have assumed that very efficient barrier implementations exist by considering the values for O_{bar} in the range $2 * C_n \leq O_{bar} \leq 6 * C_n$.[6] Even in the presence of efficient barriers the analysis indicates that the performance of the optimized program may be improved by upto 54% [7] as compared with the program which simply minimized the number of barrier synchronizations. The second graph shows that even with the help of extremely efficient barrier synchronizations ($O_{bar} = 2*C_n$), the optimizations will yield significant performance improvements as the average block time is increases.

5 Conclusion

In this paper, we have addressed the issue of reducing synchronization costs when implementing a data-parallel language on an asynchronous architecture.

---

[5] These assumptions are based on a 25MHz clock, hence 0.64 μsecs to perform an assignment, and a 128 μsecs message transmission time to a neighbor[SSS88]

[6] The lower bound of $2 * C_n$ represents the implementation where each processor sends a ready signal to a control processor which, in turn, informs all processors of arrival at the barrier. The upper bound of $6 * C_n$ assumes $p = 64$ processors and a $\log p * C_n$ overhead.

[7] Percentage improvement for $O_{bar} = 3C_n$.

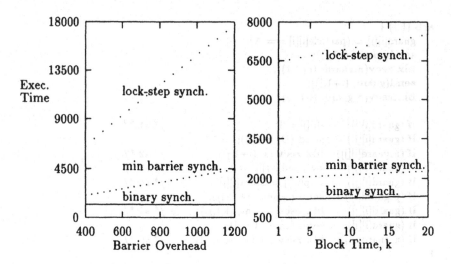

Fig. 8. Performance Comparison

The synchronization issue has been addressed from two perspectives: first, we have described language constructs that allow the programmer to specify that different parts of a data-parallel program be synchronized at different levels of granularity. This allows the programmer to take on the burden of explicit data management to reduce synchronization costs. It also supports an iterative approach to program design where programs are initially designed assuming operation level synchronization and may be later refined to use a weaker synchronization granularity. Secondly, we have shown how existing tools and algorithms for data dependency analysis can be used by the compiler to both reduce the number of barriers and to replace global barriers by cheaper clustered synchronizations. Although the techniques presented in the paper are general purpose, we have described them in the context of a data-parallel language called UC developed at UCLA.

References

[ABCD93] V. Austel, R. Bagrodia, M. Chandy, and M. Dhagat. Reductions + Relations = Data-Parallelism. Technical report, University of California, Los Angeles, CA 90024, April 1993.

[AK87] R. Allen and K. Kennedy. Automatic Translation of FORTRAN Program to Vector Form. *ACM Transactions on Programming Languages and Systems*, 9(4):491–543, October 1987.

[BA92] R. Bagrodia and V. Austel. *UC User Manual.* Computer Science Department, University of California at Los Angeles, 1992.

[BENP93] U. Banerjee, R. Eigenmann, A. Nicolau, and D.A. Padua. Automatic Program Parallelization. *Proceedings of the IEEE*, 81(2):1–33, February 1993.

[For92] High Performance Fortran Forum. High Performance Fortran Language Specification. DRAFT, November 1992.

[FOW87] J. Ferrante, K. Ottenstein, and J.D. Warren. The program dependence graph and its use in optimization. *ACM TOPLAS*, 9(3), July 1987.

[Gav72] F. Gavril. Algorithms for minimum coloring, maximum clique, minimum covering by cliques, and maximum independent set of a chordal graph. *SIAM Journal on Computing*, 1(2):180–187, 1972.

[Gup89] Rajiv Gupta. The fuzzy barrier: A mechanism for high-speed synchronization of processors. In *Proceedings of the 3rd International Conference on Architectural Support for Programming Languages and Operating Systems*, pages 54–64, April 1989.

[HQL+91] P. Hatcher, M. Quinn, A. Lapadula, B. Seevers, R. Anderson, and R. Jones. Data-parallel programming on MIMD computers. *IEEE Trans. on Parallel and Distributed Systems*, July 1991.

[MA87] S. K. Midkiff and Padua D. A. Compiler Algorithms for Synchronization. *IEEE Transactions on Computers*, C-36(12):1485–1495, December 1987.

[MR90] P. Mehrotra and J. Van Rosendale. Programming distributed memory architectures using Kali. Report 90-69, Institute for Computer Application in Science and Engineering, Hampton, VA, 1990.

[PW86] D.A. Padua and M.J. Wolfe. Advanced Compiler Optimizations for Supercomputers. *Communications of the ACM*, 29(12):1184–1201, December 1986.

[QHS91] M. Quinn, P. Hatcher, and B. Seevers. Implementing a Data Parallel Language on a Tightly Coupled Multiprocessor. In A. Nicolau, D. Gelernter, Gross T., and Padua D., editors, *Advances in Languages and Compilers for Parallel Processing*, chapter 20, pages 385–401. MIT Press, Cambridge, Massachusetts, 1991.

[RS87] J.R. Rose and G.L. Steele. C*: An Extended C Language for Data Parallel Programming. PL-87.5, Thinking Machines Corporation, March 1987.

[RSW91] M. Rosing, R. B. Schnabel, and R. B. Weaver. The DINO Parallel Programming Language. *Journal of Parallel and Distributed Computing*, 13:30–42, 1991.

[SSS88] C. L. Seitz, J. Seizovic, and W. K. Su. The C Programmer's Abbreviated Guide to Multicomputer Programming. Technical Report Caltech-CS-TR-88-1, Caltech, January 1988.

[Wol89] Michael Wolfe. *Optimizing Supercompilers for Supercomputers*. MIT Press, 1989.

ZPL: An Array Sublanguage *

Calvin Lin and Lawrence Snyder

Department of Computer Science and Engineering, FR-35

Abstract. The notion of isolating the "common case" is a well known computer science principle. This paper describes ZPL, a language that treats data parallelism as a common case of MIMD parallelism. This separation of concerns has many benefits. It allows us to define a clean and concise language for describing data parallel computations, and this in turn leads to efficient parallel execution. Our particular language also provides mechanisms for handling boundary conditions. We introduce the concepts, constructs and semantics of our new language, and give a simple example that contrasts ZPL with other data parallel languages.

1 Introduction

A variety of languages have been proposed that generally provide data parallel or array semantics, including C* [15], Fortran 90 [1], NESL [4], and HPF [8]. One characteristic of these languages is that data parallelism is the only model provided. This fact introduces a certain pressure to support a wide range of general purpose facilities. Though this has resulted in rich and interesting languages, it has not always served the goals of simplicity, cleanliness or efficiency. ZPL is a different kind of language.

ZPL is an array sublanguage of the Orca family of parallel programming languages [11, 12]. The Orca languages provide a general MIMD programming model [2, 6, 17], allowing programmers to write efficient, portable and scalable parallel programs. For many tasks, such as initializing an array A to all 0's, a full MIMD programming model is overly general. For other tasks, such as summing the elements of the array A, the best parallel solution is generally well understood, but somewhat machine sensitive. So, to simplify the programmer's job without limiting expressiveness, the Orca languages provide a set of facilities to perform data parallel operations, such as A := 0; and standard parallel abstractions, such as sum reduction (+\A). These convenience facilities, together with some control-flow operations, make up ZPL. Thus, ZPL is the "non-MIMD" component of the Orca languages. (Further discussion of the relationship between full Orca and ZPL is given in Section 4.)

ZPL can be thought of as a stand-alone parallel programming language. Though the Orca languages are explicitly parallel, the ZPL subset is implicitly parallel. The fact that ZPL is a sublanguage of a larger, more general language

---

* This research was supported in part by ONR Grant N00014-89-J-1368, ARPA Grant N00014-92-J-1824 and NSF Grant CDA-9211095

has been a critical advantage in its design because it has relieved the pressure to solve everything using the data parallel paradigm. That is, if the inclusion of some complex capability seemed to do violence to ZPL's clean semantics, there was always the option of leaving it out since that capability could be realized by the MIMD part of the language, albeit less conveniently.

Without the need to be fully general it has been possible to design a language that is simple and expressive, with seemingly few complicating characteristics. The simplicity will be evident in the description presented below. The expressiveness is justified by the fact that ZPL is sufficient to program the SIMPLE benchmark [11] and other standard data parallel applications, including the Ising model, the Floyd-Steinberg dithering model, Cypher *et al.*'s recursive connected component labeling algorithm [5], a median threshold filtering, and the game of Life. Examples of computations not sensibly programmed in ZPL would be the FFT (due to the butterfly-based data motion), LU Decomposition (due to the manipulation of the pivot), as well as more typically MIMD computations such as multipole methods for N-body simulation. Perhaps the most important aspect of ZPL, however, is that it provides a clean and uncomplicated context in which to study compilation techniques for data parallel and array languages. In this paper, we present the language, outline the semantics and explain the guiding principles behind this language.

The structure of the remainder of the paper is as follows. Section 2 uses the Jacobi example to highlight some differences between ZPL and other data parallel languages. Section 3 then presents ZPL's design goals and describes the major language features. We then discuss the relation of ZPL to the more general Orca languages. Finally, we briefly compare ZPL to other data parallel languages before concluding.

2   A Brief Comparison

Before presenting the features of ZPL it is useful to consider how different languages express data parallel computation. The goal is to point out the distinctive features of the languages in general terms rather than to give a tedious comparison of individual constructs. As an illustrative example, consider the 4-point Jacobi computation on an array A[1..N, 1..N] in which each value in the array is to be replaced by the average of its four nearest neighbors. The boundary values are taken to be 0 except at the southern edge, where their value is 50.

In ZPL the initial values and main body of the Jacobi computation can be defined as shown below, where [R] is a user declared index set called a region; and **north, east, west** and **south** are programmer-defined vector constants called *directions*. For now we assume that the values of the above directions are [-1,0], [0,1], [0,-1], and [1,0], respectively.[2]

```
region R = [1..N, 1..N];
```

---

[2] While the directions **north, east, west** and **south** can be defined by the programmer, they have the default values that are used in this example.

```
        [north of R] A := 0;        /* Set boundary conditions */
        [east  of R] A := 0;
        [west  of R] A := 0;
        [south of R] A := 50;
        [R]          A := 100;
```

The kernel of the computation would be specified as follows:

```
        [R]    A := (A@north + A@east + A@west + A@south)/4;
```

The body of the above statement computes, for a given array element, the average of its four neighbors. Each neighbor is specified by the @ operator as an offset from a given element. For example, A@north refers to the element whose index is [-1,0] relative to the given element. The scope of this statement is defined by the region, [R]. That is, the body of the statement is applied (in parallel) to each element whose index is in [R].

If it is possible to distinguish the semantic approaches to data parallel computations by the terms "single point-based" and "array-based," then ZPL is clearly an array-based approach. The array is the basic unit of reference and the "at" operation replaces the more general array indexing operator with a disciplined method of accessing neighboring array values. Region descriptors are used to designate the scope over which data parallel operations will be applied. These regions can be specified where they are used and thus be different for every statement, but the assumption (borne out so far by our limited experience) is that scientific codes will generally sweep over a modest set of regions. This implies that there is not enormous diversity and that these regions have logical meaning worthy of names, i.e., naming provides useful mnemonic information. Accordingly, ZPL anticipates a mode of use that emphasizes setting up basic regions ahead of time as a means of avoiding tedious and error prone specification of a program's invariant information.

Jacobi in C*. C* employs a point-based approach. The Jacobi initialization and kernel statement are given below.

```
    shape [N][N] cell;

    with (cell) {
        /* Set boundary conditions */
        where ((!pcoord(0)) || (!pcoord(1)) ||
               (pcoord(1) == (N-1))) {
            active = 0;
            oldA = newA = 0.0;
        } else where (pcoord(0) == (N-1)) {
            active = 0;
            oldA = newA = 50.0;
        } else {
```

```
        active = 1;
        newA = 100.0;
    }

    /* The Jacobi kernel */
    where (active) {
        oldA = newA;
        newA = ([.-1][.]oldA + [.+1][.]oldA +
                [.][.+1]oldA + [.][.-1]oldA)/4.0;
    }
}
```

The above kernel is specified using indices relative to each data element. For example, [.-1][.]oldA is equivalent to A@[-1,0] in ZPL. Because the above code applies to every point in the data space, there is the need to define "active" and "inactive" points. The boundary values never change and are therefore marked as "inactive." Notice that the nested logic obfuscates the specification of the boundary conditions, yet it is desirable for efficiency reasons. By contrast, the ZPL region descriptors allow different code to be applied to different portions of the data space. For this reason, boundary condition definitions are cleaner and more concise in the ZPL program. In addition, the point-based view of C* forces the programmer to explicitly define "new" and "old" copies of the data; this is not necessary in ZPL. Finally, the access of neighbor values is similar to that in the ZPL program except that ZPL allows neighbor values to be represented as named vectors.

Jacobi in HPF. There are several ways to implement Jacobi in HPF. We present two variants below.

```
! Variant 1: use FORALL

REAL a(0:n+1,0:n+1)
!HPF$ DISTRIBUTE a(BLOCK,BLOCK)

! Initialize boundary conditions
FORALL (i=0,   j=1:n) a(i,j) =   0.0
FORALL (i=n+1, j=1:n) a(i,j) =  50.0
FORALL (i=1:n, j=0)   a(i,j) =   0.0
FORALL (i=1:n, j=n+1) a(i,j) =   0.0
FORALL (i=1:n, j=1:n) a(i,j) = 100.0

! The Jacobi kernel
FORALL (i=1:n, j=1:n)   a(i,j) = (a(i-1,j)+a(i+1,j)+
                                  a(i,j-1)+a(i,j+1))/4
```

```
! Variant 2: use array assignment

REAL a(0:n+1,0:n+1)
!HPF$ DISTRIBUTE a(BLOCK,BLOCK)
    ...
! Set boundary conditions
a(0,   1:n) =    0.0
a(n+1, 1:n) =   50.0
a(1:n, 0)   =    0.0
a(1:n, n+1) =    0.0
a(1:n, 1:n) = 100.0


! The Jacobi kernel
a(1:n, 1:n) = (a(0:n-1,1:n) + a(2:n+1,1:n) +
               a(1:n,0:n-1) + a(1:n,2:n+1))/4
```

The HPF programs are closer in spirit to ZPL than the C* program. The first variant uses explicit iterators and thus takes the point-based approach, while the latter uses an array-based approach. In both cases, the indices must be specified in both the boundary condition initialization and the kernel computation. This is an error prone situation for two reasons. First, the heavy use of explicit indices provides many opportunities to make a mistake, while ZPL's use of named directions is self-documenting. Second, the HPF approach duplicates the specification of indices in the boundary condition code and in the kernel code, which further increases the potential for error. The ZPL approach reduces repetition by defining direction vectors once and using these for both the boundary conditions and the kernel specification.

Jacobi in Fortran 90.

```
REAL a(n,n)
    ...
a = (EOSHIFT(a,-1,DIM=1,BOUNDARY= 0.0) +  &
     EOSHIFT(a, 1,DIM=1,BOUNDARY=50.0) +  &
     EOSHIFT(a,-1,DIM=2,BOUNDARY= 0.0) +  &
     EOSHIFT(a, 1,DIM=2,BOUNDARY= 0.0)) / 4
```

The Fortran 90 example[3] is closest in style to the ZPL program. Rather than deal with explicit indices, the EOSHIFT function is a higher level operation that shifts the array reference in a particular direction. Besides being more verbose than the ZPL "at" operator, EOSHIFT separates the dimension from the magnitude and direction of the shift, while ZPL's direction vectors convey all of this information in a single entity. Thus, for example, when using the EOSHIFT function it's easy to imagine confusing a "-1" with a "1" or "DIM=1" with "DIM=2."

---

[3] Since HPF is a superset of Fortran 90, this Fortran 90 example can also be considered an HPF program.

Such errors are still possible in ZPL but the use of named vectors reduces their likelihood since "east" and "west" are more syntactically distinct than "1" and "-1." As a performance issue, notice that because each call to EOSHIFT can specify a different boundary value as a parameter, each invocation of EOSHIFT must include a test to determine whether the data points reside on a process boundary.

Jacobi in NESL. NESL [4] is an applicative language that is based on vector operations such as scan and reduce. NESL supports nested parallelism and distinguishes itself from most other data parallel languages by its functional nature. Below is NESL code that applies to both regular and irregular meshes. Each Jacobi iteration is a matrix-vector product, where a sparse matrix is represented as a nested sequence. Most of the code is used to set up the initial conditions.

```
function sparse_MxV(mat,vect) =
  {sum({val * vect[i] : (i,val) in row}): row in mat} $

% Each Jabobi iteration is just a matrix vector product. %
% This will repeat it n times. %

function Jacobi_Iterate(Mat,vect,n) =
  if (n == 0) then vect
  else Jacobi_Iterate(Mat,sparse_MxV(Mat,vect),n-1) $

% The following two functions are mesh-specific.         %
% Each is called once to initialize the mesh and vector %

function make_2d_n_by_n_mesh(n) =
  let
    % A sequence of indices of the internal cells. %
    internal_ids = flatten({{i + n*j: j in [1:n-1]}: i in [1:n-1]});

    % Creates a matrix row for each internal cell.
      Each row points left, right, up and down with weight .25 %
    internal = {(i,[((i+1), .25), ((i-1), .25),
                    ((i+n), .25), ((i-n), .25)]):
                    i in internal_ids};

    % Creates a default matrix row (used for boundaries).
      Each points to itself with weight 1 %
    default = {[(i,1.0)]: i in [0:n^2]}

  % Insert internal cells into defaults %
  in default <- internal $

% Assumes mesh is layed out in row major order %
```

```
function make_initial_vector(n) =
  dist(0.0,n^2) <- { i, 50.0: i in [n^2-n:n^2]} $

% invoke it %
function test(n, steps) =
let matrix = make_2d_n_by_n_mesh(n);
    vector = make_initial_vector(n);
in Jacobi_Iterate(matrix,vector,steps) $
```

The main contributor to the NESL code's length is the manipulation of 1D vectors to implement 2D abstractions. For example, it is cumbersome to modify the interior of the 2D problem state separately from the borders. In fact, for convenience, the above code initializes the interior points to the value 0.0 instead of 100.0.

As a test of ZPL's expressiveness, we have written the SIMPLE computational fluid dynamics benchmark in our new language. We have no comparison against other data parallel implementations, but we can compare our ZPL version against those written in other paradigms. A parallel implementation written in a MIMD message passing style was about 5000 lines of C code [10]. A sequential implementation from Cornell was about 2400 lines of Fortran code. Meanwhile, our ZPL version was less than 500 lines. While comparing lines of code is admittedly a poor metric of clarity, the large disparity, along with our own experience with the C version, point out the superiority of the ZPL formulation with respect to readability.

We conclude this discussion of data parallel languages by briefly considering compilation issues. Optimizing compilers typically stumble because they must be conservative in the face of uncertainty. This uncertainty can have many sources, such as pointer references or functions in external modules with unknown side effects. Our language makes it difficult for the compiler to stumble because so much information is known at compile time. In ZPL there are no arbitrary array indices, no pointers, and no goto's. Moreover, ZPL's high level abstractions provide semantic information that the compiler can exploit. For example, the use of regions provides a way to recognize subportions of arrays and to perform finer grained data dependency analysis on arrays than is typically feasible. Thus, we are confident that ZPL can be very efficiently compiled.

3 Language Definition

By limiting the scope of ZPL to purely data parallel aspects we are following the creed of giving special treatment to the "common case." Given this premise, our design goals are as follows.

- *Allow users to program at a high level*, namely, by using arrays.
- *Provide an extremely efficient language.* The use of high level abstractions can supply information to optimizing compilers that lower level languages

cannot. For example, communication is only induced by operators such as scan and "at." It is not possible to generate irregular communication.

- *Provide a clean language with only a few central concepts.* This, too, is intended to help both the ZPL compiler writer and the applications programmer by reducing feature interaction. There are no explicitly parallel constructs.
- *Provide support for boundary conditions* since they are the most tedious aspect of data parallel computing.
- *Provide freedom to the MIMD aspects of Orca.* Although ZPL can be viewed as a stand-alone language, ZPL must also fit in the framework of the Orca languages where programmers will write their own MIMD phases. This integration is possible because ZPL makes few assumptions regarding parallelism.

The ZPL design can be divided into a sequential component and a data parallel component. In essence, any sequential language can form the basis for ZPL – we choose one that is similar to Modula-2. The remainder of this section focuses on the data parallel aspects of ZPL.

Array Operations. ZPL has two classes of variables – arrays and scalars – that can serve as basic units of computation. All of the standard scalar operators that are typically found in sequential procedural languages exist in ZPL and can be applied to either class of variables. In the case of array operands, the operator is applied to each element of the array to produce an array result. For this reason, array operators can only be applied to conformable arrays – arrays with the same size, shape and base type. For example, the binary addition operator (+), when applied to arrays, sums the corresponding elements of two arrays.

When scalars and arrays are combined in an expression, scalars are promoted to conformable arrays. Similarly, functions can be promoted, which allows scalar code to be re-used without making source code changes. For example, a `sqrt()` library routine can be promoted by passing it an array argument, as shown below. The result of this function call is an array of the same size and shape as A containing the square roots of each element of A.

```
                    /* A and B are arrays. */
 B := sqrt(A);      /* Promote the scalar sqrt() function. */
```

Regions. Conformability of arrays is specified at the statement level through the use of regions. A region is an index set that is prepended to statements and qualifies all arrays in the statement that have the same rank as the prepended region. Regions can have an arbitrary number of dimensions and are defined in a manner similar to the way arrays are declared in most languages:

```
region    R = [x1..x2, y1..y2];
```

The above declaration defines a two dimensional region whose points are the cross product of (x1..x2) and (y1..y2). The values of all regions are fixed at load time. They typically will depend on some runtime parameter that describes the problem size. Once defined, regions can be applied to statements as shown below, where we assume that A, B and C are 2D arrays.

```
[R]  A := B + C;
```

The effect of the above statement is to compute A[i][j] = B[i][j] + C[i][j] for $x1 \leq i \leq x2$ and $y1 \leq j \leq y2$. In other words, the region [R] defines an index set for all 2D arrays to which the region is applied. This example applies a region to a single statement, but in general, regions provide scope in a block structured manner. They can be applied to blocks of statements, and regions can be nested within other regions. The following code fragment illustrates this point.

```
[R1] A := B + C;       /* use Region R1 for this statement */

[R2] begin
     A := B + 5*C;  /* use Region R2 for this statement */
[R1] B := A;        /* use Region R1 for this statement */
     foo(A);        /* use Region R2 for this function call */
     end
```

The above uses of regions assume that all array operands have been declared to include at least the points in their respective regions. Arrays can be declared using regions as shown below:

```
var        A: real [R];
           B: real [R];
           C: real [R];
```

By applying regions to entire statements, ZPL programs are syntactically clean since they are not muddled by complicated indices. Significantly, region scopes are the *only* way to reference arrays. In particular, explicit array indexing is not allowed, since this would allow or even encourage programmers to use ZPL for applications that are not strictly data parallel.[4]

Directions. A direction is a vector that can be used to access neighboring array values with the At operator (@) and to define new regions from existing regions. Like regions, directions have an associated rank, and their values are initialized once at load time and do not change during the execution of a program. Examples of direction declarations are shown below.

```
direction  north = [-1,0];
           east  = [0, 1];
           west  = [0,-1];
           south = [1, 0];
           se    = [1, 1];
```

---

[4] It is, however, possible to initialize arrays through I/O statements.

The At operator (@) is used to access neighboring array elements. For example, **A@east** refers to the array that has the same shape as **A** – as defined by the region scope that applies to this expression – but is displaced from **A** by the vector **east**, which in this case is **[0,1]**.

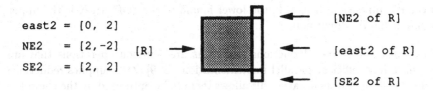

east2 = [0, 2]   [R] →   [NE2 of R] ←

NE2 = [2,-2]   [east2 of R] ←

SE2 = [2, 2]   [SE2 of R] ←

Fig. 1. Illustration of "Of" Regions.

All regions can be defined using explicit upper and lower bounds for each dimension, as shown above for region **R**. For example, the region consisting of the two columns to the right of **R** could be defined in the following manner:

```
region   R    = [1..N, 1..N];
         East2 = [1..N, N+1..N+2];
```

However, ZPL provides a less tedious solution that uses the Of operator and the **east2 vector**, shown below. (See also Figure 1.)

```
direction east2 = [0,2];
          SE2   = [2,2];

region    East2 = [east2 of R];
```

The Of operator takes two operands – a vector v and a region R – and describes a new region that is adjacent to R. The size of this new region is defined by the direction and magnitude of v and its location relative to R is defined by the direction of v. For example, **[east2 of R]** refers to the region that is offset from R by the vector [0,2], whose height is the same as R's height (as specified by the special value 0), and whose width is 2. As another example, **[SE2 of R]** refers to the 2×2 square that is adjacent to the southeast corner of region R.

Mathematically, if vector $v = (v_1, v_2, ... v_n)$ and
region $R = (l_1, u_1) \times (l_2, u_2) \times ... \times (l_n, u_n)$,

[v of R] defines an array of size $v_1' \times v_2' \times ... \times v_n'$,
where $v_i' = | v_i |$ if $v_i \neq 0$,
or
$v_i' = u_i - l_i + 1$ if $v_i = 0$.

This array is located such that it is adjacent to R at $(r_1, r_2, ... r_n)$,

$$\text{where } r_i = l_i \quad \text{if } v_i < 0$$
$$\text{or}$$
$$r_i = u_i \quad \text{if } v_i > 0.$$

In other words, if $v_i < 0$, the upper bound of the "Of" array is the lower bound of the ith dimension. If $v_i > 0$, the lower bound of the "Of" array is the upper bound of the ith dimension.

Reductions and Scans. Reductions and scans are common operations that are known to have efficient parallel implementations [3, 9]. ZPL supplies reductions and scans as operators because this allows them to be optimized by the compiler. For example, if reductions are not provided by the hardware, the messages needed to implement consecutive reductions can be combined to reduce communication latency.

Reductions are operations applied to the elements of an array to produce a scalar result. For example, the sum reduction of an array is the sum of the array's elements. The following reductions are defined as operators in ZPL:

+\	– Sum reduction	max\	– Maximum reduction
*\	– Product reduction	min\	– Minimum reduction
and\	– And reduction	or\	– Or reduction

Each of the above reduction operators has an analogous scan operator. The syntax for scans uses \\ instead of \. Scan operators take an array argument and return an array containing the parallel prefix of the given array: Each element of the returned array is the reduction of all elements whose indices are less than its own. For multidimensional arrays each element is assigned an index in row-major order. That is, the last (rightmost) dimension's indices vary fastest.

Partial reductions and scans are also allowed. For example, row reductions can be performed across each row of a 2D array, returning a vector result. Partial reductions and scans are expressed by using an optional parameter that specifies the dimensions across which the reduction or scan should take place. Dimensions are specified by placing numbers in brackets, with [1] indicating the first dimension and [d] indicating the dth dimension. The code fragment below, where v is a vector and s is a scalar, shows examples of partial reductions.

```
[R]   v := +\[1] A;      -- reduce A along columns, assign to v
[R]   s := +\[1][2] A;   -- full reduction of A
[R]   s := +\ A;         -- full reduction of A
```

The Where Statement. The Where statement is the array analog of an If statement. Its form is given below, where cond is a conditional expression involving array values, and s1 and s2 are statements.

```
where (cond)
then  s1;
else  s2;
```

The statement **s1** is executed for those index values that evaluate to true in the Where's conditional expression. Statement **s2** is executed for all other index values. Semantically, **s1** and **s2** are allowed to execute concurrently. A Where statement can only be qualified by a single region scope. That is, the statements in the body of the Where cannot be modified by additional region scopes. Given these constraints, Where statements are allowed to nest.

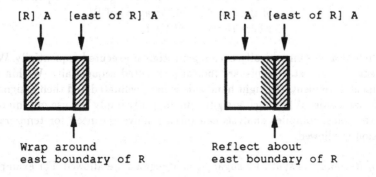

Fig. 2. The Reflect and Wrap Operators.

Reflect and Wrap. ZPL provides specific support to two common types of boundary conditions: the case where a set of values is reflected across some boundary of an array, and the case where a set of values is wrapped around from the other side of an array as in a torus. These operations are supported by the Reflect and Wrap operators, respectively.

Reflect and Wrap are syntactic sugar for initializing two common types of boundary conditions. They are particularly useful for boundary conditions that are wider than a single row or column. The Reflect operator assigns values by mirroring them across some point of reference, while the Wrap operator is used to set boundary conditions that wrap around as if the array were a torus.

The Reflect operator takes a region, [v of R], and a variable (or list of variables), X, and sets the value of X in the region [v of R] to the values of X that are reflected across the boundary between [R] and [v of R]. The region is a no-op if it does not contain an Of operator. The Reflect operator can be applied to multiple variables at once. For example, the following code sets, for variables **A**, **B**, and **C**, the column to the east of **R** to have the value of the eastern-most column of **R**. This is illustrated in Figure 2, which corresponds to the program text below.

```
[east of R]    reflect A, B, C;    -- reflect across east border
[R]            reflect A;          -- no-op, no border specified
```

Imagine that the boundary between [R] and [v of R] is connected to the opposite boundary of [R] as in a torus. The Wrap operator then sets the values of X in the region [v of R] such that this torus is emulated. The Wrap operator is illustrated in Figure 2. The semantics of Wrap are defined mathematically as follows.

if vector $v = (v_1, v_2, ... v_n)$ and
region $R = (l_1, u_1) \times (l_2, u_2) \times ... \times (l_n, u_n)$,

[v of R] Wrap X;   sets the values of X in the region [v of R] to the value
of the conformable array [v' of R],
where $v'_i = (u_i - l_i) + v_i$.

Execution Order. Semantically, each region scope is executed sequentially. Within each region scope, statements are logically executed sequentially. Within each assignment statement, the right hand side is first evaluated and then assigned to the left hand side. While such assignments logically imply the use of temporary array variables, compiler analysis can often remove the need for temporaries. Recursion is allowed.

Lists of Regions. As syntactic sugar, lists of regions are allowed. For example, a region named **border** can be defined as shown below.

```
region      R       = [x1..x2, y1..y2];
            border = [north of R][east of R]
                     [west of R] [south of R];

[border]
    b1;        /* b1 represents a block of code. */
```

When this region is then used to qualify a block of statements, **b1**, the block of statements is logically executed once for each of the regions in the list.

Syntax and Other Details. The current implementation of ZPL uses modified Modula-2 syntax. All Modula-2 constructs are preserved except there are no Case statements, no goto's, and no pointers. Recursion is allowed. In addition, ZPL uses two-level scoping, i.e. procedures are not allowed to be defined inside the scope of other procedures. This detail stems from the fact that our implementation is based on the Parafrase-2 [13] source to source translator for the C language. However, as in Modula-2, a block of statements (bracketed by **begin** and **end**) is itself considered a statement.

4   Discussion

4.1   Support for Boundary Conditions

ZPL gives support for boundary conditions in the form of the Reflect and Wrap statements described above. In addition to these two special forms, ZPL provides general support for boundary conditions through the use of regions.

Regions describe geometric areas of the data space. Because the computations on the various regions can be specified independently, the initialization of boundary conditions can be separated from the rest of the code. This modularization simplifies both the boundary condition code and the "main" body of code. From the Jacobi example we see that other languages also allow for the isolation of boundary condition code, but in these languages the separation is contingent upon the programmer's good programming style. For example, in HPF the individual indices of each array (or the individual indices of each forall statement) must be inspected to determine what portions of the data space are being manipulated.

An advantage of applying regions to entire blocks of statements is that the separation among different portions of the data space is clearly manifested. For example, the typical structure of a ZPL program is shown below, and it's immediately apparent which parts of the computation apply to which portions of the data space.

```
[border]
  begin ...
  end

[R]
  begin ...
  end
```

4.2   Relationship to Orca C

As a first approximation, a program written using the full capabilities of the Orca C language [12] will utilize one of four types of statements:

```
[R]    A := sqrt(A);          -- data parallel assignment

err := max\ Delta;            -- "standard" parallel abstraction

if err < 10**-6 then. . .     -- control construct
   else  . . .

PivotExchange();              -- phase invocation
```

The first three types, data parallel operations, "standard" parallel abstractions and control operations, form the ZPL sublanguage. The fourth statement type, phase invocation, provides access to the full MIMD capabilities of Orca C. By limitation, these can also be regarded as SPMD capabilities.

Collectively, the four statement types are said to define programming at the "problem level" of Orca C. This name emphasizes the fact that these statement types express the high level solution of the programmer's problem. For historical reasons, the problem level is also known as the *Z level* [17]. The problem level text describes the main logic of the problem solution. If the solution is sufficiently simple, ZPL constructs alone may suffice to express the program. But for complex algorithms or certain performance-critical situations, the full MIMD capabilities of the language may be needed.

A phase is a user-defined parallel computation composed of concurrently executing processes. (Phases can also be library defined.) An example might be an FFT computation. Phases have a characteristic communication structure induced by the data dependencies of the problem, e.g. the butterfly for the FFT. The language constructs provided in Orca C for defining phases are referred to, again for historical reasons, as the *Y level* of programming. And the constructs provided for defining the processes, out of which phases are defined, are known as the *X level* of programming. Further description of the phase abstractions programming model can be found in the literature [18].

Though a full introduction of the Y and X programming facilities of Orca C, and a careful introduction to the phase abstractions concepts would be beyond the scope of this paper, a brief description of the phase definition approach is appropriate. Phases are defined using an abstraction called *ensembles*. Three kinds of ensembles are required to define a phase. *Data ensembles* are partitioned data structures, *code ensembles* are partitioned sets of process instances, and *port ensembles* are partitioned graphs, the edges of which define the channels for interprocessor communication. To create a phase, the user defines the necessary ensembles so that they have the same partitioning. (See Figure 3.) This allows the partitions of the three types of ensembles to be put into one-to-one correspondence. In each partition there will be the following: a process instance, the portions of the partitioned data structures the process is to operate on, and a vertex of the partitioned graph that defines the neighbors with which the process communicates. Collectively, the ensembles define a parallel computation whose logical concurrency is given by the number of partitions.

The ZPL language has been presented (and can be used) as if it were a stand-alone language, but it is simply a language convenience: The phase abstractions programming model dictates that Z level statements are either control statements, such as an **if** statement, or they are phase invocations. A literal implementation of this requirement would force users to program all of the concurrent activity of the computation explicitly, a potentially tedious task given how simple certain aspects of parallel computation can be.

Accordingly, ZPL's data parallel constructs and "standard" parallel abstractions are small compiler generated phases, or *phaselets*. That is, logically, each data parallel statement or "standard" operation is converted by the compiler into a phase composed of generated processes that execute the operation on the portion of the array stored locally in the processor. The data layout is not specified in the ZPL portion of the language, but is inherited from whatever data ensemble is declared as part of the user defined phases. If no data layout has been specified by the user, e.g. if ZPL is simply treated as a stand alone language, then a default block layout is used for ZPL arrays.

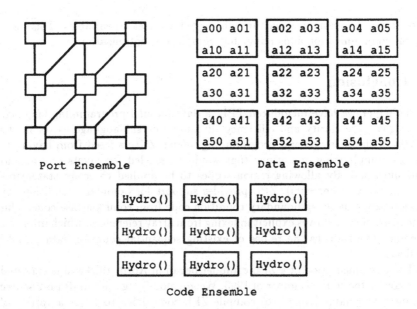

Fig. 3. Illustrations of Ensembles for the Hydro Phase of SIMPLE.

Logically, there is a barrier synchronization following each statement in the Z level language. Since in most cases the barrier is unnecessary, i.e. the computation is correct without actually synchronizing, the compiler eliminates barriers when possible. Also, phase invocation overhead can be eliminated by combining the phaselets into larger, more completely optimized phases. Indeed, when ZPL is used as a stand alone language, without true phase invocations, then only one phase per processor is generated. This gives ZPL a greater efficiency than might be apparent if the literal interpretation of phase abstractions – every line is a control structure or a phase invocation – were strictly enforced.

5 Other Related Work

ZPL inherits the notion of regions from Spot [19], a language designed to support stencil-based computations on distributed memory computers. The two languages are syntactically similar, but Spot presents a point-based view which leads to a certain awkwardness. For example, *history values* are introduced to maintain multiple values of variables across iterations.

Numerous other data parallel languages exist, including C*, Fortran 90, HPF, and NESL, which were briefly discussed in Section 2. Here we point out a few others. Broadly speaking, these languages are more general than ZPL since ZPL is an attempt to trade off expressiveness for improved clarity and efficiency. On the other hand, these other languages do not provide the same support for boundary conditions that ZPL does. C* and Dataparallel C [7] have SIMD execution semantics and provide pointers. Dino [16] programs can specify arbitrary point-to-point communication through tagged accesses to variables. This more general communication adds power but complicates optimizations.

6 Conclusion

In this paper we have introduced ZPL, a data parallel programming language whose goals are clarity and efficiency. Because this sublanguage exists in the context of the more general programming model, ZPL is freed from having to support complicating operations that would be needed for pivots or irregular communication. By allowing region scopes to be applied to entire statements (and blocks of statements), ZPL provides support for boundary conditions by syntactically separating boundary condition code from common case code. This same mechanism removes explicit indexing from array references, which improves readability and allows the re-use of existing sequential code for data parallel applications.

The implementation of a ZPL compiler began in April, 1993 and is expected to be completed in the summer of 1993. We are modifying the Parafrase-2 source to source translator [13, 14] to compile ZPL code down to C for a variety of parallel computers. We believe that this system will provide an ideal testbed to experiment with novel compiler optimizations for parallel computers.

Acknowledgments. We thank Alex Klaiber, Chuck Koelbel, and Guy Blelloch for providing C*, HPF, and NESL implementations of Jacobi. We are grateful to Brad Chamberlain, George Forman, and Derrick Weathersby for writing ZPL programs for the Floyd-Steinberg algorithm, the game of Life, and the Ising model, respectively, and to Bill Griswold and Sungeun Choi for comments on an early draft. Finally, we are indebted to George Forman for many fruitful conversations regarding the ZPL language implementation.

References

1. Jeanne C. Adams, Walter S. Brainerd, Jeanne T. Martin, Brian T. Smith, and Jerrold L. Wagener. *Fortran 90 Handbook*. McGraw-Hill, New York, NY, 1992.
2. Gail Alverson, William Griswold, David Notkin, and Lawrence Snyder. A flexible communication abstraction for nonshared memory parallel computing. In *Proceedings of Supercomputing '90*, November 1990.
3. Guy E. Blelloch. *Vector Models for Data-Parallel Computing*. MIT Press, Cambridge, MA, 1990.
4. Guy E. Blelloch. NESL: A nested data-parallel language. Technical Report CMU-CS-92-103, School of Computer Science, Carnegie Mellon University, January 1992.
5. R. E. Cypher, J. L. C. Sanz, and L. Snyder. Algorithms for image component labeling on simd mesh connected computers. *IEEE Transactions on Computers*, 39(2):276–281, 1990.
6. William Griswold, Gail Harrison, David Notkin, and Lawrence Snyder. Scalable abstractions for parallel programming. In *Proceedings of the Fifth Distributed Memory Computing Conference*, 1990. Charleston, South Carolina.

7. Philip J. Hatcher, Michael J. Quinn, Ray J. Anderson, Anthony J. Lapadula, Bradley K. Seevers, and Andrew F. Bennett. Architecture-independent scientific programming in Dataparallel C: Three case studies. In *Proceedings of Supercomputing '91*, pages 208–217, 1991.

8. High Performance Fortran Forum. *High Performance Fortran Specification.* January 1993.

9. Richard E. Ladner and Michael J. Fischer. Parallel prefix computation. *Journal of the Association for Computing Machinery*, 27(4):831–838, October 1980.

10. Jinling Lee. Extending the SIMPLE program in Poker. Technical Report 89–11–07, Department of Computer Science and Engineering, University of Washington, 1989.

11. Calvin Lin and Lawrence Snyder. A portable implementation of SIMPLE. *International Journal of Parallel Programming*, 20(5):363–401, 1991.

12. Calvin Lin and Lawrence Snyder. Data ensembles in Orca C. In *5th Workshop on Languages and Compilers for Parallel Computing*, New Haven, CT, August 1992.

13. Constantine Polychronopolous, Milind Girkar, Mohammad Reza Haghighat, Chia Ling Lee, Bruce Leung, and Dale Schouten. Parafrase-2: An environment for parallelizing, partitioning, synchronizing, and scheduling programs on multiprocessors. In *Proceedings of the International Conference on Parallel Processing*, volume 2, pages 39–48, August 1989.

14. C. D. Polychronopoulos, M. B. Girkar, M. R. Haghighat, C. L. Lee, B. P. Leung, and D. A. Schouten. The structure of parafrase-2: an advanced parallelizing compiler for c and fortran. In *Workshop on Languages and Compilers for Parallel Computing*, pages 423–453.

15. J.R. Rose and Guy L. Steele Jr. C*: An extended C language for data parallel programming. Technical Report PL 87-5, Thinking Machines Corporation, 1987.

16. M. Rosing, R. Schnabel, and R. Weaver. The Dino parallel programming language. Technical Report CU-CS-457-90, Dept. of Computer Science, University of Colorado, April 1990.

17. Lawrence Snyder. The XYZ abstraction levels of Poker-like languages. In David Gelernter, Alexandru Nicolau, and David Padua, editors, *Languages and Compilers for Parallel Computing*, pages 470–489. MIT Press, 1990.

18. Lawrence Snyder. Foundations of practical parallel programming languages. In *Proceedings of the Second International Conference of the Austrian Center for Parallel Computation.* Springer-Verlag, 1993.

19. David Grimes Socha. *Supporting Fine-Grain Computation on Distributed Memory Parallel Computers.* PhD thesis, University of Washington, Department of Computer Science and Engineering, 1991.

A   Fragments of the SIMPLE Code

There is not enough space to show the entire SIMPLE code, so this appendix contains fragments of the SIMPLE program.

```
direction ne    = [-1,1];                    /* declare directions */
         . . .

region    R     = [minX..maxX, minY..maxY];  /* declare regions */
```

```
var       Rho, P, Q    : real [R];              /* declare arrays */
          Delta_tau    : real [R];
          . . .
                                                /* define functions */
function Jacobian();
var   Tmp_J1, Tmp_J2 : real[R];
begin
  Tmp_J1 := (X.r * (X.z@south - X.z@west)
           + X.r@west * (X.z - X.z@south)
           + X.r@south * (X.z@west - X.z)) / 2.0;

  Tmp_J2 := (X.r@west * (X.z@south - X.z@sw)
           + X.r@sw * (X.z@west - X.z@south)
           + X.r@south * (X.z@sw - X.z@west)) / 2.0;

  J := Tmp_J1 + Tmp_J2;
  Old_S := New_S;
  New_S := ((X.r + X.r@west + X.r@south) * Tmp_J1 +
           (X.r@west + X.r@sw + X.r@south) * Tmp_J2) / 3;
end

function main()                                 /* Main body */
[R]
begin
  /* Hydro Phase */
  [west of R]  P := west_bound_p;
  [north of R]
  [NE of R]
  [east of R]  reflect Rho, P, Q, J;

  Jacobian();
  . . .

  En_error := Int_en + Kin_en - Work + Heat;
  En_error := +\ En_error;              /* implicit temporary variable */
end;
```

Event-based Composition of Concurrent Programs*

Raju Pandey   James C. Browne

Department of Computer Sciences
University of Texas at Austin
Austin, TX 78712
{raju, browne}@cs.utexas.edu

Abstract. This paper presents a model for concurrent programming, where programs (concurrent program structures) are represented as composition expressions over component programs with suitably defined operators. In this model of programming, called Composition bY Event Specification (C-YES), a composition of programs specifies that all events (individual occurrences of named operations, called actions) of component programs can execute in parallel, except for a set of events that interact with each other. Interactions among such events can be specified by establishing execution orderings among them. This paper presents a mechanism, where such interactions are specified by constructing algebraic expressions from a set of primitive interaction expressions and interaction operators. The primitive expressions model interactions at the fundamental level of computations, namely, events. The interaction operators model nondeterministic interactions and interaction over sets of events.

A mechanism for the representation of concurrent programs, called *interacting blocks*, is also given. The interface of an interacting block contains, in addition to the conventional parameters, references to events that may interact with events of other interacting blocks. The implementation of an interacting block contains definitions of its computations and mappings between internal events, and references to these events. Examples illustrating the properties of the C-YES model are presented in the paper.

1   Introduction

A concurrent program is a composition of a set of component programs. The components represent certain aspects of a problem that the composite program models. During an execution of the composite program, the components execute in parallel and contribute to the overall result by solving sub-problems. They cooperate and share information and resources with each other. Such cooperation, called *interaction*, among the component programs arises due to semantic

---

* This work was supported by Texas Advanced Research Program under grant 003658-445.

dependencies such as data dependency, resource consistency, resource fairness, etc., among certain operations of the component programs. The dependencies impose constraints on how such operations can be executed. A correct execution of a concurrent program is one where executions of these operations satisfy any semantic constraints associated with the interactions of the component programs.

Concurrent programming is difficult because asynchronous and concurrent executions of component programs introduce nondeterminism in the way interacting operations can affect each other. It is possible that semantic constraints associated with interactions are not preserved over different executions of a concurrent program. One of the outcomes is that different executions may produce different results. Mechanisms are needed to ensure that semantic constraints are preserved during the executions of the component programs. Such mechanisms, called *interaction specification mechanisms*, are very important aspects of a concurrent programming model. They influence how programs are designed, implemented, and reasoned with (during verification and debugging).

Many models for concurrent programming have been proposed [And91]. In most of these models, the components of a concurrent program contain two kinds of operations: i) simple operations denoting certain computations, and ii) synchronization operations of the form

```
if <condition> <operation> else <delay>
```

The execution of a synchronization operation delays the executing program if the <condition> is not true. The program starts to execute again once the <condition> becomes true. A concurrent program execution, thus, consists of parallel executions of the component programs, where each component repeatedly executes a simple operation or a synchronization operation. Interaction among the components is realized by a set of synchronization operations. The following characterize the interaction specification mechanisms in these models:

- Indirect: Semantic dependencies among operations are specified indirectly through a set of synchronization operations. Conditions in synchronization operations determine if a component program might violate any semantic constraints by executing a synchronization operation. If it does so, the program is delayed until other component programs execute a set of operations in order to ensure that the delayed program may proceed to execute the operation without violating the semantic constraints. Programs, therefore, affect each other *indirectly* by accessing and modifying elements that affect the validity of synchronization conditions.
- Operational: Synchronization operations are embedded within the definitions of component programs. One must reason with the logic associated with the implementation of a program in order to determine how synchronization operations are used in the program and how they affect the executions of other programs.
- Noncompositional: The interaction specification mechanisms identify a set of synchronization operations and their semantics. All interactions must

only be realized through these synchronization operations only. There is no separate mechanism for combining the synchronization operations order to construct more powerful and abstract synchronization operations. Most languages use sequential compositional mechanisms (such as if–then–else, procedure or function composition operators, etc.,) to combine synchronization operations.

All of these characteristics make it difficult to design, implement, and reason with concurrent programs.

This paper presents a model of concurrent programming, called Composition bY Event Specification (C-YES). The C-YES model is based on the observation that concurrency and interaction represent specific kinds of semantic relationships among operations of programs. The relationships underline semantic independence or dependence among these operations. Semantically independent operations can execute in parallel. Executions of dependent operations should occur in an order that preserves any semantic constraints associated with the interaction.

The C-YES model identifies individual occurrences of operations, called *events*, as the basis for specifying concurrency and interaction relationships. Concurrent events are not ordered and, therefore, can execute in parallel. Our interaction specification mechanism identifies the interaction between two events as the fundamental interaction. It models such an interaction by specifying an execution ordering between the two events. The interaction specification mechanism represents other interactions by combining fundamental interactions among different events with suitable operators, called *interaction operators*. The interaction operators model nondeterministic interactions as well as interactions over sets of events. The following are the characteristics of the interaction specification mechanism:

- Interactions are specified directly and precisely by establishing ordering relations among events.
- The interaction specification mechanism is compositional: it defines mechanisms for specifying fundamental interactions, and for combining interaction expressions in order to represent more powerful and abstract interactions.
- The interaction specification mechanism is algebraic. It is possible to reason with interaction expressions in order to determine how programs affect each other.
- The interaction specification mechanism captures only the abstractions associated with interactions. The primitives and the operators do not depend on the semantics of their operands (events); it is, therefore, possible to use the interaction specification mechanism for both shared and distributed memory programming models.

This paper also presents a mechanism, called an *interacting block*, for representing concurrent programs. A program represented using this mechanism contains two elements: the first is the specification of its computations, and the second is the identification of certain execution points, called *interaction points,* where the program may interact with other programs. Interaction points are abstractions of execution points of a program: they capture those execution points that may have semantic relationships with the interaction points of other programs. A concurrent program, therefore, is defined by specifying its component programs and an interaction expression. The latter determines execution orderings among the interaction points of the component programs.

Our model separates interaction specifications from program specifications. It is, therefore, possible to reuse a program definition in many concurrent program compositions. Also, the model separates how interaction points are used and how they are defined. This allows one to localize changes in either program implementations or interaction behaviors without affecting each other in certain cases.

The paper is organized as follows: Section 2 contains definitions of basic terms, and their notations. In Section 3, we present the C-YES model. It first describes how programs can be composed and how their interactions can be specified. The representation mechanism of concurrent programs is then presented. We develop the classical producer and consumer problem, and a problem from numerical analysis (Gaussian elimination algorithm) to illustrate the C-YES model. We briefly survey the different synchronization mechanisms in section 4. Section 5 contains final remarks and ongoing work.

2 Basic Definitions

We define two sets of terms we used in this paper. The first denotes terms that are used while specifying the representation of programs, whereas the second contains terms used during the execution of programs.

2.1 Structures

Definition 2.1 (Program) *A program is a composition of operations and other programs.* ◁

Definition 2.2 (Action) *An action labels operations that will be performed during the execution of a program.* ◁

Actions represent the alphabet that a programmer can use to compose a program. At a certain level of abstraction, the notions of program and action coincide. We will not distinguish between the two and will use them interchangeably.

2.2 Executions

Definition 2.3 (Computation) *A computation denotes a specific execution of a program.* ◁

Each program has a set of computations associated with it.

Notation: Let terms $\xi_s(C)$ and $\xi(C)$ respectively denote the set of computations and some computation of program C.

Definition 2.4 (Event) *An event is a specific occurrence of an action during a computation.* ◁

The relationship between actions and events can be described by the following program:

```
for (i = 0; i < 5; i = i+1)
    sum();
```

In the above, sum() denotes an action. It is executed five times when the above program is executed. Each execution of sum() denotes a unique event occurrence during the above computation.

Definition 2.5 (Event Ordering) *The event ordering relation $\otimes$ between two events is an asymmetric, nonreflexive, and transitive relation. The relation $e_1 \otimes e_2$ specifies that e_1 occurs before e_2.* ◁

Relation $\otimes$ models the execution ordering between events.

Definition 2.6 (Concurrent Event) *Events e_1 and e_2 are concurrent if there is no ordering relation between the two events.* ◁

Notation: We use $(e_1 \|_e e_2)$ to denote concurrency between events e_1 and e_2. Concurrency is modeled by the lack of any execution orderings.

A concurrent computation is a set of events such that some of the events are not ordered with respect to each other, and hence, can be executed in parallel. We will use two mathematical entities, pomsets [Pra86] and event dependency graphs, to represent a concurrent computation.

Definition 2.7 (Pomset) *A labeled partial order is a 4-tuple $(V_c, \Sigma, \otimes, \mu)$ consisting of i) a set V_c of events, ii) an alphabet Σ of actions, iii) a partial order $\otimes$ on set V_c, and iv) a labeling function $\mu : V_c \rightarrow \Sigma$ assigning symbols to events, each labeled event representing an occurrence of the action labeling it.* ◁

Notation: We will write $(V_c, \otimes)$ for pomsets when Σ and μ can be derived from the context.

Notation: We will use $e \in V_c$ to mean that e is an event in computation $(V_c, \otimes)$.

Definition 2.8 (Event Dependency Graph) *An event dependency graph $G = (V_c, E_c)$ is a directed graph such that i) V_c is a set of events, and ii) $(e_1, e_2) \in E_c$ iff $e_1 \otimes e_2$.* ◁

3 C-YES Model

3.1 Model of Concurrent Programming

In most conventional concurrent programming models, a concurrent program is composed from a set of component programs, each containing a set of both simple as well as synchronization operations. During the execution of the composite program, the components form separate threads of executions, and execute in parallel. A thread of execution is delayed if it attempts to execute a synchronization operation and the condition associated with the operation is not true. It remains blocked until the condition becomes true. A correct execution of the composite program is one where the executions of the components satisfy all semantic constraints associated with the interactions of the components.

We take an alternate, and direct, view of the composition of concurrent programs: here, the role of a concurrent composition mechanism is to establish two kinds of relationships among operations of programs. The first, called *concurrency*, represents semantic independence among these operations. Such operations can execute in parallel. The second, called *interaction*, underlines semantic dependencies among operations. Semantic dependencies arise because an operation may rely on information produced by another operation (data dependency), operations must access a resource in an ordered manner (resource consistency and fairness), or operations must satisfy other application specific semantic considerations. Unlike existing programming models, where interaction and concurrency are represented indirectly through the executions of concurrent threads and synchronization constraints, our compositional model represents the two relationships directly.

Our model is based on the Pomset model [Pra86] in that concurrency and interaction among operations are represented by specifying the presence or absence of execution orderings among the operations. Concurrency is specified by the lack of execution orderings, whereas interaction is represented by specifying the order in which interacting operations must be executed. For instance, if an operation e_1 utilizes information produced by an operation e_2, their interaction is specified by the relation

$$e_2 \oslash e_1$$

The relation states that e_1 executes only after e_2 has terminated. Other semantic dependencies such as consistency and fairness can also be represented by establishing proper execution orderings among operations.

3.2 Event-based Concurrent Program Composition

We now present our concurrent composition mechanism. We choose "event" as the basis for specifying concurrency and interaction relations: concurrency is specified by the lack of execution orderings among events, whereas interaction is represented by specifying constraints on the execution orderings of interacting events. The composition mechanism is defined below:

Definition 3.1 (Constrained Concurrent Composition) *The constrained concurrent composition*

$$(C_1 \parallel C_2 \parallel \ldots \parallel C_n) \text{ where } \mathcal{E}$$

of programs $C_1, C_2, \ldots, C_n$ *denotes a program* C *such that during an execution* $\xi(C)$ *of* C,

$$\langle \, \forall \, i, j : i, j \in \{1 \ldots n\} \wedge i \neq j :$$
$$\langle \, \forall \, e_k, e_l : e_k \in \xi(C_i) \wedge e_l \in \xi(C_j) \wedge \neg(Ordered(\mathcal{E}, e_k, e_l)) :$$
$$e_k \parallel_e e_l) \rangle$$

where $Ordered(\mathcal{E}, e_k, e_l)$ *is true if the event ordering constraint expression* $\mathcal{E}$ *specifies an ordering relation between* e_k *and* e_l. *Computations* $\xi(C_i)$ *and* $\xi(C_j)$ *respectively are specific executions of program* C_i *and* C_j *and occur during the computation* $\xi(C)$. ◁

Intuitively, the above composition expression defines a program C such that during its execution, all events in the computations of C_1, C_2, $\ldots$, and C_n occur in parallel with respect to each other, except for a small set of events (compared to the number of events in the composite program). Events in this set must be executed in an order that satisfies the ordering constraints imposed by the event ordering constraint expression $\mathcal{E}$. The focus of a composition, therefore, is on the identification of interacting events, and on the derivation of an event ordering constraint expression.

3.2.1 Interaction specification. Interaction among programs in our model is specified by an algebraic expression, called *event ordering constraint expression*. It is used to represent semantic dependencies among the events of component programs by specifying execution orderings — deterministic or nondeterministic — among the events. An event ordering constraint expression (eoce) is constructed from a set of *primitive ordering constraint expressions* and a set of *interaction operators*. A primitive ordering constraint expression captures the interaction between two events, whereas the interaction operators are used to represent nondeterministic interactions as well as interactions among sets of events.

Syntax: The BNF expression for generating an event ordering constraint expression (eoce) is shown in figure 1.

In the BNF definition, the term `<event_id>` denotes a unique event. Since most programming languages do not define any syntactic mechanisms for differentiating the different occurrences of actions, we use the notation (`<ActionId>`, `<Selector>`) to denote events in this paper. Here `<ActionId>` denotes an action, and `<Selector>` is one of the following:

- **Occurrence number:** We associate a number with each occurrence of an action, starting with the number 1. A unique event can be selected by identifying its occurrence number.

```
<eoce>  ::=  event_id ⊗ event_id
          | <eoce> Ⓥ <eoce>
          | <eoce> Ⓐ <eoce>
          | forall <iterator> in <set>
              <eoce>
          | exists <iterator> in <set>
              <eoce>
          | (<eoce>)
```

Fig. 1. BNF expression for event ordering constraint expressions

- **Boolean condition:** The boolean condition selector specifies a condition that must be true during the execution of an action. Note that it is the programmer's responsibility to specify a boolean condition that uniquely identifies an event.

The term <iterator> in figure 1 is a mechanism used to iterate over a set denoted by the term <set>.

Semantics: We develop the semantics associated with event ordering constraint expressions by defining two terms, *Ordering Constraint Set* and *Satisfy.*

Definition 3.2 (Ordering Constraint Set) *An ordering constraint set S is a set of sets of ordered pairs (a, b) such that a and b are events and $a \otimes b$.* ◁

Notation: We use $\mathcal{O}(E)$ to denote the ordering constraint set associated with the event ordering constraint expression E.

Definition 3.3 (Sat) *For a computation $(V, \otimes_v)$ and an event ordering constraint expression E, the term $Sat((V, \otimes_v), E)$ is true if*

$$(\exists \, s : s \in \mathcal{O}(E) :$$
$$(\forall \, (e_i, e_j) : (e_i, e_j) \in s :$$
$$(e_i \in V) \wedge (e_j \in V) \wedge (e_i \otimes_v e_j) \,))$$

We say that $(V, \otimes_v)$ satisfies E. ◁

Intuitively, if $\mathcal{O}(E) = \{l_1, l_2 \ldots l_n\}$, a computation satisfies E if all orderings specified in at least one of $l_j, j \in \{1 \ldots n\}$ are preserved in the computation.

The constrained concurrent composition

$$C = (C_1 \parallel C_2 \parallel \ldots \parallel C_n) \text{ where } \mathcal{E}$$

of programs $C_1, C_2, \ldots, C_n$, therefore, denotes a program C such that

$$(\forall \, (V, \otimes_v) : (V, \otimes_v) \in \mathcal{X}_s(C) : Sat((V, \otimes_v), \mathcal{E}) \,)$$

We now define the semantics of the primitive event ordering constraint expression and the interaction operators by specifying the corresponding ordering constraint sets:

1. For expression <eoce>::= event_id1 ⊗ event_id2

$$\mathcal{O}(\texttt{<eoce>}) = \{\{\texttt{event\_id1, event\_id2}\}\}$$

The above expression models the interaction relationship between two events. The order of execution between the events is determined by issues such as data dependency, safety, and progress properties. Primitive ordering constraint expressions allow one to capture such interactions when they are translated to the most primitive level of computations, that is, events.

2) **And constraint operator** ($\bigotimes$): The operator $\bigotimes$ is used for combining a set of event ordering expressions in order to represent interactions among sets of events. For expression $\texttt{<eoce>::=} E_1 \bigotimes E_2$

$$\mathcal{O}(E_1 \bigotimes E_2) = \bigcup_{s_i \in \mathcal{O}(E_1)} (\bigcup_{s_j \in \mathcal{O}(E_2)} s_i \cup s_j)$$

Intuitively, the above expression specifies that a computation satisfies $(E_1 \bigotimes E_2)$ if it satisfies both E_1 and E_2.

Example 3.1 *($\bigotimes$ operator)* For expression $E = (a \bigotimes b) \bigotimes (c \bigotimes d)$

$$\mathcal{O}(E) = \{\{(a,b),(c,d)\}\}$$

A computation satisfies E if event a occurs before event b *and* event c occurs before event d in the computation. ◁

3) **Or Constraint Operator** ($\bigovee$): The operator $\bigovee$ is used to incorporate nondeterminism in the orderings of events. For expression $\texttt{<eoce>::=} E_1 \bigovee E_2$

$$\mathcal{O}(E_1 \bigovee E_2) = \mathcal{O}(E_1) \cup \mathcal{O}(E_2)$$

Intuitively, the above expression specifies that a computation satisfies $(E_1 \bigovee E_2)$ if it satisfies *at least one* of E_1 or E_2.

Example 3.2 *($\bigovee$ operator)* For expression $E = (a \bigotimes b) \bigovee (b \bigotimes a)$

$$\mathcal{O}(E) = \{\{(a,b)\}, \{(b,a)\}\}$$

A computation satisfies E if a occurs before b or b occurs before a in the computation. Expression E specifies mutual exclusion between the events a and b. ◁

Assume that F and G denote ordered (with respect to an index) sets of events $\{f_1, f_2, \ldots, f_n\}$ and $\{g_1, g_2, \ldots, g_n\}$ respectively. Terms f_i and g_j denote the ith and jth events of F and G respectively. Note that sets F and G may include any kind of events, including events that are occurrences of different actions.

4) **forall**: The expression

$$\texttt{forall } i \texttt{ in } \{1 \ldots n\}$$
$$P(f_i, g_i)$$

is equivalent to the expression

$$P(f_1, g_1) \bigotimes P(f_2, g_2) \bigotimes \cdots \bigotimes P(f_n, g_n)$$

Here $P(f_i, g_i)$ is an event ordering constraint expression between the events denoted by f_i and g_i.

5) exists: The expression

$$\textbf{exists } i \textbf{ in } \{1 \ldots n\}$$
$$P(f_i, g_i)$$

is equivalent to the expression

$$P(f_1, g_1) \bigovee P(f_2, g_2) \bigovee \cdots \bigovee P(f_n, g_n)$$

Operators forall and exists are extensions of operators $\bigotimes$ and $\bigovee$ respectively.

Example 3.3 *(Event ordering constraint expression)* For expression E,

$$E = ((a \otimes b) \bigovee (c \otimes d)) \bigotimes ((a \otimes c) \bigovee (b \otimes d))$$

the ordering constraint set is

$$\mathcal{O}(E) = \{\{(a, b), (a, c)\}, \{(a, b), (b, d)\}, \{(c, d), (a, c)\}, \{(c, d), (b, d)\}\}$$

◁

3.3 Representation of Programs

There are two unique aspects in our model of concurrent programming: the first is the separation of interaction definitions from programs specifications, and the second is the choice of "events" as the basis for interaction. We now examine how the two aspects affect representations of programs.

Concurrent programs aim to model applications where entities exist and perform independently. During an execution, an entity performs certain operations. Occasionally, it interacts with its environment at certain points. We call such execution points *interaction points*. Programming languages such as CSP[Hoa78] model such entities as processes and model their interactions with other entities by sending and receiving messages on channels of communications. Sends and receives, therefore, form the interaction points of processes.

We observe that there are two elements of an interaction point: the first is its identification. This underlines the fact that a program may interact at the interaction point. In CSP, for instance, names of communication channels along with the send and receive operations identify the interaction points of a process. The second is its *role* in an interaction. The role of an interaction point determines the manner in which a program participates in an interaction at the interaction point. For instance, the role associated with a "receive" interaction point determines a process's behavior at the interaction point, that is, the process is delayed until a message arrives.

In our model of programming, the two elements of an interaction point — its identification and its role — are separated. Interaction points of a program are identified when the program is specified. However, the roles of the interaction points are determined (by event ordering constraint expressions) when the program is composed with other programs by the composition operator. Since "events" form the basis for defining event ordering constraint expressions, we choose events to represent interaction points. We now present a representation for programs, which contains, in addition to its composition definition, definitions of interaction points.

In sequential imperative programming languages, programs are represented by blocks [CK89]. A block, say f_s, has two components: i) interface of the form $f_s(p_1, p_2, \ldots, p_n)$, where variables $p_1, p_2, \ldots, p_n$ parameterize the execution behavior of f_s; and ii) composition of operations, specifying the computations of f_s. A block identifies — implicitly — two interaction points: i) *entry* point, where control and values of the parameters are passed and ii) *exit* point, where the block terminates and returns any values. All other execution points are encapsulated by the block abstraction.

We extend the notion of sequential blocks. We call such entities *interacting blocks*. The following are the elements of an interacting block:

1. **Interface**: An interacting block f_c has an interface of the form

$$f_c(p_1, \ldots, p_n \; ; \; i_1, \ldots, i_m)$$

Here $p_1, p_2, \ldots,$ and p_n are parameter variables. Interaction parameters $i_1, i_2, \ldots,$ and i_m denote interaction points of f_c.

2. **Implementation**: The implementation of an interacting block is partitioned into two. The first specifies the sequential and concurrent composition of a program. It determines the execution behaviors of the program. The second contains a mapping between the interaction parameters $i_1, i_2, \ldots,$ and i_m and the events of the program.

The composition of two interacting blocks $f_c(v_1, \ldots, v_n \; ; \; i_1, \ldots i_m)$ and $g_c(w_1, \ldots, w_l \; ; \; j_1, \ldots, i_k)$ is, thus, specified by the expression:

$$f_c(v_1, \ldots, v_n) \parallel g_c(w_1, \ldots, w_l)$$
$$\textbf{where}$$
$$\mathcal{E}(e_1, \ldots, e_p)$$

Here, the event ordering expression $\mathcal{E}$ is over a set of events $\{e_1, \ldots, e_p\}$ such that every event in this set is an interaction point of either f_c or g_c.

3.4 Examples

This section contains two examples, each highlighting aspects of the C-YES model. The emphasis in the first example is on the composition and interaction specification mechanisms. In the second example, it is on the representation of concurrent programs by interacting blocks. The language that we use here contains features from C [KR78] and a few extensions in order to present our ideas. We explain these extensions where they are used.

3.4.1 Example 1: Producer/Consumer. Let **Producer** and **Consumer** be two programs, whose abstract representations are:

```
Producer(Prod(int i)) = {          Consumer(Cons(int j)) = {
  while (1) {                        while (1) {
      :                                  :
    Produce(Buf);                      Consume(Buf);
      :                                  :
  }                                  }
  Prod(int i) = (Produce, i)        Cons(int j) = (Consume, j)
}                                  }
```

Interaction parameters **Prod(i)** and **Cons(j)** are interaction points of **Producer** and **Consumer** programs respectively. Parameter **Prod(i)** names all **Produce** events. It denotes a set of events such that **Prod(k)** denotes (**Produce, k**) (kth occurrence of **Produce**) in the **Producer** program. Parameter **Cons(j)** is similarly defined. We will write (**Prod, i**) and (**Cons, j**) for **Prod(i)** and **Cons(j)** respectively.

We now derive a composition of the **Producer** and **Consumer** programs. The actions **Produce** and **Consume** interact with each other. All other actions are non-interacting and hence execute in parallel during the execution of the composite program. The following is such a composition of the two programs:

$$\text{Comp} = (\text{Producer} \parallel \text{Consumer}) \text{ where ConsExp}$$

The above expression specifies that during an execution of **Comp**, all events in **Producer** and **Consumer** execute in parallel except for those that must satisfy the ordering constraints imposed by the event ordering constraint expression **ConsExp**.

The simplest interaction arises from the mutual exclusion constraint between the actions: no occurrences of **Produce** and **Consume** should execute in parallel. The following event ordering constraint expression captures the mutual exclusion constraint between the ith and jth occurrences of **Produce** and **Consume** actions:

$$((\text{Prod, i}) \otimes (\text{Cons, j})) \; \text{\textcircled{V}} \; ((\text{Cons, j}) \otimes (\text{Prod, i}))$$

The expression for mutual exclusion among all occurrences of **Produce** and **Consume**, therefore, is:

```
ConsExp = forall i in {1...}
          forall j in {1...}
              ((Prod, i) ⊗ (Cons, j)) ⓥ ((Cons, j) ⊗ (Prod, i))
```

There are many possible executions of **Comp** that satisfy the event ordering constraint expression **ConsExp**. One such execution is shown in figure 2. Only the interacting events are shown in the figure. Here all occurrences of **Produce** dominate the first occurrence of **Consume**, thereby causing the starvation of **Consumer**. The interaction in the figure is captured by the following event ordering constraint expression:

```
ConsExp1 =   forall i in {1...}
                (Prod, i) ⊗ (Cons, 1)
```

Note

$$\langle \forall v : v \in \xi_s(\text{Comp}) : Sat(v, \text{ConsExp1}) \Rightarrow Sat(v, \text{ConsExp}) \rangle$$

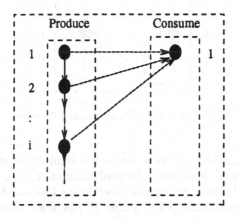

Fig. 2. Domination of Produce events over Consume events

A different interaction semantics for the **Producer** and **Consumer** programs can be specified by constructing a different event ordering constraint expression. For instance, assume that **Producer** and **Consumer** access a buffer of size one. The semantic constraints on accessing and modifying the buffer are: i) No data is consumed until it is produced, and ii) No data is produced until the previously produced data has been consumed. The following event ordering constraint expression captures these constraints:

```
ConsExp2 = forall i in {1...}
              ((Prod, i) ⊗ (Cons, i)) ⊗ ((Cons, i) ⊗ (Prod, i+1))
```

Figure 3 shows the event dependency graph of the computation of the composition. Note that there are no starvations or deadlocks.

3.4.2 Example 2: Gaussian Elimination.
We develop below a concurrent program for the Gaussian elimination algorithm. The purpose here is to highlight the important ideas inherent in the notion of interacting blocks, and to discuss their usefulness in the representation of concurrent programs.

For a $n \times n$ matrix A, the Gaussian elimination algorithm [Ste73] solves the linear equation

$$Ax = b$$

There are two distinct steps in the algorithm. The first step, called *forward elimination*, transforms A into an upper triangular matrix, whereas the second

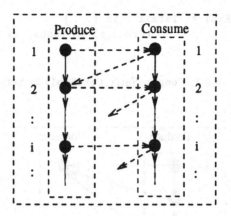

Fig. 3. Single buffer interaction between Producer and Consumer

step uses the transformed matrix to derive the solutions of the unknowns. We will focus our attention here on the forward elimination step.

There are $(n-1)$ steps, each called *pivot*, in the forward elimination step. In the ith pivot step, elements $A[i+1, i]$ through $A[n, i]$ are reduced to zero, while modifying certain other elements of A. We represent each pivot by an interacting block. The forward elimination program is a constrained concurrent composition of the $(n-1)$ pivot programs. The event ordering constraint expression associated with the composition represents the interaction among the pivot steps.

A motivation for structuring the forward elimination program in this manner is to show that i) there is concurrency among the different pivot steps, and ii) this concurrency can be easily expressed by our composition and interacting block mechanisms. The interacting block associated with the ith pivot step is shown in figure 4. The details of the definition in figure 4 are :

```
P(int i; Access(int aIndJ, int aIndK), Change(int cIndJ, int cIndK)) = {
   int j, k;
   { /*implements functionality of P(i) */
     for (j = i+1; j < n; j = j + 1)
        for (k = i+1; k < n; k = k+1)
           A[j, k] = A[i, k] - (A[j, k]*(A[i, i]/A[j, i]));
   }
   /* Map interaction points to internal execution points*/
   Access(int aIndJ, int aIndK) = (read.A[j, k], 1);
   Change(int cIndJ, int cIndK) = (write.A[j, k], 1);
}
```

Fig. 4. Representation of the ith Pivot step

1. Interface: The interface of P(i) defines three parameters. The first, i, identifies the ith pivot. The interaction parameters, Access(int aIndJ, int

aIndK) and `Change(int cIndK, int cIndK)`, denote the interaction points of `P(i)`.

2. Implementation: The first part of the implementation specifies the computations of the ith pivot. The implementation shown here is sequential. Most implementations of the forward elimination step focus on exploiting parallelism inherent within each pivot step.

The second part specifies how interaction parameters are mapped to the actual events of `P(i)`. The parameter `Access(int aIndJ, int aIndK)` denotes a set of `P(i)`'s *first* read events of elements of *A*. For instance, term `P(i).Access(2, 3)` denotes the *first* read of element `A[2, 3]` that `P(i)` executes. Since all such *first* reads in the ith pivot step interact with the writes to the corresponding elements of the $(i-1)$th pivot steps, we include these read events in the set denoted by `Access` by the following definition:

$$\text{Access(int aIndJ, int aIndK)} = (\text{read.A[j, k]}, 1);$$

The variables `j` and `k` in the above definition refer to the variables `j` and `k` of the implementation of `P(i)`. The parameters `aIndJ` and `aIndK` are used to select unique events from the set that `Access` denotes. The other interaction parameter `Change(cIndJ, cIndK)` is defined similarly.

The forward elimination program can now be specified as a constrained concurrent composition of the $(n-1)$ pivot steps. Let us look at the interaction between the ith and $(i+1)$th pivot steps: Pivot `P(i+1)` should not read or write to any `A[j, k]` until `P(i)` has modified this `A[j, k]`. There is an explicit ordering between the reads and writes of the two steps and the event ordering constraint expression must capture this data dependency. The following expression represents such a dependency:

$$
\begin{aligned}
&(\textbf{forall } aj, ak \text{ in } P(i+1).Access \\
&\qquad P(i).Change(aj, ak) \otimes P(i+1).Access(aj, ak)) \\
&\qquad\qquad \oslash \\
&(\textbf{forall } cj, ck \text{ in } P(i+1).Change \\
&\qquad P(i).Change(cj, ck) \otimes P(i+1).Change(cj, ck))
\end{aligned}
$$

In the above expression, `aj`, `ak`, `cj` and `ck` are variables that range over the sets that `Access` and `Change` denote. The expression captures the orderings among the interacting reads and writes of `P(i)` and `P(i+1)`. The forward elimination program is shown in figure 5.

3.5 Discussion

We now examine the characteristics of our program composition and program representation mechanisms.

```
ForwardElimination = {
   ||ⁿ⁻¹ᵢ₌₁  P(i) where
      forall i in {1, ..., (n-2)}
         (forall aj, ak in P(i).Access
               P(i).Change(aj, ak) ⊘ P(i+1).Access(aj, ak) )
                          ⊘
         (forall cj, ck in P(i).Change
               P(i).Change(cj, ck) ⊘ P(i+1).Change(cj, ck))
}
```

Fig. 5. Forward elimination program

3.5.1 Event Based Program Composition.

The constrained concurrent composition of programs specifies two kinds of relationships among the events of component programs: concurrency and interaction. The notion of concurrency is assumed to be universal, that is, events are concurrent by default. Interaction among events is modeled by interaction expressions, which determine execution orderings among the events. The model contains several unique ideas such as separation of program and interaction specifications, "events" as the basis for interaction, abstraction of interaction, and algebraic interaction expressions. We discuss each in detail below.

The composition mechanism separates interaction specifications from program specifications. A program in our model does not include any synchronization information; it merely specifies what its computations are. Since programs interact with other programs only when they are composed, interaction specifications are elements of concurrent compositions. They are defined when such compositions are defined.

One of the implications of the above separation is that a program specification can be used in many concurrent compositions, each defining different event ordering constraint expressions. The interaction behavior of the program may be different in each of the compositions. For instance, the two event ordering constraint expressions **ConsExp** and **ConsExp2** specify different interaction semantics for the same **Producer** and **Consumer** programs.

Interaction is specified at the "event" level. The composition mechanism is based on the observation that fundamental interaction occurs between two events. All other interactions can be represented by suitable combinations of primitive interaction expressions. The name space in our model, therefore, is fine-grained, since it contains names for actions as well as their individual occurrences.

One of the implications of such a fine-grained name space is that interaction relationships can be defined among all events directly. This is unlike other approaches, where the name space contains a fixed set of named actions. Also, the interaction among the occurrences of these actions is predetermined, and cannot be changed.

Our concurrent constrained composition mechanism, in conjunction with the choice of "events" as the basis for interaction, allows one to represent programs that are highly concurrent. We show this by extending the producer-consumer example. Assume that **Producer** and **Consumer** programs access a buffer such that

$$\text{Produce} = \text{P(buffer[0])}; \ \text{P(buffer[1])}$$
$$\text{Consume} = \text{C(buffer[0])}; \ \text{C(buffer[1])}$$

Here, every **Produce** event creates information in **buffer[0]** and **buffer[1]** and every **Consume** event retrieves information from **buffer[0]** and **buffer[1]**. Note that **Produce** and **Consume** here are not atomic actions anymore; they are composed (with the sequential operator ';') from actions **P** and **C** respectively.

Expression **ConsExp2** can be used here to specify an interaction between **Produce** and **Consume**. However, it overconstrains the executions of **P** and **C** events. It introduces unnecessary ordering among events when there should be none. In order to derive an event ordering constraint expression that does not impose any ordering constraints among the events that occur at different buffers, we need to identify **P** and **C** as the basis of interaction — not **Produce** and **Consume**. The redefined interaction points **Prod** and **Cons**, therefore, are:

$$\text{Prod(i)} = \text{(P, i)}$$
$$\text{Cons(j)} = \text{(C, j)}$$

The derivation first specifies single buffer interactions at **buffer[0]** and **buffer[1]**, and then combines the two expressions to construct an expression for both the buffers.

For all $i \in \{\,1\ldots\,\}$, let

$$\text{(P1, i)} = \text{(Prod, 2i-1)} \tag{3.5.1}$$
$$\text{(P2, i)} = \text{(Prod, 2i)} \tag{3.5.2}$$
$$\text{(C1, i)} = \text{(Cons, 2i-1)} \tag{3.5.3}$$
$$\text{(C2, i)} = \text{(Cons, 2i)} \tag{3.5.4}$$

$\mathcal{E}_1$

= {Single buffer interaction at Buf[0]}
  forall i in $\{1\ldots\}$
    (P1, i) ⊘ (C1, i) ⊗
    (C1, i) ⊘ (P1, $i+1$)

= { eqn 3.5.1, eqn 3.5.3 }
  forall i in $\{1\ldots\}$
    (Prod, $2i-1$) ⊘ (Cons, $2i-1$) ⊗
    (Cons, $2i-1$) ⊘ (Prod, $2i+1$)

= { $k = 2i - 1$ }
  forall k in $\{1, 3, \ldots\}$
    (Prod, k) ⊘ (Cons, k) ⊗

$\mathcal{E}_2$

= {Single buffer interaction at Buf[1]}
  forall j in $\{1\ldots\}$
    (P2, j) ⊘ (C2, j) ⊗
    (C2, j) ⊘ (P2, $j+1$)

= { eqn 3.5.2, eqn 3.5.4 }
  forall j in $\{1\ldots\}$
    (Prod, $2j$) ⊘ (Cons, $2j$) ⊗
    (Cons, $2j$) ⊘ (Prod, $2j+2$)

= { $l = 2j$ }
  forall l in $\{2, 4, \ldots\}$
    (Prod, l) ⊘ (Cons, l) ⊗

$$(\text{Cons}, k) \otimes (\text{Prod}, k+2) \qquad\qquad (\text{Cons}, l) \otimes (\text{Prod}, l+2)$$

$$\{ \text{ Combine } \mathcal{E}_1 \text{ and } \mathcal{E}_2 \ \}$$
$$\text{ConsExp3} = \mathcal{E}_1 \otimes \mathcal{E}_2 =$$
$$\text{forall } i \text{ in } \{1 \dots\}$$
$$(\text{Prod}, i) \otimes (\text{Cons}, i) \oslash$$
$$(\text{Cons}, i) \otimes (\text{Prod}, i+2)$$

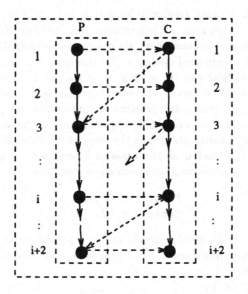

Fig. 6. Two buffer interaction between **Producer** and **Consumer**

Figure 6 shows the event dependency graph associated with an execution of **Comp**. Observe that

$$\langle\, \forall\, i : i \in \{\, 1 \dots \} :\, (\text{P}, i+1)\, \|_e\, (\text{C}, i)\, \rangle$$

Intuitively, it means that **Consumer** can access **buf[0]** while **Producer** is modifying **buf[1]**. Also, the above interaction expression can be extended to define interaction over a buffer of size **N**:

$$\mathcal{E} = \text{forall } i \text{ in } \{1 \dots\}$$
$$(\text{Prod}, i) \otimes (\text{Cons}, i) \oslash (\text{Cons}, i) \otimes (\text{Prod}, i+N)$$

The interaction specification mechanism captures the fundamental abstractions of interaction. It specifies interaction by suitable ordering relations among the interacting events of programs. It does not depend on the semantics of these events. Hence, the model can be used for both shared and distributed memory programs. For instance, the event ordering constraint expressions **ConsExp1** and **ConsExp2** in the producer-consumer example specify interaction in accessing a buffer. The buffer can be a shared memory structure or a distributed resource. Implementations of the **Produce** and **Consume** actions determine the shared or distributed nature of the buffer.

The interaction expressions are algebraic in nature. They are composed from a set of primitive ordering constraint expressions and the interaction operators. The approach is constructive in that one first identifies the events that interact, and represents their interaction through a set of primitive ordering constraint expressions. An event ordering constraint expression is then constructed from the primitive expressions and the interaction operators. This facilitates *modular* [Blo79] construction of event ordering constraint expressions. For instance, in the two-buffer producer-consumer example, we derive separate event ordering constraint expressions for the two buffers and then use the $\bigotimes$ operator to combine the two expressions.

Since the properties of the basic primitives and the operators are well defined, it is possible to reason with the interaction specifications in a rigorous manner. For instance, it is possible to prove that

$$\langle \forall v : v \in \xi_s(\texttt{Comp}) : Sat(v, \texttt{ConsExp2}) \Rightarrow Sat(v, \texttt{ConsExp}) \rangle$$

which states that the interaction expression **ConsExp2** guarantees mutual exclusion between the **Produce** and **Consume** actions.

3.5.2 Concurrent Program Representation.

An interacting block extends the notion of sequential block by incorporating mechanisms to identify a set of events as interaction points. The interface of an interacting block includes interaction parameters denoting interaction points of the block. The implementation defines the mappings between the interaction parameters and the events of the block.

The separation between the interaction parameters (defined at the interface) and their mappings (defined in implementation) provides a powerful mechanism for isolating the definition of the interaction behavior of a program from the implementation of the program. It is, therefore, possible to change the implementation, the interaction parameters, or the interaction parameter mappings without changing other aspects of the program definition. We explore how these changes can be made and what they mean in terms of design and implementation of concurrent programs.

It is possible to change a program's implementation without changing any composition expressions that include this program. This is possible because of the separation between how interaction points are defined (in implementations) and how they are used (in event ordering constraint expressions). Note, however, that changes in the implementation should not affect the semantic nature of the interaction points and their participation in the composition definition. We clarify this by showing that it is possible to modify **P(i)**'s implementation without changing either the definitions of the interaction points or the **ForwardElimination** program.

The idea is to change those aspects of the program that do not affect either the interaction points or the orderings between the interaction points of the different pivots. In P(i), it is easy to do so, since we can parallelize one or some aspect of the pivot without changing either the interaction points (reads and writes) or the ordering constraints between them. The implementation in figure 7 is one such realization.

```
P(int i; Access(int aIndJ, int aIndK), Change(int cIndJ, int cIndK)) = {
    int j, k;
    { /*implements functionality of P(i) */
       ||_{j=i+1}^{j=n-1}
          ||_{k=i+1}^{k=n-1}
                A[j, k] = A[i, k] - (A[j, k]*(A[i, i]/A[j, i]));
    }
    /* define interaction points*/
}
```

Fig. 7. Parallel implementation of P(i)

The body of P(i) now utilizes the parallelism inside each pivot step. The definitions of Access, Change, and ForwardElimination remain unchanged, since there are no changes either in the interaction points or in the orderings among interacting events. The above algorithm is optimally concurrent in that no event is delayed unless it is semantically dependent on some other event.

Another implication of the separation between the interaction parameter and an interacting block's implementation is that the interaction behavior of a program can be changed by modifying either the mappings between the interaction parameters and the internal events, or the event ordering constraint expressions, or both. This is useful in determining those interaction points and interaction expressions that provide optimal performance for a given algorithm by balancing the costs involved in computation and interaction.

In the Gaussian elimination example, the interacting block P(i) waits for P(i+1) to modify an element A[j, k] before it can read or write this element. The different pivot steps, therefore, interact at the level of single elements of the matrix. In many systems (e.g., message passing systems), such closely coupled interactions can be very inefficient. A modified version of ForwardElimination is shown in figure 8. In this implementation, the interaction between the pivots occurs at the level of rows: P(i+1) reads or writes a given row j only after P(i) has modified this row.

The above defines an ordering between the writes to the last element of a row by P(i) and reads and writes to the first element of a row by P(i+1). The composition relies on the fact that a row j is modified sequentially within P(i). It exploits the ordering relationships between the reads and writes in a single row. The above composition expression, therefore, cannot be used if the rows are not modified sequentially in P(i) (as is the case in figure 7).

```
ForwardElimination = {
    {
        ‖ⁿ⁻²ᵢ₌₁ P(i) where
            forall i in {1, ..., (n-2)}
                ( forall aj in P(i+1).Access
                        P(i).Change(aj, n) ⊘ P(i+1).Access(aj, i+1))
                        ⊗
                ( forall cj in P(i+1).Change
                        P(i).Change(cj, n) ⊘ P(i+1).Change(cj, i+1) )
    }
}
```

Fig. 8. Row level interaction among pivots of forward elimination program

4 Related work

We now look at the interaction mechanisms that different concurrent programming languages use. We classify two broad classes of interaction mechanisms on the basis of how common information is manipulated by concurrent programs in these languages.

4.1 Unstructured

In unstructured approaches, programming models do not impose any constraints on how shared information can be manipulated or exchanged inside programs. The models identify a set of synchronization primitives, which are used to synchronize accesses to shared information or to access distributed information. The interaction between the synchronization primitives is defined at the "action" level. All interactions are constructed from suitable combinations of these primitives. Examples of unstructured synchronization primitives are semaphores [Dij65, Dij68], message-passing primitives [Hoa78, Per87], and write-once shared variables [Sha89, FT89] of logic programming languages.

Interactions among programs in these languages are realized indirectly through the executions of suitable synchronization primitives. The synchronization primitives are at a low level of abstraction, which makes it difficult to define concurrent programs. Also, since the synchronization primitives are embedded within the specifications of the programs, one must reason, operationally, with the logic of these programs.

4.1.1 Structured Approaches
In structured approaches, a module $M = (I_1, I_2, \cdots, I_n)$ provides a set of services through interfaces $I_1, I_2, \ldots, I_n$. Any accesses or modifications to the data structures of M must be made through the interfaces. Examples of structured approaches are Monitor [Hoa74], abstract data types with Path Expressions [CH74, And79] or abstract expressions [AHV85],

Mediators [GC86], rendezvous–based models [Geh84, GR86], remote–procedure call models [BN84], and concurrent object–oriented models [Ame87, YBS87, TS89, CK92, WKH92].

There are two possible sources of concurrency and interactions among programs in such models: i) External interaction and concurrency: these arise when a program C requests for a service through an interface I_k. The requested service and C can both execute in parallel and interact. ii) Internal interaction and concurrency: these arise because of the concurrent invocations of services within M. The concurrent requests interact because they share the data structures that M encapsulates.

Models based on structured approaches support hierarchical and modular software development methodologies and hence should be a basis for software development in the concurrent domain as well. However, support for concurrency and interaction in these models is weak. The reasons are the following:

1. The external interaction in most languages such as ADA [Geh84] and Monitors [Hoa74] is based on synchronous call-return semantics. This limits the possible concurrency between the calling and called computations.
2. Models that do allow for external concurrency among the calling and called computations employ ad-hoc mechanisms such as **future** [YBS87] for specifying external interaction between the two computations. There is no general mechanism for specifying arbitrary external interactions.
3. Many programming models such as Monitors [Hoa74] and ADA [Geh84] do not support internal concurrency.
4. Models such as Mediator [GC86] do allow concurrent executions within a module. However, they either support only non-interacting concurrent executions or use unstructured primitives to specify interactions. Such models inherit the problems associated with the unstructured primitives.

5 Conclusions and Future Work

There are two elements in a program definition in our model: the first specifies its computations (what the program does when it is executed), and the second identifies its interaction points (places where the program may interact with its environment). Interaction points are abstractions of a subset of execution points of the program. A constrained concurrent composition combines a set of programs by specifying both ordering relationships among their interaction points as well as concurrency among all other execution points.

In our model, "events" form the basis for identifying interaction points as well as for specifying interaction among programs. The latter is specified by constructing an algebraic expression from a set of primitive interactions and interaction operators.

Our programming model isolates a program's specification from its interaction behaviors. The separation between the interaction and program specifications allows one to reuse the program definition in many concurrent compositions. Also, the notion of interacting block separates how interaction points are defined (within a program's implementation) and how they are used (in interaction expressions). Hence, it is possible to change a program's implementation without changing any composition expressions as long as certain semantic properties of the interaction points are preserved. In addition, the separation allows one to experiment with different interaction expressions in order to examine different interaction behaviors of the program. This provides a flexible mechanism for finding those interaction points that try to balance the cost involved in computation and interaction.

The choice of "events" as a basis for interaction and the algebraic mechanism for interaction specifications allow direct and precise formulation of interaction definitions among programs. The interaction expressions are modular and algebraic. Also, it is possible to rigorously analyze interaction expressions in order to determine certain classes of properties of programs.

The programming model, therefore, supports the specification of concurrent programs, which are i) highly concurrent and asynchronous, ii) portable across both shared and distributed memory architectures, and iii) represented as expressions over component programs. The composition also supports precise and direct specifications of interactions.

We are investigating a number of issues that deal with the theoretical, language design, and implementation aspects of our model. Active work is proceeding on the integration of our concurrent programming model within the object–oriented framework. The issues that we consider here deal with the representation of concurrent and interacting objects, method compositions, inheritance of methods and interactions expressions, and association between events and method activations. Further, we aim to extend an existing object–oriented programming language to define a concurrent programming language. We also plan to define execution semantics for this language. In addition, we are looking at extending the set of interaction operators and their associated semantics. One of the interesting operators is conditional ordering operator. We are examining its semantics and its relationship with the ∨ and **exists** operators.

References

[AHV85] F. Andre, D. Herman, and J. P. Verjus. *Synchronization of Parallel Programs*. The MIT Press, Cambridge, MA, 1985.

[Ame87] Pierre America. POOL-T: A Parallel Object–Oriented Language. In A. Yonezawa and M. Tokoro, editors, *Object-Oriented Concurrent Programming*, pages 199–220. The MIT Press, 1987.

[And79] S. Andler. Predicate Path Expression. In *Proc. Sixth ACM Symposium on Principles of Programming Languages*, pages 226–236, 1979.

[And91] Gregory R. Andrews. *Concurrent Programming*. The Benjamin/Cummings Publishing Company, Redwood City, CA, 1991.

[Blo79] Toby Bloom. Evaluating Synchronization Schemes. In *Proc 7th Symposium on Operating Systems Principles*, pages 24–32. ACM, 1979.

[BN84] Andrew Birrell and B. J. Nelson. Implementing Remote Procedure Calls. *ACM Transactions on Computer Systems*, 2(1):39–59, 1984.

[CH74]   R. H. Campbell and A. N. Habermann. The Specification of Process Synchronization by Path Expressions. In *Lecture Notes on Computer Sciences*, volume 16, pages 89–102. Springer Verlag, 1974.

[CK89]   Gianna Cioni and Antoni Kreczmar. Modules in High Level Programming Languages. In *Advanced Programming Methodologies*, pages 247–340. Academic Press, Ltd., 1989.

[CK92]   K. Mani Chandy and Carl Kesselman. Compositional C++: Compositional Parallel Programming. Technical Report Caltech-cs-tr-92-13, Cal Tech, 1992.

[Dij65]   E. W. Dijkstra. Solution of a Problem in Concurrent Programming Control. *Communication of the ACM*, 8(9):569, 1965.

[Dij68]   E. W. Dijkstra. The Structure of the THE Multiprogramming System. *Communication of the ACM*, 11(5):341–346, 1968.

[FT89]   Ian Foster and Stephen Taylor. *Strand: New Concepts in Parallel Programming*. Prentice Hall, Englewood Cliffs, N. J., 1989.

[GC86]   J. E. Grass and R. H. Campbell. Mediators: A Synchronization Mechanism. In *Sixth International Conference on Distributed Computing Systems*, pages 468–477, 1986.

[Geh84]   Narain H Gehani. *Ada: Concurrent Programming*. Prentice Hall, Englewood Cliffs, N.J., 1984.

[GR86]   Narain H Gehani and W. D Roome. Concurrent C. *Software – Practice and Experience*, 16(9):821–844, 1986.

[Hoa74]   C. A. R. Hoare. Monitor: An Operating System Structuring Concept. *Communication of the ACM*, 17(10):549–557, 1974.

[Hoa78]   C. A. R. Hoare. Communicating Sequential Processes. *CACM*, 21(8):666–677, 1978.

[KR78]   Brian W. Kernighan and Dennis M. Ritchie. *The C Programming Language*. Prentice-Hall, Englewood Cliffs, New Jersey, 1978.

[Per87]   Brinch Hansen Per. Joyce - A Programming Language for Distributed Systems. *Software – Practice and Experience*, 17(1):29–50, 1987.

[Pra86]   Vaughan Pratt. Modeling Concurrency with Partial Order. *International Journal of Parallel Programming*, pages 33–71, 1986.

[Sha89]   Ehud Shapiro. The Family of Concurrent Logic Programming Languages. *ACM Computing Surveys*, 21(3):413–510, 1989.

[Ste73]   G. W. Stewart. *Introduction to Matrix Computations*. Academic Press, New York, 1973.

[TS89]   Chris Tomlinson and Mark Scheevek. Concurrent Object Oriented Programming Languages. In Won Kim and F. H. Lochovsky, editors, *Object Oriented Concepts, Databases, and Applications*, pages 79–124. ACM Press, 1989.

[WKH92] Barbara B. Wyatt, K. Kavi, and Steve Hufnagel. Parallelism in Object-Oriented Languages: a Survey. *IEEE Software*, 9(6), 1992.

[YBS87]   A. Yonezawa, J. Briot, and E. Shibayama. Modeling and Programming in Object-Oriented Concurrent Language ABCL/1. In A. Yonezawa and M. Tokoro, editors, *Object-Oriented Concurrent Programming*, pages 55–89. The MIT Press, 1987.

Adaptive Parallelism on Multiprocessors: Preliminary Experience with Piranha on the CM-5

Nicholas Carriero, Eric Freeman, and David Gelernter*

Department of Computer Science, Yale University, New Haven, CT 06520

Abstract. Mechanisms for sharing multiprocessors among users are still in their infancy—typical approaches include simple space-sharing and inefficient, restricted forms of time-sharing. In this work we investigate a new alternative: *adaptive parallelism* [2]. Adaptively parallel programs can execute over a *dynamically changing* set of processors; many such codes can easily and dynamically share a multiprocessor by individually adapting to execute in separate groups of processors that may vary with time. Adaptive parallelism has been successfully used in *Piranha*, an execution model for Linda[2] programs that turns idle networked workstations into a significant computing resource [4]. This work explores Piranha on the Connection Machine CM-5 multiprocessor. Our preliminary results suggest that adaptive parallelism can provide an attractive alternative to traditional methods for sharing multiprocessors among users.

1 Introduction

Large, scalable, multiprocessor computers are the emerging dominant species of supercomputer. How do we share such a machine among its users? Solutions are still in their infancy—space-sharing through static partitions and inefficient, restricted forms of time-sharing are currently common.

In this paper we explore the *adaptive parallelism* [2] alternative. Adaptive parallelism refers to a parallel application that executes over a set of dynamically changing processors. Adaptive parallelism has been used successfully in *Piranha*, an execution model that harnesses the computing power of idle network workstations [4].

Specifically we discuss Piranha on the CM-5[3] multiprocessor [3]. Our results suggest that adaptive parallelism can provide an alternative to traditional methods of sharing multiprocessors.

* This work is supported by Air Force Grant AFOSR-91-0098 and NASA Graduate Research Fellowship NGT-50858. CM-5 resources were provided by the Pittsburgh Supercomputing Center and the National Center for Supercomputing Applications.

[2] A registered trademark of Scientific Computing Associates, New Haven.

[3] Thinking Machines Corporation Disclaimer: these results are based upon a test version of the CM-5 software where the emphasis was on providing functionality and the tools necessary to begin testing the CM-5. This software release has not had the benefit of optimization or performance tuning and, consequently, is not necessarily representative of the performance of the full version of this software.

2 Adaptive Parallelism

A program exhibiting "adaptive parallelism" executes on a dynamically changing set of processors: processors may join or withdraw from the computation as it proceeds.

In any computing environment (including a dedicated multiprocessor), an adaptively parallel program is capable of taking advantage of new resources as they become available, and of gracefully accommodating diminished resources without aborting. Our previous work has focussed on workstation networks (conventional UNIX workstations with standard LAN interconnects). Workstations at most sites tend to be idle for significant fractions of the day, and those idle cycles may constitute in the aggregate a powerful computing resource. Although the Ethernet and comparable interconnects weren't designed for parallel applications, they are able in practice to support a significant range of production parallel codes. Ongoing trends will make "aggregate LAN waste" an even more attractive target for recycling: desktop machines continue to grow in power; better interconnects will expand the universe of parallel applications capable of running well in these environments. For these reasons and others, we believe that adaptive parallelism is assured of playing an increasingly prominent role in parallel applications development over the next decade.

Work on the Piranha system (discussed in the next section) has shown that a variety of coarse-grain parallel applications can indeed be run effectively as adaptive applications on LANs [4]. In some cases, supercomputer-equivalents of computing power can be achieved merely by recycling the garbage.

3 Piranha

The Piranha programming model is an adaptive version of master-worker parallelism [1]. Programmers specify in effect a single general purpose worker function, called piranha(). They do not explicitly create processes and their applications do not rely on any particular number of active processes. When a processor becomes available, a new process executing the piranha() function is created there; when a processor withdraws, a retreat() function is invoked, and the local piranha process is destroyed. Thus there are no "create process" operations in the user's program, and the number of participating processes varies with available processors.

Workers perform *tasks*. A task consists of a set of input data from which a worker function produces a set of output data and possibly a collection of new tasks. Tasks may be ordered or unordered, depending on the logical requirements of the application.

Piranha applications may use Linda's shared, associative object memories ("tuple spaces") to store descriptors and other data in distributed data structures accessible to all worker processes. The underlying Piranha system itself uses another tuple space to coordinate user and system activity.

The Piranha system is discussed in greater detail and compared to alternative models in [2].

4   Adaptive Parallelism on Multiprocessors

How should large distributed-memory multiprocessors be shared?

Most current approaches to the sharing of such machines center on space-sharing. The machine's nodes are typically paritioned into disjoint sets. A user grabs one set to run his job. Jobs "share" the machine by running in separate sets. But there are problems with this approach. If the machine is shared among several jobs running in fixed partitions, left-over nodes may be wasted if they don't correspond to the static partition requirements of any waiting application. If parallel job J is sharing the machine with another job that completes, J is confined to its initial partition despite the existence of idle nodes freed up by the terminated job. Even if more jobs are queued, they may not need or want as large a partition as the just-completed job occupied; or, J might be a higher-priority job, more deserving of newly-available resources. But current programming approaches don't allow for dynamic expansion and contraction of parallel programs.

Time sharing is always a possibility in principle: many jobs share a single partition or the entire machine, with each being given a time slice now and then. Time sharing as currently implemented on the CM-5 is "all-or-nothing" in time and space. A particular job controls all the nodes for an entire quantum, if it needs less than the full partition or some processes block for some reason before the end of the quantum, resources go idle. This policy is a reasonable fit to the SIMD programming model commonly used on the CM-5, but it is inflexible and inefficient when it comes to asynchronous MIMD codes (like Linda programs). Processes can block at independent times and the "geometry" of a code may not fit the available partition or may even change dramatically during execution. A more flexible time-sharing strategy would pose hard problems involving co-scheduling of processes with inter-dependencies.

Piranha represents a different approach. Under Piranha, a large multiprocessor is treated as a pool of resources to be dynamically allocated among competing jobs. Suppose a new job is dropped into the pool but all nodes are currently in use. If the priority of the job warrants, currently running jobs may be forced to back off dynamically, freeing nodes for the new job. When a job terminates and leaves the machine, existing jobs may dynamically expand to fill the available space. A long running job might (for example) maintain a toe hold on a small number of nodes during particularly busy periods, and expand to fill a much greater number of nodes during relatively less busy times. Piranha doesn't in itself dictate the scheduling policy under which a node decides which available job it should be executing (research on such scheduling policies is ongoing): Piranha does provide a framework under which such schedulers become plausible and useful.

Clearly, some parallel jobs won't be amenable to this kind of dynamic treatment; they will require a fixed number or configuration of nodes. We do know at present that a broad collection of useful applications *can* be Piranhafied. Our intention is to allow conventional fixed-partition jobs to be embedded in a dynamic Piranha environment.

5 CM-5 Piranha: Design and Implementation

Ideally we would like the Piranha runtime system to be a scheduler for all programs, allowing Piranha programs and native fixed-topology CM-5 programs to co-exist. Native CM-5 jobs would request specific resources from the Piranha scheduler. Piranha jobs would contract and expand around the native jobs to recycle previously unused machine time into Piranha computations. In addition, multiple Piranha jobs could expand and contract relative to each other to use available resources more efficiently.

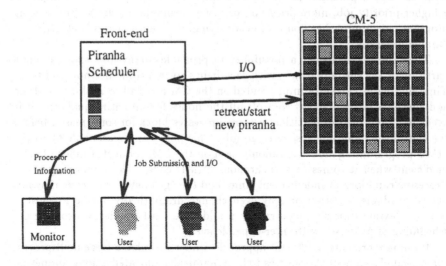

Fig. 1. CM-5 Piranha Design.

We currently only manage adaptively parallel codes with our Piranha system (because of the current CM-5 OS design). Adding native CM-5 jobs is only a small logical step beyond—they are in concept Piranha jobs that never expand or retreat. In addition, the current CM-5 OS does not allow processors in different "traditional" partitions to communicate so our current system manages multiple Piranha jobs within one partition rather than over the whole machine. This is not a serious impediment to our work, however, because a partition provides the same interface as the whole machine, so we can perform our experiments as if we were using the whole machine —although if all we (and the system managers) cared about were Piranha codes, that partition could be the whole machine.

Figure 1 is an overview of the runtime system. The runtime system consists of a job submission and scheduling process on the CM-5 front-end, which we call the "scheduler." The scheduler accepts requests to start user jobs, and assigns those jobs to subsets of nodes on the partition. The scheduler directs each node to reboot and reload itself with the new job's executable. If the node was not idle, its retreat function is called first.

Scheduling is currently handled in a simple way by allocating a "fair" portion of processors to each job. Figure 2 illustrates this scheduling behavior. Initially there are no jobs in the system and all processors are idle. Job 1 enters the system and consumes all processors that are available. At timestep 20, job 2 enters with job 1 still present. Job 1 is asked to give up some nodes, and both jobs proceed with half the processors available in the system each. At time step 60, job 2 leaves and job 1 reclaims those processors. Job 3 then enters the system and we have the same situation as before, each job computing on half the processors. Finally job 4 enters the system, and both jobs 1 and 3 are asked to give up processors, resulting in each process computing with roughly one-third of the total processors.

One can envision (and we will soon be implementing) a more general system. For instance, when a job no longer needs some of its processors, they can be allocated to another process. Under this scheme jobs do not always acquire $1/n$ processors, where n is the number of jobs in the system; they acquire as many processors as are available without exceeding what they can use.

5.1 CM-5 Piranha Scheduler: Implementation

The Piranha scheduler controls the execution of multiple Piranha jobs by accepting requests from users and from Piranha processes to perform various tasks, and making scheduling decisions based on a processor table that maps CM-5 processors to Piranha jobs.

Figure 3a shows a state diagram for the scheduler. This scheduler sits in a dispatch loop waiting for requests. Three types of requests are possible: user requests, piranha requests, and master requests. The only user request currently supported is to execute a Piranha job. When this request is made the scheduler assigns processors to the new job by first recording the new system state in the processor table. The scheduler then goes through the table and signals all processors allocated to the new job. The selected processors are then "rebooted" (a process described in detail later) and sent the new executable. The scheduler then returns to the dispatch loop.

Masters send a request to the scheduler when they have completed their computations. Not only does this notify the scheduler that the master's node can be reused, but also that all the piranha computing for that master can be recycled. The scheduler goes through the same process above, reassigning processors to the remaining jobs and then sending executables.

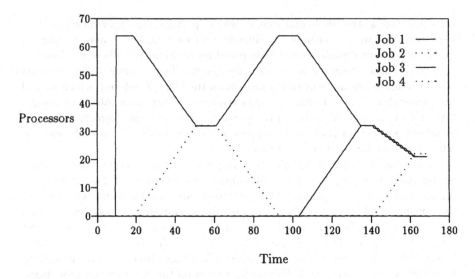

Fig. 2. Runtime Characteristics of Piranha on a 64 node system.

The piranha request is sent from an individual piranha that has finished computing tasks. This situation occurs, for instance, when a piranha application computes in two phases and the second phase requires less piranha (workers) than the first. By notifying the scheduler, the existing piranha's processor can be reassigned to another job. This functionality currently requires the programmer to tell a piranha to finish (this can be done, for instance, through a "poison" task). We are exploring ways that the piranha runtime system itself can recognize when a piranha is idle. In addition there is a subtle problem reassigning a processor. Should we reassign it to any job, including the original job? There are circumstances where doing so is appropriate. But a reasonable default is to reassign it to one of the other jobs. We are exploring a variety of scheduling methods to improve this situation.

If the respective piranha job is at the end of its computation then it doesn't need additional processors, however the piranha may have stopped because it was at the end of one phase of a computation, and in this case we want to possibly assign the processor to the original job. We are currently exploring solutions to this problem.

5.2 CM-5 Piranha Loader: Implementation

Because the CM-5 supports only the single program, multiple data (SPMD) programming model, a small bootstrapping loader is needed to provide a multiple

program, multiple data (MPMD) environment for Piranha. The Piranha loader
resides on each node and loads executables broadcast from the scheduler. After
loading the executables into memory, the loader starts the new program.

In the event that the scheduler reassigns a node to a new job, the node
is rebooted by interrupting the node and returning control to the loader. The
loader then executes a code segment that calls the retreat function, cleans up
the stack, and waits for the next executable.

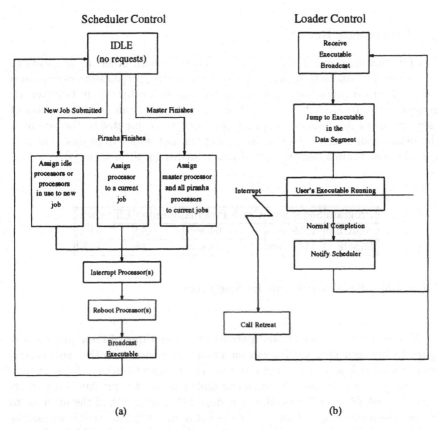

(a)   (b)

Fig. 3. Scheduler and Loader Control.

Figure 3b shows the state diagram of the loader. The loader initially receives
an executable from the scheduler and then jumps to the entry address of the
executable. At this point the user's Piranha code takes control of the processor. If
the Piranha code finishes normally, control returns to the loader and notification
is sent to the scheduler. If the processor is interrupted to run another Piranha
executable, the retreat handler executes and control returns to the loader at the
top level.

6 Evaluation

Is Piranha effective at sopping up idle resources and gracefully making room for new jobs without introducing excessive overhead? We used the following as a preliminary test. Consider some applications that "don't fit" on our experimental 64-node partition: they keep every node busy only part of the time. If Piranha is effective, running many such jobs simultaneously should be more efficient than running many sequentially in batch mode: Piranha should make it possible to put the nodes that are wasted in batch mode to good use.

6.1 Preliminary Results

Two Piranha programs developed in collaboration with other departments at Yale are used in our tests: a physics code for computing propagation of neutrinos and an electrical engineering code for finding dipole localization in biomagnetic imaging; both are described in [4]. The neutrino code is an "unordered bag of tasks" program. A number of tasks are generated and computed by the piranhas. The dipole code is also a bag of tasks program, but with two phases. The first phase locates minima and the second phase further localizes them [4].

Program	Sequential	CM-5 Piranha	Speedup	Efficiency
Neutrino	2729 secs	64 secs	43	68%
Dipole	1144 secs	75 secs	15	24%

Fig. 4. CM-5 Piranha Test suite for Single Runs.

We present the sequential and parallel execution times of these programs in figure 4. The sequential version ran on a Sparc processor with the same performance as a CM-5 node. The piranhafied version ran on a 64-node CM-5 partition. Neutrino generates 96 tasks of equal size and thus uses the machine fully to execute the first 64 tasks (one task per node), then uses only half the machine to execute the remaining 32 tasks. Over the entire run, neutrino is able to use the 64 nodes with 68% efficiency. With dipole it is harder to use the CM-5 efficiently (and harder to analyze its performance because it uses two phases where the second phase is computationally longer but requires less piranha): it fully uses the machine in the first pass, but in the second pass it generates only 4 tasks, using 1/16th of the machine; over the entire run it uses the 64-node partition with 24% efficiency. Both codes are good candidates for our Piranha system insofar as they both waste resources: the neutrino code because it is impossible

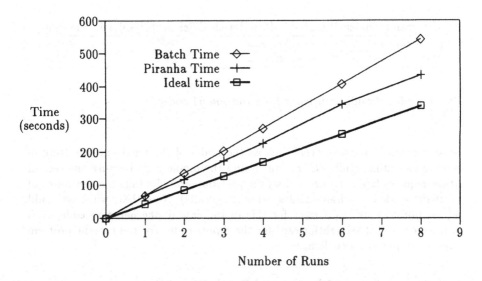

Fig. 5. Neutrino Performance in Piranha (64 nodes).

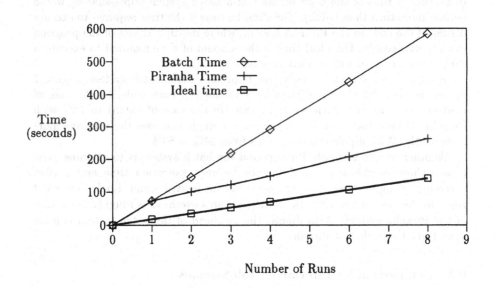

Fig. 6. Dipole Performance in Piranha (64 nodes).

Program	Batch	Piranha	Ideal	Batch Efficiency	Piranha Efficiency
Neutrino	544 secs	436 secs	341 secs	68%	78%
Dipole	584 secs	263 secs	142 secs	24%	54%

Fig. 7. CM-5 Piranha Efficiency for 8 runs on 64 nodes.

to load-balance its tasks evenly across the nodes of the partition (resulting in some nodes idling while others work), and the dipole code because the second phase requires fewer resources than the partition provides (again a mismatch of available work to available nodes, so some go idle). Note that, while we could adjust problem size to correct for this in the case of the neutrino code, such adjustment is not straightforward for the dipole code. For the current problem sizes, both present a challenge.

6.2 Comparison of Piranha and Batch Execution

Figure 5 shows data for 1 to 8 *simultaneous* runs of neutrino in Piranha and 1 to 8 *successive* runs of neutrino in the batch system. Figure 6 shows the same information for dipole. Batch time in both cases is the amount of time required to execute n runs of the code in the CM-5 batch system (time-sharing would require more time than batch). The Piranha time is the time required to execute n runs of the code in the Piranha system, where multiple copies of the program run simultaneously. The ideal time is the amount of time required to execute n runs of the program with perfect speedup.

In both cases Piranha does better than the native batch system. Figure 7 shows the detailed results of running 8 versions of each code. In the case of neutrino we raise the efficiency from 68% (in the case of batch) to 78% with Piranha. Dipole does even better, because a single run uses the machine more inefficiently. With dipole efficiency rises from 24% to 54%.

Another way to compare Piranha and the batch system is to examine overhead (where overhead is the difference between execution time and perfect speedup). In figure 8 we show the overhead for neutrino and dipole over eight runs. In the case of neutrino, the batch system's overhead is roughly twice that of the Piranha system. With dipole, the overhead of the batch system is more than three times that of Piranha.

6.3 Comparison for Intermixed Job Streams

Figure 9 shows data for intermixed job streams of the dipole and neutrino codes. Each data point represents a job stream where dipole and neutrino are each run five times in an intermixed and random fashion. Each job stream was run on a clean CM-5 (there were no other processes running) and run so that the Piranha system was always busy (there was always at least one Piranha job executing).

Program	Batch Overhead	Piranha Overhead	Ratio
Neutrino	203 secs	95 secs	2.14
Dipole	442 secs	121 secs	3.6

Fig. 8. Comparison of Piranha and batch overhead for 8 runs on 64 nodes.

Note that this does not imply that all processors were always busy because, for example, we could have the case where only one Piranha job is in the system and the job doesn't use of all 64 processors. The horizontal axis represents the job stream's "load average". This load average is computed by averaging over the number of jobs running in the Piranha system over the course of the run. The horizontal line at approximately 655 seconds[4] is the time it would take to execute five runs of dipole and neutrino in the batch system (the time is constant regardless of the order of jobs).

At a load average of 1 we have the equivalent of the batch system—there is only one job in the Piranha system at a time—and as a result the piranha and batch execution times are the same. As we move in the direction of increasing load average, the machine is used more efficiently until we reach a load average of approximately three, when there is no additional benefit to packing jobs more tightly. Note that in the neighborhood of a 1.1 load average we can actually do worse than the native batch system due to Piranha system overhead. This overhead is in the form of lost computation that occurs when retreating a process.

If we again consider the ratio of the runtime overheads, the overhead of the batch system is roughly twice that of the Piranha system. In this calculation the perfect speedup time for the job streams would be 302 seconds, the batch overhead is a constant $655 - 302 = 353$ seconds, and we use the roughly asymptotic runtime value of 484 for Piranha (in the case of a 4.0 load average) to compute an overhead of $484 - 302 = 182$ seconds and a ratio of $353/182 = 1.9$.

7 Conclusions

Adaptive parallelism provides a novel method for sharing multiprocessors. Our Piranha system has the advantage that it can be used to run multiple programs concurrently without the disadvantages of current multiprocessor time-sharing systems. In addition, our preliminary results suggest that CM-5 Piranha is more efficient than the CM-5 batch system. Future work will include thorough testing of a more diverse set of Piranha programs and dynamic scheduling methods. Our

---

[4] Based on the data in figure 4 you might expect the batch execution time to be 695 seconds, however the job stream tests were conducted after additional improvements were made to the operating system and message passing libraries by Thinking Machines.

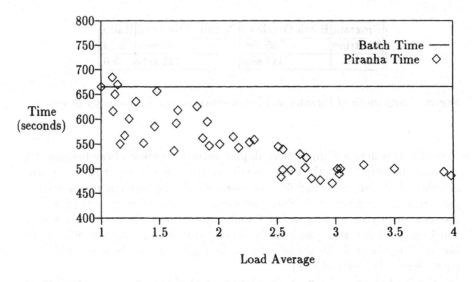

Fig. 9. Random streams of jobs consisting of five runs of dipole and five runs of neutrino intermixed.

goal is to integrate Piranha fully into the CM-5 environment, so that Piranha applications can co-exist with native CM-5 applications.

8 Acknowledgments

We wish to thank David Kaminsky and Rob Bjornson for their invaluable help during this project. We also wish to thank the fine technical support of Thinking Machines Corporation—in particular Mike Flanigan and Adam Greenberg. Alan Klietz of the Minnesota Supercomputer Center was also of great help.

151

References

1. Nicholas Carriero and David Gelernter, *How to write parallel programs: A first course*. (Cambridge: MIT Press, 1990).
2. Nicholas Carriero, David Gelernter, David Kaminsky, and Jeffery Westbrook. "Adaptive Parallelism with Piranha", YALEU/DCS/RR-954, February 1993.
3. The Connection Machine CM-5 Technical Summary, Thinking Machines Corporation, Cambridge, MA, 1992.
4. David Gelernter and David Kaminsky. "Supercomputing out of Recycled Garbage: Preliminary Experience with Piranha", Proceedings of the ACM, International Conference on Supercomputing, July 19-23, 1992.

Slicing Analysis and Indirect Accesses to Distributed Arrays

Raja Das[1] and Joel Saltz[1] and Reinhard von Hanxleden[2]

[1] Department of Computer Science, University of Maryland, College Park, MD20742.
E-mail: {raja|saltz}@cs.umd.edu
[2] Center for Research on Parallel Computation, Rice University, Houston, TX 77251.
E-mail: reinhard@rice.edu

Abstract. An increasing fraction of the applications targeted by parallel computers makes heavy use of indirection arrays for indexing data arrays. Such *irregular access patterns* make it difficult for a compiler to generate efficient parallel code. Previously developed techniques addressing this problem are limited in that they are only applicable for a single level of indirection. However, many codes using sparse data structures access their data through *multiple levels of indirection*.

This paper presents a method for transforming programs using multiple levels of indirection into programs with at most one level of indirection, thereby broadening the range of applications that a compiler can parallelize efficiently. A central concept of our algorithm is to perform *program slicing* on the subscript expressions of the indirect array accesses. Such slices peel off the levels of indirection, one by one, and create opportunities for aggregated data prefetching in between. A *slice graph* eliminates redundant preprocessing and gives an ordering in which to compute the slices. We present our work in the context of High Performance Fortran; an implementation in a Fortran D prototype compiler is in progress.

1 Introduction

In distributed memory machines, large data arrays are frequently partitioned between local memories of processors. We will refer to such partitioned data arrays as *distributed arrays*. Recently, there have been major efforts in developing programming language and compiler support for distributed memory machines. Based on initial projects like Fortran D [5, 11] and Vienna Fortran [1, 20], the High Performance Fortran Forum has proposed the first version of High Performance Fortran (HPF) [9], which can be thought of as Fortran 90 enhanced with data distribution annotations. Long term storage of distributed array data is assigned to specific memory locations in the parallel machine. HPF offers the promise of significantly easing the task of programming distributed memory machines and making programs independent of a single machine architecture. Current prototypes of compilers for HPF-like languages produce Single Program Multiple Data (SPMD) code with message passing and/or runtime communication primitives.

Reducing communication costs is crucial in achieving good performance [12, 10]. While current systems like the Fortran D project [11] and the Vienna Fortran Compilation system [1] have implemented a number of optimizations for reducing communication costs (like message blocking, collective communication, message coalescing and aggregation), these optimizations have been developed mostly in the context of regular problems (*i.e.*, for codes having only regular data access patterns). Special effort is required in developing compiler and runtime support for applications that do not have such regular data access patterns.

In irregular problems, communication patterns depend on data values not known at compile time, typically because of some indirection in the code. Indirection patterns have to be preprocessed, and the elements to be sent and received by each processor must be precomputed in order to

- reduce the volume of communication,
- reduce the number of messages, and
- prefetch off processor data to hide communication latencies.

In earlier work, we have developed runtime support, analysis techniques, and compiler prototypes designed to handle loops where distributed arrays are accessed through a single level of indirection [17, 3, 8, 7, 6]. Compiler transformations can handle loops with indirectly referenced distributed arrays by transforming the loops into two constructs called an inspector and executor [15, 14]. During program execution, the *inspector* examines the data references made by a processor and calculates what off-processor data need to be fetched and where these data will be stored once they are received. The *executor* loop then uses the information from the inspector to implement the actual computation.

```
                    SUBROUTINE simple(x, y, col, m, n)

                    INTEGER i, m, n, col(m)
                    REAL x(n), y(n)
        !HPF$ DISTRIBUTE(BLOCK) :: col, x, y

        !HPF$ EXECUTE (i) ON_HOME x(i)
        !HPF$ INDEPENDENT
    K1          DO i = 1, n
    K2              x(i) = x(i) + y(col(i))
    K3          ENDDO
    K4          END
```

Fig. 1. Kernel with single level of indirection.

An example for the class of kernels that can be handled by the techniques developed so far is the irregular kernel in Fig. 1. In this example, data arrays *col*, x, and y are block distributed between processors. The i-loop iterations are partitioned using the HPF-directive **ON_HOME**, which in this case is equivalent to the *owner computes rule* that assigns the computation of an assignment statement to the processor that stores the left hand side reference. A single level of indirection arises because the data array y is indexed using the array *col* in statement K2.

While we can handle such simple indirection patterns, many application codes have code segments and loops with more complex access functions that go beyond the scope of current compiling techniques. In many cases, a chain of distributed array indexing is set up where values stored in one distributed array are used to determine the indexing pattern of another distributed array, which in turn determines the indexing pattern of a third distributed array. Such loops with multiple levels of indirection are very common and appear, for example, in unstructured and adaptive applications codes associated with particle methods, molecular dynamics, sparse linear solvers, and in some unstructured mesh CFD solvers.

This paper develops techniques that can be used by compilers to transform loops with array accesses involving more than a single level of indirection into loops where array references are made through at most one level of indirection. We present this transformation technique in the context of distributed memory machines and therefore often refer to prefetching as "communication" or "message blocking." However, our method is likely to be useful on any architecture where it is profitable to prefetch data between different levels of a memory hierarchy.

The rest of this paper is organized as follows. Sect. 2 gives an overview of our technique by transforming an example code that shows two levels of indirection. Sect. 3 introduces some terminology that used in Sect. 4, which gives a formal description of our algorithms and illustrates how the transformation shown in Sect. 2 was derived. Sect. 5 concludes with a brief discussion and an overview of the status of our implementation.

2   Example Transformation

This section illustrates the effect of applying our transformation to the HPF subroutine *CSR* shown in Fig. 2. This code is based on a sparse matrix vector multiply kernel and uses the Compressed Sparse Row format [16]. An n by n sparse matrix is multiplied by an n-element array x, the results are stored in an n-element array y. The matrix values are all assumed to be equal to zero or one. The columns associated with non-zero entries in row i are specified by $col(j)$, where $ija(i)+1 \leq j \leq ija(i+1)$. For simplicity, all distributed arrays are distributed blockwise in this example; our techniques apply equally well to other, potentially irregular decompositions. The indexing of y by array *col* causes a first level of indirection. The dependence of the loop bounds of the inner j-loop on the distributed array *ija* causes an additional level of indirection. This double

```
                SUBROUTINE CSR(x, y, col, ija, m, n)

                INTEGER i, j, m, n, col(m), ija(n)
                REAL x(n), y(n)
           !HPF$DISTRIBUTE(BLOCK) :: col, ija, x, y

           !HPF$EXECUTE (i) ON_HOME x(i)
           !HPF$INDEPENDENT
     R1        DO i = 1, n
     R2           x(i) = 0
     R3           DO j = ija(i) + 1, ija(i + 1)
     R4              x(i) = x(i) + y(col(j))
     R5           ENDDO
     R6        ENDDO
     R7        END
```

Fig. 2. CSR kernel – original version.

indirection becomes clear when rewriting the computation as

$$x(i) = \sum y(col(ija(i) + 1 : ija(i + 1)))$$

for $i = 1 \ldots n$.

All references to the distributed array x are indexed by the loop induction variable i. The HPF ON_HOME construct partitions the iteration space of the DO (INDEPENDENT) loop such that iteration i is performed on the processor that owns $x(i)$, so there is no communication required for referencing x. For the other three arrays, ija, col, and y, data communication is required. As already mentioned, keeping the total number of these communication steps down is key to high performance on a distributed memory machine. Therefore, we want to perform only a small number of aggregate prefetch operations, instead of communicating each reference individually. This requires a significant amount of preprocessing to determine what data need to be prefetched and in what order that has to be done. We will transform the code such that the compiler runtime support will have access to the subscripts of all elements of ija, col, and y that need to be prefetched from other processors. This information makes it possible to carry out the communications optimizations described in Sect. 1; *i.e.*, to reduce the volume of communication, reduce the number of messages and to prefetch off-processor data to hide communication latencies.

The transformed version of subroutine *CSR* is shown in Figs. 3 and 4. For ease of presentation, we use a variation of HPF that contains additional directives BEGIN LOCAL and END LOCAL indicating *local variables*. These variables do not reside in the global name space inhabited by the other HPF variables, but instead they exist independently in the local name space of each processor. In

```
                    SUBROUTINE CSR(x, y, col, ija, m, n)

                    INTEGER i, j, m, n, col(m), ija(n)
                    REAL x(n), y(n)
              !HPF$ DISTRIBUTE(BLOCK) :: col, ija, x, y

              !HPF$ BEGIN LOCAL
                    INTEGER v4, v5
                    INTEGER, ALLOCATABLE(:) ::
                    . v1arr, v2arr, v3arr
              !HPF$ END LOCAL

              C     COUNTING SLICE D
              C     Count local iterations of outer loop
              C     to determine size of v1arr.
        T1          v4 = 0
        T2    !HPF$ EXECUTE (i) ON_HOME x(i)
              !HPF$ INDEPENDENT
        T3          DO i = 1, n
        T4             v4 = v4 + 1
        T5          ENDDO

              C     COLLECTING SLICE A
              C     Collect "i + 1" into v1arr(1:v4).
        S1          ALLOCATE (v1arr, v4)
        S2          v4 = 0
        S3    !HPF$ EXECUTE (i) ON_HOME x(i)
              !HPF$ INDEPENDENT
        S4          DO i = 1, n
        S5             v4 = v4 + 1
        S6             v1arr(v4) = i + 1
        S7          ENDDO
        S8    C     Prefetching ija(v1arr(1:v4)) goes here

              C     COUNTING SLICE E
              C     Count local iterations of inner loop to
              C     determine size of v2arr and v3arr.
        T6          v4 = 0
        T7          v5 = 0
        T8    !HPF$ EXECUTE (i) ON_HOME x(i)
              !HPF$ INDEPENDENT
        T9          DO i = 1, n
        T10            v4 = v4 + 1
        T11            DO j = ija(i) + 1, ija(v1arr(v4))
        T12               v5 = v5 + 1
        T13            ENDDO
        T14         ENDDO
```

Fig. 3. CSR kernel – transformed version (Part 1).

```
        C      COLLECTING SLICE B
        C      Collect "j" into v2arr(1:v5).
S9             ALLOCATE (v2arr, v5)
S10            v4 = 0
S11            v5 = 0
S12  !HPF$     EXECUTE (i) ON_HOME x(i)
     !HPF$     INDEPENDENT
S13            DO i = 1, n
S14              v4 = v4 + 1
S15              DO j = ija(i) + 1, ija(v1arr(v4))
S16                v5 = v5 + 1
S17                v2arr(v5) = j
S18              ENDDO
S19            ENDDO
S20  C      Prefetching col(v2arr(1:v5)) goes here

        C      COLLECTING SLICE C
        C      Collect "col(j)" into v3arr(1:v5).
S21            ALLOCATE (v3arr, v5)
S22            v4 = 0
S23            v5 = 0
S24  !HPF$     EXECUTE (i) ON_HOME x(i)
     !HPF$     INDEPENDENT
S25            DO i = 1, n
S26              v4 = v4 + 1
S27              DO j = ija(i) + 1, ija(v1arr(v4))
S28                v3arr(v5) = col(v2arr(v5))
S29                v5 = v5 + 1
S30              ENDDO
S31            ENDDO
S32  C      Prefetching y(v3arr(1:v5)) goes here

        C      ACTUAL COMPUTATION
E1             v4 = 0
E2             v5 = 0
E3   !HPF$     EXECUTE (i) ON_HOME x(i)
     !HPF$     INDEPENDENT
E4             DO i = 1, n
E5               x(i) = 0
E6               v4 = v4 + 1
E7               DO j = ija(i) + 1, ija(v1arr(v4))
E8                 v5 = v5 + 1
E9                 x(i) = x(i) + y(v3arr(v5))
E10              ENDDO
E11            ENDDO
E12            END
```

Fig. 4. CSR kernel – transformed version (Part 2).

strict HPF, such variables could be emulated by either adding another dimension of size *n$proc* (the total number of processors) and referencing this dimension with *my$proc* (the id of each processor), or by manipulating them only through so called extrinsic functions. Except for these local variables, the whole code is presented in global name space, and for simplicity it is here assumed that all global to local address translations will be handled by the HPF compiler. Note, however, that this index translation in the presence of indirect addressing and perhaps further complications like irregular decompositions is a nontrivial task; the code actually generated by our implementation assists in this process.

In our example, the distributed array *ija* is distributed conformable to the array *x*. Since the reference *ija(i)* in statement R3 occurs in a DO loop whose iteration space is aligned to the index space of *x*, this reference does not generate any communication. It is also assumed that the back end compiler recognizes the use of induction variable *i* in this reference and does not require any preprocessing for performing the global to local name space conversion.

The references $ija(i+1)$, $col(j)$, and $y(col(j))$, however, may require preprocessing. In general, for a reference of the form $arr(sub_{ast})$, this preprocessing may perform the following:

- It has to collect all values of sub_{ast} in order to prefetch the data referenced in $arr(sub_{ast})$ en bloc. In some cases, preprocessing is also carried out to reduce communication volume through recognition of duplicated references in sub_{ast}.
- It has to provide a mechanism to access the prefetched data in the actual computation.

Here sub_{ast} stands for the Abstract Syntax Tree (AST) index of the subscript. Note that while this index is different for each reference in the program, the value numbers of these references may be identical, even for subscripts that might textually look different.

In the transformed code, the statements proceeding the actual computation (in E1...E12) perform this preprocessing. Statements S8, S20, and S32 indicate opportunities for aggregated prefetching of the data required for references $ija(i + 1)$, $col(j)$, and $y(col(j))$, respectively. For our *CSR* kernel, we assume that subscript reuse is relatively low. Therefore we perform the prefetching and indexing via temporary trace arrays that store global indices and are themselves indexed through counters that are incremented with each reference. Alternative mechanisms are described in Sect. 4.2.

The first prefetch statement, S8, brings in all $ija(i+1)$'s referenced by statement R3 in the original code. Statements T1...T5 and S1...S7 perform the preprocessing necessary for S8. Since in our example we are basing the prefetching mechanism on temporary trace arrays that have to be allocated dynamically, we first have to determine the size of the trace, *i.e.*, the number of references. This size is computed into *v4* by statements T1...T5. Statement S1 then allocates the local array *v1arr*, which has been declared ALLOCATABLE. Statements S2...S7 generate and store the trace into *v1arr*. Finally, the prefetching operation in S8 brings in all the non-local data and stores them in the right locations of the array *ija*. This might require resizing the array *ija* to store the off-processor data. For the purpose of this example, we assume that storing of the off-processor data in the resized *ija* array is such that they can be referenced in global coordinates.

The next potential communication is generated by the prefetching statement S20, which collects on each processor the off-processor references to *col(j)* in statement R4. Statements S10...S19 collect the trace of the values *j* indexing the array *col* into the local array *v2arr*. Note that in the expression for the upper bound of the *j*-loop, array *ija* is no longer indexed by $(i + 1)$ but by the trace vector *v1arr* generated in statements S4...S7. The statements T6...T14 in Fig. 3 compute the size of the array *v2arr* into the local scalar *v5*. The array *v2arr*, that like *m1arr* has been declared to ALLOCATABLE, is allocated in statement S9.

The values of *y* that are required on each processor at statement R4 are communicated in the prefetching statement S32. The trace of the values that index *y* is done in statements S22...S31, it is stored in the dynamic local array *v3arr*. Note that the number of references to *y(col(j))* is the same as the number of references to *col(j)*, therefore the size of *v3arr* is the same as the size of *v2arr*. Hence we do not need any additional code to find out the size of *v3arr*, instead we can reuse the already computed local variable *v5* that stores the size of *v2arr*. Note also that in statement S28, the array *col* is referenced by the local array *v2arr* which stores global indices, instead of being referenced by *j*. After the execution of the statement S32, all processors have the required values of *y* in their local memories.

The actual loop computation is performed in statements E1...E11. During this computation no communication is required because everything that is necessary on each processor has already been fetched.

To summarize, the original code shown in Fig. 2 has been transformed into the code shown in Figs. 3 and 4. The transformed code performs all the necessary data communication in phases after several preprocessing steps. Within the different loops in the transformed code, all distributed arrays are referenced by at most one level of indirection and require no data communication.

3 Definitions

This section introduces some concepts that will be used in the algorithms in Sect. 4.

A *Slice* is a tuple

$$s = \left(s_{vn}, s_{target}, s_{code}, s_{ident}, s_{dep\_set}[, s_{cnt\_vn}]\right)$$

that contains a value number s_{vn}, a designated program target location s_{target}, a sequence of statements s_{code}, an identifier s_{ident}, a dependence set s_{dep_set}, and optionally another value number s_{cnt_vn}. Slices come in two flavors:

– A *collecting slice* stores the sequence of values (a trace) that will be assigned to a subscript during the execution of the program in some data structure identified by s_{ident}. The type of the data structure is determined by the degree of subscript reuse within the trace of the subscript, as described in Sect. 4.2.

– *Counting slices* are created from the collecting slices, they calculate the size of the subscript trace that will be generated during the execution of the collecting slice. A counting slice is needed if the collecting slice has to know the size of the trace it has to record, for example for preallocating a data structure to store the trace, and the size of the trace is not known at compile time.

Each of the slices has the following properties with respect to the original program P:

– Inserting s_{code} at s_{target} in P is legal; *i.e.*, it does not change the meaning of P. The s_{code} is similar to a dynamic backward executable slice [19].

– After executing s_{code}, s_{ident} will have stored the values of s_{vn}.

– If s is a *collecting slice*, then s_{vn} will be the value number of a subscript s_{ast} of a nonlocal array reference $arr(sub_{ast})$ in P, and s_{ident} will store the sequence of all subscripts occurring during the run of P. Note that the length of this sequence depends on the location in the program, which is given by s_{target}. For example, if s_{target} is the statement of the reference itself, then the sequence consists of only a single subscript. If s_{target} is the header of a loop enclosing the reference, then the sequence contains the subscripts for all iterations of the loop.

– If we compute counting slices, then s_{cnt_vn} will be the value number of the counter indexing s_{ident} after execution of s_{code} is finished; *i.e.*, the value of s_{cnt_vn} will be the size of the subscript trace computed in s_{ident}.

– If s is a *counting slice*, then there exists a collecting slice t for which $s_{vn} = t_{cnt\_vn}$ and $s_{target} = t_{target}$. s_{ident} will store the size of the subscript trace computed in t_{ident}. Since s_{ident} corresponds to a single value, s_{cnt_vn} will be the value number corresponding to the constant "1." Note that s_{target} must equal t_{target} because otherwise we might count too many (for s_{target} preceding t_{target}) or too few (for s_{target} succeeding t_{target}) subscripts.

– The s_{dep_set} stored in each slice is a set of AST indices of subscripts of references of that need runtime processing. Only the references in s_{code} that require runtime processing are considered when the s_{dep_set} is created.

A *Slice Graph* is a directed acyclic graph

$$G = (S, E)$$

that consists of a set of slices S and a set of edges E. For $s, t \in S$, an edge $e = (s, t) \in E$ establishes an ordering between s and t. The presence of e implies that t_{code} contains a direct or indirect reference to s_{ident} and therefore has to be executed after s_{code}. G has to be acyclic to be a valid slice graph. Note that the edges in the slice graph not only indicate a valid ordering of the slices, but they also provide information for later optimizations. For example, it might be profitable to perform *loop fusion* across slices; the existence of an edge between slice nodes, however, indicates that these slices cannot be fused.

A *Subscript Descriptor*

$$sub_{ast} = (sub_{vn}, sub_{target})$$

for the subscript sub_{ast} of some distributed array reference consists of sub_{vn}, which is the value number of sub_{ast}, and of sub_{target}, which is the location in P where a slice generated for sub should be placed. Our algorithm will generate a slice for each unique subscript descriptor corresponding to a distributed array reference requiring runtime preprocessing. Identifying slices by subscript descriptors is efficient in that it allows a slice to be reused for several references, possibly of different data arrays, as long as the subscripts have the same value number. It is conservative in that it accounts for situations where different references might have the same subscript value number but different constraints as far as prefetch aggregation goes, which corresponds to different target nodes.

4 The Algorithm

This section gives a description of the algorithm to do the transformation shown in Sect. 2. The algorithm consists of two parts. The first part, described in Sect. 4.1, analyses the program and generates the slices and the slice graph. The second part, described in Sect. 4.3, uses the slice graph to do the code generation.

4.1 Slice Graph Construction

The procedure **Generate_slice_graph()** shown in Fig. 5 is called with the program P and the set of subscripts R of the references that need runtime preprocessing, *i.e.*, the irregular references. It returns a slice graph consisting of a set of slices S and edges E. This procedure first generates all the necessary slices and then finds the edges between these slices.

A subscript descriptor (sub_{vn}, sub_{target}) for each subscript AST index sub_{ast} is computed in A4...A8. We assume that P has an associated value number table that maps AST indices to value numbers. **Lookup_val_number()** uses this table to compute sub_{vn} from sub_{ast}. **Gen_target()** maps the AST index sub_{ast} to the target node sub_{target} for the slice generated starting from that AST index. The constraints on sub_{target} are the following.

- In the Control Flow Graph (CFG), sub_{target} predominates the reference sub_{ast}; *i.e.*, it is guaranteed that sub_{target} will be executed before sub_{ast} is used to reference its data array arr.
- There are no modifications of the data array arr between sub_{target} and sub_{ast}.

Procedure Generate_slice_graph(P, R)

// *P: Program to be transformed*
// *R: AST indices of subscripts of references*
//   *that need runtime preprocessing*

A1 $S := \emptyset$ // *Slices*
A2 $E := \emptyset$ // *Slice ordering edges*
A3 $U := \emptyset$ // *Subscript descriptors*

// *Compute subscript descriptors.*
A4 **Foreach** $sub_{ast} \in R$
A5 $sub_{vn} :=$ Lookup_val_number(sub_{ast})
A6 $sub_{target} :=$ Gen_target(sub_{ast})
A7 $U := U \cup \{(sub_{vn}, sub_{target})\}$
A8 **Endforeach**

// *Compute slices.*
A9 **Foreach** $sub \in U$
A10 $s :=$ Gen_slice(sub)
A11 $S := S \cup \{s\}$

// *The following steps are executed*
// *iff counting slices are required.*
O1 $t :=$ Lookup_slice(S, (s_{cnt_vn}, s_{target}))
O2   **If** $t = \emptyset$ **Then**
O3 $t :=$ Gen_slice(s_{cnt_vn}, s_{target})
O4 $S := S \cup \{t\}$
O5 $E := E \cup \{(t, s)\}$
O6   **Endif**

A12 **Endforeach**

// *Compute edges resulting from*
// *dependence sets of slices.*
A13 **Foreach** $s \in S$
A14   **Foreach** $sub_{ast} \in s_{dep\_set}$
A15 $sub_{vn} :=$ Lookup_val_number(sub_{ast})
A16 $sub_{target} :=$ Lookup_target(sub_{ast})
A17 $t :=$ Lookup_slice(S, (sub_{vn}, sub_{target}))
A18 $E := E \cup \{(t, s)\}$
A19   **Endforeach**
A20 **Endforeach**

A21 **Return** (S, E)

Fig. 5. Slice graph generation algorithm.

– Any code inserted at sub_{target} is executed as infrequently as possible.

Gen_target() implements these constraints using a Tarjan interval tree and array MOD information; starting at the node corresponding to the reference, it walks the interval tree upwards and backwards until it reaches a modification of *arr*.

The next Foreach statement in A9...A12 iterates through the subscript descriptors $sub \in U$ and generates for each subscript descriptor both the collecting slice *s* and, if needed, the counting slice *t*. Gen_slice() takes a subscript descriptor $sub = (sub_{vn}, sub_{target})$ and generates for location sub_{target} the slice that computes the values corresponding to sub_{vn}. The slice generation function uses the program's CFG and SSA (Static Single Assignment) information. Roughly speaking, Gen_slice() follows the use-def and control dependence chain starting in sub_{ast} until it reaches sub_{target}.

If we are interested in the size of the subscript trace recorded in *s* (*e.g.*, for allocating trace arrays), then we compute in statements O1...O6 a counting slice *t* for each *s*. However, different collecting slices can share a counting slice if they have the same counter value number sub_{cnt_vn} and target location sub_{target}. Therefore, we first examine the set of already created slices. Lookup_slice() takes as input a set of slices S and a subscript descriptor *sub* and returns the slice $t \in S$ corresponding to *sub* if there exists such an *t*; otherwise, it returns $\emptyset$. If a counting slice has not been created yet, a new counting slice *t* is generated. Since the counting slice *t* must be executed before the collecting slice *s*, a directed edge (t, s) is added to the edge set E.

The nested Foreach statements in A13...A20 are used to find the directed edges resulting from the dependence sets in each slice. The outer Foreach iterates through the slices *s*, the inner one loops through the references sub_{ref} stored in the dependence set s_{dep_set} of *s*. All the relevant information has already been generated previously, therefore these loops only have to consult tables to complete the set of edges.

The slice graph corresponding to the transformation example done in Sect. 2 is shown in Fig. 6. There are five nodes in the slice graph, out of which nodes A, B, and C contain collecting slices, while nodes D and E contain counting slices. Note that the collecting slices B and C share the counting slice E, which reflects that the number of references to $y(col(j))$ is the same as the number of references to $col(j)$.

4.2 Trace Management Schemes

The discussion so far was mostly concerned with where to precompute which subscript traces in what order. Before actually generating code, however, we have to decide what data structures to use for first recording the traces to prefetch nonlocal data and then accessing these prefetched data. The example presented in Sect. 2 used temporary trace arrays for performing both of these operations. It turns out, however, that this is just one of several options, and there are different tradeoffs involved depending on the characteristics of the subscript traces. Therefore, when generating the statements s_{code} of a slice *s*, we do not include

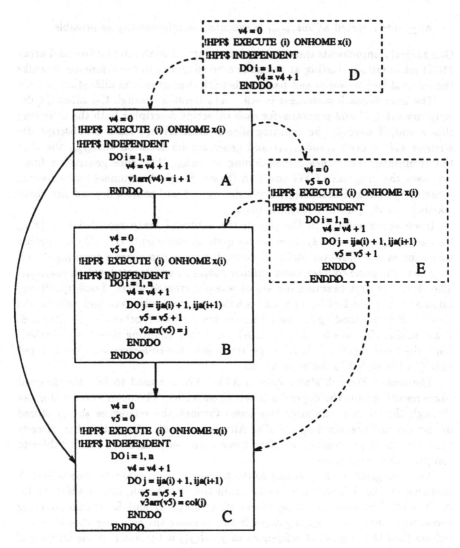

Fig. 6. Example of a Slice Graph.

the code for manipulating these data structures; *i.e.*, we do not include counter initializations and increments or the assignments into trace arrays. Instead, we include place holders for these operations and delay the generation of these statements until the slice instantiation phase during the final code generation.

Let T be the size of the trace, *i.e.*, the number of times a subscript is evaluated with respect to the target location of the slice. Let R be the number of unique elements in T, and let N be the global size of the subscripted array, *i.e.*, the number of different subscripts possible. Note that $R \le N$, $R \le T$ must hold.

Case 1: Low Subscript Reuse. In this case, which is characterized by $R \approx T$, each subscript typically appears at most once in the trace produced by the slice. A possible example is the CSR kernel described in Sect. 2. Here it is reasonable to use a *dynamically allocated array* that is indexed through a counter incremented with each reference. This array can be used both for precomputing the subscripts and for looking them up during the actual computation. Since we have to store each subscript individually, the space requirements are $\mathcal{O}(T)$. We also usually have to generate counting slices to perform the dynamic allocation of the arrays. The time per access, however, is only $\mathcal{O}(1)$.

Case 2: High Subscript Reuse. This case is characterized by $R \ll T$, each subscript typically appears several times in the trace produced by the slice. An example of this is the pair list used for the non-bonded force kernel in molecular dynamics applications [2]. Since each atom interacts with many other atoms, it appears many times in the pair list. Here some set representation, like a hash table, which collects subscripts and stores each of them at most once, would be an appropriate trace recording mechanism [13]. The space requirements are only $\mathcal{O}(R)$, and no counting slices are needed. The time per access, however, will be $\mathcal{O}(\log(R))$ for most common set representations.

As a subscripting mechanism in the actual computation, we can use some dictionary representation, like a hash table (of a different kind than the one used for representing sets), that maps global indices to local indices. This typically requires space $\mathcal{O}(N)$ and $\mathcal{O}(\log(N))$ time per access.

An alternative subscripting mechanism is a "global shuffle," where – roughly speaking – everything is translated to local coordinates, including the subscripting arrays themselves. The space requirements would be at most $\mathcal{O}(N)$, depending on how many data a processor needs locally and whether things can be shuffled in place or not. The time per access would be $\mathcal{O}(1)$.

4.3 Code Generation

The code generation algorithm is shown in Fig. 7. The procedure **Gen_code()** takes as input the original program P and the slice graph consisting of slices S and their ordering E. Gen_code() traverses the program and changes the subscripts of all the references that required runtime preprocessing. The function **Instantiate_program()** takes the program P and the set of slices S and replaces in P subscripts on which preprocessing has been performed with accesses of data structures defined in the preprocessing phase. This program instantiation depends on what type of data structure was used to store the trace of subscripts in the collecting slices, as discussed in Sect. 4.2.

Topological_sort() performs a topological sort of the slice graph so that the partial order given by the directed edges in E is maintained during generating code for the slices in S. The Foreach statement in C3...C6 iterates through the slices S. **Instantiate_slice()** is similar to Instantiate_program(), but instead of a program P it takes a slice s. However, it not only replaces subscript references,

```
                    Procedure Gen_code(P, S, E)

            C1 Instantiate_program(P, S)
            C2 Topological_sort(S, E)
            C3 Foreach s ∈ S
            C4     Instantiate_slice(s, S)
            C5     Insert_code(P, s_code, s_target)
            C6 Endforeach

            C7 Return P
```

Fig. 7. Code generation algorithm.

but also adds the code mentioned in Sect. 4.2 for collecting the subscript that s is slicing on. Therefore this instantiation, like the program instantiation, depends on the type of data structure that was used to store the subscript traces of the references that affect the computation in this slice. After s has been instantiated, Insert_code() inserts s_{code} into the program at the target location s_{target}. The transformed program is returned to the calling procedure.

In the CSR example in Sect. 2, we assume that the subscript traces are stored in dynamically allocatable arrays. The instantiation routines will add the code for maintaining and referencing these arrays to the slices of the graph presented in Fig. 6. A topological sort on the graph yields the node order to be D, A, E, B, and C; this is the same order in which the slices appear in the transformed code in Fig. 5. For each of the slices, the subscripts of the references requiring runtime preprocessing present in the slice are changed to the local array that stores a trace of the subscript. At runtime, the trace must already have been generated because there must exists an edge from the node where the trace was created to the node where it is being used. The slice is next substituted in the program before the slice target node. Note that the topological sort order is unique; this indicates, for example, that there is no loop fusion possible in the example. Note also that the transformed code in Fig. 4 would be equally valid without having the subscripts of the references $ija(i + 1)$, $col(j)$, and $y(col(j))$ replaced with references to trace arrays. However, this replacement makes the subsequent task of translating global indices to local indices simpler; instead of having to modify user declared variables and subscript arrays, it is sufficient to translate the trace arrays.

5 Conclusions

The scheme that we presented in this paper can be used by a compiler to generate parallel code for irregular problems. In combination with a communication placement dataflow framework that maximum reuse of off-processor data [8, 6], the transformation presented in this paper will allow to generate efficient parallel code for any problem where irregular data access patterns exist. We have also carried out extensive research on the design of runtime support to support the communication requirements associated with indirectly accessed distributed arrays. One of the key optimizations is to reduce the communication volume associated with a prefetch by recognizing duplicated data references [18, 4].

We are implementing the algorithm presented in Sect. 4 in the Fortran D compiler being developed at Rice University [6]. At present we handle loops with a single level of indirection. We have also implemented a program slicer to be used to generate the slice graph.

Acknowledgements

We would like to thank Ken Kennedy and Chuck Koebel at Rice University for their ongoing support of this project. Thanks to the developers of the ParaScope programming environment and the Fortran D compiler prototype, in particular to Paul Havlak, whose symbolic analysis work is a crucial component of our algorithms. We would also like to thank Alan Sussman for many useful discussions on distributed memory compiler design.

Das and Saltz were supported by ARPA under contract No. NAG-1-1485, NSF under grant No. ASC 9213821 and ONR under contract No SC292-1-22913. An IBM fellowship supported von Hanxleden.

References

1. B. Chapman, P. Mehrotra, and H. Zima. Programming in Vienna Fortran. *Scientific Programming*, 1(1):31–50, Fall 1992.
2. T. W. Clark, R. v. Hanxleden, K. Kennedy, C. Koelbel, and L.R. Scott. Evaluating parallel languages for molecular dynamics computations. In *Proceedings of the Scalable High Performance Computing Conference (SHPCC-92)*, pages 98–105. IEEE Computer Society Press, April 1992. Available via anonymous ftp from softlib.rice.edu as pub/CRPC-TRs/reports/CRPC-TR992202.
3. R. Das, R. Ponnusamy, J. Saltz, and D. Mavriplis. Distributed memory compiler methods for irregular problems – data copy reuse and runtime partitioning. In J. Saltz and P. Mehrotra, editors, *Languages, Compilers and Runtime Environments for Distributed Memory Machines*, pages 185–220. Elsevier, 1992.
4. R. Das, J. Saltz, D. Mavriplis, and R. Ponnusamy. The incremental scheduler. In *Unstructured Scientific Computation on Scalable Multiprocessors*, Cambridge Mass, 1992. MIT Press.
5. G. Fox, S. Hiranandani, K. Kennedy, C. Koelbel, U. Kremer, C. Tseng, and M. Wu. Fortran D language specification. Technical Report CRPC-TR90079, Center for Research on Parallel Computation, Rice University, December 1990.
6. R. v. Hanxleden. Handling irregular problems with Fortran D — A preliminary report. In *Proceedings of the Fourth Workshop on Compilers for Parallel Computers*, Delft, The Netherlands, December 1993. Available via anonymous ftp from softlib.rice.edu as pub/CRPC-TRs/reports/CRPC-TR93339-S.

7. R. v. Hanxleden and K. Kennedy. A code placement framework and its application to communication generation. Technical Report CRPC-TR93337-S, Center for Research on Parallel Computation, October 1993. Available via anonymous ftp from softlib.rice.edu as pub/CRPC-TRs/reports/CRPC-TR93337-S.

8. R. v. Hanxleden, K. Kennedy, C. Koelbel, R. Das, and J. Saltz. Compiler analysis for irregular problems in Fortran D. In *Proceedings of the Fifth Workshop on Languages and Compilers for Parallel Computing*, New Haven, CT, August 1992. Available via anonymous ftp from softlib.rice.edu as pub/CRPC-TRs/reports/CRPC-TR92287-S.

9. High Performance Fortran Forum. High Performance Fortran language specification, version 1.0. Technical Report CRPC-TR92225, Center for Research on Parallel Computation, Rice University, Houston, TX, 1992 (revised Jan. 1993). To appear in *Scientific Programming*, July 1993.

10. S. Hiranandani, K. Kennedy, and C. Tseng. Compiler optimizations for Fortran D on MIMD distributed-memory machines. In *Proceedings Supercomputing '91*, pages 86–100. IEEE Computer Society Press, November 1991.

11. S. Hiranandani, K. Kennedy, and C. Tseng. Compiling Fortran D for MIMD distributed-memory machines. *Communications of the ACM*, 35(8):66–80, August 1992.

12. S. Hiranandani, K. Kennedy, and C. Tseng. Evaluation of compiler optimizations for Fortran D on MIMD distributed-memory machines. In *Proceedings of the Sixth International Conference on Supercomputing*. ACM Press, July 1992.

13. S. Hiranandani, J. Saltz, P. Mehrotra, and H. Berryman. Performance of hashed cache data migration schemes on multicomputers. *Journal of Parallel and Distributed Computing*, 12:415–422, August 1991.

14. C. Koelbel and P. Mehrotra. Compiling global name-space parallel loops for distributed execution. *IEEE Transactions on Parallel and Distributed Systems*, 2(4):440–451, October 1991.

15. R. Mirchandaney, J. H. Saltz, R. M. Smith, D. M. Nicol, and Kay Crowley. Principles of runtime support for parallel processors. In *Proceedings of the 1988 ACM International Conference on Supercomputing*, pages 140–152, July 1988.

16. Y. Saad. Sparsekit: a basic tool kit for sparse matrix computations. Report 90-20, RIACS, 1990.

17. J. Saltz, H. Berryman, and J. Wu. Multiprocessors and runtime compilation. Technical Report 90-59, ICASE, NASA Langley Research Center, September 1990.

18. J. Saltz, R. Das, R. Ponnusamy, D. Mavriplis, H Berryman, and J. Wu. Parti procedures for realistic loops. In *Proceedings of the 6th Distributed Memory Computing Conference*, Portland, Oregon, April-May 1991.

19. G. A. Venkatesh. The semantic approach to program slicing. In *Proceedings of the SIGPLAN '91 Conference on Programming Language Design and Implementation*, pages 107–119, June 1991.

20. H. Zima, P. Brezany, B. Chapman, P. Mehrotra, and A. Schwald. Vienna Fortran — A language specification, version 1.1. Interim Report 21, ICASE, NASA Langley Research Center, March 1992.

Figure 1: The DozMerge operation.

kind of computation, which we refer to as a *Do&Merge*, arises frequently. For example, in the domain of image processing, such applications as edge detection and connected components can be solved using this paradigm. In the signal processing domain, we see this pattern whenever narrow-band data needs to be combined to yield broad-band data.

In most parallel programming languages, the two component operations are explicitly separate: the programmer first specifies the conversion function to be applied across the input in parallel, and then specifies the merge operator. We point out the benefit of not separating the two operations; often the programmer can combine them into a single function that is more efficient to execute.

In the remainder of this paper, we describe the semantics of the Do&Merge computation and we describe a construct, called the *Pdo* loop, for expressing the Do&Merge. Section 2 describes the basic Do&Merge semantics and describes two existing constructs for expressing the Do&Merge operation. Section 3 describes the *Pdo* loop, which allows the programmer to combine the Do&Merge operators in a more efficient manner, resulting in improved execution time and memory usage. In Section 4 we describe how a compiler can simply and efficiently compile a *Pdo* loop. Finally, Section 5 formulates several problems as Do&Merge computations and compares the *Pdo* performance with that of existing methods. We use simple example problems to help get the basic idea across. However, for many important problems (e.g., connected components) the conversion function and merge operator are complex user-defined functions.

2 Do&Merge operation

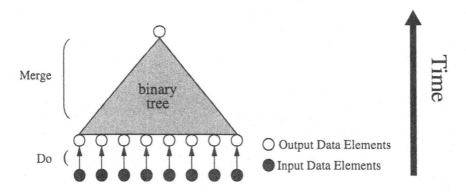

Figure 1: The Do&Merge operation.

The Do&Merge operation is illustrated in Figure 1. Conceptually, a conversion function F is applied in parallel to each of the N input elements, to form a set of partial results. Then an associative merge operator C is applied $N - 1$ times to produce the final result. The order of application of C implicitly forms a binary tree; any binary tree produces a valid result. The C operator is associative, but not necessarily commutative, with a left identity I. Formally, we have the following:

- $F : \beta \to \alpha$

- $C : \alpha \times \alpha \to \alpha$

- $C(I, \alpha) = \alpha$

There are many ways in which the Do&Merge can be implemented. Two such methods available in HPF [3] are the following:

result $= I$
 DO $k = 1, N$
     result $= C(\text{result}, F(\text{input}[k]))$
 END DO
	FORALL $(k = 1 : N)$
	     partial$[k] = F(\text{input}[k])$
	 END FORALL
	 result $=$ REDUCE$(C, \text{partial})$

Do implementation	*Forall* implementation

These two implementations of the Do&Merge differ only in the structure of the merge tree that is created. The merge tree structures are pictured in Figure 2 for $P = 2$ processors. The thick arrows represent interprocessor communication. Notice that the *Do* implementation is forced to run sequentially due to data dependences; these data dependences are mostly artificial, due to the associativity of C, although in practice, this may be difficult to determine for a compiler.

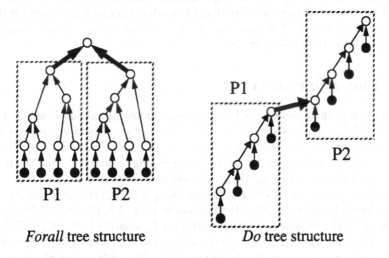

Forall tree structure   *Do* tree structure

Figure 2: Tree structures of two possible Do&Merge implementations.

We can analyze the running time of each of these implementations. Let $T(F)$ be the time required to execute F, $T(C)$ the time required to execute C, P the number of processors, and $N \gg P$. Also assume that the data is distributed across the processors in *block* fashion (i.e., a single, disjoint, contiguous block of the input data resides on each processor). The total running time for the *Do* implementation is $N \times (T(F) + T(C))$. Notice that the running time is the same regardless of P, due to the sequential nature of the *Do* loop.

The *Forall* version, on the other hand, is more clever. Since N/P input elements reside on each processor, the FORALL body executes in time $(N/P)(T(F))$. The optimal REDUCE function will apply C locally on each processor to yield one partial result per processor, in time $(N/P)(T(C))$, and then merge the partial results across the processors in time $T(C) \log P$, for a total execution time of:

$$(N/P)(T(F) + T(C)) + T(C) \log P. \tag{1}$$

Another possible Do&Merge implementation is the DOACROSS [2] loop, which allows F to proceed in parallel but still sequentializes the application of C. Yet another possibility is the DOANY [7] construct, which requires C to be both associative and commutative, allowing the loop to be sequentialized in any way. However, neither construct fully integrates the Do and the non-commutative Merge to allow maximum efficiency.

When performing the merge, many different legitimate merge tree structures are possible, due to the associativity of C. In Figure 2, processors P1 and P2 evaluate their local results using differently shaped merge trees. Both trees yield correct results. However, when generating the merge tree within one processor, most implementations typically use a single method to generate the tree, namely sweeping across from left to right, much as the way P2 executes in Figure 2. In the next section, we describe an implementation in which we combine the Do and Merge operators in such a way that left-to-right execution is required if that operator is to be used. This implementation proves to be more efficient than the *Forall* implementation in most cases.

3 The *Pdo* construct

In many cases the programmer has additional knowledge about F and C that may be difficult or impossible for the compiler to derive. This information can be encapsulated into a new operator $C' : \alpha \times \beta \rightarrow \alpha$, where $C'(\alpha, \beta) \equiv C(\alpha, F(\beta))$. The C' operator takes a partial result corresponding to inputs $i..j$ and the input $j + 1$, and produces a new partial result corresponding to inputs $i..(j + 1)$.

We have implemented the Do&Merge using a construct called the *Pdo*, in which the programmer specifies the implementation of I, C', and C. Note that defining C' and I implicitly gives a definition of F, since $C'(I, \beta) = C(I, F(\beta)) = F(\beta)$. Also note that, given implementations of F and C, a naive implementation of C' is trivial, simply by the definition of C'. The *Pdo* construct imposes a particular order on the merge tree to yield maximum parallel performance. The basic *Pdo* loop is specified in the following manner:

```
PDO i = ⟨loop bounds⟩
   FIRST: ⟨implementation of I⟩
   NEXT:  ⟨implementation of C'⟩
   MERGE: ⟨implementation of C⟩
END PDO
```

Each processor begins by executing I. Then the processor iterates from left to right through the array elements that reside on that processor, executing the C' operator, thus yielding one partial result per processor. This step requires $(N/P)(T(C'))$ time to execute. (Note that we ignore the time for executing the FIRST section, which should be relatively small since N/P is assumed to be large.) Once each processor has completed this work, the partial results are merged between processors using the C operator, yielding a single result. As in the *Forall* version, this merge step requires $T(C) \log P$ time to execute, for a total execution time of:

$$(N/P)(T(C')) + T(C) \log P. \tag{2}$$

By the definition of C', it is trivial to implement C' such that $T(C') = T(F) + T(C)$. Comparing equations (1) and (2), we find that the *Pdo* version outperforms the *Forall* version whenever:

$$T(C') < T(F) + T(C). \tag{3}$$

In Section 5 we show several examples of applications where (3) holds.

The *Pdo* representation of the Do&Merge has an additional benefit: it often gives the programmer a more intuitive way of expressing the parallelism. This intuition comes from the fact that the C' operator is inherently sequential, which reflects the way that a programmer typically approaches an algorithm. The *Pdo* construct is directly based upon the parallel looping construct in the Adapt [6] programming language, which has proven to be a useful construct suitable for efficient implementation.

The Do&Merge in general, and the *Pdo* in particular, can also be used to implement a general FORALL loop, or a general reduction operator. The FORALL can be specified simply by omitting the merge operator, in which case the compiler can trivially remove the merge phase. In a general reduction, the F function is a no-op; hence C and C' are identical.

4 Compilation of the *Pdo* loop

In addition to being simple for the programmer to specify, the *Pdo* loop is simple for the compiler writer to implement efficiently if the compiler provides a framework for executing array assignment statements.

The first step for the compiler is to partition the variables referenced within the loop into 3 sets: *induction variables*, *conversion variables*, and *merge variables*. Merge variables are variables written by the C operator, and conversion variables are variables accessed by the conversion function F that are not induction variables or merge variables. We allow F to have localized side effects, so long as no two iterations try to write to the same element of a conversion variable. To determine this partitioning, the compiler can use analysis of the access patterns, or it can rely on hints from the programmer.

To simplify the discussion of the compilation of the *Pdo*, we assume for now that we are parallelizing over a single dimension. In Section 4.4.3, we discuss relaxing this restriction. Our implementation then consists of two phases: processing the Do section, and processing the Merge section.

4.1 Do phase

To process the Do section, we use copy-in/copy-out semantics. Conceptually, the entire global data space is copied into the local data space for each iteration, with the exception of the merge variables. Then each iteration runs independently and in parallel. Finally, any conversion variables that were modified are copied out into the global data space after all iterations have completed.

Clearly, it is infeasible to copy the entire data space for each iteration. Instead, we determine which section of an array is needed for each iteration, and we redistribute the array so that each iteration has all needed data local to the processor on which that iteration is executed. This redistribution is performed by creating a temporary array with the necessary distribution, and executing an array assignment statement to insert the data into the temporary. Techniques for efficiently compiling such assignment statements are described in detail in [1, 4]. The remainder of this subsection concerns how to determine the parameters of the redistribution.

We assume that array distributions are specified using the TEMPLATE, ALIGN, and DISTRIBUTE directives from HPF. The iteration space of the *Pdo* corresponds directly to the template. Thus we will declare a single template whose size is equal to the upper bound of the *Pdo* loop index.

The distribution of *Pdo* iterations to processors corresponds directly to the distribution of the template. Thus we can use any distribution of loop iterations that the compiler can also use for distributing templates across the processors.

The access pattern of a conversion variable corresponds to the way that the variable's temporary should be aligned with the template. For example, if iteration i accesses $A(:, i)$ (i.e., column i of array A), then we generate the alignment statement: "ALIGN $A(:, i)$ WITH $T(i)$," where T is the generated template. As another example, if iteration i accesses $A(2i + 1, :)$, we generate the alignment statement: "ALIGN $A(2i + 1, :)$ WITH $T(i)$." In fact, any alignment function that can be handled within ALIGN statements corresponds to data access patterns that can be dealt with in the Do section.

After the input arrays are redistributed into temporaries, each processor must generate a loop that iterates through the *Pdo* iterations mapped to that processor. When the Do phase completes, we perform the copy-out of conversion variables that were modified (or we can wait until after the Merge phase to do the copy-out).

4.2 Merge phase

To process the Merge section, we set up a merge tree of height $\log P$ where P is the number of processors. This merge tree is a binary tree such that the merging begins at the leaves and propagates up toward the root. For each merge step, the right child processor sends its partial result to the left child, which assumes the role of the parent node for the merge step. The left child merges the results and continues, while the right child remains idle for the remainder of the $\log P$ merge steps. Finally, when the result propagates up to the root, the root processor broadcasts its result.

For the merge, each processor must allocate space for three copies of the merge variable. The three copies correspond to a node in the merge tree and its two children. The partial result is initially stored in the copy corresponding to the node. When a partial result is sent to another processor for merging, it is stored on the receiving processor in the copy corresponding to the right child, while the receiving processor copies its partial result into the left child copy, and then merges the two partial results and stores the new partial result in the node copy. In Section 4.3.3 we describe how to reduce the amount of extra storage needed.

4.3 Optimizations

Several simple optimizations can dramatically improve performance. The first optimization concerns eliminating the redistribution of conversion variables into temporary arrays. The second optimization precomputes local memory indices at compile time. The third optimization reduces the amount of memory usage (and the associated execution time for managing that memory) in the Merge phase.

4.3.1 Copy-in/copy-out optimization

Recall from Section 4.1 that for each conversion variable, we create a temporary array which is aligned in the appropriate dimension with the *Pdo* template. We redistribute the conversion variable into this temporary using an array assignment statement, and then use the temporary inside the *Pdo* body in place of the original variable. However, it is clear that this redistribution is unnecessary if the alignment and distribution of the original array already matches that of the proposed temporary. In particular, if the following conditions hold, then there is no need for the temporary:

- The template to which the conversion variable is aligned matches the *Pdo* template.

- The alignment of the conversion variable to its template matches the proposed alignment of the temporary to the *Pdo* template.

- The distribution of the template to which the conversion variable is aligned matches the distribution of the *Pdo* template.

Although the compiler has little choice in the *Pdo* template or in the alignment of the temporaries to the template, it can choose an arbitrary distribution of the template (and thus an arbitrary distribution of loop indices to processors). Thus to minimize the amount of redistribution that takes place, the compiler should choose a distribution to maximize the number of conversion variables for which all three conditions above hold.

For the Do phase, the overhead of computing the distributed loop bounds is essentially identical regardless of the distribution. Thus, provided the loop iterations are distributed evenly across the processors (providing a load balance), the only difference in execution time will come from array redistributions. However, not all array redistributions are equally costly; e.g., a nearest-neighbor communication should be cheaper than an all-to-all communication. Furthermore, as we see in Section 4.4.1, the distribution choice can have a large impact on the cost of the Merge phase. These issues combine to form an interesting optimization problem.

4.3.2 Local index computation

Figure 3 shows how global indices of an array are stored locally on a processor. The shaded boxes represent indices of an array A with a block-cyclic distribution that reside on a particular processor. These array elements are compactly stored in LM_A , as shown in Figure 3. When we access a portion of the array within the Do phase, we must translate the global index into a local index. This translation can be expensive, involving multiplication, division, and modulo operators. It is especially expensive if the translation is performed within an external procedure, as the procedure call breaks up basic blocks, thus limiting the effectiveness of the optimizer.

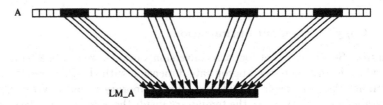

Figure 3: Array compaction.

However, a simple optimization is to compute the local memory index once per loop iteration, and avoid the repeated evaluations of the same expression. Better yet, when the stride of the loop bounds is 1, we notice that the stride of the local memory index is also 1. Thus we can compute the local memory index for only the first iteration, and simply increment it at the end of each loop iteration.

4.3.3 Merge variable memory optimization

As described in Section 4.2, the Merge phase implementation triples the amount of memory usage, to hold the left and right partial results as well as the new partial result. Since the processor corresponding to the left child performs the merge computation for itself and the right child, we clearly need to allocate memory to receive the right child's partial result. However, in many cases, we can map the left child's partial result and the new partial result to the same memory, eliminating the need for special memory for the left child and correspondingly the need to perform the copy. Within a single merge step, if we ever read the left child's partial result after we have written to the new partial result, then we cannot share the memory for the two partial results. This situation can generally be detected using simple data dependence testing techniques.

4.4 Advanced issues

Until now, we have implicitly made many assumptions regarding the specification of the Do&Merge in general, and the *Pdo* in particular. These issues are addressed and resolved here.

4.4.1 Non-block data distribution

Our analysis for merging so far has assumed that the input array is distributed across the processors in block fashion. In particular, we have assumed that each processor iterates over a contiguous section of the global iteration space. However, if we distribute the iteration space in cyclic or block-cyclic fashion, this condition no longer holds.

Due to the non-commutativity of the merge operator, we can only apply C across contiguous blocks of the global index space. Furthermore, we can also only apply C' across contiguous blocks. This presents a problem when several contiguous blocks reside on a single processor. In this case, the processor generates several partial results to be globally reduced, one per contiguous block.

The compiler can generate code to perform the correct merge in the following manner. Recall that we previously specified that the processor would begin by initializing its partial result r to the identity specified by I, then sequentially apply C' across the input, and finally perform a global merge of each processor's r value using the C operator. Now, we generalize by making r a vector of length B, where B is the number of contiguous blocks on the processor. For each block i, we initialize $r[i]$ to the identity I, and then sequentially apply C' across the block. When performing the global merge, we apply C individually to each $r[i]$ on the left and $r[i]$ on the right, yielding the new value of $r[i]$; hence two vectors of length B are point-wise merged using the C operator to yield a new vector of length B. At the end, there will be a final vector of length B on a single processor. At this point, we simply apply C across this vector, yielding a single global result.

Note that our simplified timing analysis breaks down in the general block-cyclic case. For the purpose of simplicity, we have assumed that the time required to execute I once is trivial compared to the N/P times that we execute C'. Whereas C' is still executed N/P times per processor, I will now be executed B times per processor, and the time spent doing the global merge is increased by a factor of B (in terms of both computation and amount of communication). This effect is particularly noticeable in a cyclic distribution, where B is maximized at $B = N/P$.

4.4.2 Commutative merge operator

In many cases, the C operator is commutative. Although compiler analysis might be able to determine this, the programmer might also be able to explicitly provide this information to the compiler. When C is commutative, and the input distribution is block-cyclic, a non-block data distribution no longer presents the problems described in Section 4.4.1. Since C is commutative, we can conceptually rearrange the input to be block distributed. This rearrangement could be done explicitly with a redistribution in the form of an array assignment, although this operation would most likely involve communication. A better approach is to simply apply C' across the input array, regardless of contiguity. This approach involves minimal overhead and no extra communication.

4.4.3 Nested *Pdo* loops

Our analysis to this point has assumed that in a loop nest, we are only parallelizing a single loop. This is adequate if we are certain that only that particular dimension of the input array is distributed. However, when the input array is distributed over more than one dimension, we may wish to parallelize the outermost loops.

For the remainder of this discussion, we will assume that the *Pdo* loops are perfectly nested; hence the syntax is specified in the following manner:

$$\text{PDO } (i = 1 : m, j = 1 : n) \ \ldots$$

Distributing the index space across the processors is simple: just calculate the distribution independently for each index, and take the Cartesian product of the results.

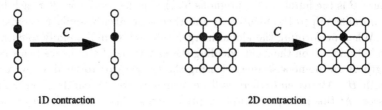

1D contraction   2D contraction

Figure 4: Merging in one and two dimensions.

The nontrivial issue involves the merge step. When the iteration space is k-dimensional, we can envision iterating over a k-dimensional mesh, with the rule that we can only apply C to two adjacent nodes in the mesh. When C is applied to the two adjacent nodes, the edge between them is contracted. One such contraction is illustrated in Figure 4 for both a 1-dimensional and a 2-dimensional index space. These contractions continue until there is only one node remaining in the graph.

However, this model of arbitrary edge contraction may in some cases place an undue burden on the programmer. For example, consider an image connected components algorithm. The F function converts a section of input to an equivalence table. However, the F function must also save the border of the image section, which is needed by the C operator for merging two equivalence tables. The C operator must create a new equivalence table, plus the boundary of the merged region. If we allow arbitrary edge contraction, the programmer must be prepared to handle arbitrary shaped boundaries. For this reason, we might choose to guarantee the programmer that edges will be contracted in some regular order, such as in rectangular order.

5 Performance results

In this section, we consider two examples of computation that benefit from using the Do&Merge construct (and the time to perform the Do&Merge loop is less than the time it takes to perform a parallel loop and a reduction separately) : a Histogram example from the domain of image processing, and a Matvec (Matrix-vector multiplication) example from the domain of regular matrix computations. For each example, we give both *Forall* and *Pdo* versions in an HPF-like notation, and we compare their performance when compiled by a parallelizing Fortran compiler on the iWarp system [5]. In each case, the *Pdo* version is significantly faster, because it allows more overlapped execution.

5.1 Histogram

The first example is a 2-dimensional histogram. The input is an $n \times n$ *image* of grayscale pixel values, where $1 \leq image(i, j) \leq G$, and the output is a vector *hist* of length G, where $hist(i)$ is the number of pixels in *image* with a value of i. We assume that the image is block-distributed by rows.

The *Pdo* version of Histogram is implemented with the following parallel loop:

```
PDO i=1,n
INPUT image(i,:)
OUTPUT result(:)
FIRST
   result = 0
NEXT
   DO j = 1,n
```

```
      result(image(i,j)) = result(image(i,j)) + 1
   END DO
MERGE
   result = LEFT(result) + RIGHT(result)
END PDO
```

The INPUT directive aligns the *ith* row of the input image to the *ith* loop iteration. The OUTPUT directive identifies the result vector that will be merged across processors. Note that in general the information in the INPUT and OUTPUT directives could be determined automatically by compiler analysis. We have included these directives merely to simplify the implementation of our compiler.

Recall from Section 3 that the FIRST section defines the I operator, the NEXT section defines the C' operator, and the MERGE section defines the C operator. The LEFT and RIGHT intrinsics identify the intermediate merge results from the left and right subtrees, respectively, of the merge tree.

The corresponding *Forall* version of Histogram consists of a separate FORALL, which computes the histogram per row, followed by a call to a reduction intrinsic.

```
local = 0
FORALL i=1,n
   DO j = 1,n
      local(i,image(i,j)) = local(i,image(i,j)) + 1
   END DO
END FORALL
result = REDUCE(SUM,0,local)
```

Notice that the body of the loop defines the F operator. Notice also that in each version, processors communicate only when results are merged.

For the Histogram example, we see that $T(F) + T(C) = O(G + n)$, while $T(C') = O(n)$. In practice, the savings is substantial, especially as G increases. This savings can be seen quite clearly in Figure 5.

5.2 Matvec

The second example is a Matvec operation, $y = Ax$, where A is a dense $m \times n$ matrix, x is an n-vector, and y is an m-vector. We assume that A is block-distributed by columns, x is block-distributed, and y is replicated.

The *Pdo* version of Matvec is implemented by applying a SAXPY operator on each column of A, and then summing the resulting vectors to form y.

```
PDO j=1,n
INPUT a(:,j),x(j)
OUTPUT y
FIRST
   y = 0.0
NEXT
```

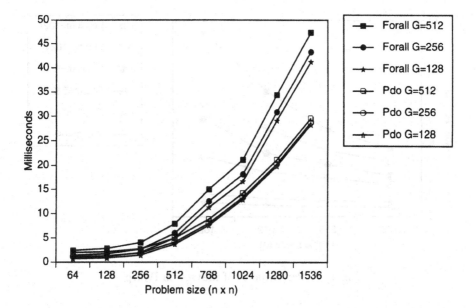

Figure 5: Performance of Histogram on iWarp.

```
    y = y + a(:,j)*x(j)
MERGE
    y = LEFT(y) + RIGHT(y)
ENDPDO
```

The corresponding *Forall* version of Matvec is implemented with a FORALL loop, followed by a call to a reduction intrinsic that merges the intermediate results:

```
FORALL j=1,n
    b(:,j) = a(:,j)*x(j)
END FORALL
y = REDUCE(SUM,0,b)
```

Again, note that processors communicate only when results are merged.

For the Matvec example, we see that while $T(F)+T(C) = O(m)$ and $T(C') = O(m)$, the C' operator performs $3m + 1$ memory accesses and the F and C operators perform a total of $5m + 1$ memory accesses. Thus we would expect the *Forall* version to run roughly a factor of $5/3$ slower than the *Pdo* version, if we neglect the global merge time, which is relatively small as n increases. The measured results in Figure 6 confirm this expectation, especially for larger values of n and m.

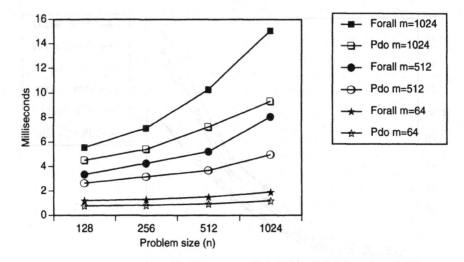

Figure 6: Performance of Matvec on iWarp.

6 Concluding remarks

We have identified a common operation, called the Do&Merge, that can be significantly optimized by integrating two previously separated operations into one common operation. This optimization of the Do&Merge, which we call the *Pdo*, is beneficial for a number of reasons: the programmer can often give the compiler a more efficient implementation of the C' operator than the compiler can derive by itself; and the C' operator is often more natural for the programmer to express than the F and C operators separately. Further, the *Pdo* can be implemented quite easily in any parallelizing compiler that supports array assignment statements.

We are currently evaluating the *Pdo* implementation within the framework of a parallelizing Fortran compiler similar to HPF. We have presented some preliminary results of that evaluation, where we found performance improvements of up to 50% for Histogram and Matvec example programs.

References

[1] S. Chatterjee, J. Gilbert, F. Long, R. Schreiber, and S. Teng. Generating local addresses and communication sets for data-parallel programs. In *Proceedings of the ACM SIGPLAN Symposium on Principles and Practice of Parallel Programming*, pages 149–158, San Diego, CA, May 1993.

[2] R. Cytron. Doacross: Beyond vectorization for multiprocessors. In *Proceedings 1986 International Conference on Parallel Processing*, pages 836–844, St. Charles, Illinois, 1986.

[3] High Performance Fortran Forum. High Performance Fortran language specification version 1.0, May 1993.

[4] J. Stichnoth. Efficient compilation of array statements for private memory multicomputers. Technical Report CMU-CS-93-109, School of Computer Science, Carnegie Mellon University, February 1993.

[5] J. Subhlok, J. Stichnoth, D. O'Hallaron, and T. Gross. Exploiting task and data parallelism on a multicomputer. In *Proceedings of the ACM SIGPLAN Symposium on Principles and Practice of Parallel Programming*, pages 13–22, San Diego, CA, May 1993.

[6] J. A. Webb. Steps toward architecture independent image processing. *IEEE Computer*, 25(2):21–31, February 1992.

[7] M. Wolfe. Doany: Not just another parallel loop. In *Conference Record, Fifth Workshop on Languages and Compilers for Parallel Computing*, pages 1–12, Yale University, August 1992.

CM2, BC1]) and the the Vienna Fortran Compilation System (VFCS), a successor of SUPERB ([ZB2], [G 1], [GZ1]), an interactive system which supports the restructuring of Vienna Fortran programs to parallel programs for execution on distributed memory multiprocessors. This system requires the user to provide a **data distribution**, i.e. a description of the way in which the program's data is to be distributed among the processors which will execute it. It then generates code for a target machine selected from a range of architectures. The work described in this paper aims to extend the functionality of the system by generating the data distribution automatically.

In the next section, we describe Vienna Fortran and the programming model underlying this language extension. Section 3 then outlines the basic compilation strategy adopted in VFCS. This is followed by a discussion of the role of data distributions in creating parallel codes. Section 5 describes the design of the distribution tool that is being constructed. Details of the system structure are given in Section 6. The paper concludes with a discussion of related work.

2 Vienna Fortran and its Programming Model

Vienna Fortran describes a set of language extensions of FORTRAN. The majority of these extensions enable the user to describe a data distribution within the program code. Vienna Fortran is based on the so-called *SPMD* (Single Program Multiple Data) or data parallel model of computation. In this model, the data arrays in the original program are each partitioned and mapped to the processors. This is known as *distributing* the arrays. The specification of the mapping of the elements of the arrays to the set of processors is called the *data distribution* of that program. A processor is then thought of as *owning* the data assigned to it; these data elements are stored in its local memory. Now the work is distributed according to the data distribution: computations which define the data elements owned by a processor are performed by it - this is known as the *owner computes* paradigm. The processors then execute essentially the same code in parallel, each on the data stored locally; parallelism is obtained by applying the computation to different parts of the data domain simultaneously.

If accesses to non-local data occur in the code, the compiler automatically inserts communication constructs to send and receive data at the appropriate positions in the code. This is called *message passing*. The compiler will also map logical processor structures declared by the user to the physical processors which execute the program. These transformations are, however, transparent to the Vienna Fortran programmer.

A major characteristic of this style of programming is that the performance of the resulting code depends to a very large extent on the data distribution selected by the programmer. It determines not only where computation will take place, but is also the main factor in deciding what communication is necessary. The total cost incurred when non-local data is accessed involves not only the actual time taken to send and receive data, but also the time delay while a processor waits for non-local data, or for other processors to reach a certain position in the code.

The Vienna Fortran language extensions include the following features:

- The **processors** which execute the program may be explicitly specified and referred to. It is possible to impose one or more structures on them.
- The **distributions** of arrays can be specified using annotations which may use processor structures introduced by the user. Intrinsic functions are provided to define the distribution of an array dimension to a corresponding processor dimension. They include block, cyclic, block cyclic and general block distributions, in which the lengths of individual blocks may vary. Data may be replicated to all or a subset of processors.
- An array may be **aligned** with another array, providing an implicit distribution.
- The distribution of arrays may be changed **dynamically**. However, a clear distinction is made between arrays which are statically distributed and those whose distribution may be changed at runtime.
- In **procedures**, dummy array arguments may inherit the distribution of the actual argument, or be explicitly distributed, possibly causing some data motion.

Care was taken during the specification of this language to ensure that it is not only suitable for a user-provided specification of a distribution of data, but also suitable for generation by an automatic tool. Vienna Fortran is the target language of the tool outlined in this paper.

3   The Basic Compilation Strategy of VFCS

In this section we describe the basic features of automatic parallelization by specifying a **source-to-source** translation from Vienna Fortran to a Fortran extension with explicit message passing constructs (MPF). We simplify the presentation by considering a proper subset of Vienna Fortran, which assumes all arrays to be distributed **statically**, in the sense that once an array has been bound to a distribution (in a declaration), this association remains invariant throughout the entire subprogram. Formal arrays in **procedures** may be explicitly distributed or they may assume the distribution of the actual argument.

This compilation strategy enforces the **owner computes paradigm**.

The translation from Vienna Fortran to MPF is described as a sequence of **phases**, each of which specifies a translation between two source codes (cf. Figure 1). Details are to be found in [ZC2].

Assume that a Vienna Fortran source program Q^0 is given. We transform Q^0 into an MPF program Q^4 in four conceptually distinct consecutive phases:

Phase 1 (Front End): Vienna Fortran Source Program $Q^0 \mapsto$ Vienna Fortran Normalized Program Q^1 The source program Q^0 is processed by a **Front End**, which performs the following three tasks: it transforms the source

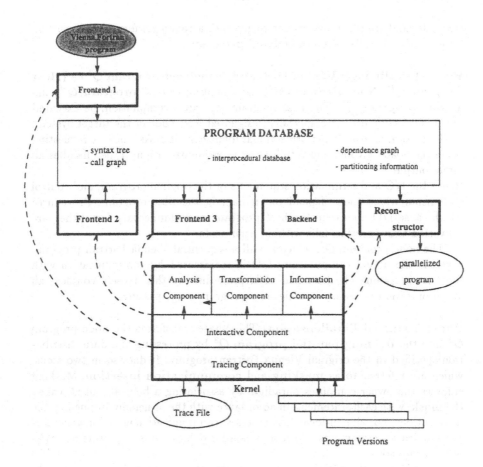

Fig. 1. Structure of VFCS

code into an *internal representation* suitable for further compiler manipulation; it performs the *initial analysis* of the program, and it *normalizes* the code. This analysis may have to be updated or recomputed during subsequent phases.

Thus Phase 1 includes syntactic and semantic analysis, control flow analysis, data flow analysis, data dependence analysis and the construction of the call graph. Such transformations as interprocedural constant propagation and dead code elimination are applied. Code normalizations are applied to simplify subsequent compiler operations. They eliminate certain program constructs (such as statement functions) move some kinds of statement to a prescribed place in the code, and transform other statements into a canonical form. The resulting program, Q^1, is called the **normalized program**.

Phase 2 (Splitting): Vienna Fortran Normalized Program $Q^1 \mapsto$ (Host Program Q^H, Node Program Q^2) Q^1 is split into a **host program**, Q^H, and a **node program**, Q^2. The host program will, after compilation, be executed on the host computer or a specially designated host node of the target system, as the **host process**. It performs global management tasks, such as requesting resources, loading code, and terminating program execution; it also handles all input/output.[2]

Hence the I/O and termination statements of the original program, and control statements which these depend on, remain in the host program. Procedures which cause I/O appear in the host program in a rudimentary form: they are converted to subroutine calls without arguments.

The node program, Q^2, which is still a sequential Vienna Fortran program, contains the actual computation; I/O is represented by communication with the host program. The host and node programs are thus loosely coupled; all synchronization necessary is achieved through message passing.

Phase 3 (Initial Parallelization) This phase transforms the node program Q^2 into the **defining parallel program** Q^3 by processing the data distribution specified in the original Vienna Fortran program. It does so in two steps, which are referred to as **masking** and **communication insertion**. Masking enforces the owner computes paradigm by associating a boolean guard, called the **mask**, with each statement, in accordance with the ownership implied by the distributions. For all non-local data accesses, communication insertion generates communication statements which copy non-local data items to *private variables* of the processor.

According to the SPMD execution model, the compiler does not generate separate node programs for each processor. Instead, each will execute the same program, receiving its parameters and initial data from the host program.

The actual performance of this code is likely to be very poor. Subsequent program manipulations convert this node program into a form which will run well on the target machine.

Phase 4 (Optimization and Target Code generation): Defining Parallel Program $Q^3 \mapsto$ Optimized Target Program Q^4 In this phase, the defining parallel program is transformed into an optimized parallel MPF target program, Q^4. Communication and masking are improved: Communication statements are moved out of loops and combined to perform aggregate communication where possible; the *strip mining* of loops [ZC1] across the processors can be achieved in many cases by propagating the information in masks to the loop bounds. A prerequisite for many optimizations is precise flow and data dependence information, as gathered in Phase 1, and overlap analysis, which

---

[2] Future versions will also have to permit individual node I/O to concurrent files.

detects regular communication patterns and re-organizes communication based upon them. Overlap analysis also helps determine the amount of storage needed for each non-trivially distributed data array in a processor's memory.

VFCS puts a good deal of effort into optimizing the target program, in particular extracting communication from loops whenever possible, and combining individual communication statements (by vectorization and fusion) to reduce the overall communication cost ([GZ1, G 2]).

4 The Role of Data Distributions in Creating Parallel Code

The specification of data partitioning is the crucial and most critical step in the parallelization process, requiring a detailed knowledge of the algorithm, the architecture, and the cost of communication in the transformed program. The penalty for a "wrong" decision may be quite high: excessive communication may be generated, resulting in an inacceptable performance degradation of the target program. Thus the user's skill in selecting data distributions in a Vienna Fortran program may have a large influence on the quality of the code produced.

The method by which the data is distributed determines the structure of the parallel program as described in Sec. 2 and, in particular, the workload for each processor; hence, the data distribution also determines the overall performance of the parallelized program. Program factors that influence the selection of a distribution include the size of the application, the ranges of do-loops, major access patterns of arrays, how the arrays are used together, and the dependences among the statements of a loop. The communication behavior of the target machine, its communication/computation ratio, cache sizes and pipelines/vector processing facilities all play a role.

Currently implemented systems do not provide adequate support to the user for the crucial task of data distribution. Automatic support for it is essential if there is to be an advance in compilation technology for DMMP systems.

Theoretical results show that there is no optimal solution to the problem of determining a data distribution for a given program, even under much simplified conditions ([M 1]). Thus there is no pure analytical solution.

The most promising approach seems to be a combination of both analytical and heuristic methods. The precise strategy adopted will depend both on the features of the actual code and the characteristics of the target machine.

The tool described here makes use of performance analysis methods where it seems reasonable to do so, but also – implicitly, via heuristics – makes use of empirical performance data ([CH1]). There are a number of known good data distributions for some important and frequent subproblems in numerics: knowledge of them flow directly into the system.

5 Design of the Distribution Tool

The approach described in this paper is suitable for arbitrary regular FORT-RAN 77 codes. It will not produce good results if the behavior of the code is very strongly dependent on the program input data. This, however, poses an equally difficult problem for the programmer. As is the case for parallelization in general, superior results are likely to be produced for loosely synchronous problems ([FJ1]).

Some methods for distributing the data of irregular problems are also being considered: these involve a combination of compile time and run time handling according to the following strategy. Such codes are generally characterized by indirect accesses to major arrays in much or all of the program.

In this case, performance data may be used to select those loops which perform much of the computation in the code. Compile time analysis aligns other data to the arrays in these loops, or provides them with explicit distributions. The distribution of the data in the loops is then performed in a run-time preprocessing phase, using a partitioning algorithm specified by the user.

Vienna Fortran provides a general definition for the concepts of data distribution and alignment. Initially, we restrict the class of distributions and alignments considered to simplify the task of selection. This restriction will be reconsidered at a later stage. In particular, the tool will generally select combinations of block and cyclic(k) distribution functions to describe the derived mappings, including partial and total replication. Arrays used as work spaces will require a list of distributions. These mappings can be easily described in Vienna Fortran syntax, as given in [ZB1].

5.1 The General Approach

Our design for a tool to distribute data is based on two foundations: advanced program analysis and knowledge-based techniques, in particular pattern matching facilities in conjunction with the explicit representation and retrieval of knowledge. We rely strongly on heuristics to make many of the decisions involved.

- **Program Analysis**
  The current generation of parallelizers perform a good deal of program analysis. Information about the structure of the program, and the patterns in which data is accessed (in particular, within loops), is also required for data distribution. Details on this analysis are found in [G 2] and [ZC1].
- **Knowledge-based Techniques**
  Heuristic rules are widely used to reduce the size of the search space and to determine constraints which a solution should satisfy. A pattern matching facility is used to recognize several different kinds of patterns in the program

code. In particular, certain kinds of constructs are detected, for which implementation details are present in the knowledge base for the target machine. A clear interface enables extension of the patterns which may be matched (see Sec. 6.2).

- **Interactivity**
  The distribution tool is an interactive system, which provides the user with the opportunity to provide distributions explicitly, to view and modify those supplied by the system.

The strategy adopted for implementation within VFCS decomposes the task of selecting a distribution into several separate stages which are described in the next section.

6 The System Structure

The general strategy for deriving a data distribution consists of five separate phases: preprocessing of the input program, performance analysis, the application of heuristics and analysis of reference patterns in the code, a subsequent pass over the program's call graph, and a final optimization phase. We are primarily concerned with the third and fourth of these phases in this work.

The initail step corresponds to the Phases 1 and 2 described in Section 3, and it is part of VFCS proper. The system performs a significant amount of program analysis.

The next phase consists of invoking the **Weight Finder**, a profiling tool, to obtain performance data, in particular for loops and subroutines in the code. This is followed by **intraprocedural alignment and pattern matching**, (Section 6.2) which performs two distinct tasks. It first determines a suitable alignment of the arrays within a procedure. A pattern matching facility then attempts to recognize a selected set of code patterns, which are marked in the code if detected.

The fourth phase in the strategy performs an **interprocedural distribution analysis**: data is propagated up the call graph so that at each call site, information is available on the amount of computation represented by the procedure call and on the suitable distributions of formal procedure parameters. In the subsequent top-down pass over the call graph, the relevant information is resolved according to simple heuristics. A formal argument may inherit the distribution of the actual arguments, or it may have a fixed distribution. Moreover, two or more versions of the original procedure may be generated, corresponding to different actual arguments.

The resulting program contains all information to generate the Vienna Fortran program output by the tool. The matched patterns are not substituted until the code generation stage, when an implementation of the pattern is selected for the target machine depending in the size and selected distributions of its arguments. This will use, wherever possible, efficient library routines on the nodes of the machine. Where there is no efficient implementation on the particular machine, the pattern can be ignored.

The logical structure of this process is outlined in Fig. 2.

6.1 The Weight Finder

The *Weight Finder* derives profiling information for the program Q_1. Computationally intensive areas are determined by a combination of static performance analysis and dynamic techniques; after suitable instrumentation, the program is compiled and executed on a sequential processor, with a characteristic set of input data provided by the user.

The output of this phase is a labelling of the program with profiling information indicating, in particular, the number of times loops and subroutines are executed, and their average execution times. In addition, true ratios for IF statements are determined. These values will play an important guiding role in the next phases, for example providing a sound basis for selecting a specific data distribution for a section of code or deciding whether redistribution is necessary.

The Weight Finder determines the relative and absolute importance of individual program sections, including single statements, basic blocks, loops and subroutines. For this purpose, the Weight Finder provides a set of sequential program parameters, including the following:

- The *profile time* for a statement S in Q_1 determines the measured time of a single instantiation of S during a single program run of Q_1.
- The *loop iteration count* of a DO-loop L is specified by the number of times the body of L is executed for a single instantiation of L. Thus each DO-loop is associated with an integer number.
- The *frequency count* of a statement S in Q_1 specifies how many times S is executed during a single program run of Q_1.

Moreover, true ratios may be determined.
Loop iteration counts and profile times for a specific statement may vary for different statement instantiations. Therefore these parameter values are derived as average values. Apart from profile times, all sequential parameters derived by the Weight Finder are machine independent[3].

A significant amount of optimization is carried out to decrease profile time and memory overhead: a number of transformations are applied to reduce the number of instrumentation statements in the code, including extracting them from loop nests. Details are to be found in [FH1] and [F 1].

Based on the sequential program parameters, the Weight Finder produces for every program statement a pair of values, the **weights**, which represent the basic execution time of the corresponding program section, and the number of times it is expected to be executed[4]. The output of the Weight Finder is the program Q_2, whose statements are annotated with weights.

---

[3] The information gathered is not only useful for automatic data distribution, but also for knowledge based program transformation systems, and performance prediction.

[4] For subroutines, these values may be specific to an instantiation.

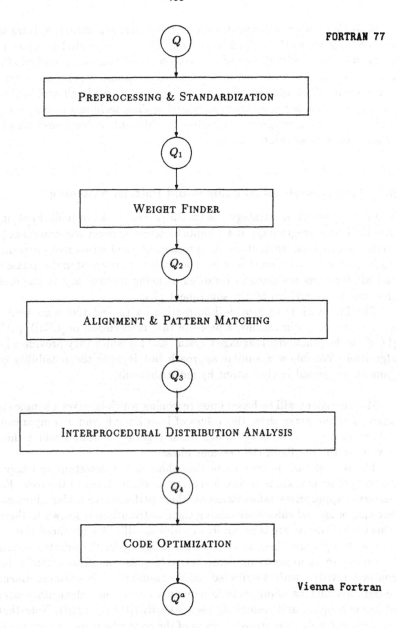

Fig. 2. The Phases in the Data Distribution Strategy

A single profile run derives the sequential program parameters. If transformations are subsequently applied to program Q_2, the sequential program parameters can be incrementally modified for a variety of program transformations, including statement reordering, loop distribution, fusion, skewing and interchange, and loop unrolling and jamming. Loop tiling can be easily allowed for by simple functions of the tile size. Interprocedural scaling techniques allow the adjustment of sequential program parameters for different problem sizes based on the original parameter values.

6.2 Intraprocedural Alignment and Pattern Matching

The next phase of the strategy has two important tasks to fulfil. First, in a pass over the entire program Q_2, it attempts to derive as many constraints as possible on the overall data distribution. For a reasonably well-structured program, major decisions can be taken on this basis. The analysis performed in this phase is local, and all decisions are initially regarded as being preliminary, in the sense that they can be overridden by the subsequent phase.

The first task is to provide information on the relative placement, or alignment, of array dimensions, a problem that is discussed in [LC1]), [CC1], and [LC2] for the functional language Crystal, and for which they provide a heuristic algorithm. We follow a similar approach but include the possibility of realignment (expressed in the output by redistributions).

Most decisions will be based upon reasoning which involves a simple syntactic analysis of the array sizes, the values of loop bounds and a comparison of the indices used to access arrays which occur together in statements within loops. It will use the results of the previous phase.

The second task performed in this phase is the detection and appropriate marking of several kinds of common array access patterns in the code. For these patterns, appropriate information on their performance under different distributions, or special rules constraining their distribution, is known to the system. This part of the system is naturally machine-specific. An advanced system might be able to optimize these sections of the program for the selected distribution, by calling an appropriate implementation (e.g. as contained within a library of routines invoked with distributed data). Standard code patterns amenable to recognition and handling include reduction operations, elementary operations of linear algebra, and commonly used stencils ([HA1], [RS1]). Note that these patterns will only be matched in areas of the code which are, in terms of the performance data, considered sufficiently important. The performance information provided for these patterns is a cost function which specifies, in dependence of the size of the arguments in an instantiation, and the target machine's configuration, the cost of its execution under different data distributions for the arrays involved.

At the end of this step, a new version of the program, Q_3, is produced. It contains information specifying the constraints on the data distribution function that were derived; this includes marking the positions in code where redistribution is to be performed and labelling arrays with local distribution and alignment information.

Note that under certain circumstances it may be possible to derive an optimal distribution for segments of code analytically (cf. [RS1],[R 1]).

6.3   Interprocedural Distribution Analysis

In contrast to the above, this is a global processing phase which uses the information contained in the program version Q_3. It assumes the call graph to be acyclic.

In a bottom-up pass over the call graph, each procedure is visited and its (weighted) do-loops are analyzed. Based on the reference patterns they contain, the loop bounds and the local alignment relations, simple heuristics are applied to select a **cost function** describing the execution time of the loop under the set of considered distributions for the arrays. For patterns which have been matched, such cost functions are provided in a knowledge base. Procedure calls (within and outside of loops) are also considered. Since the called procedure will have been previously analyzed, both a cost function for the call, which can be applied to the actual arguments, and the weight of the procedure call is available within the current program unit. Heuristics are again applied to combine the individual weights and cost functions for the loops and subroutine calls within a program unit, to derive a cost function for the distribution for the program unit. Note that loops and procedure calls with a weight below a machine-specific minimum value can generally be ignored. For procedure calls with a weight above a fixed (machine-dependent) value and a cost function which indicates that a particular distribution is to be strongly preferred, distributions will be selected for the formal arguments and local arrays at this stage. In the resulting Vienna Fortran code, such a subroutine will have explicit distributions in the specification part for all of these arrays.

The heuristics employed in this phase will be successively refined. Note that they require machine-dependent information in general.

The second half of this phase must now use the weights and cost functions to select distributions for the arrays in the program. Note that since information on the suitability of certain distributions has been propagated up the call graph via the use of cost functions, the information available in the main program already provides us with a cost function for the entire program, although it is incomplete in the sense that arrays not visible in the main program are not explicitly represented in it. The arrays in the main program, which will often include all common block arrays which may be distributed, will be distributed at this point. However, the call graph must still be processed in top down order before all distributions can be selected. The distributions are propagated successively down the call graph to each subprogram for which distributions were not selected in the previous part of this phase. In the resulting Vienna Fortran code, this will be specified as an inherited distribution. If a subprogram, for which distributions have not already been selected, is called from several different places, it is possible that in different incarnations of the subroutine, the distributions of the actual arguments of a dummy argument may differ. A further analysis compares the distributions which reach a subroutine. Under certain, rather limited, circumstances, the system may clone such a subroutine to enable optimization of the code in subsequent transformation phases. This has already been implemented in VFCS (see [G 2]).

The resulting program, Q_4, is appended with sufficient information to generate the Vienna Fortran data distribution annotations representing the selected array distributions. This information is present in each procedure of the program.

6.4 Optimization

This phase may make use of the information on selected distributions to optimize the resulting code. In particular, it may insert calls to selected routines where code patterns have been marked. It may possibly apply certain code transformations to improve the communication behavior.

Finally, it must insert the appropriate distribution annotations into the Fortran source code to produce the final output program, Q^a, in Vienna Fortran.

7 Related Work

Finding a suitable data distribution for the data belonging to a program is a topic of concern not only where distributed memory multiprocessor systems are involved, but also for SIMD systems, where processors are connected in such a way that they perform the same instruction in lock step on local data.

For the CM-2, a SIMD computer from Thinking Machines Corporation, research on optimizing communication by the appropriate allocation of arrays was performed by Knobe, Lukas and Steele ([KL1]). Although the same fundamental issues arise in this context – in particular, the need to spread data versus the need for data which is used together to be stored on the same processor – the approach taken differ significantly: on SIMD systems, there is conceptually one element of an array in a processor's local memory, and when an instruction is executed, the operands must be "aligned", i.e. data elements combined in an individual operation must be placed on the same processor. This generally involves data motion, and in fact, individual data items are frequently shifted within the available memory. One of the major tasks here is to coordinate this motion and to minimize the cost of data movement in an area of code.

In contrast, it is critical to the performance of a program on a DMMP to place sections of arrays on each processor in such a way that it can perform a significant amount of work involving these local data items and as few non-local items as possible. The data placement should also ensure a good balance of the workload among the processors. Thus - although we do permit redistribution of data - the placement of data no longer calls for a local solution, but must be seen from a global perspective.

Nevertheless, most efforts so far have gone into determining suitable placements of data for selected code patterns, usually within the context of a single Fortran do-loop. This approach is thus based on local analysis, and results cannot be generalized easily to real programs. Nonetheless, insights gained on handling code patterns amenable to this kind of analysis form part of the information a system is able to apply to a specific program.

J. Ramanujam and P. Sadayappan ([RS1]) have proposed an analytical approach to determining a data distribution for the arrays in a do-loop, introducing a matrix notation to represent their access patterns: the corresponding system of linear equations is solved to yield the distribution scheme. The scheme applies to the loop under consideration only.

David E. Hudak and Santosh G. Abraham ([HA1]) have developed techniques for generating distributions for parallel loops based on the access patterns inside the loop. They permit polygonal partitions, which are difficult to handle, and will generally be "right" for just one loop in the code. Thus their approach cannot easily form the basis for a method to handle larger programs.

A proposal which does attempt to deal with data distribution for a DMMP as a global problem is the "constraint-based" approach presented by Manish Gupta and Prithviraj Banerjee ([GB1, GB2, G 1]), in which pattern matching at statement level is used to derive constraints on a data distribution, together with "goodness measures" that approximate the communication penalty if they are not satisfied. In contrast to the previous two works, characteristics of the target machine are taken into account. This approach attempts to derive expressions which approximate the execution times for an entire program: the symbolic evaluations required could be prohibitive for larger codes. The user may be asked to provide information which cannot be derived analytically. This work has been implemented in a system which is based on the Parafrase-2 transformation system. It derives distributions for the data of programs written in a simplified Fortran 77 without subroutines, by performing a number of separate passes over the source. These attempt to separately solve sub-problems of data distribution: an alignment is found by mapping data to a logical processor array of an appropriate dimensionality, it is determined whether block or cyclic distributions are more appropriate, and block widths are derived. Finally, the processor array must be fixed. All but two dimensions of the original processor array used are collapsed: the available processors will be shared among them.

A number of other research efforts are relevant to the task of finding a data distribution for a DMMP.

In particular, Jingke Li and Marina Chen developed an alignment strategy for the functional language Crystal, based on an n-dimensional grid machine architecture. They detect communication patterns in code, mapping them to aggregate communication primitives available on the target machine ([LC1, LC2]).

At Rice and Syracuse Universities, "training sets" of code have been developed, with the the aim of assessing the communication behavior of machines. The results have been used to predict the performance of loops with explicit communication ([BF1]) which satisfy certain restrictions. The method does not, however, appear to have general applicability.

Within the context of Parallel Ellpack, Houstis and coworkers are working on the generation of data distributions for the code produced by their system ([CH1]).

References

[BF1] V. Balasundaram, G. Fox, K. Kennedy, and U. Kremer: An Interactive Environment for Data Partitioning and Distribution. Proc. DMCC5, Mar 1990, 1160-1170

[BK1] V. Balasundaram and K. Kennedy: A Technique for Summarizing Data Access and its Use in Parallelism Enhancing Transformations. SIGPLAN '89 Conf. Programming Language Design and Implementation, 1989, 43-53

[BC1] Benkner,S., Chapman,B.M., Zima,H.P.: Vienna Fortran 90. Proc. Scalable High Performance Computing Conference, Williamsburg, April 1992, 51-59

[CH1] B. Chapman, H. Herbeck and H. Zima: Automatic Support for Data Distribution. Proc. Sixth Distributed Memory Computing Conference, Portland, 51-58

[CM1] B. Chapman, P. Mehrotra and H. Zima: Vienna Fortran - A Fortran Language Extension for Distributed Memory Multiprocessors. In: J. Saltz, P. Mehrotra (Eds): Compilers and Runtime Software for Scalable Multiprocessors, Elsevier, Amsterdam (1991)

[CM2] B. Chapman, P. Mehrotra and H. Zima: Vienna Fortran. Scientific Programming, 1(1), Wiley, August 1992

[CC1] Marina Chen, Young-il Choo, and Jingke Li: Theory and Pragmatics of Compiling Efficient Parallel Code. YALEU/DCS/TR-760, December 1989

[CH1] N.P. Chrisochoides, C.E. Houstis, E.N. Houstis, P.N. Papachiou, S.K. Kortesis and J.R. Rice: DOMAIN DECOMPOSER: A Software Tool for Mapping PDE Computations to Parallel Architectures. Domain Decomposition Methods for Differential Equations, SIAM, 341-357, 1991.

[F 1] T. Fahringer: A Static Parameter Based Performance Prediction Tool for Parallel Programs for Distributed Memory Systems, Invited Paper, 7th ACM Int. Conf. on Supercomputing, Tokyo, 1993

[FH1] T. Fahringer and C. Huber: The Weight Finder, A Profiler for Fortran 77 Programs. Tech. Report, Dept. of Computer Science, University of Vienna, Sep. 1992

[FJ1] G. Fox, M. Johnson, G. Lyzenga, S. Otto, J. Salmon, and D. Walker: Solving Problems On Concurrent Processors Vol. I. 1988 Prentice-Hall International, Inc.

[G 1] H.M. Gerndt: Array Distribution in SUPERB. Proc. ACM Int.Conf. on Supercomputing, Crete,164-174 (Jun 1989)

[G 2] H.M. Gerndt: Automatic Parallelization for Distributed-Memory Multiprocessing Systems. Ph.D. Dissertation, University of Bonn, Also: ACPC/TR90-1, Austrian Center for Parallel Computation

[GZ1] H.M. Gerndt, and H.P. Zima: Optimizing Communication in SUPERB. Proc. Conpar 90 - VAPP IV, LNCS 457, 300-311

[GB1] Manish Gupta, and Prithviraj Banerjee: Automatic Data Partitioning on Distributed Memory Multiprocessors. UILU-ENG-90-2248, Coordinated Science Lab., University of Illinois

[GB2] Manish Gupta and Prithviraj Banerjee: Demonstration of Automatic Data Partitioning Techniques for Parallelizing Compilers for Multicomputers. IEEE Transactions on Parallel and Distributed Systems, 3(2), 179-193, March 1992

[G 1] Manish Gupta: Automatic Data Partitioning on Distributed Memory Multicomputers. Ph.D. Thesis, University of Illinois at Urbana-Champaign, UILu-ENG-92-2237, Coordinated Science Lab, University of Illinois, 1992

[H 1] Michael Hind: Full Interprocedural Dependence Analysis. Tech. Report, IBM T.J. Watson Research Center, 1992 (to appear)

[HA1] David E. Hudak and Santosh G. Abraham: Compiler Techniques for Data Partitioning of Sequentially Iterated Parallel Loops. Proc. ACM Int. Conf. on Supercomputing, 187-200 (1990)

[KL1] Kathleen Knobe, Joan D. Lukas, and Guy L. Steele: Data Optimization: Allocation of Arrays to Reduce Communication on SIMD Machines. Journal of Parallel and Distributed Computing 8, 102-118 (1990)

[L 1] Fung F. Lee: Partitioning of Regular Computation on Multiprocessor Systems. Journal of Parallel and Distributed Computing 9, 312-317 (1990)

[LC1] Jingke Li, and Marina Chen: Index Domain Alignment: Minimizing Cost of Cross-Referencing Between Distributed Arrays. YALEU/DCS/TR-725 November 1989

[LC2] Jingke Li, and Marina Chen: Synthesis of Explicit Communication from Shared-Memory Program References. YALEU/DCS/TR-755 May 1990

[LY1] Zhiyuan Li and Pen-Chuang Yew: Interprocedural Analysis for Parallel Computing. In Int. Conf. on Parallel Processing, Vol 2, 221-228, 1988

[M 1] M. Mace: Globally Optimal Selection of Memory Storage Patterns. Ph.D. Thesis, Duke University, Durham, USA, May 1983

[R 1] J. Ramanujam: Compile-time Techniques for Parallel Execution of Loops on Distributed Memory Multiprocessors. TR-90-09-01, Dept. Electrical and Comp. Engineering, Louisiana State University (1990)

[RS1] J. Ramanujam, and P. Sadayappan: Compile-Time Techniques for Data Distribution in Distributed Memory Machines. TR-90-09-03, Dept. Electrical and Comp. Engineering, Louisiana State University (Sept. 1990)

[ZB1] H. P. Zima, P. Brezany, B. Chapman, P. Mehrotra and A. Schwald: Vienna Fortran - A Language Specification Version 1.1. Technical Report ACPC/TR 92-4, (March 1992). Also: ICASE Interim Report 21, NASA Langley Research Center, Hampton, March 1992

[ZB2] H.P. Zima, H.-J. Bast, and H.M. Gerndt: SUPERB - a Tool for Semi-Automatic MIMD/SIMD Parallelization. Parallel Computing, 6, 1-18 (1988)

[ZC1] H.P. Zima, and B. Chapman: Supercompilers for Parallel and Vector Computers. ACM Press Frontier Series, Addison-Wesley 1990

[ZC2] H. P. Zima, and B. Chapman: Compiling for Distributed-Memory Systems. Invited paper, Proceedings of the IEEE, Special Section on Languages and Compilers for Parallel Machines, February 1993

A Compilation Approach for Fortran 90D/HPF Compilers

Zeki Bozkus, Alok Choudhary, Geoffrey Fox, Tomasz Haupt, and Sanjay Ranka

Northeast Parallel Architectures Center
3-201, Center for Science and Technology
Syracuse University
Syracuse, NY 13244-4100

Abstract. This paper describes a compilation approach for a Fortran 90D/HPF compiler, a source-to-source parallel compiler for distributed memory systems. Different from Fortran 77 parallelizing compilers, a Fortran90D/HPF compiler does not **parallelize** sequential constructs. Only parallelism expressed by Fortran 90D/HPF parallel constructs is exploited. The methodology of compilation of Fortran 90D/HPF programs such as computation partitioning, communication detection and generation are discussed. An example of Gaussian Elimination is used to illustrate the compilation techniques with performance results.

1 Introduction

Distributed memory multiprocessors are increasingly being used for providing high performance for scientific applications. Currently, distributed memory machines are programmed using a node language and a message passing library. This process is tedious and error prone because the user must perform the task of data distribution and communication for non-local data access.

There has been significant research in developing parallelizing compilers. In this approach, the compiler takes a sequential program, e.g. a Fortran 77 program as input, applies a set of transformation rules, and produces a parallelized code for the target machine. However, a sequential language, such as Fortran 77, obscures the parallelism of a problem in sequential loops and other sequential constructs. This makes the potential parallelism of a program more difficult to detect by a parallelizing compiler. Therefore, compiling a sequential program into a parallel program is not a natural approach. An alternative approach is to use a programming language that can naturally represent an application without losing the application's original parallelism. Fortran 90 [1] (with some extensions) is such a language. The extensions may include the *forall* statement and compiler directives for data partitioning, such as decomposition, alignment, and distribution. Fortran 90 with these extensions is what we call "Fortran 90D", a Fortran 90 version of the Fortran D language [8]. We developed the Fortran D language with our colleagues at Rice University. There is an analogous version of Fortran 77 with compiler directives and other constructs, called Fortran 77D. Fortran D allows the user to advise the compiler on the allocation of data to processor memories. Recently,the High Performance Fortran Forum, an informal group of people from academia, industry and national labs, led by Ken Kennedy, developed a language called HPF (High Performance Fortran) [13] based on Fortran D. HPF essentially adds extensions to Fortran 90 similar to Fortran D directives. Hence, Fortran 90D and HPF are very similar except a few differences. For this reason, we call our compiler the Fortran 90D/HPF compiler.

This paper presents the design of a prototype compiler for Fortran 90D/HPF. The compiler takes as input a program written in Fortran 90D/HPF. Its output is SPMD (Single Program Multiple Data) program with appropriate data and computation partitioning and communication calls for MIMD machines. Therefore, the user can still program using a data parallel language but is relieved of the responsibility to perform data distribution and communication.

Tremendous effort in the last decade has been devoted to the goal of running existing Fortran programs on new parallel machines. Restructuring compilers for Fortran 77 programs have been researched extensively for shared memory systems[19]. The compilation technique of Fortran 77 for distributed memory systems has been addressed by Callahan and Kennedy [4]. Currently, a Fortran 77D compiler is being developed at Rice [14]. Hatcher and Quinn provide a working version of a C* compiler. This work converts C* - an extension of C that incorporates features of a data parallel SIMD programming model- into C plus message passing for MIMD distributed memory parallel computes[12]. The ADAPT system [17] compiles Fortran 90 for execution on MIMD distributed memory architectures. The ADAPTOR [2] is a tool that transform data parallel programs written in Fortran with array extension and layout directives to explicit message passing. Li and Chen [6] describes general compiler optimization techniques that reduce communication overhead for Fortran-90 implementation on massivelly parallel machines. Many techniques especially for unstructured communication of Fortran 90D/HPF compiler are adapted from Saltz et al. [3]. Gupta et al. [11] use collective communication on automatic data partitioning on distributed memory machines. Superb [20] compiles a Fortran 77 program into a semantically equivalent parallel SUPRENUM multiprocessor. Koelbel and Mehrotra [15] present a compilation method where a great deal of effort is put on run-time analysis for optimizing message passing in implementation of Kali.

2 Compilation Overview

Our Fortran90D/HPF parallel compiler exploits only the parallelism expressed in the data parallel constructs. We do not attempt to *parallelize* other constructs, such as *do* loops and *while* loops, since they are used only as naturally sequential control constructs in this language. The foundation of our design lies in recognizing commonly occurring computation and communication patterns. These patterns are then replaced by calls to the optimized run-time support system routines. The run-time support system includes parallel intrinsic functions, data distribution functions, communication primitives and several other miscellaneous routines. This approach represents a significant departure from traditional approaches where a compiler needs to perform in-depth dependency analyses to recognize parallelism, and embed all the synchronization and low-level communication functions inside the generated code.

Given a syntactically correct Fortran90D/HPF program, the first step of the compilation is to generate a parse tree. The front-end to parse Fortran 90 for the compiler was obtained from ParaSoft Corporation. In this module, our compiler also transforms each array assignment statement and *where* statement into equivalent *forall* statement with no loss of information. In this way, the subsequent steps need only deal with *forall* statements.

The partitioning module processes the data distribution directives; namely, decomposition, distribute and align. Using these directives, it partitions data and computation among processors.

After partitioning, the parallel constructs in the node program are sequentialized since they would be executed on a single processor. This is performed by the sequentialization module. Array operations and *forall* statements in the original program are transferred into loops or nested loops. The communication module detects communication requirements and inserts appropriate communication primitives.

Finally, the code generator produces *loosely synchronous* SPMD code. The generated code is structured as alternating phases of local computation and global communication. Local computations consist of operations by each processor on the data in its own memory. Global communication includes any transfer of data among processors, possibly with arithmetic or logical computation on the data as it is transferred (e.g. reduction functions). In such a model, processes do not need to synchronize during local computation. But, if two or more nodes interact, they are implicitly synchronized by global communication.

3 Data Partitioning

Distributed memory systems solve the memory bottleneck of vector supercomputers by having separate memory for each processor. However, distributed memory systems demand high locality for good performance. Therefore, the distribution of data across processors is of critical importance to the performance of a parallel program in a distributed memory system.

Fortran D provides users with explicit control over data partitioning with both data *alignment* and *distribution* specifications. We briefly overview directives of Fortran D relevant to this paper. The complete language is described elsewhere [8]. The DECOMPOSITION directive is used to declare the name, dimensionality, and the size of each problem domain. We call it "template" (the name "template" has been chosen to describe "DECOMPOSITION" in HPF [13]). The ALIGN directive specifies fine-grain parallelism, mapping each array element onto one or more elements of the template. This provides the minimal requirement for reducing data movement. The DISTRIBUTE directive specifies coarse-grain parallelism, grouping template elements and mapping them to the finite resources of the machine. Each dimension of the template is distributed in either a block or cyclic fashion. The selected distribution can affect the ability of the compiler to minimize communication and load imbalance in the resulting program.

- **BLOCK** divides the template into contiguous chunks.
- **CYCLIC** specifies a round-robin division of the template.

The **BLOCK** attribute indicates that blocks of global indices are mapped to the same processor. The block size depends on the size of the template dimension, N, and the number of processors, P, on which that dimension is distributed (shown in the first column of Table 1).

Table 1. Data distribution function(refer to Definition 1): N is the size of the global index space. P is the number of processors. N and P are known at compile time and $N \geq P$. I is the global index. i is the local index and p is the owner of that local index i.

	Block-distribution	Cyclic-distribution
global to proc $I \rightarrow p$	$p = \frac{I*P}{N}$	$p = I \bmod P$
global to local $I \rightarrow i$	$i = I - \frac{p*N}{P}$	$i = \lfloor \frac{I}{P} \rfloor$
local to global $(p, i) \rightarrow I$	$I = i + \frac{p*N}{P}$	$I = iP + p$
cardinality	$\frac{N}{P}$	$\lfloor \frac{N+P-1-p}{P} \rfloor$

The **CYCLIC** attribute indicates that global indices of the template in the specified dimension should be assigned to the logical processors in a round-robin fashion. The last column of Table 1 shows the CYCLIC distribution functions. This also yields an optimal static load balance since the first $N \bmod P$ processors get $\lceil \frac{N}{P} \rceil$ elements; the rest get $\lfloor \frac{N}{P} \rfloor$ elements. In addition, these distribution functions are efficient and simple to compute. Although cyclic distribution functions provided a good static load balance, the locality is worse than that using block distribution because cyclic distributions scatter data.

The following example illustrates the Fortran D directives. Consider the data partitioning schema for matrix-vector multiplication proposed by Fox *et al.*[9] and shown in Figure 1. The matrix vector multiplication can be described as

$$y = Ax$$

where y and x are vectors of length M, and A is an $M \times M$ matrix. To create the distribution shown in the Figure 1, one can use the following directives in a Fortran 90D program.

```
C$    DECOMPOSITION    TEMPL(M,M)
C$    ALIGN A(I,J)  WITH TEMPL(I,J)
C$    ALIGN X(J)    WITH TEMPL(*,J)
C$    ALIGN Y(I)    WITH TEMPL(I,*)
C$    DISTRIBUTE    TEMPL(BLOCK,BLOCK)
```

If this program is mapped onto a 4x4 physical processor system, the Fortran 90D compiler will generate the distributions shown in Figure 1. Matrix A is distributed in both dimensions. Hence, a single processor owns a subset of matrix rows and columns. X is column-distributed and row-replicated. But Y is row-distributed and column-replicated.

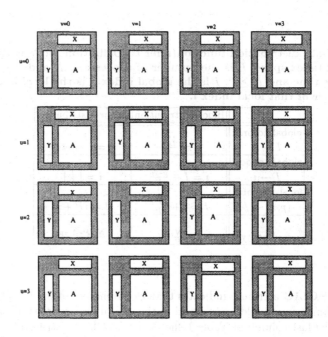

Fig. 1. Matrix-vector decomposition: each processor is assigned array section of A, X, and Y.

4 Computation Partitioning

Once the data is distributed, there are several alternatives to assign computations to processing elements (PEs) for each instance of a *forall* statement. One of the most common methods is to use the *owner computes rule*. In the owner computes rule, the computation is assigned to the PE owning the *lhs* data element. This rule is simple to implement and performs well in a large number of cases. Most of the current implementations of parallelizing compilers uses the owner computes rule [20, 4]. However, it may not be possible to apply the owner computes rule for every case without extensive overhead. The following examples describe how our compiler performs computation partitioning.

Example 1 (canonical form) Consider the following statement, taken from the Jacobi relaxation program

```
forall (i=1:N, j=1:N)
&    B(i,j) = 0.25*(A(i-1,j)+A(i+1,j)+A(i,j-1)+A(i,j+1))
```

In the above example, as in a large number of scientific computations, the *forall* statement can be written in the canonical form. In this form, the subscript value in the *lhs* is identical to the forall iteration variable. In such cases, the iterations can be easily distributed using the owner computes rule. Furthermore, it is also simpler to detect structured communication by using this form

Figure 2 shows the possible data and iteration distributions for the $lhs_I = rhs_I$ assignment caused by iteration instance I. Cases 1 and 2 illustrate the order of communication and computation arising from the owner computes rule. Essentially, all the communications to fetch the off-processor data required to execute an iteration instance are performed before the computation is performed. The generated code will have the following communication and computation order.

```
Communications   ! some global communication primitives
Computation      ! local computation
```

Example 2 (non-canonical form) Consider the following statement, taken from an FFT program

```
forall (i=1:incrm, j=1:nx/2)
&    x(i+j*incrm*2+incrm) = x(i+j*incrm*2) - term2(i+j*incrm*2+incrm)
```

The *lhs* array index is not in the canonical form. In this case, the compiler equally distributes the iteration space on the number of processors on which the *lhs* array is distributed. Hence, the total number of iterations will still be the same as the number of *lhs* array elements being assigned. However, this type of forall statement will result in either Case 3 or Case 4 in Figure 2. The generated code will be in the following order.

```
Communications   ! some global communication primitives to read
Computation      ! local computation
Communication    ! a communication primitive to write
```

For reasonably simple expressions, the compiler can transform such index expressions into the canonical form by performing some symbolic expression operations. However, it may not always be possible to perform such transformations for complex expressions.

In summary, our computation and data distributions have two implications.

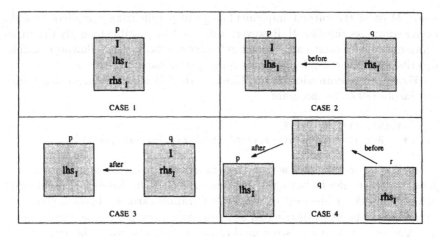

CASE 1: No communications

CASE 2: Communication before computation to fetch non-local rhs

CASE 3: Communication after computation to store non-local data lhs

CASE 4: Communication before and after computation to fetch and store non-locals

Fig. 2. I shows the processor on which the computation is performed. lhs_I and rhs_I show the processors on which the *lhs* and *rhs* of instance I reside.

- The processor that is assigned an iteration is responsible for computing the *rhs* expression of the assignment statement.
- The processor that owns an array element (*lhs* or *rhs*) must communicate the value of that element to the processors performing the computation.

5   Communication

Our Fortran 90D/HPF compiler produces calls to collective communication routines instead of generating individual processor send and receive calls inside the compiled code. The idea of using collective communication routines came from researchers involved in developing scientific application programs [9]. There are three main reasons for using collective communication to support interprocessor communication in the Fortran 90D/HPF compiler.

1. *Improved performance of Fortran 90D/HPF programs.* To achieve good performance, interprocessor communication must be minimized. By developing a separate library of interprocessor communication routines, each routine can be optimized. This is particularly important given that the routines will be used by many programs compiled through the compiler.
2. *Increased portability of the Fortran 90D/HPF compiler.* By separating the communication library from the basic compiler design, portability is en-

hanced because to port the compiler, only the machine specific low-level communication calls in the library need to be changed.

3. *Improved performance estimation of communication costs.* Our compiler takes the data distribution for the source arrays from the user as compiler directives. However, any future compiler will require a capability to perform automatic data distribution and alignments [5]. In any case, distributions of temporary arrays must be determined by the compiler. Such techniques usually require computing trade-offs between exploitable parallelism and the communication costs. The costs of collective communication routines can be determined more precisely, thereby enabling the compiler to generate better distributions.

In order to perform a collective communication on array elements, the communication primitive needs the following information 1-) send processors list, 2-) receive processors list, 3-) local index list of the source array and, 4-) local index list of the destination array.

There are two ways of determining the above information. 1) Using a pre-processing loop to compute the above values or, 2) based on the type of communication, the above information may be implicitly available, and therefore, not require pre-processing. We classify our communication primitives into *structured* and *unstructured* communication.

Our structured communication primitives are based on a logical grid configuration of the processors which is formed according to the shape of template and the number of available physical processors. Hence, they use grid-based communications such as shift along dimensions, broadcast along dimensions etc. The following summarizes some of the structured communication primitives implemented in our compiler.

- **transfer:** Single source to single destination message. This may happen that one column of grid processors communicate with another column of the grid processors.
- **multicast:** broadcast along a dimension of the logical grid.
- **overlap_shift:** shifting data into overlap areas in one or more grid dimensions. This is particularly useful when the shift amount is known at compile time. This primitive uses that fact to avoid intra processor copying of data and directly stores data in the overlap areas [10].
- **temporary_shift:** This is similar to overlap shift except that the data is shifted into a temporary array. This is useful when the shift amount is not a compile time constant. This shift may require intra-processor copying of data.

We have implemented two sets of unstructured communication primitives: 1) where the communicating processors can determine the send and receive lists based only on local information, and hence, only require pre-processing that involves local computations, [15] and 2) where to determine the send and receive lists pre-processing itself requires communication among the processors [3].

- **precomp_read:** This primitive is used to bring all non-local data to the place it is needed before the computation is performed.
- **postcomp_write:** This primitive is used to store remote data by sending it to the processors that own the data after the computation is performed. Note that these two primitives requires only local computation in the preprcessing loop.
- **gather:** This is similar to *precomp_read* except that pre-processing loop itself may require communication.
- **scatter:** This is similar to *postcomp_write* except that pre-processing loop itself may require communication.

The gather and scatter operations are powerful enough to provide the ability to read and write distributed arrays with vectorized communication facility. These two primitives are available in PARTI (Parallel Automatic Runtime Toolkit at ICASE) [7] designed to efficiently support irregular patterns of distributed array accesses. Fortran 90D/HPF compiler uses the PARTI to support these two powerful primitives.

The compiler must recognize the presence of collective communication patterns in the computations in order to generate the appropriate communication calls. Specifically, this involves a number of tests on the relationship among subscripts of various arrays in a forall statement. These tests should also include information about array alignments and distributions. We use pattern matching techniques similar to those proposed by Li and Chen [16]. Further, we extend the above tests to include unstructured communication. Table 2 shows the patterns of communication primitives used in our compiler.

Table 2. Communication primitives based on the relationship between *lhs* and *rhs* array subscript reference pattern for block distribution. (c: compile time constant, s, d: scalar, f: invertible function, V: an indirection array).

Steps	(lhs,rhs)	Comm. primitives
1	(i, s)	multicast
2	$(i, i + c)$	overlap_shift
3	$(i, i - c)$	overlap_shift
4	$(i, i + s)$	temporary_shift
5	$(i, i - s)$	temporary_shift
6	(d, s)	transfer
7	(i, i)	no_communication
8	$(i, f(i))$	precomp_read
9	$(f(i), i)$	postcomp_write
10	$(i, V(i))$	gather
11	$(V(i), i)$	scatter
12	$(i, unknown)$	gather
13	$(unknown, i)$	scatter

6 Example and Performance Results

We use Gaussian elimination with partial pivoting as an example for translating a Fortran90D/HPF program into a Fortran+MP program. The Fortran90D/HPF code is shown in Figure 3. Arrays *a* and *row* are partitioned by compiler directives. The second dimension of *a* is block-partitioned, while the first dimension is not partitioned. Array *row* is block-partitioned. This program illustrates the convenience for the programmer of working in Fortran 90D/HPF. Data parallelism is concisely represented by array operations, while the sequential computation is expressed by *do* loops. More importantly, explicit communication is not needed since the program is written for a single address space.

```
1.          integer, dimension(N) :: indx
2.          integer, dimension(1) :: iTmp
3.          real, dimension(N,NN) :: a
4.          real, dimension(N) :: fac
5.          real, dimension(NN) :: row
6.          real :: maxNum
7.    C$  PROCESSORS PROC(P)
8.    C$  DECOMPOSITION TEMPLATE(NN)
9.    C$  DISTRIBUTE TEMPLATE(BLOCK)
10.   C$  ALIGN row(J) WITH TEMPLATE(J)
11.   C$  ALIGN a(*,J) WITH TEMPLATE(J)
12.
13.         indx = -1
14.         do k = 0, N-1
15.          iTmp = MAXLOC(ABS(a(:,k)), MASK = indx .EQ. -1)
16.          indxRow = iTmp(1)
17.          maxNum = a(indxRow,k)
18.          indx(indxRow) = k
19.          fac = a(:,k) / maxNum
20.
21.         row = a(indxRow,:)
22.         forall (i = 0:N-1, j = k:NN-1, indx(i) .EQ. -1)
23.    &        a(i,j) = a(i,j) - fac(i) * row(j)
24.         end do
```

Fig. 3. Fortran90D/HPF code for Gaussian elimination.

Figure 4 shows how the Fortran 90D/HPF compiler translates Gaussian Elimination into Fortran 77+MP form. It is easy to see that the generated code is structured as alternating phases of local computation and global communication. Local computations consist of operations by each processor on the data in its own memory. Global communication includes any transfer of data among processors. The compiler partition the distributed arrays into small sizes and the parallel constructs are sequentialized into a *do* loop.

```
B= NN/P
integer indx(N)
real aLoc(N,B)
real fac(N)
real rowLoc(B)
real maxNum
integer source(1)

call grid_1(P)
do i = 1, N
  indx(i) = -1
end do
do k = 1, N
    do i = 1, N
      mask(i) = indx(i) .EQ. -1
    end do
    source(1)=(k-1)/B
    call set_DAD_2(aLoc_DAD, 1, N, N, k-my_id()*B, k-my_id()*B, B)
    call set_DAD_1(temp1_DAD, 1, N, N)
    call broadcast_R_V (temp1, temp1_DAD, aLoc, aLoc_DAD, source)
    call set_DAD_1(temp1_DAD, 1, N, N)
   .call set_DAD_1(mask_DAD, 1, N, N)
    indxRow = MaxLoc_1_R_M(temp1, temp1_DAD, N, mask, mask_DAD)
    source(1)=(k-1)/B
    call broadcast_R_S(maxNum, aLoc (indxRow, k-my_id()*B), source)
    indx(indxRow) = k
    call set_DAD_2(a_DAD, 1, N, N, k-my_id()*B, k-my_id()*B, B)
    call set_DAD_1(temp2_DAD, 1, N, N)
    call broadcast_R_V (temp2, 1, temp2_DAD, aLoc, 2, aLoc_DAD, source)
    do i = 1, N
       fac (i) = temp2 (i) / maxNum
    end do
    do i = 1, 10
       rowLoc (i) = aLoc (indxRow, i)
    end do
```

Fig. 4. Fortran 90D/HPF compiler generated Fortran77+MP code for Gaussian elimination.

The compiler generates the appropriate communication primitives depending on the reference pattern of distributed array. For example, the statement

```
      call set_BOUND(k, NN, llb, lub, 1, B)
      do j = llb, lub
        do i = 1, N
          if (indx (i) .EQ. (-1)) THEN
            aLoc (i, j) = aLoc (i, j) - fac (i) * rowLoc (j)
          end if
        end do
      end do
    end do
```

Figure 4: Fortran 90D/HPF compiler generated Fortran77+MP code for Gaussian elimination (cont.)

```
temp = ABS(a(:,k))
```

is transformed into a broadcast primitives since the array a is distributed in the second dimension. All runtime routines are classified according to data types. For example, _R(Real) specifies the data type of the communication and _V specifies that it is vector communication. The primitive set_DAD is used to fill the Distributed Array Descriptor (DAD) associated with array a so that it can be passed to the *broadcast* communication primitive at run-time. The DAD has sufficient information for the communication primitives to compute all the necessary information including local lower and upper bounds, distributions, local and global shape etc. In this way the communication routines also has an option to combine messages for the same source and destination into a single message to reduce communication overhead. This is the typical characteristic of our compiler since we are only parallelizing array assignments and forall statements in Fortran 90D/HPF, there is no data dependency between different iterations. Thus, all the required communication can be performed before or after the execution of the loop on each of the processors involved.

The intrinsic function *MAXLOC* is translated into the library routine *MaxLoc_R_M*. The suffix _R specifies the data type and _M specifies that *MAXLOC* intrinsic has optional mask array. Once again the array information passed to the runtime system with the associated _DAD data structure.

Several types of *communication* and *computation* optimizations can be performed to generate a more efficient code. In terms of *computation* optimization, it is expected that the scalar node compiler performs a number of classic scalar optimizations within basic blocks. These optimizations include common subexpression elimination, copy propagation (of constants, variables, and expressions), constant folding, useless assignment elimination, and a number of algebraic identities and strength reduction transformations. However, Fortran 90D/HPF may perform several optimizations to reduce the total cost of communication. The compiler can generate better code by observing the following:

```
15.              Tmp = ABS(a(:,k))
17.              maxNum = a(indxRow,k)
19.              fac = a(:,k) / maxNum
```

The distributed array section $a(:, k)$ is used at lines 15,17 and 19. The array a is not changed between line 15-19. Each statement causes a broadcast operation. Because the compiler performs statement level code generation for the above three statements. However, the compiler can eliminate two of three communication calls by performing the above dependency analysis. It need only generate one broadcast for line 15 which communicates a column of array a. The Lines 17 and 19 can use that data as well. The optimized code is shown in Figure 5. We generated this programs by hand since the optimizations have not yet been implemented in our compiler. Currently our compiler performs statement level optimizations. It does not perform basic-block level optimizations.

```
do k = 1, N
   do i = 1, N
      mask(i) = indx(i) .EQ. -1
   end do
   source(1)=(k-1)/B
   call set_DAD_2(aLoc_DAD, 1, N, N, k-my_id()*B, k-my_id()*B, B)
   call set_DAD_1(temp1_DAD, 1, N, N)
   call broadcast_R_V (temp1, temp1_DAD, aLoc, aLoc_DAD, source)
   call set_DAD_1(temp1_DAD, 1, N, N)
   call set_DAD_1(mask_DAD, 1, N, N)
   indxRow = MaxLoc_1_R_M(temp1, temp1_DAD, N, mask, mask_DAD)
   maxNum=temp1(indxRow)
   indx(indxRow) = k
   do i = 1, N
      fac (i) = temp1 (i) / maxNum
   end do
   do i = 1, 10
      rowLoc (i) = aLoc (indxRow, i)
   end do
   call set_BOUND(k, NN, llb, lub, 1, B)
   do j = llb, lub
      do i = 1, N
         if (indx (i) .EQ. (-1)) THEN
            aLoc (i, j) = aLoc (i, j) - fac (i) * rowLoc (j)
         end if
      end do
   end do
end do
```

Fig. 5. Gaussian elimination with communication elimination optimization.

To validate the performance of our compiler on Gaussian Elimination which is a part of the FortranD/HPF benchmark test suite [18], we tested three codes on the iPSC/860 and plotted the results. 1-) The code in given 4. This is shown as the dotted line in Figure 6, and represent the compiler generated code. 2-) The code in Figure 5. This appears as the dashed line in Figure 6 and represents the hand optimized code on the compiler generated code as discussed above. 3-) The hand-written Gaussian Elimination with Fortran 77+MP. This appears as the solid line in Figure 6. The code is written outside of the compiler group at NPAC to be unbiased.

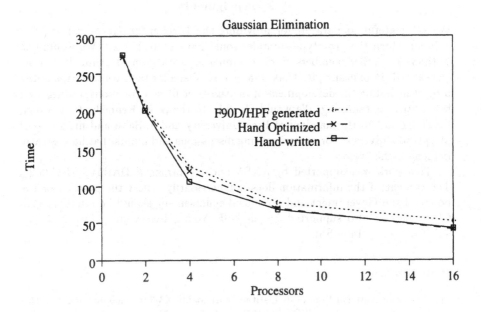

Fig. 6. Performance of three version of Gaussian Elimination. Matrix size is 1023x1024 (time in seconds).

The programs were compiled by using Parasoft Express Fortran compiler which calls Portland Group if77 release 4.0 compiler with all optimization turned on (-O4). We can observe that the performance of the compiler generated code is within 10% of the hand-written code. This is due to the fact that the compiler generated code produces an extra communication calls that can be eliminated using optimizations. The hand optimized code gives very near performance to hand-written code. From this experiment we conclude that Fortran 90D/HPF compiler which is incorporated with optimizations can compete with hand-crafted code on some significant algorithms, such as Gaussian Elimination.

7 Conclusions

Fortran 90D/HPF are languages that incorporate parallel constructs and allow users to specify data distributions. In this paper, we presented a design for Fortran 90D/HPF compiler for distributed memory machines. Specifically, techniques for processing distribution directives, computation partitioning, communication generation were presented. We believe that the methodology presented in this paper to compile Fortran 90D/HPF can be used by the designers and implementors for HPF language.

Acknowledgments

We are grateful to Parasoft for providing the Fortran 90 parser and Express without which the prototype compiler could have been delayed. We would like to thank the other members of our compiler research group I. Ahmad, R. Bordawekar, R. Ponnusamy, R. Thakur, and J. C. Wang for their contribution in the project including the development of the run-time library functions, testing, and help with programming. We would also like to thank K. Kennedy, C. Koelbel, C. Tseng and S. Hiranandani of Rice University and J. Saltz and his group of Maryland University for many inspiring discussions and inputs that have greatly influenced this work.

This work was supported by ARPA under contract # DABT63-91-C-0028. The content of the information does not necessarily reflect the position or the policy of the Government and no official endorsement should be inferred. Alok Choudhary is also supported by an NSF Young Investigator Award, CCR-9357840 and by Intel SSD.

References

1. American National Standards Institue. Fortran 90: X3j3 internal document s8.118. Summitted as Text for ISO/IEC 1539:1991, May 1991.

2. Brandes, T.: ADAPTOR Language Reference Manual. Technical Report ADAPTOR-3, German National Research Center for Computer Science, 1992.

3. Berryman, H., Saltz, J., Wu, J., and Hiranandani, S.: Distributed Memory Compiler Design for Sparse Problems. Interim Report ICASE, NASA Langley Research Center, 1991.

4. Callahan, D., and Kennedy, K.: Compiling programs for Distributed Memory Multiprocessors. The Journal of Supercomputing, pages 171–207, 1988.

5. Chatterjee, S., Gilbert, J.R., Schreiber, R., and Tseng, S.H.: Automatic Array Alignment in Data-Parallel Programs. Twentieth Annual ACM SIGACT/SIGPLAN Symposium on Principles of Programming Languages, January 1993.

6. Chen, M., and Wu, J. J.: Optimizing FORTRAN-90 Programs for Data Motion on Massivelly Parallel Systems. Technical Report YALEU/DCS/TR-882, Yale University, Dep. of Comp. Sci., 1992.

7. Das, R., Saltz, J., and Berryman, H.: A Manual For PARTI Runtime Primitives. NASA,ICASE Interim Report 17, May 1991.

8. Fox, G. C., Hiranadani, S., Kenndy, K., Koelbel C., Kremer U., Tseng, C., and Wu, M.: Fortran D Language Specification. Technical report, Rice and Syracuse University, 1992.

9. Fox, G.C., Johnson, M.A., Lyzenga, G.A., Otto, S.W., Salmon, J.K., and Walker, D.W.: In Solving Problems on Concurrent Processors, volume 1-2. Prentice Hall, May 1988.

10. Gerndt, M.: Updating distributed variables in local computations. Concurrency: Practice and Experience, September 1990.

11. Gupta, M., and Banerjee, P.: Demonstration of Automatic Data Partitioning Techniques for Parallelizing Compilers on Multicomputers. IEEE: Transaction on Parallel and Distributed Systems, pages 179–193, March 1992.

12. Hatcher, P., and Quinn, M.: Compiling Data-Parallel Programs for MIMD Architectures. 1991.

13. High Performance Fortran Forum.: High performance fortran language specification version 1.0. Draft, Also available as technical report CRPC-TR92225 from the Center for Research on Parallel Computation, Rice University., Jan. 1993.

14. Hiranandani, S., Kennedy, K., and Tseng, C.: Compiler optimization for Fortran D on MIMD distributed-memory machines. Proc. Supercomputing'91, Nov 1991.

15. Koelbel, C., and Mehrotra, P.: Supporting Compiling Global Name-Space Parallel Loops for Distributed Execution. IEEE Transactions on Parallel and Distributed Systems, October 1991.

16. Li, J. and Chen, M.: Compiling Communication -Efficient Programs for Massively Parallel Machines. IEEE Transactions on Parallel and Distributed Systems, pages 361–376, July 1991.

17. Merlin, J. H.: Techniques for the Automatic Parallelisation of 'Distributed Fortran 90'. Technical Report SNARC 92-02, Southampton Novel Architecture Research Centre, 1992.

18. Mohamed, A.G., Fox, G.C., Laszewski, G.V., Parashar, M., Haupt, T., Mills, K., Lu, Y., Lin, N., and Yeh, N.: Application Benchmark Set for Fortran-D and High Performance Fortran. Technical Report SCCS-327, Northeast Parallel Architectures Center, May 1992.

19. Padua, D., Leasure, B., Kuck, D., Kuhn, R., and Wolfe, M.: Dependence graph and compiler optimizations. Proc. of 8th ACM Symp. Principles on Programming Lang., September 1981.

20. Zima, H., Bast, H., and Gerndt, M.: Superb: A tool for semi Automatic SIMD/MIMD Parallelization. Parallel Computing, January 1988.

A Framework for Exploiting Data Availability to Optimize Communication

Manish Gupta and Edith Schonberg

IBM T. J. Watson Research Center
P. O. Box 704
Yorktown Heights, NY 10598

Abstract. This paper presents a global analysis framework for determining *the availability of data* on a virtual processor grid. The data availability information obtained is useful for optimizing communication when generating SPMD programs for distributed address-space multiprocessors. We introduce a new kind of array section descriptor, called an *Available Section Descriptor*, which represents the mapping of an array section onto the processor grid. We present an array data-flow analysis procedure, based on interval analysis, for determining data availability at each statement. Several communication optimizations, including redundant communication elimination, are also described. An advantage of our approach is that it is independent of actual data partitioning and representation of explicit communication.

1 Introduction

Distributed memory architectures are becoming increasingly popular as a viable and cost-effective method of building massively parallel computers. However, the absence of global address space, and consequently, the need for explicit message passing among processes makes such machines very difficult to program. This has motivated considerable research towards developing compilers that relieve the programmer of the burden of generating communication [15, 23, 17, 19, 18, 16, 21]. Such compilers take a sequential or a shared-memory parallel program, annotated with directives specifying data decomposition, and generate the target SPMD program with explicit message passing. Thus, the compiler performs two essential tasks:

- partitioning of computation, usually based on the *owner computes* rule [15, 23, 19], which makes the processor that owns a data item (being assigned a value) responsible for its computation, and
- generation of communication, whereby the owner of a data item (being used in a computation) sends its value to the processor performing that computation.

In order to reduce the cost of communication, the compilers perform optimizations like message vectorization [15, 23], using collective communication [13, 17], and overlapping communication with computation [15]. However, the extent to which most compilers are able to (or even attempt to) optimize communication is still limited by the following factors:

- It is always the *owner* of a data item that supplies its value when required by another processor. It may be possible to generate more efficient communication if *any* processor that has a valid copy of that data is allowed to send its value. In the special case when a processor receiving a value via communication already has a valid copy of that data item available, the communication can be recognized as being redundant, and eliminated.

- There is no global analysis performed of the communication requirements of array references over different loop nests. This precludes general optimizations, such as redundant communication elimination, or carrying out extra communication inside one loop nest if it subsumes communication required in the next loop nest.

```
DIMENSION B(100, 100), A(100, 100), D(100)
!HPF$ ALIGN B(I, J) WITH VPROCS(I, J)
!HPF$ ALIGN A(I, J) WITH VPROCS(I, J)
!HPF$ ALIGN D(I) WITH VPROCS(I, 1)
```

s_1 :   `DO I = 2, 100`
s_2 :   `DO J = 1, 100`
s_3 :   `B(I, J) = ...A(J, I) ...`
s_4 :   `ENDDO`
s_5 :   `A(100, I-1) = ...`
s_6 :   `D(I) = A(1, I)`
s_7 :   `ENDDO`

Fig. 1. Example Program

As an example, consider the program fragment in Figure 1. According to the HPF alignment directives, B and A are identically aligned to an abstract template, represented by VPROCS. The variable D is aligned with the first column of VPROCS. To enforce the *owner computes rule* at statement s_3, communication must be generated which creates a copy of A transpose aligned with B. Similarly, statement s_6 would require a second communication to align the first row of A with D. However, since D is aligned with the first column of B, the second communication is subsumed by the the first, and is therefore redundant.

Our goal is to provide a framework, based on global array data-flow analysis, for performing communication optimizations. The conventional approach to data-flow analysis regards each access to an array element as an access to the entire array. Previous researchers [12, 11, 20] have applied data-flow analysis to array sections to improve its precision. The array section descriptors, such as the *regular section descriptor* (RSD) [7], and the *data access descriptor* (DAD) [5], provide a compact representation for elements comprising certain special substructures of arrays. However, in the context of communication optimizations, these descriptors are insufficient, because they do not capture information about the processors where the array elements are available.

Granston and Veidenbaum [11] use data-flow analysis to detect redundant accesses to global memory in a hierarchical, shared-memory machine. However, they do not explicitly represent information about the availability of data on processors. Instead, they rely on simplistic assumptions about scheduling of parallel loops, which are often not applicable. Amarasinghe and Lam [4] use the *last write tree* framework to perform optimizations like eliminating redundant messages. Their framework does not handle general conditional statements, and they do not eliminate redundant communication due to different references in arbitrary statements (for instance, statements appearing in different loop nests). Von Hanxleden et al. [22] have developed a data flow framework for generating communication in the presence of indirection arrays. Their work focusses on irregular subscripts, and can be viewed as complimentary to this work, which deals with regular subscripts, and attempts to obtain more precise information.

In this paper, we first introduce a new kind of descriptor, the *Available Section Descriptor* (ASD), that describes the availability of array elements on processors in an abstract space. We apply ideas from the interval analysis method [2, 12] to develop a procedure for obtaining global data-flow information. This information is recorded using the ASDs. Finally, we describe some optimizations that can now be performed to reduce communication costs, and present an algorithm for one such optimization, eliminating redundant communication.

An advantage of our approach is that availability analysis is performed on the original program form, before any communication is introduced by the compiler. Thus, communication optimizations based on data availability analysis need not depend on detailed knowledge of explicit communication representations. Additionally, our analysis does not rely on how data is eventually partitioned onto physical processors. Availability information can therefore be valuable input for automatic data partitioning decisions.

2 Available Section Descriptor

The Available Section Descriptor is an extended version of an array section descriptor, that also records information about the availability of data items on processors. It is defined as a pair $\langle D, M \rangle$, where D is an array section descriptor, and M is a descriptor of the function mapping elements in D to virtual processors. We use the term *mapping* to convey the availability of data at processors, not simply the ownership of data by processors. Data is made available through communication.

In this paper, we shall use the *bounded regular section descriptor* (BRSD) [14], a version of RSD to represent array sections. Bounded regular sections allow representation of subarrays that can be specified using the Fortran 90 triplet notation. We represent a bounded regular section as an expression $A(S)$, where A is the name of an array variable, S is a vector of subscript values such that each of its elements is either (i) an expression of the form $\alpha * k + \beta$, where

k is a loop index variable and α and β are invariants, (ii) a triple $l : u : s$, where l, u, and s are invariants (the triple represents the expression discussed above expanded over a range) , or (iii) $\perp$, indicating no knowledge of the subscript value.

The processor space is regarded as an unbounded grid of virtual processors. The abstract processor space is similar to a *template* in High Performance Fortran (HPF) [9], which is a grid over which different arrays are aligned. The mapping function descriptor M is a pair $\langle P, F \rangle$, both P and F being vectors of length equal to the dimensionality of the processor grid. The ith element of P (denoted as P_i) indicates the dimension of the array A that is mapped to the ith grid dimension, and F_i is the mapping function for that array dimension, i.e., $F_i(j)$ returns the position(s) along the ith grid dimension to which the jth element of the array dimension is mapped.

We represent a mapping function as

$$F_i(j) = \begin{cases} (c * j + l : c * j + u : s) & \text{(Form 1)} \\ \perp & \text{(Form 2)} \end{cases}$$

In the expression for Form 1, c, l, u and s are invariants. The parameters c, l and u may take rational values, as long as $F_i(j)$ evaluates to a range over integers, over the data domain. The above formulation allows representation of one-to-one mappings (when $l = u$), one-to-many mappings (when $u \geq l + s$), and also constant mappings (when $c = 0$). The one-to-many mappings expressible with this formulation are more general than the replicated mappings for ownership that may be specified using HPF [9]. As with the usual triplet notation, we shall omit the stride, s, from the expression when it is equal to one. Form 2 represents the case when there is no information about the availability of data.

If an array has fewer dimensions than the processor grid, clearly there is no array dimension mapped to some of the grid dimensions. For each such grid dimension m, P_m takes the value $\perp$, which represents a "missing" array dimension. In that case, F_m is no longer a function of a subscript position. It is simply an expression of the form $l : u : s$ or $\perp$, and indicates the position(s) in the mth grid dimension at which the array is available.

Example. Consider a 2-D virtual processor grid VPROCS, and an ASD $\langle A(2 : 100 : 2, 1 : 100), \langle [2, 1], [F_1, F_2] \rangle \rangle$, where $F_1(j) = 1 : 100, F_2(i) = (3/2) * i + 0 : (3/2) * i + 0$. The ASD represents an array section $A(2 : 100 : 2, 1 : 100)$, each of whose element $A(2 * i, j)$ is available at a hundred processor positions given by VPROCS$(1 : 100, 3 * i)$. This ASD is illustrated in Figure 2. Figure 2(a) shows the array A, where each horizontal stripe A_i represents $A(2 * i, 1 : 100)$. Figure 2(b) represents the mapping of the array section onto the virtual processor template VPROCS, where each subsection A_i is replicated along its corresponding column.

3 Data-Flow Analysis

In this section, we present a procedure for obtaining data-flow information for a structured program. The basic item of information that we derive is the availability of data values at different processors, at each node in the control flow graph

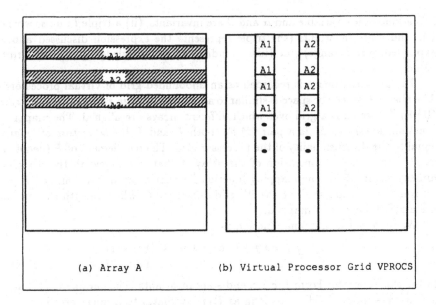

Fig. 2. ASD Illustration

of the program. This is similar to determining *available expressions* in classical data-flow analysis [1], with the difference that we also determine the processor(s) at which each expression is available. Our procedure, like the one presented in [12], is based on the interval analysis method [2], with data-flow extensions for arrays. We are assuming Fortran 77-like language constructs. However, doall loops also can be analyzed in this framework, as well as HPF forall constructs and array language after scalarization.

Let IN_i denote the availability of data at entry to statement node n_i, OUT_i denote the availability of data at exit from n_i, and K_i be the data that is unavailable at exit. The set K_i corresponds to *killed* variables. Let $Kill_i$ be the set of variables defined in the statement node n_i, and Gen_i be the set of variables along with their mapping functions made available at n_i. The sets $Kill_i$ and Gen_i can be computed locally from each statement. All of these sets are represented as ASDs. The ASD representation of any killed data always has a mapping function $\top$ associated with it, which signifies the data being killed on all processors.

The data-flow transfer functions for n_i are defined as follows:

$$K_i = (\cup_p K_p) \cup Kill_i \tag{1}$$

$$IN_i = \cap_p OUT_p$$

$$OUT_i = [IN_i - Kill_i] \cup Gen_i \tag{2}$$

where p ranges over predecessors of n_i.

The set Gen_i is dependent on the compute-rule used by the compiler in translating the source program into SPMD form. In the next section, we define a function *Avail*, which corresponds to the owner computes rule. For an assignment statement $lhs = F(rhs_1...rhs_n)$,

$$Gen_i = \cup_{rhs_i} Avail(lhs, \ rhs_i).$$

In Section 3.2, we describe our global data-flow procedure, based on interval analysis, for propagating availability data.

3.1 Compute Rule Function

The *Avail* function can easily be defined to handle various methods of assigning computation to processors [8], as long as that decision is made statically. In this work, we define this function based on the *owner computes* rule. The owner computes rule requires each item referenced on the *rhs* of an assignment statement to be sent to the processor that owns the *lhs*.

Let $\langle D^L, M^L \rangle$ represent the ASD which specifies ownership for the *lhs* variable. *Avail* calculates the mapping of the *rhs* variable $\langle D^R, M^R \rangle$ that results from enforcing the owner computes rule. The new ASD represents the *rhs* data aligned with *lhs*. The regular section descriptor D^R represents the element(s) referenced by *rhs*. The mapping descriptor $M^R = \langle P^R, F^R \rangle$ is obtained by the following procedure:

Step 1. *Align array dimensions with processor grid dimensions:*

1. For each processor grid dimension i, if the subscript expression obtained from P_i^L has the form $\alpha_1 * k + \beta_1$ and there is a *rhs* subscript expression $\alpha_2 * k + \beta_2$, for the same loop index variable k, set P_i^R to the *rhs* subscript position.
2. For each remaining processor grid dimension i, set P_i^R to j, where j is an unassigned *rhs* subscript position. If there is no unassigned *rhs* subscript position left, set P_i^R to $\perp$.

Step 2. *Calculate the mapping function for each grid dimension:*
For each processor grid dimension i, let $F_i^L(j) = c * j + l$ be the ownership mapping function of the *lhs* variable.[1] We determine the *rhs* mapping function $F_i^R(j)$ from the subscript expressions corresponding to P_i^R and P_i^L. The details are specified in Table 1.

Finally, if any *rhs* or *lhs* subscript expressions are coupled, or if any subscript expressions are non-linear, then $\langle D^R, M^R \rangle$ is set to $\perp$.

Example. Consider the assignment statement in the code fragment:

```
!HPF$ ALIGN A(I, J) WITH VPROCS(J, I+1)
...
A(I, J) = ..B(2*I)..
```

---

[1] This is the form allowed by HPF alignment directives.

P_i^L	P_i^R	$F_i^R(j)$
$\alpha_1 * k + \beta_1$	$\alpha_2 * k + \beta_2,\ \alpha_2 \neq 0$	$c * \left(\frac{\alpha_1 * (j - \beta_2)}{\alpha_2} + \beta_1 \right) + l$
$\alpha_1 * k + \beta_1$	β_2	$c * (\alpha_1 * k + \beta_1) + l$
$\alpha_1 * k + \beta_1$	$\perp$	$c * (\alpha_1 * k + \beta_1) + l$
$\perp$	$\alpha_2 * k + \beta_2$	l (c must be 0)

Table 1. Mapping Function Calculation for Owner Computes Rule

The ownership mapping descriptor M^L for the *lhs* variable A is $\langle [2,1], F^L \rangle$ where $F_1^L(j) = j$ and $F_2^L(j) = j + 1$. This mapping descriptor is derived from the HPF alignment specification. Applying Step 1 of the compute rule algorithm, P^R is set to $[\perp, 1]$. That is, the second dimension of VPROCS is aligned with the first dimension of B, and the first entry of P^R is $\perp$, since B only has one dimension. The second step is to determine the mapping function F^R. For the first grid dimension, P_1^L corresponds to the subscript expression J and P_1^R is $\perp$. Therefore, using F_1^L and the third rule in Table 1, F_1^R is set to $1*(1*J + 0) + 0 = J$. For the second grid dimension, P_2^L corresponds to the subscript expression I, and P_2^R corresponds to the subscript expression $2*I$. Using F_2^L and the first rule in Table 1, $F_2^R(j)$ is set to $\frac{j}{2} + 1$. The mapping descriptor thus obtained maps B(2*I) onto VPROCS(J, I+1).

3.2 Interval-Based Data Availability Analysis

Interval analysis is precisely defined in [6]. An interval corresponds to a program loop. Each interval has a header node h, a last node l, and a single backedge $\langle l, h \rangle$. The analysis for structured (reducible) control flow graphs is performed in two phases, an *elimination phase* and a *propagation phase*.

Elimination Phase

The elimination phase processes the program intervals in a bottom-up (innermost to outermost) traversal. The nodes of each interval are visited in a forward traversal. After each interval has been processed, its dataflow information is summarized and is associated with its header node, and the interval is logically collapsed. Thus, when an outer interval is traversed, each inner interval is treated as a single node, represented by its header.

For availability analysis, we initialize the local sets for the header node of each interval as follows:

$$OUT_h = Gen_h$$
$$K_h = Kill_h$$

Transfer functions (1) and (2) are then applied to each statement node during the forward traversal of the interval. Finally, the data availability generated for the interval last node l must be summarized for the entire interval, and associated with h. However, the data availability at l, obtained from (1) and (2), is only for a *single iteration* of the loop. Following [12], we would like to represent the availability of data corresponding to *all iterations* of the loop.

Definition. For an ASD set S, *expand*$(S, k, low : high)$ is a function which replaces all single data item references $\alpha * k + \beta$ used in any array section descriptor D in S by the triple $(\alpha * low + \beta : \alpha * high + \beta : \alpha)$, and any mapping function of the form $F_i(j) = c * k + l$ by $F_i(j) = c * low + l : c * high + l : c$.

The following equations define the transfer functions which summarize the data being killed and the data being made available in an interval for all iterations $low : high$.

$$Kill_h = \text{expand}(K_l, k, low : high)$$
$$Gen_h = \text{expand}(OUT_l, k, low : high) - (\cup_{def}\text{expand}(def, k, low : high))$$

where def ranges over definitions in the interval loop, such that each definition is the target of an anti-dependence carried by the loop [3]. If the loop is a doall loop, the range of def is empty, so that $Gen_h = \text{expand}(OUT_l, k, low : high)$.

For computing the interval kill set $Kill_h$, we simply expand the kill set generated at l over the interval loop bounds $low : high$. Computing the interval availability set Gen_h requires more work, because a variable definition in an iteration k may kill data made available in previous iterations $low : k - 1$. Therefore, we first expand the data made available in a single iteration, obtaining all data made available in any iteration, and then subtract out the data that may be killed after it is made available. A definition kills data made available in a previous iteration of a loop if it is the target of an anti-dependence carried by the loop, that is, if it defines data previous used.

Example. Table 2 shows ASD sets for the example in Figure 1, obtained during the elimination phase of interval analysis.[2]

The availability domain of the inner loop Gen_2 is the array section $A(1:100,I)$. For a single iteration I, the assignment to $A(100,I-1)$ at s_5 does not kill Gen_2. Therefore, after s_6, both $A(1:100,I)$ and $A(1,I)$ are available. Since $A(1,I)$ is a subset of $A(1:100,I)$, OUT_6 is simply $A(1:100,I)$. (See the union operation in Section 4.) The final availability set Gen_1 is obtained by: a) expanding OUT_6 into $A(1:100,2:100)$, b) expanding the definition at s_5, which is the target of an anti-dependence carried by the loop, into $A(100,1:99)$, and c) taking the difference between the resulting sets. The result of the difference operation is shown in Figure 3.

Propagation Phase

The propagation phase processes the program intervals in a top-down (outermost to innermost) traversal, and the nodes of each interval are visited in a

---

[2] Since the mapping descriptor $\langle P, F \rangle$ for variable A is identical for all availability sets, we ignore it in the discussion below.

ASD set	D	P	F
OUT_3	A(J,I)	2, 1	$F_1(j) = j,\ F_2(j) = j$
K_3	B(I,J)	T	T
Gen_2	A(1:100,I)	2, 1	$F_1(j) = j,\ F_2(j) = j$
$Kill_2$	B(I,1:100)	T	T
OUT_5	A(1:100,I)	2, 1	$F_1(j) = j,\ F_2(j) = j$
K_5	A(100,I-1)	T	T
	B(I,1:100)	T	T
OUT_6	A(1:100,I)	2, 1	$F_1(j) = j,\ F_2(j) = j$
K_6	D(I)	T	T
	A(100,I-1)	T	T
	B(I,1:100)	T	T
Gen_1	A(1:99,2:100), A(1:100, 100)	2, 1	$F_1(j) = j,\ F_2(j) = j$
$Kill_1$	D(2:100)	T	T
	A(100,1:99)	T	T
	B(2:100,1:100)	T	T

Table 2. Steps in Elimination Phase for Example in Figure 1

forward traversal. Thus, data made available outside each interval is propagated to nodes inside the interval. During this node traversal, any inner interval is treated as a single node represented by its header. Our analysis calculates the data availability for a loop iteration k. To determine the data availability of the entire loop, we set $k = high$.

For the elimination phase, the reaching set IN_h is initially empty. For the propagation phase, the initial reaching set for iteration k consists of:

1. The data made available before the loop is entered which is not killed in iterations $1 : k - 1$, and
2. The data made available on all previous iterations $1 : k - 1$, which has not been killed before iteration k.

We define IN_i^k to be the availability of data at entry to a statement i on the kth iteration of its loop. Therefore, IN_h^{low} is the available data that reaches the header node h of an interval before the interval is entered. The data that is available on entry to the kth loop iteration is given by the equation:

$$IN_h^k = [IN_h^{low} - \text{expand}(K_l, k, low : k - 1)] \cup$$
$$[\text{expand}(OUT_l, k, low : k - 1) - (\cup_{def} \text{expand}(def, k, low : k - 1))]$$

where def ranges over definitions that are targets of anti-dependences carried by the loop. Availability information is propagated within the interval using the transfer functions defined in (1) and (2).

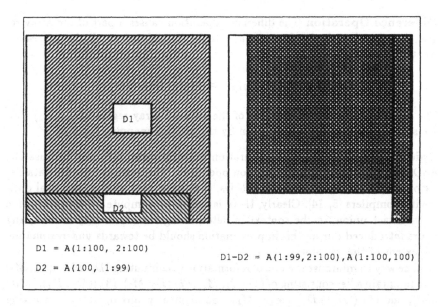

Fig. 3. Result of Difference Operation on RSD

Example. For the example in Figure 1, $IN_1^I = \langle A(1:99,2:I-1), A(1:100,I-1)\rangle$. During the forward traversal of this outer interval, we obtain:

$$OUT_2 = \langle A(1:99, 2:I), A(1:100, I-1:I)\rangle$$
$$OUT_6 = \langle A(1:99, 2:I), A(1:100, I)\rangle$$

For brevity, we have omitted the mapping function, since it is the same for all ASDs on A.

4 Operations on Available Section Descriptors

In this section, we present the algorithms for various operations on the ASDs. Each operation is described in terms of further operations on the array section descriptors and the mapping descriptors that constitute the ASDs. There is an implicit order in each of those computations. The operations are first carried out over the array section descriptors, and then over the descriptors of the mapping functions applied to the resulting array section.

Intersection Operation The intersection of two ASDs represents the elements constituting the common part of their array sections, that are mapped to the same processors. The operation is given by:

$$\langle D_1, M_1\rangle \cap \langle D_2, M_2\rangle = \langle (D_1 \cap D_2), (M_1 \cap M_2)\rangle$$

In the above equation, $M_1 \cap M_2$ represents the intersection of each of the mapping functions M_1 and M_2 applied to the array region $(D_1 \cap D_2)$.

Difference Operation The difference operation causes a part of the array region associated with the first operand to be invalidated at all the processors where it was available.

$$\langle D_1, M_1 \rangle - \langle D_2, \top \rangle = \langle (D_1 - D_2), M_1 \rangle$$

The result represents the elements of the reduced array region $(D_1 - D_2)$ that are still available at processors given by the original mapping function M_1.

Union Operation The union operation presents some difficulty because the ASDs are not closed under the union operation. The same is true for data descriptors like the DADs and the BRSDs, that have been used in practical optimizing compilers [5, 14]. Clearly, there is a need to compute an approximation to the exact union. In the context of determining the availability of data, any errors introduced during this approximation should be towards *underestimating* the extent of the descriptor.

One way to minimize the loss of information in computing $\langle D_1, M_1 \rangle \cup \langle D_2, M_2 \rangle$ is to maintain a list consisting of (1) $\langle D_1, M_1 \rangle$, (2) $\langle D_2, M_2 \rangle$, (3) $\langle (D_1 \cup D_2), (M_1 \cap M_2) \rangle$, and (4) $\langle (D_1 \cap D_2), (M_1 \cup M_2) \rangle$. Subsequently, any operations involving the descriptor would have to be carried out over all the elements in that list. The items (3) and (4) are included in the list because they potentially provide more useful information than just (1) and (2).

Example. Let $\langle D_1, M_1 \rangle = \langle A(1 : 100, 3), \langle [2, 1], F \rangle \rangle$, and let $\langle D_2, M_2 \rangle = \langle A(1 : 100, 4), \langle [2, 1], F \rangle \rangle$, where $F_1(j) = F_2(j) = j$. Figure 4(a) shows $\langle D_1, M_1 \rangle$ and Figure 4(b) shows $\langle D_2, M_2 \rangle$. Consider the subset test: $\langle A(7 : 8, 3 : 4), \langle [2, 1], F \rangle \rangle \subseteq \langle D_1, M_1 \rangle \cup \langle D_2, M_2 \rangle$. If the union is represented as the list of ASDs 4(a) and 4(b) only, this subset test will fail, which is inaccurate. The ASD for item (3) $\langle (D_1 \cup D_2), (M_1 \cap M_2) \rangle$ is shown in Figure 4(c). The subset test succeeds for 4(c).

However, this solution is too expensive, as the size of the list grows exponentially in the number of original descriptors to be unioned (the growth would be linear if only items (1) and (2) were included in the list). There are a number of optimizations that can be done to exclude redundant terms from the above list:

- If $D_1 \subset D_2$, the first term can be dropped from the list, since $\langle D_1, M_1 \rangle$ is subsumed by $\langle (D_1 \cap D_2), (M_1 \cup M_2) \rangle$. Similarly, appropriate terms can be dropped when $D_2 \subset D_1$, $M_1 \subset M_2$, or $M_2 \subset M_1$.
- If $D_1 = D_2$, only the fourth term needs to be retained, since $\langle D_1, M_1 \cup M_2 \rangle$ subsumes all other terms. If $M_1 = M_2$, the third term, that effectively evaluates to $\langle D_1 \cup D_2, M_1 \rangle$, subsumes all other terms, which may hence be dropped.

In addition to these optimizations, the compiler can use heuristics like dropping terms associated with the smaller array regions to ensure that the size of such lists is bounded by a constant. Further discussion of these heuristics is beyond the scope of this paper.

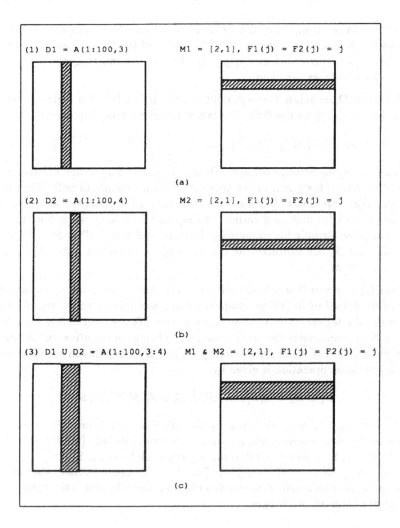

(1) D1 = A(1:100,3)   M1 = [2,1], F1(j) = F2(j) = j

(a)

(2) D2 = A(1:100,4)   M2 = [2,1], F1(j) = F2(j) = j

(b)

(3) D1 U D2 = A(1:100,3:4)   M1 & M2 = [2,1], F1(j) = F2(j) = j

(c)

Fig. 4. ASD Union Operation Example

4.1 Operations on Bounded Regular Section Descriptors

Let D_1 and D_2 be two BRSDs, that correspond to array sections $A(S_1^1, \ldots, S_1^n)$ and $A(S_2^1, \ldots, S_2^n)$ respectively, where each S_1^i and S_2^i term is a range represented as a triple. We now describe the computations corresponding to different operations on D_1 and D_2.

Intersection Operation The result is obtained by carrying out individual intersection operations on the ranges corresponding to each array dimension.

$$D_1 \cap D_2 = A(S_1^1 \cap S_2^1, \ldots, S_1^n \cap S_2^n)$$

The formula for computing the exact intersection of two ranges, S_1^i and S_2^i, expressed as triples, is given in [16]. The result of the intersection operation is another range represented as a triple. If either of the two ranges is equal to $\perp$, the result also takes the value $\perp$.

Difference Operation Conceptually, the result is a list of n regions, each region corresponding to the difference taken along one array dimension.

$$D_1 - D_2 = \text{list}(A(S_1^1 - S_2^1, S_1^2, \ldots, S_1^n), \ldots, A(S_1^1, \ldots, S_1^{n-1}, S_1^n - S_2^n))$$

When the regions corresponding to D_1 and D_2 differ only in one dimension, all except for one of the terms in the above expression evaluate to null. When there is more than one non-null term, the result may be represented as a list, and heuristics used (as discussed earlier) to keep such lists bounded in length.

Again, the formula for computing the exact difference, $R^i = S_1^i - S_2^i$, when both S_1^i and S_2^i are expressed as triples, is given in [16]. If either $S_1^i = \perp$ or $S_2^i = \perp$, then $S_i = \perp$.

Union Operation The BRSDs are not closed under the union operation. The algorithm described in [14] to compute an approximate union potentially *overestimates* the region corresponding to the union. We need a different algorithm, one that underestimates the array region while being conservative. In the special case when the array regions identified by D_1 and D_2 differ only in one dimension, say, i, the union operation is given by:

$$D_1 \cup D_2 = A(S_1^1, \ldots, S_1^{i-1}, S_1^i \cup S_2^i, S_1^{i+1}, \ldots, S_1^n)$$

In the most general case when the regions differ in each dimension, an exhaustive list of regions corresponding to $D_1 \cup D_2$ would include (1) $A(S_1^1, \ldots, S_1^n)$, (2) $A(S_2^1, \ldots, S_2^n)$, and the following n terms: $A(S_1^1 \cup S_2^1, S_1^2 \cap S_2^2, \ldots, S_1^n \cap S_2^n), \ldots, A(S_1^1 \cap S_2^1, \ldots, S_1^{n-1} \cap S_2^{n-1}, S_1^n \cup S_2^n)$. Once again, heuristics are needed to keep the lists bounded. Figure 5 describes an algorithm for computing an approximate union of two ranges.

4.2 Operations on Mapping Function Descriptors

Consider two mapping function descriptors, $M_1 = \langle P_1, F_1 \rangle$ and $M_2 = \langle P_2, F_2 \rangle$, associated with the same array $A(S)$ section. The intersection and union operations are defined as:

$$M_1 \cap M_2 = \begin{cases} \langle P_1, F_1 \cap F_2 \rangle & \text{if } P_1 = P_2 \\ \langle \perp, \perp \rangle & \text{if } P_1 \neq P_2 \end{cases}$$

$$M_1 \cup M_2 = \begin{cases} \langle P_1, F_1 \cup F_2 \rangle & \text{if } P_1 = P_2 \\ \text{list}(M_1, M_2) & \text{if } P_1 \neq P_2 \end{cases}$$

Let $F_1 = [F_1^1, \ldots, F_1^n]$, and let $F_2 = [F_2^1, \ldots, F_2^n]$. The computations of various operations between F_1 and F_2 can be described at two levels: (i) computations

```
function union-range(S₁, S₂)
    if (S₁ = ⊥) return S₂
    if (S₂ = ⊥) return S₁
    Let  S₁ = (l₁ : u₁ : s₁), S₂ = (l₂ : u₂ : s₂)
    if (s₁ mod s₂ = 0)&((l₂ - l₁) mod s₁ = 0)
        s = s₁
    else if (s₂ mod s₁ = 0)&((l₂ - l₁) mod s₂ = 0)
        s = s₂
    else return list(S₁, S₂)
    if (l₁ ≤ l₂)&(u₁ ≥ l₂)
        return (l₁ : max(u₁, u₂) : s)
    else if (l₂ ≤ l₁)&(u₂ ≥ l₁)
        return (l₂ : max(u₁, u₂) : s)
    return list(S₁, S₂)
end union-range.
```

Fig. 5. Algorithm to Compute Union of Ranges

of $F_1 \cap F_2$ and $F_1 \cup F_2$ in terms of further operations over F_1^i and F_2^i, $1 \le i \le n$, and (ii) computation of $F_1^i \cap F_2^i$, and of $F_1^i \cup F_2^i$.

The computations of the first type are identical to those described for the BRSDs. For example, the intersection operation is given by:

$$F_1 \cap F_2 = [F_1^1 \cap F_2^1, \ldots, F_1^n \cap F_2^n]$$

We now describe the intersection and union operations on the mapping functions of individual array dimensions. As mentioned in Section 2, depending on whether P_i represents a true array dimension or a "missing" dimension, F_1^i is either a function of the type $F_1^i(j) = (c_1 * j + l_1 : c_1 * j + u_1 : s_1)$, or simply a constant range, $F_1^i = (l_1 : u_1 : s_1)$. We need to describe only the results for the former case, since the latter can be viewed as a special case of the former, with c_1 set to zero. Thus, in the remainder of this section, we shall regard F_1^i and F_2^i as functions of the form $F_1^i(j) = (c_1 * j + l_1 : c_1 * j + u_1 : s_1)$, and $F_2^i(j) = (c_2 * j + l_2 : c_2 * j + u_2 : s_2)$.

Intersection Operation There are two cases:

Case 1: $c_1 = c_2$: Let $(l : u : s) = (l_1 : u_1 : s_1) \cap (l_2 : u_2 : s_2)$ as described in [16]. The result is given by:

$$(F_1^i \cap F_2^i)(j) = (c_1 * j + l : c_1 * j + u : s)$$

Case 2: $c_1 \ne c_2$: In this case, we check if one of the mapping functions completely covers the other function over the data domain, and otherwise return $\bot$. The high-level algorithm is:

$$if\ F_1^i(j) \subseteq F_2^i(j), j \in S_{P_i}$$
$$return\ F_1^i$$
$$else\ if\ F_2^i(j) \subseteq F_1^i(j), j \in S_{P_i}$$
$$return\ F_2^i$$
$$else\ return\ \perp$$

Let $S_{P_i} = (low : high : step)$. We now describe the conditions for checking if F_1^i is covered by F_2^i. For $j \in (low : high : step)$,

$$F_1^i(j) \subseteq F_2^i(j)$$
$$\Leftrightarrow \quad (c_1 * j + l_1 : c_1 * j + u_1 : s_1) \subseteq (c_2 * j + l_2 : c_2 * j + u_2 : s_2)$$

A set of sufficient conditions for the above relationship to hold is: (i) $c_1 * j + l_1 \geq c_2 * j + l_2$, $low \leq j \leq high$, (ii) $c_1 * j + u_1 \leq c_2 * j + u_2$, $low \leq j \leq high$, (iii) $[(c_1 - c_2) * low + (l_1 - l_2)]\ mod\ s_2 = 0$, and (iv) $s_1\ mod\ s_2 = 0$. In the special case when $s_1 = s_2 = 1$, the last two conditions are satisfied trivially, and conditions (i) and (ii) are both necessary and sufficient. The conditions (i) and (ii) can be further simplified to the following:

(i) $c_1 * low + l_1 \geq c_2 * low + l_2$,
(ii) $c_1 * high + u_1 \leq c_2 * high + u_2$,   if $c_1 \geq c_2$
(i) $c_1 * high + l_1 \geq c_2 * high + l_2$,
(ii) $c_1 * low + u_1 \leq c_2 * low + u_2$,   if $c_1 < c_2$

The conditions for checking if $F_2^i(j) \subseteq F_1^i(j), j \in S_{P_i}$, can be derived in a similar manner.

Union Operation Once again, there are two cases:

Case 1: $c_1 = c_2$: Let $(l : u : s)$ denote $(l_1 : u_1 : s_1) \cup (l_2 : u_2 : s_2)$ as described in Figure 5. The result is given by:

$$(F_1^i \cup F_2^i)(j) = (c_1 * j + l : c_1 * j + u : s)$$

If $(l_1 : u_1 : s_1) \cup (l_2 : u_2 : s_2)$ is actually a list, $F_1^i \cup F_2^i$ is also represented as a list, each element of which is given by the above equation.

Case 2: $c_1 \neq c_2$: We check if one of the mapping functions completely covers the other, and otherwise return a list, as shown below:

$$if\ F_1^i(j) \subseteq F_2^i(j), j \in S_{P_i}$$
$$return\ F_2^i$$
$$else\ if\ F_2^i(j) \subseteq F_1^i(j), j \in S_{P_i}$$
$$return\ F_1^i$$
$$else\ return\ \texttt{list}(F_1^i, F_2^i).$$

5 Communication Optimizations

Availability of global data-flow information enables the compiler to perform communication optimizations that improve the performance of the program as a whole. Several optimizations are briefly described below.

5.1 Redundant Communication Elimination

The most obvious optimization is the elimination of redundant messages: if the receiving processor already has a valid copy of the data being communicated, that communication can be eliminated. More precisely, let $IN_i = \langle D_1, M_1 \rangle$ be the reaching availability set and $Gen_i = \langle D_2, M_2 \rangle$ be the data made available at node n_i. Then communication for Gen_i is redundant if $\langle D_2, M_2 \rangle \subseteq \langle D_1, M_1 \rangle$, i.e., if the following conditions are satisfied:

1. $D_2 \subseteq D_1$
2. $M_2(D_2) \subseteq M_1(D_2)$.

This analysis assumes that the relevant data received during prior communication is not destroyed. In fact, the results of the analysis can be used to determine which data can be usefully cached. Data invalidation is not necessary, since the compile-time analysis ensures consistency.

5.2 Communication Placement

The placement of communication can greatly impact performance. For example, prefetching data enables optimizations such as message vectorization and overlapping communication with computation. Another reason to move the communication earlier is for subsuming subsequent communication. Consider the program:

```
do  k = 1, n
     z(k, 100) = F(d(k))
enddo
...
do  j = 1, n
   do  k = 1, n
        z(k, j) = F(d(k))
   enddo
enddo
```

In the first loop, d must be aligned with the hundredth column of z. In the second loop nest, d must be aligned with every column of z. If the communication needed for the second loop nest is performed before the first loop, then the first communication is unnecessary. Availability analysis is useful for optimizing communication placement.

5.3 Message Merging

When different messages must be sent between the same processors, it is possible to optimize the communication by merging messages. Availability information specifies when data is identically mapped across multiple statements over the whole program. This is precisely the information that is needed for merging messages.

5.4 Multiple Sender Selection

If message-send data is available on several processors, one processor may be better suited to playing the role of the sending processor than the others. A processor may be better suited if it is closer to the receiving processor, or selecting it leads to a better communication pattern. For instance, consider the well-known distributed memory algorithm for matrix multiplication $C = A * B$ in which A is distributed by rows, and B is distributed by columns [10]. The columns of the second array are to be rotated among processors as the computation proceeds. The communication can be realized using a *shift* operation if we let a processor other than the owner send the necessary data. Our analysis makes explicit when different copies of the same data are available.

6 Conclusions

We have presented a new framework for analyzing array references for distributed memory compilation. This framework has the advantage that the analysis is performed on the original program form, before it is transformed into a local SPMD node program: It is generally much harder to analyze a program once the semantic level has been lowered by inserting a lot of additional code. The availability analysis results can be used to perform various global communication optimizations, thus improving the final node program. For future work, the communication optimization algorithms briefly described in Section 5 must be further developed. Also, experience is needed with the ASDs, to design an effective union operation, and assess the cost of this analysis in practice.

References

1. A. V. Aho, R. Sethi, and J. D. Ullman. *Compilers: principles, techniques, and tools.* Addison-Wesley, 1986.
2. F. E. Allen and J. Cocke. A program data flow analysis procedure. *Communications of the ACM*, 19(3):137–147, March 1976.
3. J. R. Allen and K. Kennedy. Automatic translation of Fortran programs to vector form. *ACM Transactions on Programming Languages and Systems*, 9(4):491–542, October 1987.
4. S. P. Amarasinghe and M. S. Lam. Communication optimization and code generation for distributed memory machines. In *Proc. ACM SIGPLAN '93 Conference on Programming Language Design and Implementation*, Albuquerque, New Mexico, June 1993.
5. V. Balasundaram. A mechanism for keeping useful internal information in parallel programming tools: the data access descriptor. *Journal of Parallel and Distributed Computing*, 9(2):154–170, June 1990.
6. M. Burke. An interval-based approach to exhaustive and incremental interprocedural data-flow analysis. *ACM Transactions on Programming Languages and Systems*, 12(3):341–395, July 1990.

7. D. Callahan and K. Kennedy. Analysis of interprocedural side effects in a parallel programming environment. *Journal of Parallel and Distributed Computing*, 5:517–550, 1988.

8. S. Chatterjee, J. R. Gilbert, R. Schreiber, and S.-H. Teng. Optimal evaluation of array expressions on massively parallel machines. In *Proc. Second Workshop on Languages, Compilers, and Runtime Environments for Distributed Memory Multiprocessors*, Boulder, CO, October 1992.

9. High Performance Fortran Forum. High Performance Fortran language specification, version 1.0. Technical Report CRPC-TR92225, Rice University, Jan '93.

10. G. Fox, M. Johnson, G. Lyzenga, S. Otto, J. Salmon, and D. Walker. *Solving Problems on Concurrent Processors*. Prentice Hall, 1988.

11. E. Granston and A. Veidenbaum. Detecting redundant accesses to array data. In *Proc. Supercomputing '91*, pages 854–965, 1991.

12. T. Gross and P. Steenkiste. Structured dataflow analysis for arrays and its use in an optimizing compiler. *Software - Practice and Experience*, 20(2):133–155, February 1990.

13. M. Gupta and P. Banerjee. A methodology for high-level synthesis of communication on multicomputers. In *Proc. 6th ACM International Conference on Supercomputing*, Washington D.C., July 1992.

14. P. Havlak and K. Kennedy. An implementation of interprocedural bounded regular section analysis. *IEEE Transactions on Parallel and Distributed Systems*, 2(3):350–360, July 1991.

15. S. Hiranandani, K. Kennedy, and C. Tseng. Compiling Fortran D for MIMD distributed-memory machines. *Communications of the ACM*, 35(8):66–80, August 1992.

16. C. Koelbel. *Compiling programs for nonshared memory machines*. PhD thesis, Purdue University, August 1990.

17. J. Li and M. Chen. Compiling communication-efficient programs for massively parallel machines. *IEEE Transactions on Parallel and Distributed Systems*, 2(3):361–376, July 1991.

18. M.J. Quinn and P. J. Hatcher. Data-parallel programming on multicomputers. *IEEE Software*, 7:69–76, September 1990.

19. A. Rogers and K. Pingali. Process decomposition through locality of reference. In *Proc. SIGPLAN '89 Conference on Programming Language Design and Implementation*, pages 69–80, June 1989.

20. C. Rosend. *Incremental Dependence Analysis*. PhD thesis, Rice University, March 1990.

21. R. Ruhl and M. Annaratone. Parallelization of Fortran code on distributed-memory parallel processors. In *Proc. 1990 ACM International Conference on Supercomputing*, Amsterdam, The Netherlands, June 1990.

22. R. v. Hanxleden, K. Kennedy, C. Koelbel, R. Das, and J. Saltz. Compiler analysis for irregular problems in Fortran D. In *Proc. 5th Workshop on Languages and Compilers for Parallel Computing*, New Haven, CT, August 1992.

23. H. Zima, H. Bast, and M. Gerndt. SUPERB: A tool for semi-automatic MIMD/SIMD parallelization. *Parallel Computing*, 6:1–18, 1988.

The Alignment-Distribution Graph *

Siddhartha Chatterjee[1], John R. Gilbert[2], and Robert Schreiber[1]

[1] Research Institute for Advanced Computer Science, Mail Stop T045-1,
NASA Ames Research Center, Moffett Field, CA 94035-1000
(sc@riacs.edu, schreibr@riacs.edu)
[2] Xerox Palo Alto Research Center, 3333 Coyote Hill Road, Palo Alto, CA 94304-1314
(gilbert@parc.xerox.com)

Abstract. Implementing a data-parallel language such as Fortran 90 on a distributed-memory parallel computer requires distributing aggregate data objects (such as arrays) among the memory modules attached to the processors. The mapping of objects to the machine determines the amount of *residual communication* needed to bring operands of parallel operations into alignment with each other. We present a program representation called the *alignment-distribution graph* that makes these communication requirements explicit. We describe the details of the representation, show how to model communication cost in this framework, and outline several algorithms for determining object mappings that approximately minimize residual communication.

1 Introduction

When a data-parallel language such as Fortran 90 is implemented on a distributed-memory parallel computer, the aggregate data objects (arrays) have to be distributed among the multiple memory units of the machine. The mapping of objects to the machine determines the amount of residual communication needed to bring operands of parallel operations into alignment with each other. A common approach is to break the mapping into two stages: first, an *alignment* that maps all objects to an abstract Cartesian grid called a *template*, and then a *distribution* that maps the template to the processors. This two-phase approach separates language issues from machine issues; it is used in Fortran D [6], High Performance Fortran [8], and CM-Fortran [13].

A compiler for a data-parallel language attempts to produce data and work mappings that reduce completion time. Completion time has two components: computation and communication. Communication can be separated into intrinsic and residual communication. *Intrinsic communication* arises from operations such as reductions that must move data as an integral part of the operation. *Residual communication* arises from nonlocal data references in an operation whose operands are not mapped to the same processors. We use the term *realignment* to refer to residual communication due to misalignment, and *redistribution* to refer to residual communication due to changes in distribution.

---

* The work of the first and third authors was supported by the NAS Systems Division via Contract NAS 2-13721 between NASA and the Universities Space Research Association (USRA).

In this paper, we describe a representation of array-based data-parallel programs called the *Alignment-Distribution Graph*, or ADG for short. We show how to model residual communication cost using the ADG, and discuss algorithms [2, 3, 4] for analyzing the alignment requirements of a program. The ADG is closely related to the *static single assignment* (SSA) form of programs developed by Cytron *et al.* [5], but is tailored for alignment and distribution analysis. In particular, it uses new techniques to represent the residual communication due to loop-carried dependences, assignment to sections of arrays, and transformational array operations such as reductions and spreads. The ADG provides a detailed and realistic model of residual communication cost that accounts for a wide variety of program features; it allows us to handle alignment and distribution as discrete optimization problems.

The remainder of the paper is organized as follows. Section 2 motivates and formally describes the ADG representation of programs. Section 3 describes how the ADG is used to model the communication cost of a program. Section 4 discusses approximations that we make in the model presented in Section 2 for reasons of practicality. Section 5 outlines some algorithms for alignment analysis that use the ADG. Our previous papers [2, 3, 4] contain more details about the algorithms. Section 6 compares the ADG representation with SSA form and with the *preference graph*, another representation used in alignment and distribution analysis. Section 7 discusses open problems and future work.

2 The ADG representation of data-parallel programs

The ADG is a directed graph representation of data flow in a program. Nodes in the ADG represent computation; edges represent flow of data.

Alignments are associated with endpoints of edges, which we call *ports*. A node constrains the relative alignments of the ports representing its operands and its results. Realignment occurs whenever the ports of an edge have different alignments. The goal of alignment analysis is to determine alignments for the ports that satisfy the node constraints and minimize the total realignment cost, which is a sum over edges of the cost of all realignment that occurs on that edge during program execution.

Similar mechanisms can be used for determining distributions. In the distribution analysis method that we foresee, the template has a distribution at each node of the ADG; the alignment of an object to the template and the distribution of the template jointly define the distribution of the object onto processors at that node. The distributions are chosen to minimize an execution time model that accounts for redistribution cost (again associated with edges of the ADG) and computation cost, associated with nodes of the ADG and dependent on the distribution as well. For the remainder of this paper, however, we focus on alignment analysis.

The ADG distinguishes between program array variables and array-valued objects in order to separate names from values. An *array-valued object* (object for short) is created by every array operation and by every assignment to a section of an array. Assignment to a whole array, on the other hand, names an object. The algorithms presented in Section 5 determine an alignment for each object in the program rather than for each program variable.

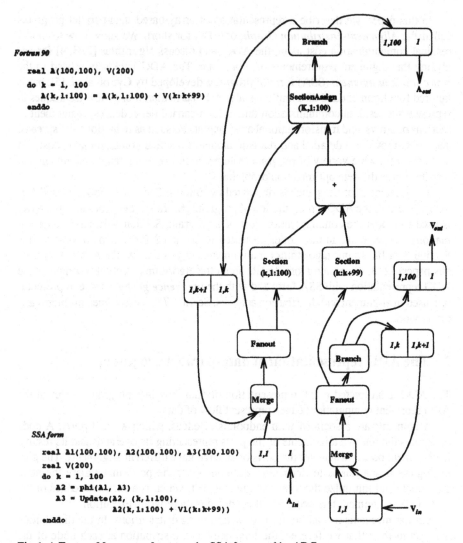

Fortran 90

```
real A(100,100), V(200)
do k = 1, 100
   A(k,1:100) = A(k,1:100) + V(k:k+99)
enddo
```

SSA form

```
real A1(100,100), A2(100,100), A3(100,100)
real V(200)
do k = 1, 100
   A2 = phi(A1, A3)
   A3 = Update(A2, (k,1:100),
              A2(k,1:100) + V1(k:k+99))
enddo
```

Fig. 1. A Fortran 90 program fragment, its SSA form, and its ADG.

2.1 A summary of SSA form

A program is in *SSA form* if each variable is the target of exactly one assignment statement in the program text [5]. Any program can be translated to SSA form by renaming variables and introducing a pseudo-assignment called a ϕ-function at some of the join nodes in the control flow graph of the program. Cytron *et al.* [5] present an efficient algorithm to compute minimal SSA form (*i.e.*, SSA form with the smallest number of ϕ-functions inserted) for programs with arbitrary control flow graphs. Johnson and Pingali [9] have recently improved the complexity of SSA-conversion.

In common usage, SSA form is usually defined for sequential scalar languages, but this is not a fundamental limitation. It can be used for array languages if care is taken to properly model references and updates to individual array elements and array sections [5, §3.1]. The ADG uses SSA form in this manner.

A major contribution of SSA form is the separation between the values manipulated by a program and the storage locations where the values are kept. This separation, which allows greater opportunities for optimization, is the primary reason for basing the ADG on SSA form. After optimization, the program must be translated from SSA form to object code. Cytron *et al.* discuss two optimizations (dead code elimination and storage allocation by coloring) that produce efficient object code [5, §7].

2.2 Ports and alignment

The ADG has a *port* for each textual definition or use of an object. Ports are joined by edges as described below. The ports that represent the inputs and outputs of a program operation are grouped together to form a *node*. Some ports are named and correspond to program variables; others are anonymous and correspond to intermediate values produced by the computation.

The principal attribute of a port is its *alignment*, which is a one-to-one mapping of the elements of the object into the cells of a template. We use the notation

$$A(\theta_1, \ldots, \theta_d) \boxplus [g_1(\theta_1, \ldots, \theta_d), \cdots, g_t(\theta_1, \ldots, \theta_d)]$$

to indicate the alignment of the d-dimensional object A to the t-dimensional (unnamed) template. The formula above has d implicit universal quantifiers to its left, one for each of the index variables θ_1 through θ_d.

When we consider an object defined or used in a nest of *do* loops with induction variables (LIVs) $\xi_1, \ldots, \xi_k$, we extend the notation to

$$A(\theta_1, \ldots, \theta_d) \boxplus_\xi [g_1(\theta_1, \ldots, \theta_d), \cdots, g_t(\theta_1, \ldots, \theta_d)],$$

where $\xi = (1, \xi_1, \ldots, \xi_k)$, and each g_k is now a function of ξ. The additional 1 at the beginning of ξ signifies that an object outside any loop nests has a position independent of any loop iteration variables. (See Section 4.2 for more details.) In this notation, the index variables are universally quantified, but the induction variables are free. Such an alignment is said to be *mobile*.

High Performance Fortran allows a program to use more than one template. We have extended our theory to use multiple templates, but in this paper, for simplicity, we assume that all array objects are aligned to a single template.

We restrict our attention to alignments in which each axis of the object maps to a different axis of the template, and elements are evenly spaced along template axes. Such an alignment has three components: *axis* (the mapping of object axes to template axes), *stride* (the spacing of successive elements along each template axis), and *offset* (the position of the object origin along each template axis). Each g_j is thus either a constant f_j (in which case the axis is called a *space axis*), or a function of a single array index of the form $s_j \theta_{a_j} + f_j$ (in which case it is called a *body axis*). There are d body axes and $(t - d)$ space axes. We allow the stride and offset components to be functions of the induction variables in the mobile case. In matrix notation, the alignment $g_A(\theta)$

of object A can be written as $g_A(\theta) = L_A\theta + f_A$, where L_A is a $t \times d$ matrix whose columns are orthogonal and contain exactly one nonzero element each, f_A is a t-vector, and $\theta = (\theta_1, \ldots, \theta_d)^T$. The elements of L_A and f_A are expressions in ξ. The nonzero structure of L_A gives the axis alignment, its nonzero values give the stride alignment, and f_A gives the offset alignment.

We also allow replication of objects. The offset of an object in a space axis of the template, rather than being a scalar, may be a set of values. We restrict our attention to sets are arithmetic sequences representable by triplets $\ell : h : s$.

2.3 Edges, iteration spaces, and control weights

An edge in the ADG connects the definition of an object with a use of the object. Multiple definitions or uses are handled with merge, branch, and fanout nodes as described below. Thus every edge has exactly two ports. The purpose of the alignment phase is to label each port with an alignment. All communication necessary for realignment is associated with edges; if the two ports of an edge have different alignments, then the edge incurs a cost that depends on the alignments and the total amount of data that flows along the edge during program execution. An edge has three attributes: data weight, iteration space, and control weight.

The *data weight* of an edge is the size of the object whose definition and use it connects. As the objects in our programs are rectangular arrays, the size of an object is the product of its extents. If an object is within a loop nest, we allow its extents, and hence its size, to be functions of the LIVs. We write the data weight of edge (x, y) at iteration ξ as $w_{xy}(\xi)$.

The ADG is a static representation of the data flow in a program. However, to model communication cost accurately, we must take control flow into account. The *branch* and *merge* nodes in the ADG are a static representation, in a data-oriented model, of the forks and joins in control flow. Control flow has two effects: data may not always flow along an edge during program execution (due to conditional constructs), and data may flow along an edge multiple times during program execution (due to iterative constructs). An *activation* of an edge is a instance of data flowing along the edge during program execution. To model the communication cost correctly, we attach *iteration space* and *control weight* attributes to edges.

First consider a singly nested *do*-loop, as in Figure 1. Data flows once along the edges from the preceding computation into the loop, along the forward edges of the loop at every iteration, along the loop-back edges after all but the last iteration, and once, after this last iteration, out of the loop to the following computation. Summing the contribution of each edge over its set of iterations correctly accounts for the realignment cost of an execution of the loop construct. In general, an edge (x, y) inside a nest of k *do*-loops is labeled with an *iteration space* $\mathcal{I}_{xy} \subset \mathbf{Z}^{k+1}$, whose elements are the vectors ξ of values taken by the LIVs. As explained above, both the size of the object on an edge and the alignment of the object at a port can be functions of the LIVs. The realignment and redistribution cost attributed to an edge is the sum of these costs over all iterations in its iteration space.

For a program where the only control flow occurs in nests of *do*-loops, iteration spaces exactly capture the number of activations of an edge. However, programming

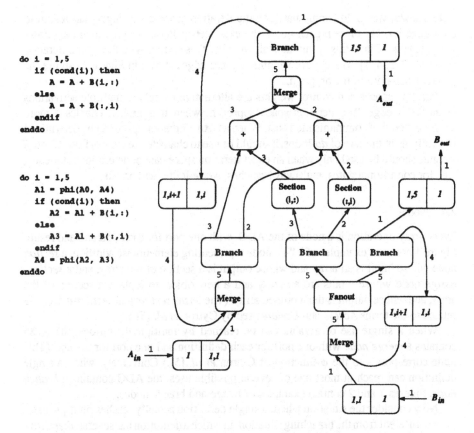

```
do i = 1,5
    if (cond(i)) then
        A = A + B(i,:)
    else
        A = A + B(:,i)
    endif
enddo


do i = 1,5
    A1 = phi(A0, A4)
    if (cond(i)) then
        A2 = A1 + B(i,:)
    else
        A3 = A1 + B(:,i)
    endif
    A4 = phi(A2, A3)
enddo
```

Fig. 2. The ADG for a program with conditional branches. The labels on the edges are their control weights, assuming that the *then* branch of the conditional is taken 60% of the time, and that the *else* branch is taken 40% of the time.

languages allow a wider variety of control flow constructs—*while-* and *repeat*-loops, *if-then-else* constructs, conditional *goto*s, and so on. Iteration spaces can both underestimate and overestimate the effect of such control flow on communication. First, consider a *do*-loop nested within a *repeat*-loop. In this case, the iteration space indicated by the *do*-loop may underestimate the actual number of activations of the edges in the loop body. Second, because of *if-then-else* constructs in a loop, an edge may be activated on only a subset of its iteration space. For this reason, we associate a control weight $c_{xy}(\xi)$ with every edge (x, y) and every iteration ξ in its iteration space. One may think of $c_{xy}(\xi)$ as the expected number of activations of the edge (x, y) on an iteration with LIVs equal to ξ. Control weights enter multiplicatively into our estimate of communication cost.

Consider the *if-then-else* construct in the code of Figure 2. In the ADG, we have introduced two *branch* nodes, since the values A1 and B can flow to one, but not both, of two alternative uses, depending on the outcome of the conditional. If the outcomes were known, we could simply partition the iteration space accordingly, and assign to each edge leaving these branch nodes the exact set of iterations on which data flows over the edge. Since this is impractical, we label these edges with the whole iteration space $\{1, 2, 3, 4, 5\}$. The control weights of these edges shown in Figure 2 capture the dynamic behavior of the program.

Iteration spaces and control weights are alternative models of multiple activations of an ADG edge. The iteration space approach, when it is usable, enables a more accurate model of communication cost. When an exact iteration space can be determined statically, as in the case of *do*-loops, it should be use to characterize control flow. Control weights should be used only when an exact iteration space cannot determined statically, *e.g.*, for conditional *gotos*, multiway branches, *while*-loops, and breaks.

2.4 Nodes

Every array operation is a node of the ADG, with one port for each operand and result. Figure 1 contains examples of a "+" node representing elementwise addition, a *section* node whose input is an array and whose output is a section of the array, and a *section-assign* node whose inputs are an array and a new object to replace a section of the array, and whose output is the modified array. (The terms *section* and *section-assign* are related to the terms *Access* and *Update* used by Cytron *et al.* [5].)

When a single use of a value can be reached by multiple definitions, the ADG contains a *merge node* with one port for each definition and one port for the use. (This node corresponds to the ϕ-function of Cytron *et al.* [5].) Conversely, when a single definition can reach at most one of several possible uses, the ADG contains a *branch node*. Figures 1 and 2 contain examples of merge and branch nodes.

Now consider the situation where a single definition actually reaches multiple uses. This is different from the branching situation, in which a definition has several *alternative* uses. Given alignments for the definition and for all the uses, the optimal way to make the object available at the positions where it is used is through a *Steiner tree* [15] in the metric space of possible alignments, spanning the alignment at the definition, the alignments at the uses, and additional positions as required to minimize the sum of the edge lengths. Determining the best Steiner tree is NP-hard for most metric spaces. We therefore approximate the Steiner tree as a star, adding one additional node, called a *fanout node*, at the center of the star. Figures 1 and 2 contain examples of fanout nodes. There remains the possibility of replacing this star by a true Steiner tree in a later pass.

Finally, for a program with *do*-loops, we need to characterize the introduction, removal, and update of LIVs, as we intend to let data weights and alignments be functions of these LIVs. Accordingly, for every edge that carries data into, out of, or around a loop, we insert a *transformer node* that enforces a relationship between the iteration spaces at its two ports. Figures 1 and 2 contain examples..

ADG nodes define relations among the alignments of their ports, as well as among the data weights, control weights, and iteration spaces of their incident edges. The relations on alignments constrain the solution provided by alignment analysis. They must be satisfied if the computation performed at the nodes is to be done without further realignment. An alignment (of all ports, at all iterations of their iteration spaces) that satisfies the node constraints is said to be *feasible*.

The constraints force all realignment communication onto the edges of the ADG. By suitably choosing the node constraints, the apparently "intrinsic" communication of such operations as transpose and spread is exposed as realignment; this enables optimization of realignment.

Only intrinsic communication and computation happens within the nodes. In our current language model, the only program operations with intrinsic communication are reduction and vector-valued subscripting (scatter and gather), which access values from different parts of an object as part of the computation.

2.5 Nodal relations and constraints

We now list the constraints on alignment (the matrix L and the vector f introduced in Section 2.2) and the relations on iteration spaces and control weights that hold at each type of node. The relations on data weights are a simple consequence of language semantics and are not stated here.

Elementwise operations and fanout nodes An elementwise arithmetic or logical operation on congruent objects A_1 through A_k produces an object R of the same shape and size. Fanout nodes behave the same way. Alignments are identical at all ports:

$$L_{A_1} = \cdots = L_{A_k} = L_R$$

and

$$f_{A_1} = \cdots = f_{A_k} = f_R.$$

Array sectioning Let A be a d-dimensional object, and S a section specifier. Then $A(S)$ is the object corresponding to the section of that object. A section specifier is a d-vector $(\sigma_1, \ldots, \sigma_d)$, where each σ_i is either a scalar ℓ_i or a triplet $\ell_i : h_i : s_i$. Array axes corresponding to positions where the section specifier is a scalar are projected away, while the axes where the specifier is a triplet form the axes of $A(S)$. Let the elements of S that are triplets be in positions $\lambda_1, \ldots, \lambda_c$ in ascending order. Let e_i be a column vector of length d whose only nonzero entry is 1 at position i.

The axis alignment of $A(S)$ is inherited from the dimensions of A that are preserved (not projected away) by the sectioning operation. Strides are multiplied by the sectioning strides. The offset alignment of $A(S)$ is equal to the position of $A(\ell_1, \ldots, \ell_d)$:

$$L_{A(S)} = L_A \cdot [s_{\lambda_1} e_{\lambda_1}, \ldots, s_{\lambda_c} e_{\lambda_c}]$$

and

$$f_{A(S)} = g_A((\ell_1, \ldots, \ell_d)^T) = f_A + L_A(\ell_1, \ldots, \ell_d)^T$$

where $\cdot$ denotes matrix multiplication.

Assignment to array sections An assignment to a section of an array, as in the Fortran 90 statement $A(1:100:2, 1:100:2) = B$, is treated in SSA form as taking an input object A, a section specifier S, and a replacement object B conformable with $A(S)$, and producing a result object R that agrees with B on $A(S)$ and with A elsewhere. The result aligns with A, and the alignment of B must match that of $A(S)$:

$$L_R = L_A, \quad f_R = f_A$$

and

$$L_B = L_{A(S)}, \quad f_B = f_{A(S)}.$$

Transposition Let A be a d-dimensional object, and let ρ be a permutation of $(1, \ldots, d)$. The array object ρA (produced by an ADG *transpose* node) is the array $\rho A(\theta_{\rho_1}, \ldots, \theta_{\rho_d}) = A(\theta_1, \ldots, \theta_d)$. (Fortran 90 uses the $reshape$ and $transpose$ intrinsics to perform general transposition.) The offset of the transposed array is unchanged, but its axes are a permutation of those of A:

$$L_{\rho A} = L_A \cdot [e_{\rho_1}, \ldots, e_{\rho_d}], \quad f_{\rho A} = f_A.$$

Reduction Let A be a d-dimensional object. Then the program operation $sum(A, dim=k)$ produces the $(d-1)$-dimensional object R by reducing along axis k of A. (The operation used for reduction is of no importance in determining alignments.) Let n_k be the extent of A in axis k. Then R is aligned identically with A except that the template axis to which axis k of A was aligned is a space axis of R. The offset of R in this axis may be any of the positions occupied by A.

$$L_R = L_A \cdot [e_1, \ldots, e_{k-1}, e_{k+1}, \ldots, e_d]$$

and

$$f_R = f_A + \beta L_A e_k, \text{ where } 0 \le \beta < n_k.$$

Spread Let A be a d-dimensional object. Then the program operation $spread(A, dim=k, ncopies=n)$ produces a $(d+1)$-dimensional object R with the new axis in position k, and with extent n along that axis. The alignment constraints are the converse of those for the dual operation, reduction. The new axis of R aligns with an unused template axis, and the other axes of R inherit their alignments from A.

$$L_A = L_R \cdot [e_1, \ldots, e_{k-1}, e_{k+1}, \ldots, e_{d+1}].$$

In order to make the communication required to replicate A residual rather than intrinsic, we require the offset alignment of A in dimension k to be replicated. This condition sounds strange, but it correctly assigns the required communication to the input edge of the *spread* node. In this view, a *spread* node performs neither computation nor communication, but transforms a replicated object into a higher-dimensional non-replicated object. Thus,

$$f_A = f_R + f_r$$

where the vector f_r has one nonzero component, a triplet in the axis spanned by the replicated dimension:

$$f_r = (0 : n-1)L_R e_k.$$

The multiplication of a vector by a triplet is defined by $(0 : h)(x_1, \ldots, x_t)^T \equiv ((0 : x_1 h : x_1), \ldots, (0 : x_t h : x_t))$.

Merge nodes Merge nodes occur when multiple definitions of a value converge. This occurs on entry to a loop and as a result of conditional transfers. Merge nodes enforce identical alignment at their ports.

The iteration space of the outedges is the union of the iteration spaces of inedges. The expected number of activations of the outedge with LIVs ξ is just the sum of the expected number of activations with LIVs ξ of the inedges. Therefore, the control weight of the outedge is the sum of the control weights of the inedges. Let the iteration spaces of the inedges be $\mathcal{I}_1$ through $\mathcal{I}_m$, and the corresponding control weights $c_1(\xi)$ through $c_m(\xi)$. Let the iteration space of the outedge be $\mathcal{I}_R$ and its control weight be $c_R(\xi)$. Extend the c_i for each input edge to $\mathcal{I}_r$ by defining $c_i(\xi)$ to be 0 for all $\xi \in \mathcal{I}_r - \mathcal{I}_i$. Then

$$\mathcal{I}_R = \bigcup_{i=1}^{m} \mathcal{I}_i$$

and

$$\forall \xi \in \mathcal{I}_R, \quad c_R(\xi) = \sum_{i=1}^{m} c_i(\xi).$$

Branch nodes Branch nodes occur when multiple mutually exclusive uses of a value diverge. Following the activation of the inedges, one of the outedges activates, with the selection made through program control flow. Branch nodes enforce identical alignment at their ports.

The relations satisfied by iteration spaces and control weights of the incident edges are dual to those of merge nodes. Let the iteration spaces of the outedges be $\mathcal{I}_1$ through $\mathcal{I}_m$, and the corresponding control weights be $c_1(\xi)$ through $c_m(\xi)$. Let the iteration space of the inedge be $\mathcal{I}_A$ and its control weight be $c_A(\xi)$. Then

$$\mathcal{I}_A = \bigcup_{i=1}^{m} \mathcal{I}_i$$

and

$$\forall \xi \in \mathcal{I}_A, \quad c_A(\xi) = \sum_{i=1}^{m} c_i(\xi).$$

Transformer nodes Transformer nodes are of two types: those that relate iterations at the same nesting level, and those that relate iterations at different nesting levels.

Transformer nodes of the first kind (*loop-back* transformer nodes) have the form

$$(1, \xi_1, \ldots, \xi_k | 1, \xi_1, \ldots, \xi_k + s),$$

corresponding to a change by the loop stride s in the value of the LIV ξ_k, and no change in any of the other LIVs in the loop nest. Let $\xi = (1, \xi_1, \ldots, \xi_k)$; define $\widehat{\xi}(\xi) = (1, \xi_1, \ldots, \xi_k + s)$. Let the alignment on the input ("ξ") port be $L\theta + f$, and let the alignment on the output ("$\widehat{\xi}$") port be $\widehat{L}\theta + \widehat{f}$, where L, f, $\widehat{L}$, and $\widehat{f}$ are all functions of ξ. Let $\mathcal{I}$ be the iteration space of the input port and $\widehat{\mathcal{I}}$ be the iteration space of the output port, Then the alignment constraints are

$$\forall \xi \in \mathcal{I}, \quad L(\xi) = \widehat{L}(\widehat{\xi})$$

and
$$\forall \xi \in \mathcal{I}, \ f(\xi) = \widehat{f}(\widehat{\xi}).$$

The relation between the iteration spaces is
$$\widehat{\mathcal{I}} = \mathcal{I} + s(0, e_k)^T.$$

Consider one of the $(1, k|1, k+1)$ transformer nodes in Figure 1. An offset alignment $f = 2k + 3$ and $\widehat{f} = 2k + 1$ satisfies the node's alignment constraints. If the input iteration space is $\mathcal{I} = \{(1, 1)^T, \ldots, (1, n-1)^T\}$, then the output iteration space is $\widehat{\mathcal{I}} = \{(1, 2)^T, \ldots, (1, n)^T\}$.

Transformer nodes of the second kind (*entry/exit* transformer nodes) have the form
$$(1, \xi_1, \ldots, \xi_{k-1}|1, \xi_1, \ldots, \xi_{k-1}, \xi_k = v)$$

or
$$(1, \xi_1, \ldots, \xi_{k-1}, \xi_k = v|1, \xi_1, \ldots, \xi_{k-1}),$$

corresponding to the introduction or removal of the LIV ξ_k in a loop nest. Let $\xi = (1, \xi_1, \ldots, \xi_{k-1})$ and define $\widehat{\xi}(\xi) = (1, \xi_1, \ldots, \xi_{k-1}, v)$. Let the alignment on the input ("ξ") port be $L\theta + f$, and let the alignment on the output ("$\widehat{\xi}$") port be $\widehat{L}\theta + \widehat{f}$. Let $\mathcal{I}$ be the iteration space of the input port and $\widehat{\mathcal{I}}$ be the iteration space of the output port, Then the alignment constraints are
$$\forall \xi \in \mathcal{I}, \ L(\xi) = \widehat{L}(\widehat{\xi})$$

and
$$\forall \xi \in \mathcal{I}, \ f(\xi) = \widehat{f}(\widehat{\xi}).$$

The relation satisfied by the iteration spaces is
$$\widehat{\mathcal{I}} = \mathcal{I} \times \{v\},$$

where $\times$ denotes the Cartesian product. Thus, the $(1|1, 1)$ transformer node in Figure 1 constrains its input position (which does not depend on k) to equal its output position for $k = 1$. An offset alignment of $f = 1$ and $\widehat{f} = 2i - 1$ satisfies the node's constraints.

3 Modeling residual communication cost using the ADG

The ADG describes the structural properties of the program that we need for alignment and distribution analysis. Residual communication occurs on the edges of the ADG, but so far we have not indicated how to estimate this cost. This missing piece is the *distance function d*, where the distance $d(p, q)$ between two alignments p and q is a nonnegative number giving the cost per element to change the alignment of an array from p to q. The set of all alignments is normally a metric space under the distance function d [3]. We discuss the structure of d in Section 4.

We model the communication cost of the program as follows. Let E be the edge set of the ADG G, and let $\mathcal{I}_{xy}$ be the iteration space of edge (x, y). For a vector ξ in $\mathcal{I}_{xy}$, let $w_{xy}(\xi)$ be the data weight, and let $c_{xy}(\xi)$ be the control weight of the edge. Finally, let π be a feasible alignment for the program. Then the realignment cost of edge (x, y) at iteration ξ is $c_{xy}(\xi) \cdot w_{xy}(\xi) \cdot d(\pi_x(\xi), \pi_y(\xi))$, and the total realignment cost of the ADG is

$$K(G, d, \pi) = \sum_{(x,y)\in E} \sum_{\xi \in \mathcal{I}_{xy}} c_{xy}(\xi) \cdot w_{xy}(\xi) \cdot d(\pi_x(\xi), \pi_y(\xi)). \qquad (1)$$

Our goal is to choose π to minimize this cost, subject to the node constraints. An analogous framework can be used to model redistribution cost.

4 Approximations

The definition of the ADG in Section 2 assumed complete knowledge of control flow, and also ignored the effect of the parameters of the model on the complexity of the optimization problem. In this section, we discuss approximations to the model to address questions of practicality. The approximations are of two kinds: those that make it possible to compute the parameters of the model, and those that make the optimization problem tractable.

4.1 Control weights

Our model of control weights as a function of LIVs is formally correct but difficult to evaluate in practice. We therefore approximate the control weight $c_{xy}(\xi)$ as an averaged control weight c'_{xy} that does not depend on ξ. We now relate this averaged control weight to the execution counts of the basic blocks of the program.

Assume that we have a control flow graph (CFG) of the program (whose nodes are basic blocks of the program, and edges are transfers of control) and an estimate of the branching probabilities of the program. (These probabilities can be estimated using heuristics, profile information, or user input.) Let p_{ij} be this estimate for edge (i, j) of the CFG; $p_{ij} = 0$ if (i, j) is not an edge of the CFG. Let there be B basic block nodes in the CFG, plus the two distinguished nodes *ENTER* and *EXIT*. We first determine the execution counts of the basic blocks by setting up and solving "conservation of control flow" equations at each basic block. The conservation equation for basic block i with execution count u_i is $u_i = \sum_{j\neq i} p_{ji} u_j$. In matrix notation, we solve the linear system $Au = v$, where $u = [u_1, \cdots, u_B]^T$ is the vector of execution counts, $v = [p_{ENTER,1}, \cdots, p_{ENTER,B}]^T$, and A is a $B \times B$ matrix with $A(i, i) = 1$ and $A(i, j) = -p_{ji}$ for $i \neq j$. The (averaged) control weight c'_{xy} of the ADG edge (x, y) coming from a computation in basic block b is then $u_b / |\mathcal{I}_{xy}|$.

4.2 Mobile alignment

So far we have not constrained the form that mobile alignments may take. In principle, they could be arbitrary functions of the LIVs. To keep the analysis tractable, we restrict mobile alignments to be affine functions of the LIVs. Thus, the alignment function for an object within a k-deep loop nest with LIVs $\xi_1, \ldots, \xi_k$ is of the form $a_0 + a_1\xi_1 + \cdots + a_k\xi_k$, where the coefficient vector $a = (a_0, \ldots, a_k)$ is what we must determine. We write this alignment succinctly in vector notation as $a\xi^T$. Both a and ξ are $(k+1)$-vectors. This reduces to the constant term a_0 for an object outside any loops.

Likewise, we restrict the extents of objects to be affine in the LIVs, so that the size of an object is polynomial in the LIVs.

4.3 Replicated alignments

In Section 2, we introduced triplet offset positions to represent the possibility of replication. In practice, we treat the replication component of offset separately from the scalar component. The alignment space for replication has two elements, called $\mathbf{R}$ (for replicated) and $\mathbf{N}$ (for non-replicated). The extent of replication for an $\mathbf{R}$ alignment is the entire template extent in that dimension. In this approximate model of replication, communication is required only when changing from a non-replicated alignment to a replicated one. Thus, the distance function is given by $d(\mathbf{N}, \mathbf{R}) = 1$ and $d(\mathbf{R}, \mathbf{R}) = d(\mathbf{R}, \mathbf{N}) = d(\mathbf{N}, \mathbf{N}) = 0$. We call the process of determining these restricted replicated alignments *replication labeling*.

4.4 Distance functions

In introducing the distance function in Section 3, we defined it to be the cost per element of changing from one alignment to another. Now consider the various kinds of such changes, and their communication costs on a distributed-memory machine. A change in axis or stride alignment requires unstructured communication. Such communication is hard to model accurately as it depends critically on the topological properties of the network (bisection bandwidth), the interactions among the messages (congestion), and the software overheads. Offset realignment can be performed using shift communication, which is usually substantially cheaper than unstructured communication. Replicating an object involves broadcasting or multicasting, which typically uses some kind of spanning tree. Such broadcast communication is likely to cost more than shift communication but less than unstructured communication.

We could conceivably construct a single distance function capturing all these various effects and their interactions, but this would almost certainly make the analysis intractable. We therefore split the determination of alignments into several phases based on the relative costs of the different kinds of communication, and introduce simpler distance functions for each of these phases.

We determine axis and stride alignments (or the matrix L of Section 2.2) in one phase, using the *discrete metric* to model axis and stride realignment. This metric, in which $d(p, q) = 0$ if $p = q$ and $d(p, q) = 1$ otherwise, is a crude but reasonable approximation for unstructured communication.

We determine scalar offset alignment in a separate phase, using the *grid metric* to model shift realignment. In this metric, alignments are the vectors f of Section 2.2, and $d(f, f')$ is the Manhattan distance between them, i.e., $d(f, f') = \sum_{i=1}^{t} |f_i - f_i'|$. Note that the distance between f and f' is the sum of the distances between their individual components. This property of the metric, called *separability*, allows us to solve the offset alignment problem independently for each axis [3].

Finally, we use yet another phase to determine replicated offsets, using the alignments and distance function described in Section 4.3.

The ordering of these phases is as follows: we first perform axis and stride alignment, then replication labeling, and finally offset alignment.

The various kinds of communication interact with one another. For instance, shifting an object in addition to changing its axis or stride alignment does not increase the communication cost, since the shift can be incorporated into the unstructured communication needed for the change of axis or stride. We model such effects in a simple manner, by introducing a *presence weight* of an edge for each phase of the alignment process. The presence weight multiplies the contribution of the edge to the total realignment cost for that phase. Initially, all presence weights are 1. Edges that end up carrying residual axis or stride realignment have their presence weights set to zero for the replication and offset alignment phases. Similarly, edges carrying replication communication have their presence weights set to zero for the offset alignment phase.

5 Determining alignments using the ADG

In this section, we briefly describe our algorithms for determining alignment. Full descriptions of these algorithms are in our previous papers [2, 3, 4].

5.1 Axis and stride alignment

To determine axis and stride alignment, we minimize the communication cost $K(G, d, \pi)$ using the discrete metric as the distance function. The position of a port in this context is the matrix L of the alignment function. The algorithm we use, called *compact dynamic programming* [3], works in two phases.

In the first phase, we traverse the ADG from sources to sinks, building for each port a cost table indexed by position. The cost corresponding to position p gives the minimum cost of evaluating the subcomputation up to that port and placing the result in position p. The cost table at a node can be computed from the cost tables of its inputs and the distance functions. This recurrence is used to build the cost tables efficiently. At the end of the first phase, we examine the cost tables of the sinks of the ADG and place the sinks at their minimum-cost positions. In the second phase, we traverse the ADG from sinks to sources, placing the ports so as to achieve the minimum costs calculated in the first phase.

Compact dynamic programming is based on the dynamic programming approach of Mace [12]. The "compact" in the name refers to the way we exploit properties of the distance function to simplify the computation of costs and to compactly represent the cost tables. The method is exact if the ADG is a tree, but in general it is an approximation.

5.2 Offset alignment

For offset alignment, a position is the vector f of the alignment function, and the Manhattan metric is the distance function. As the distance function is separable, we can solve independently for each component of the vector. For code where the positions do not depend on any LIVs, the constrained minimization can be solved exactly using linear programming [2, 4]. With mobile alignments, the residual communication cost can be approximated and this approximate cost minimized exactly using linear programming.

5.3 Replication labeling

For replication labeling, the position space has two positions for each template axis, called R (for replicated) and N (for non-replicated). The distance function is as given in Section 4.3. Note that this distance function is not a metric. The sources of replication are *spread* operations, certain vector-valued subscripts, and read-only objects with mobile offset alignment. As in the offset alignment case, each axis can be treated independently.

A minimum-cost replication labeling can be computed efficiently using network flow [2].

6 Comparison with other work

In this section, we compare the ADG representation with SSA form and with the *preference graph*, another representation that has been used for automatic determination of alignments.

6.1 SSA form

While our ADG representation is based on SSA form, it has a number of extra features. All of the differences stem from the fact that the ADG representation was designed to manipulate positions of objects, while SSA form was designed to manipulate values. In fact, an SSA form based on a nonstandard "position semantics" would probably look exactly like the ADG formalism.

The ADG representation annotates the ports and edges with data weights, control weights, and iteration spaces, none of which are present in SSA form. However, the substantive difference between the two representations lies in the nodes. Every ϕ-function of SSA corresponds to a merge node in ADG, but certain merge nodes (*e.g.*, for read-only objects within a loop) do not correspond to any ϕ-functions in SSA. Similarly, fanout and branch nodes have no analog in SSA form.

The fanout and branch nodes of the ADG resemble similar nodes in the Program Dependence Web representation developed by Ballance *et al.* [1]. However, the motivations behind them are very different.

6.2 The preference graph

Another representation that has been used in alignment analysis is the *preference graph*, which has several variants [7, 10, 11, 14]. The preference graph is an undirected, weighted graph constructed from the reference patterns in the program. The nodes of the preference graph correspond to dimensions of array occurrences in the program, the edges reflect beneficial alignment relations, and the weights reflect the relative importance of the edges. The edges of the preference graph encode axis alignment, while additional node attributes are used to encode stride and offset alignment.

The preference graph has two kinds of edges, corresponding to the two sources of alignment decisions. Each statement considered in isolation provides some relations among nodes that avoid residual communication in computing the given statement. The edges corresponding to these relations are called *conformance preference edges*. A conformance preference edge between two array occurrences indicates that if they are not aligned, residual communication will be needed to align them in preparation for the operation.

The second kind of alignment preference comes from relating definitions and uses of the same array variable. The edges corresponding to these relations are called *identity preference edges*. An identity preference edge between two array occurrences indicates that if they are not positioned identically, residual communication will be needed to make the values from the definition available at the use.

Alignment decisions are made by contracting graph edges. At each step, an edge is chosen, and if the two nodes connected by the edge satisfy certain conditions, the edge is contracted and one of the nodes is merged into the other. When an edge is contracted, we say that the alignment preference it carries has been *honored*. The contraction process stops when no more edges can be contracted. An acyclic preference graph can be contracted to a single node, guaranteeing a communication-free implementation. If, however, there are cycles in the preference graph, some alignment preferences may remain unhonored and will result in residual communication. In this case, we must decide which preferences to honor and which to break. There are two principal variants of this general framework.

The Knobe-Lukas-Steele algorithm Knobe, Lukas, and Steele [10] call the nodes of the preference graph *cells*. They introduce an additional attribute of cells (called *independence anti-preference*) to model the constraint that a dimension occurrence has sufficient parallelism and should not be serialized.

An alignment conflict can only occur within a cycle of the preference graph. We therefore need to locate a cycle, determine whether it causes a conflict, and resolve the conflict if it exists. Actually, we only need to examine and resolve conflicts in a set of fundamental cycles of the preference graph, since if such a cycle basis is conflict-free, then all cycles in the graph are conflict-free. A cycle basis can be easily determined from a spanning tree of the graph: each non-tree edge determines a unique fundamental cycle of the graph with respect to the spanning tree. This ignores the fact that the preference graph is weighted. Given a choice between honoring two preferences, we would choose to honor the preference with higher weight. The Knobe-Lukas-Steele algorithm uses the nesting depth of an edge as its weight and constructs a maximum-weight spanning tree.

An unhonored identity preference implies that an object will live in distinct location in different parts of the program. An unhonored conformance preference implies that not all of the operations in a statement are necessarily performed in the location of the "owner" of the LHS. In other words, breaking a conformance preference is the mechanism for improving the "owner-computes rule".

The Li-Chen algorithm Li and Chen [11] use the preference graph model to determine axis alignment. Their algorithm was developed in the context of the Crystal language, which allows more general reference patterns than we have considered, for instance, a pattern like $A(i, j) = B(i, i)$. This indicates conformance preferences between the first axis of A and both axes of B; such sets of preferences that are generated from the same reference pattern and are incident upon a common node are said to be *competing*.

Li and Chen call the preference graph the *Component Affinity Graph* (CAG), and call preferences *affinities*. Competing edges have weight ϵ, while noncompeting edges are unit-weight. The quantities ϵ and 1 are incommensurate, with $\epsilon \ll 1$. The axis alignment problem is framed as the following graph partitioning problem:

> Partition the node set of the CAG into n disjoint subsets $V_1, \ldots, V_n$ (where n is the maximum dimensionality of any array) with the restriction that no two axes of the same array may be in the same partition, so as to minimize the sum of the weights of edges connecting nodes in different subsets of the partition.

The idea here is to align array dimensions in the same subset of the partition, with edges between nodes in different partitions corresponding to residual communication. Hence the condition that we minimize the sum of the weights of such edges.

The graph partitioning problem stated above is NP-complete [11]. Li and Chen therefore solve it heuristically by finding maximum-weight matchings of a sequence of bipartite subgraphs of the CAG.

Discussion We now compare the ADG approach with the preference graph approach with regard to semantics, cost modeling, and the treatment of control flow.

- The conformance preferences, while similar to the node constraints of our approach, are not clearly related to the data flow and the intermediate results of the computation. Intermediate results have no explicit representation in the conformance graph model. They could, however, be made explicit by preprocessing the source.
- The preference graph model distinguishes between objects at different levels of a loop nest, but does not consider the size of an object, or the shift distance, in computing the cost of moving it. In fact, it can be thought of as using the unweighted discrete metric to model all communication cost.
- Knobe *et al.* [10] discuss handling control flow by introducing alignments for arrays at merge points in the program. Our use of static single assignment form provides a sound theoretical basis regarding the placement of merge nodes.
- To the best of our knowledge, the preference graph method has not been used to determine when objects should be replicated.

7 Conclusions

We have motivated and described a representation of data-parallel programs called the alignment-distribution graph, which provides a mechanism for explicitly representing and optimizing residual communication cost. The representation is based on a separation of variables and values, extended from the static single assignment form of programs.

The communication requirements of the program are faithfully modeled by carefully representing realignment communication due to control flow, loop-carried dependences, assignment to sections of arrays, and transformational array operations.

The ADG provides a more detailed model of residual communication than the preference graph, another representation that has been used for the same analysis. We have developed algorithms in the ADG framework to determine axis alignment, mobile stride and offset alignment, and replication. We have devised a scheme for generating the ADG from program text, which we are presently refining and implementing. We are also implementing the algorithms mentioned in Section 5 to test the validity of this approach.

We are currently studying several interesting problems that remain unsolved. These include developing algorithms for distribution analysis using the ADG framework, understanding the interactions between the alignment and distribution phases, developing interprocedural optimization techniques in this framework, finding better algorithms for solving the alignment problem in the discrete metric, and allowing for the possibility of skew alignments.

References

1. R. A. Ballance, A. B. Maccabe, and K. J. Ottenstein. The Program Dependence Web: A representation supporting control-, data-, and demand-driven interpretation of imperative languages. In *Proceedings of the ACM SIGPLAN'90 Conference on Programming Language Design and Implementation*, pages 257–271, White Plains, NY, June 1990.

2. S. Chatterjee, J. R. Gilbert, and R. Schreiber. Mobile and replicated alignment of arrays in data-parallel programs. In *Proceedings of Supercomputing'93*, Portland, OR, Nov. 1993. To appear.

3. S. Chatterjee, J. R. Gilbert, R. Schreiber, and S.-H. Teng. Optimal evaluation of array expressions on massively parallel machines. In *Proceedings of the Second Workshop on Languages, Compilers, and Runtime Environments for Distributed Memory Multiprocessors*, Boulder, CO, Oct. 1992. Published in SIGPLAN Notices, 28(1), January 1993, pages 68–71. An expanded version is available as RIACS Technical Report TR 92.17 and Xerox PARC Technical Report CSL-92-11.

4. S. Chatterjee, J. R. Gilbert, R. Schreiber, and S.-H. Teng. Automatic array alignment in data-parallel programs. In *Proceedings of the Twentieth Annual ACM SIGACT/SIGPLAN Symposium on Principles of Programming Languages*, pages 16–28, Charleston, SC, Jan. 1993. Also available as RIACS Technical Report 92.18 and Xerox PARC Technical Report CSL-92-13.

5. R. Cytron, J. Ferrante, B. K. Rosen, M. N. Wegman, and F. K. Zadeck. Efficiently computing static single assignment form and the control dependence graph. *ACM Trans. Prog. Lang. Syst.*, 13(4):451–490, Oct. 1991.

6. G. C. Fox, S. Hiranandani, K. Kennedy, C. Koelbel, U. Kremer, C.-W. Tseng, and M.-Y. Wu. Fortran D language specification. Technical Report Rice COMP TR90-141, Department of Computer Science, Rice University, Houston, TX, Dec. 1990.

7. M. Gupta. *Automatic Data Partitioning on Distributed Memory Multicomputers*. PhD thesis, University of Illinois at Urbana-Champaign, Urbana, IL, Sept. 1992. Available as technical reports UILU-ENG-92-2237 and CRHC-92-19.

8. High Performance Fortran Forum. High Performance Fortran language specification version 1.0. Draft, Jan. 1993. Also available as technical report CRPC-TR 92225, Center for Research on Parallel Computation, Rice University.

9. R. Johnson and K. Pingali. Dependence-based program analysis. In *Proceedings of the ACM SIGPLAN'93 Conference on Programming Language Design and Implementation*, pages 78–89, Albuquerque, NM, June 1993.

10. K. Knobe, J. D. Lukas, and G. L. Steele Jr. Data optimization: Allocation of arrays to reduce communication on SIMD machines. *Journal of Parallel and Distributed Computing*, 8(2):102–118, Feb. 1990.

11. J. Li and M. Chen. The data alignment phase in compiling programs for distributed-memory machines. *Journal of Parallel and Distributed Computing*, 13(2):213–221, Oct. 1991.

12. M. E. Mace. *Memory Storage Patterns in Parallel Processing*. Kluwer international series in engineering and computer science. Kluwer Academic Press, Norwell, MA, 1987.

13. Thinking Machines Corporation, Cambridge, MA. *CM Fortran Reference Manual Versions 1.0 and 1.1*, July 1991.

14. S. Wholey. *Automatic Data Mapping for Distributed-Memory Parallel Computers*. PhD thesis, School of Computer Science, Carnegie Mellon University, Pittsburgh, PA, May 1991. Available as Technical Report CMU-CS-91-121.

15. P. Winter. Steiner problem in networks: A survey. *Networks*, 17:129–167, 1987.

An Overview of a Compiler for Scalable Parallel Machines

Saman P. Amarasinghe, Jennifer M. Anderson,
Monica S. Lam and Amy W. Lim

Computer Systems Laboratory
Stanford University, CA 94305

Abstract. This paper presents an overview of a parallelizing compiler to automatically generate efficient code for large-scale parallel architectures from sequential input programs. This research focuses on loop-level parallelism in dense matrix computations. We illustrate the basic techniques the compiler uses by describing the entire compilation process for a simple example.

Our compiler is organized into three major phases: analyzing array references, allocating the computation and data to the processors to optimize parallelism and locality, and generating code.

An optimizing compiler for scalable parallel machines requires more sophisticated program analysis than the traditional data dependence analysis. Our compiler uses a precise data-flow analysis technique to identify the producer of the value read by each instance of a read access. In order to allocate the computation and data to the processors, the compiler first transforms the program to expose loop-level parallelism in the computation. It then finds a decomposition of the computation and data such that parallelism is exploited and the communication overhead is minimized. The compiler will trade off extra degrees of parallelism to reduce or eliminate communication. Finally, the compiler generates code to manage the multiple address spaces and to communicate data across processors.

1 Introduction

A number of compiler systems, such as SUPERB[21], AL[17], ID Noveau[15], Kali[11], Vienna FORTRAN[3], FORTRAN D[8, 16] and HPF[7], have been developed to make effective use of scalable parallel machines. These systems simplify the compilation problem by soliciting the programmer's help in determining the data decompositions. The goal of our research is to fully automate the parallelization process. We are currently developing a compiler to automatically translate sequential scientific programs into efficient parallel code.

This research was supported in part by DARPA contracts N00039-91-C-0138 and DABT63-91-K-0003, an NSF Young Investigator Award and fellowships from Digital Equipment Corporation's Western Research Laboratory and Intel Corporation.

Our compilation techniques are applicable to all machines with non-uniform memory access times. Our target machines include both distributed address space machines such as the Intel iPSC/860[9], and shared address space machines such as the Stanford DASH multiprocessor[12]. Our research focuses on dense matrix computations written in sequential FORTRAN-77, though many of the techniques presented are also applicable to optimizations within and especially across FORTRAN-90 statements.

Our techniques are applicable to programs with arbitrary nestings of parallel and sequential loops. The loop bounds and array subscripts must be affine functions of the loop indices and symbolic constants. Our techniques can also handle conditional statements, although less precise analysis techniques must be used in these cases. We characterize parallel machines by their message passing overhead, message latency and communication bandwidth; machine topology is not considered significant. Currently, our compiler operates on each procedure individually, and cannot handle function calls.

We have decomposed the complex problem of compiling for large-scale parallel machines into several well-defined subproblems: extracting precise array data-flow information from the program, mapping the data and computation onto the processors and generating efficient code. Algorithms to solve these subproblems have been developed and implemented in our SUIF (Stanford University Intermediate Format) compiler. This paper presents an overview of our parallelizing compiler, concentrating on how the various components fit together. We explain the steps taken in the compiler by showing how they operate on a simple example. We assume that readers are familiar with the literature on parallelizing compilers. Details and related work on individual algorithms can be found in our other papers[1, 2, 14, 18, 19].

An optimizing compiler for scalable parallel machines needs more sophisticated program analysis than the traditional data dependence analysis. Exact array data-flow analysis determines if two dynamic instances of an array access refer to the same *value*, and not just to the same *location*. This information is useful for array privatization, an important optimization for increasing parallelism. It is also important for generating efficient code for distributed address space machines.

Reducing the frequency of synchronization is critical to minimizing communication overhead. Our first step in the parallelization process is to expose the maximum degree of coarse-grain parallelism in the code. Loop transforms such as unimodular transforms (combinations of loop interchange, skewing and reversal), loop tiling and array privatization are used to achieve this goal.

The decomposition phase maps the data and computation onto the processors of the machine. We observe that the choice of parallelism can affect the communication cost. In addition to aligning the data and computation to minimize communication, our algorithm will also choose to trade off excess parallelism if necessary.

Our parallelization and decomposition algorithms treat the code within the innermost loop as an atomic unit. It is possible to improve the parallelization by expanding our scope to include optimizations that can alter the composition of these atomic units. Such transformations include loop reindexing, fission and fusion.

The final phase of the compiler generates an SPMD (single program multiple data) program from the decompositions produced in the previous phase. For distributed address space machines, this phase needs to generate the necessary receive and send instructions, allocate memory locally on each processor and translate global data addresses to local addresses. Using exact data-flow information, our compiler is capable of more aggressive communication optimizations than compilers that rely on data dependence analysis. Our code generation algorithms can also be used to enhance the memory system performance of machines with a shared address space.

2 Array Data-Flow Analysis

Previous research on parallelizing compilers is based primarily on data dependence analysis. The domain of data dependence analysis is that the array index function and the loop bounds must be integer affine functions of loop indices and possibly other symbolic constants. The traditional formulation of the data dependence problem can best be described as memory disambiguation. That is, data dependence checks if *any* of the dynamic instances of two array accesses in a loop nest refers to the same *location*. Consider the following example:

for $i := 0$ **to** N **do**
  for $j := 3$ **to** N **do**
    $X[j] := X[j-3]$;

Data dependence analysis of this program will produce the dependence vectors $\{[+,3],[0,3]\}$, meaning that the read access in iteration $[i_r,j_r]$ may be data dependent on all iterations $[i_w,j_w]$ such that $j_w = j_r - 3$ and $i_w \leq i_r$. There are two sources of inaccuracy in this result. First, data dependence does not contain *coverage* information. For this example, the fact that the data *value* used by the read is produced in the same i iteration $(i_w = i_r)$ cannot be found using data dependence analysis. Second, data dependence information lacks the *identity* of the dependence. That is, the fact that the first three iterations of i use data defined outside the loop nest is not captured by the data dependence analysis. Unlike data dependence analysis, exact array data-flow analysis determines if two dynamic instances refer to the same value, and not just to the same location. This information is found for every dynamic read-write access pair. Thus, exact data-flow analysis does not have the inaccuracies of the traditional data dependence analysis.

The problem of finding exact array data-flow information was first formulated by Feautrier[4, 5, 6]. Feautrier proposed a parametric integer programming algorithm that can find such exact information in the domain of loop nests where the loop bounds and array indices are affine functions of loop indices. We have developed an algorithm that can find the same exact information for many common cases more efficiently. The data-flow information generated by our array data-flow analysis is captured by a representation called a *Last Write Tree* (LWT)[13, 14]. The LWT is a function that maps an instance of a read operation to the very write instance that produces the value read, provided such a write exists. We denote a read and a write instance by the values of their loop indices, i_r and i_w, respectively. The domain of the LWT function is the set of read iterations i_r that satisfy the constraints imposed by the loop bounds. Each internal node in the tree contains a further constraint on the value of the read instance i_r. It partitions the domain of read instances into those satisfying the constraint, represented by its right descendants, and those not satisfying the constraint, represented by its left descendants. We define the *context* of a node to be the set of read iterations that satisfy the constraints of a node's ancestors. The tree is constructed such that either all the values read within the context of a leaf are written within the loop, or none of them are. In the former case, the leaf node defines a *last-write relation* that relates each read instance i_r within the context to the write instance i_w that produces the value read. All the read-write pairs share the same dependence levels. If the instances within a context do not read any value written within the loop, we denote the lack of a writer by $\perp$.

As another example, consider the code for a single stage of an Alternating Direction Implicit (ADI) integration shown in Figure 1.

(1) **for** $i_1 := 1$ **to** N **do**
    for $i_2 := 0$ **to** N **do**
        $X[i_1,i_2] := f_1(X[i_1,i_2], X[i_1 - 1,i_2], Y[i_1,i_2])$;

(2) **for** $i_1 := 0$ **to** N **do**
    for $i_2 := 1$ **to** N **do**
        $X[i_1,i_2] := f_2(X[i_1,i_2], X[i_1,i_2 - 1], Y[i_1,i_2])$;

Fig. 1. ADI integration code.

We will use this code as a example throughout the paper. Loop nest 1 sweeps along the first dimension of the array X and loop nest 2 sweeps along the second dimension. This kernel is representative of the computation used in the heat conduction phase of the benchmark SIMPLE from Lawrence Livermore National Laboratory. The LWT information for the read access $X[i_1 - 1, i_2]$ with respect to the write access $X[i_1, i_2]$ of loop nest 1 of the example is given in Figure 2. Let (i_{1r}, i_{2r}) be the loop index values of an instance of a read access. The root node represents the domain of the read iterations. The single internal node divides the read iterations into two sections. If $i_{1r} \geq 2$ then the read iterations use a value produced by the instance (i_{1w}, i_{2w}) of the write access, where $i_{1w} = i_{1r} - 1$ and

$i_{2w} = i_{2r}$. This is represented by the right leaf. If $i_{1r} < 2$ then the value read is defined outside the loop nest and is denoted by $\perp$ in the left leaf.

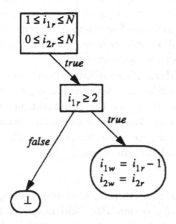

Fig. 2. The Last Write Tree for the read access $X[i_1 - 1, i_2]$ with respect to the write access $X[i_1, i_2]$ in loop nest 1.

We have developed an array privatization algorithm based on the LWT analysis[14]. The algorithm first parallelizes the loops by considering only the *data-flow* dependence constraints. If the parallelized loop carries any anti or output dependences, privatization is necessary. On machines with a shared address space, the compiler needs to create a private copy of the data for every processor. The private copies may need to be initialized and the final results may need to be written back to the original array. On machines with a distributed address space, where every processor must keep a local copy of the data accessed, privatized arrays are treated no differently from any other data. The compiler will not generate any communication unless there is a data-flow dependence.

In addition to enabling optimizations such as array privatization, LWTs are also useful for generating efficient code for distributed address space machines, as discussed in Section 4.

3 Data and Computation Decompositions

This section describes our compiler algorithm to find data and computation decompositions that maximize parallelism and minimize communication. First a local, loop-level analysis phase transforms the code to expose the maximum degree of parallelism. Then a global analysis determines the best mapping of data and computation across the processors of the machine.

3.1 Loop Transformations for Maximizing Parallelism

The compiler first transforms the code to expose the maximum degree of loop-level parallelism, while minimizing the frequency of communication. It tries to generate the coarsest granularity of parallelism by placing the largest degree of parallelism in the outermost positions of the loop nest. Since no communication is needed between iterations of a parallel loop, pushing the parallel iterations outermost reduces the frequency of communication.

The scope of our loop transformations is interchange, skewing, reversal and tiling. All but the tiling transformations are unified as unimodular matrix transforms on the iteration space representing the computation. The problem thus reduces to finding the best combination of a unimodular matrix transform and tiling that yields the maximum degree of coarse-grain parallelism, while satisfying the data flow or data dependence constraints.

Choices of Parallelism. Our algorithm for maximizing loop-level parallelism is based on the concept of *fully permutable* loop nests. A loop nest is fully permutable if any arbitrary permutation of the loops within the nest is legal[10, 19]. Fully permutable loop nests can be easily transformed to contain coarse-grain parallelism. In particular, every fully permutable loop nest of depth k has at least $k - 1$ degrees of parallelism. In the degenerate case where the loop nest has no loop-carried dependences, it has k degrees of parallelism.

A loop nest with only distance vectors has the property that it can always be transformed into a fully permutable loop nest. Loop nests with direction vectors, however, cannot always be converted into a single fully permutable loop nest. The compiler uses unimodular transformations to transform the code into the canonical format of a nest of fully permutable subnets, such that each subnet is made as large as possible starting with the outermost loops. Within each subnet, loops that are already *doall* loops in the source program are placed in the outermost positions. A *doall* loop has no loop-carried dependences and can thus execute in parallel with no communication. The maximum degree of (outermost) parallelism for the entire loop nest is simply the sum of the degree of parallelism contained in each of the fully permutable subnets.

For the example from Figure 1, the compiler interchanges the loops in the first loop nest to produce the code shown in Figure 3. The outer loops are *doall* loops, and both loop nests are fully permutable. The resulting dependence vectors are shown to the right of each loop nest.

The parallelism in a fully permutable loop nest can be exploited in many ways. Consider the first loop nest in the ADI example. Since the *doall* (outer) loop accesses columns of arrays X and Y, iterations of the *doall* loop can run in parallel with no communication if columns of the array are distributed across the processors. The original 2-D iteration space is shown in Figure 4(a) and Figure 4(b) shows the 1-D parallel execution of the *doall* loop.

When iterations of a loop with loop-carried dependences are allocated to different processors, explicit synchronization and communication are required

(1) **for** $i_2 := 0$ **to** N **do**   /* doall */
    for $i_1 := 1$ **to** N **do**
        $X[i_1,i_2] := f_1(X[i_1,i_2], X[i_1 - 1,i_2],Y[i_1,i_2]);$ Dependences $= \{(0,1)\}$

(2) **for** $i_1 := 0$ **to** N **do**   /* doall */
    for $i_2 := 1$ **to** N **do**
        $X[i_1,i_2] := f_2(X[i_1,i_2], X[i_1,i_2 - 1],Y[i_1,i_2]);$ Dependences $= \{(0,1)\}$

Fig. 3. ADI integration code, after parallelization.

within the computation of the loop. Opportunities for *doacross* parallelism occur when a fully permutable loop nest contains at least two loops. *Doacross* parallelism is also available in the first loop nest of the ADI code. The loop with the loop-carried dependence (the inner loop) accesses rows of the arrays. For example, if each processor calculates an iteration of this loop, and rows of the arrays are distributed across the processors, then point-to-point communication is required between neighboring processors. Figure 4(c) shows the 1-D parallel execution of the loop nest using *doacross* parallelism.

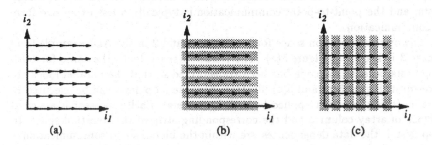

Fig. 4. (a) Original iteration space. (b)-(c) Iteration spaces showing parallel execution of the first loop nest in the ADI example. The arrows represent data dependences, and the iterations in each shaded region are assigned to the same processor.

In Figure 4(b) we allocated iterations along the direction $(1,0)$ to each processor, whereas in Figure 4(c) we allocated iterations along the direction $(0,1)$. In fact, it is possible to exploit parallelism by allocating to each processor iterations along any direction within these two axes.

It is possible to reduce the communication volume and frequency by tiling (also known as blocking, unroll-and-jam and stripmine-and-interchange)[18, 20]. In general, tiling transforms a loop nest of depth k into a loop nest of depth $2k$. The inner k loops iterate over a fixed number of iterations, while the outer loops iterate across the inner blocks of iterations. By tiling and then parallelizing only the outer loops, the synchronization frequency and communication volume are reduced by the size of the block. A fully permutable loop nest has the property that it can be completely tiled. Since the compiler first transforms the loop nests into the canonical form of nests of fully permutable subnets, the tiling transformation is easily applied.

Global Considerations. If we look at each loop nest individually, then distributing the iterations in the direction of the *doall* loops is preferable, as no communication is necessary. However, this is not always the case when we analyze multiple loop nests together. In the ADI example, consider what happens if we only try to exploit the parallelism in the *doall* loops. The *doall* loop in the first loop nest accesses columns of arrays X and Y, whereas iterations of the *doall* loop in the second loop nest accesses rows of the arrays. Communication will occur between the loop nests because the data must be completely reorganized as the data distribution switches between rows and columns.

We can avoid redistributing the arrays between the first and second loop nest by using *doacross* parallelism in one of the loop nests. For example, in the second loop nest the loop with the loop-carried dependence (the inner loop), accesses columns of the array. If iterations of this loop are distributed across the processors, then point-to-point communication is required between neighboring processors. However, no data reorganization is needed between the two loop nests, and the point-to-point communication is typically a less expensive form of communication.

The original iteration space for loop nests 1 and 2 in the ADI example from Figure 3 is shown in Figure 5(a). The iteration space looks the same for both loop nests because the code has been transformed so that the parallel loops are outermost. Figure 5(b) and 5(c) illustrate how the loop nests can be executed in parallel (tiling has been applied to both loop nests). Each processor is assigned a block of array columns and the corresponding strip of the iteration space. In loop nest 1, the data dependences are within the blocks so no communication is necessary. In loop nest 2, there are dependences across the blocks and explicit synchronization is used to enforce the dependences between the blocks.

As this example illustrates, only exploiting the parallelism in the *doall* loops may not result in the best overall performance. In general, there may be tradeoffs between the best loop-level decompositions, and the best global decompositions. Thus the loop-level analysis in our compiler transforms the code to expose the maximum degree of parallelism, but does not make decisions as to how that parallelism is to be implemented. The loop-level analysis leaves the code in a canonical format of fully permutable loop nests, from which the coarsest degree of parallelism can be easily derived.

3.2 Maximizing Locality

Effective utilization of a machine's memory hierarchy is important for achieving high performance. Since interprocessor communication is the most expensive

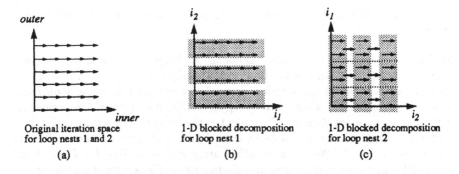

Fig. 5. (a) Original iteration space. (b)-(c) Iteration spaces showing the parallel execution of tiled loops for the ADI example. The arrows represent data dependences.

form of data movement in the memory hierarchy of a multiprocessor, minimizing such communication is therefore the most critical locality optimization. This is achieved by transforming the code to maximize the coarsest granularity of parallelism. The next step is to optimize for the memory hierarchies in a single processor, such as caches and registers. We have developed a data locality optimizing algorithm within our unified loop transformation framework[18]. We apply this uniprocessor algorithm to the subset consisting of the distributed parallel loops and their inner loops. The original loop structure differs from this subset by having additional sequential loops outside the parallel loops. Since these sequential loops must be placed outermost due to legality reasons, the uniprocessor data locality is not compromised by parallelization.

3.3 Finding Decompositions

We model decompositions as having two components. The computation and data are first mapped onto a virtual processor space using affine functions. The virtual processor space has as many processors as is needed to fit the number of loop iterations and the sizes of the arrays. Next a folding function is used to map the virtual processor space onto the physical processors of the target machine. The physical processor mapping takes load-balance considerations into account, and reduces the communication cost by placing blocks of communicating virtual processors onto the same physical processor. This two-step model is able to capture a wide range of computation and data assignments. For example, our model represents a superset of the decompositions available to HPF[7] programmers.

Virtual Processor Mapping. The objective of the virtual processor mapping phase is to minimize communication while maintaining sufficient parallelism. This phase eliminates communication in two ways. First, it explicitly chooses which loops to distribute across the processors – it will consider trading off excess parallelism to reduce or eliminate communication. Also, for a given degree of parallelism, it aligns the arrays and loop iterations to reduce nonlocal data accesses.

Modeling Decompositions. In this discussion, all loops are normalized to have a unit step size, and all arrays subscripts are adjusted to start at 0. A loop nest of depth l defines an iteration space $\mathcal{I}$. Each iteration of the loop nest is identified by its index vector $\mathbf{i} = (i_1, i_2, \ldots, i_l)$. An array of dimension m defines an array space $\mathcal{A}$, and each element in the array is accessed by an integer vector $\mathbf{a} = (a_1, a_2, \ldots, a_m)$. Similarly, an n-dimensional processor array defines a processor space $\mathcal{P}$. We write an affine array index function $\mathbf{f} : \mathcal{I} \to \mathcal{A}$ as $\mathbf{f}(\mathbf{i}) = F\mathbf{i} + \mathbf{k}$, where F is a linear transformation and $\mathbf{k}$ is a constant vector.

Definition 1. For each index $\mathbf{a}$ of an m-dimensional array, the *data decomposition* of the array onto an n-dimensional processor array is a function $\delta(\mathbf{a}) : \mathcal{A} \to \mathcal{P}$, where

$$\delta(\mathbf{a}) = D\mathbf{a} + \mathbf{d}$$

D is an $n \times m$ linear transformation matrix and $\mathbf{d}$ is a constant vector.

Definition 2. For each iteration $\mathbf{i}$ of a loop nest of depth l, the *computation decomposition* of the loop nest onto an n-dimensional processor array is a function $\gamma(\mathbf{i}) : \mathcal{I} \to \mathcal{P}$, where

$$\gamma(\mathbf{i}) = C\mathbf{i} + \mathbf{c}$$

C is an $n \times l$ linear transformation matrix and $\mathbf{c}$ is a constant vector.

Let the computation decomposition for loop nest j be $\gamma_j = C_j(\mathbf{i}) + \mathbf{c}_j$ and the data decomposition for array x in loop j be $\delta_{xj} = D_{xj}(\mathbf{a}) + \mathbf{d}_{xj}$. Furthermore, let $\mathbf{f}_{xj}$ be an array index function for array x in loop nest j. No communication is required if it is possible to define a computation decomposition for each loop nest j and a data decomposition for each array x such that the following equation holds for all iterations $\mathbf{i}$:

$$D_{xj}(\mathbf{f}_{xj}(\mathbf{i})) + \mathbf{d}_{xj} = C_j(\mathbf{i}) + \mathbf{c}_j \tag{1}$$

If it is possible to find a single non-trivial, decomposition with no communication, then there exist many equivalent decompositions with the same degree of parallelism and no communication. For example, given a communication-free decomposition we could always transpose all the data and computation and still have no communication. We make the observation that the property shared by equivalent communication-free decompositions is the data and computation that is assigned to the same processor. We use this observation to reduce the complexity of finding the decomposition functions. Our approach is to first solve for the data and computation that are mapped onto the same processor. A simple calculation can then be used to find an assignment of data and computation to specific processors[2].

The data decompositions $\delta(\mathbf{a}) = D\mathbf{a} + \mathbf{d}$ and computation decompositions $\gamma(\mathbf{i}) = C\mathbf{i} + \mathbf{c}$ have two components. The linear transformation matrices D and

C describe the mapping between the axes of the array elements and loop iterations, and the processors. The constant vectors $\mathbf{d}$ and $\mathbf{c}$ give the displacement of the starting position of the data and computation. Communication due to mismatches in the linear transformation component of a decomposition is considered expensive, since it requires a reorganization of the entire array. In contrast, communication at the displacement level is inexpensive since the amount of data transferred is significantly reduced by blocking. Thus the priority is in finding the best linear transformation, and we focus on the version of Eqn. 1 that omits displacements. Letting $\mathbf{f}_{xj}(\mathbf{i}) = F_{xj}(\mathbf{i}) + \mathbf{k}_{xj}$,

$$D_x F_{xj}(\mathbf{i}) = C_j(\mathbf{i}) \tag{2}$$

Algorithm Overview. This section presents a brief overview of the decomposition algorithms we have developed. The details of the algorithms can be found in a related paper[2].

Each loop nest has been transformed into canonical form to expose the maximum degree of coarse-grain parallelism. The loop nests with parallelism may be nested within outer sequential loops. The outer sequential loops are considered in order from innermost to outermost. At each sequential loop level, the decomposition algorithm tries to eliminate communication by aligning the data and computation and also by reducing the degree of parallelism where necessary. If it cannot eliminate communication while still maintaining at least one degree of parallelism, then communication is necessary.

Finding decompositions that minimize communication while allowing at least one degree of parallelism is NP-hard[2]. We thus use a greedy algorithm to eliminate the largest amounts of potential communication first. To model the potential communication in a program, the compiler uses a *communication graph*. The nodes in the graph correspond to the loop nests with parallelism in the program, and the edges are labeled with worst-case estimates of the communication cost between the nodes.

We use a greedy algorithm that examines the edges in order of decreasing weights. For each edge, it looks at the two loop nests connected by the edge. The algorithm first tries to find a decomposition that only distributes the completely parallel, or *doall*, loops of the two loop nests, such that there is no data reorganization communication. If such a decomposition cannot be found that still has at least one degree of parallelism, the algorithm then expands the search to also consider *doacross* parallelism. Finally, if communication is required between the loop nests, the algorithm tries to find a decomposition with the minimum communication volume across the two loops nests.

We want to avoid making unnecessary choices in our greedy algorithm. If there is no non-displacement communication, then equivalent decompositions have the same data and computation assigned to a single processor. Thus each step of the greedy algorithm first collects constraints that specify which array elements and loop iterations must be mapped onto the same processor. These constraints are represented in terms of constraints on each individual array and loop nest with respect to itself. Mathematically, the constraints form the nullspace of the linear transformation matrices D and C for each array and loop nest, respectively.

After the nullspaces have been found, the full linear transformation matrices (D and C) and displacements($\mathbf{d}$ and $\mathbf{c}$) are then calculated to specify the complete virtual processor mapping. If there exist non-trivial decompositions that do not require any communication beyond the displacement level, our algorithm is optimal in that it will find the decomposition with the maximum degree of parallelism[2]. Once the algorithm finds the decompositions for a single instance of the current enclosing sequential loop, it then finds decompositions for all instances of that outer loop using the same greedy strategy.

Consider the ADI example from Figure 3. The algorithm first tries to find decompositions for loop nests 1 and 2 with no data reorganization communication using only the *doall* loops. Since the only such decomposition is to run the loops sequentially by placing all the data and computation on a single processor, the algorithm next considers using *doacross* parallelism. The loop nests in the example are fully permutable, so the algorithm then considers all the loops as candidates for distribution. The resulting computation decompositions the compiler finds (shown in Figures 5(b) and 5(c)) are $C_1 = \begin{bmatrix} 1 & 0 \end{bmatrix} \begin{bmatrix} i_2 \\ i_1 \end{bmatrix}$ and $C_2 = \begin{bmatrix} 0 & 1 \end{bmatrix} \begin{bmatrix} i_1 \\ i_2 \end{bmatrix}$. The corresponding data decompositions are $D_X = \begin{bmatrix} 0 & 1 \end{bmatrix} \begin{bmatrix} a_1 \\ a_2 \end{bmatrix}$ and $D_Y = \begin{bmatrix} 0 & 1 \end{bmatrix} \begin{bmatrix} a_1 \\ a_2 \end{bmatrix}$.

Physical Processor Mapping. After finding the affine virtual processor mapping, the compiler then determines the physical processor mapping. The goal of this step is to effectively utilize the limited physical resources and to further optimize communication for the target architecture.

Currently, our compiler only considers three discrete mapping functions for each distributed dimension; they correspond to the choices of "block", "cyclic" and "block-cyclic" in the HPF terminology. It is possible to specify the the mapping function by simply specifying the block size. Let N be the number of loop iterations and P is the number of processors, the block sizes for the three mappings are, respectively, $\lceil \frac{N}{P} \rceil$, 1, and b where $1 < b < \lceil \frac{N}{P} \rceil$ and b is determined based on the performance parameters of the machine. (N and P need not be compile-time constants in the program).

The choice of physical mapping is influenced by several factors. First, the affine decomposition phase might decide to block a loop (and arrays used in the loop) to exploit *doacross* parallelism efficiently. Second, if the execution time of each iteration in a parallel loop is highly variable, a cyclic mapping is needed to obtain good load balance. An example of such code is if the parallel loop contains an inner loop whose iteration count is a function of the index of the parallel loop. Finally, to reduce communication, it is desirable to use the same data mapping for the same array across different loops. The compiler tries to satisfy all these constraints using an iterative algorithm similar to the affine decomposition algorithm. For example, if an array has a block constraint for one loop nest, and a cyclic constraint in another loop nest, then the compiler will choose a block-cyclic physical mapping. When no constraint is imposed on a loop, the default is to distribute by blocks of size $\lceil \frac{N}{P} \rceil$. For the ADI example, all the distributed loops and arrays are distributed by blocks of size $b = \lceil \frac{N}{P} \rceil$.

4 Code Generation

After finding the decompositions, the next phase in our compiler is to transform and optimize the code allotted to each processor. For a machine with a shared address space, this phase is straightforward. However, if the machine has a distributed address space, the compiler must also manage the memory and communication explicitly. This section describes how to generate correct and efficient code for distributed address space machines.

4.1 When and Where to Communicate

While exact data-flow information is useful in determining the necessary communication, the information may not be available due to, for example, non-affine loop bounds or conditional control flow. Our algorithm uses data-flow information whenever it is available.

Our compiler preprocesses the program and identifies those contiguous regions of code where exact data-flow information is available. It further divides the rest of the program into regions, such that the code with different data decompositions belongs to different regions. Thus, a region either has a uniform data decomposition, or exact data-flow information is available. There are two forms of communication: communication at the boundaries of different regions, and communication within a region. Massive data movements between regions can be optimized by mapping them to hand-tuned collective communication routines.

If data-flow information is not available, we plan to use an algorithm similar to that used in FORTRAN D to generate communication [16]. In our case, however, both the computation and data decomposition are specified by our compiler. Communication is necessary whenever the processor executing an operation does not own the data used. The compiler uses data dependence analysis to perform communication optimizations such as message aggregation.

If data-flow information is available, our communication generation algorithm uses the given data decompositions only as boundary conditions for the region[1]. This allows for more flexible data decompositions within a region including data replication and data migration across different processors. Communication within the region is captured by all the non-$\perp$ contexts in the LWT generated by our data-flow analysis algorithm. The LWT specifies the exact write instance that produces the *value* used by each read instance. Communication is necessary if the producer and consumer instances are to be executed by different processors. The LWT groups the read instances into contexts, such that all the instances within a context have the same distance or direction vector. This structure facilitates optimizations such as message aggregation and hiding the latency of communication with communication.

4.2 Communication Code Generation

We have developed a uniform mathematical framework to solve the problems of communication code generation[1]. We represent data decompositions, computation decompositions and the array access information all as systems of linear inequalities.

For the ADI example from Figure 3, the earlier compiler phase decides to block the second dimension of both arrays X and Y (Section 3.3). That is, the array element $[a_1, a_2]$ resides in processor p if and only if $bp \leq \begin{bmatrix} 0 & 1 \end{bmatrix} \begin{bmatrix} a_1 \\ a_2 \end{bmatrix} < bp + b$, where b is the block size. The computation decomposition decision is to block the outer loop in the first loop nest and to block the inner loop in the second loop nest. Thus, iteration (i_2, i_1) in the first loop nest executes on processor p if and only if $bp \leq \begin{bmatrix} 1 & 0 \end{bmatrix} \begin{bmatrix} i_2 \\ i_1 \end{bmatrix} < bp + b$, where b is the block size. Similarly, iteration (i_1, i_2) in the second loop nest executes on processor p if and only if $bp \leq \begin{bmatrix} 0 & 1 \end{bmatrix} \begin{bmatrix} i_1 \\ i_2 \end{bmatrix} < bp + b$, where b is the block size.

We also represent a set of communication by a system of linear inequalities. We derive the receiving and sending code for each communication set by projecting the polyhedra represented by the system of linear inequalities onto lower-dimensional spaces in different orders[1].

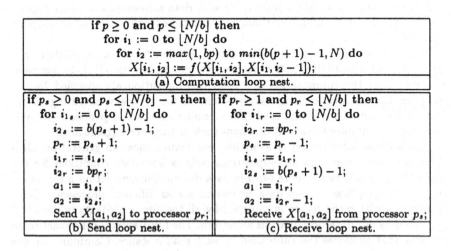

Fig. 6. Loop nests generated for computation and communication.

In the ADI example, communication is necessary only for the second loop nest and only for the array X. Figure 6 shows the three components of code that each processor has to execute in the second loop. We concentrate on array X as it is the only array that needs communication. These components are merged together to form a single SPMD program after optimizations.

4.3 Communication Optimization

Our compiler performs several communication optimizations. These optimizations include eliminating redundant messages, aggregating messages, and hiding communication latency by overlapping the communication and computation. The data-flow information enables the compiler to perform these optimizations more aggressively than would otherwise be possible using data dependence information[1].

The compiler uses the LWT information to eliminate redundant data transfers. While accessing the same location may require multiple data transfers since the value at the location may or may not have changed, each value needs to be transferred once and only once.

The perfect producer and consumer information enables the compiler to issue the send immediately after the data are produced and to issue the receive just before the data are used. This maximizes the chances that the communication is overlapped with computation. However, there is a tradeoff between this optimization and message aggregation. Maximum overlapping of communication and computation generates a large number of messages, creating a very high message overhead.

Thus, based on estimates using the performance parameters of the architecture, the compiler may create a single message for a block of iterations to achieve a balance between parallelism and communication overhead. For the ADI example, the outer loop is blocked and messages are aggregated within each block, as shown in Figure 7.

4.4 Local Address Space

Typically, a processor on a parallel machine touches only a part of an array. Since data sets processed by these programs are often very large, it is essential that the compiler only allocates, on each processor, storage for the data used by that processor.

The following is a simple approach to the memory allocation problem. We allocate on each processor the smallest rectangular region covering all the data read or written by the processor, and we copy all the received data from the communication buffer to their home locations in the local array before they are accessed. If there are multiple accesses to the same array, we simply find the bounding box of the rectangular boxes for all the accesses to the same array. Note that this formulation allows local data spaces on different processors to overlap. The computation loop nest with the local address of X is given in Figure 8.

```
if p ≥ 0 and p ≤ ⌊N/b⌋ then
  for i'₁ := 0 to ⌊N/t⌋ do
    for i₁ := ti'₁ to min(t(i'₁ + 1) - 1, N) do
      for i₂ := max(1, bp) to min(b(p + 1) - 1, N) do
        X[i₁, i₂] := f(X[i₁, i₂], X[i₁, i₂ - 1]);
```
(a) Computation loop nest.

```
if p ≥ 0 and p ≤ ⌊N/b⌋ - 1 then
  for i'₁ := 0 to ⌊N/t⌋ do
    p_r := p + 1;
    initialize(msg);
    for i₁ₛ := ti'₁ to min(t(i'₁ + 1) - 1, N) do
      i₂ₛ := b(p + 1) - 1;
      enqueue(msg, X[i₁ₛ, i₂ₛ]);
    Send msg to processor p_r;
```
(b) Send loop nest.

```
if p ≥ 1 and p ≤ ⌊N/b⌋ then
  for i'₁ := 0 to ⌊N/t⌋ do
    pₛ := p - 1;
    Receive msg from processor pₛ;
    for i₁ᵣ := ti'₁ to min(t(i'₁ + 1) - 1, N) do
      i₂ᵣ := bp;
      X[i₁ᵣ, i₂ᵣ - 1] = dequeue(msg);
```
(c) Receive loop nest.

Fig. 7. Blocking the outer loop for message aggregation with block size t.

```
double X[N, b + 1];
if p ≥ 0 and p ≤ ⌊N/b⌋ then
  for i'₁ := 0 to ⌊N/t⌋ do
    for i₁ := ti'₁ to min(t(i'₁ + 1) - 1, N) do
      for i₂ := max(1, bp) to min(b(p + 1) - 1, N) do
        X[i₁, i₂ - (bp - 1)] = f(X[i₁, i₂], X[i₁, i₂ - 1 - (bp - 1)]);
```

Fig. 8. Local address space mapping (from Figure 7(a)).

Further optimizations to reduce the local address space are possible if data-flow information is available. A processor can operate on the communication buffer directly, and it is not necessary to find the smallest rectangular box covering the data used throughout the entire program.

4.5 Merging Loop Nests

Our code generation algorithm creates separate code for each of the three components of an SPMD program: the computation, the receiving side of the communication and the sending side of the communication. Each of these components specify the actions to be performed in a subset of the source iterations. The final step is thus to merge these components together so that the operations are performed at the correct time[1]. The final SPMD program for our ADI example is given in Figure 9.

5 Conclusion

In this paper, we showed how the complex problem of compiling for distributed memory machines can be divided into several well-defined subproblems: array data flow analysis, data and computation decomposition and code generation.

Compilers for distributed memory machines require the more sophisticated analysis of exact data-flow analysis on individual array elements. This information allows the compiler to perform more advanced optimizations than with traditional data dependence analysis. In particular, our compiler uses array dataflow information to perform array privatization, as well as communication code generation and optimization.

The parallelism and communication in a program are inter-related; opportunities for parallelism must be weighed against the resulting communication cost. The parallelization phase of the compiler transforms the code to expose the maximum degree of parallelism and minimize the frequency of communication for each loop nest. The decomposition phase then selects among the degrees of parallelism to find computation and data decompositions that reduce communication.

For the given decompositions, the final phase of the compiler generates an SPMD program. By using exact data-flow information, our communication code generation algorithm gains several advantages over the traditional approach based on data dependence. First, it supports more flexible data decomposition schemes; data do not require a static home, data may be replicated, and the owner-computes rule can be relaxed. Code generation also involves allocating local space on each processor for distributed data, translating the global data addresses to local addresses and generating all the necessary receive and send instructions.

We model each stage of the compilation mathematically. The parallelization phase uses a framework that unifies transformations such as loop skewing, reversal and permutation by representing them as unimodular matrix transformations. The decompositions are represented as the composition of two functions: an affine function mapping the computation and data onto a virtual processor space, and a folding function mapping the virtual space onto physical processors of the target machine. By using this model, our algorithm avoids expensive searches through the program transformation space by solving for these mappings directly. The code generation algorithms represent communication as systems of linear inequalities. The various code generation and communication optimization problems are solved within this framework.

The next step of this research is to run experiments with real programs. We need to gain experience with the compiler system, and to test its effectiveness and practicality. In the future, we plan to extend the parallelization phase to

```
double X[N, b + 1];

if p = 0 then
  for i'₁ := 0 to ⌊N/t⌋ do
    /* Computation */
    for i₁ := ti'₁ to min(t(i'₁ + 1) − 1, N) do
      for i₂ := max(1, bp) to min(b(p + 1) − 1, N) do
        X[i₁ − (bp − 1), i₂ − (bp − 1)] := f(X[i₁ − (bp − 1), i₂ − (bp − 1)],
                                              X[i₁ − (bp − 1), i₂ − 1 − (bp − 1)]);
    /* Send */
    pᵣ := p + 1;
    initialize(msg);
    for i₁ₛ := ti'₁ to min(t(i'₁ + 1) − 1, N) do
      i₂ₛ := b(p + 1) − 1;
      enqueue(msg, X[i₁ₛ − (bp − 1), i₂ₛ − (bp − 1)]);
    Send msg to processor pᵣ;

if p ≥ 1 and p ≤ ⌊N/b⌋ − 1 then
  for i'₁ := 0 to ⌊N/t⌋ do
    /* Receive */
    pₛ := p − 1;
    Receive msg from processor pₛ;
    for i₁ᵣ := ti'₁ to min(t(i'₁ + 1) − 1, N) do
      i₂ᵣ := bp;
      X[i₁ᵣ − (bp − 1), i₂ᵣ − 1 − (bp − 1)] = dequeue(msg);
    /* Computation */
    for i₁ := ti'₁ to min(t(i'₁ + 1) − 1, N) do
      for i₂ := max(1, bp) to min(b(p + 1) − 1, N) do
        X[i₁ − (bp − 1), i₂ − (bp − 1)] := f(X[i₁ − (bp − 1), i₂ − (bp − 1)],
                                              X[i₁ − (bp − 1), i₂ − 1 − (bp − 1)]);
    /* Send */
    pᵣ := p + 1;
    initialize(msg);
    for i₁ₛ := ti'₁ to min(t(i'₁ + 1) − 1, N) do
      i₂ₛ := b(p + 1) − 1;
      enqueue(msg, X[i₁ₛ − (bp − 1), i₂ₛ − (bp − 1)]);
    Send msg to processor pᵣ;

if p = ⌊N/b⌋ then
  for i'₁ := 0 to ⌊N/t⌋ do
    /* Receive */
    pₛ := p − 1;
    Receive msg from processor pₛ;
    for i₁ᵣ := ti'₁ to min(t(i'₁ + 1) − 1, N) do
      i₂ᵣ := bp;
      X[i₁ᵣ − (bp − 1), i₂ᵣ − 1 − (bp − 1)] = dequeue(msg);
    /* Computation */
    for i₁ := ti'₁ to min(t(i'₁ + 1) − 1, N) do
      for i₂ := max(1, bp) to min(b(p + 1) − 1, N) do
        X[i₁ − (bp − 1), i₂ − (bp − 1)] := f(X[i₁ − (bp − 1), i₂ − (bp − 1)],
                                              X[i₁ − (bp − 1), i₂ − 1 − (bp − 1)]);
```

Fig. 9. The SPMD code for the example.

perform transformations such as loop reindexing, fission and fusion to expose greater degrees of parallelism. Currently, the compiler operates on each procedure individually. We plan to extend our algorithms to do interprocedural analysis.

References

1. S. P. Amarasinghe and M. S. Lam. Communication optimization and code generation for distributed memory machines. In *Proceedings of the SIGPLAN '93 Conference on Programming Language Design and Implementation*, June 1993.

2. J. M. Anderson and M. S. Lam. Global optimizations for parallelism and locality on scalable parallel machines. In *Proceedings of the SIGPLAN '93 Conference on Programming Language Design and Implementation*, June 1993.

3. B. Chapman, P. Mehrotra, and H. Zima. Programming in Vienna Fortran. *Scientific Programming*, 1(1):31–50, Fall 1992.

4. P. Feautrier. Parametric integer programming. Technical Report 209, Laboratoire Methodologie and Architecture Des Systemes Informatiques, January 1988.

5. Paul Feautrier. Array expansion. In *International Conference on Supercomputing*, pages 429–442, July 1988.

6. Paul Feautrier. Dataflow analysis of scalar and array references. *Journal of Parallel and Distributed Computing*, 20(1):23–53, February 1991.

7. High Performance Fortran Forum. *High Performance Fortran Language Specification*, January 1993. Draft Version 1.0.

8. S. Hiranandani, K. Kennedy, and C.-W. Tseng. Compiling Fortran D for MIMD distributed-memory machines. *Communications of the ACM*, 35(8):66–80, August 1992.

9. Intel Corporation, Santa Clara, CA. *iPSC/2 and iPSC/860 User's Guide*, June 1990.

10. F. Irigoin and R. Triolet. Supernode partitioning. In *Proceedings of the SIGPLAN '88 Conference on Programming Language Design and Implementation*, pages 319–329, January 1988.

11. C. Koelbel, P. Mehrotra, and J. Van Rosendale. Supporting shared data structures on distributed memory architectures. In *Proceedings of the Second ACM/SIGPLAN Symposium on Principles and Practice of Parallel Programming*, pages 177–186, March 1990.

12. D. Lenoski, K. Gharachorloo, J. Laudon, A. Gupta, J. Hennessy, M. Horowitz, and M. Lam. The Stanford DASH Multiprocessor. *IEEE Computer*, 25(3):63–79, March 1992.

13. D. E. Maydan. *Accurate Analysis of Array References*. PhD thesis, Stanford University, September 1992. Published as CSL-TR-92-547.

14. D. E. Maydan, S. P. Amarasinghe, and M. S. Lam. Array data flow analysis and its use in array privatization. In *Proc. 20th Annual ACM Symposium on Principles of Programming Languages*, January 1993.

15. A. Rogers and K. Pingali. Compiling for locality. In *Proceedings of the 1990 International Conference on Parallel Processing*, pages 142–146, June 1990.

16. C.-W. Tseng. *An Optimizing Fortran D Compiler for MIMD Distributed-Memory Machines*. PhD thesis, Rice University, January 1993. Published as Rice COMP TR93-199.

17. P.-S. Tseng. *A Parallelizing Compiler for Distributed Memory Parallel Computers.* PhD thesis, Carnegie Mellon University, May 1989. Published as CMU-CS-89-148.

18. M. E. Wolf and M. S. Lam. A data locality optimizing algorithm. In *Proceedings of the SIGPLAN '91 Conference on Programming Language Design and Implementation*, pages 30–44, June 1991.

19. M. E. Wolf and M. S. Lam. A loop transformation theory and an algorithm to maximize parallelism. *Transactions on Parallel and Distributed Systems*, 2(4):452–470, October 1991.

20. M. J. Wolfe. *Optimizing Supercompilers for Supercomputers.* MIT Press, Cambridge, MA, 1989.

21. H. P. Zima, H.-J. Bast, and M. Gerndt. SUPERB: A tool for semi-automatic MIMD / SIMD parallelization. *Parallel Computing*, 6(1):1–18, January 1988.

Toward a Compile-Time Methodology for Reducing False Sharing and Communication Traffic in Shared Virtual Memory Systems

Elana D. Granston*

High Performance Computing Division, Dept. of Comp. Science, Leiden University
Niels Bohrweg 1, 2333 CA Leiden, The Netherlands

Abstract. To date, page management in shared virtual memory (SVM) systems has been primarily the responsibility of the run time system. However, there are some problems that are difficult to resolve efficiently at run time. Chief among these is false sharing. In this paper, a loop transformation theory is developed for identifying and eliminating page-level sharing between processors at compile-time. Loop nests of one and two dimensions (before blocking) with single-level doall style parallelism are discussed.

1 Introduction

In large-scale multiprocessors, whether loosely or tightly coupled, there is typically some memory that is cheaper to access than other memory. To ease programming of such systems, much research effort has been directed toward providing the programmer with a shared virtual memory (SVM) interface [1, 2, 3, 4]. To date, proposed and implemented page-management strategies have relied heavily on the operating system, and secondarily on the hardware, to effect page placement decisions. However, it is generally agreed upon that there are several problems that are difficult to handle if ignored until run time. Chief among these problems is false sharing of pages, which arises when two or more processors are accessing distinct data on a page and at least one of the accesses is a write. To maintain coherence in a typical SVM system, a falsely-shared page will either be bounced between processors or be frozen to one place. In either case, this can result in unacceptably high communication costs, traffic levels and memory access delays.

In this paper, a loop transformation theory is presented for identifying and eliminating page-level sharing between processors at compile time. Loop nests of

---

* While at Leiden University, this work was supported by the Esprit Agency DG XIII under Grant No. APPARC 6634 BRA III. Part of this work was done while the author was a Research Scientist at the Center for Research on Parallel Computation at Rice University, supported by a National Science Foundation Postdoctoral Research Associateship in Computational Science and Engineering under grant no. CDA-9310307 and by the Center for Research on Parallel Computation under grant no. CCR-9120008.

one and two dimensions (before blocking) with single-level doall style parallelism
are discussed. The remainder of this paper is organized as follows. Section 2
provides an overview of page-level sharing. Section 3 discusses the handling of
one-dimensional arrays with subscripts that are linear functions of a single loop
index. Sections 4 and 5 extend the techniques to two-dimensional loop nests
and multi-dimensional arrays, respectively. Section 6 discusses related research.
Section 7 concludes this paper.

2 Page-Level Sharing

Consider the following simple *doall* loop before (left) and after (right) blocking
for locality:

Loop Nest 1

```
    doall I = 0 to N-1
        A[I] = A[I] + 0.5
    enddoall
```

Loop Nest 2

```
    doall II = 0 to ⌈N/b⌉ - 1
        do I = II*b to min((II+1)*b-1, N-1)
            A[I] = A[I] + 0.5
        enddo
    enddoall
```

Assume that a page can hold precisely μ array elements.

Example 1. If the *blocking factor b* in Loop Nest 2 is not a multiple of μ, multiple
processors will be simultaneously writing to different elements of A on the same
page, thus resulting in false sharing. Depicted below is the mapping between
pages and doall loop iterations that results when $\mu = 4$ and $b = 5$.[2]

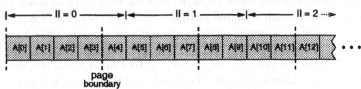

Example 2. For this same loop, false sharing also results when b is a multiple
of μ, if $A[0]$ is not aligned with the beginning of a page. Depicted below is the
mapping between pages and doall loop iterations that results when $\mu = b = 4$,
but $A[0]$ is positioned in the middle of a page.

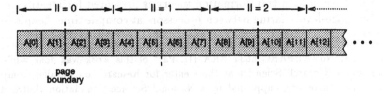

---

[2] In practice, page sizes are clearly much larger. Small page sizes are used throughout
many of the examples here to simplify illustrations.

When false sharing occurs, no two processors are accessing the same datum, so no classical, processor-crossing dependence exists. Therefore, such sharing generally does not get considered in traditional dependence-analysis based optimization frameworks. (An exception to this is discussed in Section 6.)

In Examples 1 and 2 above, page-level sharing arose from multiple references to the same page within a single execution of a doall loop. Suppose instead that a doall loop were enclosed within a serial loop. Then page-level sharing could also arise if there were overlap between the sets of pages accessed during distinct executions of the doall loop (equivalently, distinct iterations of the enclosing loop). In this paper, we target the elimination of this type of page-level sharing as well.

When pages are read-shared, no synchronization is necessary. In theory, read-sharing can be easily handled by replicating pages. In practice, however, read sharing can tax the limitations of processors' local memories and lead to unacceptably high traffic levels. Although we only discuss the elimination of write-sharing in this paper, the techniques presented in this paper can be used to alleviate the analogous cases of read sharing as well [5].

3 Detecting and Eliminating False Sharing in One-Dimensional Loop Iteration Spaces

Consider the following loop nest containing a reference R to $A[c\,I + \lambda]$, where I is the index of the enclosing loop, and $c, \lambda \in \mathbb{Z}$ are invariant with respect to the loop. [3]

Loop Nest 3
```
        doall I = 0 to N-1
 R:         A[c*I+λ] = ···
        enddoall
```

In this loop nest, as in all other loop nests in this paper, it is assumed that standard optimizations to remove processor-crossing dependences (e.g., as scalar expansion) and those to improve locality have already been applied where possible and profitable.

In this section, we discuss constraints on *blocking factors* and *alignment factors* that are needed to eliminate page-level sharing. While the presentation may seem unnecessarily formal for the relatively straightforward in the case of one-dimensional loop nests, the results presented in this section form a foundation that is necessary for extending these ideas to two-dimensional loop nests (Sect. 4).

---

[3] In this paper, we use the following set notation: $\mathbb{P} = \{1, 2, \ldots, \infty\}$, $\mathbb{N} = \{0, 1, \ldots, \infty\}$, $\mathbb{Z}$ is the set of integers, and $\mathbb{Q}$ is the set of rational numbers.

3.1 Preliminaries

Let $m(A[expr])$ be the offset of $A[expr]$ on a page, $0 \leq m(A[expr]) < \mu$. Let $\rho(A[expr])$ be the number of the page containing $A[expr]$. $m(A[0])$ can be determined directly from the starting address of A. Arbitrarily let $\rho(A[0]) = 0$.

Lemma 1. *Based on the above assumptions,*
(a) $m(A[expr]) = (m(A[0]) + expr) \bmod \mu$.
(b) $\rho(A[expr]) = \lfloor \frac{m(A[0]) + expr}{\mu} \rfloor$.

Let $sign(c)$ be 1 if $c > 0$, -1 if $c < 0$, and 0 otherwise. Let $s = sign(c)$ and let $s^- = max(-s, 0)$. (Recall that c is the coefficient of I in the above loop.)
Consider the layout of A with respect to reference R in Loop Nest 3.

Definition 2. A is *perfectly aligned* with respect to R if either

- $c \geq 0$ and array A is laid out across pages so that the element of A accessed in iteration $I = 0$ is located at the *beginning* of a page ($m(A[expr]) = (-s^-) \bmod \mu = 0$),

- or $c < 0$ and array A is laid out across pages so that the element of A accessed in iteration $I = 0$ is located at the *end* of a page ($m(A[expr]) = (-s^-) \bmod \mu = \mu - 1$).

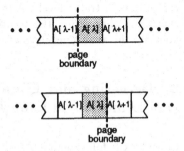

3.2 Computing Blocking Factors

Suppose that Loop Nest 3 has been stripmined to exploit spatial locality: [4]

Loop Nest 4
```
        doall II = 0 to ⌈N/b⌉ - 1
          do I = ⌈II * b⌉ to min(⌈(II + 1) * b⌉-1, N-1)
  R:         A[c*I+λ] = ···
          enddo
        enddoall
```

Let $i \in I$ denote a value that variable I can take on during execution of the loop nest. Let $i \in I(II = ii)$ denote a value that variable I can take on when index II of the enclosing loop has value ii.

How can false-sharing be eliminated? Intuitively, the goal is to constrain the selection of blocking factors so that I loop iterations are partitioned into blocks of "pages". This in turn ensures that the same processor executes all iterations that map to a given page. This idea was informally introduced in a previous paper [6]. In this section (Sect. 3.2), we review some of these results more formally.

---

[4] In the following loop nest, it is assumed that b may be rational. The reason for this will become apparent later in Sect. 3.2.

Definition 3. An iteration $i \in I$ **maps** to a page ρ with respect to a reference R, if the element of A referenced at R during i is located on page ρ.

Lemma 4. *When $c \neq 0$, the iterations of the I loop that map to a given page fall within an interval of size $\mu/|c|$.*

Consider the reference R to $A[c\,I + \lambda]$ in Loop Nest 4.

Lemma 5. *One of three sharing patterns exists, depending on the magnitude of c in relation to μ.*

Case 1: $c = 0$: *Illegal.*
Case 2: $0 < |c| < \mu$: *There may be false sharing.*
Case 3: $|c| \geq \mu$: *There is no page-level sharing of any kind between processors.*

Because Case 1 is illegal, it is henceforth assumed that $c \neq 0$. The remainder of this section focuses on eliminating page-level sharing between processors that arises in Case 2. The theory presented here is sufficiently robust to encompass Case 3 as well, as this will become useful when analyzing two-dimensional loop nests (Sect. 4).

Theorem 6. *Assuming that A is perfectly aligned with respect to R, employing a blocking factor of*

$$b \in block(c, \mu) = \begin{cases} \{\, b(k) = k\,b^{min} \mid k \in \mathbf{P}, \; b^{min} = \frac{\mu}{|c|} \,\} & 0 < |c| < \mu \\ (0 : \infty]_\mathbb{Q} & |c| \geq \mu. \end{cases}$$

will prevent page-level sharing (if any) between processors during the execution of Loop Nest 4.[5]

Proof. First consider the case when $b = b(k)$. Assume that $ii, ii' \in II$, $ii < ii'$, and that $i \in I(II = ii)$ and $i' \in I(II = ii')$. When $c > 0$, by the definition of perfect alignment, there exists $t \in \mathbb{Z}$ such that $m(A[0]) + \lambda = t\,\mu$. Therefore, $m(A[0]) + c\,i + \lambda \; < \; m(A[0]) + c\,(ii' \cdot b) + \lambda \; = \; (ii' \cdot k + t)\,\mu \; \leq \; m(A[0]) + c\,i' + \lambda$, so

$$\rho(A[c\,i + \lambda]) \; = \; \left\lfloor \frac{m(A[0]) + c\,i + \lambda}{\mu} \right\rfloor \; < \; ii' \cdot k + t \; \leq \; \left\lfloor \frac{m(A[0]) + c\,i' + \lambda}{\mu} \right\rfloor \; = \; \rho(A[c\,i' + \lambda]).$$

When $c < 0$, $m(A[0]) + \lambda = t\,\mu - 1$, so $\rho(A[c\,i + \lambda]) > \rho(A[c\,i' + \lambda])$. Therefore, no pages are accessed during more one doall loop iteration. The remainder of the theorem follows directly from Lemma 5.

---

[5] The notation $(mn : mx]$ denotes the set $\{r \mid mn < r \leq mx, r \in \mathbb{R}\}$. $(mn : mx]_S$ denotes the set $(mn : mx] \cap S$, where $S \in \{\mathbb{Z}, \mathbb{P}, \mathbb{N}, \mathbb{Q}\}$.

Observation 1 *When A is perfectly aligned with respect to R, choosing a blocking factor of $b = b(k)$ ensures that the I-loop iterations that are accessed during a given iteration of the II loop are precisely those that map to some k-page block. During any two distinct iterations of the II loop, distinct k-page blocks are accessed.*

A discussion on choosing the parameter k can be found in [6].

Example 3. Consider a reference R to $A[3i]$. Assume that A is perfectly aligned with respect to R and that $\mu = 4$. [6] We arbitrarily choose $k = 2$, so that $b = b(2) = 8/3$. Depicted below is the mapping between pages and doall loop iterations that results when Loop Nest 4 is executed under these conditions. Note that during distinct doall loop iterations, distinct 2-page blocks are accessed.

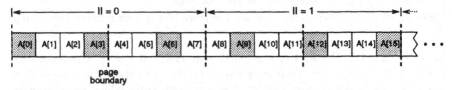

3.3 Compensating for Imperfect Alignment

Suppose that A is not perfectly aligned. Because iteration $I = 0$ maps to the middle of a block, employing a blocking factor of $b = b(k)$ is insufficient to eliminate false sharing, if any. When false sharing exists, in addition to blocking by a multiple of b^{min}, the interval of iterations that is executed during the first doall loop iteration must be shortened to compensate for the initial partial page.

The resulting code looks as follows:

Loop Nest 5

```
        doall II = 0 to ⌈(N + φ)/b⌉-1
            do I = max(⌈II*b − φ⌉, 0) to min(⌈(II+1)*b − φ⌉-1, N-1)
    R:          A[c*I+λ] = ···
            enddo
        enddoall
```

Definition 7. This optimization is known as **processor-page alignment**.

The goal of processor-page alignment as presented here is the same that originally presented in [6]. However, the technique itself differs somewhat. The modified version presented here has the advantages of being simpler and introducing less overhead.

Definition 8. Two loop nests are **equivalent** if executing one loop nest yields the same result as executing the other.

---

[6] An unrealistically small page size has been chosen to simplify pictorial representation.

Lemma 9. *Given any $\phi \in [0 : b)_\mathbb{Q}$, Loop Nest 5 is equivalent to Loop Nest 3 (the original loop).*

Proof. See [5].

Definition 10. Let $b \in block(c, \mu)$. $\phi \in [0 : b)_\mathbb{Q}$ is an alignment factor for reference R if and only if using that value of ϕ in Loop Nest 5 in combination with blocking factor b suffices to eliminate page-level sharing between processors with respect to R.

Lemma 11. *If $m(A[-c\phi + \lambda]) = (-s^-) \bmod \mu$, then page-level sharing (if any) is eliminated from Loop Nest 5 with respect to R, and ϕ is an alignment factor for R.*

Proof. Let $ii, ii' \in II$, $ii < ii'$, and $i = I(II = ii)$ and $i' = I(II = ii')$. Using similar reasoning as in the proof of Theorem 6, it can be shown that if $m(A[-c\phi + \lambda]) = (-s^-) \bmod \mu$, then $\rho(A[c\,i + \lambda]) \neq \rho(A[c\,i' + \lambda])$. Therefore, no pages are accessed during more than one doall loop iteration.

Theorem 12. *Possible alignment factors for R include*

$$\phi \in align(m(A[0]) + \lambda, c, k, \mu) = \begin{cases} \{\phi(n) \mid n \in [0 : k)_\mathbb{N} & 0 < |c| < \mu \\ [0 : b)_\mathbb{Q} & |c| \geq \mu, \end{cases}$$

where $\phi(n) = \dfrac{(s(m(A[0]) + n\mu + \lambda + s^-)) \bmod (k\mu)}{|c|}$.

Proof. For any $n \in \mathbb{N}$, $m(A[-c \cdot \phi(n) + \lambda]) = (-s^-) \bmod \mu$. Therefore, by Lemma 11, any $\phi(n) \in align(m[0] + \lambda, c, k, \mu)$ is an alignment factor. The remainder of the proof follows from Lemma 5 and the definition of alignment factor.

Corollary 13. *If $\phi(n)$ is an alignment factor, so is $\phi(t\,k + n)$.*

Proof. $\phi(n) = \phi(t\,k + n)$.

Observation 2 *There are k distinct partionings of pages into k-page blocks. The choice of n determines which partitioning is effected by $\phi = \phi(n)$.*

Without loss of generality, we restrict ourselves to values of n such that $0 \leq n < k$.

Let $m_k^n(A[expr])$ be the offset of $A[expr]$ within the k-page block containing it. Let $\rho_k^n(A[expr])$ be the number of that k-page block.

Lemma 14. *Suppose* $b = b(k)$ *and* $\phi = \phi(n)$.
(a) $m_k^n(A[0]) = m(A[0]) + n\mu$.
(b) $m_k^n(A[expr]) = (m_k^n(A[0]) + expr) \bmod (k\mu)$.
(c) $\rho_k^n(A[expr]) = \lfloor \frac{m_k^n(A[0]) + expr}{k\mu} \rfloor$.

Proof. (a) Let $ii \in II$. When an alignment factor of $\phi(n)$ is employed, pages are partitioned into k-page blocks such that, if $c > 0$ $(c < 0)$, $A[c\,(ii \cdot b - \phi(n)) + \lambda]$ is the first (last) element in a k-page block. Therefore, $m_k^n(A[c\,(ii \cdot b - \phi(n)) + \lambda]) = (-s^-) \bmod (k\mu)$. Solving for $m_k^n(A[0])$ completes the proof.

(b),(c) Substituting $k\mu$ for μ, the remainder of the proof follows directly from part (a) and Lemma 1.

Example 4. Consider a reference R to $A[-3i + 60]$. Assume that $\mu = 4$, and that $m(A[0]) = 1$, so that A is not perfectly aligned with respect to R. We arbitrarily choose $k = 2$ and $n = 0$. Below is a diagram of the mapping between pages and doall loop iterations that results (1) after blocking by $b = b(k) = 8/3$ only and (2) after blocking by $b = 8/3$ and aligning by $\phi = \phi(0) = 2/3$.

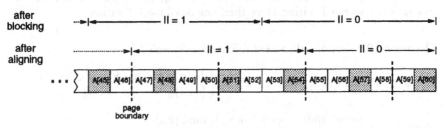

Theorem 15. *Lemma 11 presents a condition that is sufficient but not necessary for ϕ to qualify as an alignment factor.*

Proof. See [7].

Whenever $b = b(k)$ is an integer, a commonly occuring case, it is possible to find an alignment factor ϕ that is also an integer and effects the same mapping as $\phi(n)$ [7].

3.4 Multiple References

Suppose we wish to eliminate page-level sharing for a set of references simultaneously. The primary distinction between this and the single reference case is that blocking factors and alignment factors must meet the constraints imposed by each reference individually *and* by any dependences or "page" dependences between the references. For example, suppose that a loop contained references R^A and R^B to $A[c^A I + \lambda^A]$ and $B[c^B I + \lambda^B]$, respectively. Assume that $c^A, c^B \neq 0$. To eliminate page-level sharing with respect to both references, we must select a blocking factor $b \in block(c^A, \mu^A) \cap block(c^B, \mu^B)$. If there is a dependence between the two references, they must both be aligned by same alignment factor $\phi \in align(m(A[0]) + \lambda^A, c^A, k^A, \mu^A) \cap align(m(B[0]) + \lambda^B, c^B, k^B, \mu^B)$. Otherwise, they can each be aligned by different factors. If a blocking factor and alignment factor that meet this criteria cannot be found, it may still be possible to eliminate false sharing for both references by using loop distribution.

4 Detecting and Eliminating False Sharing in Two-Dimensional Loop Iteration Spaces

Assume that array subscripts have the form $c_1 I_1 + c_2 I_2 + \lambda$, where I_1 and I_2 are indices of the outer and inner loops, respectively, and $c_1, c_2, \lambda \in \mathbb{Z}$ are invariant with respect to both loops.

Loop Nest 6
```
do I₁ = 0 to N₁-1
    do I₂ = 0 to N₂-1
        A[c₁ * I₁ + c₂ * I₂ + λ] = ···
    enddo
enddo
```

In this section, we analyze the case where the inner loop is parallelized and stripmined as shown below. Other cases are discussed in [5].

Loop Nest 7
```
do I₁ = 0 to N₁-1
    doall II₂ = 0 to ⌈N₂/b⌉ - 1
        do I₂ = ⌈II₂ * b⌉ to min(⌈(II₂ + 1) * b⌉-1, N₂ - 1)
            A[c₁ * I₁ + c₂ * I₂+λ] = ···
        enddo
    enddoall
enddo
```

Eliminating page-level sharing between processors is accomplished in two steps. First, we apply the techniques from the previous section to eliminate the sharing that results during a single execution of the doall loop (equivalently, a single iteration of the I_1 loop). Then, we build on this to eliminate sharing across executions of the doall loop (equivalently, across iterations of the I_1 loop).

4.1 Step 1: Eliminating Page-level Sharing within a Single Doall Loop Execution

Because the expression $c_1 I_1 + \lambda$ is constant within an iteration of the I_1 loop, the distinctions between this case and that presented in the previous section are that (1) the constant expression with respect to the inner loop is now $c_1 I_1 + \lambda$, rather than λ, and (2) the set of possible alignment factors depends on the value of I_1.

Observation 3 *Within a single doall loop execution, (equivalently, a single iteration of the i_1 loop) page-level sharing between processors may exist only when $0 \leq |c_2| < \mu$.*

As in the previous section, we again address only those cases where the coefficient of the inner loop index is non-zero.

Theorem 16. *Page-level sharing between processors can be eliminated by employing a blocking factor $b \in block(c_2, \mu)$ and an alignment factor $\phi_{I_1} \in align(m(A[0]) + c_1 I_1 + \lambda, c_2, k, \mu)$.*

The proof follows directly from Theorems 6 and 12. The resulting loop nest is presented below:

Loop Nest 8
```
     do I₁ = 0 to N₁-1
        φ = φ_I₁
        doall II₂ = 0 to ⌈(N₂ + φ)/b⌉-1
           do I₂ = max(⌈II₂ * b - φ⌉, 0) to min(⌈(II₂ + 1) * b - φ⌉-1, N₂-1)
R :            A[c₁ * I₁ + c₂ * I₂ + λ] = ···
           enddo
        enddoall
     enddo
```

Example 5. Consider a reference to $A[-2I_1 - 3I_2 + 60]$. Let $\mu = 4$ and $m(A[0]) = 1$. Suppose we choose $k = 2$ and $n = 0$. Then, $b = 8/3$, and $\phi_{I_1}(n) = ((2 I_1 + 2) \bmod 8)/3$. The mapping between pages and doall loop iterations that results when executing Loop Nest 8 under these conditions is displayed in Fig. 1. Note that during any given execution of the doall loop, page-level sharing is eliminated. However, this does not hold across doall loop executions.

4.2 Step 2: Eliminating Page-level Sharing across Doall Loop Executions

Consider the memory reference pattern that arises from the reference R during the execution of Loop Nest 8. Within a single execution of this doall loop, footprint of R is a range of length $c_2(N_2 - 1) + 1$ and stride c_2. This footprint moves across A at a rate of c_1 locations per iteration of loop i_1.

When analyzing the page level sharing generated by A, two cases can arise. These are depicted in Fig. 2.

Case 1: $|c_1| > |c_2|(N_2 - 1) + \mu$. If b and ϕ meet the requirements of Theorem 16 and n is invariant with respect to the I_1 loop, there is no page sharing between processors across executions of the doall loop.

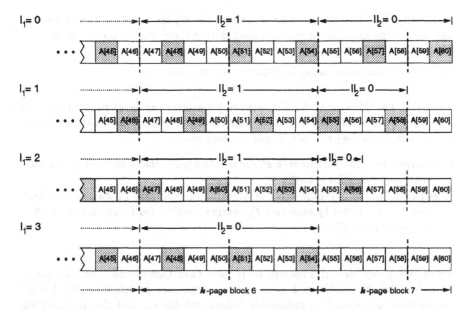

Fig. 1. Example of eliminating page-level sharing between processors within a single doall loop execution R is a reference to $A[-2i_1 - 3i_2 + 60]$.

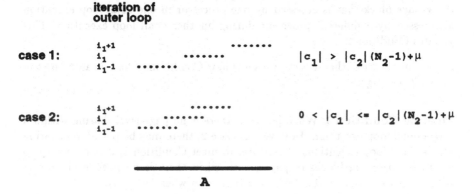

Fig. 2. Footprint of reference to $A[c_1 I_1 + c_2 I_2 + \lambda]$.

Case 2: $0 \leq |c_1| \leq |c_2|(N_2 - 1) + \mu$.

The same page might be accessed during two or more executions of the doall loop. In this case, the goal is to distribute pages amongst processors so that the processor that executes the iterations associated with a given page during one execution of the doall loop executes the iterations associated with that page during any other executions of the doall loop in which that page is accessed.

Before this approach can be presented, the concepts of *consistent partitioning* is needed.

Definition 17. The partitioning of pages into k-page blocks is **consistent** if and only if the same partitioning is used during every doall loop execution.

Example 6. The partitioning in Figure 1 is consistent.

Theorem 18. *Page-level sharing between processors can be eliminated with respect to R (both within a single doall loop execution and across doall loop executions) if the following two conditions are both met:*

Condition 1: *the partitioning of pages into k-page blocks is consistent across doall loop executions, and*

Condition 2: *if a k-page block is accessed by processor P_j during one doall loop execution and by processor $P_{j'}$ during another doall loop execution, then necessarily $j = j'$.*

Proof. We prove that if Theorem 18 is false then Conditions 1 and 2 cannot both be true. If Condition 1 is met, then pages are partitioned into k-page blocks that are treated as indivisible "pages" of size $k\mu$ and this partitioning is the same across every execution of the doall loop. During any given doall loop execution, only one processor can execute iterations that map to pages in that block. Therefore, page-level sharing between processors can occur only if the k-page block that is accessed by one processor in one doall loop execution is accessed by a different processor during another doall loop execution. This violates Condition 2.

In the remainder of this section, we show how Conditions 1 and 2 can be met in Case 2 from Fig. 2.

Meeting Condition 1 When $|c_2| \geq \mu$, there is no page-level sharing within a single doall loop execution. However, in Case 2, there may be page-level sharing across doall loop executions. Therefore, to meet Condition 1, it is necessary to assign iterations in blocks of pages, even when there is no page-level sharing within one execution of the doall loop (i.e., even when $|c_2| \geq \mu$).

Definition 19. ϕ is a **consistent alignment factor** if ϕ is an alignment factor and a consistent partition is effected in Loop Nest 8 when ϕ is used in combination with a blocking factor of $b = b(k), k \in \mathbf{P}$.

Theorem 20. *Assume that $b = b(k)$, $k \in \mathbf{P}$. If n is invariant with respect to the I_1 loop, then $\phi_{I_1}(n)$ is a consistent alignment factor.*

Proof. The value of n determines the partitioning of pages into k-page blocks. If n is invariant with respect to the I_1 loop, then the partitioning of pages into k-page blocks is the same during every iteration of the I_1 loop.

Meeting Condition 2 To meet Condition 2, we must ensure that every time a k-page block is accessed, it is accessed by the same processor. Within a doall loop execution this is ensured once a consistent partitioning is effected, because each k-page block is treated as an indivisible unit, and during each iteration of the II_2 loop iteration a single k-page block is accessed.

To ensure this across iterations of the outer loop, we define a surjective mapping from k-page blocks to processors:

$$\rho_k \longrightarrow P_{\pi(\rho_k)}.$$

Then we ensure that during each I_1 loop iteration, any II_2 loop iterations that access k-page block ρ_k are assigned to processor $P_{\pi(\rho_k)}$. The mapping that we choose is

$$\pi(\rho_k) = \rho_k \bmod P,$$

where P is the number of processors allocated to the loop nest.

Example 7. Consider the reference $A[-2I_1 - 3I_2 + 60]$ again, under the same conditions as in Ex. 5. Figure 3 shows the assignment of k page blocks to processors that results when the above mapping is used. Note that page-level sharing between processors is now eliminated.

We now derive the transformation needed to effect this mapping.

Lemma 21. *If the k-page block accessed during iteration $ii_2 \in II_2(I_1 = i_1)$ maps to processor P_{pid}, then the k-page block accessed during iteration $ii_2 + P \in II_2(I_1 = i_1)$ also maps to processor P_{pid}.*

Proof. During any given iteration of the II_2 loop, a single k-page block is accessed. Suppose that k-page block ρ_k^n, which maps to processor P_{pid}, is accessed during iteration $ii_2 \in II_2(I_1 = i_1)$. If $c_2 > 0$, k-page block $\rho_k^n + P$ is accessed during iteration $ii_2 + P \in II_2(I_1 = i_1)$. If $c_2 < 0$, k-page block $\rho_k^n - P$ is accessed. $\pi(\rho_k^n + P) = \pi(\rho_k^n - P) = \pi(\rho_k^n)$.

Lemma 22. *The lowest numbered iteration $firstIterForPid \in II_2(I_1 = i_1)$ that maps to processor P_{pid} is $firstIterForPid = (s_2 (pid - \rho_k^n(A[c_1 I_1 + \lambda]))) \bmod P$.*

Proof. See [5].

The transformed loop nest is shown below:

Loop Nest 9

```
b = b(k)
do I₁ = 0 to N₁-1
    φ = φ_{I₁}(n)
    doall II'₂=0 to P-1
        pid = GetPid()
        firstIterForPid = (s₂ (pid − ρᵏⁿ(A[c₁ I₁ + λ])) mod P
        do II₂= firstIterForPid to ⌈(N₂ + φ)/b⌉ − 1 by P
            do I₂ = max(⌈II₂ * b − φ⌉, 0) to min(⌈(II₂ + 1) * b − φ⌉-1, N₂-1)
R :             A[c₁ * I₁ + c₂ * I₂ + λ] = ···
            enddo
        enddo
    enddoall
enddo
```

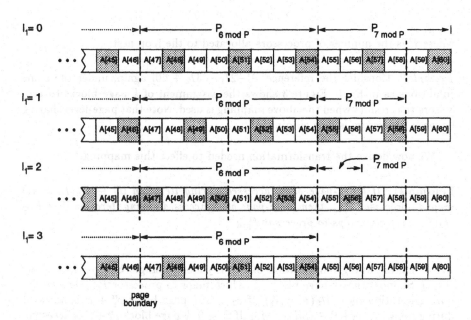

Fig. 3. Example of meeting Conditions 1 and 2 for loop nest containing reference $A[-2I_1 - 3I_2 + 60]$.

P is the number of processors allocated to the loop nest. The function $GetPid()$ returns an identifier between 0 and $P-1$ that represents the id of the processor to which a doall loop iteration is mapped. If a doall loop with P iterations is executed, it is also assumed that each distinct doall loop iteration is mapped to a distinct processor. Because there are at most $\lceil N_2/b \rceil + 1$ k-page blocks accessed during any doall loop execution, at most $\lceil N_2/b \rceil + 1$ processors can be productively used.

Lemma 23. *Loop nest 9 is equivalent to Loop Nest 8. .*

Proof. See [5].

Theorem 24. *Loop Nest 9 meets Conditions 1 and 2.*

The proof follows directly from Lemmas 21–23.

Note that the scheduling of doall loop iterations in Loop Nest 9 is static. Alternatively, a consistent surjective mapping could have been effected while allowing doall loop iterations to be dynamically scheduled.

5 Eliminating Page-level Sharing of Multi-Dimensional Arrays

Consider the case of a two-dimensional loop nest enclosing a d-dimensional array with linear subscripts:

Loop Nest 10
```
      do I₁ = 0 to N₁-1
        do I₂ = 0 to N₂-1
          A[c₁⁰ * I₁ + c₂⁰ * I₂ + λ⁰, ..., c₁^{d-1} * I₁ + c₂^{d-1} * I₂ + λ^{d-1}]
        enddo
      enddo
```

Assume $c_1^0, \ldots, c_1^{d-1}, c_2^0, \ldots, c_2^{d-1}, \lambda^0, \ldots, \lambda^{d-1} \in \mathbb{Z}$ and row-major order. Let the lower bound of dimension j be 0 and the upper bound be $D^j - 1$, $0 \le j < d$. The linearized subscript expression of the reference to A is

$$c_1 I_1 + c_2 I_2 + \lambda,$$

where $c_1 = \sum_{j=0}^{d-1} \left(c_1^j \prod_{l=j+1}^{d-1} D^l \right)$, $c_2 = \sum_{j=0}^{d-1} \left(c_2^j \prod_{l=j+1}^{d-1} D^l \right)$, and $\lambda = \sum_{j=0}^{d-1} \left(\lambda^j \prod_{l=j+1}^{d-1} D^l \right)$.[7] Once the linearized version is obtained, the theory from Sect. 4 can be directly applied.

6 Related Research

The potential performance degradation that can be caused by false sharing has been studied by several researchers. Based on this research, several data layout optimizations such as the padding of array rows has been proposed [1, 8, 9]. Spatial locality optimizations [10, 11, 12] generally eliminate some false sharing as a side effect.

The problem of eliminating false sharing of cache lines at compile time has been studied by Breternitz et al. [13]. Their approach has the advantage over

---

[7] $\prod_{l=d}^{d-1} D^l = 1$.

ours that they do not rely on knowledge of array offsets, and the disadvantage that, even in the case of an individual reference, extra synchronization must be inserted.

Recent operating systems' efforts have focused on improving memory management through the use of data annotations and programmer hints to allow application programmers to help the operating system tailor page management and memory allocation policies to individual data [2, 3].

The problem of alleviating the impact of false sharing has been more directly attacked from the operating system end by [8, 14] who propose to provide the user with directives for designating a program region during which weak coherency is to be applied to a particular subset of pages. Modifications are merged only at the end of the time period. Although the weak coherency directives are an improvement in handling false sharing over the alternatives of bouncing or freezing pages, this solution entails significant overhead. Therefore, it is still preferable to eliminate false sharing whenever possible.

7 Summary and Future Research

The purpose of this paper has been to present a loop transformation theory that deals with the identification and elimination of page-level sharing. Most importantly, we have developed a set of constraints on blocking factors, alignment factors and iteration scheduling techniques that, when met, guarantee the elimination of page-level sharing between processors. In the future, we plan to incorporate these transformations into a restructuring compiler, and to study the tradeoffs between optimizing to eliminate page-level sharing and balancing loads.

Acknowledgements

The author would like to thank Arjan Bik, Francois Bodin, William Jalby, Thierry Montaut, David Sehr and Olivier Temam for insightful comments on an early drafts of this paper.

References

1. W. J. Bolosky, R. P. Fitzgerald, and M. L. Scott, "Simple But Effective Techniques for NUMA Memory Management," in *Proceedings of the 12th ACM Symposium on Operating Systems Principles*, pp. 19–31, Dec. 1989.
2. J. B. Carter, J. K. Bennett, and W. Zwaenepoel, "Implementation and Performance of Munin," in *Proceedings of the 13th ACM Symposium on Operating Systems Principles*, pp. 152–164, Oct. 1991.
3. R. LaRowe Jr., J. T. Wilkes, and C. S. Ellis, "Exploiting Operating System Support for Dynamic Page Placement on a NUMA Shared Memory Multiprocessor," in *Proceedings of the Third ACM SIGPLAN Symposium on Principles and Practice of Parallel Programming*, pp. 122–132, Apr. 1991.

4. Z. Lahjomri and T. Priol, "KOAN: A Shared Virtual Memory for the iPSC/2 Hypercube," Tech. Rep. 597, IRISA/INRIA, July 1991. Submitted to *Journal of Parallel and Distributed Computing*.

5. E. D. Granston, "Toward a Compile-Time Methodology for Eliminating False Sharing and Reducing Communication Traffic in Shared Virtual Memory Systems," Tech. Rep. 93-12, Computer Science Department, Leiden University, 1993.

6. E. D. Granston and H. A. G. Wishoff, "Managing Pages in Shared Virtual Memory Systems: Getting the Compiler into the Game," Tech. Rep. 92-19, Computer Science Department, Leiden University, Dec. 1992. Revised July 1993.

7. E. D. Granston, "Computing Blocking and Alignment Factors for References Whose Subscripts Are Functions of a Single Loop Index," Tech. Rep. 93-22, Computer Science Department, Leiden University, 1993.

8. T. Priol and Z. Lahjomri, "Trade-offs Betweeen Shared Virtual Memory and Message-Passing on an iPSC/2 Hypercube," Tech. Rep. 637, IRISA/INRIA, Feb. 1992.

9. J. Torrellas, M. S. Lam, and J. L. Hennessy, "False Sharing and Spatial Locality in Multiprocessor Caches," Aug. 1992. Submitted to *IEEE Transactions on Computers*.

10. M. E. Wolf and M. S. Lam, "A Data Locality Optimizing Algorithm," in *Proceedings of the ACM SIGPLAN '91 Conference on Programming Languages Design and Implementation*, vol. 26(6), pp. 30–44, June 1991.

11. K. Kennedy and K. S. McKinley, "Optimizing for Parallelism and Data Locality," in *Proceedings of the International Conference on Supercomputing*, pp. 323–334, July 1992.

12. F. Bodin, C. Eisenbeis, W. Jalby, and D. Windheiser, "A Quantitative Algorithm for Data Locality Optimization," in *Code Generation-Concepts, Tools, Techniques*, Springer-Verlag, 1992.

13. M. Breternitz, Jr., M. Lai, V. Sarkar, and B. Simons, "Compiler solutions for the stale-data and false-sharing problems," Tech. Rep. 03.466, IBM Santa Teresa Laboratory, Apr. 1993.

14. W. Giloi, C. Hastedt, F. Schoen, and W. Schroeder-Preikschat, "A Distributed Implementation of Shared Virtual Memory with Strong and Weak Coherence," in *Distributed Memory Computing* (A. Bode, ed.), LNCS 487, pp. 23–31, Springer-Verlag, Apr. 1991.

Program Transformation for Locality Using Affinity Regions

Bill Appelbe, Charles Hardnett, and Sri Doddapaneni

College of Computing,
Georgia Institute of Technology, Atlanta, GA 30332

Abstract. Affinity regions ensure that a shared processor schedule, mapping loop iterations to processors, is used in consecutive parallel loop nests. Using affinity regions can improve locality without affecting parallelism.

Unlike loop fusion, affinity regions are always safe. Also, unlike parallel regions, affinity regions do not require explicit code for mapping loop iterations to processors. While affinity regions improve locality, there may be cases where more than one affinity region is possible for the same pair of loop nests. Also, loop transformations such as interchange and alignment can affect the profitability of affinity regions. In this paper we discuss the interaction between loop transformations and affinity regions, and the relationship between affinity regions and global optimization for parallelism and locality. The algorithms in this paper are being implemented in the parallelization tool, PAT, targeted at generating of affinity regions for the KSR-1.

1 Introduction

An *affinity region* is a sequence of parallel loop nests which share a common schedule (mapping iterations to processors)[4]. An **AFFINITY REGION** construct ensures that a shared processor scheduling, mapping iterations to processors, is used in consecutive parallel loop nests, that are declared as members of the **AFFINITY REGION**. Using affinity regions can significantly improve locality of reference, and hence performance. Many parallel programs consist of sequences of parallel loops accessing common data arrays with regular access patterns and overlapping references. The primary reason for using affinity regions is to minimize data movement between processors. Scheduling using affinity regions can ensure that processors access the same array sections in successive loop nests.

Affinity regions are targeted at shared-memory or NUMA (Non-Uniform Memory Access) multiprocessors, such as the Kendall Square KSR-1[2]. However, the algorithms used to find affinity regions are applicable to optimization for distributed memory systems as explained below.

In principle, the scheduling of parallel loops in an affinity region can use either self-scheduling or pre-scheduling strategies. Pre-scheduling specifies the iteration to processor mapping statically, whereas self-scheduling is a dynamic mapping. The shared schedule used in an affinity region can either be determined statically, or by the first loop executed in the region. Although, self-scheduling results in proper load balancing, pre-scheduling can result in better locality[6].

In practice, aside from affinity regions, there are two other ways of achieving data locality between loop nests – *loop fusion* and PARALLEL REGIONS. However, affinity regions are more general than loop fusion, and a higher level construct than parallel regions[4]. To illustrate the effectiveness of affinity regions we will use the following program fragment:

```
PARALLEL LOOP J=1,N
    PARALLEL LOOP I=1,N
        A(I,J)=0
        LOOP K=1,N
            A(I,J) = A(I,J) + B(K,I)*C(K,J)
        END LOOP
    END LOOP
ENDLOOP
PARALLEL LOOP I = 1,N
    LOOP K=1,N
        SUM(I) = SUM(I) + B(K,I)
    END LOOP
END LOOP
```

Program 1: Parallel Loop Nests

In this example we can fuse the two outer loop nests after the first loop has been distributed (to remove the initialization of A), and the resulting loop nest without the initialization has been interchanged. However, fusion would create more problems than it solves. Although fusion can obtain locality for B, the A initialization had to be distributed, so locality for A has been lost.

Alternatively, the two loop nests in Program 1 can be placed in a PARALLEL REGION, and an explicit explicit mapping of iterations to processors used:

```
PARALLEL LOOP I = 1, N
    PARALLEL LOOP J = 1, N
        A(J,I) = 0.0
    END LOOP
END LOOP
CALL PTHREAD_PROCSETINFO(NUMPROCS, IPROC_IDS, 1, ISTAT)
NUMTHREADS = NUMPROCS
PARALLEL REGION(NUMTHREADS)
MYNUM = IPR_MID()+1
LOOP I = MYNUM, N, NUMPROCS
    LOOP J = 1, N
        LOOP K = 1, N
            A(I,J) = A(I,J) + B(K,I)*C(K,J)
        ENDLOOP
    ENDLOOP
```

```
        ENDLOOP
        LOOP I = MYNUM, N, NUMPROCS
          LOOP K = 1, N
            SUM(I) = SUM(I) + B(K,I)
          ENDLOOP
        ENDLOOP
        END PARALLEL REGION
```

Program 2: Parallel Regions

To summarize, the disadvantages of using either fusion or parallel regions to obtain locality are:

fusion is possible only if the loops are adjacent (no intervening serial code that cannot be moved) and fusion of the loops will not result in the introduction of loop-carried dependences in the resulting fused loop nest.

parallel regions use explicit processor or thread to iteration mappings, which are machine dependent, difficult to maintain, and error-prone. If threads (logical processors) are used, then the program must still ensure that the threads do not migrate to a different processor within the region.

Using the affinity region construct of the KSR-1 together with PTILEs (parallel loops), we can rewrite Program 1 in KSR Fortran[1] as:

```
        DO 10 J = 1, N
          DO 20 I = 1, N
            A(I,J) = 0
20      CONTINUE
10    CONTINUE
C*KSR* AFFINITY REGION(I:1,N, K:1,N)
        DO 30 J = 1, N
C*KSR* PTILE(I,K,TILESIZE=(I:1,K:N),AFFMEMBER=1)
          DO 40 I = 1, N
            DO 50 K = 1, N
              A(I,J) = A(I,J) + B(K,I)*C(K,J)
50        CONTINUE
40      CONTINUE
30    CONTINUE
C*KSR* PTILE(I,K,TILESIZE=(I:1,K:N),AFFMEMBER=1)
        DO 60 I = 1, N
          DO 70 K = 1, N
            SUM(I) = SUM(I) + B(K,I)
70      CONTINUE
60    CONTINUE
C*KSR* END AFFINITY REGION
```

Program 3: Affinity Regions (KSR Fortran)

KSR Parallel Fortran specifies parallel loop nests using the PTILE directive, whose arguments include:

- The parallel loop indices (I and K in both loop nests above).
- The size and shape of tiles allocated to threads (TILESIZE=(I:1,K:N) in the first loop nest above).
- If the loop nest is a member of an enclosing affinity region (AFFMEMBER=1 or true).

In order to use affinity regions effectively, we need to provide answers to several questions.

Feasibility When can two loop nests be placed in an affinity region, with some gain in locality?

Profitability How can the performance gains from using affinity regions be quantified?

The answer to this question allows us to compare the performance of affinity regions to that of other transformations such as fusion.

Strategy How do affinity regions interact with other program transformations, especially intraloop transformations such as interchange and skewing?

Answers to the first two questions were provided in [4]. In summary, there needs to be a reaching dependence (including input dependences) between the two loop nests, of an array variable A, whose index is dependent upon a parallel loop index in both loops. In addition, there must be a 1-1 mapping between a subset of the ranges of the parallel loops in the two loop nests ($\mathcal{L}_{MAP}$: $\mathcal{L}^1_{Par-index} \mapsto \mathcal{L}^2_{Par-index}$) such that under the mapping identical array elements are accessed (if s^1 is the subscript expression vector of A in the first loop, and s^2 is the subscript expression vector of A in the second loop nest, then for each subscript dimension j of A: either $s^2_j \equiv \mathcal{L}_{MAP}(s^1_j)$, or s^1_j does not contain any subscripts in $Domain(\mathcal{L}_{MAP})$ and s^2_j does not contain any subscripts in $Range(\mathcal{L}_{MAP})$).

Affinity regions lead to definite performance improvements. The following table shows the relative execution time of Program 3 with and without affinity regions. The program was run on a KSR-1 with 32 nodes.

Size N	Without Affinity Regions	Affinity Regions
15	78.8	21.4
20	100.1	24.1
30	132.7	38.4
90	364.7	167.2

Profitability can be measured by the number of (possibly) non-local memory references converted to local memory references by the use of an affinity region. A complete analysis of the profitability of affinity regions requires a machine model. For example, on the KSR-1 prefetching and post-store can be used to overlap computations with data movement in order to reduce the timing overhead involved in accessing data from non-local memory to further improve locality.

This paper addresses the last question: how does the use of affinity regions interact with other transformations for parallelism?

At first sight, the question seems fairly trivial, as affinity regions can be inserted only when loop nests have already been parallelized. Thus, the insertion of affinity regions might appear to be carried out in a simple post-pass after parallelization. However, the following analysis shows that the interactions are not as simple as they appear.

The analysis below assumes a general model for affinity regions[4], which is not constrained by the limitations of the current implementations imposed by the KSR-1.

2 Transformations for Affinity

There may be more than one possible affinity region to encompass two loop nests. This in turn implies that the affinity regions may differ in the common subscripted variable being used. It would be profitable if affinity regions can be merged in some way. The merging of affinity regions can be made possible by the use of transformations in [4]. The transformations that we are discussing in this paper are chiefly *tiling*, an optimization for scheduling iterations, *alignment* (modifying the subscript expressions), and *loop distribution* and *loop skewing* (iteration space transformations).

2.1 Tiling

Iteration space tiling is a program transformation that tiles the iteration space in order to achieve better data reuse and reduce data movement. Consider the following code fragment:

```
LOOP J = 1, N
   LOOP I = 1, N
      B(I,J) = ...
   END LOOP
END LOOP

LOOP J = 1, N
   LOOP I = 1, N
      X(I,J) = B(I+1,J) + B(I,J)
   END LOOP
END LOOP
```

Program 4: Tiling

If the two loop nests, $\mathcal{L}^1$ and $\mathcal{L}^2$, are scheduled independent of each other, self-scheduling and tiling might be used for $\mathcal{L}^1$ and $\mathcal{L}^2$ respectively. Although tiling for $\mathcal{L}^2$ improves data locality, the execution of the two loop nests using different scheduling strategies results in a large amount of data movement. However, the two loop nests meet the criteria necessary to be put into an affinity region[4]. The affinity region construct insists that the same scheduling strategy be used in both loop nests. Since $\mathcal{L}^2$ requires tiling for better data locality, the same strategy will be used in $\mathcal{L}^1$ if they are both in the affinity region. Insertion of affinity regions therefore resulted in converting the self-scheduling strategy of $\mathcal{L}^1$ into one of tiling to preserve data locality between loop nests. Thus, the scheduling strategy used for an affinity region needs to be chosen based upon all loops in the nest, even if that means reducing the number of levels of parallelism.

2.2 Alignment

We initially assumed that the affinity regions were inserted after all the transformations for maximal parallelism were done.

```
LOOP J = 1, N
  LOOP I = 1, N
    A(I,J) = C(I,J)
    C(I-1,J)  = B(I,J)
  END LOOP
END LOOP
LOOP J = 1, N
  LOOP I = 1, N
    A(I,J) = ....
    B(I,J) = ....
  END LOOP
END LOOP
```

Program 5: Alignment

Consider the scenario illustrated by the above code fragment. If $\mathcal{L}^1$ is transformed for maximal parallelism, then the access to array C in the second statement of $\mathcal{L}^1$ will be aligned with the first statement resulting in the change in the subscript expression of B as shown below (ignoring peeled iterations).

```
C Peeled iterations
      LOOP J = 1, N
        LOOP I = 2, N-1
          A(I,J) = C(I,J)
          C(I,J) = B(I+1,J)
        END LOOP
      END LOOP
C Peeled iterations
```

Program 6: Aligned Loop nest 1 for Parallelism

The loop nests $\mathcal{L}^1$ and $\mathcal{L}^2$ are also *affinity adjacent* (sharing a variable with a reaching dependence [4]) based on their access to A. However, there are potentially two possible affinity regions for the above loop nests - one based on the accesses to A and the other based on the accesses to the subscripted variable B. Applying either one of these two possible affinity regions results in the movement of data of the other array resulting in a loss of data locality between the two loop nests.

To maximize the data locality between the two loop nests, we need to merge the two possible affinity regions. In order to do the merge, we align the accesses to the array B in $\mathcal{L}^2$ with the accesses to the same array in $\mathcal{L}^1$. The transformed code is shown below (ignoring peeled iterations again).

```
LOOP J = 1, N
  LOOP I = 2, N-1
    A(I,J) = C(I,J)
    C(I,J)  = B(I+1,J)
  END LOOP
END LOOP
LOOP J = 1, N
  LOOP I = 2, N-1
    A(I,J) = ....
    B(I+1,J) = ....
  END LOOP
END LOOP
```

Program 7: Aligned Loop Nest 2 for Data Locality

The alignment of accesses to B is made possible due to the absence of dependences that may have prevented maximal parallelism in $\mathcal{L}^2$. We may run into a situation where the alignment along a certain dimension for improved data locality between two loop nests reduces the degree of parallelism or more specifically, the loop nest will not be maximally parallel but can be run in parallel with synchronization points in the loop. These synchronization points in the resulting code fragment also cause messages to go form one processor to the other. The overhead incurred because of the communication to synchronize iterations can be equated to the overhead due to data movement when the loop nests are maximally parallel. We are looking into a more sophisticated performance model to make the decision in favor of one or the other.

2.3 Linear Transformation of Subscripts

It may not always be possible to use alignment for transforming the subscript expressions so that the accesses to the subscripted variables preserve data locality. For instance, consider the program fragment shown in program 8:

```
LOOP J = 1, N
  LOOP I = 1, N
    A(I,J) = ....
    B(I,J)  = ....
  END LOOP
END LOOP
```

```
LOOP J = 1, N
   LOOP I = 1, N
      A(I,J) = ....
      B(I, N-J) = FUNC(I,J)
   END LOOP
END LOOP
```

Program 8: Reverse Access

The access pattern of B in the two loop nests indicate that the data locality will be lost if the two loop nests are surrounded by an affinity region based on the accesses to the array A. Also, tiling and alignment are not appropriate transformations to preserve preserve data locality when B is a member of an affinity region based on accesses to A. There is no 1 to 1 mapping of iterations in the first loop nest to iterations in the second loop nest that will preserve locality for both A and B, although locality can be preserved for either array individually. However, the use of linear transformation on the subscript expression of B in the second loop nest, as shown in Program 9, ensures that data locality for both A and B is maintained without any loss of correctness of the program semantics.

```
LOOP J = 1, N
   LOOP I = 1, N
      A(I,J) = ....
      B(I,J) = ....
   END LOOP
END LOOP
LOOP J = 1, N
   LOOP I = 1, N
      A(I,J) = ....
      B(I,J) = FUNC(I,N-J)
   END LOOP
END LOOP
```

Program 9: Linear Transformation for Affinity

3 Transformations not affecting Subscript Expressions

We have already stated that transformations play a major role in the insertion of affinity regions only when there is more than one potentially applicable affinity region. The transformations that have been discussed so far modify the subscript expressions of the subscripted variables so that the access pattern to the subscripted variables under a specified iteration space access pattern is altered to reflect the enhancement in the data locality for the variable. In this section, we conjecture that the transformations that do not transform the subscript expressions but transform the loops alone do not improve data locality or, in other words, do not improve the possibilities of merging the potentially applicable affinity regions. Our conjecture is based on the following scenario:

- There are several potential affinity regions.
- If a potential affinity region has to be merged then the access pattern has to be transformed
- The iteration space distribution or any other transformation of the iteration space can aid in achieving the desired data locality for both the subscripted variables **A** and **B** if and only if the affinity regions can be merged with a different mapping between the iteration space of the two loop nests.

We know that loop distribution can be used to improve parallelism. Also, it has been shown that loop fusion results in better data locality in the presence of memory hierarchy[5, 6]. For example:

```
LOOP I = 1, N
    A(I) = ....
    B(I) = ....
END LOOP
LOOP J = 1, N
    A(I) = ....
    B(I+STEP) = A(I)
END LOOP
```

Program 10: Fragment for Loop Distribution

In the example program 10, there are two possible affinity regions based on the accesses to the variables **A** and **B** respectively. But the affinity regions cannot be merged by applying any of the aforementioned subscript transformations because they do not suffice to both improve locality as well as ensure correctness. Instead, we can distribute the second loop nest so that the affinity region based on **A** does not affect the accesses to **B** as shown in program 11.

```
LOOP I = 1, N
    A(I) = ....
    B(I)  = ....
END LOOP
LOOP J = 1, N
    A(I) = ....
END LOOP
LOOP J = 1, N
    B(I+STEP) = A(I)
END LOOP
```

Program 11: Distributed Loop nests

However, when we have to execute the second part of the distributed loop nest containing the accesses to **B**, the data locality for **A** will lost anyway since it also has accesses to **A**.

In general, the alignment cannot be applied to the loop nests to improve affinity because there is a cyclic dependence, either direct or indirect, in at least one of the statements in the loop nest. If the iteration space of the loop is transformed, the resultant loop nests may have more parallelism. But the distribution has not resulted in any relative change in the access pattern among the subscripted variables involved in the cycle. According to our conjecture, if there is no change in the relative data access pattern then, invariably, there is no improvement in the data locality.

4 Global Optimization for Parallelism and Locality

Finding affinity regions is based upon being able to find a 1-1 mapping between a subset of the ranges of the parallel loops in the two loop nests ($\mathcal{L}_{MAP}$: $\mathcal{L}^1_{Par-index} \mapsto \mathcal{L}^2_{Par-index}$) which preserves locality for a particular array accessed in both loops. This is related to the approach of Anderson and Lam[3], who use an explicit iteration to processor mapping $vecc$ and an explicit array to processor mapping $\mathbf{d}$. Composing these mappings yields an iteration to iteration mapping which can be equivalent to $\mathcal{L}_{MAP}$. However, there are some significant differences in the two approaches:

1. Introducing an explicit mapping for data $\mathbf{d}$ is not necessary, as the distribution of data can be deduced. In addition, it is difficult to reconcile with data migration, replication, and renaming.
2. The mappings $vecc$ and $\mathbf{d}$ are restricted to affine expressions (which can be represented by matrices).
3. Their approach is based upon putting loop nests into maximally parallel form without performing any statement transformations. A general approach must incorporate statement transformations such as those discussed in the paper. In addition, putting a loop nest into maximally parallel form with associated overheads such as skewing introduces is not always necessary as parallelism may only be exploited in a subset of the dimensions when locality is considered.

5 Conclusion

Even if a parallel programming language does not support affinity regions directly, they are still a highly desirable high-level approach to improving locality. Affinity regions are generally applied as a "post-pass" after parallelization. However, our analysis shows that they do interact subtly with other transformations for parallelism. We are currently implementing the algorithm for feasibility detection of affinity regions, and heuristics for combining them with other program transformations. Also, the mapping used in affinity regions offers promise as a new approach to global optimization for locality and parallelism.

References

1. *KSR Fortran Programming.* Kendall Square Research, Waltham, Massachusetts, 1991.

2. *KSR Parallel Programming.* Kendall Square Research, Waltham, Massachusetts, 1991.

3. ANDERSON, J., AND LAM, M. S. Global optimzations for parallelism and locality on scalable parallel machines. In *SIGPLAN Programming Language Design and Implementation* (1993), pp. 112–125.

4. APPELBE, W. F., AND LAKSHMANAN, B. Optimizing parallel programs using affinity regions. In *International Conference on Parallel Processing* (August 1993).

5. WOLFE, M. *Optimizing Supercompilers for Supercomputers.* The MIT Press, Cambridge, Massachusetts, 1989.

6. ZIMA, H., AND CHAPMAN, B. *Supercompilers for Parallel and Vector Computers.* ACM Press, New York, New York, 1990.

Maximizing Loop Parallelism and Improving Data Locality via Loop Fusion and Distribution*

Ken Kennedy[1] and Kathryn S. M[c]Kinley[2]

[1] Rice University, Houston TX 77251-1892
[2] University of Massachusetts, Amherst MA 01003-4610

Abstract. Loop fusion is a program transformation that merges multiple loops into one. It is effective for reducing the synchronization overhead of parallel loops and for improving data locality. This paper presents three results for fusion: (1) a new algorithm for fusing a collection of parallel and sequential loops, minimizing parallel loop synchronization while maximizing parallelism; (2) a proof that performing fusion to maximize data locality is NP-hard; and (3) two polynomial-time algorithms for improving data locality. These techniques also apply to loop distribution, which is shown to be essentially equivalent to loop fusion. Our approach is general enough to support other fusion heuristics. Preliminary experimental results validate our approach for improving performance by exploiting data locality and increasing the granularity of parallelism.

1 Introduction

Loop fusion transforms multiple distinct loops into a single loop. It increases the granule size of parallel loops and exposes opportunities to reuse variables from local storage. Its dual, loop distribution, separates independent statements in a loop nest into multiple loops with the same headers.

```
PARALLEL DO I = 1, N
    A(I) = 0.0                              PARALLEL DO I = 1, N
END                       ⟹                    A(I) = 0.0
                       fusion                    B(I) = A(I)
PARALLEL DO I = 1, N                        END
    B(I) = A(I)            ⟸
END                   distribution
```

In the example above, the fused version on the right experiences half the loop overhead and synchronization cost as the original version on the left. If all A(1:N) references do not fit in cache at once, the fused version at least provides reuse in cache. Because the accesses to A(I) now occur on the same loop iteration rather than N iterations apart, they could also be reused in a register. For sequential execution of this example, performance improvements of up to 34% were measured on an RS/6000 Model 540.

* This research was supported by the Center for Research on Parallel Computation, a NSF Science and Technology Center. Use of the Sequent Symmetry S81 was provided under NSF Cooperative Agreement No. CDA-8619393.

This paper examines two fusion problems. The first is to fuse a collection of parallel and sequential loops, minimizing synchronization between parallel loops without reducing the amount of parallelism. We refer to this criterion as *maximizing parallelism*. The fusion problem arises when generating efficient code for parallel architectures. We present an optimal algorithm for this problem based on a greedy algorithm.

The second problem is to maximize data locality by minimizing the number of data dependences between fused nests. We show this problem is NP-hard and present two heuristics for solving it. The first is also based on the greedy algorithm and is linear in time and space. It produces solutions of unknown precision when compared to an optimal solution. The second solution is based on the *maximum-flow/minimum-cut* algorithm and is therefore not as quick, but allows us to prove a tight worse-case bound on the precision of its solution.

All of the algorithms are flexible in that they will completely reorder loop nests to improve fusion. The two algorithms for improving reuse may also be used independently or integrated into the parallelization algorithm. Preliminary experimental results demonstrate the efficacy of our approach.

We begin with a brief technical background. We then review the technical criteria for *safe* fusion, for fusions which do not reduce parallelism, and for modeling fusion as a graph problem. The same review of loop distribution follows as well as the map of a distribution problem to one of fusion. Section 4 formally describes the graph framework for fusion we use in the remaining sections. Section 5 presents an optimal greedy algorithm which fuses to maximize parallelism. The next three sections explore fusion to improve reuse of array and scalar references, adding an explicit representation of reuse, proving it NP-hard, and presenting the heuristics. Our experimental results, a careful comparison to related work, and conclusions complete the paper.

2 Technical Background

2.1 Dependence

We assume the reader is familiar with *data dependence* [5] and the terms *true, anti, output* and *input* dependence, as well as the distinction between *loop-independent* and *loop-carried* dependences [4]. *Parallel loops* have no loop-carried dependences and *sequential loops* have at least one.

Intuitively, a *control dependence*, $S_1\delta_c S_2$, indicates that the execution of S_1 directly determines whether S_2 will be executed [10, 12]. In addition to using control dependence to describe program dependence, we will use the control dependence and postdominance relations for an arbitrary graph G. These definitions are taken from the literature [12].

Definition 1 *y postdominates x in G if every path from x to the exit node contains y.*

Definition 2 *Given two statements x, y $\in$ G, y is control dependent on x iff (1) $\exists$ a non-null path p, x $\rightarrow$ y, such that y postdominates every node between x and y on p, and (2) y does not postdominate x.*

3 Transformations

Loop fusion and distribution are *loop-reordering transformations*; they change the order in which loop iterations are executed. A *safe* reordering transformation preserves any true, anti and output dependences in the original program. (Input dependences need not be preserved for correctness.)

3.1 Loop Fusion

Safety. Consider safe loop fusion between two loops or loop nests with *compatible* loop headers. Compatible loop headers have exactly the same number of iterations, but not necessarily the same loop index expressions. It is possible to make loop headers with differing numbers of iterations compatible by using conditionals, but the additional complexity may make reuse harder to exploit in registers.

Between two candidate nests the following dependences may occur: (1) no dependence, (2) a loop-independent dependence, and (3) a dependence carried by an outer loop which encloses the candidates. Clearly, fusion is always safe for case (1). Fusion is safe in case (3) as well; any loop-carried dependence between two loops *must* be on an outer loop which encloses them and fusing them does not change the carrier. The dependence will therefore always be preserved.

In the case of a loop-independent dependence, fusion is safe if the sense of the dependence is preserved, *i.e.*, if the dependence direction is not reversed. A simple test for this case performs dependence testing on the loop bodies as if they were in a single loop. After fusion, a loop-independent dependence between the original nests can (a) remain loop-independent, (b) become forward loop-carried or (c) become backward loop-carried. Since the direction of the dependence is preserved in the first two cases, fusion is legal. Fusion is illegal when a loop-independent dependence becomes a backward carried dependence after fusion. These dependences are called *fusion-preventing* dependences [1, 25].

Since a loop is parallel if it contains no loop-carried dependences and is sequential otherwise, fusion in case (b) is safe but prevents parallelization of the resultant loop. If either one or both of the loops were parallel, fusion would reduce loop parallelism. Therefore, *maximizing loop parallelism* requires these dependences to be classified as fusion-preventing.

Model. We represent the fusion problem with a graph in which each candidate loop nest is represented by a node and each dependence from a statement in one loop to a statement in another is represented as a directed edge between the nodes. If there are fusion-preventing dependences or incompatible loop headers between two nodes, the edge between them is marked fusion-preventing. If other program fragments are interspersed between the loops and these statements are not connected by dependences to any loop, these statements can be ignored during fusion. If there are dependences, the formulation captures the program fragments by placing them in a node(s) and using fusion-preventing edges. For example, a group of statements between two loops is represented as a node in the fusion graph, and the dependence edges between the statements and a loop are marked fusion-preventing. For loops on which the statements do not depend, fusion-preventing edges are added and if possible are oriented such that the node containing the statements may move either before or after pairs of fusable loops.

Given the definition of dependence on the original loop ordering, the fusion graph is a DAG. A safe fusion partitions nodes in the graph such that:

1. a partition contains a set of loops that can be legally fused, and
2. the ordering of nodes in the partitioned graph respects all the dependences.

Achieving *maximum granularity* of loop parallelism is thus equivalent to partitioning this graph into the fewest number of partitions.

3.2 Loop Distribution

Loop distribution is the dual of loop fusion. Rather than merge loops together, it separates independent statements inside a single loop (or loop nest) into multiple loops (or loop nests) with identical headers. Loop distribution exposes partial parallelism by separating statements which may be parallelized from those that must be executed sequentially and is a cornerstone of vectorization and parallelization. Loop distribution preserves dependences if all statements involved in a recurrence (*i.e.*, dependence cycle) in the original loop are placed in the same loop [18]. Loops containing recurrences must be executed sequentially.

Loop distribution first places each set of statements involved in a recurrence in a separate sequential node. Statements without recurrences are parallel and are placed in nodes by themselves. Dependences are edges between nodes and some may be fusion-preventing. Fusion-preventing edges connect pairs of nodes that must be sequential if fused. Since the statements execute correctly, but sequentially in the same loop, the edges are not required for correctness. This graph is a DAG and therefore can always be ordered using topological sort. The construction partitions the graph to its finest possible granularity. Maximizing the granularity of loop parallelism however requires a partition of the graph with the fewest number of parallel loops, an application of fusion to the finest partition graph. Distribution may therefore be viewed as fusion with a preceding step that divides the original nest into the finest partitions. Consequently, we only discuss fusion since our results apply to distribution as well.

4 The Partition Problem

The following description formally maps fusion to a graph partitioning problem.

Partitioning problem: Given a DAG where
        nodes = loops and are marked parallel or sequential
        edges = dependence edges, some of which are fusion-preventing
  Rules: 1. *Separation constraint:* cannot fuse sequential and parallel nodes.
        2. *Fusion-preventing constraint:* two nodes connected by a fusion-preventing edge cannot fuse.
        3. *Ordering constraint:* the relative ordering of two nodes connected by an edge cannot change.
  Goal: group parallel loops together such that parallelism is maximized while minimizing the number of partitions.

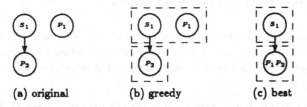

Fig. 1. Partition Example, s = sequential, p = parallel

The separation constraint contributes to *maximizing parallelism* by requiring that a particular partition contains only sequential or parallel loops. The ordering constraint is required for correctness. As discussed in Section 3, some fusion-preventing edges are necessary for correctness and others are needed to achieve an optimal solution.

Allen, Callahan and Kennedy refer to *maximal parallelism with minimum barrier synchronization* [3, 6]. By omitting the separation constraint, they arrive at an optimal greedy algorithm. Their work also tries to partition the graph into minimal sets, but uses a model of parallelism with both loop-level and fork-join task parallelism. These criteria are not equivalent to minimizing synchronization overhead when considering loop-level parallelism. Consider Fig. 1 where the edge (S_1, P_2) is an ordering constraint, S_1 is a sequential node, and P_1 and P_2 are parallel nodes.

The greedy algorithm places as many nodes as possible into a single partition without sequentializing a parallel node, but not all nodes in a partition are fused. Only nodes of the same type in the same partition are fused. For the program in Fig. 1(a), the greedy algorithm forms two partitions, $\{P_1, S_1\}$ and $\{P_2\}$, as illustrated in Fig. 1(b). S_1 and P_1 are not fused, but by using a parallel task construct, they may execute concurrently with each other. The iterations of the parallel loop P_1 also execute concurrently. Once they both complete, the parallel loop P_2 executes concurrently.

Because it ignores the node type, the greedy algorithm is provably optimal, minimizing the total number of partitions and maximizing task parallelism [3, 6]. The greedy algorithm however fails for the partition problem defined above, *i.e.* restricting it to loop-level parallelism, no task parallelism. For example, the parallel loop overhead and synchronization in the partitioning $\{S_1\}$ $\{P_1, P_2\}$ in Fig. 1(c), is half that of the partitioning in 1(b), although the amount of parallelism is equivalent. The greedy algorithm cannot achieve maximum loop-level parallelism because it unable to determine which node to select first. For example, if P_1 is selected first in Fig. 1(a), then three partitions result.

Our model considers the overhead of parallel loop startup and synchronization. The parallelization algorithm presented below maximizes the granularity and amount of loop parallelism by minimizing the number of parallel loops without sacrificing any parallelism. If task and loop parallelism are both advantageous, first using our loop parallelism algorithm and then Allen, Callahan and Kennedy may glean the benefits of both.

5 An Unweighted Fusion Algorithm

The following algorithm for maximizing the granularity of parallel loops is based on the observation that the problem may be divided based on node type because parallel and sequential nodes cannot be placed into the same partition. It consists of the following steps.

- Create a parallel component graph G_p from the original fusion graph G_o by placing all parallel nodes and edges between parallel nodes in G_o into G_p.
- Add fusion-preventing edges to G_p that preserve constraints in G_o not present in G_p.
- Partition G_p using the greedy algorithm into $G_{p'}$ and perform the partition specified by $G_{p'}$ on G_o, collapsing the original edges and forming $G_{o'}$.
- Create a sequential component graph G_s similarly from $G_{o'}$, but using sequential nodes and edges and then adding fusion-preventing edges to G_s that preserve constraints in $G_{o'}$ not present in G_s.
- Partition G_s into $G_{s'}$ with the greedy algorithm. Perform the partition specified by $G_{s'}$ on $G_{o'}$, forming the solution DAG.

This algorithm takes advantage of the constraint that sequential and parallel nodes cannot be fused by first separating the problem into a a parallel graph G_p, partitioning it, tanslating it onto G_o, and then creating the sequential graph G_s, partitioning it, and translating it. As we show in Section 5.2, partitioning the parallel graph first is required to minimize the number of parallel loops. However, because the process is the same for both of the *component graphs* G_p and G_s, we discuss them below simultaneously.

A component graph G_c represents an independent fusion problem with nodes of type c, in this case parallel or sequential. It consists of nodes of type c and the edges connecting them from G_o. These edges are not sufficient however because G_o may represent relationships that prevent nodes of the same type from being in the same partition, but that do not have an edge between them.

Example. Consider P_4 and P_7 in G_o in Fig. 2(a) where fusion-preventing dependences are marked with a slash. Although the edge (P_4, P_7) is not fusion-preventing, P_4 and P_7 may not legally fuse together without including S_6. Placing a parallel node and sequential node in the same partition however forces the partition to be executed sequentially, violating the maximal parallelism constraint. We prevent it by adding fusion-preventing dependences when we create G_p.

Transitive Fusion-Preventing Edges. The simplest way to find and preserve all the fusion-preventing relationships in G_o for G_c is to compute a modified transitive closure G_{tr} on G_o before pulling out G_c. In general, a fusion-preventing edge is needed between any two nodes of type c when a path between them contains a node not of type c. For example, if there is a path between any two parallel nodes that contains at least one sequential node, then they cannot be placed in the same partition and a fusion-preventing edge is added between them in G_p. Adding all of these edges unfortunately introduces redundant constraints.

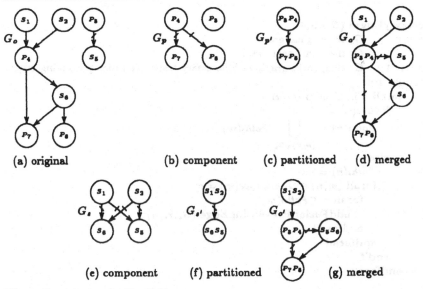

Fig. 2. Partitioning for Parallelism

Example. Assume for the moment that S_1 in Fig. 2(a) is parallel and call it P_1. Applying a full transitive closure algorithm for parallel nodes to this modified version of G_o would results in the following fusion-preventing edges: (P_1, P_7), (P_1, P_8), (P_4, P_7), (P_4, P_8). However, the edges (P_1, P_7) and (P_1, P_8) are redundant because of the original ordering edge (P_1, P_4) and the two other fusion-preventing edges (P_4, P_7) and (P_4, P_8) which together prevent P_1 from being fused with P_7 or P_8.

To simplify the discussion here, we present the algorithm *NecessaryEdges* in Section 5.1. It introduces the necessary and sufficient fusion-preventing edges to complete a component graph.

Partitioning a Component Graph. Given G_c is at most the transitive closure of a DAG, it must also be a DAG and can be partitioned optimally using the greedy algorithm into sets of loops that can be fused (see Callahan's dissertation for the proof [6]). The greedy algorithm places the roots of all the connected components into a partition and then recursively tries to add the successors in breadth-first order. A node can be added to the partition of a predecessor if it is not connected to any node in the partition by a fusion preventing edge. If a node cannot be added to an existing partition, a new partition is created for it. We call the partitioned component graph $G_{c'}$. Each node $N_{c'} \in G_{c'}$ contains one or more of N_c.

Translating a partition onto G_o. To translate the partition $N_{c'}$ onto G_o and form $G_{o'}$, we simply combine the nodes in G_o corresponding to $G_{c'}$ in the same way. The edges in G_o are inherited in the obvious way; if $(n, m) \in G_o$ then a corresponding edge between the possibly singleton partition nodes containing n

NecessaryEdges (G_o, G_c)
    INPUT: G_o the original graph
                    G_c the component graph
    OUTPUT: G_c component graph with necessary transitive fusion-preventing edges
    ALGORITHM:
        forall n in G_o in preorder
(1)   **if** $type(n) \neq c$

$$Paths(n) = \bigcup_{(m,n) \in G_o} Paths(m)$$

        else
(2) $Paths(n) = n$
(3)   **forall** $(m,n) \in G_o$ s.t. $type(m) \neq c$
            forall $r_i \in Paths(m)$
                addFusionPreventingEdge (G_c, r_i, n)
            endforall
        endforall
      endif
    endforall

Alg. 1. Adding Sufficient Transitive Fusion-Preventing Edges to G_c

---

and m is in $G_{o'}$. Edges that become redundant may be removed. Because G_o is a DAG and $G_{c'}$ contains only safe fusions, $G_{o'}$ is also a DAG.

Example. For G_o in Fig. 2(a), the algorithm begins by extracting G_p and adds two fusion-preventing edges (P_4, P_7) and (P_4, P_8) as depicted in Fig. 2(b). The greedy partitioning fuses P_3 and P_4, and P_6 and P_7 in Fig. 2(c). This partition is translated onto G_o in Fig. 2(d). Fig. 2(e) through (g) show the formation, partitioning and translation of G_s onto $G_{o'}$.

5.1 Finding the Necessary Transitive Fusion-Preventing Edges

This section describes Alg. 1 *NecessaryEdges* which adds fusion-preventing edges to a component graph G_c. Without loss of generality, consider G_p. Intuitively, a fusion-preventing edge needs only be added to G_p when there exists a path with length greater than one between two parallel nodes and all the nodes on the path are sequential. These edges are sufficient because a path containing all parallel nodes just inherits its relationships from G_o and therefore need not be augmented. This characterization encompasses all cases since a path between two parallel nodes that contains both sequential and parallel nodes is just a sequence of paths between parallel nodes that either contain all sequential nodes or all parallel nodes. Definition 3 captures this notion formally.

Definition 3 *Two nodes $node_i$ and $node_j \in G_c$ of type c require a transitive fusion-preventing edge between them in G_c iff:*

$$\forall \, path \mid node_i \rightarrow node_h^+ \rightarrow node_j \in G_o \text{ where } \forall \, h, \, type(node_h) \neq c.$$

Based on this definition, Alg. 1 *NecessaryEdges* computes transitive fusion-preventing edges to be inserted into a G_c. *NecessaryEdges* formulates this problem similarly to a data-flow problem, except that solutions along an edge differ depending on node types.

The data structure *Paths* is used to recognize paths between nodes of the same type as G_c which only contain nodes h with $type(h) \neq c$. It stores sets of initial nodes for these paths and is initialized to the empty set. The traversal is in breadth-first order and begins by creating singleton sets, $Paths(n) = n$, where n is a root of G_o and is of type c. In step (1), *NecessaryEdges* visits node n with $type(n) \neq c$ and unions all the paths of n's predecessors. Thus, $Paths(n)$ where $type(n) \neq n$ contains the set of initial nodes of type c for paths that otherwise consist of nodes h where $type(h) \neq c$. In step (3), the visit of n when $type(n) = c$ inserts a fusion-preventing edge from each of the initial nodes in $Paths(m)$ where $(m, n) \in G_o$, and $type(m) \neq c$. At step (2), it sets $Paths(n) = n$ to begin any set of paths originating at n.

5.2 Discussion

Correctness and Optimality. The correctness and optimality of this algorithm are shown as follows. With the above construction, parallel nodes and sequential nodes are never placed in the same partition, satisfying the separation constraint. Because G_p is a DAG, minimizing the number of parallel partitions is achieved using the greedy algorithm (the proof of minimality from Callahan's dissertation is directly applicable [6].)

We now show that the construction of G_p does not introduce any constraints which would cause the component solution $G_{p'}$ to be non-optimal.

Proof. All the edges which are not fusion-preventing in G_p are in G_o by construction. We therefore need only prove there are no unnecessary fusion-preventing dependences between nodes that can be fused. The proof is by contradiction. Assume there is a fusion-preventing edge in G_p which prevents two parallel loops from being fused that can be fused. If the fusion-preventing edge was in G_o, we have a contradiction. If the fusion-preventing edge was not in G_o and the nodes can be fused then either the nodes were not connected by a path in G_o or there is no path between them in G_o which contains a sequential node. In either case, *NecessaryEdges* would not insert a fusion-preventing dependence. □

Although the same proof holds for G_s, the minimality of $G_{s'}$ is for the new problem posed in $G_{o'}$. The *total* solution therefore may not be minimal because partitioning G_p constrains fusions in G_s and may increase the number of sequential partitions. As an example, consider exchanging parallel and sequential nodes in Fig. 2(a) and then applying the algorithm. Similarly, partitioning G_s and G_p simultaneously may result in inconsistent fusions.

Complexity. This algorithm takes $O(N * E)$ time and space, making it practical for use in a compiler. In the worst case, *NecessaryEdges* computes the equivalent of a transitive closure to insert fusion-preventing edges. The greedy algorithm is linear in time and space.

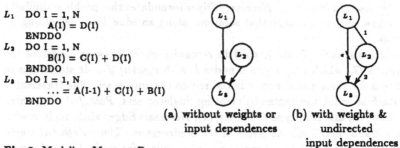

```
L₁   DO I = 1, N
          A(I) = D(I)
     ENDDO
L₂   DO I = 1, N
          B(I) = C(I) + D(I)
     ENDDO
L₃   DO I = 1, N
          ... = A(I-1) + C(I) + B(I)
     ENDDO
```

          (a) without weights or   (b) with weights &
              input dependences   undirected

Fig. 3. Modeling Memory Reuse   input dependences

This approach may be applied to other graph partitioning problems as well. The separation of concerns lends itself to problems that need to sort or partition items of different types and priority while maintaining transitive relationships. This feature has been instrumental in designing a multilevel fusion algorithm [20]. The overall structure of the algorithm also enables different partitioning and sorting algorithms to be used on the component graphs. Sections 7 and 8 present partitioning algorithms based on reuse that can be used independently or in place of the greedy algorithm.

6 Loop Fusion for Reuse

Fusion can improve reuse by moving references closer together in time, making them more likely to still be in cache or registers. For example, reuse provided by fusion can be made explicit by using *scalar replacement* to place array references in a register [7]. However, fusion may also increase working set size, negatively impacting cache and register performance.

The effects of fusion on memory access are not captured in the representation used in the loop parallelization algorithm because only true and input dependences indicate opportunities for reuse.[3] The example in Fig. 3 and its representation as an unweighted graph in Fig. 3(a) illustrate the problem. In the original formulation for maximizing parallelism, there is no representation for the reuse of D(I) between loops L_1 and L_2, nor is the reuse of both C(I) and B(I), between loops L_2 and L_3 given any importance. By adding input dependences, edge weights, and factoring in dependence type, we include these considerations.

Input dependence, like true data dependence, captures reuse. It is not required to preserve correctness and therefore should not restrict statement order. These edges are undirected and result in a graph that is not a DAG (see Fig. 3(b)).

Edge weights represent the *amount* of reuse between two loops. For simplicity, true and input dependence edges have weight of one, output and anti dependences have weight zero, and fusion-preventing dependences have weight $\epsilon \ll 1$. If there exists

---

[3] Depending on the cache hardware and coherence mechanism, the time to write to cache may not change appreciably whether the corresponding line is in cache or not, the case for output or anti dependences.

more than one edge between two nodes, the edges are collapsed and the weights are added. The cumulative edge is directed if any of the collapsed edges are, otherwise if all edges are undirected, it is undirected. Any measure of reuse which results in a single numeric value could replace this measure.

We now show that the problem of finding a fusion that maximizes reuse is NP-hard. Consider the Multiway Cut problem proven NP-hard for $k \geq 3$ by Dahlhaus *et al.*[11]. Given a graph $G = (V, E)$, a set $S = \{s_1, s_2, \ldots, s_k\}$ of k specified vertices called *terminals*[4] and undirected edges with weight $w(e) = 1$, find a minimum weight set of edges $E' \subset E$ for each edge $e \in E$ such that the removal of E' from E disconnects each terminal from all other terminals. To prove fusion for reuse NP-hard, we transform Multiway Cut to the Fusion problem. In so doing we establish that the subproblem with no input dependences is NP-hard.

Theorem 1: *Fusion for reuse is NP-hard.*

Proof. To establish the result we present a polynomial-time algorithm for reducing Multiway Cut to Fusion.

1. Select an arbitrary *terminal* $s \in V$ as a start node and number the nodes of V as follows. Initially, let the set *ready* contain all the successors of the start node. Number the start node 1. Select a vertex from *ready*, always picking a non-terminal vertex if one exists (*i.e.*, pick a terminal if only terminals are in the set). Give the selected vertex the next number and add to *ready* all its successors that are neither numbered nor in *ready*.

2. Construct a Fusion DAG G' in G by making each vertex in V be a loop node and orienting each edge from E such that the source of the edge has lower number than the sink in E'. None of these edges are fusion-preventing.

3. Let $\{s_1, s_2, \ldots, s_k\}$ be the terminals in the Multiway Cut problem, listed in order of their numbering. Add the following fusion-preventing edges oriented from lower to higher number to the DAG:

$$(s_1, s_2), \ldots (s_1, s_k), (s_2, s_3) \ldots, (s_2, s_k), \ldots (s_j, s_{j+1}), \ldots, (s_j, s_k), \ldots, (s_{k-1}, s_k)$$

The constructed Fusion problem has a minimal solution with weight m *iff* the corresponding Multiway Cut problem has the same solution.

Only If. Consider a weight m solution to the Fusion problem G' (m non-fusion-preventing dependence edges are cut). This solution corresponds to the removal of m undirected edges from the Multiway Cut problem G and is a weight m solution that disconnects terminals. Suppose the solution is not correct, *i.e.*, let $v_1, v_2, \ldots, v_p$ be a path in G from terminal $s_1 = v_1$ and terminal $s_2 = v_p$ such that no edge in the path is mapped to an edge broken in the solution to the Fusion problem. But an uncut edge in the Fusion solution, regardless of its orientation, means that the source and sink are in the same fusion group in G'. Thus all of $v_1, v_2, \ldots,$ and v_p may be fused, but this is precluded by the existence of a fusion-preventing edge between v_1 and v_p. This contradiction establishes that every undirected path between terminals in G must be cut as a part of the Fusion solution in G'.

---

[4] All other vertices are called *non-terminals*.

If. We show that the weight m solution to the Multiway Cut problem G corresponds to a correct weight m solution to the Fusion problem G'. Suppose there is a path between a terminal and a non-terminal $s_1, v_1 \in G$ after the cut but s_1 and v_2 cannot be fused in G' because there exists path from s_1 to v_2 in G' that passes through terminal s_2. In other words, the Multiway Cut solution places s_1 and s_2 in different partitions after the cut and s_1 and v_1 in the same partition, but since there is directed a path in G' from s_1 to s_2 to v_1, v_1 cannot fuse with s_1. However, this situation can never arise because of the numbering scheme.

Under the numbering scheme, if there is a path of non-terminals v_j connecting two terminals s_1 and s_2, where s_1 has the lower number, then all v_j have a smaller number than s_2 (because the numbering algorithm always numbers an available non-terminal vertex first). There can thus be no directed path from s_2 to any v_j. In particular, there can be no directed path from s_1 to v_j that passes through s_2, because each v_j has a lower number than s_2. Thus any solution of the Multiway Cut corresponds to a solution to the Fusion problem.

Minimality. Because solutions have the same weight and are correct in both, a minimal solution in one corresponds to a minimal solution in the other. □

The Fusion problem with input dependences must be NP-hard as well, because the subproblem without undirected input dependences is NP-hard; any algorithm that optimally solves the problem with input dependences must be able to solve the case without input dependences.

7 Improving Reuse with Loop Fusion: The Simple Algorithm

The simple algorithm is a straightforward modification of the greedy algorithm that moves loops to different partitions to improve reuse when legal. Like the greedy algorithm it is linear. Given a greedy solution that specifies loops in partitions, we increase the amount of reuse based on the following observation.

> In the greedy partition graph, if there exists two partitions g_1 and g_2 with a directed edge (g_1, g_2), then no node in g_2 may be legally placed in g_1 or the greedy algorithm would have put it there. However, it may be safe and profitable to move nodes in g_1 down into g_2.

We determine if it is safe and profitable to move $n \in g_l$ down into another partition g_h as follows.

Safety. A node $n \in g_l$ may move to g_h *iff* it has no successors in g_l and there is no fusion-preventing edge (n, r) such that $r \in g_h$ or $r \in g_k$ where g_k must precede g_h.

Profitability. Compute a sum of edges (m, n), $m \in g_l$, and a sum for each g_h of edges (n, p), such that $p \in g_h$ and n may be safely moved into g_h. Pick the partition g with the biggest sum. If $g \neq g_l$ move n down into g.

Simple (G_g)
    INPUT: G_g a greedy partition graph
    OUTPUT: $G_{g'}$ a partitioning with improved reuse
    ALGORITHM:
        forall partitions $g_l \in G_g$ in reverse topological order
        forall nodes $n \in g_l$ in reverse topological order
        consider g_h where $(n,p) \in G_g$ and $p \in g_h$
        if it is *safe* and *profitable* to move n to g_h
        move n to g_h
    return $G_{g'}$

Alg. 2. Simple Algorithm for Improving Reuse

Alg. 2 *Simple* applies these criteria to improve reuse. It begins by performing a bottom-up pass on the partition graph G_g formed by the greedy algorithm. For all nodes n within a partition, it performs a bottom-up pass testing if it is safe and profitable to move n down into another partition g_h. For Fig. 3, this algorithm produces a partition of $\{L_1\}$, $\{L_2, L_3\}$ correcting the initial greedy partition $\{L_1, L_2\}$, $\{L_3\}$.

Further adjusting the results of the greedy algorithm for reuse on sequential loops, we only fuse loops in a given partition if they offer reuse. Given no reuse and negligible sequential loop overhead, it is more important to keep register pressure at a minimum than to decrease loop overhead. Since all the loops in a partition may be safely fused, we fuse only those connected by true or input dependences to improve reuse. Assuming fork and join of parallel tasks is relatively expensive, we still fuse all nodes in parallel partitions.[5] This decision may differ depending on the parallel architecture.

8 Improving Reuse with Maximum-Flow/Minimum-Cut: The Weighted Algorithm

In this section, we describe a more general and powerful algorithm which is a modification of the maximum-flow/minimum-cut algorithm that seeks to maximize reuse via loop fusion.

If there is only one fusion preventing dependence ($k = 1$), the graph can be divided in two using the maximum-flow/minimum-cut algorithm [13, 16]. Maximum-flow/minimum-cut is polynomial time and makes a single minimum cut that maximizes flow in the two resultant graphs. The maximum-flow algorithm works by introducing flow at the source such that no capacity is exceeded and the capacity of the flow network to the sink is maximised. To divide the graph in two parts, a cut is taken. The minimum cut consists of the edges that are filled to capacity and can be determined with a breadth-first search originating at the source of flow. If $k = 2$, the problem is polynomial time solvable by using two applications of the 2-way cut algorithm [26].

---

[5] Simple replaces the greedy algorithm on the component graphs in loop parallelisation.

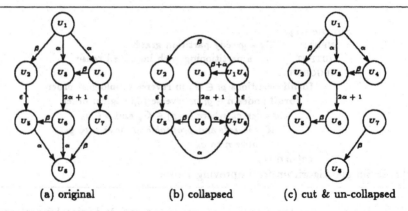

(a) original   (b) collapsed   (c) cut & un-collapsed

Fig. 4. Using Minimum-Cut for Fusion ($\beta > \alpha$)

Dahlhaus *et al.* develop an *isolation heuristic* [11] and combine it with Goldberg and Tarjan's maximum flow algorithm [16] to design a polynomial algorithm that produces a multicut that is at most (2k - 1)/k times the optimal. Goldberg and Tarjan's maximum flow algorithm is to date the most efficient with time complexity $O(nmlog(n^2/m))$ [16]. The running time of Dahlhaus *et al.*'s algorithm is $O(2^{2k}knmlog(n^2/m))$, which is polynomial for fixed k [11]. They leave open whether a more efficient algorithm with a similar optimality guarantee exists.

In the Fortran programs in our studies, k, n, and m have always been very small. The following section is devoted to the design of an $O(knmlog(n^2/m))$ algorithm for reuse problem. The algorithm is based on Goldberg and Tarjan's maximum-flow algorithm; it is guaranteed to be within k times the optimal. In some cases, it is optimal.

8.1 Structuring the Maximum-Flow/Minimum-Cut Problem

First, we perform a topological sort on the fusion-preventing edges and select the first fusion-preventing edge (*src*, *sink*) to cut. In maximum-flow/minimum-cut, *src* provides infinite flow and *sink* infinite consumption. In the minimum-cut algorithm, these additions force the fusion-preventing edge to be cut and in some cases, are sufficient to characterize the problem. For instance, infinite flow into L_1 and out of L_3 in Fig. 3(b) would cause (L_1, L_2) and (L_1, L_3) to be cut, therefore optimally fusing L_2 and L_3.

Consider breaking the fusion preventing dependence (U_4, U_7) in Fig. 4(a). Providing flow to U_4 and consumption to U_7 only cuts the fusion-preventing edge, but other edges must be cut as well to separate them. The insight is that to use minimum cut, the nodes that must precede *src* are *temporarily* collapsed into *src* and nodes that must follow *sink* are temporarily collapsed into *sink*, so that they truly represent the source and the sink of flow. However, collapsing all predecessors of *src* and all successors of *sink* can impose unnecessary ordering constraints on the resulting graph. We therefore use the control dependence relation to determine the nodes to temporarily collapse. After each application of minimum-cut, the nodes are "un-collapsed".

In the reuse graph G_r, we compute all control dependence ancestors of *src* and collapse them into *src* and *src* inherits their edges (self edges are ignored). For *sink*, we compute control dependence on the *reverse* graph of G_r, RG_r. The reverse graph simply reverses the direction of each edge in G_r. All control dependence ancestors of *sink* in RG_r are collapsed into *sink* in G_r and their edges inherited. The cut of this graph is applied to G_r the original, un-collapsed graph. The cut always includes the fusion-preventing edge and breaks the original graph into two subgraphs.

The algorithm collapses each subgraph with an uncut fusion-preventing edge, applies minimum-cut and un-collapsing as above. It repeats this process until all fusion-preventing edges are broken. For instance, one application of this process to Fig. 4(a) where $\beta > \alpha$ results first in the collapsed graph 4(b) and then in the cut graph 4(c). The next application cuts edges (U_2, U_5), (U_1, U_3) and (U_1, U_4).

Optimality. Given a graph with a single fusion-preventing edge, this algorithm performs optimally. For the general problem, given there will be at most k cuts and each cut is minimal, the total of the multicut will be at most k times greater than the optimal. This bound is a tight worst case, as illustrated by Fig. 4 where the total cost of the cuts made by our algorithm is 4α when $\beta > \alpha$. However, the optimal cut is (U_2, U_5), (U_3, U_6) and (U_4, U_7) with cost $2\alpha + 1$.

One solution to this inaccuracy would be to collapse all the sources of fusion-preventing dependences that have control dependence ancestors in common and cut all the corresponding sinks at once. Instead of multicuts, this construction would always make a single cut of the middle edge in Fig. 4(a). However, if the edge (U_3, U_6) has a weight greater than 4α then the multicut is better and this construction cannot find it. Differentiating between multicuts of degree 1, l and $l + 1$ makes these tradeoffs very difficult.

Complexity. This algorithm applies the $O(nmlog(n^2/m))$ maximum-flow algorithm k times splitting the graph at each application. For these types of graphs, computing control dependence is linear [10]. The complexity of our algorithm is therefore $O(knmlog(n^2/m))$ time.

9 Results

As our experimental vehicle we used the ParaScope Editor [21], an interactive parallelization tool which provides source-to-source program transformations using dependence analysis. We implemented the tests for correctness and the update of the source program and dependence information for fusion between two adjacent loops. We also implemented the correctness tests and updates for distribution to the finest granularity. We selected only programs which contained candidates for fusion or distribution to explore the impact on performance. In each program, performance improves.

9.1 Maximizing Parallelism

We performed the fusion algorithm for maximizing parallelism using ParaScope on 3 programs, Erlebacher, Seismic and Ocean. Both the fused and original hand-coded versions were compiled with the standard Fortran compiler and then executed in parallel on 19 processors of a Sequent Symmetry S81. The improvements due to fusion appear in Fig. 5.

program	parallel execution time in seconds without fusion	with fusion	% improvement
Erlebacher	6.67	6.20	7%
Seismic	17.05	12.59	26%
Ocean	116.6	79.3	32%

Fig. 5. Improving Parallel Performance with Fusion

Erlebacher is an ADI benchmark program with 835 non-comment lines written by Thomas Eidson of ICASE. It performs tridiagonal solves on all dimensions of a three dimensional array ($50\times50\times50$). In the original version, many of the loops consisted of a single statement. Twenty-six loop nests benefit from fusion, improving parallel performance by 7% as illustrated in Fig. 5. Multiple fusions were performed which reduced the twenty-six nests to eight with fusion groups of size 2, 3, 4 and 5 loops. In the fusion problems posed, three consisted of seven loop nodes with two fusion-preventing dependences. In six of the eight, fusion improved reuse as well increased granularity.

Seismic is 1312 non-comment lines and performs 1-D seismic inversion for oil exploration. It was written by Michael Lewis at Rice University. In this program, there was one opportunity to fuse four loops into a single nest which improved parallel performance by 26%. The original nests were connected by data dependence (*i.e.*, contained reuse) and accounted for a significant portion of the total execution time. These nests were fused across procedure boundaries using *loop extraction* to place the nests in the same procedure [17, 22]. Loop extraction pulls a loop out of the called routine and into the caller, actually increasing procedure call overhead. The increased reuse and decreased parallel loop synchronization resulting from fusion more than overcame the additional call overhead.

Ocean is 3664 non-comment line program from the Perfect benchmark suite [9]. Fusion improved parallel performance by 32 % on Ocean. Thirty-one nests benefit from fusion across procedure boundaries [17, 22]. Some of the candidates were exposed after constant propagation and dead code elimination. Loop extraction enabled fusion. (Again, extraction's only effect is to increase total execution time because of increased call overhead.) The fused nests consisted of between two and four parallel loops from the original program and increased both reuse and granularity. As Seismic and Ocean indicate, fusion is especially effective across procedure boundaries.

Erlebacher	seconds		% improvement
	original	fused	
IBM RS6000	.813	.672	4.25 %
Intel i860	.548	.518	5.47 %
Sun Sparc2	.400	.383	17.34 %

Fig. 6. Effect of Fusion on Erlebacher for Uniprocessors

9.2 Improving Reuse on Uniprocessors

In this section, we illustrate the benefits of fusion and of loop distribution to improve uniprocessor performance.

Erlebacher. In this experiment, we applied loop fusion only to loop nests with reuse using the simple algorithm. For two fusion graphs, the greedy algorithm was optimal for reuse. One required the simple fusion algorithm to obtain maximum reuse and in three, the algorithms reordered the loops to achieve better reuse. In Fig. 6, we compare the fused and original versions of the same nests on three modern microprocessors. Improvements due to fusion ranged from 4 to 17 percent.

Gaussian Elimination. This kernel illustrates that distribution and fusion should not be considered only in isolation; the improvements due to fusion and distribution will be enhanced by using them in concert with other transformations. In Gaussian Elimiation, the benefit of loop distribution comes from its ability to enable loop permutation. In the original KIJ form in Fig. 7, the J loop has poor data locality for Fortran 77 where arrays are stored in column-major order. Placing the I loop innermost for statement S_2 would instead provide stride-one access on the columns. Using loop distribution enables the interchange and the combination significantly improves the execution time. The algorithm that evaluates and applies loop permutation with distribution appears elsewhere [8].

Loop Distribution & Interchange

```
        { KIJ form }                    ⇒              { KJI form }
      DO K = 1,N                                     DO K = 1,N
        { select pivot, exchange rows }                { select pivot, exchange rows }
        DO I = K+1,N                                   DO I = K+1,N
S₁        A(I,K) = A(I,K) / A(K,K) - 1.1                 A(I,K) = A(I,K) / A(K,K) - 1.1
          DO J = K+1,N                                 DO J = K+1,N
S₂          A(I,J) = A(I,J) - A(I,K)*A(K,J)             DO I = K+1,N
                                                         A(I,J) = A(I,J) - A(I,K)*A(K,J)
```

Processor	256 × 256		% improvement
	original	distribution & interchange	
Sun Sparc2	12.23	5.22	57 %
Intel i860	8.35	2.63	69 %
IBM RS6000	27.29	4.84	82 %

Performance Results in Seconds

Fig. 7. Gaussian Elimination

9.3 Discussion

The fusion problems we encountered were fairly simple indicating that the complexity of the weighted algorithm is perhaps unnecessary. This preliminary evidence also indicates that the flexibility of the simple algorithm is required, *i.e.* the greedy algorithm is not sufficient. For example, reordering the loops in *Erlebacher* and improving on the greedy solution were both necessary to fully exploit reuse. Our results for these programs show a performance improvement every time fusion was applied to improve reuse or increase the granularity of parallelism.

Fusion is especially important for Fortran 90 programs because of the array language constructs. To compile Fortran 90 programs, the array notation is expanded into loop nests containing a single statement, providing many opportunities for fusion. Fusion and distribution also enable loop interchange, making them an important component for many optimization strategies.

10 Related Work

In the literature, fusion has been recommended for decreasing loop overhead, improving data locality and increasing the granularity of parallelism [2, 23]. Abu-Sufah and Warren have addressed in depth the safety, benefits and simple application of loop fusion [1, 25]. Neither presents a general algorithm for loop fusion that supports loop reordering or any differentiation between fusion choices. Goldberg and Paige [15] address a related fusion problem for stream processing, but their problem has constraints on fusions and ordering that are not present in the general fusion problem we address. Allen, Callahan, and Kennedy consider a broad fusion problem that introduces both task and loop parallelism, but does not address improving data locality or granularity of loop parallelism [3, 6]. Our algorithm for maximizing loop parallelism and its granularity is a new result.

Sarkar and Gao present an algorithm to perform loop fusion and array contraction to improve data locality on uniprocessors for single assignment languages [24]. This work is limited because it does not account for constraints imposed by data dependence [14, 24]. Their more recent work on loop fusion for uniprocessors and pipelining [14] takes into consideration data dependence constraints and also is based on the maximum-flow/minimum-cut algorithm. (Our work was developed independently.) Our algorithm is distinguished because of its tight worst-case bound. Both of our reuse algorithms reorder loop nests which is not possible in their formulation. The results indicate this flexibility is necessary. In practice, our preliminary experimental results also indicate that the additional complexity of the maximum-flow/minimum-cut algorithms is probably not necessary. Our overall approach is more flexible because it optimizes for both multiprocessors and uniprocessors.

For parallel code generation for shared-memory multiprocessors, this work extends our previous work by providing comprehensive fusion and distribution algorithms [19, 22]. In Carr, Kennedy, McKinley and Tseng, they combine loop permutation with fusion and distribution to improve data locality on uniprocessors [8]. The algorithms presented here are complementary to this work.

11 Summary

This paper presents an optimal algorithm for performing loop fusion and its dual, loop distribution, to maximize the granularity of loop parallelism, therefore minimizing sychronization. We prove that finding a fusion that results in maximum reuse is NP-hard and describe two heuristics to perform fusion and distribution based on reuse. The reuse algorithms work independently or as elements in the parallelization algorithm. The first algorithm for improving data locality uses a variant of the greedy algorithm and is linear in time. In practice, it may be that this algorithm is sufficient. However, the more ambitious algorithm may be beneficial for languages such as Fortran 90 that can pose difficult fusion problems. These algorithms are flexible and allow loop reordering to achieve a desired and safe partition. This paper also provides a general framework for solving loop fusion and loop distribution problems.

Acknowledgments

While pursuing the research on the weighted partition problem, we thank Alejandro Schaffer and Mark Krentel for their advice and expertise during several fruitful discussions. We also acknowledge Chau-Wen Tseng, Preston Briggs, Amer Diwan, Mary Hall and Nathaniel McIntosh for their valuable comments on numerous drafts of this paper.

References

1. W. Abu-Sufah. *Improving the Performance of Virtual Memory Computers*. PhD thesis, Dept. of Computer Science, University of Illinois at Urbana-Champaign, 1979.
2. F. Allen and J. Cocke. A catalogue of optimizing transformations. In J. Rustin, editor, *Design and Optimization of Compilers*. Prentice-Hall, 1972.
3. J. R. Allen, D. Callahan, and K. Kennedy. Automatic decomposition of scientific programs for parallel execution. In *Proceedings of the Fourteenth Annual ACM Symposium on the Principles of Programming Languages*, Munich, Germany, Jan. 1987.
4. J. R. Allen and K. Kennedy. Automatic translation of Fortran programs to vector form. *ACM Transactions on Programming Languages and Systems*, 9(4):491–542, Oct. 1987.
5. A. J. Bernstein. Analysis of programs for parallel processing. *IEEE Transactions on Electronic Computers*, 15(5):757–763, Oct. 1966.
6. D. Callahan. *A Global Approach to Detection of Parallelism*. PhD thesis, Dept. of Computer Science, Rice University, Mar. 1987.
7. D. Callahan, S. Carr, and K. Kennedy. Improving register allocation for subscripted variables. In *Proceedings of the SIGPLAN '90 Conference on Program Language Design and Implementation*, White Plains, NY, June 1990.
8. S. Carr, K. Kennedy, K. S. McKinley, and C. Tseng. Compiler optimizations for improving data locality. Technical Report TR92-195, Dept. of Computer Science, Rice University, Nov. 1992.

9. G. Cybenko, L. Kipp, L. Pointer, and D. Kuck. Supercomputer performance evaluation and the Perfect benchmarks. In *Proceedings of the 1990 ACM International Conference on Supercomputing*, Amsterdam, The Netherlands, June 1990.

10. R. Cytron, J. Ferrante, and V. Sarkar. Experiences using control dependence in PTRAN. In D. Gelernter, A. Nicolau, and D. Padua, editors, *Languages and Compilers for Parallel Computing*. The MIT Press, 1990.

11. E. Dahlhaus, D. S. Johnson, C. H. Papadimitriou, P. D. Seymour, and M. Yannakakis. The complexity of multiway cuts. In *Proceedings of the 24th Annual ACM Symposium on the Theory of Computing*, May 1992.

12. J. Ferrante, K. Ottenstein, and J. Warren. The program dependence graph and its use in optimization. *ACM Transactions on Programming Languages and Systems*, 9(3):319–349, July 1987.

13. Ford, Jr., L. R. and D. R. Fulkerson. *Flows in Networks*. Princeton University Press, Princeton, NJ, 1962.

14. G. Gao, R. Olsen, V. Sarkar, and R. Thekkath. Collective loop fusion for array contraction. In *Proceedings of the Fifth Workshop on Languages and Compilers for Parallel Computing*, New Haven, CT, Aug. 1992.

15. A. Goldberg and R. Paige. Stream processing. In *Conference Record of the 1984 ACM Symposium on Lisp and Functional Programming*, pages 228–234, Aug. 1984.

16. A. V. Goldberg and R. E. Tarjan. A new approach to the maximum-flow problem. *Journal of the Association for Computing Machinery*, 35(4):921–940, Oct. 1988.

17. M. W. Hall, K. Kennedy, and K. S. McKinley. Interprocedural transformations for parallel code generation. In *Proceedings of Supercomputing '91*, Albuquerque, NM, Nov. 1991.

18. K. Kennedy and K. S. McKinley. Loop distribution with arbitrary control flow. In *Proceedings of Supercomputing '90*, New York, NY, Nov. 1990.

19. K. Kennedy and K. S. McKinley. Optimizing for parallelism and data locality. In *Proceedings of the 1992 ACM International Conference on Supercomputing*, Washington, DC, July 1992.

20. K. Kennedy and K. S. McKinley. Typed fusion with applications to parallel and sequential code generation. Technical Report TR93-208, Dept. of Computer Science, Rice University, Aug. 1993.

21. K. Kennedy, K. S. McKinley, and C. Tseng. Analysis and transformation in an interactive parallel programming tool. *Concurrency: Practice & Experience*, to appear 1993.

22. K. S. McKinley. *Automatic and Interactive Parallelization*. PhD thesis, Dept. of Computer Science, Rice University, Apr. 1992.

23. A. Porterfield. *Software Methods for Improvement of Cache Performance*. PhD thesis, Dept. of Computer Science, Rice University, May 1989.

24. V. Sarkar and G. Gao. Optimization of array accesses by collective loop transformations. In *Proceedings of the 1991 ACM International Conference on Supercomputing*, Cologne, Germany, June 1991.

25. J. Warren. A hierachical basis for reordering transformations. In *Conference Record of the Eleventh Annual ACM Symposium on the Principles of Programming Languages*, Salt Lake City, UT, Jan. 1984.

26. M. Yannakakis, P. C. Kanellakis, S. C. Cosmadakis, and C. H. Papadimitriou. Cutting and partitioning a graph after a fixed pattern. *Automata, Languages, and Programming - Lecture Notes in Computer Science*, 154:712–722, 1983.

Align and Distribute-based Linear Loop Transformations

Jordi Torres, Eduard Ayguadé, Jesús Labarta and Mateo Valero

Departament d'Arquitectura de Computadors, Universitat Politècnica de Catalunya
Campus Nord, Mòdul D6, Gran Capità s/núm. 08071 - Barcelona, SPAIN

Abstract. In this paper we generalize the framework of linear loop transformations in the sense that loop alignment is considered as a new component in the transformation process. The aim is to match the structure of loop nests with the data distribution and alignment in order to eliminate non-local references whenever possible when compiling a sequential program for a distributed memory machine. The alignment and distribution functions are assumed to be user specified or automatically generated by the compiler. The transformation process is modelled with non-singular matrices and we use the ideas recently proposed in this field to find part of the transformation matrix and generate an efficient transformed code. However, additional aspects have to be studied when the alignment and distribution functions are considered, both in the obtaining of the transformation matrix and in the generation of code.

1 Introduction

Loop transformations have been recognized to be one of the most important components of the parallelizing and vectorizing technology for current supercomputers. The aim is to transform nested-loop structures in the source program into semantically equivalent versions with more opportunities to parallelize them [1, 2].

When distributed memory machines are considered to run scientific codes, data decomposition is needed. Data have to be decomposed into pieces and distributed among all processors. Optimizing locality is crucial for this kind of architectures and for non-uniform memory architectures (NUMA) in general. As a consequence, it is important to access local data whenever possible to avoid the access to remote data. When non-local references are necessary, and in order to amortize their remote access, block transfer of data and data reuse are additional aspects to be considered and optimized to improve the efficiency.

The programming model offered by Fortran-D [3] and HPF [4] gives the programmer control over how to align and distribute data structures across processors.

The compiler has to be able to assign work to processors (the ownership rule is the simplest way to do this [5]) and restructure loop nests with the aim of avoiding non-local accesses as much as possible, and when necessary, optimize communication to transfer remote data [6]. The single-program multiple-data (SPMD) model [7] is used to generate code. Each processor runs the same program but accesses to different parts of the data.

Research in the past years has focussed at finding a matrix theory for program transformations to reveal program parallelism [8, 9] or exploit data locality and block transfers [10, 11]. From the specification of the source loop nest and the transformation matrix, a target loop nest is generated with more opportunities to exploit parallelism or for data reuse. This step has been solved when unimodular matrices are used [8, 9] and in general, when non-unimodular matrices are considered. The key point in the solutions proposed in the last case is the use of the Fourier-Motzkin elimination method and the Hermite Normal Form decomposition [12, 13, 14].

In this paper we propose to consider the set of statements in the loop body as a new component in the framework of non-singular transformations. This allows to consider loop alignment [15, 16, 17] in a unified way with other loop transformations. We assume that data alignment and distribution is either user specified or automatically generated by the compiler. From the reaching alignment and distribution functions for each array, and array references in the statements, a different transformation for each statement of the loop is derived with the aim of reducing the number of non-local accesses. In the scope of this paper we consider that the same transformation matrix is used for all the statements and add a different alignment component to each of them.

The owner computes rule is the basic mechanism to associate loop iterations to processors. Sometimes the owner computes rule can be relaxed allowing processors to compute values for data they do not own. Once computed, these values have to be send to the owners. Deciding the alignment component for a statement can be done by analyzing its multiple right-hand side and the left-hand side references to distributed arrays. In order to reduce the number of non-local accesses, the owner computes rule can be broken.

Aspects dealing with the assignment of iterations to processors and generation of synchronization or communication instructions that take care of dependences are not considered in this paper.

The rest of the paper is organized as follows. In section 2 we present the terminology and assumptions used along this paper. In section 3 we outline some previous work on loop transformations, code generation for them and obtaining of the transformation matrix when NUMA architectures are considered. Section 4 presents the alignment component in the transformation framework and code generation. In section 5 we discuss some ideas and problems to obtain the alignment component that is added to each statement. Finally, we conclude the paper and present some future work.

2 Terminology and Assumptions

Through this paper we consider perfectly nested loops $\{L_1, ..., L_n\}$ where bounds for any loop L_k ($1 \le k \le n$) are affine functions of indices of its outer loops $L_1, ..., L_{k-1}$, that is,

$$i_k \ge a_{k,0} + a_{k,1} \cdot i_1 + ... + a_{k,(k-1)} \cdot i_{k-1} = l_k$$
$$i_k \le b_{k,0} + b_{k,1} \cdot i_1 + ... + b_{k,(k-1)} \cdot i_{k-1} = u_k$$

The iteration space for this loop nest is defined as

$$IS = \{(i_1, ..., i_n) \in Z^n, l_k \le i_k \le u_k, 1 \le k \le n\}$$

and can be written following the matrix notation used in the literature

$$\alpha \cdot I \le \beta$$

where

$$\alpha = \begin{bmatrix} L - ID \\ ID - U \end{bmatrix} \quad and \quad \beta = \begin{bmatrix} -l \\ u \end{bmatrix}$$

L is constructed from the coefficients $a_{k,i}$ ($1 \le k \le n$, $1 \le i \le k-1$) of the loop indices in the lower bound expressions, U is constructed from the coefficients $b_{k,i}$ ($1 \le k \le n$, $1 \le i \le k-1$) of the loop indices in the upper bound expressions, ID is the identity matrix, and l and u are constructed from the independent coefficients $a_{k,0}$ and $b_{k,0}$ ($1 \le k \le n$) of the lower and upper bounds respectively.

For example, for the loop nest in Figure 1.a, the IS of the loop can be defined by

$$\begin{bmatrix} -1 & 0 \\ 0 & -1 \\ 1 & 0 \\ 0 & 1 \end{bmatrix} \cdot \begin{bmatrix} i_1 \\ i_2 \end{bmatrix} \le \begin{bmatrix} -1 \\ -1 \\ 10 \\ 8 \end{bmatrix}$$

Figure 1.b shows the aspect of the IS for this loop. Each point represents the execution of one iteration of the inner loop body.

In the scope of this paper we consider dense iteration spaces, i.e., spaces where all points correspond to iterations of the loop.

The loop body is composed of multiple assignment statements $\{S_1, ..., S_m\}$ that reference array variables whose subscripts are affine functions of loop indices $i_1, ..., i_n$. Let V be the set of statements in the loop body. The Statement per Iteration Space (SIS) of a loop nest is defined as the cartesian product

$$SIS = IS \times V$$

Each point in the SIS represents the execution of an iteration of a statement of the loop body.

Dependence relations between a pair of statements S_i and S_j (denoted $S_i \, \delta \, S_j$) appear when there is an execution ordering between them [18]. We do not distinguish between different kinds of data dependences because they all impose ordering constraints in the same way. When dependence relations are uniform (i.e., invariant through the SIS), they can be characterized by distance vectors $\bar{d}=(d_1, ..., d_n)$ expressing the number of iterations that the dependence extends across in each loop dimension. Dependences are lexicographically positive, that is, the leading non-zero component is always positive.

Arrays accessed during the execution of a loop are considered to be aligned among them and distributed across processors. The alignment and distribution of the arrays is assumed to be user specified or automatically generated by the compiler [19, 20]. In any case, we consider that each array accessed in the loop is affected by a set of reaching alignment and distribution functions. These functions are the standard supported by current data-partitioning languages such as Fortran-D. The ALIGN statement maps each array element onto an index domain or DECOMPOSITION. The DISTRIBUTE statement groups elements of the decomposition and maps them onto the parallel machine. Alignment can be either within or between dimensions and include offsets. Each dimension is localized or distributed in a block, cyclic or block-cyclic manner.

The sequential code in Figure 1.a shows the reaching alignment and distribution functions for the arrays referenced inside the loop. Notice that just one dimension is distributed, as specified by the : attribute in the DISTRIBUTE statement which denotes that the dimension is assigned locally. In the example, if P is the number of processors, processor p (p=1, 2, ..., P) owns rows p, p+P, p+2·P, ... of matrices A and C and p-1, p+P-1, p+2·P-1, ... of matrix B.

3   Linear Loop Transformations and Data Access Matrix

A loop transformation is a mapping between two iteration spaces (named original and target IS). In this paper we consider linear transformations, which can be modelled using non-singular integer matrices. Unimodular matrices (i.e., matrices whose determinant is ±1) are a particular case and can be used to model some basic transformations such as permutations, skewing and reversal [8, 9]. Non-unimodular matrices can be used to model other basic transformations such as scaling [12], but in general, any linear transformation represented by a non-singular integer matrix can be viewed as a composition of these four basic transformations [12].

Let I be a point of the original IS, J a point of the target IS and T the transformation matrix. The relationship among them is

$$J = T \cdot I$$

The target IS can be dense or sparse depending on the unimodularity of the transformation matrix.

In our model, the first p rows of the transformation matrix T define the spatial component of the transformation and the last n-p rows the temporal component [21].

ALIGN A, C WITH E

ALIGN B (i, j) WITH E (i+1, j-1)

DISTRIBUTE E (CYCLIC, :)

DO i_1=1, 10

    DO i_2=1, 8

        $A[i_1+2 \cdot i_2, i_1] = f(A[i_1+2 \cdot i_2, i_1], C[i_1+1, i_2], B[i_1+2 \cdot i_2-1, i_1])$

        $B[i_1+2 \cdot i_2, i_1] = g(A[i_1+2 \cdot i_2+1, i_1], B[i_1+2 \cdot i_2, i_1])$

    ENDO

ENDO   (a)

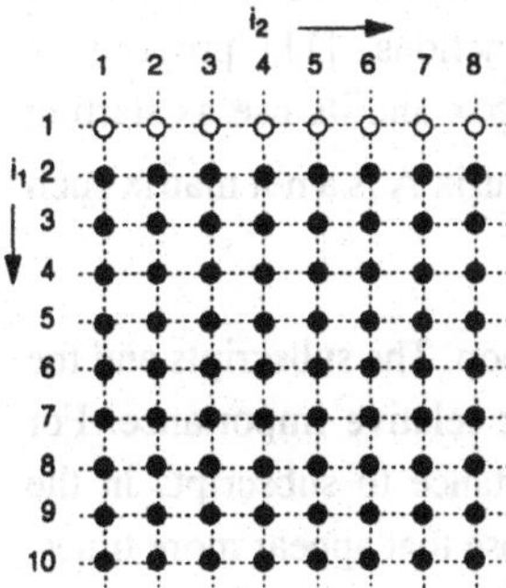

$$T = \begin{bmatrix} 1 & 2 \\ 1 & 0 \end{bmatrix}$$

(b)

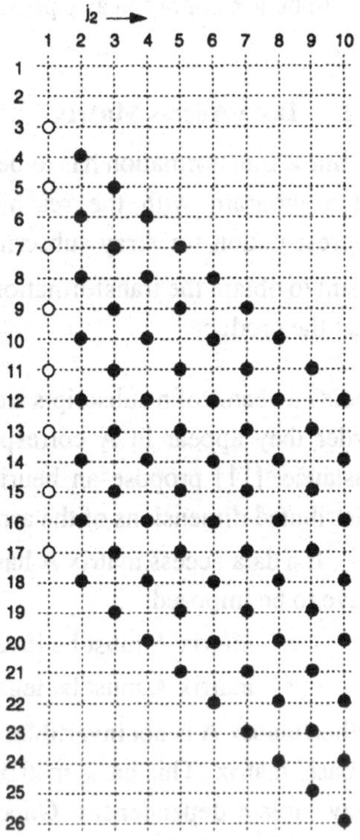

(c)

ALIGN A, C WITH E

ALIGN B (i, j) WITH E (i+1, j-1)

DISTRIBUTE E (CYCLIC, :)

DO j_1=3, 26

    DO $j_2 = j_1 + 2 \cdot \max (-8, \lceil (1-j_1)/2 \rceil), j_1 + 2 \cdot \min (-1, \lfloor (10-j_1)/2 \rfloor), 2$

        $A[j_1, j_2] = f(A[j_1, j_2], C[j_2+1, (j_1- j_2)/2], B[j_1-1, j_2])$

        $B[j_1, j_2] = g(A[j_1+1, j_2], B[j_1, j_2])$

    ENDO

ENDO

(d)

Fig. 1. Working example: (a) Source loop nest and (b) original IS. (c) Target IS when a non-singular transformation matrix T is used. (d) Transformed loop nest that scans the points in the transformed IS skipping over points that do not have to be executed.

Iterations in the outermost loops of the transformed nest are distributed among the processors while iterations the innermost loops are executed sequentially within each processor.

Let $\bar{d}$ be a distance vector in the original IS. Due to the fact that T is a linear transformation, $T \cdot \bar{d}$ is the transformed distance vector in the target IS. A transformation T is legal if

$$T \cdot \bar{d} > \bar{0}$$

for all dependence relations $\bar{d}$ in the loop. This means that each transformed dependence has to be lexicographically positive in the target IS.

3.1 Data Access Matrix

A linear transformation has to be found in order to match the structure of the loop nests in a program with the reaching data decomposition functions. [11] proposes a representation for array subscripts named Data Access Matrix and its use as starting point to obtain the transformation matrix. The data access matrix A is a n·n matrix such that the product

$$A \cdot I$$

yields a vector of n subscripts from array references in the loop. The subscripts and the order they appear in A correspond to an estimate of their relative importance. For instance, [11] propose an heuristic that gives more importance to subscripts in the distributed dimensions of the arrays and, among them, to those that appear more times.

If a data access matrix A has to be used as a transformation matrix, two conditions have to be imposed:

- matrix A must be invertible.
- matrix A must be legal, that is, it must not violate dependences in the loop.

When matrix A is not invertible, linearly dependent rows have to be eliminated yielding a basis matrix. This basis matrix has to be legal so additional rows must be deleted if they violate dependences. Once a legal basis matrix is obtained, it is padded to an invertible matrix by adding rows which are independent of the rows in the basis matrix and which do not violate dependence constraints. The transformation matrix obtained using this approach retains as many rows of the original data access matrix as possible.

Figure 1 shows the example that is used as working example along the paper. Figure 1.b shows the original IS and Figure 1.c shows the target IS when the following non-singular transformation matrix is used

$$T = \begin{bmatrix} 1 & 2 \\ 1 & 0 \end{bmatrix}$$

Different shades are used in the points to help the reader to establish the relationship between points in the original and transformed IS. This transformation matrix corresponds to the data access matrix for the array subscripts in the distributed array dimensions shown in Figure 1.a.

3.2 Code Generation

Once a legal transformation T has been defined, we have to generate a loop nest that appropriately scans the points in the target IS. In order to do that, we have to:

- generate the bounds of the target DO loops and the stride for each loop index in order to skip over points of the target IS that do not have to be executed. As we have seen, the original loop nest is defined by $\alpha \cdot I \le \beta$. Therefore, if a transformation matrix T is applied, the target IS can be obtained from the inverse matrix T^{-1}

$$\alpha \cdot T^{-1} \cdot J \le \beta$$

However, the bounds obtained by direct elimination from the above inequality might not have the structure assumed at the beginning of the previous section.

- replace the subscripts in the array references that appear in the loop body such that they are affine functions of the new loop indices (i.e., substitute I with $T^{-1} \cdot J$ in all subscript functions).

Some previous works [8, 9] have addressed the problem of code generation when unimodular matrices are used to transform the original IS. [22] includes conditional statements in order to deal with the sparseness that is introduced in the target IS when a non-unimodular matrix is used. Other authors [12, 13, 14] have made proposals to avoid these conditionals and, as a consequence, reduce the overhead introduced by them. The key point in all of them is the use of the Fourier-Motzkin elimination method and the Hermite Normal Form decomposition [23] to obtain the target loop nest.

Figure 2.a summarizes the procedure when the source IS is dense and the transformation matrix is unimodular. With these conditions, the target IS is also dense. If the transformation matrix is non-unimodular, then a sparse IS is obtained. Figure 2.b shows the procedure applied to obtain the target code. The basic idea, as proposed in [12] is to decompose the matrix T into the product of a lower triangular matrix H with positive diagonal elements (Hermite matrix of T) and a unimodular matrix U (reflecting column transformations performed on T to obtain H) such that

$$T = H \cdot U$$

Applying U to the original IS, and using Fourier-Motzkin elimination, the bounds of a dense auxiliary IS are obtained. Because of the sparseness of the target IS, two things have to be done: adjust loop bounds and skip over points that do not have to be executed. Matrix H is used to obtain the bounds of the sparse target loop nest by direct elimination. The diagonal elements of matrix H are the strides of each loop index variable in the target loop nest.

Figure 1.d shows how the original loop nest shown in Figure 1.a is transformed applying the procedure outlined in this section.

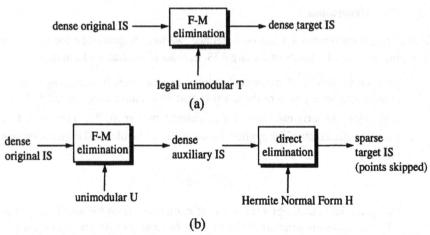

Fig. 2. Transforming a dense IS using Fourier-Motzkin elimination. (a) When a unimodular matrix T is used and (b) when a non-unimodular matrix T is used.

4   The Alignment Component

Before presenting the general framework we present the underlying idea in our working example. Assume that iterations of the outermost loop in Figure 1.d are distributed among P processors in such a way that processor p (p=1, 2, ..., P) is involved in the execution of an iteration j_1 if (j_1-1) mod P = (p-1). With this assignment, the accesses to matrices A and B are local in the execution of statement S_1 but non-local in the execution of statement S_2. For instance and assuming P=4, processor p=1 executes iterations j_1=5, 9, ..., 25 and accesses

$$A(5, j_2), A(9, j_2), ..., A(25, j_2)$$
$$B(4, j_2), B(8, j_2), ..., B(24, j_2)$$

in the execution of S_1 which are stored in its local memory and accesses

$$A(6, j_2), A(10, j_2), ..., A(26, j_2)$$
$$B(5, j_2), B(9, j_2), ..., B(25, j_2)$$

in the execution of S_2 which are stored in the local memory of processor p=2. In fact, to make local the accesses to matrices A and B in statement S_2, we would have had to distribute iterations in such a way that j_1 mod P = (p-1). In order to make local all the accesses to A and B, it is necessary to align the execution of statements S_1 and S_2, as shown below.

Consider that each statement in the loop is represented with a hyperplane in the SIS and that we apply a different transformation to each statement in such a way that the resulting target IS is the one shown in Figure 3. Different shades are used to identify the different hyperplanes. If processor p executes iterations j_1 so that (j_1-1) mod P = (p-1), then all the accesses to matrices A and B are local. For instance, processor p=1 executes j_1=5, 9, ..., 25 and accesses

$$A(5, j_2), A(9, j_2), ..., A(25, j_2)$$
$$B(4, j_2), B(8, j_2), ..., B(24, j_2)$$

in the execution of both S_1 and S_2.

Due to the alignment of the hyperplanes, most of the iterations in the target loop execute both statements but others just execute one of them. The new bounds of the target loop nest have to be the union of the bounds for each statement. The body has to include the appropriate conditional statements to ensure that each statement is executed within its bounds.

In this section we generalize the framework of linear transformations to include loop alignment. Some additional aspects have to be considered in the generation of the target loop nest, such as the generation of conditional guards to preserve the semantics of the original loop nest and the optimization of these conditional guards to reduce as much as possible the execution overhead introduced.

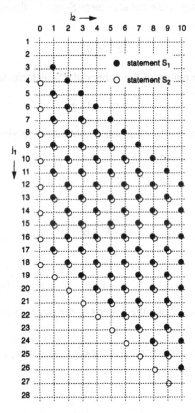

Fig. 3. Target SIS assuming that each statement of the loop is transformed with a different transformation.

4.1 Bounds for each statement

We can consider that the SIS is the composition of several hyperplanes, one for each statement in the loop body. Consider that the hyperplane associated to a statement S_i is transformed using the following transformation

$$J^i = T \cdot (I + D^i)$$

where D^i is the displacement applied to the S_i hyperplane. Notice that all the statements are transformed using the same transformation matrix T.

Let $T = H \cdot U$ be the decomposition of matrix T into a unimodular matrix U and the Hermite upper triangular matrix H. Therefore, the transformed IS for statement S_i is

$$J^i = H \cdot U \cdot (I + D^i) = H \cdot K^i$$

being K^i the auxiliary IS of the statement S_i

$$K^i = U \cdot (I + D^i)$$

The bounds of the auxiliary space for statement S_i can be derived from the bounds of the original IS

$$\alpha \cdot I \le \beta$$

and using U^{-1}, the inverse matrix of the unimodular transformation,

$$I = U^{-1} \cdot K^i - D^i$$

So the bounds of the auxiliary IS of S_i can be obtained applying the Fourier-Motzkin elimination method to

$$(\alpha \cdot U^{-1} \cdot K^i) - (\alpha \cdot D^i) \le \beta$$

or more clearly to

$$\alpha' \cdot K^i \le \beta^i$$

where

$$\alpha' = \alpha \cdot U^{-1} \qquad \text{and} \qquad \beta^i = \beta + \alpha \cdot D^i$$

Using the matrix H, we can obtain the bounds of the target IS for each statement S_i by direct elimination.

For instance, consider that we transform each statement hyperplane in the working example in the following way:

$$J^1 = T \cdot I$$

$$J^2 = T \cdot \left(I + \begin{bmatrix} -1 \\ 1 \end{bmatrix} \right)$$

The decomposition of T in the Hermite Normal Form is given by

$$T = \begin{bmatrix} 1 & 2 \\ 1 & 0 \end{bmatrix} \qquad H = \begin{bmatrix} 1 & 0 \\ 1 & 2 \end{bmatrix} \qquad U = \begin{bmatrix} 1 & 2 \\ 0 & -1 \end{bmatrix}$$

The bounds of the auxiliary space of each statement can be obtained from

$$\begin{bmatrix} -1 & -2 \\ 0 & 1 \\ 1 & 2 \\ 0 & -1 \end{bmatrix} \cdot K^1 \le \begin{bmatrix} -1 \\ -1 \\ 10 \\ 8 \end{bmatrix} \qquad \text{and} \qquad \begin{bmatrix} -1 & -2 \\ 0 & 1 \\ 1 & 2 \\ 0 & -1 \end{bmatrix} \cdot K^2 \le \begin{bmatrix} 0 \\ -2 \\ 9 \\ 9 \end{bmatrix}$$

and are,

$$\text{DO } k_1^1 = 3, 26$$
$$\text{DO } k_2^1 = \max (-8, \lceil (1-k_1^1)/2 \rceil), \min (-1, \lfloor (10-k_1^1)/2 \rfloor)$$

for statement S_1, and

$$\text{DO } k_1^2 = 4, 27$$
$$\text{DO } k_2^2 = \max (-9, \lceil -k_1^2/2 \rceil), \min (-2, \lfloor (9 -k_1^2)/2 \rfloor)$$

for statement S_2. Due to the sparseness of the target SIS, we have to modify or adjust these bounds using matrix H. Since H is lower triangular, we can derive the relationship between both spaces

$$j_1^i = k_1^i \qquad j_2^i = k_1^i + 2 \cdot k_2^i$$

and finally obtain the bounds

$$\text{DO } j_1 = 3, 26$$
$$\text{DO } j_2 = j_1 + 2 \cdot \max (-8, \lceil (1-j_1)/2 \rceil), j_1 + 2 \cdot \min (-1, \lfloor (10-j_1)/2 \rfloor), 2$$

for statement S_1, and

$$\text{DO } j_1 = 4, 27$$
$$\text{DO } j_2 = j_1 + 2 \cdot \max (-9, \lceil -j_1/2 \rceil), j_1 + 2 \cdot \min (-2, \lfloor (9 - j_1)/2 \rfloor), 2$$

for statement S_2. Notice that the elements in the diagonal of matrix H are the strides in each loop dimension.

4.2 Cover Bounds

Now we have to obtain the bounds of the union of the two statement hyperplanes in order to obtain the target loop nest. We define the cover bounds as the bounds of a space that includes all the statement hyperplanes. The cover bounds can be obtained by elimination from

$$\alpha' \cdot K^{cover} \le max_{\forall i} \{\beta^i\}$$

where the maximum function is applied to each component of the vectors β^i. In our working example we have to solve

$$\begin{bmatrix} -1 & -2 \\ 0 & 1 \\ 1 & 2 \\ 0 & -1 \end{bmatrix} \cdot K^{cover} \leq \begin{bmatrix} 0 \\ -1 \\ 10 \\ 9 \end{bmatrix}$$

obtaining the following target loop nest

DO $j_1 = 2, 28$

DO $j_2 = j_1 + 2 \cdot \max (-9, \lceil -j_1/2 \rceil), j_1 + 2 \cdot \min (-1, \lfloor (10-j_1)/2 \rfloor), 2$

From now on, and for reasons of clarity, we denote with $lower_i^k$ and $upper_i^k$ the lower and upper bounds for each hyperplane S_k in loop dimension L_i, with $step_i$ the stride for loop dimension L_i, and with $lower_i^{cover}$ and $upper_i^{cover}$ the lower and upper bounds of the cover in loop dimension L_i.

With this notation, the basic structure of the target loop nest and body can be written as shown in Figure 4. The key point to note here is that this code is expensive in terms of run-time overhead. In each iteration of the loop, the guard conditionals that control the execution of each statement have to be evaluated. In general, there is a part of the SIS where all the statements of the loop body are executed and it encompasses a large part of the cover.

4.3 Core Bounds

We define the core bounds as the bounds of a space where all the statements of the loop body are executed. The core bounds can be obtained by elimination from

$$\alpha' \cdot K^{core} \leq \min_{\forall i} \{\beta^i\}$$

where the minimum function is applied to each component of the vectors β^i. In our working example we have to solve

$$\begin{bmatrix} -1 & -2 \\ 0 & 1 \\ 1 & 2 \\ 0 & -1 \end{bmatrix} \cdot K^{core} \leq \begin{bmatrix} -1 \\ -2 \\ 9 \\ 8 \end{bmatrix}$$

obtaining the following loop nest

DO $j_1 = 5, 25$

DO $j_2 = j_1 + 2 \cdot \max (-8, \lceil (1-j_1)/2 \rceil), j_1 + 2 \cdot \min (-2, \lfloor (9-j_1)/2 \rfloor), 2$

```
DO j₁ = lower₁ᶜᵒᵛᵉʳ , upper₁ᶜᵒᵛᵉʳ , step₁
    ...
    DO jₖ = lowerₖᶜᵒᵛᵉʳ , upperₖᶜᵒᵛᵉʳ , stepₖ
        ...
        DO jₙ = lowerₙᶜᵒᵛᵉʳ , upperₙᶜᵒᵛᵉʳ , stepₙ
            ...
            IF (lower₁ᵏ ≤ j₁ ≤upper₁ᵏ ) and (...) and (lowerₙᵏ ≤ jₙ ≤upperₙᵏ ) THEN {statement Sₖ}
            ...
        ENDDO
        ...
    ENDDO
    ...
ENDDO
```

Fig. 4. Basic Structure of the code with guard conditionals.

Again we denote with $lower_i^{core}$ and $upper_i^{core}$ the lower and upper bounds of the core in each loop dimension L_i. Notice that this core part can be executed without guard conditionals at the statement level, reducing the run-time overhead introduced by them.

4.4 Code Generation

Let us consider again our working example. Figure 5 shows the skeleton of the target SIS and the expressions of the boundaries for each of the spaces considered.

In general, the code has three parts, namely prolog, core and epilog parts. The prolog and epilog parts are defined as the parts of the cover not included in the core that are executed before or after the core part, respectively. We have to include guard conditionals in these two parts in order to control the execution of each statement.

For instance consider what happens when $j_1=10$ in Figure 5. In this case, first we have to execute the iteration $j_2=0$ of S_2 (prolog part), then the iteration $j_2=2$, 4 and 6 of both statements (core part) and finally the iteration $j_2=8$ of S_1 (epilog part). Not always these three parts are executed. For example, observe that for $j_1=15$ only points in the core part have to be executed, and that for $j_1=4$ no points have to be executed in the core part.

The structure of the code can be written using our notation as shown in Figure 6. In this code, and depending on the original loop bounds, transformation and alignment components, the compiler has a lot of opportunities to simplify the conditionals generated and make the code less run-time expensive.

In particular, the code that is obtained for our working example is shown in Figure 7. For instance, the compiler can recognize that just one iteration is executed in the prolog and epilog parts due to the values of the alignment components. Therefore, loops in these parts can be substituted by conditional statements. The compiler can also recognize that statement S_1 is never executed in the prolog part and statement S_2 is never executed in the epilog part.

4.5 Dependence Relations in the Target Space

Let d_{ij} be a dependence relation between two different statements S_i and S_j (i.e., $S_i \delta S_j$). The distance vector $\overline{d}_{ij}$ is the number of iterations the dependence extends across in each loop dimension. So

$$\overline{d}_{ij} = I_2 - I_1$$

where I_1 and I_2 are two points in the original IS directly dependent because of the dependence d_{ij}.

If T is the transformation matrix applied,

$$T \cdot (I_1 + D^i) \qquad \text{and} \qquad T \cdot (I_2 + D^j)$$

are the corresponding points in the target SIS. Therefore, due to the fact that T is a linear

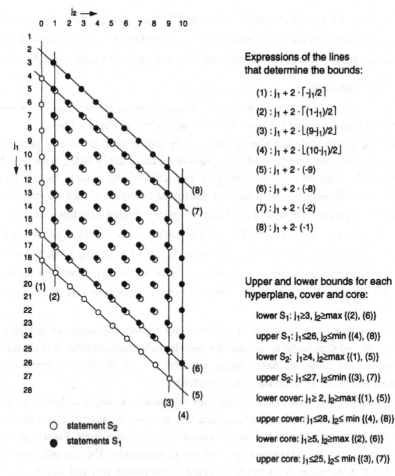

Expressions of the lines that determine the bounds:

$(1): j_1 + 2 \cdot \lceil -j_1/2 \rceil$

$(2): j_1 + 2 \cdot \lceil (1-j_1)/2 \rceil$

$(3): j_1 + 2 \cdot \lfloor (9-j_1)/2 \rfloor$

$(4): j_1 + 2 \cdot \lfloor (10-j_1)/2 \rfloor$

$(5): j_1 + 2 \cdot (-9)$

$(6): j_1 + 2 \cdot (-8)$

$(7): j_1 + 2 \cdot (-2)$

$(8): j_1 + 2 \cdot (-1)$

Upper and lower bounds for each hyperplane, cover and core:

lower S_1: $j_1 \geq 3$, $j_2 \geq \max \{(2), (6)\}$

upper S_1: $j_1 \leq 26$, $j_2 \leq \min \{(4), (8)\}$

lower S_2: $j_1 \geq 4$, $j_2 \geq \max \{(1), (5)\}$

upper S_2: $j_1 \leq 27$, $j_2 \leq \min \{(3), (7)\}$

lower cover: $j_1 \geq 2$, $j_2 \geq \max \{(1), (5)\}$

upper cover: $j_1 \leq 28$, $j_2 \leq \min \{(4), (8)\}$

lower core: $j_1 \geq 5$, $j_2 \geq \max \{(2), (6)\}$

upper core: $j_1 \leq 25$, $j_2 \leq \min \{(3), (7)\}$

○ statement S_2

● statements S_1

Fig. 5. Basic skeleton of the SIS for our working example and expressions for the lines that determine each bound.

transformation, the transformed distance is

$$T \cdot (\overline{d_{ij}} + D^j - D^i)$$

The transformation matrix and alignment components must be legal in the sense that they have to respect all data dependences d_{ij} in the loop.

5 Obtaining the Alignment Components

In this section we present some ideas about how to obtain the alignment component for each statement in the loop body. The aim of the process is to reduce interprocessor communication when parallelizing for a coarse-grain MIMD system. With the alignment components we try to minimize the number of non-local data references in the execution of the code assigned to each processor.

In the same way [11] constructs the Data Access Matrix from the subscripts in array references, we obtain the alignment components for each statement in the loop body. Constants in the set of subscripts that make up the Data Access Matrix and the alignment functions for the arrays subscripted by them contribute to find the alignment components. In fact, just those subscripts that correspond to the spatial part of the transformation matrix have to be analyzed.

Assume that we are analyzing the reference to a matrix M in a statement of the loop. Let σ be a vector with the independent coefficients of the subscripts in the spatial part

DO j_1 = lower$_1^{cover}$, upper$_1^{cover}$, step$_1$

    DO j_2 = lower$_2^{cover}$, lower$_2^{core}$ - step$_2$, step$_2$ **prolog part**

       ...

       IF (lower$_1^k \le j_1 \le$ upper$_1^k$) and (lower$_2^k \le j_2 \le$ upper$_2^k$) THEN {statement S_k}

       ...

    ENDDO

    IF (lower$^{core} \le j_1 \le$ upper^{core}) THEN

       DO j_2 = lower$_2^{core}$, upper$_2^{core}$, step$_2$ **core part**

        ...

        {statement S_k}

        ...

       ENDDO

       low = upper$_2^{core}$ + step$_2$ **epilog part**

    ELSE

       low = lower$_2^{core}$

    ENDIF

    DO j_2 = low, upper$_2^{cover}$, step$_2$

       ...

       IF (lower$_1^k \le j_1 \le$ upper$_1^k$) and (lower$_2^k \le j_2 \le$ upper$_2^k$) THEN {statement S_k}

       ...

    ENDDO

ENDDO

Fig. 6. Target code generated with prolog, core and epilog parts (for two-dimensional loops).

of the transformation matrix used in the reference to M. For instance, consider the reference $B[i_1+2 \cdot i_2-1, i_1]$ in statement S_1 in the example shown in Figure 8.a. Assume the same transformation matrix T used along the paper in which the first row corresponds to the spatial part of the transformation. In this case, the subscript term is $i_1+2 \cdot i_2$ and the independent coefficient is $\sigma=[-1]$.

Let ϕ be a vector whose components are the offsets of the ALIGN function for array M in the dimensions where the correspondent subscripts are used. In the same example, the align function for matrix B is

$$\text{ALIGN } B(i, j) \text{ WITH } E(i+1, j-1)$$

and therefore $\phi=[1]$ as indicated in the first component of the decomposition.

If we denote with T_s the spatial part of the transformation, the alignment component D for the reference analyzed can be obtained from

$$T_s \cdot D = \sigma + \phi$$

For the reference we are analyzing, we have to solve

$$\begin{bmatrix} 1 & 2 \end{bmatrix} \cdot \begin{bmatrix} D_1 \\ D_2 \end{bmatrix} = \boxed{0} \qquad \rightarrow \qquad d_1 + 2 \cdot d_2 = 0$$

Due to the fact that this equation has several integer solutions, we select the one that maximizes the size of the core part in the resulting code. In this case, this means that the minimum value for D_2 is chosen, so [0, 0] is the alignment vector obtained.

The alignment component D^i for a statement S_i is the alignment component that appears more times in all the array references in S_i.

Applying this procedure to all the references in the loop shown in Figure 8.a, we obtain $D^1=[0, 0]^t$ for statement S_1 and $D^2=[-1, 1]^t$ for statement S_2. The code obtained in this case is shown in Figure 8.b. Now references $B[j_1-1, j_2+1]$ and $A[j_1, j_2+1]$ in statement S_2 are local and references $B[j_1-2, j_2+1]$ and $C[j_2+2, (j_1-j_2-2)/2]$ are non-local, reducing the number of remote accesses.

If no alignment components had been added to the transformation, the code shown in Figure 8.c would have been obtained. Analyzing the data accesses performed, one can see that references $A[j_1, j_2]$ and $B[j_1-1, j_2]$ in the statement S_1 and reference $B[j_1-1, j_2]$ in statement S_2 are local. Other references are remote. However, observe that the access to $C[i_1+1, i_2]$ in statement S_2 does not require a remote access because it is reusing the same value that has been accessed in statement S_1. So in this case just accesses to $B[j_1, j_2]$ and $A[j_1+1, j_2]$ are non-local. In conclusion, the same number of remote accesses are performed.

In general it is necessary to consider the reuse of the array elements in order to find the alignment components.

6 Conclusions and Future Work

In this paper we have proposed the inclusion of loop alignment as a new component in the framework of non-singular transformations. This allows the compiler to match the structure of loop nests according to data alignment and distribution specifications. The aim is to reduce the number of remote data accesses in distributed-memory machines.

We have used some ideas recently published in the literature to generate code that controls the correct execution of each statement in each iteration of the transformed loop nest and body. In this case it is more difficult to generate code and we have shown how to reduce the overhead due to conditionals that appear in the loop body [24].

We have presented a simple method to obtain the alignment component for each statement of the loop body. It is based on the analysis of constants in the set of subscripts that make up the data access matrix (in the spatial part of the transformation) and the alignment functions for the arrays subscripted by them. Data reuse has not been considered in the method we have proposed. A more precise formulation of the problem of finding the alignment components where data reuse is considered is part of our future work.

A possible extension to the work presented in this paper is the use of a different transformation for each statement. From array references in each loop statement, a different data access matrix or transformation matrix T and alignment component can be obtained to increase locality. The target loop nest obtained with this approach has the same structure as the one we have presented in this paper. In general, the transformed dependence distances become non-uniform and as a consequence, it is more difficult to generate the associated synchronization/communication instructions. The study of the legality of all the transformation matrices is more complex because of this non-uniform characteristic of dependences in the target space.

```
DO j₁ = 2, 28
        lcover = j₁ + 2 · max (-9,⌈(-j₁) /2⌉)
        ucover = j₁ + 2 · min (-1, ⌊(10-j₁)/2⌋)
        lcore = j₁ + 2 · max (-8,⌈(1-j₁) /2⌉)
        ucore = j₁ + 2 · min (-2, ⌊(9-j₁)/2⌋)
        IF lcover < lcore THEN
                B[ j₁-1,  lcover+1] = g(A[ j₁,  lcover+1], B[ j₁-1,  lcover+1])
        DO j₂ = lcore, ucore, 2
                A[ j₁,  j₂] = f(A[ j₁,  j₂], C[ j₂+1, ( j₁- j₂)/2], B[ j₁-1,  j₂])
                B[ j₁-1,  j₂+1] = g(A[ j₁,  j₂+1], B[ j₁-1,  j₂+1])
        ENDDO
        IF ucore < ucover THEN
                A[ j₁,  ucover] = f(A[ j₁,  ucover], C[ ucover+1,( j₁- ucover)/2], B[ j₁-1,  ucover])
ENDDO
```

Fig. 7. Target loop nest obtained for the example in Figure 1.a when a different transformation is applied to each statement of the loop body.

338

```
ALIGN A, C WITH E
ALIGN B (i, j) WITH E (i+1, j-1)
DISTRIBUTE E (CYCLIC, :)
DO i₁=1, 10
    DO i₂=1, 8
        A[i₁+2·i₂, i₁] = f(A[i₁+2·i₂, i₁], B[i₁+2·i₂-1, i₁], C[i₁+1, i₂])
        B[i₁+2·i₂, i₁] = g(A[i₁+2·i₂+1, i₁], B[i₁+2·i₂-1, i₁], C[i₁+1, i₂])
    ENDO
ENDO
```
(a)

```
DO j₁=2, 28
    ...
    DO j₂ = lcore,ucore, 2
        A[ j₁, j₂] = f(A[ j₁, j₂], B[ j₁-1, j₂], C[ j₂+1, ( j₁- j₂)/2] )
        B[ j₁-1, j₂+1] = g(A[ j₁, j₂+1], B[ j₁-2, j₂+1], C[ j₂+2, ( j₁- j₂-2)/2])
    ENDO
    ...
ENDO
```
(b)

```
DO j₁=3, 26
    DO j₂ = j₁ + 2 · max (-8, ⌈(1-j₁)/2⌉), j₁ + 2 · min (-1, ⌊(10-j₁)/2⌋), 2
        A[ j₁, j₂] = f(A[ j₁, j₂], B[ j₁-1, j₂], C[ j₂+1, ( j₁- j₂)/2])
        B[ j₁, j₂] = g(A[ j₁+1, j₂], B[ j₁-1, j₂],C[ j₂+1, ( j₁- j₂)/2] )
    ENDO
ENDO
```
(c)

Fig. 8. (a) Original loop nest. Two different options for the alignment components: (b) $D^1=[0, 0]^t$ and $D^2=[-1, 1]^t$ and (c) $D^1=D^2=[0, 0]^t$.

Acknowledgments

This work has been supported by the Ministry of Education of Spain under contract TIC-880/92, by the ESPRIT Basic Research Action 6634 APPARC and by the CEPBA (European Center for Parallelism of Barcelona).

References

1. Polychronopoulos C., *Parallel Programming and Compilers*, Kluwer Academic Publishers, 1988.
2. Wolfe M., *Optimizing Supercompilers for Supercomputers*, The MIT Press, 1989.
3. Fox G. et al., Fortran-D Language Specification, Technical Report TR90-140, Dept. of Computer Science, Rice University, revised January 1992.

4. David Loveman (ed.), Draft High Performance Fortran Language Specification Version 1.0, Technical Report TR92-225, CRPC, Rice University, January 1993.

5. Callahan D. and Kennedy K., Compiling Programs for Distributed-Memory Multiprocessors, *Journal of Supercomputing*, vol. 2, no. 2, October 1988.

6. Hiranandani S., Kennedy K. and Tseng C., Evaluation of Compiler Optimizations for Fortran D on MIMD Distributed-Memory Machines, in *Proceedings of the 1992 ACM International Conference on Supercomputing*, July 1992.

7. Karp A.H., Programming for Parallelism, *Computer*, vol. 20, no. 5, May 1987.

8. Banerjee U., Unimodular Transformations of Double Loops, chapter 10 of *Advances in Languages and Compilers for Parallel Processing*, The MIT Press, 1991.

9. Wolf M.E. and Lam M.S., A Loop Transformation Theory and an Algorithm to Maximize Parallelism, *IEEE Transactions on Parallel and Distributed Systems*, vol. 2, no. 4, October 1991.

10. Wolf M.E. and Lam M., A Data Locality Optimizing Algorithm, in *Proceedings of the ACM SIGPLAN Conference on Programming Language Design and Implementation*, June 1991.

11. Li W. and Pingali K., Access Normalization: Loop Restructuring for NUMA Compilers, in *Proceedings of the Fifth Int. Conference on Architectural Support for Programming Languages and Operating Systems*, October 1992.

12. Li W. and Pingali K., A Singular Loop Transformation Framework Based on Non-Singular Matrices, in *Proceedings of the Fifth Workshop on Languages and Compilers for Parallel Computers*, August 1992.

13. Fernández A., Systematic Transformation of Systolic Algorithms for Programming Distributed Memory Multiprocessors, Ph.D. Thesis, Department of Computer Architecture, Polytechnic University of Catalunya (Spain), November 1992.

14. Ramanujam J., Non-unimodular Transformations of Nested Loops, in *Proceedings of the Supercomputing'92*, November 1992.

15. Padua D.A., Multiprocessors: Discussions of some theoretical and practical problems, Technical Report DCS UIUCDCS-R-79-990, Ph.D. dissertation, University of Illinois at Urbana-Champaign, November 1979.

16. Peir J-K., Program Partitioning and Synchronization on Multiprocessor Systems, Ph.D. Thesis, University of Illinois at Urbana-Champaign, 1986.

17. Allen R., Callahan D. and Kennedy K., Automatic Decomposition of Scientific Programs for Parallel Execution, in *Proceedings of the 14th ACM Symposium Principles of Programming Languages*, January 1987.

18. Banerjee U., *Dependence Analysis for Supercomputing*, Kluwer Academic Publishers, 1988.

19. Kennedy K. and Kremer U., Automatic Data Alignment and Distribution for Loosely Synchronous Problems in an Interactive Programming Environment, Technical Report TR91-155, Dept. of Computer Science, Rice University, April 1991.

20. Li J., Compiling Crystal for Distributed-Memory Machines, Ph.D. Thesis, Dep. of Computer Science, Yale University, December 1991.

21. Moldovan D.I. and Fortes J.A.B., Partitioning and Mapping Algorithms into Fixed Size Systolic Arrays, *IEEE Transactions on Computers*, vol. 35, no.1, January 1986.

22. Lu L. and Chen M., New Loop Transformation Techniques for Massive Parallelism, Research Report TR-833, Department of Computer Science, Yale University, October 1990.

23. Schrijver A., *Theory of Linear and Integer Programming*, John Wiley and Sons, 1986.

24. Ayguadé E. and Torres J., Partitioning the Statement per Iteration Space Using Non-singular Matrices, in *Proceedings of the 1993 ACM International Conference on Supercomputing*, July 1993.

Extending Software Pipelining Techniques for Scheduling Nested Loops [*]

Guang R. Gao[1], Qi Ning[2] and Vincent Van Dongen[2]

[1] McGill University, School of Computer Science, Montréal PQ H3A 2A7, CANADA
[2] Centre de recherche informatique de Montréal, Montréal PQ H3A 2N4, CANADA

Abstract. In this paper, we extend software pipelining techniques for scheduling nested loops. Under this framework, a periodic scheduling function, called *r-periodic schedule*, is associated with each operation of the loop body for the entire iteration space. We present a simple problem formulation as well as efficient solutions which give provable, asymptotically time-optimal schedules for nested loops under our program model. It also provides some useful insights on the interplay between unimodular loop transformations and fine-grain scheduling under a unified framework.

1 Introduction

Software pipelining has been successfully applied to high-performance pipelined processor architectures, as well as superscalar and VLIW architectures [1, 2, 3, 16, 17, 23, 26, 30, 33]. However, most proposed methods for software pipelining have been focused on a single-level (the inner-most loop of a nested loop). Since it is primarily targeted to uniprocessor architectures, the available instruction level parallelism is quite limited, and little attention has been paid to software pipelining for nested loops.

The goal of this paper is to develop a methodology for fine-grain loop scheduling which extends software pipelining technique to nested loops. In this approach, we define a scheduling function for each operation of the loop body in the entire iteration space. In the case of single-level loops, the schedule is of the form:

$$t(i, v) = \lfloor \frac{T \cdot i + A[v]}{r} \rfloor,$$

where the parameters T, r and $A[v]$ are integers, and $t(i, v)$ is the starting time of the ith occurrence of the vth statement of the loop body[3]. In this form, the schedule is periodic with periodicity r, period T and offset time $A[v]$. This formulation does not have the restriction that the schedule of each individual iteration must be the same. In fact, the schedule of two consecutive iterations

---

[*] This work was supported by the EPPP project, financed by Industry Science Canada, Alex Parallel Computers, Digital Equipment Canada, IBM Canada and CRIM (Centre de recherche informatique de Montréal).

[3] Here, $\lfloor \frac{a}{b} \rfloor$ denotes the floor of $\frac{a}{b}$, while $\lceil \frac{a}{b} \rceil$ is the ceiling of $\frac{a}{b}$.

may not be the same, but repeat every r iterations; hence is called *r-periodic*. This is based on the work pioneered by Reiter on scheduling of Karp-Miller style computation graphs [31]. In [34], we have demonstrated the use of such simple scheduling in software pipelining of one-level loops.

In [29], a vectorized version of r-periodic schedules is used for scheduling uniform recurrences in the context of systolic array design; T and i are n-dimensional vectors where n is the dimension of the recurrence equation. In this paper, we demonstrate that such r-periodic scheduling can be used for nested loops of depth n. For loops under our program model,

- We show that, using the form of r-periodic scheduling, the time-optimal software pipelining can be formulated into a linear programming problem of n variables only.
- We demonstrate that r-periodic scheduling is *near-optimal*; that is it is asymptotically as good as the best schedule — the *free* schedule where statements can be scheduled as early as possible subject only to data dependence constraints.
- When the nesting level n is small, we present an efficient polynomial time solution method. This surprisingly efficient solution is based on a vectorized extension of the solution of the *minimum cost-to-time ratio cycle* (MCTRC) problem [24]. The key intuition leading to this efficient solution is the observation that the time-optimal computation rate of a nested loop is dominated by its *critical dependence cycles*.
- For reasons to be discussed in the paper, it may be desirable to use a small fixed periodicity r in the schedule. In [15], we show that the optimal scheduling for a fixed r solution is NP-complete. However, in real-life applications, the dimension of loops to be scheduled is small, hence an efficient solution is possible. We present such a solution in this paper.

For the past few years, substantial progress has been made in parallelizing nested loops. The following two areas are most relevant to the work described in this paper. First, unimodular transformations of nested loops have been proposed as a method to exploit parallelism for parallelizing compilers [5] and for systolic array design (see [7, 8]). These transformations provide a framework to combine other loop transformation techniques such as *loop interchange, loop skewing* and *loop reversal*. However, the focus has not been on loop scheduling and, as a result, statement timing has not been considered explicitly as a parameter in the problem formulation. The second related area is the application of periodic scheduling for parallelizing nested loops. In [12, 13], Darte, Risset, and Robert have proposed a periodic scheduling scheme, called *affine-by-statement loop scheduling*. In [18], Feautrier has proposed another interesting scheme which may apply different scheduling functions to different parts of index domain if necessary. All of this work has been focused on theoretical framework and methods that are exact in nature. Although, the methods are very powerful and interesting from a research perspective, an efficient implementation in conventional compilers remains to be a challenging task. Compared with the above work, our main objective is to develop methods which are both theoretically sound and can feasibly be implemented in practical parallelizing compilers.

This paper is organized as follows. We give some examples in Section 2 to motivate our approach. We introduce our program model in Section 3. In Section 4, we introduce the concepts of periodic schedules and show that, based on such schedules, software pipelining for nested loops can be formulated into a simple linear programming problem. We also demonstrate that periodic scheduling is asymptotically optimal, i.e., its difference from a free scheduling is only a constant which is independent of the loop bounds. In Section 5, we propose an efficient algorithm to solve the optimal periodic scheduling problem, based on a novel vectorized extension of the solution of the MCTRC problem. Section 6 focuses on the problem with a fixed periodicity r, and presents an efficient solution when the loop nesting level is small. Finally, in Section 7, we discuss the generalization of this work and give a comparison of our work with other related work. Section 8 gives the conclusions.

2 Motivating Examples

In this section, we use three examples to illustrate the notion of r-periodic scheduling and how it can handle software pipelining for nested loops. All of these loops contain multiple statements in their bodies.

The first example is taken from [6]. It illustrates how useful it might be to consider both loop parallelization and statement scheduling in a unified framework. In Example 2, the optimal scheduling of the loop cannot be obtained through a unimodular loop transformation only. Instead, it requires a unimodular transformation followed by instruction scheduling[4] to obtain the optimal schedule. We demonstrate, in intuitive terms, that the r-periodic scheduling proposed in this paper captures both loop transformation and instruction scheduling in a unified mathematical framework.

In Example 3, we present a loop for which even performing the unimodular transformation plus instruction scheduling together cannot reach the optimal schedule. Intuitively, the time-optimal schedule of the loop is dominated by the critical dependence cycle [19], which is not treated by the traditional instruction scheduling technique. We show that such cycle constraints are captured elegantly by the periodicity in the framework of the proposed r-periodic scheduling.

Example 1. Consider the following loop taken from [6].

$$
\begin{aligned}
&\text{for } i = 0 \text{ to } N_1 - 1 \\
&\quad \text{for } j = 0 \text{ to } N_2 - 1 \\
&\qquad \text{begin} \\
&S_1: \quad a(i,j) = b(i,j-1); \\
&S_2: \quad b(i,j) = a(i-1,j) + a(i-1,j-1); \\
&\qquad \text{end}
\end{aligned}
\tag{1}
$$

---

[4] For our purpose, the terms "statement" and "instruction" are interchangeable here.

In [6], the loop is first transformed into a parallel form and then instruction scheduling is performed. The final code is unfortunately not optimal because loop parallelization and instruction scheduling are not considered together.

In this paper, we present a systematic technique to compute the optimal schedule in one step. The corresponding schedule is always periodic. For loop (1), we can prove that the optimal periodic schedule is:

$$t((i,j),v) = 2i + A(v),$$

with $A(1) = 1$ and $A(2) = 0$. Here, $t((i,j),v)$ represents the starting time of statement S_v at iteration (i,j). After rewriting, the loop becomes:

$$
\begin{aligned}
&\text{for } i = 0 \text{ to } N_1 - 1 \\
&\quad \text{forall } j = 0 \text{ to } N_2 - 1 \\
&\qquad \text{begin} \\
&\qquad\quad b(i,j) = a(i-1,j) + a(i-1,j-1); \\
&\qquad\quad a(i,j) = b(i,j-1); \\
&\qquad \text{end}
\end{aligned}
$$

In this case, a simple reordering of S_1 and S_2 transforms the nested loop into one in which the inner loop is parallel. In addition to being optimal, this loop is much simpler to implement than the one derived in [6].

Example 2. Consider the following loop. Let λ be any constant positive integer.

$$
\begin{aligned}
&\text{for } i = 0 \text{ to } N \\
&\quad \text{for } j = 0 \text{ to } N \\
&\qquad \text{begin} \\
&S_1: \quad a(i,j) = f_1(b(i-1,j-\lambda), c(i-1,j+\lambda), ...); \\
&S_2: \quad b(i,j) = f_2(a(i,j-1), ...); \\
&S_3: \quad c(i,j) = f_3(a(i,j-1), ...); \\
&\qquad \text{end}
\end{aligned}
\tag{2}
$$

We assume that each of the statements S_1, S_2 and S_3 takes one unit of time to execute. In this paper, we present a method which formulates the problem of deriving the ultimate time-optimal schedule in a unified mathematical framework. We propose a periodic schedule of the form (for a two-dimensional loop)

$$t((i,j),v) = \lfloor \frac{T_i \cdot i + T_j \cdot j + A(v)}{r} \rfloor, \tag{3}$$

that minimizes the total execution time. Here, $t((i,j),v)$ represents the starting time of statement S_v at iteration (i,j); T_i and T_j are integers, $A(v)$ is a non-negative integer and r is a positive integer. Let us illustrate the meaning of these parameters using Example 2.

In terms of (3), a unimodular transformation makes use of a schedule of the form:

$$t((i,j),v) = T_i \cdot i + T_j \cdot j,$$

where T_i and T_j are relatively prime integers. That is, the effect of unimodular transformation is captured by $\mathbf{T}$ — the affine scheduling vector. This form, clearly a restriction of (3), ignores both r and the $A(v)$ parameters. Intuitively, the $A(v)$'s specify the relative offset of the statements of the body in a periodic schedule. That is, they capture exactly what the instruction scheduling phase is trying to optimize in our example. Therefore, the $A(v)$'s are essential in order to fully exploit the fine-grain parallelism of a multiple-statement loop. For our example, the best schedule is given by:

$$t((i,j),v) = 2 \cdot i + A(v),$$

with $A(1) = 0$ and $A(2) = A(3) = 1$. Clearly, the schedule in the form of (3) expresses the unimodular transformation and the scheduling of the loop statements together in a unified mathematical form. The above example also illustrates the fact that the amount of parallelism gained by using r-periodic schedules instead of unimodular transformations is unbounded. This is explained in detail in [15].

Example 3. Even combined unimodular transformations and instruction scheduling may not be sufficient to exploit all of the parallelism in loop. Consider the following loop.

$$
\begin{aligned}
&\text{for } i = 0 \text{ to } N \text{ do} \\
&\quad \text{for } j = 0 \text{ to } N \text{ do} \\
&\quad\quad \text{begin} \\
&S_1: \quad a(i,j) = a(i-1,j) + c(i-1,j); \quad\quad\quad (4)\\
&S_2: \quad b(i,j) = a(i,j) + b(i,j-1); \\
&S_3: \quad c(i,j) = b(i-1,j) + c(i-1,j); \\
&\quad\quad \text{end}
\end{aligned}
$$

It can be shown that, in terms of r-periodic scheduling, the following is the optimal schedule:

$$t((i,j),v) = \lfloor \frac{3i + 2j + A(v)}{2} \rfloor,$$

with $A(1) = 0$, $A(2) = 2$ and $A(3) = 1$.

Note that the parameter r can no longer be ignored in this example. Figure 1 shows the dependence graph of the loop. We can observe that the critical cycle has a total dependence distance of $(2,0)$. Intuitively, this suggests the fact that the optimal schedule should contain two instances of each statement on the first coordinate (i).

In the next two sections, we formalize the intuition developed through these examples, and present efficient solutions to compute the optimal schedule.

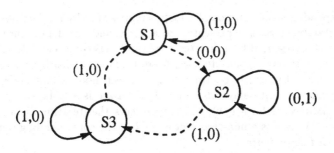

Fig. 1. The dependence graph for the loop (4) and its critical cycle shown in dash.

3   Program Model

In this section, we introduce the program model for loops treated in this paper. Basically, we can deal with nested loops which are defined over a rectangular domain and whose dependence distance vectors have non-negative constant coefficients.[5] More precisely, we require that the loops are *normalized* and have the form:

$$\text{for } i_1 = 0 \text{ to } N_1$$

$$\vdots$$

$$\text{for } i_n = 0 \text{ to } N_n$$
$$\text{begin}$$
$$S_1;$$

$$\vdots$$

$$S_m;$$
$$\text{end}$$

The loop has the following properties:

- Each of the m statements in the loop body, S_v $(1 \le v \le m)$, is an assigment statement defining an array element. Let $\mathbf{i}$ be the index vector $(i_1, i_2, ..., i_n)$. Then all of the statements in the body are of the form:

$$a(\mathbf{i}) = f(b(\mathbf{i} - \delta), ...) \tag{5}$$

where
  - a and b are n-dimensional arrays.
  - δ is a constant integer vector with non-negative components.
  - f is some *elementary* function (unary or binary) whose arguments are either external inputs or are of the form $b(\mathbf{i} - \delta)$.

---

[5] In section 7, we will see how this model can be extended.

The dependence information of a loop is represented by its *dependence graph* (DG). A statement S_v is represented as a node, and the dependence between statements is represented by a directed edge (arc) between them. We will assume that the DG is strongly connected. Each arc (u, v) is labeled by a delay $d(u, v)$ which represents the execution time delay between node u and node v. When all statements are unit-delays, $d(u, v) = 1$. Each arc is also labeled with a *dependence distance vector* $\delta(u, v)$, which represents the iteration distance of this dependence. When δ is a non-zero vector, we call the corresponding dependence a *loop-carried dependence*.

4 Periodic Scheduling and its Optimality

4.1 Periodic schedules

Given a nested loop whose index $(i_1, i_2, \cdots, i_n)$ is of dimension n, and whose body has m instructions, we use the notation $t((i_1, i_2, \cdots, i_n), v)$ to indicate the starting time to schedule statement S_v in the iteration indexed by $(i_1, i_2, \cdots, i_n)$. We are interested in finding a schedule of the following form:

$$t((i_1, i_2, \cdots, i_n), v) = \lfloor \frac{T_1 \cdot i_1 + T_2 \cdot i_2 + \cdots + T_n \cdot i_n + A(v)}{r} \rfloor,$$

whose parameters $T_1, T_2, \cdots T_n$ are integers, $A(1), A(2), \cdots, A(m)$ are non-negative integers, and r is a positive integer. In vector form, the schedule is written as:

$$t(\mathbf{i}, v) = \lfloor \frac{\mathbf{T} \cdot \mathbf{i} + A(v)}{r} \rfloor, \tag{6}$$

where $\mathbf{i} = (i_1, i_2, \cdots i_n)$ and $\mathbf{T} = (T_1, T_2, \cdots, T_n)$.

We will define a schedule of the form (6) as *r-periodic*, and call $\mathbf{T}$ and r its *period* and *periodicity*, respectively. This class of schedule was first introduced by Quinton in the context of systolic array design [29]. See Section 2 for an example of periodic schedules.

For one-dimensional loops, the scheduling vector degenerates to a scalar, as does the iteration vector. The readers are referred to Section 7 for a discussion of related work.

4.2 A Linear Programming Formulation

In this section, we formulate the optimal r-periodic scheduling problem into a linear programming problem of n variables only.

Among the starting times of all statements, let $max_{\mathbf{i}, v}(t(\mathbf{i}, v))$ and $min_{\mathbf{i}, v}(t(\mathbf{i}, v))$ denote the latest and earliest, respectively. Let ΔT be $max_{\mathbf{i}}(\frac{\mathbf{T} \cdot \mathbf{i}}{r}) - min_{\mathbf{i}}(\frac{\mathbf{T} \cdot \mathbf{i}}{r})$ and let ΔA be $max_v(\frac{A(v)}{r}) - min_v(\frac{A(v)}{r})$. Let Δt be total execution time of a periodic schedule. Then we have:

$$\Delta t = \Delta T + \Delta A - \epsilon,$$

where $\epsilon \in [0, 1]$. One can easily see that ΔT depends on the size of the domain of i while ΔA does not. Therefore, asymptotically for large domains, it is important to minimize ΔT. Let us define the **fastest periodic schedule** as the one that minimizes ΔT. The following theorem formulates the problem of finding the fastest periodic schedule into a linear programming problem.

Theorem 1. *Given a loop as defined in Section 3, the fastest periodic schedule can be found by minimizing*

$$\sum_{i=1}^{n} T_i \cdot N_i / r, \tag{7}$$

under the constraints:

$$\sum_{i=1}^{n} T_i \cdot \delta_i(u, v) + A(v) - A(u) \geq r \cdot d(u, v), \ \forall \delta(u, v) \tag{8}$$

$$T_j \geq 0, \ \forall j \in [1, n] \tag{9}$$

The proof is given in [15]. At this point, one should compare this result to the related work. In [22], it is shown in the context of systolic array design, that the optimal r-periodic schedule can be found by solving a set of linear programs of $n + m$ variables. In [13], a single linear programming formulation is given with a number of variables that depends not only on the loop body but also on the shape of the domain. In both cases, their program model is more general than ours. (For instance, the domain is not restricted to be rectangular.) On the other hand, our linear programming formulation is much simpler. In addition, we provide a very efficient method for solving it and its integer counterpart.

4.3 Asymptotic Optimality

This section shows that periodic schedules not only have a simple linear programming formulation, but also achieve asymptotic optimality as defined below.

Let $N = (N_1, N_2, ..., N_n)$, let ΔT_f be the total time it takes to execute a loop when using the free schedule (i.e., the statements are executed as soon as possible) and let ΔT_p be the total time it takes to execute a loop when using the fastest periodic schedule. We will say that a periodic schedule is *asymptotically time-optimal* if and only if $(\Delta T_p - \Delta T_f)$ is a constant independent of N; i.e. this periodic schedule is as fast as the free schedule for a sufficiently large value of N.

The optimality of the periodic scheduling method is stated in the following theorem.

Theorem 2. *Given a loop as defined in Section 3, its fastest periodic schedule is asymptotically time-optimal.*

Proof: The proof is quite long and can be found in [15]. Here we give some hints.

- The basic intuition and observation behind the proof is that there exists a critical dependence path along which the affine schedule cannot be improved over the free schedule by more than a constant. Such a critical dependence path is captured by *dependence cycles* in the dependence graph.
- Furthermore, the direction of optimization, which determines the objective function of the optimal solution, can also be related with the dependence cycles. In its most general form, it may be specified as a linear combination of n critical cycles. □

5 Solution for Periodic Scheduling

The optimal value of $\mathbf{T}/r$ can be found by means of established solution method of linear programming such as the simplex method. Note that the number of variables is $m + n$, where m denotes the number of statements in the loop and n is the depth of the loop nest. In practice, n is small (e.g. usually, there is a nesting level of 1, 2 or 3). Therefore, in this section, we propose a solution method which is very efficient for small n. The key observation is that in the linear program formulation (see Theorem 4.1), the optimal value of $\mathbf{T}/r$ in the linear constraint (8) is bounded by the maximum computation rate of the so-called *critical cycles* in the dependence graph. Such a bound can be derived efficiently by solving a generalized version of the so-called *minimum cost-to-time ratio cycle (MCTRC) problem* [24]. This generalization is inspired by our previous work for solving the one-dimensional problem [34]. In this section, the technique is first developed for the case when there is no *a priori* constraint on r. In Section 6, we generalize this technique to the case when r is fixed.

Without loss of generality, let us present our solution method for the case $n = 2$. An extension to cases for n greater than 2 is left as an exercise. The basic observation of our solution method is that we can perform a systematic search along one dimension. Each step of this search can be reduced to a MCTRC problem along another dimension which we can solve efficiently.

Let δ be the largest value of $\delta(u, v)$ and let d be the largest value of $d(u, v)$; that is,

$$\delta = \max_{(u,v) \in DG} \{\delta(u, v)\},$$

$$d = \max_{(u,v) \in DG} \{d(u, v)\}.$$

Given a loop as defined in Section 3 but with $n = 1$, let us first introduce the main results of [34] for computing the optimal $\mathbf{T}/r = T/r$ and the overall solution. (We use lower case letter T to denote the fact that it is a scalar value).

1. The optimal value of T/r is in $[0, md]$.
2. The minimum distance between two distinct values of T/r is $1/(m\delta)^2$. The value of r is in $[1, m\delta]$.

3. One can test that there exists a particular schedule of a given T/r by solving a shortest path problem, which will, in fact, give valid values for each $A(v)$. When using the Bellman-Ford algorithm, the complexity for doing so is in $\mathcal{O}(m^2)$. Using Gabow-Tarjan's algorithm, it is $\mathcal{O}(m \lg m \sqrt{m})$. (Here, we consider the number of dependences per statement to be constant.)

4. There are a maximum of $md(m\delta)^2$ distinct values for T/r to test. A binary search can be used to find the optimal value of T/r. After $(3 \lg m + \lg d + 2 \lg \delta)$ shortest path problems, the distance to the optimal value is smaller than the minimal distance between two distinct values of T/r. Let T'/r be this near-optimal value.

5. The optimal value can be found from this near-optimal solution by solving one additional shortest path which will detect the critical cycle of the DG. By using $T/r = T'/r - 1/(m\delta)^2$, one detects a negative cycle which is the critical cycle.

6. Given the critical cycle c, the optimal value of T/r can be found by solving $T/r = \sum_c d(u,v) / \sum_c \delta(u,v)$.

7. Valid $A(v)$ can finally be found by means of one additional shortest path problem using the optimal value of T/r.

The complexity of this method to compute T/r, when using Bellman-Ford, is therefore $\mathcal{O}(m^2 (3 \lg m + \lg d + 2 \lg \delta + 1)) = \mathcal{O}(m^2 \lg m)$.

We now generalize this to the case $n = 2$ to compute the optimal $\mathbf{T}/r$. As in the one dimensional case, our new algorithm performs a search of the optimal value of $\mathbf{T}/r$ through a bounded solution space. However, $\mathbf{T}/r$ is now a vector and the solution space is a two-dimensional region as illustrated in Figure 2. Consider Figure 2(a) first. The two axes represent T_1/r and T_2/r — the two components of $\mathbf{T}/r$. As explained in [14], there is one linear constraint per simple cycle C of the DG, which is of the form:

$$\mathbf{T}/r \cdot \delta_c \geq d_c,$$

where δ_c is the summation of the dependence vectors along C and d_c is the sum of the associated delays. For simplicity, only three such constraints on $\mathbf{T}/r$ are shown in the figure. Note that the length of a cycle is at most m and the maximum value of a delay is d, $d_c \in [0, md]$. Furthermore, all components of δ_c are positive. Therefore, each constraint cuts the axes T_1/r and T_2/r between 0 and md. The optimal value of $\mathbf{T}/r$ is at the intersection of two constraints and is therefore always within the dashed box shown in Figure 2(a).

The cost to minimize is $\mathbf{T}/r \cdot \mathbf{N}$ — a linear function which increases along $\mathbf{N}$. As shown in the figure, we use a set of parallel lines perpendicular to $\mathbf{N}$ to represent the solution points for $\mathbf{T}/r$ with equal cost.

Consider Figure 2(b) now. The axes of this diagram are T_1/r and the minimum "cost" of $\mathbf{T}/r$ for a particular value of T_1/r. Clearly, this cost is unimodal: it decreases first up to the point where it reaches its minimum and then increases. One key idea of the new algorithm is to perform a Fibonacci search [10] along T_1/r to find the optimal solution. For each point in the Fibonacci search, we need to compute the minimal cost for a given value of T_1/r and the corresponding

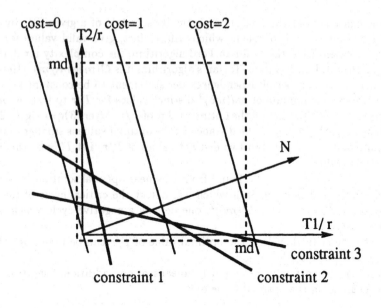

(a)

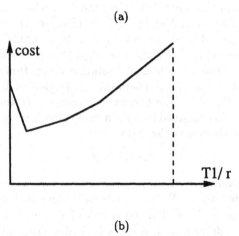

(b)

Fig. 2. The basis for extending MCTRC to the case when $n = 2$.

value of T_2/r. As we will show below, this subproblem can be easily transformed and solved efficiently using the method developed for the case $n = 1$, (i.e. a binary search to solve the MCTRC problem).

Let us now explain how a 2D problem is transformed into the 1-D problem once T_1/r is fixed. When $n = 2$, the constraints are of the form:

$$T_1\delta_1(u, v) + T_2\delta_2(u, v) + A(v) - A(u) \geq rd(u, v), \tag{10}$$

where $d(u, v)$ represents the delay for the dependence (u, v) and $(\delta_1(u, v), \delta_2(u, v))$

is its associated dependence distance. We want to transform this constraint into the familiar 1-D form:

$$T_2\delta_2(u,v) + A(v) - A(u) \geq rd'(u,v).$$

By doing so, we can solve T_2/r by means of MCTRC. Let us see how this can be done. Clearly (10) can be rewritten as:

$$T_2\delta_2(u,v) + A(v) - A(u) \geq rd(u,v) - T_1\delta_1(u,v) = r(d(u,v) - T_1/r\delta_1(u,v)). \quad (11)$$

The problem is that we want $d'(u,v)$ to be an integer constant. In order to obtain this, we do variable substitution:

$$r_0 = r/r_1,$$

and

$$T_1' = T_1/r_0.$$

Then we obtain:

$$T_1/r = T_1/(r_0 \cdot r_1) = T_1'/r_1 = r_0 T_1'/(r_0 \cdot r_1).$$

By doing so, (11) becomes:

$$T_2\delta_2(u,v) + A(v) - A(u) \geq r_0(r_1 d(u,v) - T_1'\delta_1(u,v)).$$

That is:

$$d'(u,v) = r_1 d(u,v) - T_1'\delta_1(u,v). \quad (12)$$

The algorithm MCTRC performs a binary search over the range $[0, md]$, where d is the maximal delay. In (12), d' is a function of r_1, but clearly $d' \leq r_1 d$. So now the binary search can be performed over $[0, mr_1 d]$.

Knowing how to solve the subproblem, we now return to the Fibonacci search procedure. The Fibonacci search will be along T_1'/r_1, and for each fixed value of T_1'/r_1, an optimal value of T_2/r_0 will be computed by means of MCTRC. The corresponding value of T/r will then be $(r_0 T_1', T_2)/(r_0 \cdot r_1)$.

When can the Fibonacci search terminate and return the optimal solution? From the theory of linear programming, the optimal T/r is at a vertex of the convex polyhedron defined by the set of linear constraints. Because r is at most the determinant of the matrix formed by the coefficients of two equations, the value of r is in $[1, (m\delta)^2]$. (The coefficients of the equations are in $[0, m\delta]$.) We want to do a Fibonacci search along T_1'/r_1 up to a point where the interval contains only one vertex. Because of the maximal value of r, the minimum distance between two distinct vertices is $1/(m\delta)^4$. This tells us how far we must go in the Fibonacci search. It also tells us how large r_1 can be and the complexity of the associated MCTRC.

At the end of the Fibonacci search, one is left with a very small interval for T_1'/r_1 within which the optimal solution resides. At the left of this interval, MCTRC detects a critical cycle, say C_1; and at the right of this interval, MC-TRC detects another critical cycle, say C_2. The optimal T/r is the intersection of these two constraints. So the optimal $\mathbf{T}/r$ can be computed by solving the corresponding system of equations.

Here is a summary of the basic outline of our algorithm.

Algorithm 5.1

1. **Step I**: Perform a Fibonacci search on T_1'/r_1 in the range $[0, md]$ until the size of the interval is smaller than $1/(m\delta)^4$. The cost function to minimize is $(T_1'/r_1, T_2/(r_0 \cdot r_1)) \cdot (N_1, N_2)$. For each particular value of T_1'/r_1 do the following.
   (a) Transform the problem into the lower dimension.
   (b) Perform MCTRC to compute T_2/r_0 in the range $[0, r_1 md]$.
2. **Step II**: Find the final exact solution:
   (a) Detect the critical cycles defining the optimal solution.
   (b) Find the exact solution of $\mathbf{T}/r$ with the critical cycles.

The next theorem states the complexity of the algorithm.

Theorem 3. *The complexity of the algorithm is*

$$\mathcal{O}((5\lg m + \lg d + 4\lg\delta) \cdot m^2(7\lg m + \lg d + 6\lg\delta + 1)) = \mathcal{O}(m^2(\lg m)^2). \quad (13)$$

Proof: There are $md(m\delta)^4$ values of T_1/r_1 to consider.

Thus, there are $\lg(md(m\delta)^4) = (5\lg m + \lg d + 4\lg\delta)$ iterations for the Fibonacci search of $\mathbf{T}_1'/r_1$. For each value of T_1'/r_1, a particular MCTRC has to be performed over the range $[0, r_1 md]$. The complexity, when using Bellman-Ford to solve the shortest path problem, is $\mathcal{O}(m^2(\lg r_1 + 3\lg m + \lg d + 2\lg\delta + 1))$. Because $r_1 \in [0, (m\delta)^4]$, it is in the worst case $\mathcal{O}(m^2(7\lg m + \lg d + 6\lg\delta + 1)) = \mathcal{O}(m^2(\lg m))$. Thus, the complexity of the overall algorithm is as stated in Theorem (13). $\square$

6 Periodic Scheduling with Given Periodicity

There are several programmatic, yet important, reasons that a small periodicity r is chosen for the scheduling. First, the code size of the result loop after rewriting is directly dependent on r, as illustrated in the previous section. Large code size may increase the program storage requirement, and degrades the effectiveness of the instruction cache. Secondly, large code size may also tend to increase the *register pressure* and affects the overall performance. Unfortunately, the optimal value r derived using methods described in the previous sections can become very large.

To avoid code explosion, we may need to choose a small r to begin with. In this section, we discuss how to derive a periodic schedule with a fixed periodicity.

The optimal r-periodic schedule for a given r can be solved by using the formulation given in Theorem 1. Unfortunately, the problem is now an integer programming problem and is generally much harder than ordinary linear programming problems. In particular, even for a fixed value of n, it is unclear from this formulation that the problem can be solved in polynomial time for any value of m. In [15], we show that the general problem of optimal periodic scheduling with a fixed periodicity is NP-complete, when both n and m are parameterized. Here, we prove that the problem canbe solved in polynomial-time when n is fixed and m is parameterized. The algorithm is similar to the one presented for finding the asymptotically time-optimal periodic schedule (i.e., without r fixed). The difference is that now the search is on an integer grid and not on a continuous interval. Another difference is that Fibonacci search can only be used as a first approximation. From this approximation, a complete search has to be done until we are sure that we have the correct optimal solution. However, the key point is that it remains polynomial because the domain of the search is bounded. This idea is illustrated on figure 3.

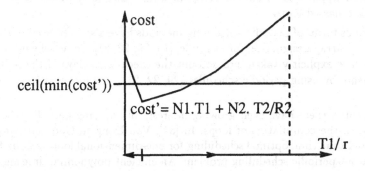

Fig. 3. Illustration of the polynomial search when r is fixed.

7 A Discussion of Related and Future Work

Machines built on advanced VLSI microprocessor architectures must take advantage of the ample resources provided by the hardware to aggressively exploit fine-grain parallelism in nested loops: both within a uniprocessor and between multiple processors. Software pipelining has been successfully applied as a fine-grain loop scheduling method in compilers for high-performance pipelined processor architectures, as well as multiple-issue architectures such as super-scalar and VLIW architectures [1, 2, 3, 16, 17, 23, 26, 30, 33]. However, most of these existing methods only handle one-dimensional loops.

Unimodular transformation has been proposed as a method to exploit parallelism in nested loops for parallelizing compilers [5] and for systolic array design (see for example [7, 8]). It provides a framework to combine other loop transformation techniques such as *loop interchange, loop skewing* and *loop reversal*. However, unimodular transformations treat the loop body (with multiple statements) as a single unit in the transformation. As a result, individual statement timing has not been considered explicitly as a parameter in the problem formulation.

In Section 2, we demonstrated that simply performing unimodular transformation (according only to the dependence structure) followed by instruction scheduling (considering instruction timing) may not be enough to obtain the best possible schedule for a loop. We have argued that it is essential to formulate the time-optimal scheduling problem in a unified framework where the dependence structure as well as statement timing constraints can be fully represented. The r-periodic scheduling scheme proposed in this paper is designed to provide such a framework.

Cyclic scheduling problems, a class of task scheduling problems where tasks are only constrainted by uniform precedence relations, have been studied by Chretienne [9]. He proved that the earliest schedule (free schedule) is optimal and that the optimal asymptotic behavior is r-periodic. Recently, these results have been applied in a number of applications. But their model is yet to be applied to nested loops.

Various forms of periodic scheduling methods have also been used in the area of systolic array design. See, for example, [14, 29, 22, 21]. Some scheduling techniques have explicitly taken into account the execution delays of the individual statements by using periodic schedules [29, 22, 21]. Our model is based on this work.

Recently, there have been growing interests in applying periodic scheduling method in the compilation of loops. In [34], Van Dongen, Gao and Ning have suggested that time-optimal scheduling for one-dimensional loops can be formulated as a r-periodic scheduling problem. An efficient polynomial time algorithm has been presented to solve it based on the MCTRC method. The same technique was developed independently and presented at the same time in [20]. In [27], Ning and Gao have applied the periodic scheduling method to solve register allocation problem for time-optimal software pipelining. The work along this line was in part inspired by the work on the scheduling of Karp-Miller style computation graphs [31], pioneered by Reiter.

This paper extends the r-periodic scheduling presented in [34] to nested loops. To do so, we have restricted ourselves to nested loops defined on a rectangular domain, whose dependence vectors have non-negative coefficients and whose DG is strongly connected. For this class of loops, we have proven that r-periodic periodic schedules are asymptotically optimal and that efficient solutions can be developed based on extensions of the MCTRC solution method. The model can easily be extended to loops whose DG is not strongly connected. In such cases, a *loop distribution* can be performed to separate a loop into a set of loops with strongly connected DGs. A more challenging generalization is when some components of the dependence vectors are negative, and the domain is a convex polyhedron instead of rectangular. In general, one can first transform the loop (e.g. using unimodular transformation) such that the dependence vectors become non-negative [23]. If the transformed loop is defined on a rectangular domain, one can successfully apply our search technique developed in previous sections. However, the resulting index domain may no longer be rectangular. Optimization techniques based on linear programming were proposed in [22, 21] to find the optimal schedule. One open problem is to prove that periodic schedules are still asymptotically optimal, and that the MCTRC algorithm can remain a basic building block to efficiently find the optimal schedule. We leave this for future work.

In [11], periodic schedules are proven to be asymptotically optimal when the loop contains only one statement and the domain index is a sufficiently "fat" polyhedron. In [32], periodic scheduling was used for nested loops and it was demonstrated that it combines three previously known loop transformations: a unimodular change of basis, the *index shift method* [25], and cycle shrinking [28]. By means of an example, it was also proven that the gain of parallelism from the one obtained only with unimodular transformations may become unbounded.

In [12, 13], Darte, Risset, and Robert proposed a periodic scheduling scheme, called *affine-by-statement loop scheduling*. A major feature of their method is that each statement in the loop body may be associated with a different *affine schedule* (e.g. a different T/r for each statement). Compared with the r-periodic scheduling method used in this paper, the affine-by-statement scheduling framework can handle a more general class of loops; e.g., non-perfect loops, loops with arbitrary index domain, loops with more than one strongly connected component, and loops with negative components in their distance vectors. In [18], Feautrier proposed another interesting scheme which may apply different scheduling functions to different parts of index domain, if necessary. These piecewise-affine schedules have proven to be powerful enough to express the free schedule of regular dependence graphs defined on a cone [4]. Both affine-by-statement and piecewise-affine schedules are more powerful than the model proposed in this paper, and hence are more computationally expensive to solve. It remains to be demonstrated to what extent such added power can be efficiently utilized in compiling real programs.

8 Conclusions

The efficient exploitation of fine-grain parallelism in loops is a major challenge in the design of next-generation high-performance computers. This paper investigates the extension of *software pipelining* for nested loops. We have proposed the use of r-periodic scheduling as a framework and derived a simple linear programming formulation of the problem as well as an efficient solution.

One important application is to extend this framework to handle resource constraints. Also, we are studying automatic data partitioning and distribution for SIMD/MIMD distributed memory machines. In particular, we are investigating a problem formulation for automatic data partitioning which permits a smooth integration of both data partitioning and periodic loop scheduling. This capability, essential for loops in which arrays are recursively defined by loop-carried dependences, may require the extension of the data parallel paradigm.

References

1. A. Aiken. Compaction-based parallelization. (PhD thesis), Technical Report 88–922, Cornell University, 1988.

2. A. Aiken and A. Nicolau. Optimal loop parallelization. In *Proceedings of the 1988 ACM SIGPLAN Conference on Programming Languages Design and Implementation*, June 1988.

3. A. Aiken and A. Nicolau. A realistic resource-constrained software pipelining algorithm. In *Proceedings of the Third Workshop on Programming Languages and Compilers for Parallel Computing*, Irvine, CA, August 1990.

4. W. Backes, U. Schwiegelshohn, and L. Thiele. Analysis of free schedule in periodic graphs. In *SPAA '92*, pages 333–339. ACM, 1992.

5. U. Banerjee. Unimodular transformations of double loops. In *Proceedings of the Third Workshop on Programming Languages and Compilers for Parallel Computing*, Irvine, CA, August 1990. Also published in *Monographs in Parallel and Distributed Computing*, Pages 192–219, Pitman, 1991.

6. C.J. Brownhill and A. Nicolau. A hierarchical parallelizing compiler for VLIW/MIMD machines. In *Proceedings of the 5-th Workshop on Languages and Compilers for Parallel Computing*, August 1992.

7. P.R. Cappello and K. Steiglitz. Unifying VLSI array design with linear transformations of space-time. In F.P. Preparata, editor, *Advances in Computing Research*, Greenwich, U.K., 1984. JAI Press Inc.

8. M.C. Chen. Synthesizing systolic designs. In *1985 International Symposium on VLSI Technology, Systems and Applications*, 1985.

9. P. Chretienne. *Les réseaux de Petri temporisés*. PhD thesis, Thèse d'état, Université P. et M. Curie, 1983.

10. L. Cooper and D. Steinberg. *Introduction to methods of optimization*. W.B. Saunders Company, 1970.

11. A. Darte, L. Khachiyan, and Y. Robert. Linear scheduling is nearly optimal. *Parallel Processing Letters*, 1(2):pp. 73–81, 1991.

12. A. Darte, T. Risset, and Y. Robert. Loop nest scheduling and transformations. In *Proc. of Environments and Tools for Parallel Scientific Computing, J.J. Dongarra and B. Tourancheau eds., North Holland (1993)*, July 1992.

13. A. Darte and Y. Robert. Scheduling uniform loop nests. Rapport 92-10, Laboratoire de l'Informatique du Parallélisme, Ecole Normale Supérieure de Lyon, February 1992.

14. J.M. Delosme and I.C.F. Ipsen. Efficient systolic arrays for the solution of Toeplitz systems: an illustration of a methodology for the construction of systolic architectures for VLSI. In *Systolic Arrays*, 1986.

15. V. Van Dongen, G.R. Gao, and Q. Ning. Extending software pipelining to nested loops. Technical Report Acaps Memo 53, School of Computer Science, McGill University, December 1992.

16. K. Ebcioğlu. A compilation technique for software pipelining of loops with conditional jumps. In *Proceedings of the 20th Annual Workshop on Microprogramming*, December 1987.

17. K. Ebcioğlu and A. Nicolau. A global resource-constrained parallelization technique. In *Proceedings of the ACM SIGARCH International Conference on Supercomputing*, June 1989.

18. P. Feautrier. A collection of papers on the systematic construction of parallel and distributed programs. Technical Report Hors-série, Lab. MASI, Université P. et M. Curie, 4 Place Jussieu 75252 Paris Cédex 05, June 1992.

19. G. R. Gao, Y. B. Wong, and Qi Ning. A Petri-Net model for fine-grain loop scheduling. In *Proceedings of the '91 ACM-SIGPLAN Conference on Programming Language Design and Implementation*, pages 204–218, Toronto, Canada, June 1991.

20. F. Gasperoni and U. Schwiegelshohn. "Scheduling Loops on Parallel Processors: a Simple Algorithm with Close to Optimum Performance," Proc. Int. Conf. CONPAR 92, G. Goos and J. Hartmanis Editors, *Lecture notes in Computer Science* 634, pp. 625–636, Springer Verlag 1992,.

21. H.V. Jagadish, S.K. Rao, and T. Kailath. Array architectures for iterative algorithms. *Proceedings of the IEEE*, 1987.

22. B. Joinnault. Conception d'algorithmes et d'architectures systoliques. Thèse de l'Université de Rennes I, Sept 1987.

23. Monica Lam. Software pipelining: An effective scheduling technique for VLIW machines. In *Proceedings of the 1988 ACM SIGPLAN Conference on Programming Languages Design and Implementation*, pages 318–328, Atlanta, GA, June 1988.

24. Eugene L. Lawler. *Combinatorial Optimization: Networks and Matroids*. Saunders College Publishing, Ft Worth, TX, 1976.

25. L.S. Liu, C.W. Ho, and J.P. Sheu. On the parallelism of nested for-loops using index shift method. In *Proc. of International Conf. on Parallel Processing*, pages II–119–II–123, Aug. 1992.

26. A. Nicolau, K. Pingali, and A. Aiken. Fine-grain compilation for pipelined machines. Technical Report TR-88-934, Department of Computer Science, Cornell University, Ithaca, NY, 1988.

27. Q. Ning and G.R. Gao. A novel framework of register allocation for software pipelining. In *Proceedings of 20th Annual ACM SIGPLAN-SIGACT Symposium on Principles of Programming Languages (POPL '93)*, pages 29–42, Charleston, South Carolina, January 10–13 1993.

28. Constantine Polychronopoulos. Toward auto-scheduling compilers. Technical report, University of Illinois-CSRD, May 1988. CSRD Rpt. No. 789.

29. P. Quinton. Automatic synthesis of systolic arrays from uniform recurrent equations. In *Proc. IEEE 11-th Int. Sym. on Computer Architecture*, 1984.

30. B. R. Rau and C. D. Glaeser. Some scheduling techniques and an easily schedulable horizontal architecture for high performance scientific computing. In *Proceedings of the 14th Annual Workshop on Microprogramming*, pages 183–198, 1981.

31. R. Reiter. Scheduling parallel computations. *Journal of ACM*, 15:590–599, October 1968.

32. Y. Robert and S. Song. Revisiting cycle shrinking. *Parallel Computing*, pages pp. 481–496, 1992.

33. R. F. Touzeau. A FORTRAN compiler for the FPS-164 scientific computer. In *Proceedings of the ACM SIGPLAN '84 Symposium on Compiler Construction*, pages 48–57, June 1984.

34. V. Van Dongen, G. Gao, and Q. Ning. A polynomial time method for optimal software pipelining. In *Proceedings of CONPAR '92*, Lecture Notes in Computer Science 634, Paris, France, September 1992.

A Methodology for Generating Efficient Disk-Based Algorithms from Tensor Product Formulas*

S. D. Kaushik[1], C.-H. Huang[1], R. W. Johnson[2] and P. Sadayappan[1]

[1] Department of Computer and Information Science, Ohio State University
[2] Department of Computer Science, St. Cloud State University

Abstract. In this paper, we address the issue of automatic generation of disk-based algorithms from tensor product formulas. Disk-based algorithms are required in scientific applications which work with large data sets that do not fit entirely into main memory. Tensor products have been used for designing and implementing block recursive algorithms on shared-memory, vector and distributed-memory multiprocessors. We extend this theory to generate disk-based code from tensor product formulas. The methodology is based on generating algebraically equivalent tensor product formulas which have better disk performance. We demonstrate this methodology by generating disk-based code for the fast Fourier transform.

Keywords: Tensor product, stride permutation, disk-based algorithm, fast Fourier transform.

1 Introduction

During the last decade, processor speeds have increased significantly and several strides in the development of high performance architectures have been made. While tremendous progress has been made in providing raw processing speed and large main memories, the I/O systems lag behind in bandwidth and access time capabilities. With the increase in main memory and secondary storage, the data sizes involved in various problems have also grown. Many scientific application operate on data matrices that are too large to fit entirely into main memory. For instance, out-of-core fast Fourier transforms operate on data arrays of sizes over a few gigabytes. The disk becomes a potential bottle-neck in the system. As a result algorithms designed to operate on data present in main memory perform unsatisfactorily. Thus the need to design disk-based algorithms arises. The objective of disk-based algorithms is to minimize the number of disk accesses, reduce the volume of data transferred from the disk to main memory, and to increase the reuse of data in main memory.

---

* This work was supported in part by DARPA, order number 7898, monitored by NIST under grant number 60NANB1D1151, DARPA, order number 7899, monitored by NIST under grant number 60NANB1D1150.

Several disk-based algorithms for specific scientific applications have been presented in the literature. Special attention has been given to permutation algorithms, the focus being on matrix transposition [1, 4, 8, 9, 11, 23, 25, 27]. Methods for performing generalized permutations of matrices stored in external memory using limited high-speed storage have been proposed by Fraser [10]. Vitter and Shriver [29] addressed the issue of performing general permutations on parallel disk systems and present asymptotically tight bounds on the number of parallel I/O operations needed to perform a general permutation. Cormen [7] extends the result to show how BPC (bit-permute/complement) permutations, can be performed with fewer parallel I/O operations than general permutations. Disk-based algorithms for performing the fast Fourier transform have been presented in [3, 5, 26, 28].

In this paper, we present a methodology based on tensor products for automatically generating disk-based algorithms. Tensor products have been used for expressing block recursive algorithms such as fast Fourier transform and Strassen's matrix multiplication [15, 17, 18]. Tensor product formulation of these algorithms has been used for the automatic generation of efficient parallel and vector programs for shared-memory multiprocessors. Tensor products are also used for automatically generating data distributions for distributed-memory machines [13] and modeling interconnection networks [20, 21]. In this paper, we extend the framework of tensor products to synthesize efficient out-of-core algorithms.

We first present a brief overview of the tensor product notation for representing algorithms in Sect. 2. In Sect. 3, we present the methodology for generating disk-based code for a tensor product formula representing an algorithm. The basic idea is to generate algebraically equivalent forms which have better disk performance. These forms correspond to the grouping of consecutive factors and the introduction of data rearrangements on disk at appropriate stages of the computation. In a typical computer system, the size of main memory is fixed while the data size varies from problem to problem. Section 4 addresses this problem and presents an algorithm for generating efficient code for a fixed main memory size. We demonstrate this methodology by generating code for the fast Fourier transform. Conclusions and directions of future work are presented in Sect. 5.

2   An Overview of Tensor Products

In this section, we give an overview of the tensor product notation. We first present the mathematical properties of the tensor product and then demonstrate the use of this notation in representing algorithms. For details of this theory, the reader is referred to [12, 14].

Let A be an $m \times n$ matrix and B an $p \times q$ matrix. The *tensor product* $A \otimes B$, is the block matrix obtained by replacing $a_{i,j}$ by the matrix $a_{i,j}B$, i.e.,

$$A \otimes B = \begin{bmatrix} a_{0,0}B & \cdots & a_{0,n-1}B \\ \vdots & \ddots & \vdots \\ a_{m-1,0}B & \cdots & a_{m-1,n-1}B \end{bmatrix}$$

A *matrix basis* $E_{i,j}^{m,n}$ is an $m \times n$ matrix with a one at position (i,j) and zeros elsewhere. A *vector basis* e_i^m is a column vector of length m with one at position i and zeros elsewhere. If the basis $E_{i,j}^{m,n}$ of an $m \times n$ matrix is stored by row, it is isomorphic to the tensor product of two vector bases $e_i^m \otimes e_j^n$. The tensor product of two vector bases $e_i^m \otimes e_j^n$ is equal to the vector basis e_{in+j}^{mn}. The tensor product $e_i^m \otimes e_j^n$ is called a *tensor basis*.

Consider the term $I_n \otimes B$ where B is an $m \times m$ matrix.

$$I_n \otimes B = \begin{bmatrix} B & & \\ & \ddots & \\ & & B \end{bmatrix}$$

Applying $I_n \otimes B$ to a vector X of size mn is equivalent to applying B to n consecutive segments of X each of size m. The following properties of the tensor product are used in this paper. I_n represents the $n \times n$ identity matrix, A is an $l \times m$ matrix, B a $p \times q$ matrix, C an $m \times n$ matrix, and D a $q \times r$ matrix. Also $\prod_{i=0}^{n} A_i = A_n \cdots A_0$.

1. $A \otimes B \otimes C = A \otimes (B \otimes C) = (A \otimes B) \otimes C$,
2. $(A \otimes B)(C \otimes D) = AC \otimes BD$
3. $A \otimes B = (A \otimes I_p)(I_m \otimes B) = (I_l \otimes B)(A \otimes I_q)$
4. $\prod_{i=0}^{t-1} (I_l \otimes A_i) = I_l \otimes \left(\prod_{i=0}^{t-1} A_i \right)$

One of the permutations used frequently in the tensor product formulation of various algorithms is the *stride permutation*. Stride permutation L_n^{mn} is defined as

$$L_n^{mn} \left(e_i^m \otimes e_j^n \right) = e_j^n \otimes e_i^m$$

L_n^{mn} permutes the elements of a vector of size mn with stride distance n. This permutation can be represented as an $mn \times mn$ transformation. For example, L_2^6 can be represented by the matrix

$$L_2^6 X^6 = \begin{bmatrix} 1 & 0 & 0 & 0 & 0 & 0 \\ 0 & 0 & 1 & 0 & 0 & 0 \\ 0 & 0 & 0 & 0 & 1 & 0 \\ 0 & 1 & 0 & 0 & 0 & 0 \\ 0 & 0 & 0 & 1 & 0 & 0 \\ 0 & 0 & 0 & 0 & 0 & 1 \end{bmatrix} \begin{bmatrix} x_0 \\ x_1 \\ x_2 \\ x_3 \\ x_4 \\ x_5 \end{bmatrix} = \begin{bmatrix} x_0 \\ x_2 \\ x_4 \\ x_1 \\ x_3 \\ x_5 \end{bmatrix}.$$

Clearly, $(L_n^{mn})^{-1} = L_m^{mn}$. A useful property of the tensor product used extensively in the remainder of the paper is the following theorem.

Theorem 1 Commutation Theorem. $L_p^{mp}(A \otimes B) = (B \otimes A) L_q^{nq}$, where A is an $m \times n$ matrix and B is a $p \times q$ matrix, i.e., $(B \otimes A) = L_p^{mp}(A \otimes B) (L_q^{nq})^{-1}$.

The commutation theorem can be generalized.

Corollary 2. *If A_i is an $m_i \times n_i$ matrix, then*

$$(A_{t-1} \otimes \cdots \otimes A_{i+1} \otimes A_i \otimes \cdots \otimes A_0) = \left(I_{m_{t-1} \cdots m_{i+2}} \otimes L_{m_{i+1}}^{m_{i+1} m_i} \otimes I_{m_{i-1} \cdots m_0} \right)$$
$$(A_{t-1} \otimes \cdots \otimes A_i \otimes A_{i+1} \otimes \cdots \otimes A_0)$$
$$\left(I_{n_{t-1} \cdots n_{i+2}} \otimes L_{n_i}^{n_{i+1} n_i} \otimes I_{n_{i-1} \cdots n_0} \right)$$

We now describe the use of the tensor product notation to represent algorithms. Consider the evaluation of the fast Fourier transform of an 8 element

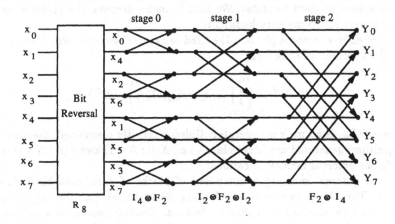

Fig. 1. Fast Fourier Transform for 8 element vector. (Bit reversal not shown)

vector $X^8 = (x_0, \ldots, x_7)^t$ as shown in Fig. 1. The tensor product representation of this algorithm is as follows.

$$Y^8 = (F_8).(X^8)$$
$$F_8 = (F_2 \otimes I_4) T_4^8 (I_2 \otimes F_2 \otimes I_2)(I_2 \otimes T_2^4)(I_4 \otimes F_2) R_8$$
$$F_2 = \begin{bmatrix} 1 & 1 \\ 1 & -1 \end{bmatrix}$$

Note that the factors of F_8 operate on the input vector X^8 from right to left. R_8 represents the bit reversal permutation. T_4^8 and $I_2 \otimes T_2^4$ represent the appropriate roots of unity also known as the twiddle factors. The algorithm consists of three stages after the bit reversal of the input vector. Stage 0 corresponds to the factor $I_4 \otimes F_2$ in which consecutive pairs of elements are combined using the operator F_2. $(I_2 \otimes F_2 \otimes I_2)(I_2 \otimes T_2^4)$ corresponds to stage 1 and $(F_2 \otimes I_4)(T_4^8)$ to stage 2. In stage 1, elements of the input vector separated by a distance of 2 are combined. In stage 2, elements separated by a distance of 4 are combined.

In general, the tensor product formula for an algorithm takes the form.

$$\prod_{j=0}^{k-1} T_j, \quad T_j = \begin{cases} I_{l_j} \otimes OP_{m_j,n_j} \otimes I_{r_j} \\ I_{l_j} \otimes L_{n_j}^{m_j \times n_j} \otimes I_{r_j} \end{cases} OP_{m_j,n_j} \text{ is an } m_j \times n_j \text{ linear transformation}$$

In this paper we only consider square operators OP_{m_j,m_j}. For details of automatically generating code from tensor product formulas refer to [15, 17].

3 Code Generation of Disk-Based Algorithms

In this section, we develop a methodology for generating disk-based programs from tensor product formulas. We first formally describe the problem and the parameters of the memory hierarchy.

Consider a vector $X(0 : N-1)$ stored in external storage. We consider tensor product formulas of the form

$$Y^N = \left(\prod_{i=0}^{t-1} (I_{l_i} \otimes OP_{m_i} \otimes I_{n_i}) \right) \cdot (X^N) \tag{1}$$

where OP_{m_i} is an $m_i \times m_i$ operator. Unless explicitly mentioned, the disk-based algorithms generated are "dual-place", i.e., $X(0 : N-1)$ and $Y(0 : N-1)$ occupy different external memory locations.

The external memory is composed of blocks of data, each block of size b bytes. The blocks can be accessed using *direct access*, i.e., the beginning of a block can be accessed in a random fashion. However, access to a byte of data within a block requires sequential access of all preceding bytes in that block. An access to external memory specifies the block address and the number of elements following this address to be read into main memory. The external memory access time t_a is composed of two components - access setup time t_s, and the total element access time. If n elements are to be accessed then $t_a = t_s + n * t_e$, where t_e is the time required per element transfer after access setup. The setup time is often the dominating component of external memory access time as $t_s \gg t_e$. For instance, the typical setup time is $10ms$. The element transfer rate is approximately $100Mb/s$ [16] which yields an element transfer time of $0.01\mu s$. The main memory size is M bytes and we assume that $b|M$, i.e., the main memory can store an integer number of external memory blocks. Also the main memory size is smaller than the total data size, i.e., $M < N$.

The total number of passes, i.e., the number of times the entire matrix is read from and stored back to the disk, has been previously used as a measure of goodness. While the number of passes reflects the volume of data movement and becomes significant for large matrices, it does not completely reflect the total disk time required. The total execution time for the algorithm is dominated by the time spent in data transfer between main memory and external memory, i.e., the computation time is expected to be negligible compared to the total time spent in disk operations. The total number of disk accesses will be used along with the number of passes as the measure of goodness.

In the following section, we examine various forms of tensor product factors and determine efficient methods for evaluating these factors. We first consider factors which can be executed with a minimum number of disk accesses for the available main memory. We call such factors *disk-optimal factors*. For the other tensor product factors, we provide algebraically equivalent forms which have better disk performance. The equivalent forms correspond to a grouping of consecutive factors, or the rearrangement of data on the disk followed by a disk-optimal evaluation and another data rearrangement, or a combination of the grouping of factors and data rearrangements. The benefit of using the equivalent forms depends on the disk seek and element transfer times, the main memory size, the input data size, the operator size, and the efficiency with which the data rearrangement can be performed. We present analytical expressions to evaluate the potential benefits of these optimizations and evaluate these benefits for the computation of a fast Fourier transform on a fixed main memory size.

3.1 Single-Pass Disk-Based Algorithms

Consider a factor of the form $I_{2N/M} \otimes OP_{M/2}$. The disk-based code for $X^N = (I_{2N/M} \otimes OP_{M/2}).(X^N)$ operates upon the input vector as follows. The program loads the vector into half of the main memory in blocks of size $M/2$. The operation $OP_{M/2}$ is performed on each block in main memory. This block is stored back to the corresponding block of X on external storage. Fig. 2 illustrates the operation on the first block of the input vector. The code is as shown in Fig. 3. The main memory is represented by the arrays $M_1(0 : M/2-1)$ and $M_2(0 : M/2-1)$. The code for the statement S, shown in Fig. 3, can be generated using the standard code generation techniques for tensor products.

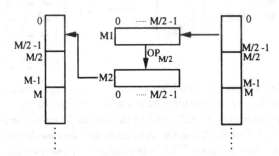

Fig. 2. Disk-based evaluation for $X^N \leftarrow (I_{\frac{2N}{M}} \otimes OP_{\frac{M}{2}}).(X^N)$.

The generated code requires a single pass over the vector and requires $2N/M$ disk read accesses and $2N/M$ disk write accesses - totally $4N/M$ disk accesses.

```
    B ← M/2
    do i = 0, 2N/M − 1
        /*Read the ith block of X into main memory*/
        M₁(0 : B − 1) ← X(iB : (i + 1)B − 1)
        /* Perform OP in main memory */
        S :  Code(M₂(0 : B − 1) ← (OP).(M₁(0 : B − 1)))
        /* Store result back to the i-th block of X */
        X(iB : (i + 1)B − 1) ← M₂(0 : B − 1)
    enddo
```

Fig. 3. Disk-Based Code for $X^N \leftarrow \left(I_{\frac{2N}{M}} \otimes OP_{\frac{M}{2}}\right).(X^N)$.

The generated program is "in-place", i.e., the input and the output vectors occupy the same external memory space. The generated code requires a minimum number of disk accesses for the available main memory. We call such factors *disk-optimal factors* and the associated code, *disk-optimal code*.

3.2 Multiple-Pass Disk-Based Algorithms

We now consider factors of the form $I_l \otimes OP_m \otimes I_n$ where $mn > M/2$. (If $mn < M/2$ then the factor is disk-optimal). As an example, consider performing the operation $Y_{512} = (I_2 \otimes F_8 \otimes I_{32}).(X_{512})$, when 32 elements can fit into main memory. The operation is shown below.

$$
\begin{bmatrix} Y_0 \\ \vdots \\ Y_{511} \end{bmatrix} = \begin{bmatrix} F_8 \otimes I_{32} & 0 \\ 0 & F_8 \otimes I_{32} \end{bmatrix} \begin{bmatrix} X_0 \\ \vdots \\ X_{511} \end{bmatrix}, \text{ where } F_8 = \begin{bmatrix} 1 & 1 & 1 & 1 & 1 & 1 & 1 & 1 \\ 1 & \omega & \omega^2 & \omega^3 & \omega^4 & \omega^5 & \omega^6 & \omega^7 \\ 1 & \omega^2 & \omega^4 & \omega^6 & 1 & \omega^2 & \omega^4 & \omega^6 \\ 1 & \omega^3 & \omega^6 & \omega & \omega^3 & \omega^7 & \omega^2 & \omega^5 \\ 1 & \omega^4 & 1 & \omega^4 & 1 & \omega^4 & 1 & \omega^4 \\ 1 & \omega & \omega^2 & \omega^7 & \omega^4 & \omega & \omega^6 & \omega^3 \\ 1 & \omega^6 & \omega^4 & \omega^2 & 1 & \omega^6 & \omega^4 & \omega^2 \\ 1 & \omega^7 & \omega^6 & \omega^5 & \omega^4 & \omega^3 & \omega^2 & \omega \end{bmatrix}
$$

We first consider a direct method for evaluating $F_8 \otimes I_{32}$. Evaluation of one element of the output vector requires that eight elements of the input vector be available in main memory. To fully utilize the available main memory we load in eight subvectors of X each of size two into main memory as shown in Fig. 4. This will require eight disk accesses. The data available in main memory can be used to evaluate eight output subvectors each of size two. Writing these subvectors back to main memory will require eight disk writes. This load-evaluate-store process will be repeated 16 times to produce the entire output vector. Performing $F_8 \otimes I_{32}$ would require 8×16 reads and 8×16 writes - totally 256 disk accesses. Thus, $I_2 \otimes F_8 \otimes I_{32}$ will require totally 512 disk accesses and a single pass over the input vector, when performed using the direct method.

Data Rearrangement. Using the commutation theorem, we have $I_2 \otimes F_8 \otimes I_{32} = (I_2 \otimes L_8^{256})(I_{64} \otimes F_8)(I_2 \otimes L_{32}^{256})$. Code for this equivalent form corresponds to rearranging the data on the disk according to the permutation $I_2 \otimes L_{32}^{256}$, performing the disk optimal code for $I_{64} \otimes F_8$ and rearranging the data according to the permutation $I_2 \otimes L_8^{256}$. The two permutations can be performed using totally 384 disk accesses and eight passes over the input vector [19]. Since $I_{64} \otimes F_8$ can be performed using 64 disk accesses and one pass, totally 448 disk accesses are required which is a significant reduction. Thus *data rearrangement* reduces the number of disk accesses for some tensor product factors. However, the number of passes over the input vector has increased to nine. Also, data rearrangement may not always lead to a reduction in the number of disk accesses. Consider performing $F_2 \otimes I_{32}$ using a main memory of size 16 - the direct method requires 32 disk accesses, while using the data rearrangement requires 88 disk accesses. In this case, the cost of performing a data rearrangement overrides the gain in executing disk-optimal code.

If data rearrangements are used, the code for the factor $I_l \otimes OP_m \otimes I_n$ is generated by first pre-permuting the data, performing the operation $I_l \otimes I_n \otimes OP_m$ and post-permuting the data. The pre-permutation is $I_l \otimes L_n^{mn}$ and the post-permutation is $I_l \otimes L_m^{mn}$. The code is as shown in Fig. 5.

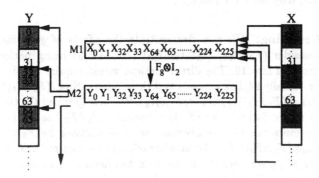

Fig. 4. Direct evaluation of $Y^{256} \leftarrow (F_8 \otimes I_{32}).(X^{256})$.

We now formulate the number of disk accesses required by the direct method. Consider $I_l \otimes OP_m \otimes I_n$, where $mn > M/2$. The computation of $I_l \otimes OP_m \otimes I_n$ corresponds to I_l copies of $OP_m \otimes I_n$ acting on the vector. The direct method for computing $OP_m \otimes I_n$ loads m subvectors, each of size $M/(2m)$, and evaluates m output vectors, each of size $M/(2m)$. Totally $2m^2n/M$ disk read and $(2m^2n)/M$ disk write accesses are required - totally $(4m^2n)/M$ disk accesses are required to compute $OP_m \otimes I_n$. Thus performing $I_l \otimes OP_m \otimes I_n$ will require $(4lm^2n)/M = 4Nm/M$ disk accesses. The number of disk accesses is m times those required for disk optimal code. The larger the operator size the greater the penalty incurred by the direct method.

Performing $I_l \otimes L_m^{mn}$ requires at most $\frac{3 log_2(m)N}{M}$ disk accesses and $log_2(m)$

```
B ← mn
do i = 0, l - 1
      /* Perform disk-based L_n^{mn} on i-th block of X*/
      X(iB : (i + 1)B - 1) ← (L_n^{mn}).(X(iB : (i + 1)B - 1))
enddo
Code(X^N ← (I_l⊗I_n⊗OP_m).(X^N))
do i = 0, l - 1
      /* Perform disk-based L_m^{mn} on i-th block of X */
      X(iB : (i + 1)B - 1) ← (L_m^{mn}).(X(iB : (i + 1)B - 1))
enddo
```

Fig. 5. Disk-Based Code for $X^N \leftarrow (I_l \otimes OP_m \otimes I_n)X^N$.

passes over the vector [19]. Similarly, performing $I_l \otimes L_n^{mn}$ requires at most $\frac{3log_2(n)N}{M}$ disk accesses and $log_2(n)$ passes over the vector. Performing the computation $I_l \otimes I_n \otimes OP_m$ requires $(4N)/M$ disk accesses and a single pass. Thus, computing $I_l \otimes OP_m \otimes I_n$ using data rearrangement requires totally $\frac{3log_2(mn)N}{M} + \frac{4N}{M}$ disk accesses and $log_2(mn) + 1$ passes.

Factor Grouping. We now demonstrate the effects of *grouping* consecutive factors. Consider $(F_2 \otimes I_{32}) (I_2 \otimes F_2 \otimes I_{16}) (I_4 \otimes F_2 \otimes I_8)$ being performed with a main memory of size 16. The direct method would require 32 disk accesses for each factor - totally 96 disk accesses and three passes. Now, $(F_2 \otimes I_{32}) (I_2 \otimes F_2 \otimes I_{16})$ $(I_4 \otimes F_2 \otimes I_8) = (F_2 \otimes I_{32})(I_2 \otimes (F_2 \otimes F_2) \otimes I_8)$. We have grouped the two trailing factors into a single factor. The effective operator $F_2 \otimes F_2$ has a size of four. The resulting formula can now be executed with 32 accesses for $F_2 \otimes I_{32}$ and 64 accesses for $I_2 \otimes (F_2 \otimes F_2) \otimes I_2$. The number of accesses required is still 96, however, the number of passes over the input data has decreased to two, improving the disk performance. Grouping may not always lead to better performance. Grouping all the three factors gives the factor $(F_2 \otimes (F_2 \otimes F_2) \otimes I_8)$ which requires 128 disk accesses and 1 pass. Improvement of disk performance in this case would depend on the relative values of the seek and transfer times, and the vector and main memory sizes.

Factor Grouping and Data Rearrangement. We now demonstrate the effects of grouping factors combined with data rearrangement of the input vector, referred to as *grouping with rearrangement*. $(F_2 \otimes I_{32})(I_2 \otimes F_2 \otimes I_{16}) (I_4 \otimes F_2 \otimes I_8)$ $= (F_2 \otimes F_2 \otimes F_2) \otimes I_8 = L_8^{64}(I_8 \otimes F_2 \otimes F_2 \otimes F_2) L_8^{64}$. Performing the algebraically equivalent form requires 72 disk accesses for the disk rearrangement and 16 disk accesses for the disk optimal factor - totally 88 disk accesses. However, the number of passes has increased to seven. Grouping with data rearrangement is beneficial if the additional cost of data rearrangement can be offset by the gain of grouping the factors.

We now evaluate the effect of these optimizations on the disk performance of an entire formula. Since we are only interested in the data access pattern of the fast Fourier transform, we exclude the factors corresponding to the twiddle factors. The resulting tensor product formula for data size $N = 2^n$ on main memory size $M = 2^m$ is given by

$$F_{2^n} = \prod_{i=0}^{n-1} (I_{2^{n-i-1}} \otimes F_2 \otimes I_{2^i}) = \prod_{i=m-1}^{n-1} (I_{2^{n-i-1}} \otimes F_2 \otimes I_{2^i}) \prod_{i=0}^{m-2} (I_{2^{n-i-1}} \otimes F_2 \otimes I_{2^i}).$$

Note that the first $m - 1$ factors are all disk-optimal factors. We group these factors into a single disk-optimal factor and apply the optimizations to the remaining $len = n - m + 1$ factors. For the grouping optimization, we consider groups of size k, $2 \leq k < m$. The group size is bound above by $m - 1$, as the effective operator size should be less than $\frac{M}{2}$. For the group and rearrange optimization, the largest possible group of factors is used. Any smaller group will require additional disk accesses and passes. We show the following analytical expressions for the total disk time - t_{nogrp} refers to the direct method, $t_{grp,k}$ refers to the grouping optimization with groups of size k, and t_{rearr} refers to the group and rearrange optimization.

$$t_{nogrp} = (2 * len + 1) * \frac{4N}{M} * t_s + 2 * (len + 1) * N * t_e$$

$$t_{grp,k} = \left(\frac{len}{k} * 2^k + d * 2^{len \bmod k} + 1 \right) * \frac{4N}{M} * t_s + 2 * \left(\frac{len}{k} + d + 1 \right) * N * t_e$$

$$t_{rearr} = \left[\frac{4Ns}{M} + \frac{5(m-1)N}{2M} * \left(\frac{s(s+1)}{2} - 1 \right) + r * \left(\frac{4N}{M} + \frac{5Nn}{2M} \right) \right] * t_s +$$

$$2 * \left[s + \frac{m-1}{2} * \left(\frac{s(s+1)}{2} - 1 \right) + r * \left(1 + \frac{n}{2} \right) \right] * N * t_e$$

$$\text{where } d = \begin{cases} 0 & \text{if } k|len, \\ 1 & \text{otherwise,} \end{cases} \quad r = \begin{cases} 0 & \text{if } (m-1)|len, \\ 1 & \text{otherwise,} \end{cases} \quad s = \frac{len}{m-1} + 1.$$

The disk times for each strategy are evaluated for input vectors of size $N = 16M, 64M, 256M, 4G, 64G$ and main memory size is $M = 2M$ using $t_s = 30ms$ and $t_e = 0.01\mu s$ [16]. The disk times are shown in Tables 1, 2, and 3. Table 1 presents the total disk times. The seek times and element transfer times are shown in Tables 2, and 3, respectively. Observing the total disk times we note that grouping of two factors has the best performance at low input data sizes and is always better than no grouping. Grouping with rearrangement has the best performance for data sizes over $64G$. This trend is observed for larger data sizes with an improvement in disk performance for grouping with data rearrangement with increasing data size. Also the element transfer times form a small fraction of the total disk time.

Table 1. Total Disk times for various groupings.

N	No Groups	Grouping (group size)						Group & Arrange
		2	3	4	5	6	7	
16M	10.3	9.6	11.6	17.0	-	-	-	21.0
64M	59.3	55.3	69.3	84.7	138.4	252.3	-	90.2
256M	309.4	288.0	344.0	523.0	645.9	1076.0	2028.3	385.4
4G	7620.7	6745.3	8539.6	12385.8	17301.0	31960.7	39825.1	6952.9
64G	153126.0	142131.0	178704.0	262462.0	396156.0	575661.0	1031790.0	123826.9

Table 2. Seek times for various groupings.

N	No Groups	Grouping (group size)						Group & Arrange
		2	3	4	5	6	7	
16M	8.6	8.6	10.6	16.3	-	-	-	16.3
64M	49.9	49.9	65.3	80.6	134.4	249.6	-	70.1
256M	261.1	261.1	322.6	506.9	629.8	1059.8	2012.2	299.5
4G	6144.0	6144.0	8110.1	12042.2	16957.4	31703.0	39567.4	5406.7
64G	129761.0	129761.0	169083.0	255590.0	389284.0	570163.0	102629.0	96337.9

Table 3. Total element transfer times for various groupings.

N	No Groups	Grouping (group size)						Group & Arrange
		2	3	4	5	6	7	
16M	1.7	1.0	1.0	0.7	-	-	-	4.7
64M	9.4	5.4	4.0	4.0	4.0	2.7	-	20.1
256M	48.3	26.8	21.5	16.1	16.1	16.1	16.1	85.9
4G	1116.7	601.3	429.5	343.6	343.6	257.7	257.7	1546.2
64G	23364.6	12369.50	9620.7	6871.9	6871.9	5497.6	5497.6	27487.8

4 Optimizing Disk Performance

In Section 3, we have demonstrated the benefits of grouping tensor product factors of the input formula and rearranging data on the disk. Typically the size of the main memory is fixed and the data size varies from problem to problem. In this section, we address the problem of finding the appropriate groups of tensor product factors and the necessary data rearrangements such that the total disk time is reduced for a fixed main memory size and data size. We focus on tensor product formulas of the form

$$Y^N = \left(\prod_{i=0}^{n-1} (I_{m^{n-i-1}} \otimes OP_m \otimes I_{m^i}) \right) \cdot (X^N) \tag{2}$$

where OP_m is an $m \times m$ operator. The main memory size is M. We first analyze the grouping of consecutive tensor product factors and determine the largest group size until which grouping of factors (without introducing rearrangements) decreases the total disk time. Using this group size and the time estimate for grouping and grouping with rearrangement, we present an algorithm for finding an efficient method for executing the formula.

4.1 Factor Grouping

The grouping optimization groups consecutive factors of the tensor product formula. The grouping results in an increase in the number of disk accesses but reduces the number of passes required. For the tensor product formula in Eq. 2, the largest number of factors which can be grouped is l where $m^l \leq M/2 < m^{l+1}$. The effective operator size after grouping k tensor product factors is m^k. Thus the grouped factor would require $\frac{4Nm^k}{M}$ disk accesses. The increase in the number of disk accesses due to grouping is given by $\frac{4N(m^k-km)}{M}$. The grouped factor requires a single pass over the input vector reducing the number of passes by $k-1$. Thus grouping of k factors would decrease the disk time if

$$\frac{4N(m^k - km)}{M} t_s < 2N(k-1)t_e \equiv \frac{2(m^k - km)}{k-1} < \frac{Mt_e}{t_s}.$$

The change in disk time due to grouping is independent of the size of the input vector. Since m^k grows exponentially with k we have the following.

$$\exists\, k' \geq 1 \ s.t. \ \frac{2(m^{k'} - k'm)}{k'-1} < \frac{Mt_e}{t_s} \ \text{ and } \ \frac{2(m^{k'+1} - (k'+1)m)}{k'} \geq \frac{Mt_e}{t_s}.$$

The term $\frac{Mt_e}{t_s}$ is dependent only on the configuration and I/O characteristics of the system . Grouping of any $k < k'$ consecutive tensor product factors will decrease the disk time. This decrease in the disk time is position independent, i.e., the decrease is the same irrespective of the position of the grouped factors within the entire tensor product formula.

4.2 Factor Grouping and Data Rearrangement

The grouping with rearrangement optimization groups k tensor product factors and introduces a data rearrangement before and after the grouped factor such that it can be executed in an optimal fashion. The cost of the data rearrangement can be evaluated as described in Sect. 3. The cost of the data rearrangement depends on the position of the grouped factors within the tensor product formula.

4.3 Dynamic Program Formulation

We now formulate the problem of determining the groups of factors and the necessary data rearrangements as a dynamic programming problem. Let $C(p,q)$ be the minimum disk time for evaluating $\prod_{i=p}^{q} (I_{m^{n-i-1}} \otimes OP_m \otimes I_{m^i})$. Let $G(k)$ (group) represent the disk time for evaluating a grouped factor consisting of k consecutive factors, and $GR(p,k)$ (group and rearrange) represent the disk time for evaluating k factors starting at the factor p, preceded and followed by a data rearrangement. Then we have the following relation

$$C(p, p) = G(1)$$

$$C(p, q) = min \begin{cases} min_{(1 \leq k \leq min(k', q-p+1))} C(p+k, q) + G(k) \\ \qquad\qquad\qquad\qquad\qquad /*\text{ grouping } */ \\ min_{(1 \leq k \leq min(l, q-p+1))} C(p+k, q) + GR(p, k) \\ \qquad\qquad\qquad\qquad\qquad /*\text{ group and rearrange } */ \end{cases}$$

Typically k' will be a small integer. $C(l+1, n)$ gives the lowest disk time and the resulting grouped factors and intermediate data rearrangements can be found in a straightforward fashion. The dynamic program has got $O(n^2)$ space complexity and $O(n^3)$ time complexity.

We now demonstrate this code generation strategy by synthesizing disk-based code for the fast Fourier Transform.

Consider a 2^{40}-point fast Fourier transform being computed on a machine with main memory size 4 Mb. Let $t_s = 30 ms$ and $t_e = 0.01 \mu s$. We have $\frac{M t_s}{t_s} \approx$ 1.25 which gives $k' = 2$. We are interested only in the data access pattern of the fast Fourier transform. We assume that the twiddle factors are computed dynamically [5] and do not consider the $(I_{2^n-i} \otimes T_{2^i-1}^{2^i})$ factors. The resulting formula is given by Eq. 3

$$F_{2^{40}} = \prod_{i=0}^{39} (I_{2^{40-i-1}} \otimes F_2 \otimes I_{2^i}) \tag{3}$$

The group and rearrange optimization for the trailing 19 tensor product factors has the lowest disk time. The resulting formula can be expressed as follows.

$$F_{2^{40}} = L_{2^{19}}^{2^{40}} \left(I_{2^{21}} \otimes \prod_{i=0}^{18} (I_{2^{19-i-1}} \otimes F_2 \otimes I_{2^i}) \right) L_{2^{21}}^{2^{40}} \left(I_{2^{19}} \otimes \prod_{i=0}^{20} (I_{2^{21-i-1}} \otimes F_2 \otimes I_{2^i}) \right)$$

The generated code is shown in Fig. 6. $M_1(0 : 2^{20} - 1)$ and $M_2(0 : 2^{20} - 1)$ represent the available main memory. $PtrM_1$ and $PtrM_2$ are pointers to the arrays M_1 and M_2, respectively.

5 Conclusions

Efficient disk-based algorithms for specific scientific applications have been previously presented in the literature. However, the issue of automatically generating efficient-disk based code has not been addressed. In this paper, we have presented a methodology based on tensor products for automatically generating efficient disk-based algorithms. The methodology is based on generating algebraically equivalent formulas which have better disk performance. Execution of the equivalent forms corresponds to grouping consecutive factors, rearranging

```
Float M₁(0 : 2²¹ − 1), M₂(0 : 2²¹ − 1), *PtrM₁, *PtrM₂
```

$$/* \text{ Perform } I_{2^{19}} \otimes \prod_{i=0}^{20} (I_{2^{21-i-1}} \otimes F_2 \otimes I_{2^i}) * /$$

```
do i = 0, 2¹⁹ − 1
    PtrM₁(0 : 2²¹ − 1) ← X(i * 2²¹ : (i + 1) * 2²¹ − 1)
    do j = 0, 20
        PtrM₂(0 : 2²¹ − 1) ← (I₂²¹⁻ʲ⁻¹ ⊗ F₂ ⊗ I₂ⱼ) (PtrM₁(0 : 2²¹ − 1))
        Interchange PtrM₁ and PtrM₂
    enddo
    X(i * 2²¹ : (i + 1) * 2²¹ − 1) ← PtrM₁(0 : 2²¹ − 1)
enddo
```

$$/* \text{ Perform disk-based stride permutation } L_{2^{21}}^{2^{40}} \text{ on } X \ */$$

$$Y(0 : 2^{40} − 1) \leftarrow (L_{2^{21}}^{2^{40}})(X(0 : 2^{40} − 1))$$

$$/* \text{ Perform } I_{2^{21}} \otimes \prod_{i=0}^{18} (I_{2^{19-i-1}} \otimes F_2 \otimes I_{2^i}) \ */$$

```
do i = 0, 2²¹ − 1
    PtrM₁(0 : 2¹⁹ − 1) ← Y(i * 2¹⁹ : (i + 1) * 2¹⁹ − 1)
    do j = 0, 18
        PtrM₂(0 : 2¹⁹ − 1) ← (I₂¹⁹⁻ʲ⁻¹ ⊗ F₂ ⊗ I₂ⱼ) (PtrM₁(0 : 2¹⁹ − 1))
        Interchange PtrM₁ and PtrM₂
    enddo
    Y(i * 2¹⁹ : (i + 1) * 2¹⁹ − 1) ← PtrM₁(0 : 2¹⁹ − 1)
enddo
```

$$/* \text{ Perform disk-based stride permutation } L_{2^{19}}^{2^{40}} \text{ on } Y \ */$$

$$X(0 : 2^{40} − 1) \leftarrow (L_{2^{19}}^{2^{40}})(Y(0 : 2^{40} − 1))$$

Fig. 6. Disk-Based Code for Eq. 3.

the data on the disk and executing the remaining operations in an efficient fashion. We demonstrate this methodology by generating efficient disk-based code for the fast Fourier transform.

With the advent of parallel I/O systems [2, 6, 22, 24] exploiting the parallelism of the parallel disk systems is an objective to be considered. Work in this direction is currently in progress.

References

1. W. O. Alltop. A computer algorithm for transposing nonsquare matrices. *IEEE Transactions on Computers*, C-24(10):1038–1040, 1975.
2. R. Alverson, D. Callahan, D. Cummings, B.Koblens, A. Porterfield, and B. Smith. The Tera computer system. In *1990 International Conference on Supercomputing*, pages 1–6, 1990.
3. G. L. Anderson. A stepwise approach to computing the multidimensional fast Fourier transform of large arrays. *IEEE Transactions on Acoustics and Speech Signal Processing*, ASSP-28(3):280–284, 1980.

4. M. B. Ari. On transposing large $2^n \times 2^n$ matrices. *IEEE Transactions on Computers*, C-27(1):72–75, 1979.

5. D. H. Bailey. FFTs in external or hierarchical memory. *Journal of Supercomputing*, 4:23–35, 1990.

6. P. M. Chen and D. A. Patterson. Maximizing performance in a striped disk array. In *Proceedings of the 17th Annual International Symposium on Computer Architecture*, pages 322–331, 1990.

7. T. H. Cormen. Fast permuting on disk arrays. *Journal of Parallel and Distributed Computing*, 17:41–57, Jan.-Feb. 1993.

8. L. G. Delcaro and G. L. Sicuranza. A method on transposing externally stored matrices. *IEEE Transactions on Computers*, C-23(9):801–803, 1974.

9. J. O. Eklundh. A fast computer method for matrix transposing. *IEEE Transactions on Computers*, 20(7):801–803, 1972.

10. D. Fraser. Array permutation by index-digit permutation. *Journal of ACM*, 23(2):298–309, 1976.

11. G. C. Goldbogen. Prim : A fast matrix transpose method. *IEEE Transactions on Software Engineering*, SE-7(2):255–257, 1981.

12. A. Graham. *Kronecker Products and Matrix Calculus: With Applications*. Ellis Horwood Limited, 1981.

13. S. K. S. Gupta, S. D. Kaushik, C.-H. Huang, J. R. Johnson, R. W. Johnson, and P. Sadayappan. A methodology for the generation of data distributions to optimize communication. In *Fourth IEEE Symposium on Parallel and Distributed Processing*, pages 436–441, 1992.

14. R. A. Horn and C. R. Johnson. *Topics in Matrix Analysis*. Cambridge University Press, Cambridge, 1991.

15. C.-H. Huang, J. R. Johnson, and R. W. Johnson. Generating parallel programs from tensor product formulas: A case study of Strassen's matrix multiplication algorithm. In *Proc. International Conference on Parallel Processing 1992*, pages 104–108, 1992.

16. Paragon XP/S product overview. Intel Corporation, 1991.

17. J. R. Johnson, R. W. Johnson, D. Rodrigues, and R. Tolimieri. A methodology for designing, modifying and implementing fourier transform algorithms on various architectures. *Circuits Systems Signal Process*, 9(4):449–500, 1990.

18. R. W. Johnson, C.-H. Huang, and J. R. Johnson. Multilinear algebra and parallel programming. *Journal of Supercomputing*, 5:189–218, 1991.

19. S. D. Kaushik, C.-H. Huang, J. R. Johnson, R. W. Johnson, and P. Sadayappan. Efficient transposition algorithms for large matrices. In *Supercomputing '93*, 1993. To appear.

20. S. D. Kaushik, S. Sharma, and C.-H. Huang. An algebraic theory for modeling multistage interconnection networks. *Journal of Information Science and Engineering*. To appear.

21. S. D. Kaushik, S. Sharma, C.-H. Huang, J. R. Johnson, R. W. Johnson, and P. Sadayappan. An algebraic theory for modeling direct interconnection networks. In *Supercomputing '92*, pages 488–497, 1992.

22. D. A. Patterson, G. Gibson, and R. H. Katz. A case for redundant arrays of inexpensive disks. In *Proceedings of the ACM International Conference on Management of Data (SIGMOD)*, pages 109–116, June 1988.

23. H. K. Ramapriyan. A generalization of Eklundh's's algorithm for transposing large matrices. *IEEE Transactions on Computers*, C-24(12):1221–1226, 1975.

24. A. Reddy and P. Banerjee. Evaluation of multiple-disk I/O systems. *IEEE Transactions on Computers*, 38:1680–1690, December 1989.

25. U. Schumann. Comment on 'a fast computer method for matrix transposing'. *IEEE Transactions on Computers*, C-22(5):542–543, 1973.

26. R. C. Singleton. A method for computing the fast Fourier transform with auxiliary memory and limited high-speed storage. *IEEE Transactions on Audio and Electroacoustics*, AU-15(2):91–98, 1967.

27. R. E. Twogood and M. P. Ekstrom. An extension of Eklundh's matrix transposition algorithm and its application to digital signal processing. *IEEE Transactions on Computers*, C-25(12):950–952, 1976.

28. C. Van Loan. *Computational framework for the Fast Fourier Transform*. SIAM, 1992.

29. J. S. Vitter and M. Shriver. Optimal disk I/O with parallel block transfer. In *Twenty Second Annual ACM Symposium on Theory of Computing*, pages 159–169, May 1990.

Loop Transformations for Prolog Programs

David C. Sehr[1]
Laxmikant V. Kale[2]
David A. Padua[3]

Abstract

Parallel execution models for Prolog have generally focused on either AND or OR parallelism. In both cases the largest speedups come from recursive computations similar to procedural language loops. Parallel models to date, however, have neither treated this *loop* parallelism by a common implementation nor provided speedups comparable to automatic parallelizers for procedural languages. In this paper we present a framework for the use of loop transformations on Prolog programs. We show by critical path timing of several benchmarks that our transformations give a significant improvement over existing parallelization methods.

1 Introduction

Prolog provides a number of advantages for the development of high-level descriptions of algorithms. Its built-in support of pattern-matching (unification) and backtracking search make it well suited to a range of computations from expert systems and database query processing to compilation and natural language processing. Another advantage often cited is Prolog's high degree of implicit parallelism, although parallel Prolog systems have yet to prove this claim by producing speedups across a range of real applications. Existing models tend to focus on very specific forms of parallelism, usually either OR [3,10,17] or AND [5,8,16] or some combination of the two [6,11,18]. As a rule, this has led to parallel systems effective for one application domain, yet producing little improvement for others.

---

[1]Software Technology Laboratory, Intel Corporation, 2200 Mission College Blvd., MS RN6-18, Santa Clara, CA 95052
[2]Department of Computer Science, University of Illinois at Urbana-Champaign, 1304 W. Springfield Ave., Urbana, IL 61801
[3]Center for Supercomputing Research and Development, University of Illinois at Urbana-Champaign, 465 CSRL, 1308 W. Main St., Urbana, IL 61801

Focusing on these types of parallelism alone has obscured a deeper connection between them. This connection lies in the fact that both AND and OR parallel systems obtain their best speedups on algorithms that perform similar computations repetitively. For OR parallel algorithms, this is usually the recursive process of a search problem that selects a successor state, tests its legality, updates the state, and repeats. For AND parallel algorithms the sequence is the recursive process of decomposing a problem into sub-problems, processing one of the sub-problems recursively, and then processing the others. Both of these processes are very similar to loops in procedural languages, which have long been the object of parallelizing transformations [4,13,19].

In this paper we describe an abstract interpretation based data flow analysis framework for the detection of opportunities to convert recursion to *loops* in Prolog programs. The framework relies upon abstract interpretation to expose and convert recursion to loops. Once converted to loops, traditional dependence analysis and parallelization techniques [4,13,19] can be applied to the program. An added benefit is that once converted to loops, sequential execution is often more efficient. The dataflow analysis techniques described herein have been implemented in an abstract interpreter for Prolog. The information computed by this interpreter was used to hand-transform a number of programs, the results of which are presented here.

This paper consists of six sections. The remainder of section one briefly describes the terminology used in the paper and several *normalizing* transformations used to eliminate awkward control structures. In section two we present the data flow analysis techniques used to expose loops in Prolog procedures. Section three presents the target language constructs and the method for converting a procedure to them. Section four describes the use of dependence analysis to parallelize the loops. Section five presents the results of applying our techniques to a number of benchmark programs. Finally, section six suggests some conclusions and future work.

1.1 Terminology

A Prolog program consists of a *top-level query* and a set of *clauses*. A query is a sequence of *literals*; the top-level query is either present in the source program or entered by the user at the run-time system's read prompt. A literal is a *compound term* consisting of a *predicate name* and some number of *subterms* or *arguments*. The number of arguments of a literal is its *arity*. A clause has a *head literal* and zero or more *body literals*. A clause with no body literals is a *fact*, otherwise it is a *rule*. Clauses are grouped into *procedures* by the predicate name and arity of their head literals.

The execution of a Prolog program traverses the implicit OR tree (SLD tree) of the program. Each node N in the OR tree is labeled with a query $Q(N)$. The first literal $L(N)$ of $Q(N)$ is called the *literal at N*. The root node is labeled with the top level query. One child of N is produced for each clause C whose head unifies with $L(N)$. The child is labeled with a query formed from $Q(N)$ by replacing $L(N)$ by the body of C and applying the variable substitutions computed during the unification. The children of a node N are ordered left-to-right by the lexical order of the clauses applied to produce them. A node having an empty query is a *success*. Sequential Prolog systems traverse the OR tree depth-first and left-to-right.

Determinism in a logic program is the property of having one solution. Since Prolog procedures compute *relations* rather than *functions*, some procedures may compute more than one result for the same input. In the run time system these are enumerated in sequence and other computations depending upon them may be invoked many times based upon the different results. Most built-in predicates in Prolog are deterministic, as are many user-defined procedures. Our methods perform best for deterministic procedures, but are able to optimize those that are not.

1.2 Normalizing Transformations

To simplify our loop analysis methods our analyzer performs three normalizing transformations on procedures before data flow analysis begins. First, each procedure is rewritten to eliminate *if-then-else* and to use *cut* as the only control predicate. Second, non-variable unifications in the term of each clause are moved into the body of that clause. Third, the construction of non-variable arguments of body literals is moved out of those literals. The latter two transformations simplify converting a recursive procedure to loops by making more explicit the reads and writes of variables.

2 Data Flow Analysis

Identifying loops in Prolog procedures requires analysis to solve three problems. First, the control structure of a procedure does not follow statement sequencing as with procedural languages, nor any syntactic evaluation order as with most functional languages. Instead, control may pass from one literal to another with successful unification, pass to a literal from a called procedure, or pass back to a literal through failure. Because of this, the first step of data flow analysis is to construct a *control flow graph* (CFG) that can be used to propagate data flow values. Second, once the CFG is constructed we attempt to identify *deterministic recursive calls* (DRCs) in a procedure. Third, data flow analysis is used to determine termination conditions for the identified recursive call and identify one or more *control induction variables* (CIVs). This involves finding exit branches in the CFG and the conditions that govern their execution.

2.1 Constructing the CFG

The control flow graph used here is an extension of that used by Debray [7]. Our extension is to represent failure explicitly so as to allow the optimization of OR parallel procedures by the same techniques as AND parallel ones. The CFG for a procedure p contains two special nodes, the start node S and the failure node F, and a set of nodes for each clause. Each clause $C(i)$ has a head node $H(i)$, a node $B(i,j)$ for each body literal, and an end node $E(i)$. There are three sorts of edges in the CFG. *Success edges* indicate the path of control flow after successful execution of the node at the tail of the edge. *Failure edges* indicate the path of control flow when the literal at the tail of the arc fails (that is, when a sequential interpreter would backtrack). *Recursive edges* represent the flow of control from one invocation to another of a recursive procedure. There are edges representing flow of control into and out of a recursive instance. It is through recursive edges that loops are most often exposed.

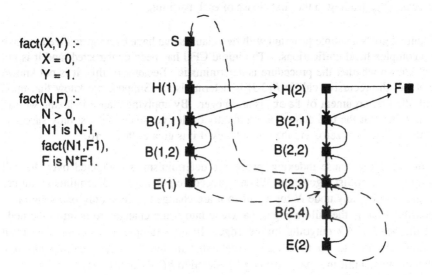

Fig. 2. The CFG for a simple procedure

The CFG is built from the subgraphs for each of P's clauses. There is a success edge from $H(i)$ to the node for the first body literal $B(i,1)$, from each $B(i,j)$ to $B(i,j+1)$, and from the last body literal node $B(i,n)$ to $E(i)$. If there are no body nodes, then there is a success edge from $H(i)$ to $E(i)$. There is a failure edge leading from $E(i)$ to the last body literal node $B(i,n)$, and from each literal node $B(i,j)$ to its immediate predecessor node $B(i,j-1)$. If there are no body nodes, there is no failure edge in the clause subgraph.

A clause subgraph is connected to the subgraph for the lexically next clause by a failure edge from each head node $H(i)$ and first body node $B(i,1)$ to $H(i+1)$. For the last clause, these edges lead to the failure node F. Also, if there are no body literals in $C(i)$, then the edges come from $H(i)$ and $E(i)$. There is a success edge from the start node S to the node $H(1)$ for the head literal of the first clause. This represents entry to the entire procedure. There is a recursive edge from the node R for a recursive call literal to S, and a recursive edge from each $E(i)$ to R.

The analysis to find DRCs depends upon accurate variable type information. This is obtained by the use of abstract interpretation to determine procedure argument call and success types. The type lattice used is fairly simple, classifying arguments into list, integer, variable, ground[4], and non-ground. These types are used to perform *indexing*, or changing edges to avoid failures that can be determined at compile time. For instance, if an argument is known to be of type integer, any clause head that attempts to unify a non-integer term with that variable is guaranteed to fail and need not be tried. Often the type of a variable is not known exactly at compile time, but clauses can be partitioned by what types they can succeed for. This can be done in the CFG by inserting an index node as the successor of S and having one outgoing success edge leading to the first clause of each partition.

Figure 2 gives a simple program with two clauses that have been normalized to have no complex head unifications. The initial CFG has been constructed, and it is not yet known whether the procedure is deterministic. Because of this, it is not known whether the recursive call in $B(2,3)$ is deterministic. Suppose we know that upon call the first argument of fact is an integer. By applying clause indexing we can determine that the two clauses are mutually exclusive, since the first only succeeds if the argument is zero, and the second only if it is greater than zero.

After applying clause indexing, procedure determinism is computed over the call graph by a worklist algorithm. When a procedure p is marked deterministic, failure edges entering any node N for a call to p are changed. Since only one solution is possible from p, the failure edges that came into N are changed to point to the node at the head of N's outgoing failure edge. In the example, the failure edge from $B(2,4)$ changes to go to $B(2,2)$. Since this makes the edge again point to a deterministic built-in, is, the edge is routed to $B(2,1)$, and so on.

Figure 3 shows the result of applying these transformations to the CFG of Figure 2. First, a new *indexing node I* has been introduced just after the start node. This is to signify the fact that the two clauses are mutually exclusive because of the disjoint integer conditions on the first argument. There are several varieties of indexing

---

[4]A ground term is one guaranteed to contain no unbound variables. Non-ground is any term not fitting a previously listed type.

nodes, corresponding to the usual indexing done by Prolog compilers [2]. The failure edges changed to reflect determinism, and there are no longer any cycles involving failure edges, which simplifies the finding of deterministic recursive calls.

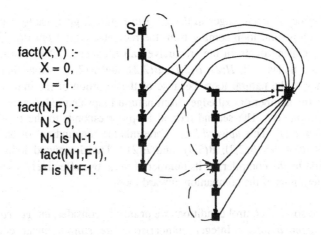

fact(X,Y) :-
    X = 0,
    Y = 1.

fact(N,F) :-
    N > 0,
    N1 is N-1,
    fact(N1,F1),
    F is N*F1.

Fig. 3. Determinism and indexing in the CFG

A DRC is *mutually exclusive* of any other recursive call in the procedure. This ensures that one recursive call will execute in a given instance. This is true if there is no control flow path from one to the other that does not involve at least one recursive edge. If this is not the case, some recursive calls are made indirectly recursive by creating a dummy procedure and renaming the call. Our method handles multiple DRCs in a procedure, although space does not permit full discussion.

If there is a path from a recursive call node N to itself not involving a recursive edge, then multiple recursive calls per invocation can be made. Whereas in a functional language a recursive call site computes a linear sequence, such a cycle in Prolog implies a possible tree-structured computation. By construction such a cycle in the CFG implies one or more predecessor nodes of N must be non-deterministic. To expose a DRC we apply inline expansion [13] to the lowest non-deterministic node M and tail duplication on the nodes after M. This creates multiple recursive calls through tail duplication, but often one of these is not involved in a cycle. The others are renamed, and the node containing the chosen call is the DRC.

2.2 Identifying Control Conditions

The recursive edge from DRC node N to the start node S of the procedure defines a *natural loop* [1] in the CFG, and it is this which we wish to first convert to a *do* loop in our target language. Nodes in the natural loop are identified by a simple depth first algorithm. Edges between nodes in the natural loop are part of the loop body. Edges leading from a node in the natural loop to a node outside it are *exit edges*, and are used to determine the control conditions for the loop.

Two of the three recursive edges in the CFG in Figure 2 give rise to natural loops. First, there is a natural loop coming from the recursive edge from $B(2,3)$ to S, and represents increasing depth in the recursive call sequence. This *downward loop* consists of the nodes S, I, $H(2)$, $B(2,1)$, $B(2,2)$, and $B(2,3)$. Note that $H(1)$ and $B(1,1)$ are not in the natural loop, because of the insertion of the indexing node I. This reduces the number of exit edges from natural loops and reduces the size of the control condition set. The second natural loop corresponds to the recursive edge from $E(2)$ to $B(2,3)$. This *upward loop* represents the "unwinding" of the recursion, and consists of nodes $B(2,3)$, $B(2,4)$, and $E(2)$. The downward loop should be processed first by the compiler, as its number of iterations effectively determines the number of iterations of the companion upward loop.

There are two sorts of control conditions we primarily consider, *integer comparisons* and *list/nil comparisons*. Integer comparisons are simple linear equalities or inequalities applied to variables known to be of type integer. List/nil comparisons are unifications of the atom [] (nil in Lisp) or [X|Y] (a cons cell with car=X and cdr=Y) with a variable known to be of type list. These control conditions are combined with induction variable information to form iterators for the do loops being constructed. These two types of control conditions are the primary sort of control seen in a large number of Prolog programs.

2.3 Induction Variable Recognition

An *induction variable* in a recursive procedure is a syntactic name for a sequence of cells with linearly changing value. By linearly changing value we mean that if it is an integer, it differs from one recursive instance to the next by the addition or subtraction of a constant. If it is a list variable, then the length of that list either increases or decreases by a constant number of cons cells between recursive invocations. The detection of the latter form often allows the conversion of a list recursion to an array by creating a new integer induction variable and changing references to cons cells to references to array elements.

Finding induction variables in Prolog is complicated significantly by the *logical variable*. All variables in Prolog are single assignment, but may be used freely in terms before they are bound to a value. This gives unparalleled ability to create aliases, but is a very powerful tool for building linked data structures. In the simplest case a variable can be an induction variable in the downward loop and in the upward loop; this is done by binding the variable in the downward loop. Since the two loops traverse the same set of values in opposite directions, the two loops obviously see the induction variable as having opposite increments. Another possibility, however, is that a variable may be passed through the downward loop without being assigned and then assigned in the upward loop. There can of course be references to such a variable in the downward loop, where the value is not known. To effectively handle both cases, the downward and upward loops are analyzed separately.

The analysis of downward loops associates a lattice value with each actual parameter at the recursive call site. These values are used to relate the actual parameter in a given position with the formal parameter in that same position. The initial value is to *bottom*. Non-top, non-bottom lattice values are pairs: the *family*, or formal parameter position to which the variable is related, and the *increment*, or amount that is added on each recursive invocation. Propagating the relationship between clause variables and formal parameter positions uses the same lattice. Each node in the control flow graph has a vector of values, one for each variable in the current clause[5]. Beginning with the start node, values are propagated through the CFG according to rules for integer and list variables.

Integer variables are assigned lattice values through unification (the = predicate) and through the arithmetic assignment predicate, is. Unification only has an effect when it involves an integer variable X whose data flow value is *bottom*. If X is unified against a term other than a variable, then X's data flow value becomes *top*, since this implies it is being assigned to a constant or structure. Otherwise X's data flow value is the data flow value of the other variable.

The is predicate in Prolog computes the value of the right-hand expression and unifies it with the left-hand term. There is no data flow effect if the term on the left is not a variable. For variables, the effect is the result of a unify between the variable and the data flow value of the right hand expression. This expression is assigned the lattice value *top* if it is anything other than a variable plus or minus a constant expression.[6] Moreover, if the variable V in the expression has value *top*, then so does the expression. Otherwise, the data flow value of the expression is the pair $<f,i+c>$, where $<f,i>$ is the value for V and c is the constant added (negative if subtracted) from V.

These values are propagated to the recursive call site, where the value of the variable V to be passed in each position i is combined with the corresponding actual parameter data flow value A. This operation combines values, because there may be more than one DRC. The join is formed by four rules. If V is *bottom* or *top*, or V has a family other than i, A is assigned *top*. This is to represent the possibility that V may have a value unrelated to the i-th formal parameter. This being the case, the i-th parameter does not constitute a simple induction variable. If V's increment

---

[5]Sparse dataflow representations such as SSA or DFGs could also be used.
[6]Although more complex expressions may sometimes be useful, Prolog's use of integers seems restricted to fairly simple induction variables.

value differs from A's, then A is again assigned `top`. This is only the case with multiple recursive call sites. Any other combination results in V's value being copied to A.

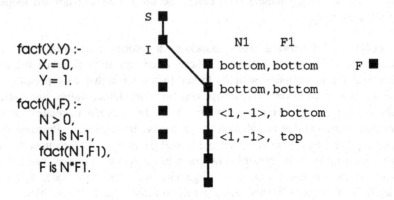

```
fact(X,Y) :-
    X = 0,
    Y = 1.

fact(N,F) :-
    N > 0,
    N1 is N-1,
    fact(N1,F1),
    F is N*F1.
```

Fig. 4. Integer induction variable detection

Figure 4 illustrates the propagation of data flow values to detect integer induction variables in the downward loop. Initially the values for N and F are $<1,0>$ and $<2,0>$ respectively, and $N1$ and $F1$ are `bottom`. The head node $H(2)$ has no effect on this, nor does $B(2,1)$. $B(2,2)$ sets $N1$'s value to $<1,-1>$, since $N1$'s value is formed from N's by subtracting one. Both actual positions are merely assigned the results of the propagation, since there is only one call site. The first formal is thus an induction variable with increment -1. Since $F1$ is unbound at the time of call, the second actual is `top`.

Propagating upward is the reverse of downward, with a vector of values for the formals that are computed from the DRC's actuals. This is because there can be unbound variables as formals to the procedure being processed, as is the case with the second parameter to `fact` in Figure 4. However the upward analysis determines in the example that F is `top`, since it is not a linearly changing value.

List variables require defining the data flow effects of `unify` calls involving list terms. This is done by relating the list lengths to the length of the *tail variable*, if there is one. Using lisp terminology once again, `tailvar(L)` is the variable in the cdr element of the cons cell arrived at by applying as many cdr operations to L as possible. For instance, the list *[1,2|X]* consists of two cons cells: one with car=1 and cdr pointing to the second cell, and one with car=2 and cdr=X, where X is a variable. The tail variable is X, and its *tail depth*, `taildepth(L)`, is the number of cdr operations required to reach what X points to; in this case, 2. Any list without a variable in the last position has an undefined tail variable and tail depth.

Unification goal:

$$[1,X,3|U] = [1|V]$$
$$s \qquad\qquad t$$

Storage layout:

Lattice values before:

$$U = <1,5>$$
$$V = bottom$$

Fig. 5. List variables and unification

To unify two list terms s and t, the tail variables U and V are first examined. If either is undefined, then the tail variable of the other term is given data flow value top. If at least one tail variable (say U) has a non-bottom, non-top data flow value[7], then after unification the length of s is the length of U plus taildepth(s). Since the lengths of s and t match after unification, the symbolic lengths must also have the same value. Thus the length of V is the length of U plus taildepth(s) minus taildepth(t). List lengths, just as with integer values, are propagated as increments from a formal parameter. Therefore unifying s and t is a data flow pair with U's family and increment plus taildepth(s) minus taildepth(t). List data flow pairs are otherwise propagated by the same rules as for integer unification.

Figure 5 shows a unification between two list terms, s and t. The first is a list s of at least length three, with tailvar(s)=U. U has been determined to be in the family of the first formal, and to be five cells longer than it. The other term is a list t of at least one cell, with tailvar(t)=V, which has lattice value bottom. The length of the whole term s is U's length plus the tail depth of s, which is three. Thus s has the approximation $<1,8>$, and so must t after unification. Since V is one cell deep in t, after unification is that V gets $<1,7>$. The computation of list lengths for lists allows us to refer to cons cells by an integer index, which often allows the replacement of the usual implementation of a list by an array.

2.4 Control Induction Variables

Finding induction variables and exit constraints in the downward loop enables us to derive the set of *control induction variables* for a procedure p. An induction variable I has an initial value N when called from outside p, and changes by the computed increment S on recursive invocation. This allows us to rewrite I as $N+S*i$, where and i is the depth of recursive invocation. This expression spans an infinite set of integer values starting at the initial value N. The exit conditions also

---

[7]Since in practice the relationships are quite simple, the constraint solving ability required for more general cases does not seem motivated.

define integer sets, and we build iterators by intersecting the two types of sets. We then determine the minimum (maximum if S is negative) value M of the resulting set and construct a Fortran-90 style triplet $N{:}M{:}S$. For list induction variables this triplet is a new parameter; for integer induction variables, it replaces one. Some other variables may also be computed as one of an induction variables plus the previously computed increment.

3 Converting to Loops

Having identified loops in the CFG and iterators for those loops, most recursive procedures are converted to use a target language extension called *do*. Conversion requires finding variables are live across the recursive call site and applying scalar expansion [13]. Expanded scalars are a language extension representing single-dimensioned, single assignment arrays of known size. The resulting procedure is recursion split [9] into two loops. For lack of space we omit discussing the handling of recursive procedures with cuts [14] in the upward loop.

```
do(IV=lower:upper:stride,
    [local_variables],
    [body_literals],
    [left_literals],
    [right_literals]).
```

Fig. 6. The do form

The target language is extended with a new built-in predicate *do*, shown in Figure 6. The *do* predicate has five arguments: an *iterator*, a list of local variables, the *body*, and *left* and *right*. The iterator is an induction variable together with a Fortran-90 style triplet. The local variables are those requiring a separate instance for each iteration because of the single assignment nature of Prolog. The body of the loop is the set of literals which precede the tail of the recursive edge in the natural loop being converted. Loops resulting from recursion splitting of Prolog procedures are a generalization of procedural language loops, because of non-determinism in procedures. Because of this, the *do* built-in predicate has two final arguments. Left contains the bodies of alternative clauses lexically before the recursive call; right is those lexically after. For deterministic procedures *left* and *right* are empty.

Do loops have a simple operational semantics based upon a single tail recursive procedure. Intuitively, a loop executes one time for each element in the iteration space. Two parts are executed in each iteration in order: first *left*, then *body*. Then each instance of *right* is executed, in the opposite order, since in SLD tree order the leftmost (sequentially, the first) of these tree regions is the last iteration of the loop. This is required to correctly execute procedures that may have infinite recursions in the *right* portion. Programmers write procedures such that there are seldom clauses both in *left* and *right*, so the execution order is simpler than it sounds. Moreover, for parallel execution we assume a preemptive scheduler that gives preference to *left* or *body*, which allows a simple iteration order creation of threads.

```
fact(N,F) :-
    alloc_scalar(Fs, 0:N),
    Fs[N] =F,
    Fs[0] = 1,
    do(I=1:N:1, [],
        Fs[I] is Fs[I-1] * I,
        [],[]).
```

Fig. 7. Example after Loop Conversion

Figure 7 shows the running example after conversion to loops. There are two variables live across the recursive function call, N and F. N is the control induction variable and is replaced. F is converted to the expanded scalar Fs which has subscripts running from zero to N. The initial value of F is copied into the topmost element $Fs[N]$. Since F is typically unbound at call, this creates an alias between $Fs[N]$ and F. The first parameter went downward by ones, and the control condition is that it must be greater than zero; the triplet for is hence $N:1:-1$. This would be used in the iterator for the downward loop; the upward loop is the same bounds with opposite stride. Since the downward loop only contains a literal that computes the value of N (which was replaced by the iteration variable), there is no downward loop in the resulting procedure. The basis of the recursion is the clause that assigns F the value one when N is zero. In the transformed program this becomes the unification $Fs[0] = 1$. Since *fact* is a deterministic procedure, there are no clauses in *left* or *right*.

4 Dependence Analysis and Parallelization

Prolog loops differ from procedural language loops for two reasons: non-determinism and unclear read and write locations. Because each clause constitutes an alternative solution to a problem, variable bindings computed for one clause of a procedure are not reflected in those variables when other clauses are tried. In sequential systems this is done by backtracking. Once a clause fails, any variable bindings it may have caused are undone. Handling such alternative bindings (for OR parallel execution) has been the subject of much research. Such mechanisms are a sort of automatic localization or privatization of variables to remove some anti- and all output dependences. With such an underlying OR parallel binding environment to handle loops that have non empty *left* or *right* parts, we can treat data dependence analysis in a uniform manner.

Prolog obscures the location of reads and writes of a variable v, because unification involving v may read it, write it, do both, or do neither. Hence any syntactic method is inherently inexact. Traditional Prolog dependence analysis has not addressed this question adequately for the entire language, because it ignores anti-dependences stemming from meta-logical and I/O predicates. To parallelize Prolog we must accurately locate reads from these predicates as well. To this end, an abstract interpretation is done to get sets of variables read at each location. Writes are found by another abstract interpretation called *mode inference* that infers approximate bindings for variables taking aliasing into account [14]. In contrast to the traditional approach, mode inference is not used alone to compute dependences. Rather, the read and write sets are intersected to compute dependence in a fashion more similar to procedural language techniques.

The OR parallel binding environment eliminates *output* dependences, but leaves *flow* and *anti* dependences. Suppose a literal U executes before a literal V. There is a flow dependence arc between U and V if U writes a variable and V reads it. There is an anti-dependence arc between U and V if U reads a variable and V writes it. The dependence graph of a program is a graph with the node set of the CFG and arcs between pairs of dependent nodes.

Converting a procedure to a loop converts one or more recursive paths in the OR tree to iterative traversal. The *left* and *right* parts of a loop are branches off the recursive path, and control flow from them only returns to that path through backtracking. Because of this any variables they may bind do not affect the execution of the body. Hence literals in *left* and *right* may only be the sinks of loop carried data dependence arcs. *Body* may be the source of dependence arcs to *body*, *left*, or *right*.

A loop with no *left* or *right* may be parallelized by procedural language methods. The parallel execution of these loops is *speculative*, however, because of the possibility of failure. Therefore, the run time system must ensure that priority is given to earlier iterations to ensure termination. The highest priority task must always be worked upon by the scheduler [12], but there is otherwise considerable flexibility. In the future we hope to extend our analysis to detect non-speculative loops. The dependence graph for the converted example program in Figure 6 has one dependence, from the is literal to itself one iteration later. Therefore the loop contains a recurrence (a product reduction), and it would probably be parallelized by replacement by a parallel recurrence solver such as parallel prefix.

A loop with clauses in *left* or *right* is a doacross loop, since solutions must be printed as in a sequential Prolog system: as if traversing the OR tree left to right, displaying solutions as encountered. These nodes may, however, be produced in any order. We implement this by assigning priority to tasks in left to right order by maintaining a linked list of tasks in the scheduler [10]. Each iteration of a loop having clauses in *left* adds one or more scheduling nodes to the left of (with higher priority than) the current loop iteration. Similarly, each iteration with clauses in *right* adds nodes to the right of (with lower priority than) all following loop iterations. The parallel run time system processes an iteration by creating scheduling nodes for *left*, *right*, and *body*, and then executing the *left* task.

5 Experimental Results

Program Name	OR (w/o loops)	AND/OR (w/o loops)	OR (w/loops)	AND/OR (w/loops)
factorial	1.0	1.3	3.4	6.8
queen (1)	25.6	69.3	53.4	127.0
queen (all)	441.0	1060.0	918.0	2210.0
serialise	1.4	1.9	1.3	2.9
sum	1.0	1.2	13.3	26.1
tak	1.1	686.0	161.0	822.0
zebra (1)	453.0	481.0	784.0	879.0
zebra (all)	959.0	1020.0	1660.0	1860.0

Table 1. Results of applying transformations

The data flow analysis techniques described here have been implemented in an abstract interpreter. Using this information a number of programs were hand-transformed using our techniques. These transformed programs were then instrumented to measure inherent parallelism under OR and AND/OR parallel execution paradigms [15]. These instrumentation programs were extended to encompass expanded scalars and the loop forms *do*, *doall*, and *doacross*. The resulting instrumented programs were then executed sequentially to measure inherent parallelism with unlimited and limited numbers of processors. Our results show that loop transformations typically expose two to three times the original parallelism. Additionally, the transformed programs are often better suited to small numbers of processors than the originals.

Table 1 shows the results of applying the transformations to six programs, two of which are presented in first and all solutions form. For each program we present the best achievable speedup under OR and AND/OR parallel execution with and without loop transformations. From the four programs with little or no OR parallelism (factorial, serialise, sum, and tak), we see that loop transformations generally exploit more parallelism than either OR or AND/OR parallel execution alone. This is because exposing most of these programs' AND parallelism requires recurrence recognition. serialise's major recursive routines were not transformed because they were indirectly recursive and had no recognizable induction variables. Because of this the overheads of expanded scalars for the small transformed routines produced a small slowdown. Another interesting point is that loop transformations were able to expose 50-150 percent more parallelism from the two search problems, queens and zebra. This is due to both having recursive list traversal procedures for testing for state consistency. These procedures were easily converted to manipulate array through induction variable analysis and related techniques [14].

6 Conclusions and Future Work

We presented a method for the data flow analysis and transformation of Prolog programs using loop transformations. The development of these techniques opens the possibility of applying the entire range of parallelizing transformations developed for procedural languages. Over a small sample of programs ranging from those with little or no parallelism under OR or AND/OR to embarrassingly parallel search we were able to demonstrate a better than two fold average increase over the best possible OR and AND/OR parallel speedups.

In the future we hope to fully automate these loop techniques to compile Prolog programs. This will enable further development and testing of transformations on more and larger programs. We would also like to build timing tools to measure how much parallelism that would be extracted by adding parallel loops to a sequential Prolog system such as SICStus. As these loop constructs are less complicated than most existing parallel Prolog models, they should be relatively simple to implement on a shared-memory parallel machine. Moreover, we believe that we can extract the majority of AND parallelism in a program and a sizable fraction of the OR parallelism in a program through the use of parallel loops.

References

[1] A. V. Aho, R. Sethi, and J. D. Ullman. *Compilers: Principles, Techniques, and Tools*. Addison-Wesley, March 1986.

[2] H. Ait-Kaci. The WAM: A (Real) Tutorial. Technical Report, Digital Equipment Corporation, Paris Research Laboratory, January 1990.

[3] K. A. M. Ali. The Muse OR-Parallel Prolog Model and its Performance. In *Proceedings of the 1990 North American Logic Programming Conference*, pages 757-776, 1990.

[4] U. Banerjee. *Loop Transformations for Restructuring Compilers: the Foundations*. Kluwer Academic Publishers, 1993.

[5] J. Chang, A. M. Despain, and D. DeGroot. AND-Parallelism of Logic Programs Based on a Static Data Dependency Analysis. In *Proceedings of COMPCON '85*, 1985.

[6] J. S. Conery and D. F. Kibler. AND Parallelism and Nondeterminism in Logic Programs. *New Generation Computing*, 3:43-70, 1985.

[7]   S. K. Debray. A Simple Code Improvement Scheme for Prolog. In *Proceedings of the Sixth International Conference on Logic Programming,* pages 17-32. MIT Press, 1989.

[8]   M. Hermenegildo. An Abstract Machine for Restricted AND-Parallel Execution of Logic Programs. In *Proceedings of the Third International Conference on Logic Programming,* pages 25-39. Springer-Verlag, 1986.

[9]   W. L. Harrison, III. Compiling Lisp for Evaluation on a Tightly Coupled Multiprocessor. Technical report, University of Illinois at Urbana-Champaign, March, 1986. CSRD Report No. 565.

[10]   L. V. Kale, D. A. Padua, and D. C. Sehr. OR Parallel Execution of Prolog Programs with Side Effects. *The Journal of Supercomputing,* 2(2):209-223, October 1988.

[11]   L. V. Kale. The REDUCE OR Process Model for Parallel Execution of Logic Programs. *Journal of Logic Programming,* Vol. 11, Number 1, July 1991, pp. 55-84.

[12]   L. V. Kale, and V. Saletore. Parallel State-space Search for a First Solution. *International Journal of Parallel Programming,* Vol. 19, 1990, pp. 251-293.

[13]   D. Padua and M. Wolfe. Advanced Compiler Optimizations for Supercomputers. *Communications of the ACM,* pages 1184-1201, December 1986.

[14]   D. C. Sehr. *Automatic Parallelization of Prolog Programs.* PhD thesis, University of Illinois at Urbana-Champaign, October 1992. CSRD Report 1288.

[15]   D. C. Sehr and L. V. Kale. Estimating the Inherent Parallelism in Prolog Programs. In *Proceedings of the International Conference on Fifth Generation Computer Systems 1992,* pages 783-790, June 1992.

[16]   Y.-W. Tung and D. I. Moldovan. Detection of AND Parallelism in Logic Programs. In *Proceedings of the 1986 International Conference on Parallel Processing,* pages 984-991, August 1986.

[17]   D. H. D. Warren. The SRI Model for OR Parallel Execution of Prolog - Abstract Design and Implementation. In *Proceedings of the 1987 Symposium on Logic Programming,* pages 92-103. IEEE Computer Society Press, September 1987.

[18]   M. Wise. *Prolog Multiprocessors.* Prentice-Hall International Publishers, 1986.

[19]   M. J. Wolfe. *Optimizing Supercompilers for Supercomputers.* The MIT Press, 1989.

A Multithreaded Implementation of Id using P-RISC Graphs

Rishiyur S. Nikhil

Digital Equipment Corporation, Cambridge Research Laboratory
One Kendall Square, Building 700, Cambridge MA 02139, USA
Email: nikhil@crl.dec.com

Abstract. P-RISC graphs are parallel, structured, executable control-flow graphs that model locality properties of distributed memory machines. P-RISC graphs have coarse grain parallelism for distribution of work to processors, and fine grain parallelism to overlap latencies of remote accesses and synchronization. These properties support dynamic and irregular parallelism. In this paper, we describe P-RISC graphs, how they are used to implement the implicitly parallel programming language Id, and how they are implemented on distributed memory machines. We also contrast our approach to Berkeley's TAM, a similar system.

1 Introduction

HPF [4] is an example of a trend back towards shared memory programming models, even though massively parallel machines are implemented with distributed memories. This approach is regaining popularity because it is now widely recognized that writing explicit message-passing programs is extremely hard even for a fixed configuration, and even harder if it is to be portable and tunable. However, for good performance on distributed memory systems, locality is very important. Today, it is infeasible to achieve completely automatic distribution of data and processes for good locality. The HPF solution is to rely on the programmer to specify data distribution of arrays. The compiler analyzes this information and uses it to distribute loop iterations close to their data; to batch communications (reducing overhead), and to overlap communication with computation (reducing idling) [5].

We are interested in more general shared memory programs where data structures may be irregular (trees, graphs, sparse arrays, ...), may be dynamically allocated, and may have data-dependent shapes and sizes. Further, such programs obtain much parallelism from producer-consumer situations, where a data structure is consumed by one process even as it is being built by another. In this environment, the compiler cannot orchestrate process and data placement in the manner of HPF compilers. Almost any individual data accesses may be remote, and may need synchronization.

Our general approach is based on multithreading. Since it is generally not known until runtime whether a particular data access is local or remote, or whether it will block (consumer ahead of producer), the processor must be prepared to multiplex efficiently to another thread instead of idling. But this raises the following questions: How can this level of parallelism be expressed conveniently by the programmer? How can this level of parallelism be modeled and implemented by the compiler and runtime system?

To answer the first question, we express programs in Id, a parallel, mostly-functional programming language [9]. Parallelism is not specified explicitly by the programmer, but is implicit in that all sub-expressions whose control dependences are satisfied may execute in parallel, subject only to data dependencies. All local variables and most data structures are single-assignment, and synchronization is implicit in access to individual data structure components.

To answer the second question, our compiler uses P-RISC graphs as the principal intermediate language. These are parallel, structured, executable control-flow graphs that model locality in distributed memory parallel machines. They are a suitable target for many source languages, including Id. Parallelism in P-RISC graphs occurs both at a coarse grain, where each procedure and loop iteration is a unit of parallelism that may be distributed across processors, and at a fine grain, within basic blocks. The latter (fine grain parallelism) allows function calls and global accesses to occur in parallel, and allows these operations, which possibly involve remote computation and synchronization, to be overlapped with local computation. These properties support dynamic and irregular parallelism.

In this paper, we describe aspects of the implementation of Id using P-RISC graphs. In Section 2 we briefly describe P-RISC graphs by way of an example recursive Id procedure. In Section 3 we describe the implementation of P-RISC graphs on distributed memory machines. In Section 4 we describe various optimizations. In Section 5.1, we draw comparisons with the TAM approach [1], which is quite close in spirit to ours. Finally, in Section 6 we close with some remarks about implementation status and plans.

Although we use Id for concreteness, the emphasis in this paper is on the multithreaded implementation of P-RISC graphs. The discussions and techniques are equally relevant for other source languages.

2 P-RISC graphs

To set the stage, we first describe the P-RISC machine model and runtime state, since variables in P-RISC graphs refer to components of the runtime state, and the graphs themselves reflect the locality assumptions of the machine model.

2.1 P-RISC machine model and runtime state

Figure 1 shows the abstract machine model for P-RISC graphs. Each processor can access its attached local memory as usual, and can send messages (non-blocking) to other processors via the communication network. Global memory accesses are *split phase*: they involve separate request and response messages, may have long latencies, and are not ordered, *i.e.*, a processor can issue multiple requests, and responses may arrive in any order. Global Memory also supports synchronized accesses, which we will describe in more detail later.

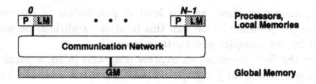

Fig. 1. P-RISC abstract machine model

It is important to emphasize that this is an abstract machine model only. It may be implemented on a multicomputer, with each node's physical local memory partitioned into the (logical) Local Memory and a part of the (logical) Global Memory.

Figure 2 shows the runtime state for P-RISC graphs. Each processor runs a number of micro-threads concurrently (logically; in practice, the processor is multiplexed amongst them). Each microthread has an Instruction Pointer (IP) that points at code, and a register set, including a Frame Pointer (FP) that points at a Frame.

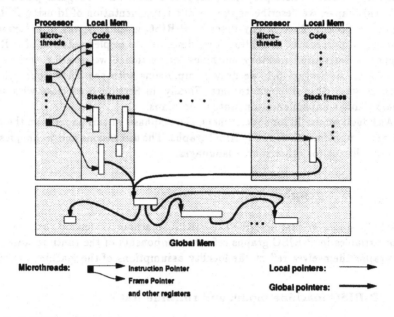

Fig. 2. P-RISC runtime state

There are two flavors of pointers. A Local Pointer is a normal address in local memory and is meaningful only within a processor. A Global Pointer identifies an arbitrary object in Global Memory or an arbitrary frame on any processor. We leave the exact coding of Local vs. Global pointers unspecified.

A microthread always points to local code and a local frame. Frames never cross node boundaries, and microthreads never cross frame boundaries. Frames contain local variables (like stack frames) and, using Global Pointers, are organized into a tree structure, due to parallelism (like cactus stacks).

The granularity of parallelism in P-RISC is small. In traditional thread models, each thread is associated with one stack and vice versa, and a stack may encompass many frames. In P-RISC, microthreads are local to a frame and there may be many microthreads in a frame.

2.2 Representing code in P-RISC graphs

Consider the following Id procedure.

```
def traverse  T  H  = if leaf?(t)
                      then  { i = t.Leaf_val;
                             H![i] = H![i] + 1 }
                      else  { traverse  T.Left   H;
                             traverse  T.Right  H } ;
```

The procedure has two arguments, a binary tree T and a histrogram array H (assumed to initially contain zero everywhere). The tree is structured recursively as follows: either it is a leaf containing an integer, or it is an internal node with two sub-trees Left and Right. The function descends the tree, fanning out in parallel at every internal node (the two recursive calls to traverse occur in parallel). At each leaf, it increments the corresponding histogram slot.

Each histogram array slot, in addition to containing data, also has a FULL/ EMPTY state. The rhs expression H![i] is called a *take* operation which waits for the slot to be FULL, reads out the value, and leaves it EMPTY. The assignment H![i] = ... is called a *put* operation, which writes back into an EMPTY slot and marks it FULL. This ensures that the increment is atomic with respect to other attempted increments on the same slot.

Figure 3 shows a P-RISC graph for the procedure. Some nodes are familiar three-address instructions, such as "hi1 = hi1 + 1" and "b = leaf?(T)." A node such as "cfp,cip,T,H = entry" is, conceptually, the recipient of a message. The contents of the message are extracted into the local variables cfp, cip, T and H, respectively. These local variables hold the *continuation frame pointer* (typically the frame pointer of the callee), the *continuation instruction pointer* (the return address), and (global) pointers to the tree and the histogram. The switch operation is simply a conditional jump that either follows the left thread if b is true or the right thread otherwise.

On the true side, we start with a gload to read the integer (i) in the leaf. This is a global load instruction, since T points at a structure in Global Memory. The dashed line below the gload indicates (a) that this thread halts after issuing a global load request, and (b) that the corresponding entry will receive the response (containing i) from Global Memory.

Once i is received, we issue a gtake request for the corresponding histogram slot, whose response is received below in hi. Note, if the slot were EMPTY, the

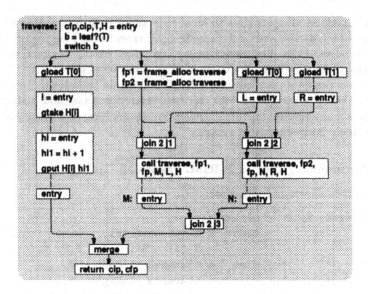

Fig. 3. P-RISC graphs: An example

Global Memory holds on to the request until some other thread puts a value back, *i.e.*, it is not the responsibility of *this* code to test for that condition.

Once hi is received, we increment it and use a gput to put it back into Global Memory. The acknowledgement from Global Memory (which carries no data) arrives at the entry below, and we finally execute the return to initiate the continuation of this procedure. (The merge performs no operation; it merely structures the graph during analysis and optimization).

On the false side, we fork three microthreads, all within the same frame. The first thread allocates two new frames for the traverse procedure, for the two recursive calls. Note, these frames may be on other processors, *i.e.*, fp1 and fp2 hold Global pointers to the new frames. Concurrently, the second and third threads initiate Global loads to fetch the left and right sub-tree components of this tree node; these are later received into the local variables L and R.

A instruction such as "join 2 j1" synchronizes two microthreads. Each microthread executing it increments the local variable (here, j1) and dies if the result is less than the terminal count (2). Thus, only the second microthread to arrive will proceed past the join. In general, joins may be *n*-way, not just binary.

The first call instruction initiates a new thread at traverse with the new frame fp1, passing as arguments, the current frame pointer fp, the label M as the return address, the sub-tree L and the histogram array H. When that recursive call terminates, the thread at M will be initiated. The second call instruction is similar. Note that the two recursive calls may execute concurrently and on different processors. The final join synchronizes both returns, after which this invocation, in turn, returns to its caller.

The reader may imagine that there is some loss in concurrency in waiting for a gput acknowledgement on the true side and for the procedure returns at M and N on the false side. After all, these entrys do not receive any data, so presumably this procedure could return earlier. However, there are good reasons for structuring it this way. Consider a top-level caller of traverse. When would it be safe for the caller to read the histogram? As it stands, the return from traverse can be seen, using an inductive argument, as a guarantee that the entire histogram construction has completed whereas, had we not waited for the acknowledgments, there would be no easy way of knowing. Thus, this structure serves as a *compiled-in barrier*, which also has the advantage that it is re-entrant, *i.e.*, we could perform many independent tree traversals concurrently, with no interference between their "barriers".

3 Implementing P-RISC graphs on Distributed Memory machines

The abstract P-RISC machine model permits many microthreads to run simultaneously on each node of a parallel machine. Further, there is conceptually a single Global Memory that contains all objects. In most real distributed memory multiprocessors, each node contains only a uniprocessor and local memory. Thus, a node's uniprocessor must be multiplexed amongst the available microthreads, and the logical Global Memory must be mapped into the nodes' local memories.

Thread multiplexing implies scheduling, for which there are many choices. In this section we describe our implementation; we will contrast it with TAM, which makes different choices, in Section 5.1.

P-RISC's logical Global Memory is simply partitioned across all nodes' local memories, with each node responsible for a chunk of the Global Memory address space. A Global Pointer, then, is simply an encoding of the pair: node number, local address.

Figure 4 describes the state in each node of a distributed memory multiprocessor. There is a queue for all incoming messages. The first slot in each message is an instruction pointer, which refers to the code that is the message-handler for that message. We leave unspecified here exactly how messages are deposited into the queue on arrival. They may placed there by an interrupt handler, by special hardware (as in the J-Machine [2] or Fujitsu AP-1000 [7]), or by periodic polling as in the TAM implementation on the CM-5 [14].

3.1 Multiplexing among microthreads

The stack is unconventional— it is not used for local variables or for call-return information (we have already seen that frames serve this role). Instead, the stack is merely used as a scheduling queue for multiplexing amongst microthreads. The top-level action of a node, then, is:

```
node_top_level_loop:    push  node_top_level_loop
                        jump  msgqh[0]
```

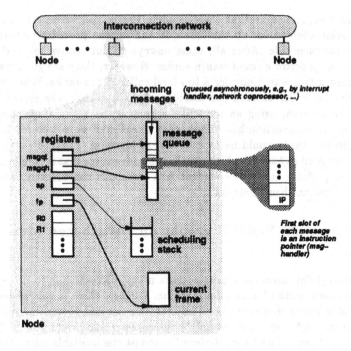

Fig. 4. State in each node of a distributed memory multiprocessor

i.e., after pushing the label node_top_level_loop on the stack, it "executes" the first message by jumping to the code that the message points to. As this execution proceeds, it may push more labels on the stack (due to forked microthreads). When a microthread completes, it pops a label from the stack and jumps to it. Eventually, it will pop node_top_level_loop and jump to it, which repeats the process with the next message.

Using a stack implies a certain scheduling order. The choice is simply a matter of expedience, since stacks can be implemented efficiently. Fortunately, since there is no notion of thread suspension in our model, the choice of a stack *vs.* a queue, or something else, cannot introduce any deadlock (of course, it can affect how the computation unfolds and can therefore affect available parallelism).

Figure 5 shows the implementation of some P-RISC control instructions. We have already mentioned that a halt, which ends a microthread, jumps to the next microthread by popping its label off the stack. Similarly, a fork simply pushes the label of one microthread on the stack and falls through to the other microthread. When this microthread halts, it will pop the stacked label and execute that microthread (assuming no more microthreads were pushed in the interim). A join, as expected, increments a local variable (which is always in the current frame) and compares it to the terminal count. If the join succeeds, it falls through; otherwise it executes the next microthread (by popping its label off the stack).

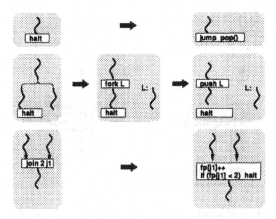

Fig. 5. Implementation of some P-RISC control instructions

It should be clear that P-RISC microthreads are very lightweight. Scheduling microthreads involves just a few instructions, and there is no operating system involvement.

3.2 Procedure calls

Figure 6 shows the implementation of a call instruction and its corresponding *entry* instruction. The call sends a message that contains the entry instruction's label (L), the new frame pointer, and any other arguments. The destination node's top-level loop will eventually begin executing at L; this code picks up its frame pointer and arguments from the message. The return instruction implementation is similar, involving a message in the reverse direction (not shown).

Doing two message-sends per procedure call/return may appear expensive. However, it is the minimum necessary for a remote call, and in Section 4 we describe optimizations that eliminate message-sending for local procedure calls.

3.3 Global accesses

Figure 7 shows the implementation of a gload, and its corresponding *entry*. The gload sends a message to a standard piece of code available at each node, the gload_handler, after which it halts. The destination node (based on address A) executes gload_handler, which reads the location and sends a response message containing the value. Arriving back at the source node, this message starts execution at L, where the frame pointer is restored and the value is extracted from the message into x. In Section 4 we describe optimizations that eliminate message-sending for local loads.

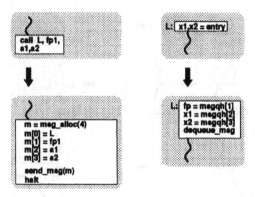

Fig. 6. Implementation of a call

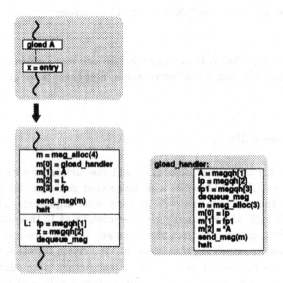

Fig. 7. Implementation of a gload

4 Dealing with locality

4.1 Frame and global object allocation

For frames and small global objects, the question arises as to where they must be allocated. This is a load balancing issue— global objects must be allocated on different nodes to keep global memory utilisation balanced across the machine, and frames must be allocated to distribute work evenly.

Our approach is to let the user annotate a constructor or function call to specify where the object or the frame is to be allocated. These annotations may be relative; in the following example, the annotations ensure that the frame for each recursive call is allocated at the machine node that contains the corresponding tree node object, ensuring that its fields will be read using local accesses.

```
def traverse  T  H  = if leaf?(t) then
                  then   { i = t.Leaf_val;
                           H![i] = H![i] + 1 }
                  else   { L = T.Left;
                           R = T.Right;
                           (traverse  L   H)@(nodeof L);
                           (traverse  R   H)@(nodeof R) } ;
```

When there is no annotation, we use a simple default policy such as a locally-decided round-robin allocation.

Large global objects (such as large arrays) pose a different problem. It is often advantageous to decompose such objects into columns, rows, or blocks which are then distributed across the nodes of the machine. Here, we plan to allow the user to annotate each array allocator with a data decomposition, patterned after the HPF distribution directives [4], and to generate the appropriate code automatically for the corresponding array accesses.

4.2 Local procedure calls

Figure 8 shows an alternative translation for a call and its corresponding entry. If the call is remote (as determined by the global pointer fp1), a message is sent *(a)*. The message goes to a standard code sequence in the runtime system, labelled Unpack_n. This code sequence *(e)* expects a message with n other arguments: the label of an entry, a frame pointer, and $n - 2$ procedure arguments. It sets up the frame pointer, loads the procedure arguments into registers, dequeues the message, and jumps to the entry code *(f)*, which now expects its arguments in registers, rather than in a message.[1]

If the call is local, we simply save registers and the current frame pointer *(b)*, load the arguments into registers and, set up the new frame pointer and jump to L *(c)*.[2] At some point, the callee reaches a halt, *e.g.*, because of a failed join, a remote global access, or synchronizing remote access. At this point the standard microthread scheduling will pop the stacked label M and begin execution there, restoring the frame pointer and registers *(d)* before executing other pending microthreads in this frame.

Simple analysis of the P-RISC graph for live register data can reduce the number of registers saved and restored in *(b)* and *(d)*. Even better, simple analysis may indicate that on entering the call, there cannot be any other stacked microthreads in this frame (because there are no forks leading up to this call). This would happen, for example, when we generate sequential code. In this case, sequences *(b)* and *(d)* can be omitted entirely.

---

[1] The assignments *(f)* may be omitted if x1, x2 are allocated to registers R0, R1.

[2] Again, if a1, a2 are allocated to registers R0, R1, the assignments *(c)* are omitted.

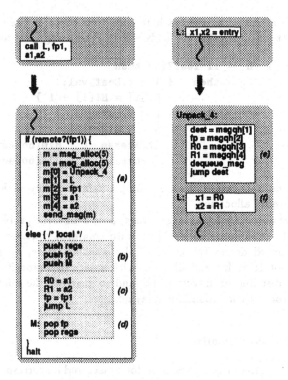

Fig. 8. Optimizing local procedure calls

Thus, for local, sequential calls, the calling convention reduces to the traditional method of passing continuations and arguments in registers. Similarly, a local return may also pass results in registers.

4.3 Access to global objects that are, in fact, local

It is also easy to optimize access to an object that is logically Global but, in fact, local. We first split the global access handler (such as gload_handler) as shown above for procedure entry points, into two parts: an unpack_n sequence handles the message and pre-loads arguments into registers, and the real handler itself. Then, the real handler can simply be inlined for local object access.

5 Related Work

5.1 TAM

Professor David Culler and his group at Berkeley have implemented a back end for the MIT Id compiler that produces code for TAM (Threaded Abstract Machine) [1] that is similar in many respects to P-RISC (indeed, both P-RISC and TAM have common roots in dynamic dataflow graphs).

As we have described, each node in our P-RISC system has a single scheduling queue— the queue of incoming messages. During execution of a message, forked threads are kept on a single, common stack. The TAM system makes different choices. Figure 9 shows a conceptual model of TAM's scheduling data structures within a node (a similar scheme was also described in [10]). TAM maintains an instruction-pointer stack in each frame, called a Remote Continuation Vector (RCV). One level up, there is an Active Frame list, containing all frames with non-empty ip stacks.

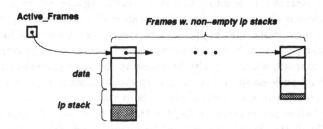

Fig. 9. TAM scheduling hierarchy, per node (concept)

When a message arrives, it is immediately executed by an "inlet", which corresponds roughly to our **entry** instruction. Recall that an **entry** instruction receives zero or more local variables fromt the message. The TAM inlet code stores this message data into the frame, and pushes an instruction pointer onto the ip stack in the frame— conceptually, it points at the **entry** instruction's successor. Further, if the ip stack was previously empty, this frame is now added to the Active Frames list. TAM inlet code often has an additional feature: if the **entry** instruction is immediately followed by a **join**, then the **join** is pulled into the inlet code; an instruction pointer is pushed on the frame's ip stack only if the **join** succeeds.

Given this scheduling data structure, a node's top-level loop is to repeatedly execute a "quantum":

- Choose a frame from the Active Frames list as the current frame.
- Execute a frame-specific initialization thread.
- Execute all microthreads from the frame's ip stack.
- Execute a frame-specific termination thread.

TAM's mechanism is analogous to sorting the message queue in the P-RISC system by frame, and executing all messages for a frame together. The intention is that this will improve usage of the local memory hierarchy. By staying in one frame for a longer period, cache behavior may improve. Further, register allocation can be performed across microthreads, with registers being restored and saved by the frame initialization and termination threads, respectively.

An early version of our P-RISC compiler also had a frame-based scheduling queue, like TAM [10, 6], although we did not have anything corresponding to TAM's inlets. We found, on our uniprocessor implementation, that the scheduling overhead dropped dramatically in going to our simpler, message-based scheduling, and the effect was much more significant than the loss in locality. At MIT, Ellen Spertus seems to have come to the same conclusion independently, based on her implementations of TAM for the J-Machine [13] (which she called the *direct* and *flattened* implementations, respectively).

The following is a more detailed comparison of the two choices.

Scheduling overhead. TAM's more complicated scheduling data structure involves more overhead. In addition to just manipulating a more complicated data structure, there is also some overhead due to atomicity concerns: Suppose a message arrives for a frame that happens to be the current frame. We must ensure that any join performed by the inlet is atomic with respect to the currently executing microthread, which may also be accessing the same join counter. Further, the inlet must push an ip on the current ip stack atomically, since the current quantum execution is also manipulating this ip stack.

Another atomicity concern in TAM is that an inlet may attempt to place a frame on the Active Frame list just as the quantum scheduler tries to select a frame off this list. There is an analogous atomicity concern in the P-RISC system: asynchronous enqueueing of arriving messages may interfere with the dequeueing of messages by the top level loop. However, this is the only atomicity concern in the P-RISC system.

Memory accesses per message arrival. In TAM, message data always travels through memory, since inlets always store message payloads into frames. Further, for messages arriving at a frame that is not the current frame, an ip must be stored into the frame's ip stack, which also means that the frame's ip stack pointer (which is in the frame) must be loaded, incremented and stored. The ip stack pointer must be tested, to check if the ip stack was previously empty, in which case, there are a few more memory accesses to place this frame on the Active Frame list.

In contrast, in P-RISC, the instruction pointer moves directly into the node's PC, and message data is loaded from the message directly into registers. The ensuing computation may consume the message data directly, without the data ever actually being stored in the frame.

However, this issue is more subtle than it appears, and depends on the underlying machine architecture. The P-RISC advantage holds only if asynchronous message queue management is "free", because of hardware support either in the network interface itself, or with a special mechanism (as in the J-Machine or Fujitsu AP-1000 [12]), or with a co-processor (as in the original MIT *T [11]).

On systems where the processor itself must copy a message out of the hardware network interface (*e.g.*, on an interrupt), the comparison is more complex (see Figure 10). In TAM, the inlet code *is* the interrupt handler, whereas P-RISC relies on a general interrupt handler. As shown in the figure, P-RISC code can therefore need an extra read and write from memory. However, this is the worst-case situation; often, the entry thread is itself the consumer thread, eliminating the extra read and write.

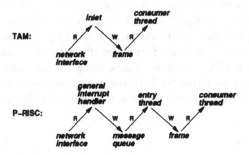

Fig. 10. Message data flow in TAM and P-RISC

Integration with local, sequential code. As described in Section 4, the P-RISC implementation allows us to optimize procedure call overhead for local calls, allowing argument- and result-passing to be done efficiently in registers, like conventional sequential code. In TAM, on the other hand, it is not clear how to achieve this, since it takes a strong position on executing all the current frame's microthreads before switching to the callee's frame; in other words, a procedure call *must* be deferred until the current frame's other threads and termination thread have been executed.

5.2   Charm

The Charm language and implementation at the University of Illinois is also a multithreaded, message-driven system [8]. A major difference is in the programming model. The Id programmer has a conventional shared memory model— multithreading, messages *etc.* are entirely within the runtime system. In Charm, on the other hand, messages and message-driven execution is explict.

The Charm programmer defines a *chare* which is an object specification— it declares local variables for the object state, and a collection of *entry* procedures that can manipulate this state. An entry is triggered by the arrival of a message, whose payload becomes its argument list. A procedure can contain arbitrary sequential code, and it can send messages to specific entry points of other chares. Chares interact with other chares *via* messages only— there is no direct access to another chare's local variables. Because of this limitation, Charm provides a library of global data structures, such as distributed associative tables. There is no general global heap containing user-defined objects.

A chare is analogous to a P-RISC codeblock (an Id function or loop iteration), and a chare *instance* corresponds to an Id function invocation, namely a P-RISC frame. A Charm entry procedure is analogous to a single microthread within an Id function, beginning at a P-RISC entry instruction.

Thus, programming in Charm is analogous to programming directly at the level of P-RISC graphs. This can be very messy and difficult, which is evident by comparing the relative complexities of the traverse function in Section 2.2 vs. its P-RISC graph in Figure 3. On the other hand, by programming at this lower level, the user may be able to produce more efficient code than is possible automatically via the P-RISC compiler. Recognizing the difficulty of programming directly at the message-driven level, Charm researchers are currently developing Dagger, a higher-level graphical notation for producing Charm code.

6 Conclusion

The P-RISC system described here is currently under construction by the author at Digital's Cambridge Research Laboratory. Our implementation compiles to C and currently runs on single and multiple workstations. A port to the CM-5 is in progress. The following table shows worst-case granularity measurements on three small test programs.

nqueens 8	paraffins 15	mat_test 20
19	17	49

Nqueens is the standard problem of finding all placements of 8 queens on a chessboard that are mutually non-threatening. Paraffins is a program to enumerate and count all unique paraffins with up to 15 carbon atoms [3]. Mat_test generates two matrices of size 20×20, multiplies them, and does a sum reduction. The table displays the average number of P-RISC instructions executed for each message taken off the message queue. It is therefore an indication of the granularity of the computation, and an indication of how efficient message-sending, receiving and queue-manipulation need to be.

The numbers in the table are unrealistic— today's parallel machines do not support efficient communication at such a fine grain. However, these are worst-case numbers, obtained by disabling the locality optimizations of Sections 4.2 and 4.3, thus forcing all procedure call/returns and all global object accesses to use messages. At the other extreme, when we run on a single processor with the optimizations of Sections 4.2 and 4.3 turned on, everything is local, and the entire program executes without generating a single message. Thus, the annotations described in Section 4.1 need to be used to strike a balance on this spectrum. In addition, the following considerations must be taken into account:

+ The table counts P-RISC instructions. Some of these are non-trivial, such as join, call and gload. The number of native instructions per message is therefore higher.

− Our compiler is rather naive at this point. Increasing the number of optimizations and generating tighter code will tend to reduce the number of instructions per message.

We expect to release our system for general use in December 1993. After that, we will be concentrating on optimizations based on detailed performance and locality studies. We hope to make detailed comparisons with the J-Machine and CM-5 implementations of TAM reported in [14].

References

1. D. E. Culler, A. Sah, K. E. Schauser, T. von Eicken, and J. Wawrzynek. Fine-grain Parallelism with Minimal Hardware Support: A Compiler-Controlled Threaded Abstract Machine. In *4th Intl. Conf. Architectural Support for Programming Languages and Operating Systems*, pages 164–175, April 1991.

2. W. Dally. *The J-Machine System*. MIT Press, 1990.

3. J. Feo (editor). *A Comparative Study of Parallel Programming Languages: The Salishan Problems*. North Holland, 1992.

4. High Performance Fortran Forum. *High Performance Fortran: Language Specification, Version 1.0*, May 3 1993. Anonymous ftp: titan.cs.rice.edu.

5. S. Hiranandani, K. Kennedy, and C.-W. Tseng. Compiling Fortran D. *Comm. ACM*, 35(8):66–80, August 1992.

6. H. S. Hochheiser. A Schezoid Compiler for P-RISC. Master's thesis, MIT, Dept. of EECS, February 1991.

7. H. Ishihata, T. Horie, S. Inano, T. Shimizu, S. Kato, and M. Ikesaka. Third Generation Message Passing Computer AP1000. In *Intl. Symp. on Supercomputing, Kyushu*, pages 46–55, November 1991.

8. L. V. Kale. Parallel Programming with CHARM: An Overview. Technical Report 93-8, Dept. of Computer Science, U. Illinois at Urbana-Champaign, 1993.

9. R. S. Nikhil. Id (Version 90.1) Reference Manual. Technical Report CSG Memo 284-2, MIT Lab for Computer Science, 545 Technology Square, Cambridge, MA 02139, USA, July 15 1991.

10. R. S. Nikhil. The Parallel Programming Language Id and its Compilation for Parallel Machines. *Intl. J. of High Speed Computing*, 5(2):171–223, 1993. Presented at Workshop on Massive Parallelism, Amalfi, Italy, October 1989.

11. R. S. Nikhil, G. M. Papadopoulos, and Arvind. *T: A Multithreaded Massively Parallel Architecture. In *Proc. 19th. Ann. Intl. Symp. on Computer Architecture, Queensland, Australia*, pages 156–167, May 1992.

12. T. Shimizu, T. Horie, and H. Ishihata. Low-latency Message Communication Support for the AP1000. In *19th. Intl. Symp. on Computer Architecture, Gold Coast, Australia*, pages 288–297, May 19-21 1992.

13. E. Spertus. Execution of Dataflow Programs on General-Purpose Hardware. Master's thesis, MIT, Dept. of EECS, August 1992.

14. E. Spertus, S. C. Goldstein, K. E. Schauser, T. von Eicken, D. E. Culler, and W. J. Dally. Evaluation of Mechanisms for Fine-Grained Parallel Programs in the J-Machine and the CM-5. In *Proc. 20th. Ann. Intl. Symp. on Computer Architecture, San Diego, CA*, May 17-19 1993.

Acceleration of First and Higher Order Recurrences on Processors with Instruction Level Parallelism

Michael Schlansker and Vinod Kathail
Hewlett-Packard Laboratories
1501 Page Mill Road, Palo Alto, CA 94304

Abstract

This paper describes parallelization techniques for accelerating a broad class of recurrences on processors with instruction level parallelism. We introduce a new technique, called blocked back-substitution, which has lower operation count and higher performance than previous methods. The blocked back-substitution technique requires unrolling and non-symmetric optimization of innermost loop iterations. We present metrics to characterize the performance of software-pipelined loops and compare these metrics for a range of height reduction techniques and processor architectures.

Keywords

recurrences, parallelism, software pipeline, loop optimization, height reduction, back-substitution, blocked back-substitution

1 Introduction

Architectures with instruction level parallelism such as VLIW and superscalar processors provide parallelism in the form of a limited number of pipelined functional units. For these architectures, recurrence height reduction techniques provide significant speedups when they are properly applied. This paper introduces a new technique, called **blocked back-substitution**, which preserves the height reduction benefits observed with symmetric back-substitution techniques but has substantially lower operation count. We analyze the impact of both the latency and the number of operations used to evaluate a recurrence on the performance of software-pipelined loops. We present speedup results on a variety of example architectures to demonstrate the utility of the techniques presented in this paper.

Recurrences appear in many forms within application programs and typically result in a performance bottleneck when executed on a processor with instruction level parallelism. A chain of operations connected through flow dependence limits program performance. Most recurrences are either first or second order where efficient acceleration techniques are best demonstrated. We believe that a broad class of recurrences can be efficiently accelerated, and we demonstrate the acceleration of one important class of recurrences within this paper.

The height reduction of arithmetic recurrences has been extensively studied in the literature; see, for example, [1-5]. The techniques used in these papers introduce computational redundancy in order to reduce the solution time of a recurrence on a parallel computer but do not carefully optimize the solution of recurrences for processors with limited instruction level parallelism. A frequently discussed solution is cyclic reduction. When cyclic reduction is applied, the operation count is of the order $n \log n$ leading to excessive operation count for large problem sizes.

The partition method was introduced by Chen et. al. [6] and studied further by H. H. Wang [7] and H. A. Van Der Vorst et. al. [8]. The partition method is amenable to parallelization and results in lower operation count (approximately 5n) when solving a first order linear recurrence. In this technique, a simple recurrence loop with trip count n is transformed into multiple nested loops with smaller innermost trip count (approximately square root of n). When a recurrence loop has mixed recurrences of different type, a loop exit, or other complex code structures, the transformation of a single innermost loop to a complex multiple loop configuration may be very difficult or impossible. The dismantling of a single loop into multiple nested loops also increases vector startup penalties and requires more load/store instructions than optimal methods.

Work by Tanaka et. al. [9] introduces a height reduction technique similar to blocked back-substitution. The technique is used to accelerate first order linear recurrences on a vector computer that has been augmented with a hardware floating point recurrence solution instruction. Our interest is in more flexible processor architectures with significant instruction level parallelism. We describe a broader family of height reduction techniques and use these techniques to efficiently process algebraic recurrences of first and higher order without the introduction of any specialized instructions.

Work by Callahan [10] introduces a fairly general class of recurrences called "bounded recurrences". A primary objective of Callahan is to establish a notational framework for the general description of recurrence acceleration techniques. The work focuses primarily on the acceleration of recurrences for multiprocessors. We treat specifically the acceleration of recurrences on uniprocessors with instruction level parallelism.

Two loop acceleration techniques are popular in the literature. In trace (or superblock) scheduling [11-13], loops are unrolled into a trace. Iterations within a single trace are overlapped, but successive traces are not. The schedule length of the trace is greater than or equal to a maximal height required by dependence over all pairs of operations in the trace. Algebraic height reductions must accommodate the distance between all operations in the trace. In software pipelining [14, 15], successive loop iterations are identical. Height reduction must minimize the relative height between each iteration and identical prior iterations In software pipelines, successive iterations overlap, and only operations on time critical dependence paths are height reduced. Blocked back-substitution combines these techniques and schedules unrolled loops in software pipelines.

Blocked back-substitution is a general algebraic height reduction technique for recurrences providing lower operation count and higher performance than prior techniques. Blocked back-substitution is also applicable to non-linear recurrences when the primitive operations in which the recurrence is expressed have the associative and distributive properties. The technique is especially advantageous for machines with a large degree of parallelism obtained through either pipelining or a large number of function units. The use of blocked back-substitution accelerates an innermost loop recurrence using a height reduced innermost loop. The preservation of the original innermost loop facilitates the scheduling of other innermost loop code in a common software pipeline with height reduced recurrence code. The fused loop has reduced vector startup penalty when compared to solutions requiring multiple fragmented loops.

The paper is organized as follows. The rest of this section provides an overview of asymmetric height reduction and introduces notation and terminology used in the rest of the paper. Section 2 provides an overview of recurrence height reduction schemas useful within software pipelines. Height reduction schema such as symmetric back-substitution and blocked back-substitution are defined for later comparison. Section 3 specializes symmetric and blocked back-substitution to the case of a first order multiply-add recurrence. Critical path lengths and operation counts allow direct performance comparison between the two approaches. Section 4 generalizes this work by providing a common technique to accelerate multiply-add recurrences of any order. Section 5 provides a detailed comparison of the performance of these techniques on selected machines. Section 6 contains concluding remarks.

1.1 Overview of Asymmetric Height Reduction

Many of the height reduction techniques found in the literature use a balanced approach in the sense that they try to minimize the length of the path from each of the inputs to the output of an expression. The balanced approach usually requires excessive redundant work, but may offer excellent speedup when the critical path length through the computation is measured. When compiling for a small number of processing elements, balanced approaches may be too computationally expensive especially when height reductions of deeply nested recurrences are required.

In this work, we have given considerable attention to minimizing the redundant work required to execute a computation. This is accomplished by evaluating expressions using asymmetric height reductions. Consider the following example:

$$s_0 = c_1 + x_1(c_2 + x_2(c_3 + x_3(c_4 + x_4(c_5 + x_5(c_6 + x_6(c_7 + x_7(c_8 + x_8(s_i))))))))$$

The evaluation of this expression is sequential requiring eight multiply and eight add operations. A height reduction goal is needed to characterize the successful parallelization of this expression. One goal is to jointly minimize the height from each of the input c_i's and s_i to the output s_0 In important cases, this goal requires excessive redundant computation and yields no additional performance benefit. A more easily met goal minimizes only a critical path (e.g. from s_i to s_0). Here, we assume that all of the c_i's are available well in advance of s_i and the evaluation latency from each c_i to s_0 is not important. We use the associative and distributive properties to derive the following expression which has a single multiplication and addition on the path from s_i to s_0 and requires seven additional multiplies as compared to the original expression.

$$s_0 = (x_1 x_2 x_3 x_4 x_5 x_6 x_7 x_8)s_i +$$
$$(c_1 + x_1(c_2 + x_2(c_3 + x_3(c_4 + x_4(c_5 + x_5(c_6 + x_6(c_7 + x_7(c_8))))))))$$

Balanced height reductions (those which jointly expedite the paths from all of the c_i's to s_0) result in substantially increased operation count yet still require at least a single multiplication and addition on the path from s_i to s_0. Such algebraic transformations have been extensively explored in techniques for the acceleration of carry look-ahead.

Another very important asymmetric evaluation principle explored within this paper is the use of blocked height reductions in the acceleration of recurrences. Here, we expedite the evaluation of a sequence of values originally calculated by repeatedly executing a recurrence expression in a loop. When a recurrence is blocked, a simple loop with recurrence is unrolled by a blocking factor. Height reduction is applied to some of the iterations within the loop body, while others are evaluated using the non-height reduced original code.

In this approach, a sequence of recurring values is separated into two categories. The timely evaluation of some of the values is expedited through height reduction with requisite computational redundancy. The evaluation of other values is not time critical and is performed using the original expression, which involves no redundant computation. This asymmetric treatment combines the height reduction benefits yielded by redundant expression evaluation with reduced operation count resulting from using redundancy as sparingly as possible.

The blocked back-substitution introduced in this paper uses associative and distributive properties to reduce the height of expressions, and it uses common sub-expression elimination to minimize the number of operations executed. In many cases, the blocked back-substitution technique provides unlimited parallelism with a corresponding increase in redundant operation count, but the increase in operation count is bounded by a constant multiplier.

1.2 Loop Recurrence Notation

The notation used to describe the flow of values between loop iterations is taken from a paper by Rau [16]. In this paper, we use the concept of the **expanded virtual register (EVR)** which is a linearly ordered set of virtual registers with a special remap operation. Note that the use of the EVR is not restricted to processors with hardware support for rotating registers. Compilation techniques using virtual rotating registers are suitable for conventional register files but require the replication of loop program text as described by Rau et. al. [17].

A scalar value s (usually calculated repeatedly within the body of a loop) can be referenced using the notation s[i]. Each time a **remap(s)** is executed, all values in the sequence shift "upward" so that each value s[i] prior to the execution of a remap is renamed as s[i+1] after the remap. Thus, the value s (identically equal to s[0]) after the execution of a single remap is renamed as s[1]. This allows multiple values from a sequence of scalar assignments to remain alive without the automatic overwrite of a value when the next member of the sequence is computed. This notation is particularly useful for the description of value usage in higher order recurrences.

We must also describe interface specifications between the code for a loop and the code that precedes or follows the loop code. For a variable s calculated in a recurrence within a loop, we introduce s_{in} and s_{out} to precisely describe loop interfaces. Out of loop code prior to the loop establishes an initial value for the s which we will call s_{in}. After loop execution has completed, the repeated evaluation of the loop body establishes a final value for the recurring value s known as s_{out}, which is referenced by out of loop code subsequent to loop execution.

1.3 Loop Performance Metrics

We use four performance metrics to help describe the advantages and disadvantages of specific recurrence acceleration methods. We define a simple metric **Ops/iter** which counts the average number of operations required to execute a single iteration of the recurrence loop. One can compare the number of operations per iteration prior to applying a height reduction technique against the number of operations per iteration after height reduction to measure redundant work introduced for the purposes of acceleration. The Ops/iter measure assumes that operations of all types are of equal cost. When a loop body has been unrolled and iterations are not treated symmetrically, the Ops/iter measure averages the number of operations required per iteration across the unrolled loop block.

When a specific processor and corresponding code for a software pipeline has been selected, we can use Ops/iter to calculate **ResMII**. ResMII and the following two metrics have been described in Dehnert et. al. [18]. ResMII establishes a resource bound on the rate of execution of loop iterations within software pipelines. In the traditional definition of ResMII, if a processor has u identical function units each capable of executing any operation, then:

$$ResMII = \left\lceil \frac{Ops / iter}{u} \right\rceil.$$

This expresses the constraint that if a schedule is developed which saturates a critical resource, the number of cycles per iteration cannot be less than the ResMII. The formula uses a ceiling function to constrain identical loop iterations in a software pipeline to take an integral number of cycles. We present techniques which use loop unrolling where the schedule for successive iterations is not identical and this constraint is pessimistic. We modify the ResMII calculation to provide a smaller (truly lower) bound for the unrolled loop case:

$$ResMII = \frac{Ops / iter}{u}.$$

Here, ResMII provides a lower (possibly non-integral) bound on the average number of iterations required per iteration across the unrolled block.

The **RecMII** of a loop describes a bound on the rate at which a software pipeline is executed based on a critical path measurement through operations within the body of the loop. Given an expression with recurrence evaluated in the body of a loop and specific hardware latencies, the RecMII is calculated as a worst case path length computation over all circuits in the program graph. Each circuit is normalized by the number of iterations spanned by the circuit to correctly calculate its impact on throughput. Once again, we have adapted RecMII to the unrolled loop case. We calculate the RecMII for the unrolled loop body and divide by the number of iterations unrolled. This provides a potentially non-integral lower bound on the number of cycles per source iteration in the case of unrolled loops.

The MII of a loop is a performance bound that takes both resource and critical path constraints into account. It is simply the maximum of ResMII and RecMII. Once again, we use a potentially non-integral form for MII derived through this maximum to better model unrolled loops.

2 Recurrence Acceleration Schemas

In this section, we illustrate three loop acceleration methods using the same program example. The example program consists of a simple associative reduction. It is commonly the case that a sequence of terms within a loop are collected into a single result using an associative operation. This action is termed associative reduction. Associative reduction can be separated into two broad classes:

1. **reduction to scalar** in which a sequence of terms calculated within the loop is reduced to a single scalar which is used after loop execution, and

2 **reduction to vector** in which terms from all iterations prior to an iteration are associatively accumulated and either stored to memory or otherwise used within the loop necessitating the correct calculation of the entire sequence of values.

These two cases require distinct treatment. In the following examples, we use the term "addition" and the operation + to represent an arbitrary associative operation and we use ℓ to represent its latency in processor cycles.

2.1 Interleaved Reduction

We first describe an interleaved reduction method which is useful in the associative reduction of a number of terms to a scalar. It has been implemented within the Cydra

5 compiler (see [18] in which the method is called "riffled" reduction) and within the Trace compiler [12]. As an example, Figure 1 shows the original code for a reduction to scalar loop side by side with the code for interleaved reduction. In this example, we assume that an initial scalar value live in to the body of the loop s_{in} is copied into s[1] and, the final value s_{out} is copied from s[1] after loop execution completes. The performance metrics for this loop are as follows: Ops / iter = 1 and RecMII = ℓ. The performance metrics indicate that only a single addition is required per cycle but no more than one iteration can be retired every ℓ cycles.

$s[1] = s_{in}$	$s[1] = s_{in}, s[2] = 0, s[3] = 0, \cdots s[b] = 0$
do i=1,n	do i=1,n
$s = s[1] + a_i$	$s = s[b] + a_i$
remap(s)	remap(s)
enddo	enddo
$s_{out} = s[1]$	$s_{out} = s[1] + s[2] + \cdots + s[b]$
(a)	(b)

Figure 1: (a) Original reduction (b) Interleaved reduction

Interleaved reduction increases the degree of parallelism without redundant work and requires no replication of the loop body and thus, is an excellent schema for the associative reduction to scalar. The single dependence chain of operations defined within the original loop is split into b independent chains thus effecting a b-fold height reduction. Interleaved reduction results in the following loop performance metrics: Ops / iter = 1 and RecMII = ℓ/b. Interleaved reduction is not suitable for associative reduction to vector because it correctly calculates only the final term in the original reduction. Interleaved reduction is also not useful when treating more complex recurrences such as first and higher order linear recurrences described later in this paper.

2.2 Symmetric Back-substitution

Symmetric back-substitution has also been implemented within the Cydra 5 compiler. The technique is more general than interleaved reduction because it handles more complex recurrences and correctly treats the reduction to vector case. However, we will show that symmetric back-substitution is frequently not the best approach.

We illustrate symmetric back-substitution in the context of the reduction to vector case. But, we focus only on the rapid evaluation of the entire stream of recurring values and don't describe in detail the means by which these values are actually used. Thus, we don't explicitly show uses of the recurring values in the examples in order to simplify the presentation. In the reduction to scalar case, the schema presented in this section must be optimized to eliminate statements whose results are not used, e.g., by using dead-code elimination.

Figure 2(a) illustrates the code for a reduction to vector example. The example is similar to the one used in the last section except that we assume that all the values of s are used (e.g., stored into the array x(i)). The performance metrics for the unmodified loop are expressed as: Ops / iter = 1 and RecMII = ℓ indicating that only a single addition is required per cycle but no more than one iteration can be retired every ℓ cycles where ℓ represents the addition latency.

s[1] = s_{in}
do i=1,n
s = s[1] + a_i /* s is stored into x(i) */
remap(s)
enddo
	s[1] = s_{in}
	do i=1,b-1 /* treat b-1 iterations
	                conventionally */
	s = s[1] + a_i
	remap(s)
	enddo
	do i=b,n /* b fold back-substitution
	             of remaining iterations */
	s = s[b] + (a_i + a_{i-1} + a_{i-2} + \cdots + a_{i-b-1})
	remap(s)
	enddo

(a)	(b)

Figure 2: (a) Original code for reduction to vector (b) Symmetric back-substitution

Performance limitations resulting from the RecMII bound are alleviated using symmetric back-substitution by substituting the expression for s computed within a previous iteration ($s[1] = s[2] + a_{i-1}$) into the expression for s computed within the current iteration. Thus we get $s = (s[2] + a_{i-1}) + a_i$. The process may be repeated to any desired depth b of back-substitution. The associative property of addition is used to asymmetrically height reduce the result (e.g. expedite the s[2] to s[0] path for b=2). This yields the expression $s = s[2] + (a_{i-1} + a_i)$. The technique produces each term in the sequence of values faithfully and can be used for both the reduction to scalar and reduction to vector cases. The computational work increases linearly in b as we expose additional parallelism. This yields inefficient solutions when highly parallelized forms of the back-substituted code are used.

The second loop in Figure 2(b) depicts code which has been parallelized through symmetric back-substitution. The back-substitution process has changed the loop from a first order recurrence to a bth order recurrence. If one enters the second loop directly this higher order recurrence uses the value s[b] which is not properly defined. The higher order recurrence is correctly initialized by executing b-1 conventional iterations within the first unmodified loop. The remaining n-(b-1) iterations are executed within the second higher order recurrence loop.

Loop performance metrics for the second loop are: Ops / iter = b and Re cMII = ℓ/b. When one applies a b-fold height reduction, a resulting b-fold increase in work is required. The linear growth in the computational requirements for symmetric back-substitution motivates the blocked back-substitution approach presented below.

We note that in the case of a reduction involving loop invariant terms, back-substitution can be streamlined. Consider the case where each of the terms a_i in the previous example are identical values, say a. Assume also that a multiplicative operation × exists such that:

$$\sum_1^n a = n \times a$$

As an example, the associative operation + could represent floating point multiplication and the multiplicative operation × could be the nth power of a. We start with the code modified to reflect the invariance of the a_i terms; see Figure 3(a).

Again, we assume that the initial value s_{in} resides in s[1] and, the final value s_{out} may be obtained in s[1] after loop execution. We now rewrite the code exactly as in the symmetric back-substitution case but pre-compute the addition of b copies of the invariant term a outside the loop; see Figure 3(b). Like the general case, this method is suitable for either reduction to scalar or reduction to vector case, but now the computational work is a constant function of the degree of height reduction. This provides an excellent method for stepping out symmetric induction variables within software pipelined loops.

(a)	(b)
s[1] = s_{in} do i=1,n s = s[1] + a remap(s) enddo	c = a × b s[1] = s_{in} do i=1,b-1 s = s[1] + a remap(s) enddo do i=b,n s = s[b] + c remap(s) enddo

Figure 3: (a) Original code with invariant terms (b) After symmetric back-substitution

The invariant case eliminates the need for redundancy in the back-substituted expression resulting in the following loop performance metrics: Ops / iter = 1 and Re cMII = ℓ/b. Note that for associative operations which have a well behaved inverse operation (e.g. additive inverse), the first loop can be eliminated and proper values for s[1], s[2], ...,s[b] can be pre-calculated before entering a back-substituted loop with trip count n.

2.3 Blocked Back-substitution

In this section, we present a new technique which unrolls loop bodies to achieve a more efficient solution. We call this technique blocked back-substitution because it uses an asymmetric treatment of code within a block of b consecutive iterations where b represents the block size or degree of unrolling. Blocked back-substitution frequently height reduces recurrences with a substantially lower increase in redundant operation count. The technique is applicable to both DO-loops and WHILE-loops, but we discuss it only in the context of DO-loops in this paper.

The schema is as follows. A loop body is unrolled b times. The first b-1 iterations of the body are simple copies of the original loop text. The final copy of the loop body is expressed using b-fold back-substitution directly in terms of values live in to the first of the b iterations. The expression for this back-substituted iteration is then height reduced. The height reduction is asymmetrically optimized to minimize the loop recurring value-in to loop recurring value-out path (s[b] to s[0]).

The b fold unrolling of loop text into a block complicates the treatment of arbitrary loop trip count. For counted loops (*e.g.*, DO loops in FORTRAN), we will post-condition the loop so that the blocked loop executes an integral multiple of b source iterations. This is achieved by defining two trip count functions: e (the epilogue count) and k (the kernel count). Both are functions of the source trip count n and the degree of blocking b. Let:

$e(n, b) = n \mod b$

$k(n, b) = n - e(n, b)$

Figure 4 shows the code obtained by post-conditioning the loop and then applying the blocked back-substitution to parallelize the recurrence. Consider the first loop in the code. In this blocked loop, we call each of the unrolled iterations a minor iteration corresponding to a single iteration of the source program. Each body of the unrolled text consisting of b minor iterations is called a major iteration. Every b^{th} minor iteration (the last minor iteration in the unrolled loop body) is calculated using b fold back-substitution. Intervening minor iterations are calculated using an unmodified, non-height reduced recurrence. This eliminates redundant work within b-1 of the b minor iterations.

```
s[1] = s_in
do i=b,k(n,b),b
s = s[1] + a_i          /* first minor iteration */
remap(s)
  ⋮
s = s[1] + a_{i+b-2}     /* (b-1)^th minor iteration */
remap(s)
s = s[b] + (a_{i+b-1} + a_{i+b-2} + a_{i+b-3} + ⋯ + a_i)  /* b^th minor iteration */
remap(s)
enddo

do i=e(n,b),n
s = s[1] + a_i          /* retire residual iterations conventionally */
remap(s)
enddo
```

Figure 4: Blocked back-substitution

It may appear superficially that this code is not very parallel in that each of the first b-1 minor iterations depends upon a result calculated within the previous minor iteration. This creates a long chain of operations linked through flow dependence. As a result of the b fold back-substitution, the bth minor iteration within the unrolled loop body depends only on values produced by that same code in the previous major iteration. Since the bth minor iteration does not depend on any of the previous b-1 minor iterations, the only recurrence cycle in the loop depends on the relationship between this b^{th} minor iteration and the same code from the previous major iteration.

Another barrier to parallelization might appear to be the remap operations positioned between each of the minor iterations; however, that is not the case. A remap operation between two minor iterations doesn't act as a barrier for code motion. An operation can be moved across a remap operation (in either direction) with a corresponding adjustment to its EVR indices. This has no detrimental effect on program semantics if all dependencies are honored. Also, multiple remap operations within a loop body don't impose any constraints on the ResMII or the RecMII of the loop. For example, it may appear that a loop body with n remaps takes a minimum of n cycles (one per remap). On processors with no hardware support for the EVR concept, this is not an issue since remaps do not appear in the generated code. The paper by Rau *et.al.* [17] describes how to generate code for such processors by using kernel-unrolling and variable-renaming. For processors that do support the EVR concept in hardware, we have two options. The first option is to generalize the concept of the remap operation so that a single operation can perform remap by multiple positions. The second is to use a single remap by 1 at the end of each major iteration and use variable-renaming to remove other remap operations.

The technique is applicable to both reduction to scalar and reduction to vector type of recurrences. Note that in the reduction to scalar case, dead code elimination should be used to eliminate unused operations in the b-1 non-height reduced minor iterations of the loop. Loop performance metrics are calculated for the reduction to vector case as follows: $\text{Ops}/\text{iter} = (2b-1)/b$ and $\text{Re cMII} = \ell/b$. In both symmetric and blocked back-substitution, additional parallelism can be exposed by increasing the degree of back-substitution b. However, while symmetric back-substitution requires work which increases linearly with the degree of back-substitution b, blocked back-substitution requires work that is bounded by a two fold increase irrespective of b.

When terms are loop invariant, blocked back-substitution may take advantage of additional savings in redundant computation as shown in Figure 5. In the case of loop invariant terms, the approach is able to provide increasing degree of parallelism with no increasing work as indicated by the loop performance metrics: $\text{Ops}/\text{iter} = 1$ and $\text{Re cMII} = \ell/b$. This technique can be used to parallelize the computation of induction variables.

```
c = a × b
s[1] = s_in
do i=1,n,b
s = s[1] + a
remap(s)
s = s[1] + a
remap(s)
⋮
s = s[1] + a    /*unroll b-1 copies of original body*/
remap(s)
s = s[b] + c    /* generate specialized final iteration*/
enddo
```

Figure 5: Blocked back-substitution with invariant terms

3 First Order Multiply-add Recurrences

We use the first order multiply-add recurrence to help illustrate the relative benefits of the height reduction approaches described above. The first order multiply add recurrence schema treat recurrences of the requisite form where primitive operations have the following properties: associative property of addition and the distributive property of multiplication over addition. While this technique is frequently applied to first order linear recurrences, the technique also applies to boolean non-linear recurrences or any other recurrence with requisite form and properties.

The code presented in Figure 6 illustrates the form of the first order multiply-add recurrence. In its unmodified form, the first order multiply-add recurrence has the following loop performance metrics: Ops / Iter = 2 and $\mathrm{RecMII} = 2\ell$. Here, we have assumed that the multiply and addition units have identical latency ℓ.

```
s[1] = s_in
do i=1,n
    s = a_i s[1] + c_i
enddo
```

Figure 6: Original first order multiply-add recurrence

3.1 Symmetric Back-substitution

The expressions shown below illustrate the derivation of the back-substituted form for the first order linear recurrence. The unmodified expression shown on the first line evaluates s directly in terms of s[1]. The second line is derived by repeatedly (for k=1,..,b) substituting the expression for s[k] into the original expression and raising the order of the recurrence. In the final line representing the bth order recurrence executed within the back-substituted loop, we have used the distributive property to isolate s[b]. This asymmetric height reduction calculates a new s from a bth previous s after only a single multiplication and addition.

$$s = a_i s[1] + c_i$$
$$s = a_i(a_{i-1}(a_{i-2}(\cdots(a_{i-b-2}(a_{i-b-1}s[b] + c_{i-b-1}) + c_{i-b-2})\cdots) + c_{i-2}) + c_{i-1}) + c_i$$
$$s = (a_i a_{i-1} \cdots a_{i-b+1})s[b] +$$
$$a_i(a_{i-1}(a_{i-2}(\cdots(a_{i-b+2}(c_{i-b+1}) + c_{i-b+2})\cdots) + c_{i-2}) + c_{i-1}) + c_i$$

The schema given in Figure 7 shows the code after symmetric back-substitution. As in section 2.2, the first loop initializes the recurrence. After initialization, the second loop repeatedly executes the back-substituted expression in order to accelerate the solution of the original recurrence. The loop performance metrics in this case are as follows: Ops / iter $= (3b - 1)$ and $\mathrm{RecMII} = 2\ell/b$. Thus, the number of operations required to execute an iteration grows linearly as the back-substitution distance is increased. This disadvantage restricts the method to a limited degree of back-substitution.

```
s[1] = s_in
do i=1,b-1          /* treat b-1 iterations conventionally */
    s = a_i s[1] + c_i
    remap(s)
enddo

do i=b,n            /* b fold back-substitution of remaining iterations */
    s = (a_i a_{i-1} \cdots a_{i-b+1})s[b] +
        a_i(a_{i-1}(a_{i-2}(\cdots(a_{i-b+2}(c_{i-b+1}) + c_{i-b+2})\cdots) + c_{i-2}) + c_{i-1}) + c_i
    remap(s)
enddo
```

Figure 7: Symmetric back-substitution for first order multiply-add recurrence

3.2 Blocked Back-substitution

The schema of Figure 8 shows the code for the first order multiply-add recurrence after blocked back-substitution. As in section 2.3, the loop is conditioned using the kernel and epilog trip count functions. The loop performance metrics in this case are as follows: $\text{Ops}/\text{iter} = (5b-3)/b$ and $\text{RecMII} = 2\ell/b$

```
s[1] = s_in
do i=b,k(n,b),b
s = a_i s[1] + c_i
remap(s)
⋮
s = a_{i+b-2} s[1] + c_{i+b-2}
remap(s)
s = (a_{i+b-1} a_{i+b-2} ⋯ a_i) s[b]
    + (a_{i+b-1}(a_{i+b-2}(a_{i+b-3}(⋯(a_{i-1}(c_i)+c_{i+1})⋯)+c_{i+b-3})+c_{i+b-2})+c_{i+b-1})
remap(s)
enddo

do i=e(n,b),n
s = a_i s[1] + c_i
remap(s)
enddo
```

Figure 8: Blocked back-substituted first order multiply-add recurrence

4 Higher Order Recurrences

In this section, we consider higher order recurrences and show how the symmetric and blocked back-substitution techniques discussed earlier can be applied to reduce the height of these recurrences. As in the last section, we phrase the description in terms of two generic operations, called add and multiply, and rely only on the following properties of these operations: associativity of addition and multiplication and the distributivity of multiplication over addition. Thus, the results apply not only to higher order linear recurrences, but to any higher order recurrence involving two operators with the required properties, *e.g.*, boolean (non-linear) recurrences.

The code in Figure 9 shows the general form of the type of recurrences that we will consider in this section. Furthermore, we will focus on the reduction to vector case, *i.e.*, the case where all n values of s are needed.

```
s[1] = s_1; ⋯ s[m] = s_m
do i = 1, n
s = a_{1,i} s[1] + ⋯ + a_{m,i} s[m] + c_i
remap(s)
enddo
```

Figure 9: Original m^{th} order recurrence

In the first few subsections, we describe a framework for handling recurrences of the form shown above. We describe schemas for symmetric and blocked back-substitution, and show how performance metrics, *i.e.*, Ops/iter and RecMII, can be computed for various schemas. These subsections don't provide any specific numbers or formulas for performance metrics. The reason is that actual numbers or formulas depend upon what one assumes about the coefficients. However, the methodology presented in these subsections can be used to calculate performance metrics for various cases.

The last two subsections present performance metrics for the most general case of an mth order recurrence, *viz.*, the case when all the coefficients are non-zero loop-variant values. We consider two different machine models, one that supports separate multiply and add operations and one that also provides a fused multiply-add operation. An extended version of this paper, published as technical report [19], contains performance formulas for several special cases of interest. These include the case when all the coefficients are loop-invariant values and the case when the coefficient c_i is 0.

4.1 Formulas for Coefficients in Back-substituted Expressions

This subsection derives formulas for coefficients in the expression that one gets after back-substitution is repeated to a certain degree. These formulas are applicable to both symmetric and blocked back-substitution techniques.

In the original program, the computation of s in the ith iteration depends upon s[1] computed in the previous iteration. The back-substitution process involves substituting the expression for s[1] in the expression that computes s, and re-arranging the terms so as to minimize the heights of recurrence paths

$$s = a_{1,i}\left(a_{1,(i-1)}s[2] + \cdots + a_{m,(i-1)}s[m+1] + c_{i-1}\right) + a_{2,i}s[2] + \cdots + a_{m,i}s[m] + c_i$$

$$s = \left(a_{1,i}a_{1,(i-1)} + a_{2i}\right)s[2] + \cdots + \left(a_{1,i}a_{(m-1),(i-1)} + a_{m,i}\right)s[m]$$
$$+ a_{1,i}a_{m,(i-1)}s[m+1] + (a_{1,i}c_{i-1} + c_i)$$

The structure of the new expression is similar to the original expression except for the structure of coefficients and the values of s used in the expression. We can repeat the process by substituting for s[2], then for s[3] and so on. In the following discussion, we denote the coefficients in the expression for s obtained after a certain number of back-substitution by $A_{1,i}^b \cdots A_{m,i}^b$ and C_i^b; the superscript denotes the degree of back-substitution. The base case, *i.e.*, the original expression with no substitution performed is denoted by b=1. Using this notation, the expression for s after (b-1) fold back-substitution can be written as follows:

$$s = A_{1,i}^{b-1}s[b-1] + \cdots + A_{m,i}^{b-1}s[b+m-2] + C_i^{b-1}$$

To derive the expression for s after b fold back-substitution, we substitute the value of s[b-1] in the above expression. In the original program, s[b-1] is computed using the following expression:

$$s[b-1] = a_{1,(i-b+1)}s[b] + \cdots + a_{m,(i-b+1)}s[b+m-1] + c_{i-b+1}$$

Substituting the expression for s[b-1] and rearranging the terms gives the following expression for s.

$$s = \left(a_{1,(i-b+1)}A_{1,i}^{b-1} + A_{2,i}^{b-1}\right)s[b] + \cdots + \left(a_{(m-1),(i-b+1)}A_{1,i}^{b-1} + A_{m,i}^{b-1}\right)s[b+m-2]$$
$$+ \left(a_{m,(i-b+1)}A_{1,i}^{b-1}\right)s[b+m-1] + \left(c_{i-b+1}A_{1,i}^{b-1} + C_i^{b-1}\right)$$

Using the notation introduced earlier, the expression for s after b fold back-substitution can also be written as:

$$s = A^b_{1,i} s[b] + \cdots + A^b_{m,i} s[b+m-1] + C^b_i$$

Comparing the above two expressions for s, we get the following recursive formulas for coefficients. In these formulas, $A^1_{1,i} \cdots A^1_{m,i}$ and C^1_i represent the base case (*i.e.*, b =1) and their values are simply the coefficients in the original expression for s.

$$A^1_{1,i} = a_{1,i} \qquad A^b_{1,i} = a_{1,(i-b+1)} A^{b-1}_{1,i} + A^{b-1}_{2,i}$$

$$\vdots \qquad\qquad \vdots$$

$$A^1_{(m-1),i} = a_{(m-1),i} \qquad A^b_{(m-1),i} = a_{m,(i-b+1)} A^{b-1}_{1,i} + A^{b-1}_{m,i}$$

$$A^1_{m,i} = a_{m,i} \qquad A^b_{m,i} = a_{m,(i-b+1)} A^{b-1}_{1,i}$$

$$C^1_i = c_i \qquad C^b_i = c_{i-b+1} A^{b-1}_{1,i} + C^{b-1}_i$$

It is important to note that these formulas don't have the same structure. Specifically, the second to last formula involves only multiplications and no additions. For a specific value of m, the formulas are used in the reverse order. For example, the first order case uses the last two formulas, the second order last three and so on.

In both symmetric and blocked back-substitution, the work involved in computing coefficients is a significant amount of the overall work. To minimize the work, it is important to recognize common sub-expressions. For example, the computation of $A^{b-1}_{1,i}$ is common to all the formulas given above. It is also important to factor common sub-expressions, *i.e.*, compute ab + ac as a(b+c). We believe the formulas given above compute coefficients using a minimum number of add and multiply operations, but we offer no formal proof of this fact.

As an example of the application of these formulas, consider the first order case. For the symmetric back-substitution with b = 3, the computation of s can be expressed using the following set of equations.

$$A^3_{1,i} = a_{1,(i-2)} A^2_{1,i}; \quad A^2_{1,i} = a_{1(i-1)} a_{1,i}$$

$$C^3_i = c_{i-2} A^2_{1,i} + a_{1i} c_{i-1} + c_i$$

$$s = A^3_{1,i} s[3] + C^3_i$$

These equations compute the same result as the one given in Section 3.1 and use the same number of operations (which is optimal). They are simply an alternate way of organizing the computation than the one given in Section 3.1.

4.2 Counting Operations

The general method to calculate the number of operations in the expression obtained after b fold back-substitution is to express number of operations as a recurrence of the following form.

$$Ops_1 = p; \quad Ops_b = Ops_{b-1} + q$$

In these equations, p is the number of operations in the original expression, b is the degree of back-substitution, and q is the number of additional operations needed to compute coefficients for b fold back-substitution given the coefficients for (b-1) fold back-substitution. In other words, q is simply the number of explicitly displayed operations in the formulas for coefficients given in Section 4.1. Recurrence relations of this form can be used not only to compute total number operations, but also to compute total number of operations of a certain type, *e.g.*, add operations.

4.3 Symmetric Back-substitution

The schema for the code generated by the symmetric back-substitution technique is shown in Figure 10. As in the previous sections, the first sequential loop initializes the recurrence by computing the first b values of s, and the second loop uses the back-substituted expression to accelerate the recurrence.

$$s[1] = s_1; \cdots s[m] = s_m$$

do i = 1, b-1 /* Treat b-1 iterations conventionally */

$$s = a_{1,i}s[1] + \cdots + a_{m,i}s[m] + c_i$$

remap(s)

enddo

do i = b, n   /* Back-substitute remaining iterations */

$$s = A_{1,i}^b s[b] + \cdots + A_{m,i}^b s[b+m-1] + C_i^b$$

remap(s)

enddo

Figure 10: Code schema for symmetric back-substitution

The RecMII of the main loop depends upon the order in which terms are added. Thus, it is important to find an order of summation that gives the minimum RecMII. Finding such an order, however, is a challenge and we don't provide a general solution that works in all cases. The general problem can be stated as follows. Suppose n_i is the number of operation on the path from s[b+i] to s. Then,

$$\mathrm{Re\,cMII} = \mathrm{Max}\left(\frac{\ell n_0}{b}, \frac{\ell n_1}{b+1}, \cdots, \frac{\ell n_{m-1}}{b+m-1}\right),$$

and we need to find the values of $n_0, n_1, \cdots$ that minimizes the RecMII. Note that the optimal solution not only depends on b and m but also on the nature of coefficients (0, 1, loop-invariant etc.) in the original expression.

The two approaches that give near optimal results are as follows. The first is to sum the terms from right to left. This gives near optimal results for small values of b, which is the important case for symmetric back-substitution. The other approach is to sum the terms using a log-tree. This works well for higher values of b, since it becomes important for higher values of b to jointly minimize the lengths of all recurrence paths.

4.4 Blocked Back-substitution

The schema for the code generated by the blocked back-substitution technique is given in Figure 11; see Section 2.3 for the definitions of k(n,b) and e(n, b). The first loop handles iterations that are multiple of b; the second loop executes the remaining iterations sequentially.

The first loop is derived from the original loop as follows. The original loop is unrolled b times. As in the last section, we call each unrolled iteration a minor iteration and call each iteration of the unrolled text consisting of b minor iteration a major iteration. The last m minor iterations are expedited using the back-substitution. The last minor iteration is calculated using b fold back-substitution, the second last using (b-1) fold back-substitution etc. Each of the last m minor iterations in a major iteration is computed as a function of last m values of s computed by the previous major iteration. Another way to view the loop is that each major iteration takes m values from the previous iteration and computes m values in a fast way for the next iteration. The remaining b-m minor iterations in a major iteration are calculated using the original recurrence, eliminating redundant work within these iterations.

$$s[1] = s_1 ; \cdots s[m] = s_m$$

do i = 1, k(n, b), b

$$s = a_{1,i}s[1] + \cdots + a_{m,i}s[m] + c_i \quad \text{/* First minor iteration */}$$

remap(s)

$\vdots$

$$s = a_{1,(i+b-m-1)}s[1] + \cdots + a_{m,(i+b-m-1)}s[m] + c_{(i+b-m-1)}$$

remap(s)

$$s = A_{1,(i+b-m)}^{b-m+1}s[b-m+1] + \cdots + A_{m,(i+b-m)}^{b-m+1}s[b] + C_{i+b-m}^{b-m+1}$$

remap(s)

$\vdots$

/* b^{th} minor iteration */

$$s = A_{1,(i+b-1)}^{b}s[b] + \cdots + A_{m,(i+b-1)}^{b}s[b+m-1] + C_{i+b-1}^{b}$$

remap(s)

enddo

do i = e(n, b), n /*Retire residual iterations conventionally*/

$$s = a_{1,i}s[1] + \cdots + a_{m,i}s[m] + c_i$$

remap(s)

enddo

Figure 11: Code schema for blocked back-substitution

An important point to note is that it is not sufficient to expedite only the last minor iteration using b fold back-substitution. The reason is that, after back-substitution, the last minor iteration uses m values of s computed in the previous major iteration. Expediting only the last minor iteration forces m-1 of these values to be computed sequentially in the previous major iteration, which forces the entire loop to run more or less sequentially.

In the code schema given above, we assume that $b \geq m$, that is the loop is unrolled at least as many times as the order of the recurrence. Applying the blocked back-substitution technique with $b < m$ seems similar to applying the symmetric back-substitution technique and then unrolling the loop. Further work is needed to see if the blocked back-substitution technique offer any advantages over the symmetric back-substitution when $b < m$.

As in the symmetric back-substitution technique, the RecMII of the main loop depends upon the order in which terms are added in each of the expedited iterations. On the other hand, the RecMII doesn't depend upon the summation order used in the first b-m minor iterations, since computation in any of these iterations is not on a critical path. Thus, we can simply use the right to left summation order for the first b - m iterations.

For expedited iterations, it is sufficient to find a summation order that minimizes the RecMII of one of the expedited iteration, since all expedited iterations calculate expressions with identical top-level structure. Consider one of the last b-m minor iteration. Suppose n_i is the number of operation on the path from s[b+i] to s. Since all values of s used in the computation are produced in the previous major iteration, the RecMII for the minor iteration is given by

$$\text{Re cMII} = \text{Max}(\ell n_0, \ell n_1, \cdots, \ell n_{m-1}).$$

And we need to find the values of $n_0, n_1, \cdots$ that minimizes the RecMII. The optimal solution depends on m and on the nature of coefficients (0, 1, loop-invariant etc.) in the original expression, but it doesn't depend upon b. The general strategy to minimize RecMII is to find a summation order in which $n_0 \cdots n_{m-1}$ are all equal. Thus, the log-tree approach for summing the terms gives near optimal results in most cases.

4.5 Performance Metrics for Multiply and Add Case

In this subsection, we present performance metrics for the case when all the coefficients in the recurrence under consideration have non-zero loop-variant values. The performance metrics are presented in the context of architectures that provides pipelined functional units capable of performing add and multiply operations. We assume that an operation can be issued on an unit at each cycle and that the operation latency is ℓ cycles.

Table 1 summarizes the performance metrics for the original program and for the programs obtained after applying the symmetric and the blocked back-substitution techniques. The formulas in the table are in terms of the following variables: the order of the original recurrence m, the degree of back-substitution b, and the latency ℓ. For blocked back-substitution, b is also the number of times the loop is unrolled and is assumed be greater than or equal to m.

Table 1: Performance metrics for the case of non-zero loop-variant coefficients in the context of architectures with + and × operations.

Technique	RecMII	Ops/iter
Original	2ℓ	$2m$
Symmetric	$\dfrac{\ell(m+1)}{b+m-1}$	$b(2m+1)-1$
Blocked $b \geq m$	$\dfrac{\ell}{b}\left(1+\lceil \log_2(m+1)\rceil\right)$	$\dfrac{1}{b}\left(\begin{array}{l}bm(2m+3)\\ -\frac{1}{2}m(m+1)(2m+1)\end{array}\right)$

In the remainder of the subsection, we describe in some detail the derivation of these formulas. For the original program, the right to left order of summing terms gives the minimum value of RecMII and is used to derive the value shown in Table 1. The number of operations performed in each iteration is simply 2m.

For symmetric back-substitution, we consider only the right to left order for summing terms. As pointed out earlier, this summation order gives near optimal results for small values of b, which are more relevant for this technique. For first and second order recurrences, there is no difference between the two approaches, i.e. the right to left order or the log-tree approach. For third order recurrences, the log-tree approach is useful for $b > 6$. For higher orders, b has to be even greater. Assuming the right to left order, RecMII is given by

$$\operatorname{RecMII} = \operatorname{Max}\!\left(\frac{2\ell}{b}, \frac{3\ell}{b+1}, \cdots, \frac{(m+1)\ell}{b+m-1}\right),$$

in which the last term is greater than or equal to all other terms for any $b > 1$. The number of operations performed in each iteration is determined using the methodology suggested in Section 4.2. The recurrence relation for this technique are

$$\operatorname{Ops}_1 = 2m; \quad \operatorname{Ops}_b = \operatorname{Ops}_{b-1} + (2m+1),$$

which are derived by simply looking at the original expression and equations for coefficients given in Section 4.1. Solving this recurrence gives

$$\operatorname{Ops}_b = (b-1)(2m+1) + 2m = b(2m+1) - 1.$$

For blocked back-substitution, the formula for RecMII assumes that terms in each of the expedited iterations are summed using the log-tree, which gives near optimal results in this case. In the formula, $\lceil \log_2(m+1) \rceil$ is the height of the log-tree with $m+1$ terms and 1 accounts for the multiplication performed on each path. The ops/iter metric is derived by summing the contribution of each of the minor iterations. The number of operations in each of the first $b-m$ iterations is identical to that in the original recurrence, which is $2m$. For back-substituted iterations, the recurrence relation used in computing the number of operations turns out to be identical to the one given above for symmetric back-substitution; the summation order has no influence on the operation count. Thus, the number of operation in each of the back-substituted iterations can be obtained by instantiating the equation for Ops_b given above with an appropriate value of b. Therefore, we get

$$\operatorname{Ops/iter} = \tfrac{1}{b}\big((b-m)2m + (b(2m+1)-1) + \cdots + ((b-(m-1))(2m+1)-1)\big),$$

which gives us the formula shown in Table 1.

4.6 Performance Metrics for Fused Multiply-add Case

In this subsection, we present performance metrics in the context of architectures that provide pipelined functional units capable of performing not only add and multiply operations but also a fused multiply-add operation. Some recent architectures provide a fused multiply-add operation for floating-point numbers, and the discussion in this subsection is appropriate for solving arithmetic recurrences on these architectures.

Table 2: Performance metrics for the case of non-zero loop-variant coefficients in the context of architectures with fused multiply-add operation.

Technique	RecMII	Ops/iter
Original	ℓ	m
Symmetric	$\dfrac{\ell m}{b+m-1}$	$b(m+1)-1$
Blocked $b \ge m$	$\dfrac{\ell}{b}\left(1 + \lceil \log_2 m \rceil\right)$	$m=1:\ \dfrac{1}{b}(3b-2)$ $m>1:$ $\dfrac{1}{b}\!\left(\begin{array}{l} bm(m+2)+m\left\lfloor \tfrac{m}{2}\right\rfloor \\ -\tfrac{1}{2}m(m^2+2m+3)\end{array}\right)$

Table 2 summarizes the performance metrics for the original program and for the programs obtained after applying the symmetric and the blocked back-substitution techniques. As in the last subsection, the performance metrics are for the case when all the coefficients in the recurrence under consideration have non-zero loop-variant values. In the formulas, m is the order of the original recurrence, b is the degree of back-substitution, and ℓ is the operation latency. The derivation of these formulas closely follows the method used for the separate multiply and add case with one exception. We carefully recognize every opportunity to collapse a multiply and an add operation into a single fused multiply-add operation. The details of the derivation are not included in this paper for lack of space but can be found in [19].

5 Performance results for selected machines

To put in perspective the results and formulas given in previous sections, we present graphs illustrating the benefits of the symmetric and blocked back-substitution techniques for machines with varying number of functional units and varying operation latency. We consider first order recurrences with non-zero loop-invariant coefficients and consider architectures with functional units capable of performing add and multiply but not fused multiply-add.

Figure 12 presents the benefits of symmetric back-substitution over the original program for machines with 1 to 6 functional units assuming the operation latency ℓ to be 3 cycles. Part (a) of the figure shows the MII of the loop as a function of the degree of back-substitution b (note that b = 1 means the original program). Each curve corresponds to a different number of functional units, which is indicated at the end of the curve. Part (b) presents the same data in terms of speedup for a given machine, that is,

$$\text{speedup} = \frac{\text{MII of the original program for machine with u units and latency } \ell}{\text{MII of the program after back substitution for the same machine}}$$

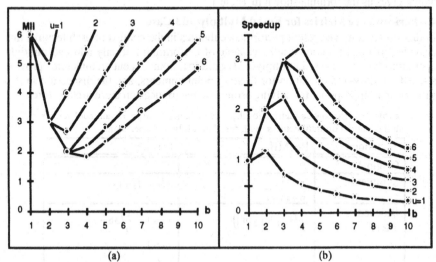

(a)   (b)

Figure 12: Graphs illustrating the benefits of symmetric back-substitution for machines with 1 to 6 functional units for the case of m = 1 and ℓ = 3. (a): MII as a function of b. (b): Speedup as a function of b.

It is evident from Figure 12(a) that, for a given machine, there is an optimal degree of back-substitution b that gives the best performance benefits. This b corresponds to the case when both RecMII and ResMII of the loop after back-substitution are nearly equal. For b less than the optimal value, the RecMII of the loop dominates, and further back-substitution helps in reducing the RecMII. For b greater than the optimal value, the ResMII dominates, and further back-substitution actually decreases the performance.

Figure 13 illustrates the benefits of blocked back-substitution for machines with varying number of functional units under the same assumptions. Again, it is evident from Figure 13(a) that there is an optimal degree of back-substitution that gives the best performance for a given machine.

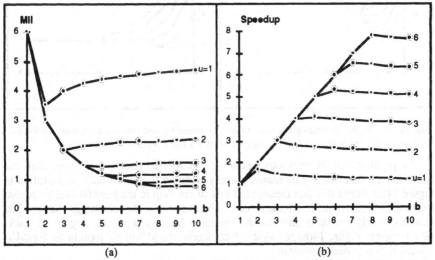

(a)   (b)

Figure 13: Graphs illustrating the benefits of blocked back-substitution for machines with 1 to 6 functional units for the case of m = 1 and ℓ = 3. (a): MII as a function of b. (b): Speedup as a function of b.

A couple of advantages of the blocked back-substitution technique are obvious from Figures 12 and 13. First, for a given machine, the blocked back-substitution technique provides better performance than the symmetric back-substitution. Second, the blocked back-substitution technique is more tolerant of over-substitution than the symmetric back-substitution. That is, for b greater than the optimal value, the performance degradation in the case of blocked back-substitution is not as large as in the case of symmetric back-substitution. Thus, exact determination of the optimal value of b is not as crucial in the case of blocked back-substitution as it is in the case of symmetric back-substitution.

Figure 14 illustrates the benefits of symmetric and blocked back-substitution techniques by varying the operation latency but keeping the number of functional units fixed at 2. The latency assumption for each curve is indicated by a number near the curve.

As in the case of varying number of functional units, there is an optimal value of b for a given latency that gives the best performance. For values of b less than the optimal value, the loop is RecMII-limited; for values of b greater than the optimal value, the loop is ResMII-limited. All the curves in Figure 14(a) or Figure 14(b) reach the same value of MII. This simply reflects the fact that the loop is ResMII-limited and the ResMII of a loop doesn't depend upon the operation latency.

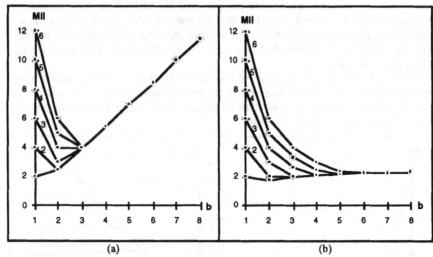

Figure 14: Graphs illustrating the benefits of symmetric (a) and blocked back-substitution (b) with latency varying from 1 to 6 for the case of m = 1 and number of units = 2.

As pointed out in previous sections, symmetric back-substitution has the disadvantage that ops/iter increases linearly with the degree of back-substitution b. Figure 14(a) shows this fact clearly; the MII of the loop in the ResMII-limited region increases linearly with b. Blocked back-substitution has the advantage that ops/iter remains nearly constant and doesn't increase linearly with the degree of back-substitution b. Figure 14(b) shows this fact clearly; the MII of the loop in the ResMII-limited region is nearly constant.

Speedup curves for symmetric and blocked back-substitution with varying latency are not shown in this paper for lack of space but can be found in [19]. Speedup curves with varying latency are very similar to speedup curves with varying functional units because techniques presented in this paper exploit parallelism independent of whether it arises from multiple function units or deeply pipelined function units.

Figure 15 is an attempt to quantify the areas of applicability of the two techniques. It plots the best speedup that can be obtained as a function of the number of functional units for first, second and third order recurrences. We assume the following: recurrences have non-zero loop-variant coefficients, architecture doesn't provide fused multiply-add capability, and operation latency is 3. Each point in the plot is annotated with the technique and the optimal value of b that achieves that speedup. In an annotation, the letter denotes the technique that gives the best speedup—O stands for the original program, S for the symmetric back-substitution, and B for the blocked back-substitution. The number in an annotation denotes the optimal value of b.

Figure 15 shows that the choice of the appropriate technique depends upon both the order of the recurrence and the parallelism provided by the machine. For first and second order recurrences, blocked back-substitution is the best technique under the assumptions mentioned above. For the third order case, the speedup curve shows that there are three distinct regions based on the parallelism in the machine; the regions are not explicitly shown in the figure but can be deduced by looking at the labels. In the first region, neither of the back-substitution techniques have much to offer. In the second region, symmetric and blocked back-substitution provide similar benefits. In the third region, blocked back-substitution is the best technique. Although the figure doesn't show it, there is also a fourth region where symmetric back-substitution performs better than blocked back-substitution. This happens when the order of the recurrence is high and the machine provide only a moderate amount of parallelism. In this case, the optimal value of b is very low (2 or 3). However, blocked back-substitution technique as defined in this paper requires b to be greater than m. Symmetric back-substitution, on the other hand, has no such limitation.

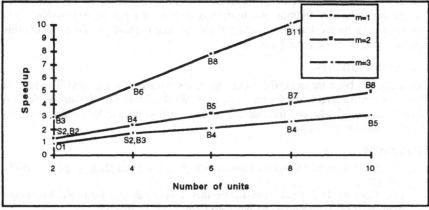

Figure 15: The best speedup that can be achieved for first, second, and third order recurrences. Each point is annotated with the technique and the optimal value of b. Operation latency is 3.

The actual speedup numbers presented in Figure 15 are, in some sense, a lower bound on speedup because they assume the most general form for coefficients, *i.e.*, non-zero loop-invariant values, and assume that the architecture provides only add and multiply operations. The actual speedup numbers would be much better if either of these assumptions are relaxed.

6 Conclusions

The graphs presented in Section 5 clearly indicate that both symmetric and blocked back-substitution techniques provide performance improvements for machines having some degree of parallelism. This is especially true for first and second order recurrences. Back-substitution techniques can exploit parallelism from either multiple or pipelined functional units.

Symmetric back-substitution may provide better performance if the order of recurrence is high and the machine has a low degree of parallelism. The penalty for back-substituting too far with symmetric back-substitution is greatly reduced performance due to rapid growth in operation count.

The blocked back-substitution technique as defined in this paper has an inherent limitation in that it requires b to be greater than m (the order of recurrence). This makes it inapplicable in the context of higher order recurrences and machines with low degree of parallelism where optimal value of b is quite small. In all other cases, the blocked back-substitution provides better performance improvement. Further work is needed to see if blocked back-substitution offers any advantages over symmetric back-substitution when b < m .

When it is useful to expose significant parallelism using a high degree of back-substitution, blocked back-substitution has significantly lower operation count than symmetric back-substitution. Blocked back-substitution allows the exposure of an arbitrary degree of parallelism from a recurrence with no more than a constant multiplier in operation count. The number of operations required for blocked back-substitution does not increase significantly with increased degree of back-substitution and, because of this, one can choose a degree of back-substitution somewhat higher than optimal with little penalty.

This work can be generalized to treat loops with conditional recurrences and loops with exits. In the context of processors that support predicated execution, if-conversion can be used to transform branching code to an algebraic expression. Such expressions can be accelerated using techniques similar to those presented within this paper and will be explored in future work.

Acknowledgments

This work has been influenced by conversations with Bob Rau, Ross Towle, and others who contributed to the Cydra 5 compiler. Work with Robbe Walstra at Hewlett Packard Laboratories helped indicate the weakness of symmetric back-substitution as a height reduction technique.

References

1. H. S. Stone. Parallel Tridiagonal Equation Solvers. ACM Trans Math. Softw 1, 4 (1975), 289-307.
2. S.-C. Chen and D. J. Kuck. Time and Parallel Processor Bounds for Linear Recurrence Systems. IEEE Transactions on Computers C-24, 7 (1975), 701-717.
3. D. Heller. Some Aspects of the Cyclic Reduction Algorithm for Block Tridiagonal Linear Systems. SIAM J. Numerical Anal. 13, 4 (1976), 484-496.
4. A. H. Sameh and R. P. Brent. Solving Triangular Systems on a Parallel Computer. SIAM J. Numerical Analysis 14, 6 (1977), 1101-1113.
5. D. J. Kuck. The structure of Computers and Computations. (Wiley, New York, 1978).
6. S. C. Chen, D. J. Kuck, and A. H. Sameh. Practical Parallel Band Triangular System Solvers. ACM Transactions on Mathematical Software 4, (1978), 270-277.
7. H. H. Wang. A Parallel Method for Tridiagonal Equations. ACM Transactions on Mathematical Software 7, 2 (1981), 170-183.
8. H. A. Van Der Vorst and K. Dekker. Vectorization of Linear Recurrence Relations. SIAM Journal on Scientific and Statistical Computing 10, 1 (1989), 27-35.
9. Y. Tanaka, et al. Compiling Techniques for First-Order Linear Recurrences on a Vector Computer. Proceedings of the Supercomputing Conference (Orlando, FL., 1988), 174-180.
10. D. Callahan. Recognizing and Parallelizing Bounded Recurrences. Proceedings of the Fourth Workshop on Languages and Compilers for Parallel Processing (Santa Clara, CA, 1991).
11. J. A. Fisher. Trace Scheduling: A Technique for Global Microcode Compaction. IEEE Transactions on Computers C-30, (1981), 478-490.
12. G. Lowney, et al. The Multiflow Trace Scheduling Compiler. The Journal of Supercomputing 7, 1/2 (1993), 51-142.
13. W.-M. W. Hwu, et al. The Superblock: An Effective Technique for VLIW and Superscalar Compilation. The Journal of Supercomputing 7, 1/2 (1993), 229-248.
14. B. R. Rau and C. D. Glaeser. Some Scheduling Techniques and an Easily Schedulable Horizontal Architecture for High Performance Scientific Computing. Proceedings of the Fourteenth Annual Workshop on Microporgramming (1981), 183-198.

15. M. S.-L. Lam, A Systolic Array Optimizing Compiler. 1987, Carnegie Mellon University:

16. B. Rau. Data Flow and Dependence Analysis for Instruction Level Parallelism. Proceedings of the Fourth Workshop on Languages and Compilers for Parallel Computing (Santa Clara, CA, 1992), 236-250.

17. B. R. Rau, M. S. Schlansker, and P. P. Tirumalai. Code Generation Schemas for Modulo Scheduled DO-Loops and WHILE-Loops. Proceedings of the 25th Annual International Symposium on Microarchitecture (Portland, Oregon, 1992), 158-169.

18. J. C. Dehnert and R. A. Towle. Compiling for the Cydra 5. The Journal of Supercomputing 7, 1/2 (1993), 181-227.

19. M. Schlansker and V. Kathail, Acceleration of Algebraic Recurrences on Processors with Instruction Level Parallelism. Technical Report HPL-93-55. Hewlett-Packard Laboratories, 1993.

Efficient Compile-Time/Run-Time Contraction of Fine Grain Data Parallel Codes *

Richard Neves[1] and Robert B. Schnabel[2]

[1] Department of Computer Science, Campus Box 430, University of Colorado, Boulder, Colorado, 80309, U.S.A. (neves@cs.colorado.edu)
[2] Department of Computer Science, Campus Box 430, University of Colorado, Boulder, Colorado, 80309, U.S.A. (bobby@cs.colorado.edu)

Abstract. This research studies the contraction problem for data parallel languages. That is, we seek to efficiently execute code written for a fine grain virtual parallel machine on a much coarser grain actual parallel machine. This paper identifies issues involved in solving this problem. Three issues are then addressed in detail: efficiently implementing tasks to emulate virtual processors, efficiently scheduling these tasks, and reducing space overhead while maintaining data consistency among these tasks. In implementing tasks, saving a reduced register state at context switches is addressed. For scheduling tasks, heuristics are proposed that minimize scheduling cost and promote data locality. Minimizing space overhead using assumptions about the communication paradigm, run-time techniques and compile-time analysis is also discussed. Finally, experimental results are presented concerning one of the main issues discussed, scheduling. The results show that the proposed scheduling heuristics are both cost efficient and promote data locality for three different problems when compared to three other scheduling policies.

1 Introduction

This research studies techniques needed to compile and execute fine grain, data parallel codes on coarser grain multiprocessors. This is known as the contraction problem. Fine grain data parallel codes are generated by programming models that assume a virtual parallel machine with many more processors than the targeted, physical machine. By allowing a language to assume a virtual parallel machine, the programmer can specify a data parallel algorithm at a granularity appropriate to an algorithm and problem, and disregard how many processors the algorithm will actually run on.

The research addresses a specific domain of languages: data parallel languages. These languages are intended mainly for numerical computation. The issues that are studied are most directly relevant to explicitly parallel languages such as PC [3], or DINO [21], but may also be relevant to implicitly data parallel languages such as Fortran D [11] or High Performance Fortran [23]. It is

---

* Research supported by NSF grants ASC-9015577 and CDA-8922510.

assumed that information regarding how data is mapped to virtual processors and how virtual processors are mapped to physical processors is provided. This assumption is generally satisfied by such languages.

Within the domain of data parallelism, the research addresses at least three communication paradigms: Block-SIMD (BSIMD) with communication points identifiable at compile-time, BSIMD with communication points only identifiable at run-time, and the general send/receive paradigm. These three paradigms span different approaches to data parallel programming. (BSIMD is sometimes referred to as loosely synchronous.) In BSIMD each piece of data is "owned" by a single virtual processor. Each processor only can modify the data that it owns, but processors can read data owned by any other processors. The language specifies a "block" (e.g. a parallel loop), and modifications of data in the current block are only viewable by other processors after the next block boundary. Semantically, data is exchanged only at block boundaries. Processors that do not own a piece of data, read the version of that data before the previous block boundary, while the processor that owns a piece of data reads the current value of that data. Kali [18], DYNO [28], Fortran D [11], and High Performance FORTRAN [23] are some examples of BSIMD. Fortran D and High Performance FORTRAN can be viewed as BSIMD in their use of loop parallelism. In most cases, communication points are identifiable at compile-time in these languages. DYNO is an example of BSIMD where communication points are determined at run-time. This is also true of Kali, Fortran D, and High performance FORTRAN when index arrays are utilized. The general send/receive paradigm is provided by vendors as the default means of programming their multiprocessors. The paradigm is also found in languages like DINO where it is augmented with distributed data mappings.

A distributed memory MIMD multiprocessor is assumed in this research. In addition, machines that support small, low latency messages are well-suited to contracting fine grain code, which will have a propensity to generate many small messages. Therefore, support for such messages [10, 20] is related to this research but it is not our focus in this paper. When a low latency interface is unavailable, aggregation of small messages becomes necessary. Though aggregation is also part of the research, it is only addressed briefly in this paper.

One possible approach to the contraction problem is for the compiler to generate an equivalent, efficient program whose number of processes matches the number of physical processors. This is done in the SIMD language Dataparallel C [13], for example, by using for-loops to emulate virtual processors. This allows several virtual processors to execute as one process on a physical processor. This contraction mechanism is possible because the SIMD semantics of the language state that no interactions between virtual processors may exist. Our assumptions are considerably less restrictive.

In fact, we do not take this purely compile-time approach to contraction in this research, for two reasons. First, it is difficult or impossible to efficiently contract parallel programs at compile-time as the complexity of the program or of the communication paradigm grows. This is particularly true for general send/receive code. Second, it may be more efficient to allow multiple virtual processors (as tasks) per physical processor to mask communication costs, even in models such as BSIMD [24].

For these reasons, we pursue a mixed compile-time/run-time approach to the contraction problem. In studying the contraction problem from this viewpoint, the goal of this research is to minimize the overhead resulting from contraction of fine grain computation. One source of overhead is the time it takes to switch between virtual processors. This includes the time needed to save the current state and restore the state of the next virtual processor. It is also important to reduce overhead due to scheduling virtual processors. It is imperative that the choice of which virtual processor to schedule next be made very inexpensively in almost all instances. Closely related to the scheduling issue is the overhead that can arise from poor use of the cache. Virtual processors executing on the same processor will have a high miss rate if the order in which virtual processors are scheduled does not account for locality of reference. Another source of overhead is the memory consumed in order to maintain consistent views of data among virtual processors. Virtual processors that communicate on the same processor will actually read and write data, as opposed to sending and receiving data over a network. One goal is to keep as few copies of this communicated data on the processor as possible. Finally, overhead may result from communication of small messages between virtual processors on different physical processors, if message latency on the parallel computer is high. Our goal is to minimize the above overhead so that it possible to contract codes where the amount of computation between context switches is as little as 20-40 flops.

The approach to task emulation taken in this research is to emulate each virtual processor with a task abstraction that is managed partly at compile time and partly at run time so that the time to switch between two tasks is minimized. The bulk of this switching cost is due to saving and restoring register state [1]. We consider two approaches to the issue of register optimization. Both of these approaches can be expressed using either continuations [9] or threads. Using different techniques, these two task implementations can result in the same register allocation, but will differ in how efficiently stack space is used.

In addition to implementing tasks, an inexpensive means of scheduling tasks is another key issue in this research. Scheduling accounts for a significant part of the overhead in contracting very fine grain tasks at run-time. We assert that, in this special context, scheduling can be performed at a fraction of the cost of traditional and more general approaches. To achieve this goal, we have designed a set of scheduling heuristics that attempt to minimize scheduling overhead by using communication patterns found in data parallel programs. Another goal of these heuristics is to maximize cache locality by scheduling tasks that share data consecutively when possible.

The proposed scheduling heuristics will be compared to scheduling policies that function independent of the application. We seek to show that the application dependent scheduling method as we propose is less costly and promotes locality as well or better than application independent methods. In fact, we seek to approach the data locality found in manually contracted code. In the "Preliminary Results" section, the proposed heuristics are compared to LIFO, FIFO, and random scheduling policies. LIFO and FIFO are inexpensive, yet provide no direct way of promoting cache locality among communicating virtual processors. A random policy will motivate the need to address data locality in contraction. By comparing with these three policies, the proposed heuristic's success in attaining the seemingly conflicting goals of low cost and good data locality will be measured.

The solution of the contraction problem requires cooperation between the compiler and run-time system. In compiling virtual processor code, information needs to be provided to the run-time system. This information includes data to virtual processor and virtual processor to physical processor mappings. If it is possible, off-processor communication points should be identified at compile-time. Information regarding how data is stored is also helpful to aid the scheduling heuristics in improving locality of reference. In this research, we assume that this information is made available by the compiler since this is a reasonable assumption for many data parallel programming languages. Our future research may seek to relax some of these assumptions.

While this paper will focus on issues of task implementation, task scheduling, and reducing space overhead, additional compile time analysis which is beneficial to contraction will be addressed in greater detail in future research. In contracting virtual processor code, varying compiler transformations will be necessary. These include creating templates for data local to virtual processor code such that virtual processor instances can access this data in the heap, reducing stack space usage (when using threads), and performing the compiler analysis to transform code to a continuation-friendly form (when using continuations). Compile-time analysis also will be necessary to reduce space overhead and promote locality. For example, dependence analysis performed by the compiler can reduce the need for run-time duplication of data. Moving block points (when it is legal to do so) and postponing duplication until necessary are two means of accomplishing this. Both compile-time and run-time analysis will be needed in performing the message aggregation necessary for multiprocessors which do not support low latency, small message communication.

This paper is primarily a preliminary discussion of the issues involved in the approach to contraction outlined above. The next three sections discuss issues and approaches for task implementation, task scheduling, and reducing space overhead respectively. The final section presents preliminary experimental results on the costs of several scheduling strategies and their effects upon data locality.

2 Implementing Tasks

As stated in section 1, the approach that appears necessary for the contraction problem considered in this research is emulate virtual processors with a task abstraction mechanism managed partly at compile-time and partly at run-time to. The term task is used abstractly to refer to the emulation mechanism (e.g.

threads or continuations) that is used. This compile-time/run-time combination is necessary because compiler involvement is needed to generate efficient context switches and reduce space overhead, while run-time involvement is essential to handle communication-dependent synchronization.

In implementing tasks, two key considerations are that context switch cost and stack space usage must be minimized. Minimal context switch cost is vital in supporting fine granularity. An important factor in reducing context switch cost is reducing the number of registers saved and restored at context switches. Minimizing stack usage is important because the potential for heavy stack space memory consumption is greater for fine granularity in multitasking models

Two interesting possibilities in implementing tasks at the user level are threads and continuations. In this paper, a thread refers to a non-preemptive, light-weight, user-level task which does not enter the operating system on a context switch. The second, continuation-based, task abstraction has its roots in the language community [7, 14, 17, 26, 27] and has recently been applied as a portable, light-weight task abstraction in the Mach kernel [9]. Unlike the use of continuations in [9], this research considers only context switching within the same address space. The use of continuation-based tasks assumes that the code is restructured by the compiler such that for every receive (potential block point), there is a corresponding function that executes all the code following the receive. This function is called the continuation of current task. If the task blocks at the receive, the continuation function represents the functional state of the task. The task also has a data state which is stored in the heap.

When implemented in the standard way, as general purpose run-time mechanisms, threads and continuations have contrasting properties. Threads have a fairly high context switch cost since register state must be saved and restored (which allows register optimization). Continuations have far lower context switch cost, but are far less advantageous for register optimization due to the fact that functions are inserted at every potential context switch. This prevents the compiler from associating the code which would normally be executed when the context switch does not occur with the code analyzed to that point. Although the approaches differ significantly when implemented as stated, both can be improved and the differences between them become far fewer, when they are modified using compile-time information available in the special context of this research.

To achieve the efficiency that is needed in the contraction context, the compiler must cooperate in implementing tasks. In the case of threads, compiler cooperation allows the thread context switch to avoid saving and restoring unused registers. For a continuation-based implementation, compiler cooperation allows the introduction of register optimization by including the code following a continuation function call in the register analysis. (This requires that continuation calls save and restore the required register state.) Additionally, in the thread-based task implementation, the compiler can move data allocated on a thread's stack to separately allocated memory, thus allowing a stack size that more closely matches that actually needed by the task. Note that a continuation-based task implementation does not require this optimization since each continuation shares a single stack. Once the compile-time register analysis is incorporated in continuations, it appears that the only difference between thread-based and continuation-based task implementations will be stack usage.

Another interesting issue is that to some extent, effective register optimization and fast context switches are conflicting goals in this research. The benefit of storing data in registers [6] may be offset by the cost of saving and restoring these registers at context switches [1]. The difficulty is that a context switch may not always occur. At compile-time, only the potential block points can be identified. Whether a context switch actually occurs may depend, for example, on how long a message takes to arrive. Because a context switch cannot be predicted, we are left with two choices. One choice is to treat the blocks of code before and after the context switch as disjoint during local register optimization. In doing so, no registers would need to be saved and restored during the context switch. Another choice is to treat the blocks of code before and after a context switch as always contiguous during execution. In this case, those registers allocated through register optimization would need to be saved at the context switch. That is, only those registers in active use would need to be saved [25]. It is likely that the best approach will be to combine the above choices by allowing the compiler to decide on a case by case basis which to use. This judgment would be made based on how well register optimization could be performed on the said code block, the cost of saving registers on the host architecture, and an assumption that context switches will occur. This will be a topic of future research.

Our research will implement and test both thread-based and continuation-based task mechanisms to assess the issues discussed above. It should be mentioned that, regardless of how tasks are implemented, some amount of compiler optimization is lost simply by programming at a fine granularity to begin with. Register optimization may prove ineffective when compared to the resulting context switch cost and frequency of context switches. Additionally, manually contracted code would make copious use of loops (in simple cases), which would allow the compiler to perform a number of loop optimizations that may not be possible in our automatic approach. Manual contraction would also attempt to promote locality directly, whereas we address this indirectly. Our research will evaluate the effects of these factors.

3 Scheduling Tasks

In addition to efficient task mechanisms, a key to efficient, automatic contraction is very efficient methods for scheduling tasks. Uniprocessor scheduling heuristics are needed that attempt to minimize scheduling cost and promote cache locality in the context of the contraction problem. It has been noted that scheduling order is important to data locality [19]. Simple scheduling heuristics such as FIFO (first in first out) and LIFO (last in first out) scheduling can be used (see e.g. [5]), but do not take advantage of the special characteristics of the scheduling problem in the contraction context, namely, the availability of information about communication partners. None of the specialized and more complex uniprocessor scheduling policies that we are aware of (such as those which are priority-based) are both applicable to this situation and computationally inexpensive. For this reason, we have designed new scheduling heuristics for use in the contraction problem.

In this section, we will motivate and describe the new scheduling heuristics for the contraction problem, and discuss how they compare to a FIFO scheduling policy. By comparing the proposed heuristics with a FIFO policy, the low cost of communication-based scheduling is illustrated. The comparison is also instructive in showing that the effort in promoting cache locality is worthwhile and need not come at a high scheduling cost. An experimental comparison with FIFO, LIFO and a random policy is given in Section 5.

To motivate our approach, first consider a FIFO ready list scheduling policy. When a task begins or resumes execution, it is removed from the ready list. If the task blocks, another task is taken from the head of the list and run. (We assume that a task blocks on exactly one receive at a time.) The former task does not return to the end of the ready list until the reason it blocked is no longer applicable (i.e. when a message the task is waiting for has been sent). This approach has two undesirable characteristics in the context of this research:

1. For each scheduling decision, the task at the head of the ready list is removed for execution. When an executing task sends data to a blocked task (which was waiting for the send), the blocked task is added to the end of the ready list. Thus, the ready list is managed twice (on average) per scheduling decision.

2. When adding tasks to the ready list, no effort is made to order the tasks such that data locality is promoted. Thus, the resulting scheduling order of tasks may be arbitrary with respect to data locality.

In the proposed heuristics, the ready list overhead found in the first point is avoided altogether in most scheduling decisions. The overhead described in the second point is reduced by attempting to consecutively schedule tasks that compute on shared data. Before describing these heuristics, we define some terminology.

The proposed heuristics differentiate between two types of tasks: external and internal. External tasks communicate at least once with tasks mapped to other (actual) processors, while internal tasks only communicate with tasks on the same processor. Note that the terminology allows external tasks to also communicate with tasks on the same processor. When a communication primitive (i.e. a send or receive) communicates off-processor, it is referred to as an external communication (e.g. an external send). Likewise, on-processor communications are referred to as internal (e.g. an internal receive). We say that an internal receive occurs when the receiving process runs and reads the new value.

The new heuristics avoid the manipulation of a run-time data structure, such as a ready list, entirely in most situations. In particular, this can be done when it is possible to switch to a task's communication partner. Suppose that task A blocks on a receive from an internal task B. If task B is scheduled next, it is possible that the send from task B that task A is blocked on will be executed when task B next executes. If this is the case, then task A will be able to resume execution any time after task B suspends execution. So, instead of choosing a task from the ready list to schedule next when task A blocks, a reasonable strategy is to schedule the task specified in task A's receive directive. Note that this scheduling decision can be made without having to manage a ready list. In fact, the only computation necessary is to determine whether B is an internal, ready task. This information can be made available at minimal computational expense during the course of internal communication by setting the status of a receiving task to "ready" when the sending task sends the required data item. A mechanism similar to I-Structures [2] can be used for this. (Issues in implementing I-Structures in similar context are discussed in [22].) This heuristic will be referred to as "scheduling the sending task", and will be the first scheduling heuristic. Clearly, it has made significant use of the special information about communications that are available in this contraction context.

"Scheduling the sending task" does not account for every scheduling decision. Suppose a task blocks on an external receive (i.e. from an off-processor task). It is not possible to schedule the sending task since the sending task resides on another actual processor. As another example, suppose a task blocks on an internal receive, but the sending task itself is blocked. It is not possible to scheduling the sending task in this case either. A possible task to schedule next, which is also a communication partner, would be a previous internal receiving task. By this we mean an internal task which the blocked task has sent data to in the past, and which has not yet received that data. Note that there could be more than one task fitting this description, so the task the blocked task sent data to most recently is chosen. This heuristic will be referred to as "scheduling a receiving task" and is the second scheduling heuristic. Its implementation cost will be discussed later.

In the discussion thus far, two scheduling approaches have been utilized: 1) scheduling the sending task and 2) scheduling a previous receiving task. Both approaches are insufficient when:

"Scheduling the sending task" is impossible because the current task is blocked on an external receive, or the current task is blocked on an internal receive and the sending task is blocked.

and

"Scheduling a previous receiving task" is impossible because all previous send partners are blocked (on other receives).

Another scheduling option is necessary when these situations occur. So far, the heuristics have neglected external tasks which have become ready due to an external communication. Such a task motivates another scheduling heuristic. By keeping external tasks on their own external ready list, the list can be used as a third scheduling option when "scheduling the sending task" or "scheduling a previous receiving task" fails. After an external task has blocked, it is added to the external ready list when the internal or external send that it blocked on has been executed. (This implies that an asynchronous receive handler for off-processor communication exists.) External tasks are removed from the external ready list when they are scheduled to run. Since this external ready list only contains external tasks, the cost of maintaining it is not as expensive as maintaining a list for every task (since this would imply managing the list at every context switch). In addition, scheduling external tasks in a separate ready list coincides with off-processor communication except in those cases where external tasks block on receiving data from internal tasks. Thus, the overhead in managing the ready list is often dominated by the cost of off-processor communication incurred when external tasks block on external receives (unless message latency is extremely low relative to managing a linked list). Also, external communications are assumed to constitute a small percentage of all communications in a fine-grain data parallel program, so this list is expected to be used for only a small portion of the scheduling decisions. Thus, the third scheduling approach is the use of an external ready list.

We expect to show in a future paper that the above three heuristics are sufficient for a broad class of data parallel codes meeting certain requirements (except in the termination phase of execution). These requirements are not formalized here, but this contention is supported by preliminary simulation results (see Section 5).

In order to account for all possible codes, however, a fourth approach is needed as a safety net. The fourth approach (referred to as lookup) involves finding ready tasks that the above heuristics were unable to uncover. It is described in more detail below. This fourth step is the most expensive, but should account for a very small minority of most scheduling decisions.

In summary, the proposed scheduling heuristics determine which task to schedule next as follows:

step #1 If the current task is blocked on an *internal receive* and the sending internal task is not blocked then switch to the corresponding *sending task*

step #2 else if there exists an internal ready task that has not yet received a message sent by the current task since the last context switch then switch to this *receiving task*

step #3 else if the external ready list is not empty then switch to the head of the external ready list

step #4 else lookup a ready task

These heuristics impose an implicit execution order on tasks that is based on communication dependencies. They attempt to utilize very inexpensive scheduling methods for most context switches, and to use the least expensive means of switching between tasks first. A goal of this research is to show that the scheduling of tasks using this approach has low overhead, and that the overhead is considerably lower than an approach which maintains a ready list of all tasks. Now we briefly discuss the cost of these heuristics relative to ready list management overhead.

Step #1 must test that the receive is internal and that the sending task is not blocked. The sending task is then scheduled. A comparison of the cost of this step to the ready list management code, on two representative workstations, shows that step #1 costs approximately 1/2 of managing a ready list.

Step #2 requires that each time a send occurs, if the corresponding receive has not occurred, then the receiving task identification be stored for future reference. Thus, when the task blocks, it need only check that this task identification refers to a ready task. Including the conditional branch in step #1, the cost, measured in the same way as for step #1, is approximately 2/3 the cost of managing a ready list.

The cost of step #3 is approximately 1/2 greater than ready list management when one includes the conditional branches in steps one and two. But since each utilization of step #3 corresponds to an external communication which has far higher overhead, this extra cost is not significant. Also, the ratio of external to internal tasks is typically quite low, meaning that step #3 is used infrequently.

Step #4 requires that a ready task be found among all tasks. It may appear that a linear search is necessary to find such a task, but in practice this is not the case. It can be shown that Step #4 will only be needed when the only ready tasks are those which have not and will not communicate with any other tasks, or when the only ready tasks are those which will not communicate with any other tasks. Our intuition from limited experience, is that these situations occur only during the final phase of most data parallel algorithms. Thus, both of these situations can efficiently be addressed by keeping track of which tasks have begun execution and which tasks have terminated, thereby reducing the computation needed to search for a ready task. Keeping track of this incurs a one-time startup cost and a one-time termination cost for each task, which is approximately equivalent to the cost of managing a ready list for each context switch in a FIFO policy. In addition to this one time cost, the cost of using step #4 is amounts to finding a ready task in this termination list. In practice we find that the first dereference yields a ready task. This research aims to show that this one time cost is easily amortized over all context switches, and that the use of step #4 is a very small percentage of all context switches for most data parallel algorithms.

In summary, we have discussed heuristics that reduce scheduling overhead by switching among tasks in a communication-based ordering. This should allow inexpensive scheduling heuristics to be used most of the time. In addition, since the proposed heuristics promote switching between communicating internal tasks and since communicating tasks often access as adjacent portions of the main data structures in parallel programs, the heuristics are likely to encourage cache locality in data references. To assess these heuristics, we are conducting experiments using a wide variety of communication patterns for the three communication paradigms considered in this research. Section 5 gives a preliminary indication of the performance of these heuristics on four applications using careful estimates of the cost of each step and simulating the resulting data locality.

4 Space Overhead

In discussing the scheduling and implementation of tasks in the previous two sections, the time overhead incurred in using tasks to emulate virtual processors was the primary concern. The critical issues included context switch time, efficiency due to register optimizations, and efficiency of the scheduling heuristics.

Contraction of a fine-grain virtual machine to a much coarser grain actual parallel machine can also imply a great deal of space overhead due to data duplication. In this section we briefly motivate this problem, and discuss some possible approaches to reducing space overhead.

Data duplication is often necessary to maintain consistent versions of distributed data among virtual processors. Assume first that in a general send/receive paradigm is being used, and consider a situation where a virtual processor (VP) sends the value of a variable to another VP on the same physical processor. Suppose the sender continues to modify the variable just sent. If only one copy of the variable were kept on the actual processor, the receiving VP would see the subsequent modifications that the sender made to the variable, which is not the intention. In this situation, one copy of the variable is not sufficient to maintain a consistent view among the sender and receiver. It is not difficult to envision a situation where n VPs communicate m pieces of data to each other and m*n copies are needed. Of course, such a situation assumes that a VP communicates a piece of data only once. An indeterminate number of copies may be needed if the VPs send/modify data over and over again.

However, the amount of data duplication that can be required is dependent on the communication paradigm. As illustrated above, a general send and receive paradigm could require enormous amounts of space to maintain consistency. On the other hand, the BSIMD model puts constraints on when virtual processors can modify distributed data, thus reducing the number of copies required. In this model, each data item is "owned" by exactly one VP. If a VP does not own a piece of data, any reads of that data item refer to the version that existed at the previous synchronization point (this version will be the same for all non-owner VPs). During a block, the owner of the data in the BSIMD model can modify its own copy of the data, but the values of this items that the other VPs use is not affected. This means that at most two copies of each piece of distributed data are needed (one pre-block copy and one local copy for the owner VP) regardless of how many other VPs read the data, as long as there is global synchronization at block boundaries.

In general, the space overhead that arises in automatically contracting a data parallel program can be reduced by adding synchronization, using dependence information to postpone duplication of a data item, and constraining the programming model. We now briefly discuss each of the first two possibilities, and then discuss the third in a a little more detail.

First, if memory is limited, the contraction system can put a limit on how much duplication is allowable by forcing the computation to synchronize. For example, suppose that one is using an unrestricted send/receive model, and that no more than six copies of any one piece of data were allowed on the actual processor. Every time a VP encountered a send, a new copy of data would need to be created. When the number of copies reaches six, the run-time system could block the sending VP until one of its previous recipients of the same data item no longer needs its copy (because it received a new version, or it terminated, etc.). The tradeoff is that eventually this limit on data duplication may become a limit on parallelism. (Also, there is a theoretical possibility of introducing deadlock through this limit, but the circumstances that would be required to cause this seem highly unlikely to occur in real parallel programs.) If all of the recipients are unable to relinquish a copy of the data in question because one of them is waiting on an off processor communication, parallelism is lost.

Second, dependence information can be used to reduce space overhead. A simplistic approach to duplicating data is to create a new version of an item each time it is sent. This insures that the sender will have a private value to modify after the send. If the run-time system knew that the sender was not going to modify the data until much later in the code, the duplication could be postponed until that point. When this point is reached, it may not be necessary to duplicate the data because the sender yielded to receiver in the interim and the receiver is no longer reading the data. In other words, the data item should only be duplicated when it is a live data item.

Third, space overhead can be reduced by constraining the programming model. BSIMD illustrates a model where synchronization restrictions reduce data duplication. Only VPs which own a specific data item can modify that data item. This keeps the number of VPs creating versions of data items to one VP per data item instead of many VPs per data item. Even without global synchronization, this constrains the maximum number of copies of a data item to the number of times the same data item is sent by a VP. As mentioned previously, if the semantic constraint imposed by BSIMD, that each VP must synchronize at block boundaries, is strictly implemented, this further reduces the number of copies of each data item to two. In this case data is exchanged between the virtual processors only at the block boundaries. VPs cannot continue into the next block until each of them has reached the block boundary and communicated the relevant data with other VPs.

It should be noted, however, that implementing this global synchronization that is semantically imposed by BSIMD, as in the more general case above, potentially reduces parallelism. Furthermore, synchronizing at block boundaries is not always necessary. A VP can continue computation past a block boundary until it first reads data:

- which it doesn't own, and
- which has not yet been written to for the last time by the owner in a previous block (when a VP modifies data for the last time in a block, it can send this data to the VPs which read the data in the next block).

Parallelism may be lost when it is possible for a VP to compute past a block boundary and it instead waits on another VP to reach that boundary.

A solution is to relax the synchronization requirement and allow VPs to continue into the next block as long as the above conditions are satisfied. It is important to require that the synchronization is relaxed only when computation in the current block by other VPs on the same actual processor is not possible. This requirement insures that data is only duplicated in those situations where duplication is necessary for the sake of parallelism. Relaxing the synchronization requirement exposes a tradeoff between space overhead and parallelism.

It should be noted that even with this tradeoff, the BSIMD programming model still reduces space overhead. Ownership of data insures that only one VP per data item need make local copies of data. More significantly, the model forces each VP to lexographically encounter the same number of block boundaries. This allows the run-time system to recognize when duplicates of data can be discarded. This problem is significantly more difficult in the send/receive paradigm.

In summary, by introducing synchronizations, taking advantage of dependence information, and using constraints inherit to the communication paradigm, the space overhead connected with contracting a massively parallel program can be reduced, and probably be kept to an acceptable level. Our research is exploring these issues, starting with the space versus parallelism tradeoff in contracting BSIMD programs that was described above. These results are not part of the preliminary results reported in this paper.

5 Preliminary Results

This section presents and analyzes results of preliminary tests that we made to asses the scheduling heuristics discussed in Section 3. Recall that the goals of the proposed scheduling heuristics are two-fold. First, the heuristics attempt to minimize the computational overhead in choosing the next task to execute. Second, the heuristics attempt to promote overall data locality such that the resulting cache miss rate is comparable to that of manually contracted code.

Three test applications were used to evaluate the scheduling overhead and cache behavior of the proposed heuristics when compared to other policies. These applications are simple Jacobi iterative solvers using these different stencils: five-point star, nine-point cross, and nine-point square. These applications are very common kernels in numerical methods, and are typical BSIMD applications. The results separated in this section are for a 100x100 grid per actual processor, with one virtual processor per grid point. Smaller grids were also tested, and led to roughly the same conclusion except for unrealistically small grids. (One grid point per virtual processor is the natural way to program these algorithms.)

In evaluating scheduling overhead, we compare the new heuristics to FIFO and LIFO scheduling policies. Both the FIFO and LIFO policies demonstrate the use of a single data structure to store ready tasks. We seek to show that maintaining such a data structure is unnecessary and that by avoiding its use, the overall scheduling overhead can be reduced significantly.

In investigating data locality, we compare the miss rates resulting from applying the new heuristics to the miss rates resulting from the use of FIFO and LIFO scheduling policies. In addition, a random scheduling policy is simulated for each application to provide worst case cache miss rates. We show that data locality doesn't suffer from the use of inexpensive scheduling heuristics.

The test applications were run within a contraction simulator that we constructed. The simulator requires as input a virtual machine, a set of virtual processors and their data, and a mapping of the data to the virtual machine. After initialization, the simulation is driven by the communication between virtual processors. A multitasking library, Awesime [12], is used to implement the virtual processors. Awesime is an object-oriented library for parallel programming and process-oriented simulation. Although Awesime provides extensive support for simulation, modifications were needed to support LIFO and random scheduling policies. The Awesime package also needed to be modified to provide the contraction simulator control over scheduling. Awesime also provides an efficient means of attaining cache miss rates for various cache configurations since it directly integrates a version of the TYCHO [15] cache simulation software.

In obtaining the results below, the following assumptions were made. First we assume that the compiler has annotated where sends and receives between virtual processors occur, and which virtual processors are internal versus external. Second, in our measurements of cache locality, we do not include the data accesses by the run-time system. We expect that their inclusion would affect all the policies about equally. (In fact they might hinder the FIFO and LIFO policies more since these policies access more data in the course of scheduling). Third, we use a tool called pixie [8] to instrument the scheduling code and analyze the resulting execution trace to obtain the cost, in cycles, for each of the scheduling steps in the new heuristics. The code used to measure this cost is a conservative estimation of the code which will actually be used in a working contraction prototype since it lacks a few planned optimizations. The cost of the ready list manipulations performed by the FIFO and LIFO policies are also measured in cycles using pixie. The code used in obtaining the FIFO and LIFO scheduling is derived from the scheduler found in [4] and the resulting cost should be considered a very optimal estimation. The costs we arrived at are 24, 32, 67, and 53 cycles for steps 1-4, respectively, and 45 cycles for the FIFO and LIFO scheduling (which includes removing and adding an elements to the ready list). In the new heuristics, Step #4 requires an additional cost which is dependent on how many searches are necessary before finding a ready task. This cost is 17 cycles per search.

Table 1 shows the frequency and cost (in cycles) for each of the steps in the proposed heuristics, for 50 iterations of the 100x100 grid on each of the three problems. As mentioned in Section 3, a major assumption in designing the heuristics is that the first steps will be used more frequently than the later steps. In particular, it is important that the last step (#4) be utilized as infrequently as possible. The results show that, for these three application, step #4 occurs less than one percent of the time for the last two problems and 1.3% for the first. It is also important that, when step #4 is used, the number of tasks examined before finding a ready task be as small as possible. As mentioned in Section 3, we attempt to minimize these searches by recognizing that step #4 is usually only utilized in the termination phase of the algorithm (for these applications, the last iteration). The number of searches is reduced by examining only the tasks which are still active. For the problems below, this approach has been successful. Two of the three problems always find a ready task without any extra searches (i.e. "searches" in Table 1 equals zero), while the 5 point test case has to examine two tasks on average every time it must use step #4. Note that even in the worst case, the first problem, step 4 accounts for only 3.9% of the total cost.

Table 1. Scheduling Statistics for Heuristics. The frequency and cost of the proposed heuristics for each stencil on a 100x100 system running for 50 iterations. The first number in each box is the number of occurrences of this heuristic; the number in parentheses is the total cost in millions of cycles.

Step	5 point	9 point cross	9 point square
Step #1 (schedule the sending VP)	375,452 (9.01)	386,889 (9.29)	468,488 (11.2)
Step #2 (schedule receiving VP)	126,521 (4.05)	171,921 (5.50)	48,905 (1.56)
Step #3 (schedule external VP)	17,112 (1.15)	40,521 (2.71)	20,540 (1.38)
Step #4 (look up ready VP)	6,898 (0.57)	4,663 (0.25)	5,152 (0.27)
Extra searches required for step #4	11,832	0	0

Tables 2, 3, and 4 show the results of comparing the data locality and scheduling cost of the FIFO and LIFO policies with the proposed heuristics on each of the problems. The cache results only address data locality for a specific cache configuration: a 16k two-way set associative configuration. A number of other cache sizes and associativities also were simulated, but their presentation here would add little in differentiating the cache behavior among scheduling policies, since the patterns in cache behavior among scheduling approaches were the same for the problem sizes tested. In the FIFO and LIFO cases it is necessary to choose a means of initializing the ready list. To this end, we show the difference in cache behavior and scheduling cost when FIFO is initialized along rows and along columns. The tables also show two results for both 2 iterations and 50 iterations. The results for two iterations clearly reflect the influence of the initialization whereas the results for 50 iterations are more indicative of the steady state.

The cache behavior presented in these tables shows that the proposed heuristics are very competitive with the miss rates that one would obtain from the expected manual contraction, using a row-wise traversal of the data structure. In addition, the cache behavior using the proposed heuristics is close to the miss

Table 2. Five Point (Dimension = 100). Comparison of scheduling policies using a 5 point stencil. (For this problem, manually contracted code yields a miss rate of 5.04%, random scheduling yields a miss rate near 40%.)

	Proposed Heuristics		FIFO (by row)		FIFO (by column)		LIFO (by row)	
Iterations	2	50	2	50	2	50	2	50
Cache Miss Rate (percent)	5.48	3.81	5.05	5.20	5.14	5.18	2.60	3.54
Scheduling Cost (millions of cycles)	1.22	14.77	1.80	23.28	1.80	23.28	3.14	42.20

rates obtained using either FIFO policy, superior on the first problem and within 31% in the other two. LIFO cache locality is very good in all cases. In LIFO, as soon as a task becomes ready (i.e. the data it was waiting for has been sent), it is put at the beginning of the ready list where it is promptly scheduled. This has the effect of scheduling neighboring communication partners (similar to the proposed heuristics). In the worst case (Table 2), the heuristics are 58% worse than the LIFO miss rate, and are within 29% in the FIFO cases. Thus, the miss rates for all approaches are roughly comparable, with some advantage to LIFO and FIFO.

Table 3. Nine Point Square (Dimension = 100). Comparison of scheduling policies using a 9 point square stencil. (For this problem, manually contracted code yields a miss rate of 2.82%, random scheduling yields a miss rate near 35%.)

	Proposed Heuristics		FIFO (by row)		FIFO (by column)		LIFO (by row)	
Iterations	2	50	2	50	2	50	2	50
Cache Miss Rate (percent)	3.32	3.75	2.82	2.86	2.87	2.93	1.45	2.38
Scheduling Cost (millions of cycles)	1.25	14.46	1.80	23.40	1.80	23.37	5.69	61.18

The scheduling cost, unlike the behavior in data locality, differs much more among the scheduling policies. The proposed heuristics are 28 - 62% faster than the FIFO policies and a factor of 2.5 - 4.6 faster than the LIFO policy. Not only is the difference in scheduling cost greater (in most cases), but this cost has a greater weight than the cache miss rate when comparing policies. For example, while performing 50 iterations in the 5 point, 9-point cross and 9-point square stencils and assuming a 13 cycle cache miss penalty (as suggested in [16]), the proposed heuristics would require miss rates of 26%, 10%, and 15% respectively (instead of the achieved 3-4% cache miss rate) to match the larger scheduling overhead of the nearest competitor, FIFO.

Table 4. Nine Point Cross (Dimension = 100). Comparison of scheduling policies using a 9 point cross stencil. (For this problem, manually contracted code yields a miss rate of 5.04%, random scheduling yields a miss rate near 45%.)

	Proposed Heuristics		FIFO (by row)		FIFO (by column)		LIFO (by row)	
Iterations	2	50	2	50	2	50	2	50
Cache Miss Rate (percent)	3.67	4.02	2.82	3.12	3.36	3.43	1.49	3.54
Scheduling Cost (millions of cycles)	1.41	17.75	1.80	23.34	1.80	23.34	5.74	82.07

These results show that the proposed scheduling heuristics do a good job of maintaining data locality by scheduling among communication partners based upon data layout information from the compiler. While having data locality comparable to manually contracted code, the heuristics are computationally inexpensive. The low cost of these heuristics (an average 45% improvement over traditional approaches on the problems tested) allows finer granularity in contracting data parallel codes and will be an important tool in our continuing research on the contraction problem.

References

1. Thomas E. Anderson, Henry M. Levy, Brian N. Bershad, and Edward D. Lazowska. The interaction of architecture and operating system design. In *Proceedings of the 18th International Symposium on Computing Architecture*, 1991.
2. Arvind, RishiYur S. Nikhil, and Keshav K. Pingali. I-Structures: Data structures for parallel computing. *ACM Transactions on Programming Languages and Systems*, 11(4):598–632, Oct 1989.
3. B. Bagheri and L. R. Scott. PC, a parallel extension of C, the PC reference manual. Technical report, Pennsylvania State University, 1990.
4. Brian N. Bershad, Edward D. Lazowska, and Henry M. Levy. PRESTO: A system for object-oriented parallel programming. *Software Practice and Experience*, 18(8):713–732, Aug 1988.
5. L. Bic and A. C. Shaw. *The Logical Design of Operating Systems*. Prentice Hall, Englewood Cliffs, NJ, 1988.
6. Fred C. Chow and John L. Hennessy. The priority-based coloring approach to register allocation. *ACM Transactions on Programming Languages and Systems*, 12(4):501–536, Oct 1990.

7. E. C. Cooper and J. G. Morrisett. Adding threads to standard ml. Technical Report 186, School of Computer Science, Carnegie Mellon University, Dec 1990.

8. Digitil Equipment Corporation. *PIXIE*, ultrix v4.2, rev 96 edition, Sep 1991. Unix-style manual page.

9. Richard P. Draves, Brian N. Bershad, Richard F. Rashid, and Randall W. Dean. Using continuations to implement thread mangement and communication in operating systems. In *Proceedings of the 13th ACM Symposium on Operating Systems Principles*, pages 122–136, Oct 1991.

10. Edward W. Felten and Dylan McNamee. Improving the performance of message-passing applications by multithreading. In *Proceedings of Scalable High Performance Computing Conference*, pages 84–89. IEEE Press, 1992.

11. G. Fox, Ken Kennedy, Charles Koelbel, Ulrich Kremer, C. Tseng, and M. Wu. Fortran D language specification. Technical Report CRPC-TR90079, Center for Research on Parallel Computation, 1990.

12. Dirk Grunwald. A user's guide to Awesime: An object oriented parallel programming and simulation system. Technical Report CU-CS-522-91, Universit of Colorado, 1991.

13. Philip J. Hatcher and Michael J. Quinn. *Data-Parallel Programming on MIMD Computers*. The MIT Press, Cambridge, MA, 1991.

14. C. T. Haynes and D. P. Friedman. Engines build process abstractions. In *Conference Record of the 1984 ACM Symposium on LISP and Functional Programming*, pages 18–23, Aug 1984.

15. Mark D. Hill. *Tycho*. University of Wisconsin. Unix-style manual page.

16. Mark D. Hill. Evaluating associativity in CPU caches. *IEEE Transactions on Computers*, 12(38):1612–1630, 1989.

17. B. W. Lampson, J. G. Mitchell, and E. H. Satterthwaite. On the transfer of control between contexts. In *Lecture Notes On Computer Science: Proceedings of the Programming Symposium*, pages 181–203. Springer-Verlag, 1974.

18. P. Mehrotra and J. Van Rosendale. Programming distributed memory architectures using Kali. Technical Report 90-69, Institute for Computer Applications in Science and Engineering (ICASE), 1990.

19. Jeffre C. Mogul and Anita Borg. The effect of context switches on cache performance. In *Proceedings of the 18th International Symposium on Computer Architecture*, 1991.

20. M. Rosing and J. Saltz. Low latency messages on distributed memory multiprocessors. Technical Report 92-95, Institute for Computer Applications in Science and Engineering (ICASE), 1992.

21. M. Rosing, Robert B. Schnabel, and Robert P. Weaver. The DINO parallel programming language. *Journal of Parallel and Distributed Computing*, 13:30–42, 1991.

22. Ellen Spertus, Seth Copen Goldstein, Klaus Erik Schauser, Thorsten von Eicken, David E. Culer, and William J. Dally. Evaluations of mechanisms for fine-grained parallel programs in the J-Machine and the CM-5. In *Proceedings of the 20th International Symposium on Computer Architecture*, 1993.

23. Guy L. Steele Jr. High performance Fortran: status report. In *Proceedings of Workshop on Languages, Compilers, and Run-Time Environments for Distributed Memory Multiprocessors, SIGPLAN Notices*, Jan 1993.

24. Thorsten von Eicken, David E. Culler, Seth Copen Goldstein, and Klaus Erik Schauser. Active messages: a mechanism for integrated communication and com-

putation. In *Proceedings of the 19th International Symposium on Computer Architecture*, May 1992.

25. D. W. Wall. Global register allocation at link time. In *ACM SIGPLAN Symposium on Compiler Construction*, Jun 1986.

26. M. Wand. Continuation-based multiprocessing. In *Conference Record of the 1980 LISP Conference*, pages 19–28, Aug 1980.

27. S. A. Ward and R. H. Halstead, Jr. A syntactic theory of message passing. *Journal of the ACM*, 27(2):365–383, Apr 1980.

28. Robert P. Weaver. *Supporting dynamic data structures at the language level on distributed memory machines*. PhD thesis, Department of Computer Science, University of Colorado at Boulder, Nov 1992.

VISTA: The Visual Interface for Scheduling Transformations and Analysis*

Steven Novack and Alexandru Nicolau

Department of Information and Computer Science
University of California
Irvine, CA 92717

Abstract. VISTA is a visually oriented, interactive environment for parallelizing sequential programs at the instruction level for execution on fine-grain architectures. Fully automatic parallelization techniques often perform well, but may not be able to achieve the strict performance and code size requirements needed for some critical applications. In such cases, manual manipulation by an expert user can often provide enough improvements in the parallelization process to meet the requirements of the application. Using VISTA, an expert user fine-tunes the parallelization process by providing rules and directives to the system in response to graphical and numeric feedback provided by the system.

1 Introduction

The Visual Interface for Scheduling Transformations and Analysis (VISTA) is a visually oriented, interactive environment for the semi-automatic parallelization of sequential programs at the instruction level for execution on fine-grain architectures. Fully automatic parallelizing compilers (e.g. [8, 7, 10, 5]) perform well on average and produce generally good results, but in some cases may fail to extract a sufficient level of parallelism from a given program to achieve the high performance required for the application while satisfying the physical constraints (e.g. allowable memory usage) of the target machine. For many applications, such as embedded systems in aircraft, meeting specific cost and performance constraints may be strictly necessary for the application to work at all. For such applications, even small improvements over fully automatic techniques obtained by manual manipulation of the parallelization process can be the enabling factor for the feasibility of a given project.

The failure of a fully automatic compiler to achieve a desired level of performance, even though such a level is in fact achievable, is usually a consequence of two problems inherent to automatic compilation: generally good heuristics for solving NP-hard problems can fail to perform adequately for some specific cases, and a lack of application specific knowledge can force the compiler to

---

* This work was supported in part by NSF grant CCR8704367 and ONR grant N0001486K0215.

make overly conservative assumptions. The NP-hard characteristic of resource-constrained scheduling and scheduling in the presence of conditional branches suggests that there is no "best" general solution for parallelizing programs for execution on actual machines. Even though the heuristics employed by fully automated compilers for dealing with these problems may perform well on average, for any particular application, an interactive tool like VISTA will often enable an expert user to produce schedules that are significantly better than those produced by the available fully automated compilers. Furthermore, a lack of application specific knowledge can greatly degrade the performance of programs by forcing the compiler to make overly conservative decisions in such areas as the disambiguation of indirect memory references needed for instruction scheduling and the estimation of path execution probabilities necessary for making good speculative scheduling choices. Clearly, manual intervention by the user to provide application specific knowledge or scheduling direction need not (and should not) be applied at every decision point during the parallelization process. The fact that even large programs spend most of their time executing in a small fraction of their code (i.e. in loops or recursive routines) suggests that such special manual attention need only be applied at relatively few stages of compilation (e.g. at loops on critical paths) and then only selectively when the compiler is not able to make an obviously superior scheduling choice or would otherwise have to make an overly conservative decision that might adversely affect the performance of the program.

The VISTA environment allows the user to fine-tune the parallelization process using problem specific knowledge, human intuition, and trial-and-error approaches, when and where needed, by providing decisions, directives and rules to the system in response to system queries or at user specified decision points. This fine-tuning can take two forms. First, the user can provide information to the parallelization system that can not always be computed efficiently (or at all), such as identification of critical paths and bottlenecks, disambiguation of pointer and indirect references, and control path execution probabilities. Second, during the parallelization process, there may be decision points at which the system is not able to determine a clearly superior course of action. Some examples are cost vs. performance trade-offs (e.g. code size and compile time vs. parallelism), high-level transformation choices (e.g. which level to pipeline[2] in a nested loop), and choosing alternative scheduling strategies (e.g. transformation ordering heuristics and speculative scheduling strategies[3]). These decisions may be different at different points in the program and at different stages of the parallelization process.

Achieving the abovementioned functionality requires three things: an ability to visualize the parallelization process, a system of parallelizing program transformations that is powerful enough to provide maximum parallelism relative to system specific constraints while remaining efficient and flexible enough to allow for arbitrary scheduling approaches and cost vs. performance trade-offs in an

---

[2] *Loop pipelining* refers to overlapping the execution of successive iterations of a loop.

[3] Determining when to move operations above conditionals.

interactive environment, and finally, mechanisms for analyzing and anticipating the effects of such transformations during parallelization to provide the user with useful information and feedback upon which to base scheduling decisions. For small programs, Control Flow Graphs (CFG's) can be graphically displayed to provide a natural, visual representation of programs upon which a system of parallelizing transformations, such as Percolation Scheduling (PS)[9], can be performed. PS parallelizes programs by repeated application of a pair of transformations, called move-op and move-cj, that move an operation or conditional jump up one instruction[4] in the CFG while preserving the semantics of control and data flow. These transformations need not be applied in any specific order or exhaustively, thus, PS provides the flexibility to implement arbitrary scheduling heuristics.[5] Performing PS on CFG's can provably extract all of the parallelism available in a program[2]). However, as program size increases, CFG's become too unwieldy and complicated, especially after parallelization, to be useful for visualization and inefficiencies inherent to straight PS can begin to have significant detrimental effects on compilation time and code size. These inefficiencies derive mainly from the strictly incremental application of transformations and significant code explosion caused by loop unrolling and parallelizing code containing multiple control paths.

To overcome these problems, VISTA incorporates a hierarchical representation of the CFG based on Hierarchical Task Graphs (HTG's)[6] and an enhancement of PS called Trailblazing PS (TiPS)[11] that overcomes the inefficiencies of PS while retaining its power and flexibility. HTG's partition the CFG into a hierarchy of subgraphs, usually with a direct correspondence to the hierarchy of the original high-level representation of the program, thus providing a visualizable and understandable structure to the instruction level representation being parallelized. TiPS also exploits this structure by extending the PS core transformations to navigate through the HTG hierarchy. At the lowest level sub-graphs in the hierarchy, TiPS is able to perform the same fine-grained transformations as normal PS, while at higher levels, TiPS is able to move operations across large blocks of code in constant time, including loops, past which normal PS is unable to move operations at all. This non-incremental code motion itself improves efficiency over PS by bypassing multiple instructions in constant time, but also allows code explosion to be controlled by splitting control paths only when necessary to extract more parallelism,[6] and then only if the cost of doing so is justified by the performance thus achieved. TiPS attempts to move operations

---

[4] A VLIW instruction is a set of risc-like operations that can be executed in parallel, possibly containing multiple conditional jumps that combine to yield a single control path.

[5] The transformations themselves ensure the preservation of correct semantics.

[6] When moving conditionals or when moving operations that can move more on one control path than on another, control paths may need to be duplicated, or *split*, in order to preserve the semantics of control flow. Normal PS will always perform such splitting when moving operations along multiple control paths, even if it is not semantically necessary (e.g. when moving an operation across an entire if-then-else block).

at the "highest" possible level, where they can bypass multiple nodes at lower levels in constant time, while moving operations to, or keeping them at, lower levels when needed to expose more parallelism. In this fashion, TiPS is able to provide efficient code motion without sacrificing the "completeness" of normal PS and even enables some code motion not directly possible in normal PS.

In order to assist the user in directing the parallelization process, VISTA provides visually-oriented analysis and (parallel) code editing capabilities. For example, VISTA can graphically portray resource (e.g. functional unit, register, or memory bandwidth) utilization by shading in nodes in the HTG by an amount proportional to the utilization at that point. This feature helps the user to monitor the effects of different transformations on resource utilization and to identify critical paths and bottlenecks within the code. Another useful analysis capability of VISTA is an integrated simulator that can be used to report dynamic speedups at successive stages of parallelization in order to gauge the effect of the transformations. This information can also be graphically represented by shading in nodes in the HTG by an amount proportional to the normalized execution time (the percentage of total time spent executing each node), thus providing a global, visual representation of the critical paths throughout the program. The visual editing capabilities of VISTA provide the user with a "point-and-click" environment for performing transformations at any level, from moving individual operations to initiating a loop pipelining transformation or parallelizing an entire routine. The remaining sections of this paper provide an overview of the VISTA interface (Section 2) and its use in fine-tuning specific applications (Section 3).

2   The VISTA Environment

This VISTA interface portrayed in Figure 1 shows the HTG representation of the Discrete Ordinates Transport loop (number 20) of the Livermore Kernels, partially parallelized for a VLIW machine with four functional units. The main window of the graphical interface consists of three regions. The first region, called the canvas[7], located in the upper right-hand corner of the display shows the entire routine represented as a tree[8] of nodes. The dashed-line rectangle surrounding a portion of the canvas is called the *slider*. The second region, the *porthole*, located at the bottom of the display shows a magnified view of the rectangular portion of the canvas enclosed by the slider.

Each rectangle shown in the porthole represents a node in the HTG and is labelled by a unique number (actually, the memory address of the node itself). HTG's were originally presented for use at the coarse-grain level but we have adapted them for use at the instruction-level. An HTG is a directed acyclic graph containing five types of node: START and STOP nodes indicating the entry and

---

[7] The reader familiar with the X environment will recognize many of these names (and regions) as being widgets from the X Athena Widget set.

[8] For the sake of simplicity, we currently use a tree representation for the program, therefore, the multiple predecessors of join-points and backedges are not explicitly shown.

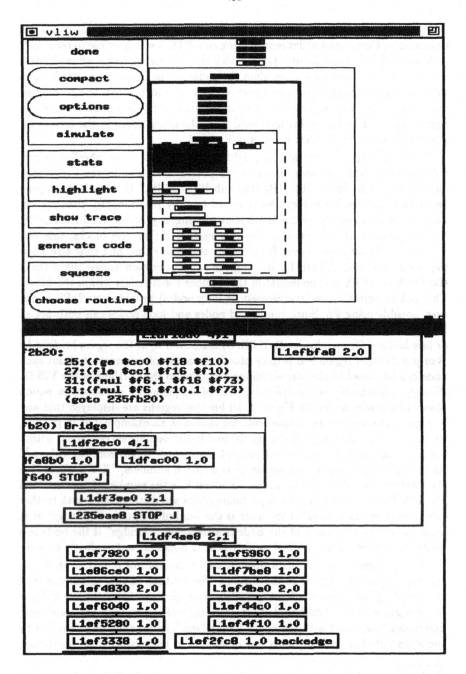

Fig. 1. HTG after automatic compaction without loop pipelining. Functional unit utilization is highlighted in the canvas.

exit of HTG's respectively, Simple nodes that, for our purposes, represent VLIW instructions, Compound nodes representing sub-HTG's which we use to represent if-then-else blocks, and finally, Loop nodes that represent loops whose bodies are sub-HTG's. Rectangles other than the slider in the canvas or porthole that contain other rectangles represent either compound or loop nodes, and rectangles that contain no others represent either simple nodes or STOP nodes. Loop nodes containing inner loops are distinguished from the other nodes in the canvas by a rectangle drawn with thick lines as in Figure 1.

When moving an operation, op, TiPS is able to determine whether or not a dependency exists between op and a compound or loop node, say B, without visiting any node within HTG(B) (the sub-HTG of B).[9] If there is no dependency or if the dependency can be removed (e.g. by renaming[3]), then op can move non-incrementally across B without visiting any nodes within HTG(B). For compound nodes containing (possibly nested) if-then-else blocks, this can provide significant savings over PS in terms of compile time and code size since the worst case cost of both for moving the same operation across the if-then-else block using PS is exponential in the number conditionals within the block. The motion across loops (represented as loop nodes) provided by TiPS is not even possible using PS. Since compound nodes and loop nodes can both act as "bridges" across their sub-HTG's, we refer to them collectively as *bridge nodes* or just *bridges*. Given a bridge B, HTG(B) is referred to as the *region bridged by B* or just *bridged region* if B is understood. A variety of information about each node can be shown in the corresponding rectangle in the porthole of the VISTA display, including the entire operation tree of simple nodes or the entire region bridged by bridge nodes. In Figure 1, all bridged regions are displayed this way and the operations of one simple node are shown as an example, but in general, we just characterize simple nodes by the number of operations contained within them and any special characteristics that distinguish them from the others.[10] At the right-hand side of each rectangle is a pair of numbers, "X,Y", where X is the total number of operations in the node and Y is the number of operations in the node that are conditional jumps. Some nodes are distinguished with further labels, such as "loop head" if the node is the head of a loop or "backedge" if at least one of the successors of the node is a backedge, "Bridge" if the node is a bridge and "Stop" if it is a STOP node (START nodes are not explicitly shown).

The final region of the main display, called the *control region*, is shown in the upper left-hand corner of the display. The buttons in this region are used to provide global control of the parallelization process when the compiler is in interactive mode. Additional, finer-grain control is provided via commands and menus associated with the nodes themselves. The functionality provided by these controls fall generally into two categories of transformations: parallelism

---

[9] This is accomplished by associating *definition* and *use* sets with B that indicate which variables are defined or used within HTG(B). If an operation shares no definitions or uses with B, then it has no dependency on any operation in HTG(B).

[10] For the purposes of this paper, the operation-level details of the code being parallelized are unimportant.

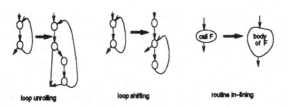

Fig. 2. Exposing Parallelism

exposing and parallelizing. Parallelism exposing transformations (see Figure 2) consist of loop unrolling (inserting one or more successive iterations of a loop into its body),[11] loop shifting ("unwinding" a loop so that its head becomes a true successor of each of its predecessors), and routine in-lining (replacing a CALL by the body of the routine being called). These transformations do not in general improve performance (although, each in-lining does eliminate a CALL and a RETURN); however, they do expose new operations that can be scheduled in parallel with existing operations, thereby allowing for improved performance at the cost of increased code size and compile time. Parallelization is affected by a hierarchy of transformations. At the lowest level are *trailblaze* (the TiPS equivalent of the PS move-op transformation) and *move-cj* (same for both PS and TiPS) which move individual operations or conditional jumps, respectively. Next higher up is the *schedule* transformation that moves operations in a user-specified order, using *trailblaze* and *move-cj*, toward the node currently being scheduled, say n, until no further operations can move into n. Operations can be prevented from moving due to data dependencies, resource constraints, and artificial limitations such as cost vs. performance trade-offs. The highest level parallelizing transformation is the *compact* transformation which traverses a specified sub-graph of the program in a top-down fashion while applying the *schedule* transformation to each node visited (the specified sub-graph may be the entire program HTG).

3 Fine-tuning parallelization

These transformations are usually performed automatically by the system; however, control is available for manually applying them as needed, at any level, in order to fine-tune specific applications. The VISTA interface can be used to provide interactive disambiguation and speculative scheduling decisions; however, in this section, we will focus on the ability of VISTA to tune cost vs. performance trade-offs. Tuning cost vs. performance trade-offs is one of the more intractable problems for fully automated parallelizing compilers since acceptable ratios of

---

[11] In our compiler, if unrolling is applied more than once, iterations from the original (rather than the current, previously unrolled) loop are inserted.

cost to performance depend entirely on the application and architecture at hand, and achieving this ratio is itself an NP-hard problem. For example, without any restrictions on program size, it is usually a good idea to fully loop-pipeline the inner loops of programs. Loop Pipelining consists of repeatedly exposing parallelism within an inner loop (using unrolling as in [10] or shifting as in [4]) and compacting the resultant loop until no more parallelism can be extracted from the loop. Loop Pipelining usually has the effect of significantly improving performance at the expense of increased program size. When there are limits on program size, VISTA allows loop pipelining to be terminated when the user determines that either enough parallelism has already been exploited or the point of diminishing returns of the cost vs. performance ratio has been reached. To facilitate the making of decisions, such as these, based on performance goals and cost vs. performance trade-offs, VISTA has mechanisms for quantitatively and graphically providing feedback to the user about the effects of transformations that have been applied to the program. Quantitative feedback can take the form of reports on program size, static speedup computed as the average degree of parallelism over a specified region of code, or dynamic speedup, the ratio of sequential to parallel execution times determined by simulating the code before and after applying any transformations. For instance, simulation (initiated by the SIMULATION button) of the schedule in Figure 1 yields a speedup of 2.41 (reported using the STATISTICS button).

While quantitative feedback is primarily useful for analyzing the effect of previously applied transformations, graphical feedback in the form of visual representations of resource utilization and normalized execution times help the user to anticipate the effect of future transformations. Graphical representation, referred to as *highlighting*, is provided by shading the rectangles in the canvas by an amount proportional to the specified resource utilization or normalized execution time at that point in the program. For example, the canvas in Figure 1 shows functional unit utilization (i.e. the percentage of functional units that are used by the operations in each node). By highlighting resource utilization, the user can determine where parallelism exposing transformations might be useful — if no resources are available, then, in general, there is no point in exposing new operations for movement.[12] For instance the availability of unutilized resources, indicated by the unshaded areas of the inner loop nodes displayed in the canvas of Figure 1, suggests that applying loop shifting and/or unrolling on the inner loop would probably improve performance. The amount of performance gained and its cost in increased code size depends on which technique is used, the architecture, and the characteristics of the loop itself. In general, when combined with a loop restructuring technique such as Perfect Pipelining[1, 10], loop unrolling can achieve maximum performance by allowing iterations to be scheduled succes-

---

[12] Although, in some cases, opportunities for redundant operation removal (e.g. load after store elimination or constant folding) might be exposed and therefore may make the parallelism exposing transformation worthwhile even in the absence of available resources.

sively until resources are utilized as well as possible,[13] but can potentially result in a significant amount of code explosion. On the other hand, loop shifting has the advantage of keeping the number of iterations constant (with somewhat less code explosion), but at the cost of arbitrarily limiting the number of operations within the loop, and therefore the maximum possible resource utilization since the fixed number of operations may not be evenly divided among the available functional units. For example, in Figure 3, the user might decide to shift rather than unroll the loop due to the lesser code explosion penalty and the likelihood that unrolling would not perform significantly better than shifting for this particular loop running on the given architecture. The intuition behind this decision is that since the architecture is relatively "narrow" with respect to the number of operations in the loop (4 functional units compared to 52 operations), then the penalty for shifting, of not being able to evenly divide the operations by the number of functional units, is likely to be small. Figure 3 shows the inner loop shifted 7 times which resulted in a 17% increase in speedup (to 2.82) at the cost of a 15% increase in code size relative to the schedule in Figure 1. While the decision to use shifting instead of unrolling may be appropriate for this particular loop running on a "four-wide" VLIW architecture, results in [10] show that for different loops and/or different architectures the performance penalty of shifting can be significant, in which case unrolling might be a better choice. Whether unrolling, shifting, or some combination of the two is best for a given application depends entirely on the characteristics of the application itself and the target architecture. Any automatic, deterministic heuristic for applying these transformations would, by necessity, be sub-optimal for some application/architecture combinations for which an expert user would nevertheless be able to find a superior solution if provided with sufficiently powerful tools for understanding and directing the parallelization process.

When multiple opportunities for parallelism exposing transformations have been identified, it may be necessary to choose from amongst them if there are limits on code size. An example of this is shown in Figure 3 wherein loop shifting and/or unrolling can be performed on either of the loop heads.[14] At this stage, it is useful to highlight the normalized execution time of the nodes in the program in order to provide a global picture of the critical paths through the code. Given this information, the user can choose which of the potential parallelism exposing and parallelizing transformations to apply based on his estimation of their likely affect on the critical paths and the relative cost vs. performance benefits of each. Then, using quantitative feedback, the user can analyze the actual costs and performance thus obtained. For example, by highlighting the normalized execution time in the canvas of Figure 3 we can see that the loop on the left is more critical than the one on the right, and therefore the next parallelism exposing transformation (and compaction) should occur on the left-most loop head. By shifting and compacting another 4 times along the left-most loop a

---

[13] Data dependencies that cross iteration boundaries can prevent full utilization.

[14] Notice that the loop has become irreducible as a result of shifting a node that contained a conditional branch.

458

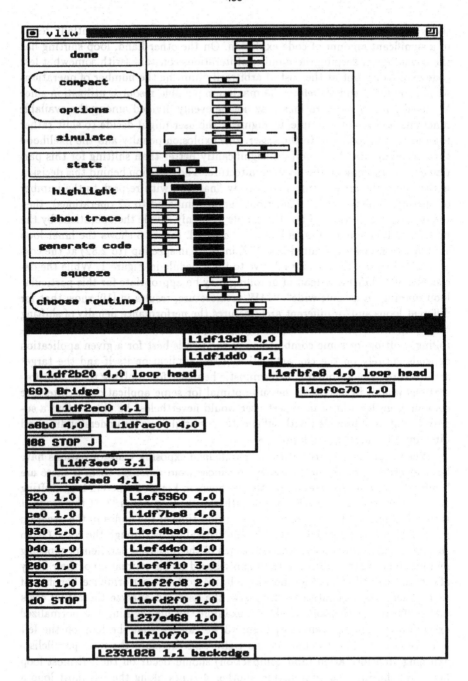

Fig. 3. HTG after user directed shifting and compaction. Normalized execution time is highlighted in the canvas.

speedup of 3.2 would be achieved, providing an incremental improvement of 14% over the schedule in Figure 3 at the incremental cost of a further 3% increase in code size. After doing this, highlighting functional unit utilization would show that resources are almost completely utilized. If it turns out that the cost vs. performance ratio is not acceptable (a determination which is entirely application dependent), then the transformations can be "undone" by replacing the outermost HTG that was affected by the transformations with a copy saved prior to performing the transformations (VISTA allows the user to save any HTG in its current state for possible restoration at a later time, but only allows restoration when semantics would be preserved by doing so).

For the example shown in Figures 1 and 3, fully automatic techniques, such as those presented in [4, 10], would usually result in much greater code explosion than obtained using VISTA, but without any significant improvements in speedup since, in the final schedule described above, resource utilization obtained with VISTA approaches 100%. In fact, depending on the choice of scheduling heuristics used by either of these (or any other) automatic techniques, speedup might actually degrade because of the added pressure on functional units caused by too much code explosion (i.e. more operations compete for the same resources). For example, the same scheduling heuristics used to create the nearly optimal results presented in [10] for some loops, would, for this particular loop, have resulted in a speedup of 2.9 at a cost in code size of over 1000 instructions (as compared to the speedup of 3.2 at a cost of 42 instructions produced using VISTA).

By selectively applying exposing and parallelizing transformations based on application-specific knowledge, intuition, and feedback from the VISTA system, the user can often fine-tune the parallelization process to provide cost vs. performance trade-offs superior to those produced by the available fully automatic systems. The problems with fully automatic techniques can be alleviated somewhat with better scheduling heuristics; however, due to the complicated interactions between the different heuristics used for dealing with the various NP-hard problems involved in compiling for fine-grain parallelism, human intervention can often be the deciding factor for achieving the necessary cost and performance goals.

References

1. A. Aiken and A. Nicolau. Perfect pipelining: A new loop parallelization technique. In *Proceedings of the 1988 European Symposium on Programming*. Springer Verlag Lecture Notes in Computer Science no. 300, March 1988.

2. A. S. Aiken. *Compaction-Based Parallelization*. PhD thesis, Cornell University, 1988.

3. R. Cytron and J. Ferrante. What's in a name? In *Proc. of the 1987 Int'l Conf. on Parallel Processing*, pages 19–27, August 1987.

4. K. Ebcioglu and T. Nakatani. A new compilation technique for parallelizing loops with unpredictable branches on a vliw architecture. In *Proceedings of the 2nd*

Workshop on Programming Languages and Compilers for Parallel Computing, Urbana, IL, 1989.

5. J. R. Ellis. *Bulldog—A Compiler for VLIW Architectures*. MIT Press, 1986.

6. M. Girkar and C. Polychronopoulos. Automatic extraction of functional parallelism from ordinary programs. *IEEE Transactions on Parallel and Distributed Systems*, 3(2):166–178, March 1992.

7. S. Moon and K. Ebcioglu. An efficient resource constrained global scheduling technique for superscalar and vliw processors. Technical report, IBM, 1992.

8. T. Nakatani and K. Ebcioglu. Using a lookahead window in a compaction-based parallelizing compiler. In *Proceedings of the 23rd Annual International Symposium on Microarchitecture*, 1990.

9. A. Nicolau. Uniform parallelism exploitation in ordinary programs. In *Proc. of the 1985 Int'l Conf. on Parallel Processing*, 1985.

10. S. Novack and A. Nicolau. An efficient global resource constrained technique for exploiting instruction level parallelism. In *Proc. of the 1992 Int'l Conf. on Parallel Processing*, St. Charles, IL, August 1992.

11. S. Novack and A. Nicolau. Trailblazing: A hierarchical approach to percolation scheduling. Technical Report TR-92-56, Univ. of Calif. at Irvine, 1992. Also appears in the *Proc. of the 1993 Int'l Conf. on Parallel Processing*, St. Charles, IL, August 1993.

Efficiently Computing ϕ-Nodes On-The-Fly
(Extended Abstract)

Ron K. Cytron[1] and Jeanne Ferrante[2]

[1] Department of Computer Science
Washington University Box 1045
St. Louis, MO 63130-4899
(Email: cytron@cs.wustl.edu)
[2] T. J. Watson Research Center
IBM Research PO Box 704
Yorktown Heights, NY 10598
(Email: ferrant@watson.ibm.com)

Abstract. Recently, *Static Single Assignment Form* and *Sparse Evaluation Graphs* have been advanced for the efficient solution of program optimization problems. Each method is provided with an initial set of flow graph nodes that inherently affect a problem's solution. Other relevant nodes are those where potentially disparate solutions must combine. Previously, these so-called ϕ-nodes were found by computing the *iterated dominance frontiers* of the initial set of nodes, a process that could take worst case *quadratic* time with respect to the input flow graph. In this paper we present an *almost-linear* algorithm for determining exactly the same set of ϕ-nodes.

1 Motivation and Background

Static Single Assignment (SSA) form [9] and the more general Sparse Evaluation Graphs (SEG) [6] have emerged as an efficient mechanism for solving compile-time optimization problems via data flow analysis [18, 10, 3, 15, 7, 5]. Given an input data flow framework, the SEG construction algorithm distills the flow graph into a set of *relevant* nodes. These nodes are then interconnected with edges suitable for evaluating data flow solutions. Similarly, SSA form identifies and appropriately interconnects those variable references that are relevant to solving certain data flow problems.

The SEG and SSA algorithms process and compute the following information:

Inputs:

Flowgraph $\mathcal{G}_f$ with nodes $\mathcal{N}_f$, edges $\mathcal{E}_f$, and root node **Entry**. If $(X, Y) \in \mathcal{E}_f$, then we write $X \in Pred(Y)$ and $Y \in Succ(X)$. We assume $\mathcal{G}_f$ is connected.

Depth-first numbering where $dfn(X)$ is the number associated with X

$$1 \le dfn(X) \le |\mathcal{N}_f|$$

in a depth-first search of $\mathcal{G}_f$.[3] We call the associated depth-first spanning tree $DFST$. Similarly, we define the inverse mapping

$$vertex(k) = X \mid dfn(X) = k$$

Dominator tree where $idom(X)$ is the immediate dominator of flow graph node X. We say that X *dominates* Y, written $X \gg Y$, if X appears on every path from flow graph **Entry** to Y; domination is both reflexive and transitive. We say that X *strictly dominates* Y, written $X \gg Y$, if $X \gg Y$ and $X \neq Y$. Each node X has a unique *immediate dominator* $idom(X)$ such that

$$idom(X) \gg X \text{ and } \forall W \gg X, W \gg idom(X)$$

Node $idom(X)$ serves as the parent of X in a flow graph's dominator tree. (An example flow graph and its dominator tree are shown in Figure 1.)

Initial nodes: $\mathcal{N}_\alpha \subseteq \mathcal{N}_f$ is an initial subset of those nodes that must appear in the sparse representation. For an SEG, such nodes represent non-identity transference in a data flow framework. For SSA, such nodes contain *definitions* of variables.

Outputs:

Sparse nodes $\mathcal{N}_\sigma$, which we compute as a property of each node:

$$\Upsilon(X) \Longleftrightarrow X \in \mathcal{N}_\sigma$$

ϕ-function nodes $\mathcal{N}_\phi \subseteq \mathcal{N}_\sigma$, which we compute as a property of each node:

$$\Phi(X) \Longleftrightarrow X \in \mathcal{N}_\phi$$

Previous SEG and SSA construction algorithms operate as follows:

1. The algorithm precomputes the *dominance frontier* $DF(X)$ for each node X:

$$DF(X) = \{ Z \mid (\exists (Y, Z) \in \mathcal{E}_f)(X \gg Y \text{ and } X \not\gg Z) \}$$

   In other words, X dominates a predecessor of Z without strictly dominating Z. The dominance frontiers for the flow graph in Figure 1 are shown in Figure 2.

2. The algorithm accepts $\mathcal{N}_\alpha \subseteq \mathcal{N}_f$.

3. The algorithm then computes the set of nodes deserving ϕ-functions, $\mathcal{N}_\phi$, as the iterated dominance frontier of the initial set of nodes:

$$\mathcal{N}_\phi = DF^+(\mathcal{N}_\alpha)$$

   In our example in Figures 1 and 2, if $\mathcal{N}_\alpha = \{ D, W \}$, then $\mathcal{N}_\phi = \{ W, X, Y, Z \}$.

4. Steps 2 and 3 can be repeated to create a forest of (related) sparse evaluation graphs. In SSA form, these graphs are usually combined, with the appropriate increase in detail and size with respect to $\mathcal{N}_\phi$.

---

[3] Here, $dfn(X)$ is assigned in order of nodes visited, starting with 1; in [2], depth first numbers are assigned starting from $|\mathcal{N}_f|$ down to 1.

5. In SEG, appropriate edges are then placed between nodes in

$$\mathcal{N}_\sigma = \mathcal{N}_\alpha \cup \mathcal{N}_\phi$$

In SSA, variables are appropriately renamed, such that each used is reached by a single definition.

These two methods have one component in common, in name as well as function: the determination of $\mathcal{N}_\phi$, where potentially disparate information combines. Consider a flow graph $\mathcal{G}_f$ with N nodes (set $\mathcal{N}_f$) and E edges (set $\mathcal{E}_f$) for a program with V variables. While computing the so-called ϕ-nodes is efficient in practice [9],

1. Constructing a single SEG (i.e., one data flow framework) by the usual algorithm [6] takes $O(E + N^2)$ time;
2. Where a data flow problem can be partitioned into V disjoint frameworks [14], constructing the associated V SEGs takes $O(EV + N^2)$ and $\Omega(EV)$ time.
3. If we bound the number of variable references per node by some constant, then construction of SSA form takes $O(EV + N^2)$ and $\Omega(E + V + N)$ time.

In comparing (2) to (3), note that SEG provides a "solution" for each edge in the flow graph, while SSA form provides a "solution" only at a program's variable references.

Our algorithm for placing ϕ-functions avoids the the computation of dominance frontiers. In doing so, we reduce the time bound for (1) to $O(E\alpha(E))$, where $\alpha()$ is the slowly-growing inverse-Ackermann function [8]. The time bound for (2) is reduced to $O(V \times E\alpha(E))$. If our algorithm places ϕ-functions for SSA form, then the time bound for (3) becomes $O(V \times E\alpha(E))$ but $\Omega(EV)$.

To summarize the above discussion, computation of dominance frontiers and their use in placing ϕ-functions can take $O(E + N^2)$ time [9], although such behavior is neither expected in general nor even possible for programs of certain structure. An example flow graph that exhibits the aforementioned worst case behavior is shown in Figure 1. The flow graph's dominance frontiers are shown in Figure 2. As this graph structure grows[4], the size of dominance frontiers of nodes along its left spine increases quadratically, while the size of the sparse data flow graph or SSA form is certainly linear in size. It is this worst case behavior brought on by precomputing the dominance frontiers that we wish to avoid.

Since one reason for introducing ϕ-functions is to eliminate potentially quadratic behavior when solving actual data flow problems, such worst case behavior during SEG or SSA construction could be problematic. Clearly, avoiding such behavior necessitates placing ϕ-functions without computing or using dominance frontiers.

In this paper we present an algorithm that computes $\mathcal{N}_\sigma$ and $\mathcal{N}_\phi \subseteq \mathcal{N}_\sigma$ from the initially specified $\mathcal{N}_\alpha$. Where previous algorithms begin with a set of nodes $\mathcal{N}_\alpha$ and use dominance frontiers (iteratively) to induct other nodes into $\mathcal{N}_\sigma$, our

---

[4] by repeating the ladder structure; the back edge is unnecessary and was added to illustrate our algorithm

algorithm does the reverse: we visit nodes in an order that allows us to determine conditions under which a given node must be in $\mathcal{N}_\sigma$. Using a similar approach, we can then determine $\mathcal{N}_\phi \subseteq \mathcal{N}_\sigma$.

In Section 2, we discuss a simple version of our algorithm and illustrate its application to the flow graph in Figure 1. The algorithm's correctness is outlined in Section 3. In Section 4, we discuss how balanced path-compression can be used to make the algorithm more efficient; it is these techniques that allow us to achieve our almost-linear time bound. Section 5 gives some preliminary experiments and section 6 suggests future work.

In related work, Johnson and Pingali describe an algorithm to construct an SSA-like representation [13] that takes $\Theta(EV)$ time. While their upper bound is slightly better than ours, our approach is more general: we construct sparse evaluation graphs for *arbitrary* data flow problems, while Johnson and Pingali construct def-use structures specific to the solution of SSA-based optimization problems such as constant propagation.

As we discuss further in Section 5, $O()$ asymptotic bounds in this area are deceptive, and one must take into account lower and expected bounds. The usual dominance-frontier-based algorithm [9] is biased toward the *average* case, in which linear behavior for constructing or consulting dominance frontiers is expected. The algorithm we present in this paper, and the algorithm due to Johnson and Pingali [13], are $\Omega(EV)$, since each edge in the flow graph is examined for each variable.

We actually present two variations of the same algorithm in this paper. The first "simple" algorithm is presented for expository reasons; the second algorithm uses balanced path-compression to achieve our improved time bound. Preliminary experiments presented in Section 5 compare the simple algorithm presented in Section 2 with the usual dominance frontier-based algorithm [9]. In fact, the usual algorithm is often faster, and so these experiments do not suggest blindly switching to the asymptotically faster algorithm. However, our algorithm does exhibit the same linear behavior as the usual algorithm. Moreover, we have not implemented the balanced path-compression presented in Section 4 which yields our better bound. These experiments give some evidence that our algorithm can yield comparable performance to the usual algorithm, while avoiding asymptotically poor efficiency.

2 Algorithm

Definition 1. *The equidominates of a node X are those nodes with the same immediate dominator as X:*

$$equidom(X) = \{ Y \mid idom(Y) = idom(X) \}$$

For example, in Figure 1,

$$equidom(A) = \{ A, V, W, X, Y, Z \}$$

More generally, the noun *equidominates* refers to any such set of nodes.

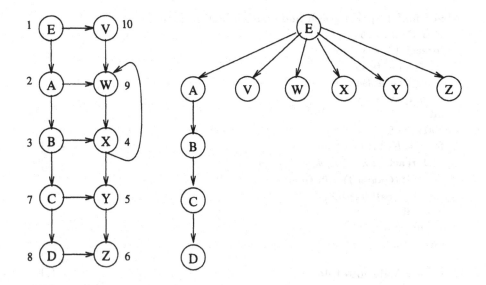

Fig. 1. Flow graph and its dominator tree.

X	$DF(X)$
A	$\{W,X,Y,Z\}$
B	$\{X,Y,Z\}$
C	$\{Y,Z\}$
D	$\{Z\}$
V	$\{W\}$
W	$\{X\}$
X	$\{W,Y\}$
Y	$\{Z\}$
Z	$\{\}$
E	$\{\}$

Fig. 2. Dominance frontiers for Figure 1.

Our algorithm essentially partitions equidominates into blocks of nodes that are in each other's iterated dominance frontiers, but without the expense of explicitly computing dominance frontiers. The relevant portions of our algorithm refer to $Cnum(X)$, $LL(X)$, or $Map(X)$; these are paraphrases of a *strongly-connected component* (SCC) algorithm [1], which we use to find (some) strongly-connected components of the dominance frontier graph (in which an edge from Y to Z implies $Z \in DF(Y)$). While the details of $Cnum(X)$ and $LL(X)$ are beyond the scope of this paper [1], we note that $Map(X)$ is the representative node for

Algorithm[1] Sparse graph node determination (simple)

```
NodeCount ← 0
foreach (X ∈ 𝒩ƒ) do
    Υ(X) ← false
    Φ(X) ← false
    Map(X) ← X
od
Cnum ← 0
for n = N downto 1 do                                        ⇐ 1
    foreach ({ Z | dfn(idom(Z)) = n }) do                    ⇐ 2
        if (Cnum(Z) = 0) then
            call Visit(Z)
        fi
    od
od

for n = N downto 1 do                                        ⇐ 3
    foreach ({ Z | dfn(idom(Z)) = n }) do                    ⇐ 4
        call Finish(Z)                                       ⇐ 5
    od
od
end


Function FindSnode(Y, P) : node
    for (X = Y) repeat(X = idom(X)) do
        if (Υ(Map(X)) or (idom(X) = P)) then
            return (Map(X))
        fi
    od
end
```

Fig. 3.

the SCC containing node X. Throughout this paper, "SCC" or "component" refers to nodes associated in this manner.

Central to this algorithm is the function $FindSnode(Y, P)$, which ascends the dominator tree from node Y, searching for a sparse graph node below P. Our proof of algorithmic correctness (Section 3) relies on the nature of $FindSnode()$ rather than its actual implementation: the function always returns

$$X \mid Z \in DF^+(X), \ Z \in Succ(Y), \ P \gg X \ggcurly Y$$

We present a straightforward, albeit inefficient, version of $FindSnode(Y, P)$ in Figure 3. The correctness of our algorithm as presented in Section 3 is based

Procedure $Visit(Z)$
    $LL(Z) \leftarrow Cnum(Z) \leftarrow ++NodeCount$
    call $push(Z)$ $\Leftarrow$ 6
    foreach $((Y, Z) \in \mathcal{E}_f \mid Y \neq idom(Z))$ **do** $\Leftarrow$ 7
        $s \leftarrow FindSnode(Y, idom(Z))$ $\Leftarrow$ 8
        if $(idom(s) \neq idom(Z))$ **then**
            call $IncludeNode(Z)$ $\Leftarrow$ 9
        else
            if $(Cnum(s) = 0)$ **then**
                call $Visit(s)$ $\Leftarrow$ 10
                $LL(Z) \leftarrow min(LL(Z), LL(s))$
            else
                if $((Cnum(s) < Cnum(Z))$ **and** $OnStack(s))$ **then**
                    $LL(Z) \leftarrow min(LL(Z), Cnum(s))$
                fi
            fi
            if $(\Upsilon(s)$ **and not** $OnStack(s))$ **then** $\Leftarrow$ 11
                call $IncludeNode(Z)$ $\Leftarrow$ 12
            fi
        fi
    od
    if $(LL(Z) = Cnum(Z))$ **then**
        repeat $\Leftarrow$ 13
            $Q \leftarrow pop()$ $\Leftarrow$ 14
            $Map(Q) \leftarrow Z$
            if $(Q \in \mathcal{N}_\alpha)$ **then**
                call $IncludeNode(Q)$ $\Leftarrow$ 15
            fi
            if $(\Upsilon(Q))$ **then**
                call $IncludeNode(Z)$ $\Leftarrow$ 16
            fi
        until $(Q = Z)$
    fi
end

Fig. 4.

on the behavior of $FindSnode()$. To obtain our almost-linear time bound, we modify our algorithm as discussed in Section 4.

    The algorithm is shown in Figures 3, 4, and 5. We now illustrate the application of the algorithm to the flow graph in Figure 1, assuming that $\mathcal{N}_\alpha = \{ B \}$. Although the full proofs appear in Section 3, we mention here that:

$$Z \in DF(X) \Rightarrow dfn(idom(X)) \geq dfn(idom(Z))$$

By ensuring that nodes with higher depth first number have already been cor-

468

Procedure *IncludeNode(X)*
  $\Upsilon(X) \leftarrow$ **true** $\Leftarrow$ ⟨17⟩
end

Procedure *finish(Z)*
  foreach $((Y, Z) \in \mathcal{E}_f \mid Y \neq idom(Z))$ **do**
    $s \leftarrow FindSnode(Y, idom(Z))$
    if $(\Upsilon(s))$ **then**
        $\Phi(Z) \leftarrow$ **true** $\Leftarrow$ ⟨18⟩
    fi
  od
  if $(\Upsilon(Map(Z)))$ **then**
    call *IncludeNode(Z)* $\Leftarrow$ ⟨19⟩
  fi
end

Fig. 5.

rectly determined to be in $\mathcal{N}_\sigma$, the algorithm can correctly determine this property for nodes of lower depth first number.

The loop at ⟨1⟩ begins with V (depth-first numbered 10 in Figure 1), but since no nodes are dominated by V, no steps are taken by ⟨2⟩; the same holds for nodes W and D. When ⟨1⟩ considers C, loop ⟨2⟩ calls *Visit* with D. The loop in *Visit* at ⟨7⟩ is empty, since the only predecessor of D immediately dominates D. Thus, $Map(D)$ is set to D in loop ⟨13⟩. Loop ⟨1⟩ then considers in turn Z, Y, and X, each of which dominates no node, so ⟨2⟩ is empty. When ⟨1⟩ considers B, *Visit* is called on C, but since C's only predecessor immediately dominates C, no action is taken by ⟨7⟩, and $Map(C)$ is set to C. When *Visit* is next called on B, $Map(B)$ is set to B; also, since $B \in \mathcal{N}_\alpha$, step ⟨15⟩ places B in $\mathcal{N}_\sigma$.

When ⟨1⟩ considers E, suppose loop ⟨2⟩ considers the nodes immediately dominated by E in order A, Y, W, X, V, and Z (although some of these will already have been processed by recursive calls to *Visit*). When *Visit* works on A, no steps of ⟨7⟩ are taken, and $Map(A)$ becomes A. When *Visit* works on Y, *FindSnode* will be called on C and X.

- For C, *FindSnode* returns B; since B and Y are not equidominates, Y is placed in $\mathcal{N}_\sigma$ by ⟨9⟩.
- For X, *FindSnode* returns X; since X and Y are equidominates, *Visit* is called recursively on X. In this invocation, loop ⟨7⟩ considers nodes B and W.
  - For B, *FindSnode* returns B, so X is placed in $\mathcal{N}_\sigma$.
  - For W, *FindSnode* returns W, so *Visit* is called recursively on W. In this invocation, loop ⟨7⟩ considers nodes A, V, and X.
    * For A, *FindSnode* returns A. Since that node has already been visited, and since A is not in $\mathcal{N}_\sigma$, nothing happens to W because of A.

* For V, $FindSnode$ returns V; $Visit$ is then called recursively for V, where $Map(V)$ becomes V.
* For X, $FindSnode$ returns X, which is already on stack, so nothing happens. In particular, $Map(X)$ is not set.

Now, $Map(W)$ and $Map(X)$ are both set to W. Since $X \in \mathcal{N}_\sigma$, W is placed in $\mathcal{N}_\sigma$.

When loop ② considers W, X, and V, each has already been visited. When $Visit$ is called for Z, nodes D and Y are considered by ⑦.

- For D, $FindSnode$ returns B, so Z is placed in $\mathcal{N}_\sigma$.
- For Y, $FindSnode$ returns Y, which has already been visited.

In contrast, previous methods [9, 6] would not only have constructed all dominance frontier sets in Figure 2, which are asymptotically quadratic in size, but would also have iterated through the dominance frontier sets of all nodes put on the worklist, namely $\{ E, B, V, W, X, Y, Z \}$.

3 Correctness

We begin with some preliminary lemmas. Omitted proofs can be found in [11].

Lemma 2.

$$(Y, Z) \in \mathcal{E}_f \implies idom(Z) \gg Y$$

Corollary 3.

$$(Y, Z) \in \mathcal{E}_f \text{ and } Y \neq idom(Z) \implies$$
$$dfn(idom(Z)) \leq dfn(idom(Y)) < dfn(Y)$$

Corollary 4.

$$(Y, Z) \in \mathcal{E}_f \text{ and } Y \neq idom(Z) \implies$$
$$idom(Z) \gg idom(Y) \gg Y$$

Lemma 5. *If X is an ancestor of $idom(Z)$ in the depth-first spanning tree DFST of $\mathcal{G}_f$, and $idom(Z) \gg Y$, then*

$$X \gg Y \implies X \gg Z$$

Theorem 6. *If X is an ancestor of $idom(Z)$ in the depth-first spanning tree DFST of $\mathcal{G}_f$, then Z cannot be in the dominance frontier of X.*

Theorem 7.

$$Z \in DF(X) \Longrightarrow dfn(X) > dfn(idom(Z))$$

Theorem 8.

$$Z \in DF(X) \Longrightarrow idom(Z) \gg X$$

Corollary 9.

$$Z \in DF(X) \Longrightarrow dfn(idom(X)) \geq dfn(idom(Z))$$

The following lemmas which formalize those properties of our algorithm that participate in our correctness proof. We omit proofs that directly follow from inspection of our algorithm.

Lemma 10. *Visit is called exactly once for each node in Flowgraph.*

Lemma 11. *During all calls to Visit, each node is pushed and popped exactly once.*

Lemma 12.

$$Y = Map(X) \Longrightarrow idom(Y) = idom(X)$$

Lemma 13. *At step* $\boxed{12}$, *node s (referenced at step* $\boxed{11}$*) has already been pushed and popped.*

Corollary 14. *Any invocation of IncludeNode(s) must already have occurred at step* $\boxed{12}$.

Lemma 15.

$$OnStack(X) \text{ and } OnStack(Y) \Longrightarrow idom(X) = idom(Y)$$

Lemma 16. *At step* $\boxed{8}$, *FindSnode() returns*

$$s \mid s = Map(S), \ Z \in DF(S)$$

Lemma 17.

$$Map(X) = Map(Y) \Longrightarrow Y \in DF^+(X) \text{ or } X = Y$$

Corollary 18.

$$s \in \mathcal{N}_\sigma \iff Map(s) \in \mathcal{N}_\sigma$$

Theorem 19. *As of step* $\boxed{3}$,

$$\varUpsilon(Map(X)) \iff Map(X) \in \mathcal{N}_\sigma$$

Theorem 20. *After the call to* finish,

$$\varPhi(Z) \iff Z \in \mathcal{N}_\phi$$

Theorem 21. *After calls to* $finish()$,

$$\varUpsilon(X) \iff X \in \mathcal{N}_\sigma$$

4 Complexity

In this section, we first show that our algorithm is $O(N + E + T)$, where N is the number of nodes and E the number of edges in the input flowgraph, and T is the total time for all calls to *FindSnode*. Unfortunately, T is not linear using *FindSnode* as written. We then provide a faster version of our algorithm and show that our correctness results still hold. In our faster algorithm, T is $O(E\alpha(E))$, obtaining our desired almost-linear complexity bound.

4.1 Analysis of Initial Algorithm

Theorem 22. *The algorithm of Figure 3 is* $O(N + E + T)$, *where* N *is the number of nodes and* E *the number of edges in the input flowgraph, and* T *is the total time for all calls to* $FindSnode$.

We now analyze the asymptotic behavior of the function $FindSnode(Y, P)$ as shown in Figure 3. Each invocation could require visiting each node on a dominator tree path from **Entry** to Y. The cost of applying $FindSnode()$ to each of N flow graph nodes is then $O(N^2)$. As such, the overall asymptotic behavior of the simple version of our algorithm is $O(E \times N)$.

Procedure *Initialize*

    $NodeCount \leftarrow 0$

    foreach $(X \in \mathcal{N}_f)$ **do**

        $\Upsilon(X) \leftarrow$ **false**

        $\Phi(X) \leftarrow$ **false**

        $Map(X) \leftarrow X$

    od

    foreach $(X \in \mathcal{N}_f)$ **do** $\Leftarrow$ [20]

        $link(X) \leftarrow \perp$

        $Label(X) \leftarrow -dfn(X)$

    od

    $Cnum \leftarrow 0$

end

Procedure *IncludeNode(X)*

    $\Upsilon(X) \leftarrow$ **true**

    call $Update(X, dfn(X))$ $\Leftarrow$ [21]

end

Fig. 6.

4.2 Faster Algorithm

Using a *path-compression* result due to Tarjan [17], we rewrite certain parts of our algorithm (shown in Figures 6 and 7) to use the instructions:

$Eval(Y)$: Using the links established by the $Link()$ instruction, $Eval()$ ascends the dominator tree from Y, returning the node of maximum label. The label initially associated with each node X is $-dfn(X)$; the link of each node is initially $\perp$.

$Link(Y, idom(Y))$: sets $link(Y) = idom(Y)$. Any $Eval()$ search that includes node Y now also includes the immediate dominator of Y.

$Update(X, dfn(X))$: changes the label associated with X to $dfn(X)$. This instruction is issued when node X becomes included in set $\mathcal{N}_\sigma$.

The path-compressing version of algorithm is obtained as follows:

1. We initialize the path-compression at steps [20] and [24].
2. Links are inserted to extend the $Eval()$ search at steps [22] and [25].
3. Path information is updated whenever a node X is added to the sparse graph, at step [21].
4. We redefine function $FindSnode()$ by:

    Function $FindSnode(Y, P)$: *node*

        return $(Map(Eval(Y)))$ $\Leftarrow$ [27]

    end

```
call Initialize
for n = N downto 1 do
    foreach ({ Z | dfn(idom(Z)) = n }) do
        if (Cnum(Z) = 0) then
            call Visit(Z)
        fi
    od
    foreach ({ Z | dfn(idom(Z)) = n }) do                    ⟸ 22
        if (Z = Map(Z)) then                                 ⟸ 23
            call Link(Z, idom(Z))
        else
            call Link(Z, Map(Z))
        fi
    od
od
foreach (X ∈ N_f) do                                         ⟸ 24
    link(X) ← ⊥
    Label(X) ← − dfn(X)
od
for n = N downto 1 do
    foreach ({ Z | dfn(idom(Z)) = n }) do
        call Finish(Z)
    od
    foreach ({ Z | dfn(idom(Z)) = n }) do                    ⟸ 25
        if (Z = Map(Z)) then                                 ⟸ 26
            call Link(Z, idom(Z))
        else
            call Link(Z, Map(Z))
        fi
    od
od
```

Fig. 7.

We must now show:

1. We use the above instructions in a manner consistent with their definition [17]: operations $Link()$ and $Update()$ are applied to nodes at the end of a "link-path".

   Lemma 23. *At steps* $\boxed{23}$ *and* $\boxed{26}$, $link(Z) = \bot$ *prior to invoking* $Link()$.

   Lemma 24. *When* $Update(X, dfn(X))$ *is invoked at step* $\boxed{21}$, $link(X) = \bot$.

2. Use of these instructions does not change the output of our algorithm.

Lemma 25. *As invoked during the course of their respective algorithms, each implementation of $FindSnode(Y, P)$ returns the same answers.*

Theorem 26. *Our faster algorithm takes $O(E\alpha(E))$ time.*

5   Preliminary Experiments

Although we have described flow graphs where the worst case, quadratic behavior of the standard algorithms does occur, previous experiments [9] have indicated this behavior is not expected in practice on real programs. We performed an experiment, wherein ϕ-functions were placed (toward construction of SSA form) in 139 Fortran procedures taken from the Perfect [4] (*Ocean*, *Spice*, *QCD*) benchmark suite and from the Eispack [16] and Linpack [12] subroutine library. In Figure 8 we compare the speed of our simple (i.e., without balanced path-compression) but asymptotically faster algorithm given in Section 2 with the speed of the usual algorithm [9]; these execution times were obtained on a SparcStation 10, and they represent only the time necessary to compute the location of ϕ-functions.

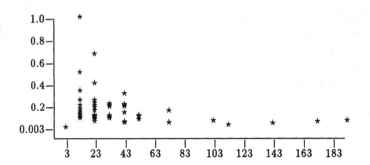

Fig. 8. Speedup of our algorithm vs. execution time (in milliseconds) of usual ϕ-placing algorithm

Most of the runs show that the execution time of our algorithm is linear (with a small constant) in the execution time of the usual algorithm, and so can be expected to also exhibit linear behavior in practice on the same programs. Because each of these runs took under 1 second, both algorithms are fast on this collection of programs. We have not implemented the balanced path-compression, and so these experiments did not reflect any improvements that might be gained by this theoretically more efficient algorithm.

Though not represented in Figure 8, we also experimented with a series of increasingly taller "ladder" graphs of the form shown in Figure 1, where worst-case behavior is expected. Our algorithm demonstrated better performance when these ladder graphs had 10 or more rungs, though smaller graphs take scant execution time anyway. Our algorithm is twice as fast as the usual algorithm for a ladder graph of 75 rungs, taking 20 milliseconds while the usual algorithm took 40 milliseconds.

In summary, comparison of our simple algorithm to the usual algorithm shows

- linear performance for the same cases as the usual algorithm, although our median test case exhibited performance degradation of a factor of 3;
- a factor of 2 better performance for some artificially generated cases.

Thus, preliminary evidence indicates comparable expected performance using our simple algorithm.

6 Conclusions and Future Work

In this paper we have shown how to eliminate the potentially costly step of computing dominance frontiers when constructing Sparse Evaluation Graphs or SSA form. By directly determining the conditions under which a node is a ϕ-node, rather than by iterating through the dominance frontiers, we obtain a worst case almost-linear bound for constructing SEG's and a worst case almost-quadratic bound for constructing SSA form. In both cases, we have eliminated the $O(N^2)$ behavior associated with computing and using dominance frontiers. We have also given preliminary experimental evidence that our simple algorithm's behavior, though slower in many cases, is comparable in practice to the usual algorithm.

Future work will incorporate balanced path-compression into our simple algorithm, and compare the results on real and artificially generated cases.

Acknowledgements

We thank Dirk Grunwald and Harini Srinivasan for their suggestions as we began work on this paper. We are grateful to our referees, especially the one who found a mistake in our proofs.

References

1. Alfred Aho, John Hopcroft, and Jeffrey Ullman. *The Design and Analysis of Computer Algorithms.* Addison-Wesley, 1974.
2. A.V. Aho, R. Sethi, and J.D. Ullman. *Compilers: Principles, Techniques, and Tools.* Addison-Wesley, 1986.
3. Bowen Alpern, Mark N. Wegman, and F. Kenneth Zadeck. Detecting equality of variables in programs. *Fifteenth ACM Principles of Programming Languages Symposium*, pages 1–11, January 1988. San Diego, CA.

4. M. Berry,
   D. Chen, P. Koss, D. Kuck, S. Lo, Y. Pang, R. Roloff, A. Sameh, E. Clementi,
   S. Chin, D. Schneider, G. Fox, P. Messina, D. Walker, C. Hsiung, J. Schwarzmeier,
   K. Lue, S. Orszag, F. Seidl, O. Johnson, G. Swanson, R. Goodrum, and J. Martin.
   The perfect club benchmarks: Effective performance evaluation of supercomputers
   the performance evaluation club (perfect). Technical report, U. of Ill–Center for
   Supercomputing Research and Development, November 1988.

5. Jong-Deok Choi, Michael Burke, and Paul Carini. Efficient flow-sensitive inter-
   procedural computation of pointer-induced aliases and side effects. *Conference
   Record of the Twentieth Annual ACM Symposium on Principles of Programming
   Languages*, January 1993.

6. Jong-Deok Choi, Ron Cytron, and Jeanne Ferrante. Automatic construction of
   sparse data flow evaluation graphs. *Conference Record of the Eighteenth Annual
   ACM Symposium on Principles of Programming Languages*, January 1991.

7. Jong-Deok Choi, Ron Cytron, and Jeanne Ferrante. On the efficient treatment of
   preserving definitions. Technical report, IBM Research, 1991. Research Report
   RC17065.

8. Thomas H. Cormen, Charles E. Leiserson, and Ronald L. Rivest. *Introduction to
   Algorithms*. The MIT Press, 1990.

9. Ron Cytron, Jeanne Ferrante, Barry K. Rosen, Mark N. Wegman, and F. Kenneth
   Zadeck. Efficiently computing static single assignment form and the control de-
   pendence graph. *ACM Transactions on Programming Languages and Systems*,
   October 1991.

10. Ron Cytron, Andy Lowry, and Ken Zadeck. Code motion of control structures
    in high-level languages. *Conf. Rec. of the ACM Symp. on Principles of Compiler
    Construction*, 1986.

11. Ron K. Cytron and Jeanne Ferrante. Efficiently computing ϕ-nodes on-the-fly.
    Technical report, IBM T.J. Watson Research Labs, 1993. Order as RC19099. Also
    available as technical report WUCS 93-24 from Washington University in St. Louis
    and wuarchive ftp.

12. J. J. Dongarra, J. R. Bunch, C. B. Moler, and G. W. Stewart. *Linpack Users'
    Guide*. SIAM Press, 1979.

13. Richard Johnson and Keshav Pingali. Dependence-based program analysis. *Pro-
    ceedings of the ACM SIGPLAN '93 Conference on Programming Langauge Design
    and Implementation*, 1993. Published as SIGPLAN Notices Volume 28 Number 6.

14. Thomas J. Marlowe. *Data Flow Analysis and Incremental Iteration*. PhD thesis,
    Rutgers University, October 1989.

15. Barry K. Rosen, Mark N. Wegman, and F. Kenneth Zadeck. Global value num-
    bers and redundant computations. *Fifteenth ACM Principles of Programming
    Languages Symposium*, pages 12–27, January 1988. San Diego, CA.

16. B. T. Smith, J. M. Boyle, J. J. Dongarra, B. S. Garbow, Y. Ikebe, V. C. Klema,
    and C. B. Moler. *Matrix Eigensystem Routines – Eispack Guide*. Springer-Verlag,
    1976.

17. Robert Tarjan. Applications of path compression on balanced trees. *JACM*,
    26(4):690–715, October 1979.

18. Mark Wegman and Ken Zadeck. Constant propagation with conditional branches.
    Conf. Rec. Twelfth ACM Symposium on Principles of Programming Languages,
    pages 291–299, January 1985.

Construction of Thinned Gated
Single-Assignment Form*

Paul Havlak

Center for Research on Parallel Computation,
Rice University, Houston TX 77251-1892 USA

Abstract. Analysis of symbolic expressions benefits from a suitable program representation. We show how to build thinned gated single-assignment (TGSA) form, a value-oriented program representation which is more complete than standard SSA form, defined on all reducible programs, and better for representing symbolic expressions than program dependence graphs or original GSA form. We present practical algorithms for constructing thinned GSA form from the control dependence graph and SSA form. Extensive experiments on large Fortran programs show these methods to take linear time and space in practice. Our implementation of value numbering on TGSA form drives scalar symbolic analysis in the ParaScope programming environment.

1   Introduction

Analysis of non-constant values yields significant benefits in a parallelizing compiler. The design of a symbolic analyzer requires careful choice of a program representation, that these benefits may be gained without using excessive time and space.

In symbolic analysis, we need to represent and compare both constant and non-constant expressions. This aids dependence testing, when we compare array subscripts; and dead code elimination, when we try to evaluate comparisons for branches. If our expression representation is self-contained, we can re-use the symbolic analysis system in multiple contexts, independent of other program representations or their absence.

Merges of program execution paths complicate the construction of symbolic expressions. In straight-line or branching code, we can simply replace each reference to a variable with the expression assigned at the unique reaching definition of that variable. This process of forward substitution yields a complete expression, in the usual form, with constants or external inputs at the leaves. Introduce merging, and we must find a way to represent the combination of values from multiple, conditionally executed assignments, or else give up on these cases.

* This work was supported in part by ARPA contract DABT63-92-C-0038 and NSF Cooperative Agreement No. CCR-9120008. Use of a Sun Microsystems Sparc 10 was provided under NSF Cooperative Agreement No. CDA-8619893. The content of this paper does not necessarily reflect the position or the policy of the Government and no official endorsement should be inferred.

Consider the problem of representing the value of I printed by the program in Figure 1.[2] The control flow graph (G_{CF}) provides complete information, but is inconveniently organized. We have the choice of running the program (if the input is available) to see the output, or of augmenting or replacing G_{CF} with another program form.

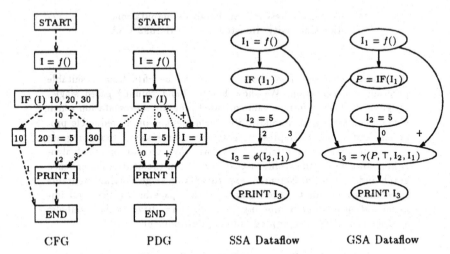

CFG   PDG   SSA Dataflow   GSA Dataflow

Fig. 1. Program Representations

One candidate representation is the program dependence graph (PDG). There are actually several varieties of PDG used in compilers and other program transformation systems [14, 18]. The PDG variant shown in Figure 1 was introduced by Cartwright and Felleisen [7]. The solid arrows represent the flow of data and the dotted arrows execution decisions.

This PDG may be interpreted by allowing each node to execute when it receives a control token from a control-dependence predecessor and for each variable reference, a data token from a data-dependence predecessor [7]. Assignments distribute data tokens to all their successors, but each branch sends control tokens only on edges whose labels correspond to the value of the predicate.[3]

While the PDG is a complete replacement for G_{CF}, its structure clashes with the requirements for a symbolic expression representation. It is far from clear how to write an expression for the merge that produces the printed value of I. And though the merge and the branch that controls it are close together in this example, in general they can be arbitrarily far apart in the PDG.

---

[2] We use the subscripted name V_i to indicate definition i of variable V or the value of that definition.

[3] We generalize the traditionally Boolean notion of predicate to include the multiway tests common in Fortran and C; e.g., the branch in Figure 1 depending on I's being negative ($-$), zero, or positive ($+$).

A second possibility is static single assignment (SSA) form [3]. In Figure 1, we give the def-use chains built on the SSA form of the program, where *pseudo-assignments* have been added at merges of values. $I_3 = \phi(I_2, I_1)$ looks like a nice expression for the merge. However, the ϕ function is not referentially transparent; its result depends not only on its inputs but also on which control flow edge (2 or 3) executes. Were we to encounter a ϕ function with the same inputs elsewhere in the program, we could not assume their equivalence.

Gated single-assignment (GSA) form solves these problems by extending SSA form with new functions that encode control over value merges. GSA form was introduced as part of the program dependence web, and descends from the high-level variant of SSA form (defined only for structured code) [5, 3].

In Figure 1, the γ function takes the predicate controlling the merge as an explicit input. Depending on whether I_1 is zero or positive, the new value for I_3 is I_2 (5) or I_1, respectively. If I_1 is negative, then I_3 represents an unexecutable expression, denoted by $\top$. We can treat a $\top$ value as equivalent to any other when it executes, because it never does.

Handling of merges with referentially transparent functions and the resulting independence from G_{CF} together make GSA form an adequate representation for symbolic expressions. However, because original GSA form was designed with other purposes in mind, it contains some control information that we consider extraneous to symbolic analysis. We introduce thinned gated single-assignment (TGSA) form with the extra information deleted.[4] We show how to build TGSA form using SSA form and the unfactored control dependence graph.

Section 2 describes the control and data-flow information needed to build TGSA form. Thinned GSA form is defined in Section 3. The algorithms given in Section 4, for building TGSA form, are shown in Section 5 to require linear time and space under reasonable assumptions and throughout extensive experiments. Section 6 describes current and future uses for TGSA form, Section 7 covers related work, and and we conclude in Section 8.

2 Background and Notation

Building TGSA form for a procedure requires its control flow graph, control dependences and def-use chains for SSA form. This section describes the preliminary graphs and our notation.

2.1 Control Flow

The nodes of the control-flow graph G_{CF} are basic blocks, each containing zero or more statements in straight-line sequence. Control flow can branch or merge only between basic blocks; wherever execution can flow from one block to another, a

---

[4] Our thinning consists of using fewer functions to replace a given ϕ than original GSA form. It should not be confused with *pruning*, which refers to the elimination of dead ϕ assignments in SSA form—those that reach no uses [8].

G_{CF} edge goes from the former block to the latter. A unique START node has no in-edges and an out-edge to every procedure entry; a unique END node has no out-edges and an in-edge from every procedure exit.

A node with multiple out-edges is a *branch*, with each out-edge labeled by the corresponding value of the branch predicate. A node with multiple in-edges is a *merge*, and its inedges are ordered.

From this graph we derive trees for dominator and loop nesting relationships. The immediate predominator of a block B, denoted $B.Ipredom$, is the last of the nodes ($\neq B$) that lie on every path from START to B. B's immediate postdominator, $B.Ipostdom$, is the first of the nodes ($\neq B$) lying on every path from B to END [21]. $B.Header$ lies on every path into and around the most deeply nested loop containing B.[5]

For some purposes we ignore back-edges (from a node to the header of a surrounding loop), leaving us with the forward control-flow graph F_{CF}. In this paper, *structured* applies to code for which F_{CF} has the fork-join property: each merge is the immediate postdominator of exactly one branch *and* all paths from a branch remain distinct until they join at the merge which immediately post-dominates the branch. (Note that C-style **break** and **continue**, as well as **goto**s, can produce unstructured code.)

2.2 Control Dependence

The control dependence graph G_{CD} consists of the basic blocks from G_{CF} with a different set of edges.[6] Given a G_{CF} edge e with label L from a branch node B, control dependence edges, also labeled L, go from B to every node that must execute if e is taken [12].

Loop-carried control dependence edges run from conditional branches out of a loop to the header block of the loop. Ignoring these edges leaves the acyclic forward control-dependence graph F_{CD} [11].

2.3 Static Single-Assignment (SSA) Form

We focus on SSA form as an improved version of def-use chains. The nodes of the SSA-form def-use graph G_{DU}^{SSA} are the original program references plus pseudo-assignments, called ϕ nodes.

SSA construction entails adding the ϕ nodes at the beginning of merge blocks, so that only they, and no original references, are reached by multiple definitions [12]. The source and sink of each def-use chain (G_{DU}^{SSA} edge) are subscripted in examples with the definition number of the source.

Each chain e into a ϕ node is also tagged with the last control flow edge ($e.CfEdge$) by which its definition reaches the merge. The ϕ serves as a merge

---

[5] Our loops are Tarjan intervals (nested strongly-connected regions), computed with minor extensions to Tarjan's test for flow-graph reducibility [24]. Irreducible loops are handled conservatively.

[6] The original presentation of GSA form uses a factored control dependence graph with added region nodes [5, 14].

function, as in Figure 1, denoting that if G_{CF} edge 3 into the merge executes, then $I_3 = \phi(I_2, I_1)$ assumes the value from definition I_1.

Loop-carried G_{DU}^{SSA} edges go from a definitions inside a loop to a ϕ node at the loop header. Ignoring these edges leaves the forward def-use graph F_{DU}^{SSA}. Each node n in the graph is annotated with the basic block (G_{CF} node) containing it, $n.Block$.

3 Definition of TGSA Form

Alpern *et al.* introduced the first gated version of static single-assignment form as high-level SSA form [3]. Ballance *et al.* introduced the terminology of gated single-assignment form [5]. TGSA form is an extension of high-level SSA form to unstructured code, for which we use the more convenient GSA-form notation. Detailed comparisons with the prior versions are given in Section 7.

Building TGSA form involves adding pseudo-assignments for a variable V:

(γ) at a control-flow merge when disjoint paths from a conditional branch come together and at least one of the paths contains a definition of V;
(μ) at the header of each loop that contains at least one definition of V; and
(η) at every exit from each loop that contains at least one definition of V.

The first two cases, merges in forward control flow and at loop entry, are handled with ϕ nodes in SSA form. The third case, merging iterative values at loop exit, is ignored by SSA form.

3.1 Structure

Gamma: Merge with Predicate. The pseudo-assignment inserted for a data-flow merge in forward control flow employs a γ function. In a simple case, the fragment

$V_1 := ...$
if (P) **then** $V_2 := ...$

is followed by $V_3 := \gamma(P, V_2, V_1)$. This indicates that if control flow reaches the merge and P was true, then V has the value from definition V_2.

We insert γ functions only to replace ϕ functions at merges of forward control flow. Whenever otherwise disjoint F_{CF} paths from an n-ary conditional branch (with predicate P) come to a merge, and at least one path redefines a variable V, we insert a definition $V' := \gamma(P, V_1, ..., V_n)$ at the merge point. Each of the V_i is the last definition (possibly another pseudo-assignment) occurring on a path from subprogram entry, through the branch, to the merge. The V_i are called the value inputs, P the predicate input. A γ is strict in its predicate input only; when the predicate has value i, the quantity from the ith value input is produced.

In unstructured code, paths from multiple branches may come together at a single merge. Replacing the ϕ then requires multiple γ functions, explicitly arranged in a dag. Such a γ dag is structured so that the immediate predominator of the merge provides the predicate for the root of the dag, and paths in the dag from the root to the leaves pass through γ functions with predicates from branches in the same order that F_{CF} paths from the immediate predominator to the merge pass through the branches themselves.

If some edges from a branch cannot reach a merge, then the corresponding locations in γ functions are given as $\top$, indicating that no value is provided. We disallow the case where all non-predicate arguments save one are $\top$, as in $\gamma(P, \top, ..., \top, V_i, \top, ..., \top)$ — if execution reaches the merge, then definition V_i must be providing the value. This simplification is one difference between *thinned* GSA form and original GSA form, which we exploit in our algorithms for building TGSA form.

Mu: Loop Merge. A pseudo-assignment at the header of a loop uses a μ function. For each variable V defined in a loop body, we insert a definition $V' := \mu(V_{init}, V_{iter})$ at the loop header, where V_{init} is the *initial input* reaching the header from outside (I_0 in Figure 2) and V_{iter} is the *iterative input*, reaching along the back-edge (I_2). If every loop header has one entry edge and one back-edge, then every ϕ at a loop header can be replaced exactly by one μ (otherwise, a γ dag may also be required to assemble one or both of the two inputs).

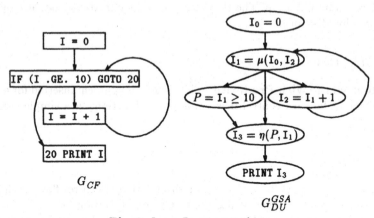

Fig. 2. Loop Representations

Since TGSA form is organized for demand-driven interpretation, there is no control over values flowing around a loop. A μ function can be viewed as producing an infinite sequence of values, one of which is selected by an η function at loop exit. (In original GSA form, μ functions have a predicate argument controlling iteration.)

Eta: Loop Value Selection. Pseudo-assignments inserted to govern values produced by loops use η functions. Given a loop that terminates when the predicate P is true, we split any def-use edge exiting the loop and insert a node $V' := \eta(P, V_{final})$, where V_{final} is the definition (I_1 in Figure 2) reaching beyond the loop. In general, a control-flow edge may exit many loops at once; for a variable that has been modified in the outermost L loops exited, we must insert a list of L η functions at the sink of the edge. The η function in TGSA form corresponds to the η^T function in original GSA form.

Loop-variance Level. The *level* of a node in G_{DU}^{GSA} is the nesting depth of the innermost loop with which it varies (or zero, for loop-invariant values). The level of a μ function equals the depth of the loop containing it; the depth of an η function equals the depth of the loop exited less 1. For any other function, the level is the maximum level over all its inputs.

Level information is required to distinguish μ functions that vary with different loops in a nest. For other nodes, level information is just a convenient annotation.

3.2 Interpretation

We give no formal semantics for the interpretation of TGSA form, but define a structural notion of congruence. Under certain conditions, congruent nodes can be assumed to have equivalent values.

Congruence. Structural congruence is a form of graph isomorphism, defined on a value graph which combines G_{DU}^{GSA} with expression trees [3]. Initially, we can view the value graph as copied from these two forms, so that values flow from definitions to uses through G_{DU}^{GSA} edges and from uses to definitions through expression trees.

Collapsing uses of variables with their reaching definitions is the equivalent of forward substitution. When this is done, the value graph is an expression dag or forest, as in [3].[7] Leaf nodes are constants and external inputs, and internal nodes are program operations (*e.g.*, arithmetic) and TGSA functions.

Leaf nodes are congruent if they are the same; other value graph nodes are structurally congruent if they have the same function (remembering to distinguish μ functions with different levels) and congruent inputs.[8] Program expressions are called congruent if their corresponding value graph nodes are congruent.

---

[7] In our implementation, G_{DU}^{GSA} is attached to G_{CF}. We also keep a map from each G_{DU}^{GSA} node to its corresponding value graph node.

[8] Two methods of discovering congruence are value numbering by hashing [1] and partitioning [3]. Partitioning can discover congruent cycles that hashing cannot; however, hashing is better suited to arithmetic simplification and lazy evaluation. We use hashing in our implementation, with extensions for inductive value recognition.

Equivalence. TGSA form is designed so that congruence of expressions can be detected regardless of their execution context. However, care is needed in inferring equivalence of expressions from congruence of their corresponding value graph nodes.

In loop-free code, every expression executes once or not at all. Congruent expressions have the same value if both execute. In code with loops, congruent loop-variant expressions with level L can be treated as equivalent only when they both execute for the same iteration of their outer L surrounding loops. Valid applications of this principle include:

- Common subexpression elimination: If two level-L program expressions are congruent and have their outermost L loops in common, L surrounding loops in common, then they assume the same value on the each iteration of the common loops. If, for example, the G_{CF} block containing one expression predominates that containing the other, we may save the result of the first expression to replace the second.
- Test elision: If congruent subexpressions are tested for equality, then they execute in synchrony and the test must always yield **true**. The **false** G_{CF} edges from the branch may be deleted, along with any code that becomes unreachable.
- Dependence testing: when analyzing subscripts to test for dependence carried at level L, assume that all loops shallower than L are frozen at some arbitrary iteration. Congruent subexpressions with level less than L may be treated safely as equivalent.

4 Construction of TGSA Form

We present algorithms for the two crucial steps in converting from SSA form to TGSA form: replacing a ϕ function with a directed acyclic graph of γ functions and building the controlling predicate of a loop for use in its η functions.

4.1 Augmenting G_{CF} and G_{DU}^{SSA}

For convenience, we assume that every G_{CF} node is reachable from START and reaches END (neither unreachable nor dead-end code exists). Loops are assumed reducible, so that all cycles pass through a unique header. (In the implementation, irreducible loops are conservatively left alone.) We build tree representations of loop nesting and of the pre- and post-dominator relations [21, 24]. By saving a preorder numbering of each tree, we can test for transitive as well as immediate loop nesting and dominance in constant time.

We augment loops, as shown in Figure 3, to provide suitable places for the placement of μ and η nodes. For each loop we add a preheader node (PH), if the header has multiple forward in-edges, and a postbody node (PB), if the header has multiple backward inedges or if the source of the back-edge is in an inner loop. The postbody node for each loop then terminates each complete iteration, and is post-dominated by the header. Wherever the sink of a loop-exit edge has other in-edges, we split the loop-exit edge with the addition of a postexit node (PE) [11]. These changes cause threefold growth in G_{CF} at worst.

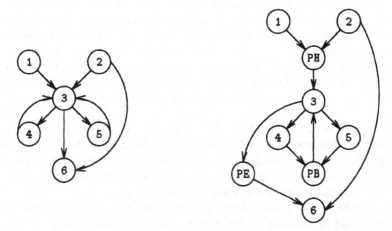

Fig. 3. Insertion of Preheader, Postbody and Postexit Nodes

The dominance and loop nesting trees are easily updated, and control dependence construction proceeds normally on the augmented G_{CF} [10]. As none of the new nodes are branches, control dependence edges among the original G_{CF} nodes are unaffected.

Construction of SSA form proceeds normally except for tweaks to the ϕ placement phase. Having ensured that each loop header has exactly two inedges, we place μ nodes at loop headers instead of ϕ nodes. Every μ node added represents a variable modified in the loop, and we immediately add an $\bar{\eta}$ definition for the same variable at the postexit node for the loop.[9] These trivial pseudo-assignments $(V' := \bar{\eta}(V))$ hold the place for later creation of η functions with predicates, and ensure proper placement of ϕ assignments for merges of values from different exits.

Once ϕ, μ, and $\bar{\eta}$ assignments have been placed, the linking of definitions to uses (often referred to as *renaming* in the SSA literature) proceeds as for standard SSA form, producing a variant of G_{DU}^{SSA}.

4.2 Data Structures

With μ and $\bar{\eta}$ assignments out of the way, the main work of building TGSA form lies in converting the remaining ϕ functions to dags of γ functions, and building

---

[9] If the postexit node is shared with a surrounding loop, we add nothing, as the appropriate $\bar{\eta}$ will be added for the outer loop.

other γ dags to represent loop-termination conditions.[10] Our solutions for these similar problems share many data structures, described below.

The procedure *replace_ϕs()*, shown in Figure 4, examines one ϕ function at a time and replaces it with a dag of γ functions. The γ dag has the same dataflow predecessors and successors as the original ϕ, except that each γ function also takes the result of a branch predicate as input. All of the γ functions in the dag replacing a ϕ are placed at the beginning of the basic block where the merge happens (ϕ.*Block*).

Likewise, *build_loop_predicate()* proceeds one loop at a time. The γ functions making up the dag for the loop-termination condition are placed at the postbody for the loop.

Branch.*Choices*: for a G_{CF} node *Branch*, a vector of one choice per out-edge. Each choice represents a value that will reach the merge if the branch goes the right way. A choice is either a leaf definition (pointing to a value computed at another G_{CF} node), another branch (representing the value chosen there), or $\top$ (indicating a choice to avoid the merge node).

In ϕ-replacement, a leaf definition is the choice if all the paths through the corresponding out-edge to the ϕ merge point pass through the same final definition. This chosen definition may occur before or after *Branch*. If there are instead multiple final definitions on these paths, then the branch choosing between them is specified as the choice for this out-edge. Such a branch must lie between *Branch* and the ϕ merge point. If no path through an out-edge reaches the ϕ merge point, then its corresponding choice entry is $\top$.

When building loop predicates, a leaf choice is **true** if an outedge must lead to the postbody or **false** if it cannot. If some paths through the outedge lead to the postbody and some do not, then a branch choice involved in the decision is specified.

Selectors: a set of G_{CF} branch nodes whose predicates will be used in building the γ dag for the current loop predicate or ϕ.

In ϕ-replacement, a branch is added to *Selectors* if and only if it affects, directly or indirectly, the choice of definition reaching the control flow merge. We add the branch to *Selectors* when we detect that two of its *Choices* are different and not $\top$. More precisely, the selectors of a ϕ assignment comprise the set of $n \in N_{CF}$ such that (1) $\exists$ at least two paths in F_{CF}, from n to ϕ.*Block*, disjoint except for their endpoints, and (2) $\exists$ such a path containing a definition of the ϕ's variable not at n or at ϕ.*Block*.

When building loop predicates, *Selectors* contains all branches inside the loop whose immediate postdominator is outside the loop (i.e., the nodes within the loop on which the postbody is transitively control dependent).

Branch.*FirstChoice*: used only in *replace_ϕs()*; it saves the first choice propagated back to the branch. Each choice propagated back to *Branch* is compared against this field. If the *FirstChoice* field already holds a different

---

[10] These algorithms are described in terms of building G_{DU}^{GSA}; they also can be used to build the GSA-form value graph on the fly.

procedure *replace_φs*(*Merge*):
    Predom := *Merge.lpredom*;
    foreach φ **at** *Merge* **do**
        foreach *CfEdge* entering *Merge* in F_{CF} **do** *init_walk*(*CfEdge.Source*);
        Selectors := {};
        foreach *DefEdge* entering φ in F_{DU} **do**
            CfEdge := *DefEdge.CfEdge*;   *Def* := *DefEdge.Source*;
            process_choice(*Def*, *CfEdge.Label*, *CfEdge.Source*);
        recursively build a dag γ from *Predom.Choices*;
        replace φ with γ;

procedure *init_walk*(*Node*):
    if (*Node.Fanout* > 1) **then**
        Node.Visits++;
        if (*Node.Visits* == 1) **then** *Node.Choices*[*] := *Node.FirstChoice* := ⊤;
        if (*Node* == *Predom*) **or** (*Node.Visits* ≠ 1) **then return**;
    /* on our first visit to non-*Predom* */
    foreach edge *Cd* entering *Node* in F_{CD} **do** *init_walk*(*Cd.Source*);

procedure *process_choice*(*Choice*, *Label*, *Node*):
    NewChoice := *Choice*;
    if (*Node.Fanout* > 1) **then**
        Node.Choices[*Label*] := *Choice*;   *Node.Visits*−−;
        if (*Node.FirstChoice* == ⊤) **then** *Node.FirstChoice* := *Choice*;
                        else **if** (*Node.FirstChoice* ≠ *Choice*) **then**
                                  Selectors += *Node*;
        if (*Node* == *Predom*) **or** (*Node.Visits* ≠ 0) **then return**;
        if (*Node* ∈ *Selectors*) **or**
          ((**not** *Thinned*) **and** (*Merge* ∉ *postdominators(Node)*)) **then**
          NewChoice := *Node*;
    /* on our last visit to non-*Predom* */
    foreach edge *Cd* entering *Node* in F_{CD} **do**
        process_choice(*NewChoice*, *Cd.Label*, *Cd.Source*);

Fig. 4. Replacing a φ with a dag of γs

value besides ⊤, then another choice has already been propagated, and we add *Branch* to *Selectors*.

Node.Visits: a counter, used only in replacing a φ. Initialized to zero, the multiple calls to *init_walk* increment *Visits* for branch nodes until it reaches the number of edges from branch that can lead to the merge. Later, calls to *process_choice* decrement *Visits* each time an edge from the branch node is processed. When *Visits* reaches zero again, then all paths from the branch to the merge have been examined. We then propagate the appropriate choice to the branch's G_{CD} predecessors: the branch itself, if it is a selector, else the one non-⊤ value from its choices.

CfNode.Exits This is the γ dag representing when the loop exits. While we could compute distinct conditions for each exit, it is sufficient to determine termination test for the entire loop.

Miscellaneous:

CfNode.Ipredom = immediate predominator;

SsaDuEdge.CfEdge = final G_{CF} edge along which a definition reaches a ϕ;

CfEdge.Label distinguishes edges sourced in the same conditional branch;

CfNode.FanOut = the number of outedges from a G_{CF} node.

Thinned is true for all examples given here; when false, extra $\top$ entries are left in γ functions.

4.3 γ Conversion

The routines in Figure 4 show how to replace a ϕ function with a dag of γ functions. We call *replace_ϕs()* for each node in topological order on F_{CF}, and it replaces any ϕ functions located there. The replacement proceeds one ϕ at a time. Auxiliary routines visit each control-dependence ancestor of F_{CF} predecessors of ϕ.*Block* in two passes. Consider their effects during *replace_ϕs(A3)* for the only ϕ assignment in Figure 5.

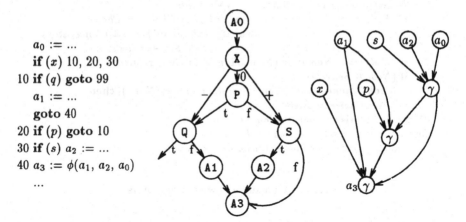

$a_0 := \dots$

if (x) 10, 20, 30

10 **if** (q) **goto** 99

$a_1 := \dots$

goto 40

20 **if** (p) **goto** 10

30 **if** (s) $a_2 := \dots$

40 $a_3 := \phi(a_1, a_2, a_0)$

$\dots$

Fig. 5. SSA-form Source, G_{CF}, and γ dag for Example

The first pass, by recursive calls to *init_walk()*, initializes fields for each node that might be a branch point for distinct paths to the merge. *Node.Visits* counts the number of visits in this walk; we will count back down on the next walk. At the end of this pass, the values for *Visits* in the example are: 1 for Q (because the other outedge cannot reach A3), 2 for S, 2 for P, and 3 for X. All choice vectors and *FirstChoice* fields are $\top$.

The second walk routine, *process_choice()*, propagates each reaching definition backwards from the ϕ until a branch is encountered. It is then entered as a choice for that branch. If another, different choice has already been entered (*Node.FirstChoice*), then the branch *Node* is added to *Selectors* for this ϕ. When we have finished all visits to a branch, we then push a choice (the branch itself, if it has been marked a selector) upwards from this branch to its controlling branch.

If we process G_{DU} edge (a_1, a_3) first, we execute *process_choice(* a_1, **nil**, **A1***)*. As this recurses, we decrement Q.*Visits* to 0, and continue propagating a_1 as the choice, since that was Q's first and only choice. When we return to the top level, we have P.*Choices* = $[a_1, \top]$ with one visit left, and X.*Choices* = $[a_1, \top, \top]$ with two visits left. (However, *Visits* is not always the same as the number of $\top$ choices left.)

If we next process G_{DU} edge (a_2, a_3), we execute *process_choice(* a_2, **nil**, **A2***)*. We then call *process_choice(* a_2, **true**, S*)*. We return having S.*Choices* = $[a_2, \top]$, with one visit one visit left.

The last edge processed at the top level is (a_0, a_3), and causes us to call *process_choice(* a_0, **true**, S*)*. This finishes off S's visits and makes it a selector, and finishes off P and X directly. We are left with *Selectors* = $\{S, P, X\}$, with their choice vectors $[a_2, a_0], [a_1, S]$, and $[a_1, P, S]$, respectively.

When the second walk is done, *Node.Choices* is fully defined for each selector. We then read off the γ dag starting at *Predom*. The γ function at the root of the dag takes its predicate input from the predicate controlling *Predom*'s branching, and its value inputs from the corresponding entries in the choice vector. Choices that are leaf definitions are made direct data inputs to the γ; a choice that is a selector is replaced with a γ function built recursively, in the same fashion, from the predicate and choice vector for the selector. The resulting γ dag for a_3 is shown rightmost in Figure 5.

We give no formal proof for the correctness of this procedure. Informally, one can easily show that *Selectors* is properly computed. To show correctness of the γ dags, we prove a one-to-one correspondence between paths in the γ dag replacing a ϕ and sequences of selectors encountered in execution paths reaching ϕ.*Block* in G_{CF}, based on the labels produced by the predicates at the selectors. The last definition on a G_{CF} path from START to ϕ.*Block* is the same as the leaf definition selected by the corresponding path through the γ dag.

4.4 η Construction

Figure 6 shows the procedures to build the γ dag for a loop-termination predicate. For each loop header, we pass its unique back-edge predecessor (its post-body node) to *build_loop_predicate()*. The γ dag built represents the negation of its control conditions, which correspond to the conditions for loop exit. We store this condition as *Loop.Exits*.

We now expand each $\tilde{\eta}$ — inserted earlier, one per loop-exit G_{CF} edge — so that there is one η per loop exited, and make the predicate input of each η refer to the loop-termination predicate for the corresponding loop. Each η takes input from the η from the next-inner loop exited on the same G_{CF} edge, and

```
procedure build_loop_predicate(End):
    Loop := End.Header;    Selectors := {};
    process_cds(End);
    Predom := Loop;
    while (Predom.Ipostdom predominates End) do Predom := Predom.Ipostdom;
    recursively build a dag from Predom.Choices;
    save negated dag as Loop.Exits;

procedure process_cds(Node):
    foreach edge Cd entering Node in F_CD do
        Pred := Cd.Source;
        if (Pred == Loop) or (Loop predominates Pred) then
            if (Pred ∉ Selectors) then /* assume all branches exit */
                Pred.Choices[*] := true;
                Selectors += Pred;
                process_cds(Pred);
            if (Node == End) then Pred.Choices[Cd.Label] := false; /* non-exit */
                                else /* possible exit path */
                                    Pred.Choices[Cd.Label] := Node;
```

Fig. 6. Building a loop-termination predicate

feeds the η for the next-outer loop exited, except that the innermost η gets the input of the original $\check{\eta}$ and the outermost η feeds the original uses of the $\check{\eta}$.

5 Theoretical and Experimental Complexity

We implemented these algorithms in the ParaScope programming environment [20] and tested them on 1227 procedures from 33 programs in the NAS, Perfect, SPEC, and RiCEPS benchmark suites [4, 9, 25, 22].[11] All told, these Fortran applications contain around 70,000 executable statements. The 23 largest procedures have over 400 G_{CF} nodes; the largest has 812.

5.1 Performance Parameters

The time and space required to build TGSA form are closely related to the size of SSA form, especially if reasonable bounds hold for a few program control-flow characteristics: the fan-out of conditional branches (c_b), the depth of loop nesting (c_l), the number of exits from any single loop (c_x), and the length of any F_{CD} path from the immediate predominator of a merge node to an F_{CF} predecessor of the merge (also referred to here as "the depth of unstructured control," c_u).

---

[11] RiCEPS is available for anonymous ftp at cs.rice.edu in the directory public/riceps.

Our notation reflects the belief that these quantities can be treated as small constants.

Our experiments indicate that these metrics usually have small values. The gross outliers from linear time and space requirements also exhibited large values for c_b, c_x, or c_u.

Auxiliary Analyses and Data Structures. Efficient methods exist for computing each of pre- and post-dominators, Tarjan intervals and control dependences [21, 24, 12, 10]. While the asymptotic time bounds range from almost linear to quadratic, for practical purposes, these methods are linear in the number of G_{CF} edges (E_{CF}).

The addition of blocks and edges to G_{CF} is bounded by the number of loop headers and loop-exit edges. The total observed growth in G_{CF} nodes was eight percent; the maximum growth in any procedure was a factor of two.

The addition of ϕ functions for SSA form affects the size of the dataflow graph. While the number of additional ϕ assignments *can* be quadratic in the number of original references, it is linear throughout extensive practical experiments [12]. The number of edges in G_{DU}^{SSA} is linear in the number of references if the arity of merges is constant. In practice, G_{DU}^{SSA} should be far smaller than traditional def-use chains, which are often quadratic in the number of references. Our results agree with the prior literature here.

Auxiliary data structures required to build GSA form from SSA form, such as the vectors of choices, are reused by different calls to *build_loop_predicate()* and *replace_ϕs()*. Their total size is $O(E_{CF})$.

μ and η Functions. There is one μ per loop per variable defined in the loop, which is exactly the number of ϕ functions at loop headers in standard SSA form. There are two cases of η functions. For variables defined in a loop, we need create only one η per level exited, so those η functions are at most $c_x c_l$ times as numerous as the μ functions. Other η functions must be created for predicates, when multiple loop-exit branches merge outside the loop. At the very worst, there are $c_x c_l$ of these η functions per γ dag (*i.e.*, per old ϕ). So the total number of η functions is $O(c_x c_l(\#\mu))$. Our experiments confirm this tight linear relationship, with an average of 1.5 η functions per μ. However, there is wide variation in the number of μ and η functions per loop, presumably because of differences in loop size.

The predicate input of an η refers to the corresponding loop's termination predicate, a γ dag with at most $(c_b - 1)$ γ functions for each block in the loop. (This worst case would require that every block end with a a multi-way loop exit.) The termination predicate is built in time proportional to its size. Since each block can be in at most c_l loops, the total size of all loop-termination predicates is $O(c_b c_l N_{CF})$. Our measurements do not distinguish γ functions in loop predicates from those replacing ϕs.

γ **Functions.** In structured code, there is only one merge point for each branch (i.e., paths from a branch merge only at its postdominator). In this situation, the γ dag replacing each ϕ has exactly the same inputs and space requirements as the ϕ, except for the addition of the predicate inputs.

In unstructured code, every branch between a ϕ's merge point and its predominator can potentially contribute to the size of the γ dag. A coarse bound for the maximum dag size in this case is $min(N_{CF}, c_b{}^{C_u})$. Therefore, the time and space to replace all the ϕ functions is linear for structured code and quadratic ($O(N_{CF} * N_{DU}^{SSA})$) for the worst case.

5.2 Overall Performance

Figure 7 plots the total size of G_{DU}^{SSA} (nodes and edges, with μ and $\check{\eta}$, but with not γ conversion) against the number of plain variable references (ordinary definitions and uses). While there is some spread, the relationship appears to be linear. The significant outlier is **master** from the RiCEPS program **boast**, with over 30 SSA nodes and edges per plain references. This routine contains one loop with an exceptionally large number of loop exit branches and edges.

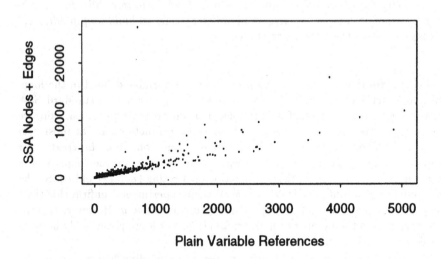

Fig. 7. SSA size vs. Plain References

Figure 8 compares the total size (nodes and edges) of G_{DU}^{GSA} and G_{DU}^{SSA}. The total growth over all procedures was 18 percent. The outlier **mosfet**, from the

SPEC version of `spice`, had a high maximum depth of unstructured control (c_u) — although a high c_u did not always cause such growth.

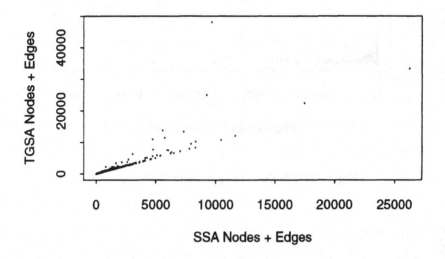

Fig. 8. Comparing size of TGSA and SSA forms

Figure 9 plots the total size of G_{DU}^{GSA} divided by the number of plain variable references. Only a very few small procedures have more than 20 TGSA elements per plain reference. The trend on this graph seems flat, implying a linear relationship between the size of TGSA form and the size of the program.

The total time required to build everything from G_{CF} to G_{DU}^{GSA} is plotted as milliseconds per G_{CF} node and edge in Figure 10. This graph is also quite flat, suggesting a linear relationship between analysis time and program size. The average time required per G_{CF} element on the entire sample was 2.4 ms; the average of the procedure averages was 3.1 ms.[12]

6 Applications and Future Work

We use TGSA form mostly in the analysis of scalar symbolic values, such as array subscripts and branch predicates. The implementation includes a conservative representation of array operations, which is used by other researcher [13].

---

[12] These measurements were taken inside the ParaScope programming environment, optimized with gcc version 2.4.5, running on a Sun MicroSystems Sparc 10 with 64 Mbytes of memory.

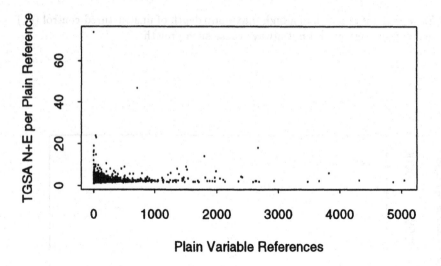

Fig. 9. TGSA Elements per Plain Reference

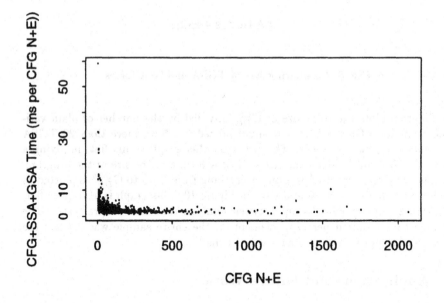

Fig. 10. Total Analysis Time per CFG Element

6.1 Symbolic Analysis

We have implemented value numbering by hashing on TGSA form in the Para-Scope programming environment [20]. The symbolic analyzer builds portions of the hashed value graph when requested by the dependence analyzer. The TGSA-form value graph represents symbolic expressions with a minimal amount of control information, which helps in comparing expressions from different contexts. However, extensions are needed to compute differences, such as dependence distances.

As expression dags are built, they are normalized on the fly by distributing multiplication over addition, extracting constant terms and coefficients, and sorting. Expressions are compared by constructing their difference, simplifying, and checking for a constant result. The power of this method subsumes that of the forward substitution used in earlier vectorizers [2], once further extensions are made for inductive value recognition [26]. While we have yet to complete our experiments with symbolic analysis, we can expect at least a 13 percent increase in dependences disproven, based on prior experience [16].

Related work on symbolic analysis has emphasized symbolic expressions [17] or linear inequalities [19]. The excessive worst-case bounds (cubic to exponential to undecidable) of symbolic analysis make experimental comparisons vitally important. Preliminary experiments with our implementation indicate that it takes time linear in the number of expressions analyzed.

6.2 Semantics

Recent work by John Field gives a formal treatment of graph rewriting on a representation resembling original GSA form [15]. The program representation graph of Horwitz *et al.* also resembles GSA form [27]. Further work is needed to establish a comparably solid formal foundation for TGSA form.

7 Related Work

7.1 High-level SSA form

Alpern *et al.* presented SSA form and proposed extensions to improve handling of conditional merges and loops [3]. For structured programs, their ϕ_{if}, ϕ_{enter}, and ϕ_{exit} are exactly equivalent to the TGSA-form versions of γ, μ, and η, respectively. They showed how to find the partition of nodes in a *value graph* based on SSA form that gives the maximum number of congruent nodes (equivalent expressions) without rewriting the graph.

TGSA form is identical to high-level SSA form for structured code. The same value partitioning methods apply to TGSA form, extending these results to unstructured programs.

7.2 Original GSA form

Ballance *et al.* introduced GSA form as a component of their program dependence web (PDW) [5]. GSA form seems to have been inspired both by high-level SSA form [3] and PDGs with valve nodes [7].

Original GSA form has an third input to the μ function, the loop-continuation predicate. In addition, it allows γ functions to have a single non-$\top$ value input, as in Figure 11.[13]

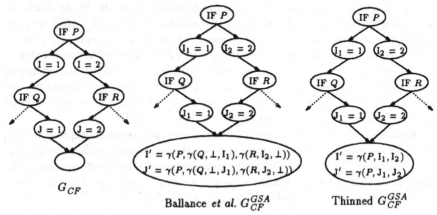

$$I' = \gamma(P, \gamma(Q, \bot, I_1), \gamma(R, I_2, \bot))$$
$$J' = \gamma(P, \gamma(Q, \bot, J_1), \gamma(R, J_2, \bot))$$

$$I' = \gamma(P, I_1, I_2)$$
$$J' = \gamma(P, J_1, J_2)$$

G_{CF}

Ballance *et al.* G_{CF}^{GSA} Thinned G_{CF}^{GSA}

Fig. 11. Different versions of GSA form on G_{CF}

Ballance *et al.* need this additional information to drive the insertion of switches, creating the data-driven form of their PDW. For symbolic analysis, it is sufficient to control values flowing out of a loop, and the predicates for η functions in thinned GSA form satisfy this purpose. Omitting the predicates on μ functions clarifies the independence of iterative sequences, such as induction variables, from the iteration count.

Extra γ functions can obscure equivalences. The original form's γ dags include both the predicates determining which definition reaches the merge *and* those determining whether or not the merge would execute.[14] In Figure 11, if I_1 and I_2 were equal, it would be much easier to notice the simplification for I' in TGSA form than in the original GSA form.

Original GSA form can be converted to thinned GSA form by globally simplifying the extra γ functions and ignoring the predicate inputs to μ functions.

---

[13] Actually, they use $\bot$, which makes sense in their dataflow interpretation, where unexecutable expressions are treated as divergent. In a demand-driven interpretation, unexecutable expressions can be assumed to have any value ($\top$), since that value will never be demanded.

[14] Because conditions for branches preceding the predominator of the merge are implied through the predicate of the γ, the extra functions occur only for unstructured merges.

While both algorithms for building GSA form seem to have the same asymptotic complexity, ours is simpler to implement, especially when working with an unfactored control dependence graph.

The Program Dependence Web researchers have recently developed another revised definition of GSA form, which retains the major differences between with thinned GSA form described above [6].

7.3 Program Dependence Graphs

Ferrante, Ottenstein and Warren introduced the program dependence graph, comprising data dependences and their now-standard formulation of control dependence [14]. Groups at Wisconsin and Rice have developed semantics for PDGs [18, 7, 23]. Selke gives semantics for programs with arrays and arbitrary control flow, and shows how to insert valve nodes efficiently.

Despite the greater maturity of PDGs as a program representation, they are inferior to TGSA form for value numbering. The inputs to each node include the control dependences under which that node executes, which would make value numbering overly conservative for dependence testing. However, ignoring control dependences in value numbering would produce results similar to those for SSA form; we would be unable to compare merged values from different parts of the program.

Perhaps rewriting systems can be defined for PDGs that have the same power as value numbering, but the practical efficiency of such an approach is uncertain.

8 Conclusion

We have introduced thinned gated single-assignment form, which is superior to previous program forms for value numbering. Our original algorithms for building TGSA form take linear time, asymptotically under reasonable assumptions and experimentally on large suite of Fortran applications. Value numbering on our implementation of TGSA form serves as the backbone of cheap yet powerful scalar symbolic analysis in the ParaScope programming environment.

Acknowledgements

I would like to thank Ken Kennedy and my other colleagues on the PFC and ParaScope projects at Rice. Bwolen Yang helped refine the algorithms through his persistent implementation efforts and questions. Robert Cartwright, Rebecca Parsons, and Mary Hall provided substantial help through discussions and comments on earlier drafts of this paper. Karl Ottenstein thoughtfully fielded my questions while attempting to refine the comparison between full and thinned GSA form.

References

1. Alfred V. Aho, Ravi I. Sethi, and Jeffrey D. Ullman. *Compilers: Principles, Techniques, and Tools*. Addison-Wesley, Reading, MA, second edition, 1986.

2. J. R. Allen. *Dependence Analysis for Subscripted Variables and Its Application to Program Transformations*. PhD thesis, Rice University, April 1983.

3. B. Alpern, M. N. Wegman, and F. K. Zadeck. Detecting equality of variables in programs. In *Conference Record of the Fifteenth ACM Symposium on the Principles of Programming Languages*, pages 1–11, San Diego, CA, January 1988.

4. David Bailey, Eric Barszcz, Leonardo Dagum, and Horst Simon. NAS parallel benchmark results. Technical Report RNR-92-002, NASA Ames Research Center, February 1993.

5. R. Ballance, A. Maccabe, and K. Ottenstein. The Program Dependence Web: a representation supporting control-, data-, and demand-driven interpretation of imperative languages. In *Proceedings of the SIGPLAN '90 Conference on Programming Language Design and Implementation*, pages 257–271, White Plains, New York, June 1990.

6. Philip L. Campbell, Ksheerabdhi Krishna, and Robert A. Ballance. Refining and defining the Program Dependence Web. Technical Report TR 93-6, Department of Computer Science, University of New Mexico, 1993.

7. Robert S. Cartwright and Matthias Felleisen. The semantics of program dependence. In *Proceedings of the SIGPLAN '89 Conference on Programming Language Design and Implementation*, Portland, Oregon, June 1989.

8. Jong-Deok Choi, Ron Cytron, and Jeanne Ferrante. Automatic construction of sparse data flow evaluation graphs. In *Conference Record of the Eighteenth ACM Symposium on the Principles of Programming Languages*, pages 55–66, January 1991.

9. G. Cybenko, L. Kipp, L. Pointer, and D. Kuck. Supercomputer performance evaluation and the Perfect benchmarks. In *Proceedings of the 1990 ACM International Conference on Supercomputing*, Amsterdam, The Netherlands, June 1990.

10. R. Cytron, J. Ferrante, and V. Sarkar. Compact representations for control dependence. In *Proceedings of the SIGPLAN '90 Conference on Programming Language Design and Implementation*, pages 337–351, White Plains, New York, June 1990.

11. R. Cytron, J. Ferrante, and V. Sarkar. Experience using control dependence in PTRAN. In D. Gelernter, A. Nicolau, and D. Padua, editors, *Languages and Compilers for Parallel Computing*. The MIT Press, 1990.

12. Ron Cytron, Jeanne Ferrante, Barry K. Rosen, Mark N. Wegman, and F. Kenneth Zadeck. Efficiently computing static single assignment form and the control dependence graph. *ACM Transactions on Programming Languages and Systems*, 13(4):451–490, October 1991.

13. Raja Das, Joel Saltz, and Reinhard von Hanxleden. Slicing analysis and indirect accesses to distributed arrays. In *Preliminary Proceedings of the Sixth Workshop on Languages and Compilers for Parallel Computing*, Portland, OR, August 1993.

14. J. Ferrante, K. J. Ottenstein, and J. D. Warren. The program dependence graph and its use in optimization. *ACM Transactions on Programming Languages and Systems*, 9(3):319–349, July 1987.

15. John Field. A simple rewriting semantics for realistic imperative programs and its application to program analysis. In *Proceedings of the ACM SIGPLAN Workshop on Partial Evaluation and Semantics-Based Program Manipulation*, pages 98–107, San Francisco, California, June 1992.

16. G. Goff, K. Kennedy, and C. Tseng. Practical dependence testing. In *Proceedings of the SIGPLAN '91 Conference on Program Language Design and Implementation*, Toronto, Canada, June 1991.

17. M. R. Haghighat and C. D. Polychronopoulos. Symbolic program analysis and optimization for parallelizing compilers. In *Preliminary Proceedings of the Fifth Workshop on Languages and Compilers for Parallel Computing*, New Haven, CT, August 1992.

18. S. Horwitz, J. Prins, and T. Reps. On the adequacy of program dependence graphs for representing programs. In *Conference Record of the Fifteenth ACM Symposium on the Principles of Programming Languages*, pages 146–157, San Diego, CA, January 1988.

19. Francois Irigoin. Interprocedural analyses for programming environments. In J. J. Dongarra and B. Tourancheau, editors, *Environments and Tools for Parallel Scientific Computing*. Elsevier Science Publishers, 1993.

20. K. Kennedy, K. S. McKinley, and C. Tseng. Analysis and transformation in the ParaScope Editor. In *Proceedings of the 1991 ACM International Conference on Supercomputing*, Cologne, Germany, June 1991.

21. T. Lengauer and R. E. Tarjan. A fast algorithm for finding dominators in a flowgraph. *ACM Transactions on Programming Languages and Systems*, 1:121–141, 1979.

22. Allan Porterfield. *Software Methods for Improvement of Cache Performance on Supercomputer Applications*. PhD thesis, Rice University, May 1989. Available as Rice COMP TR88-93.

23. Rebecca P. Selke. *A Semantic Framework for Program Dependence*. PhD thesis, Rice University, 1992.

24. R. E. Tarjan. Testing flow graph reducibility. *Journal of Computer and System Sciences*, 9:355–365, 1974.

25. J. Uniejewski. SPEC Benchmark Suite: designed for today's advanced systems. SPEC Newsletter Volume 1, Issue 1, SPEC, Fall 1989.

26. Michael Wolfe. Beyond induction variables. In *Proceedings of the SIGPLAN '92 Conference on Programming Language Design and Implementation*, pages 162–174, San Francisco, California, June 1992.

27. Wuu Yang, Susan Horwitz, and Thomas Reps. Detecting program components with equivalent behaviors. Technical Report 840, Computer Sciences Department, University of Wisconsin-Madison, April 1989.

Automatic Array Privatization *

Peng Tu and David Padua

Center for Supercomputing Research and Development
University of Illinois at Urbana-Champaign

Abstract. Array privatization is one of the most effective transformations for the exploitation of parallelism. In this paper, we present a technique for automatic array privatization. Our algorithm uses data flow analysis of array references to identify privatizable arrays intraprocedurally as well as interprocedurally. It employs static and dynamic resolution to determine the last value of a lived private array. We compare the result of automatic array privatization with that of manual array privatization and identify directions for future improvement. To enhance the effectiveness of our algorithm, we develop a goal directly technique to analysis symbolic variables in the present of conditional statements, loops and index arrays.

1 Introduction

Enhancing parallelism, balancing load and reducing communication is among the major tasks of today's parallelizing compilers. Memory-related dependence can severely limit the potential parallelism of a program. Privatization is a technique that allows each concurrent thread to allocate a variable in its private storage such that each thread accesses a distinct instance of the variable. By providing a distinct instance of a variable to each processor, privatization can eliminate memory related dependence. Previous studies on the effectiveness of automatic program parallelization show that *privatization* is one of the most effective transformations for the exploitation of parallelism [8]. A related technique called *expansion* [13] transforms each reference to a particular scalar into a reference to a vector element in such a way that each thread accesses a different vector element. When applied to an array, expansion creates a new dimension for the array.

Because the access to a private variable is inherently local, privatization reduces the communication and facilitates data distribution. Since private instances of a variable are spread among all the active processors, privatization provides opportunities to spread computation among the processors and improve load balancing [16].

* The research described was supported by Army contract DABT63-92-C-0033 and CSRD affiliate program from Motorola Corporation. This work is not necessarily representative of the positions or policies of the Army or the Government.

Previous work on eliminating memory-related dependence focused on scalar expansion [19], scalar privatization [3], scalar renaming [6], and array expansion [13] [9]. Recently there have been several papers on array privatization [11][12][16].

We present an algorithm for automatically generating an annotated parallel program from a sequential program represented by a control flow graph. In the target parallel program, each loop is annotated with its privatizable arrays and their last value assignment conditions. The algorithm has been implemented in the POLARIS parallelizing compiler. Our work on automatic array privatization presents the following new results:

- We use data flow-based analysis for array reference. Compared with the dependence analysis-based approach [12], which has to employ parametric integer programming in its most general case, our approach is more efficient and can handle nonlinear subscripts that cannot be handled by integer programming.
- The algorithm proceeds from the bottom up, which allows us to easily extend the algorithm to program call trees for interprocedural analysis. Our experience shows this interprocedural array reference analysis is necessary in many cases for successful array privatization in real applications.
- We distinguish private arrays whose last value assignments can be determined statically from those whose last values have to be assigned dynamically at runtime. This work can potentially identify more private arrays than other algorithms can identify.
- To evaluate its effectiveness, we test the algorithm on the programs in the Perfect Benchmarks. We compare the automatic privatization with manual privatization described in a previous study[8]. We find that for further improvement, more sophisticated symbolic analysis techniques are needed.
- To facilitate further improvement, we develop a goal-directed technique to analyze symbolic variables in the present of conditional statements, loops, and index arrays.

The rest of the paper is organized as follows. Section 2 is an overview of the issues in automatic array privatization and gives an example that motivates this work. Section 3 presents the algorithm. The algorithm is divided into two parts: private array identification and last-value assignment resolution. Section 4 contains the experiments of automatic privatization of the Perfect Benchmarks and presents a comparison of automatic privatization with manual privatization. Section 5 presents a goal-directed technique that uses the SSA form of a program to determine symbolic values in the presence of conditional statements, loops, and index arrays. Section 6 presents the conclusion.

2 Background

Data dependence [2] specifies the precedence constraints in the execution of statements in a program due to data producer and consumer relationships. *Anti-*

dependence and *output dependence* are memory-related or *false* dependence because they are not caused by the flow of values from one statement to another, but by the reuse of memory locations. Consider the loop:

```
S1:  DO I = 1, N
S2:     A(1) = X(I,J)
S3:     DO J = 2, N
S4:        A(J) = A(J-1)+Y(J)
S5:     ENDDO
S6:     DO K = 1, N
S7:        B(I,K) = B(I,K) + A(K)
S8:     ENDDO
S9:  ENDDO
```

Because every iteration of loop *S1* accesses the same elements of array *A*, loop *S1* cannot be executed in parallel. However, there is no flow of value across iterations. The conflict can be resolved by declaring *A* to be private to each iteration of loop *S1*. We add the following directives to the loop:

```
C$DIR  INDEPENDENT
C$DIR  PRIVATE A(1:N)
C$DIR  LAST VALUE A(1:N) WHEN (I.EQ.N)
```

The *INDEPENDENT* directive is borrowed from HPF [10]. It specifies that the iterations of loop *S*1 are independent. There are two directives for a private array. The *PRIVATE* directive associates the privatizable arrays with each iteration of a loop. The *LAST VALUE* statement specifies the conditions when a processor should copy its private array value to the global array. The interpretation of the directives is as follows:

- Each processor cooperating in the execution of the loop allocates the private arrays in its local storage before executing any statement in the loop.
- During the entire execution of an iteration, references to a private array are directed to the processor's local instance.
- After the execution of an iteration has completed, the processor checks the last-value assignment condition. If the condition is satisfied, the processor copies the private array to the corresponding global array. This operation is called *copy-out*.

The results of our research on manual array privatization of Perfect Benchmarks didn't provide any case where a privatizable array needs both a local value and a global value. Hence our model does not have *copy-in*, that is, we do not allow values to be copied from the global array to the private array. Under this assumption, our definition of privatizable array is as follows.

Definition 1. Let *A* be an array that is referenced in a loop *L*. We say *A* is privatizable to *L* if the following conditions are satisfied.

1. Every fetch to an element of A in L must be preceded by a store to the element in the same iteration of L.
2. Different iterations of L may access the same location of A. □

The conditions for copying out the value of a private array to a global array are also determined by the compiler. In simple cases such as the one above, the algorithm can find a closed form for the condition. We call these cases *static last-value assignment*. In the more complicated cases, such as in the following loop, the last-value assignment has to be determined at run time:

```
C$DIR   INDEPENDENT
C$DIR   PRIVATE A(1:N)
C$DIR   LAST VALUE A(1) WHEN (I.EQ.N)
C$DIR   LAST VALUE A(2:N) WHEN DYNAMIC
S1:   DO I = 1, N
S2:      A(1) = X(I,J)
S3:      IF (A(1).GT.0) THEN
S4:         DO J = 2, N
S5:            A(J) = A(J-1)+Y(J)
S6:         ENDDO
S7:      ENDIF
S8:   ENDDO
```

In this example, the array section $A(2:N)$ is conditionally assigned. A is still privatizable because it satisfies the privatizability conditions, but its last-value assignment cannot be determined at compile time. We use the key word *DYNAMIC* to specify that run-time resolution techniques such as *synchronization variable* [20] will have to be used for the array section $A(2:N)$. These cases are termed *dynamic last-value assignment*. For instance, the compiler can associate the subarray $A(2:N)$ with a synchronization variable *last-iteration*, which stores the last iteration that was written to $A(2:N)$. Every iteration that defines $A(2:N)$ will atomically compare its iteration number with the last iteration. If its iteration number is larger than the last iteration, the processor stores its iteration number into the last-iteration variable and copy-out $A(2:N)$. Otherwise, the assignment is ignored, because a later iteration has already written to $A(2:N)$. Note that because all the iterations are independent, the number of copy-out operations can be reduced by scheduling the loop backward from the last iteration to the first iteration.

3 Algorithm for Array Privatization

We consider the problem of identifying privatizable arrays in a data flow framework. From this point of view, to determine if an array is privatizable in a loop is to determine whether all its reaching definitions are coming from the same iteration of the loop.

3.1 Data Flow Framework

Problem Formulation. Data flow analysis examines the flow of values through a program and solves data flow problems by propagating information along the paths of a control flow graph. Because private arrays are associated with *DO* loops in the program, we must extend the traditional program flow graph with information about the scope of do loops.

Definition 2. $G = (N, E, s)$ be a program flow graph where N are nodes, E are arcs, and $s \in N$ is the initial node. Let L be a subflowgraph corresponding to a do loop (including all loops nested within it). We define as $control(L) \subset L$ the subset of nodes in L corresponding to the loop entry, increment and test of the loop index. $control(L)$ identifies the loop index, its limits and its step. We define the $body(L)$ as $L - control(L)$. ◻

When a program has nested loops, the control and body of the inner loop are included in the loop body of the outer loop. When the control flow of an inner loop is not important for the analysis of an outer loop, we can use abstraction for the inner loop and simplify the flowgraph by collapsing the subflowgraph corresponding to the inner loop into one node.

Definition 3. Let $G = (N, E, s)$ be a flow graph and L be a do loop in G. The $COLLAP(G, L)$ is a flow graph with the subflowgraph L collapsed into one node. ◻

Given a subflowgraph L corresponding to a loop, we want to determine if for every iteration of the loop, all reaching definitions to an array use come from the same iteration. We can do this through *def-use* analysis. The data values to be analyzed include both scalar values and array values. They are *scalar variable*, *subscripted variable*, and *subarray*. A subscripted variable consists of an array identifier and a list of subscript expressions. It is a special case of scalar variables. A subarray consists of a subscripted variable and one or more *ranges* for some of the indices in the subscript expression. A range includes expressions for the lower bound, upper bound, and stride. The notion of subarray we use in this paper is an extension at the *regular section* used by others[4]. Using subarray, we can represent the triangular region and banded region, as well as the strip, grid, column, row, and block of an array. For instance, the following examples respectively represent a dense upper triangle, grids in the upper triangle, and diagonal of array A.

```
(A(I,I:N),[I=1:N])
(A(I,I:N:2),[I=1:N:2])
(A(I,I),[I=1:N])
```

A range in a subarray is interpreted as a *FORALL*, `(A(I,I:N),[I=1:N])` is interpreted as `FORALL (I=1:N) A(I,I:N)`. Here the *FORALL* is just an assertion, no operational constraint, such as the order of assignment to different elements, is imposed.

We now describe the algorithm to do def-use analysis involving arrays. We start by computing *outward exposed* definitions and uses for each basic block S in the loop body. A definition of variable v in a basic block S is said to be outward exposed if it is the last definition of v in S. A use of v is outward exposed if S does not contain a definition of v before this use [22].

Definition 4. Let S be a basic block and VAR be the set of scalar variables, subscripted variables, and subarrays in the program. Henceforth these are called variables.

1. $DEF(S) := \{v \in VAR : v \text{ has an outward exposed definition in } S\}$
2. $USE(S) := \{v \in VAR : v \text{ has an outward exposed use in } S\}$
3. $KILL(S) := \{v \in VAR : v \text{ has a definition in } S\}$ □

For the flow information of a basic block S, we define $MRD_{in}(S)$ as the set of variables that are always defined upon entering S, $MRD_{out}(S)$ as the set of variables that are always defined upon exiting S. Let $pred(S)$ be the set of immediate predecessors of S in the loop's flow graph ignoring all the back edges, $MRD_{in}(S)$ can be computed using the following equations:

$$MRD_{in}(S) = \cap_{t \in pred(S)} MRD_{out}(t) \tag{1}$$

$$MRD_{out}(S) = (MRD_{in}(S) - KILL(S)) \cup DEF(S) \tag{2}$$

We start from a conservative initial solution, with each MRD_{in} an empty set ϕ. The back edges in the graph are removed because $MRD(S)$ is only concerned with the values that are defined in the statements prior to S in the flow graph. Because back edges are deleted, the algorithm actually works on the DAG of the flow graph. Since back edges for inner loops do carry information for the analysis of the outer loop, they are handled by abstraction and aggregation in the next section.

The value of each set defined above such as DEF, USE, $KILL$, and MRD, is a subset of VAR. Hence the domain of the data flow information set is the powerset $\mathcal{P}(VAR)$. The effect of a $\cup$ (union) operation is to form a union of its operands. It is precise in the sense that it will not summarize two sets unless the summary set has exactly the same members as the two sets. For instance, $\{A(I) \cup A(1 : N)\}$ will return $\{A(I), A(1 : N)\}$ unless $I \in [1 : N]$, but $\{A(1 : N : 2) \cup A(2 : N - 1 : 2)\}$ will return $A(1:N)$. The effect of a $\cap$ (join) operation is to form a join of its operands. It is conservative in the sense it will return an empty set ϕ if it cannot determine the join of its operands. For instance, $\{A(I) \cap A(1 : N)\}$ will return ϕ unless $I \in [1 : N]$. Because the join is conservative, there will be some potential loss of information at each join point of the flow graph. The effectiveness of the algorithm will hence depend on the system's ability to determine the relationship between symbolic variables. This issue will be discussed in Sec. 4.

An iterative algorithm for solving the MRD equation is shown in Fig. 1 as phases 1 and 2. Phases 3 and 4 are explained below.

Algorithm Privatize
  $privatize := func(L)$
  Input: flowgraph for loop L with back edges removed
  Output: $DEF(L), USE(L), PRI(L)$

Phase 1: Collect local information
  foreach statement $S \in body(L)$ in rPostorder do
    if $S \in control(M)$ for some loop M nested in L then
      ! S is in an inner loop, visit M first
      $[DEF(S), USE(S)] \leftarrow privatize(M)$
      ! collapse all nodes in M onto S
      $L \leftarrow COLLAP(L, M)$
    else
      compute local $DEF(S), USE(S)$
    endif
  endfor

Phase 2: Solve the MRD Data Flow Equations for each statement
  forall $S \in body(L)$ initialize $MRD(S) \leftarrow \phi$
  foreach $S \in body(L)$ in rPostorder do
    $MRD_{in}(S) \leftarrow \cap_{t \in pred(S)} MRD_{out}(t)$
    $MRD_{out}(S) \leftarrow (MRD_{in}(S) - KILL(S)) \cup DEF(S)$
  end

Phase 3: Compute Summary Sets for the Loop Body
  $DEF_b(L) \leftarrow \cap_{t \in exits(body(L))}(MRD_{out}(t))$
  $USE_b(L) \leftarrow \cup_{t \in body(L)}(USE(t) - MRD_{in}(t))$
  $PRI_b(L) \leftarrow (\cup_{t \in body(L)} USE(t)) - USE_b(L)$
  $PRI_b^{st}(L) \leftarrow DEF_b(L) \cap PRI_b(L)$
  $PRI_b^{dy}(L) \leftarrow PRI_b(L) - PRI_b^{st}(L)$

Phase 4: Return aggregated set $DEF(L)$ and $USE(L)$
  test if it is profitable to privatize $PRI_b(L)$
  determine last value assignment
  $[PRI^{st}(L), PRI^{dy}(L)] \leftarrow aggregate(PRI_b^{st}, PRI_b^{dy}, control(L))$
  $[DEF(L), USE(L)] \leftarrow aggregate(DEF_b(L), USE_b(L), control(L))$
  return $[DEF(L), USE(L)]$

Figure 1. Algorithm for Identifying Privatizable Arrays

Abstraction for Inner Loop. When the algorithm finds a loop nested inside a loop body, it will recursively call itself on the inner loop. To hide the control flow of an inner loop, we introduce some abstraction and extend the previous definition from a basic block to a complete loop. We start by defining the information for one iteration of the loop.

Definition 5. Let L be a loop and VAR be the variables in the program. We define the following set as *summary set* for $body(L)$.

1. $DEF_b(L) := \{v \in VAR : v \text{ has a } MRD \text{ reaching all exits node of } body(L) \}$
2. $USE_b(L) := \{v \in VAR : v \text{ has an outward exposed use in } body(L) \}$
3. $KILL_b(L) := DEF_b(L)$
4. $PRI_b(L) := \{v \in VAR : \text{every use of } v \text{ has a reaching } MRD \text{ in } body(L) \}$
   $\square$

The summary set is an abstraction of the effect of a loop iteration on the data flow values. Using the summary set, we can ignore the structure of the inner loops in the analysis of the outer loop. The trade-off is that we have to make a conservative approximation and may lose information in the process.

- $DEF_b(L)$ is the *must define* variables for one iteration of L; i.e. the must define variables upon exiting the iteration:

$$DEF_b(L) = \cap(MRD_{\text{out}}(t) : t \in exits(L)) \qquad (3)$$

- $USE_b(L)$, the *possibly outward exposed use* variables, is the set of variables that are used in some statements of L, but do not have an MRD_{in} in the same iteration:

$$USE_b(L) = \cup(USE(t) - MRD_{\text{in}}(t)) : t \in body(L) \qquad (4)$$

- The *privatizable variables* are the variables that are used and not exposed to definitions outside the iteration:

$$PRI_b(L) = \cup\{USE(t) : t \in body(L)\} - USE_b(L) \qquad (5)$$

In the analysis of the outer loop, we must consider the total effect of an inner loop on data flow values. That is, we need to account for the effect of back edges and index domain of the loop. We can do this by listing the summary set for each iteration of the loop. We will use an approximation called *aggregated set* to compute $DEF(L)$, $USE(L)$, $KILL(L)$, and $PRI(L)$. The aggregation computes the region spanned by each array reference in $USE_b(L)$, $DEF_b(L)$, $KILL_b$, and $PRI_b(L)$ across the iteration space. Because we only consider do loops, the aggregation is a relatively straightforward interpretation of loop index and boundaries in the do-entry of the loop. In our representation of variables, a subarray is represented as a subscripted variable together with a subscript range. To aggregate a subarray, we just need to concatenate the loop index and boundaries with the subscripted variable of subarray. For instance, if I is a loop index or an induction variable with value [1:N:1], then A(I,J) will be aggregated as (A(I,J),[I=1:N]) = A(1:N,J) and A(I,1:I) will be aggregated as (A(I,1:I),[I=1:N]).

Because one iteration's use may only be exposed to the definitions in some previous iterations of the same loop, a naive aggregation of $USE_b(L)$ may exaggerate the exposed use set. The reason is that the uses covered by the definitions in previous iterations are not exposed to the outside of the loop, and therefore they should be excluded from the aggregated $USE(L)$ set. For instance, in

```
    DO I = 2, N
S1:    A(I) = A(I-1) + B(J)
    ENDDO
```

the information for one iteration is $USE_b(L) = \{A(I-1), B(J), J\}$ and $DEF_b(L) = \{A(I)\}$, the region aggregately defined in all iterations prior to the ith iteration is $A(2:I-1)$, and $A(I-1)$ is exposed to definitions outside the loop only in the first iteration, that is, $USE(L) = \{A(1)\}$.

Profitability of Privatization. After an array is identified as privatizable in a loop, we need to determine if different iterations of a loop will access the same location of the array. For instance, in the following loop:

```
S1:  DO I = 1, N
S2:     A(I) = ...
S3:     ... = A(I)
S4:  ENDDO
```

the algorithm will identify that $A(I)$ is privatizable. We can privatize $A(I)$ using a private scalar as follows:

```
C$DIR INDEPENDENT
C$DIR PRIVATE X
C$DIR LAST VALUE A(I) = X
S1:  DO I = 1, N
S2:     X   = ...
S3:     ... = X
Sn:  ENDDO
```

This transformation is useful for conventional compiler optimization. Today's optimizing compilers usually will not allocate a register to a subscripted variable $A(I)$ in the original program because they have very limited capability to disambiguitize the array reference. In the transformed program, it is easy for them to allocate a register to a scalar X. The transformation can also reduce the amount of *false sharing* in multiprocessor caches. In a distributed memory system with *owner computes* rule [21][5] [14], the transformed program effectively transfers the ownership of $A(I)$ to iteration I; hence the processor scheduled to execute the iteration I can execute operations in S2 even if it does not own $A(I)$. This transformation can facilitate data distribution to reduce communication and improve load balance [16].

For the purpose of eliminating memory-related dependence in this paper, the array A in the previous example need not be privatized. The condition for privatization exists when different iterations of the loop access same location. This can be determined by examining $PRI_b(L)$. We will call the test the *profitability test*. Let $A(r)$ be a reference to array A where r is a subscript expression if $A(r)$ is a subscripted variable, or a range list if $A(r)$ is a subarray.

If $A(r)$ is a subscripted variable and r is a monotonic function of loop index i, then different iterations of i will access different locations of $A(i)$; hence it is not profitable to privatize $A(r)$, otherwise it is profitable. When there is more than one subscript of A in $PRI_b(L)$, we need to test if there is dependence between each pair of subscripted variables. We can use the Banerjee Test [2] to determine if within the loop boundaries two references referred to the same location. If $A(r)$ is a subarray, we need to determine if there is an iteration $j \neq i$ such that $A(r) \cap A(r[i/j]) \neq \phi$, where $r[i/j]$ represents r after we substitute each appearance of loop index i with j. Again one has to test for each pair of occurrences if there is more than one occurrence of subarrays. This discussion is summarized in the algorithm shown in Fig. 2.

Algorithm Profitability Test
   Input: PRI_b for loop L: with index $i \in [p : q : t]$
   Output: PRO, arrays profitable for privatization

   $PRO \leftarrow \phi$
   foreach $A \in PRI_b$ do
      $ALL_A \leftarrow \{A(r) : A(r) \in PRI\}$
      foreach pair $A(x), A(y) \in ALL_A$ — where x and y can be the same
         let $X \leftarrow$ set of values in x
         let $Y \leftarrow$ set of values in y
         if $(\exists j \in [p : q : t] | j \neq i, X[i/j] \cap Y \neq \phi)$
            $PRO \leftarrow PRO + A$
         !Notice that if $x = y$ and x does not contain i, the test is satisfied.
      endfor
   endfor

Figure 2. Profitability Test

3.2   Last Value Assignment

Live Analysis. *Live analysis* is needed to determine if a privatizable variable is live after exiting the loop. If it is live, the last-value assignment will be necessary to preserve the semantics of the original program; otherwise no last-value assignment is needed for that variable. A last-value assignment statement can be ignored when the private array is not used after the loop, or there are subsequent definitions of the array before any use.

Definition 6. Let S be a node in the flowgraph. The live variables at the bottom of S are the set of variables that may be used after control passes the bottom of S. We define

1. $LVBOT(S) := \{v \in VAR : v$ may be used after $S \}$
2. $LVTOP(S) := \{v \in VAR : v$ may be used after S or in $S \}$ $\qquad\qquad$ □

Let $succ(S)$ be the set of immediate successors of S in the program flowgraph. The equations for $LVTOP$, $LVBOT$ are

$$LVBOT(S) = \cup_{t \in succ(S)} LVTOP(t) \tag{6}$$

$$LVTOP(t) = (LVBOT(S) - KILL(S)) \cup USE(S) \tag{7}$$

The algorithm traverses the flow graph backward and uses the aggregated set for each loop. This algorithm is just the natural extension of scalar live analysis to include array references.

Static and Dynamic Last-Value Assignment. After live analysis, we can ignore the last-value assignments for private arrays that are not live at the bottom of the loop. However, the remaining live private arrays have to be copied to their global counterparts. Two problems prevent static determination of iteration that copies its private array to the global array. One, as shown in our early example, is due to conditional definition. Without information about which branch the program will take at runtime, it is impossible to determine which iteration shall assign the last value. Another problem is that some complicated subscript expressions make it inefficient to compute at compile time which iteration will assign the last value. In these cases, we will use well-known run-time techniques such as [20] to resolve the output dependence.

Our first step is to identify the private arrays that need dynamic last-value assignments because of conditional definition. PRI_b contains all the array uses that are covered by some definition in the same iteration of the loop; some of the uses are conditional, where they are covered by some conditional definition. DEF_b contains all the variables that must be defined in every iteration of the loop. Therefore, $PRI_b^{st} = PRI_b \cap DEF_b$ contains the privatizable arrays that are unconditionally defined. Hence $PRI_b^{dy} = PRI_b - PRI_b^{st}$ contains the conditionally defined privatizable arrays.

Because of the profitability test, at least one element of the array in PRI_b^{st} is defined in several iterations. To determine for each iteration what element has to be copied back to the global array, we define a *write back set* as the sections of private array that have to be copied back to the global array for iteration i.

Definition 7. Let L be a loop body and PRI^{st} be the static private arrays. The Write Back Set (WBS) of L for iteration i is defined as the sections of arrays in PRI^{st} that are written in the ith iteration, but are not written thereafter. □

From the definition we can compute the WBS by comparing the set defined in iteration i and the set defined in the iterations after i. The algorithm is shown in Fig. 3.

Note that the last iteration of loop L will always write back all its static private arrays. When we cannot find a closed form for WBS, we can move the array to PRI_b^{dy} and use run-time resolution. Actually the algorithm itself can be linked into the program to perform a run test for each iteration. In most cases, the algorithm will find a closed form and therefore WBS can be determined at

Algorithm Write Back Set

   Input: PRI_b^{st} for loop L: with index $i \in [p : q : t]$

   Output: WBS, for iteration i

$WBS \leftarrow \phi$

foreach array $A \in PRI_b^{st}$ do

   $ALL_A \leftarrow \{A(r) : A(r) \in PRI_b^{st}\}$

   $WBS \leftarrow ALL_A - \cup_{j \in [i+t:q:t]} ALL_A[i/j]$

endfor

Figure 3. Compute Write Back Set

compile time. The following example shows how the algorithm in Fig. 3 works in two different situations.

```
S1:   DO I = 1, N
S2:      DO J = 1, M
S3:         A(J) = ...
S4:         B(I+J) = ...
S5:      ENDDO
         ...
Sn:   ENDDO
```

For loop S1, $PRI_b^{st} = \{A(1 : M), B(I + 1 : I + M)\}$. $A(1:M)$ will be accessed in all iterations after a given $I<N$ because $A(1:M)$ does not depend on I. Hence WBS for A in iteration $I \neq N$ is ϕ, the empty set. Only the last iteration of loop S1 will copy out $A(1:M)$. For B, $B(I+1:I+M)$ is in ALL_B for iteration I, $B((I+1)+1:M+N)$ is modified in iterations from $I+1$ to N, hence the WSB for B is $B(I+1)$.

3.3 Interprocedural Analysis of Privatizable Arrays

In many cases, we need to do interprocedural analysis for array privatization. We can find more deeply nested loops by looking at the loops in the subroutines. To use the algorithm for interprocedural analysis, we generalize the loop flow graph to incorporate subroutine bodies.

Definition 8. Let R be a subroutine and VAR be the variables in the subroutine. We define the *subroutine summary set* for R as follows:

1. $DEF(R) := \{v \in VAR : v$ has a MRD reaching all exits node of $R \}$
2. $USE(R) := \{v \in VAR : v$ has an outward exposed use in $R \}$
3. $KILL(R) := DEF(R)$ □

The algorithm to find the *subroutine summary set* is the same used above to compute DEF_b, USE_b, and $KILL_b$. The input to the algorithm is now the flowgraph of the subroutine. We run the algorithm in bottom-up order on the program call tree, such that each time we encounter a subroutine call in a program, the summary set for the subroutine has already been computed. When the algorithm finds a subroutine call node, it reads the summary set of the subroutine, simplifies the summary set to get rid of variables that are not visible to the caller, and maps the formal parameters and common variables in the summary set to the corresponding actual parameters and common variables at the caller. Because array reshaping usually occurs in programs written in FORTRAN, the array defined in the subroutine may have a different shape. Our interprocedural mapping program will linearize an array in the subroutine if it has a different number of dimensions as in the caller. After the specialization, the algorithm will use the subroutine summary set for the call statement.

We implemented the algorithm with interprocedural analysis in the PO-LARIS system. It allows us to do automatic array privatization in loops with subroutine calls.

4 Automatic versus Manual Array Privatization

To evaluate the effectiveness of the algorithm, we ran the automatic array privatization on the Perfect Benchmarks. We compared the number of private arrays found by the algorithm with that of the manual array privatization reported in [8]. The result is shown in Table 1. The first column reports the number of private arrays identified by both manual and automatic privatization. The second column reports the number of private arrays identified by manual privatization but not by automatic privatization. The third column reports the number identified by automatic privatization but not by manual privatization. By comparing

Table 1. Number of Private Arrays

Program	Automatic and Manual	Manual Only	Automatic Only
ADM (AP)	2	12	0
ARC2D (SR)	0	2	0
BNDA (NA)	12	3	4
DYFESM (SD)	0	1	11
FLO52 (TF)	0	0	4
MDG (LW)	17	1	1
MG3D (SM)	1	4	0
OCEAN (OC)	4	3	0
QCD (LG)	22	7	0
SPEC77 (WS)	25	14	0
TRACK (MT)	20	2	0
TRFD (TI)	4	0	0

the results of automatic privatization and manual privatization, we found that the algorithm is sufficient to discover most of the privatizable arrays. The lattice for array references is also adequate for representing the array use and definition in the programs of Perfect Benchmarks. Where our algorithm failed, we found that in most instance it is due to lack of information about symbolic variables. Some of the ambiguities can be resolved by a more powerful forward substitution algorithm than that available in our current system. For instance, our algorithm failed to identify private array XE in subroutine *solvhe* of *DYFESM*. In this case, XE is defined in the *geteu* subroutine as a two-dimensional array XE(NDDF,NNPED) and used in *solvhe* as a one dimensional array XE(NDFE). It turns out that NDFE = NDDF*NNPED after interprocedural forward substitution.

Some of the ambiguities can be resolved by enhancing the traditional scalar constant propagation and forward substitution. For instance, a common difficulty is conditionally defined loop boundaries. Such a situation occurs in subroutine *initia* of *ARC2D* code. Two common variables JLOW and JUP are defined as follows:

```
IF (.NOT.PERIDC) THEN
    JLOW = 2
    JUP = JMAX - 1
ELSE
    JLOW = 1
    JUP = JMAX
ENDIF
```

These two common variables are then used in subroutine *filerx, filery* as loop boundaries:

```
L1: DO N = 1, 4
L2:     DO J = JLOW, JUP
            DO K = KLOW, KUP
                WORK(J,K,1) = ...
            ENDDO
        ENDDO
        IF (.NOT.PERDIC) THEN
L3:         DO K = KLOW, KUP
                WORK(1,K,1) = WORK(2,K,1) + ...
                WORK(JMAX,K,1) = WORK(JMAX-1,K,1)
            ENDDO
        ENDIF
        ...
    ENDDO
```

For the array WORK to be privatized in loop L1, we need to determine the reference WORK(2,K,1) and WORK(JMAX-1,K,1) in loop L3 are defined in L2. If we inspect the condition in the *IF* statement, we can determine that when L3 is executed the condition is (.NOT.PERDIC). Under the same condition, JLOW=2, JUP=JMAX-1;

hence the use is covered by the definition in L2. A simpler method is to propagate the upper bound of JLOW=2 and lower bound of JUP=JMAX-1, and we do not need to interpret the condition of *IF* statement.

A problem of similar nature happens in *BDNA*. It involves the bound of an induction variable L:

```
L1: DO I = 2, NSP
L2:     DO J = 1, I-1
            XDT(J) = ...
        ENDDO
        L = 0
L3:     DO J = 1, I-1
            IF (IND(J).NE.0) THEN
                L = L+1
            ENDIF
        ENDDO
L4:     DO J = 1, L
            ... = XDT(J)
        ENDDO
    ENDDO
```

For XDT to be private to loop L1, the use in L4 must be covered by definition in L2, i.e., we need to know if L<=I-1. Computing the upper bound for L in loop L3, the validity of this condition in L4 can be confirmed.

The idea of keeping more than one possible value for scalars can be generalized to propagate the value for each element of an array. This is very useful in the case of subscripted subscripts. For instance, in *ARC2D*, array JPLUS and JMINU are used to store the neighboring element on a ring of size JMAX. That is, JPLUS(I) = I+1 mod JMAX, and JMINU(I) = I-1 mod JMAX. These values are used throughout the program. By propagating the value of the whole array, we can use our algorithm to compute the range defined and used.

Another interesting case arises in MDG, where we must inspect the condition of an *IF* statement to determine whether the array RL can be privatized in subroutine *poteng* and *interf*:

```
    DO I = 1, NMOL1
L2:     DO J = I+1, NMOL
            KC = 0
            DO K = 1, 9
                RS(K) = ...
C1:             IF (RS(K).GT.CUT2) THEN
                    KC = KC + 1
                ENDIF
            ENDDO
            DO K = 2, 5
C2:             IF (RS(K).LE.CUT2) THEN
                    RL(K+4) = ...
```

```
            ENDIF
            ENDDO
C3:         IF (KC.EQ.0) THEN
               DO K = 11, 14
                  ... = RL(K-5)
               ENDDO
            ENDIF
         ENDDO
      ENDDO
```

Note that whenever (KC.EQ.0) in C3 is true, (RS(K).LE.CUT2) must also be true, because if (RS(K).GT.CUT2), then KC must be greater than 0 due to the increment in C1. Hence RL(6:9) is privatizable in L2 because whenever RL(6:9) is used, it refers to the values defined in the same iteration.

In some rare cases, user direction is needed to determine if an array is privatizable. This happens in *OCEAN*, where it cannot be statically determined if the array C and CA are defined in subroutine *in*. The *in* writes to the C and CA, but the definitions are surrounded by an error condition test. Without knowing whether the error condition will abort the program, the algorithm has no way of knowing those arrays are defined whenever the program returns from subroutine *in*.

5 Demand Driven Symbolic Analysis

In the last section, we showed that to determine the region of an array that is used in a program, a major task is to determine the relationship between symbolic variables. In this section, we present a demand-driven technique to determine the value relationship between symbolic variables. This technique is based on the Static Single Assignment (SSA) form. SSA is an intermediate representation of a program that has two useful properties:

1. Each use of a variable is reached by exactly one definition to that variable.
2. The program contains PHI functions that merge the values of a variable from a distinct incoming control-flow graph.

[1, 15, 17] present various applications of SSA, and [7] deals with efficiently transforming programs into SSA form.

5.1 Determine Symbolic Value on Demand

The SSA form can be used to track the value of symbolic variables on demand. For instance, from the following SSA representation of a piece of code in *DYFESM*, we can determine that the value of NDFE_1 used in L3 is NDDF_1*NNPED_1 since NDFE_1 is assigned in S1.

```
S1: NDFE_1 = NDDF_1 * NNPED_1
    ...
    DO K_1 = 1, N_1
L1:    DO I_1=1, NDDF_1
L2:       DO J_1=1, NNPED_1
             XE(I_1,J) = ...
          END DO
       END DO
L3:    DO I_2 = 1,NDFE_1
          ... = XE(I_2)
       END DO
    END DO
```

The loop boundaries for L1,L2 are the same NDDF_1 and NNPED_1. Hence the use of XE in L3, which is XE(1:NDFE_1)=XE(1:NDDF_1*NNPED_1), is covered by the definition XE(1:NNDF_1,1:NNPED_1) in L1. Because in a SSA representation, each use of a variable can be reached by exactly one assignment to that variable, it is very easy to track the value of a variable by its name.

In the traditional forward substitution, because it is difficult to know which variable should be forward substituted, it usually substitutes all the variables in a program and rolls back later to avoid redundant computation. In contrast, the backward tracking of a value through SSA variable name is done on demand.

5.2   Dealing with Conditionals

One difficulty in dealing with a conditional statement is to propagate the condition from the assignment of a variable to the use of the variable. For the example code from *ARC2D*, it is difficult to know that the condition guarding the assignment to JLOW_1 is the same condition guarding the use of JLOW_1. In situation like this, the unique variable name in the SSA representation serves as a handle to link the scattered information.

The SSA representation for the *ARC2D* example is as follows (we only show in SSA form for variables involved in loop boundaries):

```
    IF (.NOT.PERIDC) THEN
       JLOW_1 = 2
       JUP_1 = JMAX - 1
    ELSE
       JLOW_2 = 1
       JUP_2 = JMAX
    ENDIF
    JLOW_3 = PHI(Cond(.NOT.PERIDC),JLOW_1,JLOW_2)
    JUP_3 = PHI(Cond(.NOT.PERIDC),JUP_1,JUP_2)

L1: DO N = 1, 4
L2:    DO J = JLOW_3, JUP_3
```

```
          DO K = KLOW, KUP
             WORK(J,K,1) = ...
          ENDDO
       ENDDO
S1:    IF (.NOT.PERDIC) THEN
L3:       DO K = KLOW, KUP
             WORK(1,K,1) = WORK(2,K,1) + ...
             WORK(JMAX,K,1) = WORK(JMAX-1,K,1)
          ENDDO
       ENDIF
       ...
    ENDDO
```

Note that the PHI functions for JLOW_3 and JUP_3; it is inserted in the program to distinguish values of a variable from different branches of the control flow graph, in this case the different branches of a conditional statement. We use an extended PHI function to include the predicate for the conditional statement. Cond(.NOT.PERIDC) specifies the condition in the IF statement, if Cond(.NOT.PERIDC) is true, JLOW_3 will take the value of the second parameter of the PHI function which is JLOW_1, if Cond(.NOT.PERIDC) is false, it will take the value of the third parameter, JLOW_2.

We will first show how to interpret the conditional statement and then show how to compute the upper and lower bounds for the variables. For loop L3 to be executed, the condition (.NOT.PERDIC) must be true since L3 is control dependent on the S1. Tracing the values of JLOW_3, JUP_3 to the PHI function we know that they will have value JLOW_1, JUP_1. Tracing the value of JLOW_1, JUP_1 further, we have JLOW_3=JLOW_1=2, JUP_3=JUP_1=JMAX-1. Since now the value of JLOW_3=2, JUP_3=JMAX-1 matches the value for the subscript of the WORK(2,K,1) and WORK(JMAX-1,K,1), we do not need to trace back the value for JMAX any further. At this point we can compare the array region WORK(JLOW_3:JUP_3, KLOW:KUP, 1) defined in loop L2, which is WORK(2:JMAX-1, KLOW:KUP, 1), with the array regions WORK(2, KLOW:KUP, 1) and WORK(JMAX-1, KLOW:KUP, 1). The definition covers the uses, and WORK array is privatizable to loop L1.

As discussed before, in this example it is sufficient to prove WORK is privatizable just by showing the lower bound of JUP_3 is greater than or equal to JMAX-1 and the upper bound of JLOW_3 is less than or equal to 2. To compute the bounds for a variable, we can make a conservative choice at each PHI function and ignore the predicate for the conditional statement. We start by tracing back the values for variables until they are unified. Then we take the max or min on the second and third parameter of a PHI function and ignore the predicate.

$$max(JLOW\_3) = max(PHI(Cond(.NOT.PERIDC), JLOW\_1, JLOW\_2))$$
$$= max(PHI(Cond(.NOT.PERIDC), 2, 1)) = max(2,1) = 2$$

$$min(JUP\_3) = min(PHI(Cond(.NOT.PERIDC), JUP\_1, JUP\_2))$$
$$= min(PHI(Cond(.NOT.PERIDC), JMAX-1, JMAX)) = JMAX-1$$

In addition to being goal directed and on demand, the backward tracing scheme can stop the tracing when the symbolic expressions in question are *unified*, i.e., when the variables in the expressions are the same. After that, the additional unwinding of values will not gain any more information. In a forward propagation scheme, everything must start from the most primitive variables and in the case of several levels of conditionals, the number of branches may quickly explode and complexity may grow out of control. Because the backward tracing is goal directed and incremental, we can easily set complexity constraints such as the maximum backward tracing level to a fix number of nested PHI functions. After that, the algorithm can give up and degrade gracefully to reduce compile time.

5.3 Bounds for Monotonic Variables

The value of an induction variable or a monotonic variable depends on the structure of the loop in which it is assigned. Induction variable's last value can be determined using induction variable substitution technique such as presented in [18]. In this section, we will show a technique to estimate the bounds of monotonic variable.

Using SSA form of loop L3 in the example from *BDNA*, we have:

```
      L_1 = 0
L3:   DO J = 1, I-1
          L_2 = PHI(L3,L_4,L_1)
          IF (IND(J).NE.0) THEN
              L_3 = L_2 + 1
          ENDIF
          L_4=PHI(Cond(IND(J).NE.0),L_3,L_2)
      ENDDO
```

The original loop L4 will use L_2 as the value of L. In this example, we extend the PHI function to include loop label L3 in it to identify the loop control. Following the terminology used by Wolfe on induction variables[18], L_2 will appear as a *Strongly Connected Region (SCR)* that includes a loop header PHI function and some conditional PHI functions. To find the upper bounds of L_2, we need to find the cycle with maximum increment to L_2 in the SCR. Similarly, for the lower bound of a monotonic variable, we need to find the cycle with minimum increment to L_2 in the SCR. This can be accomplished by backward tracing and compute bounds on PHI function as follows:

$$L\_2 = PHI(L3,L\_1,L\_4) = PHI(L3,PHI(Cond(IND(J).NE.0),L\_3,L\_2),0)$$
$$= PHI(L3,PHI(Cond(IND(J).NE.0),L\_2+1,L\_2),0)$$

Hence the maximum value for L_2 will be:

```
max(L_2)=max(PHI(L3,PHI(Cond(IND(J).NE.0),L_2+1,L_2),0))
    = 0+(I-1)*max_inc(PHI(Cond(IND(J).NE.0),L_2+1,L_2))
    = (I-1)*max(0,1)=I-1
```

The way to handle loop PHI function is to take its trip count and multiply the trip count to the maximum increment in the SCR. To find the maximum increment for a loop, we will choose the branch with maximum increment in a conditional PHI function. In the example, the monotonic variable is L_2 and its maximum increment for each iteration is 1. Lower bound for monotonic variables can be computed by taking a minimum function over the PHI functions.

5.4   Index Arrays

The use of the index array in the program makes it difficult to determine the array reference region in a program. ARC2D uses an index array JPLUS. It is assigned as follows:

```
L1:  DO J=1, JMAX
         JPLUS(J) = J+1
     END DO
     JPLUS(JMAX)=JMAX
     ...
L2:  DO J = 1, JMAX
         ... = ... FLUX(JPLUS(J),K,N)
     END DO
```

We can use the SSA representation to find out the value of JPLUS(J) in loop L2. We will extend the SSA representation to array in the following way: (1) create a new array name for each array assignment; (2) use the subscript to identify which element is assigned; (3) replace the assignment with a special PHI function that will be written as MU((subscript),assignment,old). The assignment A(I) = exp is converted to A_1 = MU((I), exp, A_0), which is interpreted as element A_1(I) will take the value of exp in the assignment while other elements of A_1 will take the value in the A_0 as before the assignment. Using this extension, our example can be transformed into the following SSA form:

```
L1:  DO J=1, JMAX
         JPLUS_2 = PHI(L1,JPLUS_1,JPLUS_0)
         JPLUS_1 = MU((J),J+1,JPLUS_2)
     END DO
     JPLUS_3 = MU((JMAX),JMAX,JPLUS_2)
     ...
L2:  DO J = 1, JMAX
         ... = ... FLUX(JPLUS_3(J),K,N)
     END DO
```

For subscript expression JPLUS_3(J) in loop L2, it can be evaluated as follows.

```
JPLUS_3(J) = (MU((JMAX),JMAX,JPLUS_2))(J)
         = (MU((JMAX),JMAX,PHI(L1,JPLUS_1,JPLUS_0)))(J)
         = (MU((JMAX),JMAX,PHI(L1,MU((J),J+1,JPLUS_2),JPLUS_0)))(J)
         = (MU((JMAX),JMAX,MU(([1:JMAX]),J+1,JPLUS_0)))(J)
```

The expression can be interpreted as

```
JPLUS_3(J) = IF J=JMAX THEN
                JMAX
             ELSEIF J in [1:JMAX] THEN
                J+1
             ELSE
                JPLUS_0(J)
             ENDIF
```

Note that the PHI function for loop L1 defines an aggregated region of the index array.

6 Conclusion

We presented an algorithm to automatically identify privatizable arrays in sequential FORTRAN programs to eliminate memory-related dependence. The algorithm has been implemented in the POLARIS system to perform interprocedural array privatization. Our experiments have thus far indicated that the algorithms can privatize most of the arrays privatized by hand in [8]. To increase the coverage of the algorithms, it seems necessary to use more sophisticated techniques for determining the equivalence of symbolic variables, and interprocedural symbolic values and bounds propagation. To this purpose, we proposed a goal-directed technique that uses the SSA form of a program to determine the values and bounds of symbolic variables in the presence of conditional statements, loops, and index arrays. We are currently implementing the symbolic analysis technique and studying the application of array privatization to data distribution for greater local access and better load balancing.

References

1. B. Alpern, M. N. Wegman, and F. K. Zadeck. Detecting Equality of Variables in Programs. In *Proc. of the 15th ACM Symposium on Principles of Programming Languages*, pages 1–11, 1988.
2. Utpal Banerjee. *Dependence Analysis for Supercomputing*. Kluwer Academic Publishers, 1988.
3. M. Burke, R. Cytron, J. Ferrante, and W. Hsieh. Automatic generation of nested, fork-join parallelism. *Journal of Supercomputing*, pages 71–88, 1989.
4. D. Callahan and K. Kennedy. Analysis of interprocedural side effects in a parallel programming environment. *Journal of Parallel and Distributed Computing*, 5:517–550, 1988.

5. D. Callahan and K. Kennedy. Compiling programs for distributed-memory multi-processors. *Journal of Supercomputing*, 2:151–169, October 1988.

6. Ron Cytron and Jeanne Ferante. What's in a Name? or The Value of Renaming for Parallelism Detection and Storage Allocation. In *Proc. 1987 International Conf. on Parallel Processing*, pages 19–27, August 1987.

7. Ron Cytron, Jeanne Ferrante, Barry K. Rosen, Mark N. Wegman, and F. Kenneth Zadeck. Efficiently computing static single assignment form and the control dependence graph. *ACM Transactions on Programming Languages and Systems*, 13(4):451–490, October 1991.

8. R. Eigenmann, J. Hoeflinger, Z. Li, and D. Padua. Experience in the automatic parallelization of four Perfect-Benchmark programs. In *Proc. 4-th Workshop on Programming Languages and Compilers for Parallel Computing*. Pitman/MIT Press, August 1991.

9. P. Feautrier. Array expansion. In *Proc. 1988 ACM Int'l Conf. on Supercomputing*, July 1988.

10. High Performance Fortran Forum. High performance fortran language specification (draft). Technical report, High Performance Fortran Forum, January 1993.

11. Zhiyuan Li. Array privatization for parallel execution of loops. In *Proc. of ICS'92*, pages 313–322, 1992.

12. D. E. Maydan, S. P. Amarasinghe, and M. S. Lam. Data dependence and data-flow analysis of arrays. In *Proc. 5rd Workshop on Programming Languages and Compilers for Parallel Computing*, August 1992.

13. D. Padua and M. Wolfe. Advanced compiler optimizations for supercomputers. *Communications of the ACM*, 29(12):1184–1201, December 1986.

14. A. Rogers and K. Pingali. Process decomposition through locality of reference. In *Proc. the SIGPLAN '89 Conference on Program Language Design and Implementation*, June 1989.

15. B. K. Rosen, M. N. Wegman, and F. K. Zadeck. Global Value Numbers and Redundant Computation. In *Proc. of the 15th ACM Symposium on Principles of Programming Languages*, pages 12–27, 1988.

16. Peng Tu and David Padua. Array privatization for shared and distributed memory machines. In *Proc. 2nd Workshop on Languages, Compilers, and Run-Time Environments for Distributed Memory Machines, to appear on ACM SIGPLAN Notices 1993*, September 1992.

17. M. N. Wegman and F. K. Zadeck. Constant propagation with conditional branches. *ACM Transactions on Programming Languages and Systems*, 13(2):181–210, April 1991.

18. Michael Wolfe. Beyond induction variables. *ACM PLDI'92*, 1992.

19. Michael Joseph Wolfe. Optimizing supercompilers for supercomputers. Technical Report UIUCDCS-R-82-1105, Department of Computer Science, University of Illinois, October 1982.

20. Chuan-Qi Zhu and Pen-Chung Yew. A scheme to enforce data dependence on large multiprocessor systems. *IEEE Transactions on Software Engineering*, 13(6):726–739, June 1987.

21. H. Zima, H.-J. Bast, and M. Gerndt. Superb: A tool for semi-automatic MIMD/SIMD parallelization. *Parallel Computing*, 6:1–18, 1988.

22. Hans Zima and Barbara Chapman. *Supercompilers for Parallel and Vector Computers*. ACM Press, 1991.

FIAT: A Framework for Interprocedural Analysis and Transformation

Mary W. Hall[1] John M. Mellor-Crummey[2] Alan Carle[2] René G. Rodríguez[2]

[1] Center for Integrated Systems, Stanford University, Stanford, CA 94305
[2] Center for Research on Parallel Computation, Rice University, Houston, TX 77251

Abstract. The FIAT system is a compiler-building tool that enables rapid prototyping of interprocedural analysis and compilation systems. FIAT is a *framework* because it provides parameterized templates and common drivers to support interprocedural data-flow analysis and procedure cloning. Further, FIAT provides the complex underlying support required to collect and manage information about the procedures in the program. FIAT's reliance on system-independent abstractions makes it suitable for use in systems with distinct intermediate code representations and enables sharing of system software across research platforms. Demand-driven analysis maintains a clean separation between interprocedural analysis problems, enabling tools built upon FIAT to solve only the data-flow problems of immediate interest. FIAT drives interprocedural optimization in the ParaScope programming tools at Rice University and the SUIF compiler at Stanford University. FIAT has proven to be a valuable aid in development of a large number of interprocedural tools, including a data race detection system, a static performance estimation tool, a distributed-memory compiler for Fortran D, an interactive parallelizing tool and an automatic parallelizer in the SUIF compiler.

1 Introduction

To effectively exploit modern multiprocessor architectures, compilers and programming tools require deep analysis and program transformations to expose coarse-grain parallelism and manage the memory hierarchy. A difficulty for such tools is that procedure boundaries can obscure their understanding of a program and interfere with transformations on loop nests spanning multiple procedures. Since large scientific codes typically contain many procedures, compilers and tools must employ *interprocedural* techniques to adequately support such programs. *Interprocedural data-flow analysis* crosses procedure boundaries to expose information about a procedure's calling context and the side-effects of its procedure calls. *Interprocedural transformations* restructure a program to reveal more precise data-flow information or move code across procedure boundaries.

Many researchers have demonstrated significant performance improvements on shared-memory multiprocessors by manually applying interprocedural analysis and transformation techniques to enhance parallelism or memory hierarchy utilization [2, 30]. Techniques that have proven useful for this purpose include scalar and array side-effect analysis [6, 33, 32], interprocedural constant propagation [12, 26], array KILL analysis [2, 30], and transformations to expose loop nests to parallelization [17]. In addition to automatic parallelization, many problem domains in high-performance computing can greatly benefit from exploiting interprocedural information. For example, compiling for distributed-memory architectures and automatic detection of data races in shared-memory codes each involve program transformations that depend upon the solutions of domain-specific interprocedural problems for the generation of efficient code. Although interprocedural analysis and transformation have been shown to be important, few compilers employ these techniques due to two major obstacles:

- Compilation and analysis must be fundamentally restructured to support interprocedural analysis and transformation. Interprocedural optimization of a procedure requires information gleaned from other procedures; thus, procedures cannot be compiled and optimized in isolation. Moreover, considerations of space and time complexity may make straightforward extension of intraprocedural approaches infeasible for large programs.
- A large programming effort is required to make effective use of interprocedural optimization. Without some common framework, solving each interprocedural data-flow problem would require a substantial amount of duplicated effort.

We are building FIAT to address these obstacles. FIAT provides an effective architecture for program analysis and restructuring in an interprocedural setting and serves as a vehicle for experimenting with interprocedural optimization and its applications. Moreover, FIAT's general framework greatly reduces the programming effort needed to incorporate new interprocedural data-flow analyses and transformations. FIAT currently supports interprocedural optimization in two very different host systems — the ParaScope programming tools at Rice University [8] and the Stanford SUIF Compiler [31]. This paper describes the following key aspects of FIAT.

Abstract representations. The representation of programs used within FIAT is decoupled from the representation used by any host system in which FIAT will be applied. This decoupling made it possible to extract FIAT from Rice's ParaScope system and retarget it to Stanford's SUIF compiler with only a small amount of recoding, resulting in sharing of analysis code across research projects. Further flexibility arises from the use of abstract annotations as the principal representation of intermediate and final results of interprocedural data-flow analysis.

Demand-driven analysis framework. All solutions to interprocedural problems are computed by FIAT on a demand-driven basis. Benefits of this strategy include facilitating modular software development by providing a clean separation between interprocedural problems and eliminating the need for clients to know about the ordering of interprocedural problems.

Parameterized data-flow analysis template. FIAT provides a template for interprocedural data-flow analysis problems. From the programmer's standpoint, using this template minimizes the effort needed to specify a new interprocedural data-flow problem. This feature facilitates rapid prototyping of new interprocedural techniques.

Analysis for interprocedural transformations. FIAT provides a framework suitable to investigate the efficacy of interprocedural transformations. Since FIAT deals only with abstract representations of programs, its role in supporting interprocedural transformations is limited to identifying opportunities and assessing the profitability of applying transformations; actual source code transformations are the responsibility of tools that consume FIAT's analysis results.

The next section presents background material on FIAT's architecture, interprocedural analysis and interprocedural transformation. Section 3 describes FIAT's principal representations. Section 4 discusses how FIAT's demand-driven analysis engine manipulates these representations. Section 5 presents the parameterized data-flow analysis framework and how a user of the system incorporates a new data-flow analysis problem. Section 6 describes existing and planned frameworks for exposing opportunities for interprocedural transformations. Section 7 presents several applications of the system. The paper concludes with a brief discussion of our experiences with FIAT and future plans for the system.

2 Background

To provide some context for the remainder of the paper, here we describe the architecture of whole-program analysis systems for which FIAT was designed and introduce some terminology for interprocedural data-flow analysis and interprocedural transformation.

2.1 Three-Phase Approach to Whole-Program Analysis

FIAT has been designed for use in whole-program analysis systems based on a three-phase strategy [8, 10, 14]:

1. **Local Analysis.** Essential information describing each procedure in a module is collected and saved. This information describes the formal parameters and call sites defining the procedure's interface. In addition, immediate interprocedural effects relevant to particular data-flow problems are collected for use in initializing interprocedural propagation.
2. **Interprocedural Propagation.** FIAT's interprocedural analysis engine examines the local information collected for each procedure and uses its call site information to build a call graph. An iterative data-flow solver then computes solutions to requested interprocedural data-flow problems. Each data-flow problem can use any of the results of local analysis. A data-flow

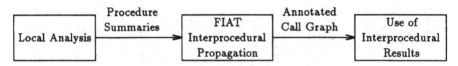

Fig. 1. A three-phase strategy for whole-program anslysis.

problem can also use results from other data-flow problems as long as dependences between data-flow problems are acyclic. Local analysis results and data-flow solutions may both be used to make decisions about interprocedural transformations.

3. **Use of Interprocedural Results.** Tools that incorporate FIAT's analysis engine can use the results it calculates for display or to direct optimizing transformations of the program.

This three-phase organization supports whole-program analysis while preserving much of the efficiency of separate compilation of procedures. The separate local analysis phase means that there is no need to examine the source code for each procedure during interprocedural propagation. Furthermore, since the initial information for a module does not depend on interprocedural effects, it only needs to be collected once when the module changes rather than every time interprocedural analysis involving that module is performed. This property is true even if the module is used as part of several programs. Using this three phase analysis strategy along with a technique called recompilation analysis, a whole-program compiler could restrict recompilation to only those modules to which interprocedural optimizations that are no longer valid [3] were applied.

The FIAT system supports the interprocedural propagation phase. This phase is independent of the intermediate representation of source code used by the other phases. FIAT's input consists of local information for each procedure represented using a system-independent abstraction that is described in the next section. From this information, FIAT computes a call graph annotated with analysis results and interprocedural transformation decisions. Tools inspect interprocedural information available from FIAT's annotated call graph and apply it as appropriate to the tool's purpose. This organization is shown in Figure 1.

2.2 Interprocedural Data-Flow Analysis

Interprocedural data-flow analysis can be described as either *flow insensitive* or *flow sensitive*. Flow-insensitive analysis calculates data-flow effects at program locations without considering the control flow paths that will be taken through individual procedures [19]. In contrast, flow-sensitive analysis derives the effects common to each distinct control-flow path that reaches a location [27].

We use several flow-insensitive data-flow problems as examples throughout the paper:

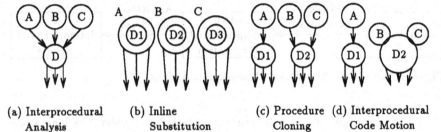

(a) Interprocedural   (b) Inline   (c) Procedure (d) Interprocedural
     Analysis   Substitution   Cloning   Code Motion

Fig. 2. Graphical comparison of interprocedural optimization techniques.

- MoD(c): the set of variables that may be modified following procedure call c, either by the called procedure or its descendants in the call graph [19].
- REF(c): the set of variables that may be referenced as a result of a procedure call c [19].
- ALIAS(p): the set of variable pairs that may refer to the same memory location in procedure p, resulting from Fortran's call-by-reference parameter-passing mechanism [19].
- CONSTANTS(p): the set of pairs $\langle v, c \rangle$ representing that variable v has constant value c across all calls to procedure p [5].

We use the following example of a flow-sensitive problem in Section 5, where the node n represents either a procedure or a block of code.

- LIVE(n): the set of variables v that may be used prior to any redefinition [27].

2.3 Interprocedural Transformations

Figure 2(a) displays a portion of a call graph where procedures A, B and C all invoke procedure D. D contains three calls to procedures not shown. Interprocedural analysis derives information about the *calling context* for D as well as the side-effects of its three call sites, but there are two limitations: (1) Data-flow analysis summarizes information when paths in the call graph merge; and (2) the compiler cannot move code across the call boundary. Interprocedural transformations can sometimes be used to overcome these limitations.

Inline substitution. This transformation replaces a procedure call with a copy of the invoked procedure. In Figure 2(b), by inlining the calls to D, each version of D may be fully optimized in the context of its caller. However, inlining can sometimes lead to unmanageable code explosion, resulting in prohibitive increases in compile time [29, 9]. Moreover, execution-time performance may degrade when optimizers fail to exploit the additional context inlining exposes or when the code size exceeds register, cache or paging system limits [9, 11, 24, 29].

In light of the limitations of both inline substitution and interprocedural data-flow analysis, our research has explored additional techniques that provide some of the power of inlining but with less associated costs.

Procedure cloning. To perform this transformation, the compiler replicates a procedure and tailors the procedure and its copy to distinct calling environments [7, 10]. In Figure 2(c), procedure D is cloned, inheriting distinct calling context information from A. Procedures B and C both invoke the same copy D2. Cloning thus avoids summarization of information inherited from callers. Procedures do not increase in size, and by sharing clones among multiple callers, the compiler can mitigate program growth.

Interprocedural code motion. This transformation moves some portion of code across the procedure boundary. In addition to inline substitution, two other forms of code motion have been explored: *loop embedding* and *loop extraction* [17]. The former moves a loop surrounding a call into the invoked procedure; the latter moves an outer enclosing loop across a call and into the caller. These transformations partially inline the code. However, since the compiler controls the code movement, it is possible to share transformed procedure bodies via cloning. In Figure 2(d), a small amount of code from procedure D has been moved into B and C, and both procedures invoke the same modified version D2.

3 Abstractions

FIAT's analysis engine manipulates three key abstractions: a summary representation of individual procedure bodies, a program call graph, and annotations on the call graph components.

3.1 Procedure Representation

An abstraction we call ProcSummary is FIAT's representation of a procedure body. Local analysis generates a ProcSummary abstraction for each procedure that serves as input to FIAT's analysis engine. It contains any information about the procedure that will be needed for interprocedural analysis. There are two principal advantages to using this abstraction rather than the procedure body itself. First, the ProcSummary abstraction contains only the local facts pertinent to interprocedural analysis and enables FIAT to avoid having the full representation of each procedure body in memory during analysis. Second, the simplicity of the ProcSummary abstraction makes it independent of both source-code language and procedure representation. This property makes FIAT easily retargetable to different systems.

The ProcSummary abstraction needed to support flow-insensitive analysis is very simple. It contains identifying information about the procedure such as its name and its formal parameters, information about the call sites in the procedure, and annotations representing immediate effects for particular data-flow problems. The information for each call site includes identifying information about the invoked procedure and its actual parameters.

To also support flow-sensitive analysis, we have extended **ProcSummary** to include a representation of the procedure's control flow graph, which serves as the basis for propagation of flow-sensitive information in the interprocedural phase. This graph is augmented with special *entry, exit, call* and *return* nodes, representing procedure entries, procedure exits, call sites and their return points. This additional structure enables us to record immediate effects at a finer granularity as annotations of nodes in the control flow graph. Our early experiences indicate that, at least for Fortran, the control flow graph is much smaller than the code so even our expanded **ProcSummary** representation remains relatively compact.

3.2 Call Graph

A *call graph* is the principal representation of a program manipulated by FIAT. Nodes in the call graph represent procedures in the program; edges represent invocation relationships that arise through call sites in the program.

Constructing the call graph. To construct the call graph, FIAT first introduces a node for each procedure in the program. Next, FIAT examines the call site information for each procedure. For each call site that is a direct invocation of a user-defined procedure, FIAT introduces an edge from the node representing the caller to the node representing the callee. To handle calls through procedure-valued formal parameters, FIAT first adds a *representative node* for each of the formals in the program, with an edge from the procedure in which the formal is declared to the formal's representative node. FIAT then performs *call graph analysis* to compute, for each procedure-valued formal f, the set *Boundto(f)* containing the possible procedure constants that may be passed to f at run time [16]. Finally, for each formal f, the system adds an edge from f's representative node to each procedure b in *Boundto(f)*. Representative nodes serve as a location to summarize, during interprocedural analysis, interprocedural information from all of the procedures potentially invoked through a procedure-valued formal. Summarization is required to report correctly the results of interprocedural analysis, and representative nodes provide a convenient mechanism to obtain this effect without any special accommodations to the data-flow analysis framework or queries on the results of analysis.

Representation. Each node and edge in the call graph contains a table to hold its associated annotations. Initially, each node in the call graph is annotated with its corresponding **ProcSummary** structure. Each edge contains a structure describing parameter bindings, used during data-flow analysis to translate variable names across the call. The binding structure has two components. The forward component is a one-to-many mapping from variables passed as actual parameters by the caller to the corresponding formal parameter(s) in the callee. The backward component is a one-to-one mapping from formal parameters in the callee to the corresponding actual parameters passed at the call.

3.3 Annotations

Annotations are the mechanism for associating arbitrary information with nodes and edges in the call graph. Annotations play an important role in FIAT. They are used to represent the intermediate and final results of interprocedural data-flow analysis and to convey interprocedural information from FIAT's driver to tools that use its analysis results.

All annotations are named entities derived from a base class; each annotation must support a basic set of methods for creating, destroying, reading, and writing the annotation. Annotations that represent data-flow sets must also support a method to test for equality with another annotation; this method is used by FIAT's data-flow solver to determine if the solution to a data-flow problem has converged. Annotations may support additional methods to manipulate conveniently the information they maintain.

FIAT completely separates the specification of an annotation representation from the specification of how it is computed, allowing opportunities for the reuse of annotation representations. As one important example, a representation of variable sets is shared by a number of interprocedural data-flow problems. The separation also makes it possible to define alternate implementations of the same data-flow analysis problem, for example, to study the use of problem formulations of different precision.

3.4 Example

Figure 3 shows an example program with three subroutines, P, Q and R, and their associated representations. The ProcSummary abstraction for P contains its name and, in the *callsites* field, the call to R with the names and types of the actual parameters. The tuple [16, 4] indicates the data of length 4 bytes starting at an offset of 16 bytes from the beginning of array A. The ProcSummary abstraction for R is similar, with field *formals* listing the formal parameters and their types. The *annotations* field in ProcSummary contains immediate effects for flow-insensitive data flow problems gathered during local analysis. Shown are annotations of the immediate effects needed for MOD and REF analysis.

The bindings for the call to procedure-valued formal X in R are resolved during call graph construction. In the graph, the representative node R.X represents this formal, and the edge from R.X to Q represents the binding of X to Q. Call site information is associated with the corresponding call graph edge. Edge P → R shows in its parameter binding structure that I in P is passed to both I and J in R. Annotations on call graph edges and nodes (not shown) represent final solutions to data-flow problems.

4 Interprocedural Analysis Driver

FIAT's interprocedural analysis engine is based upon a demand-driven paradigm. A tool using FIAT first initializes FIAT's driver to construct a call graph. The tool

530

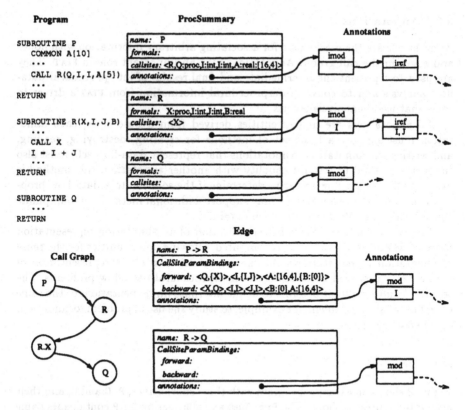

Fig. 3. FIAT's abstractions.

may obtain the solution to an interprocedural problem at any node (or edge) in the call graph by demanding the annotation corresponding to the problem solution. If the solution has not been computed already, the driver initiates its computation, caches the computed solution so that it is available for future requests, and returns the requested value. FIAT's demand-driven approach has the following desirable properties:

- The solution to any interprocedural data-flow problem can be obtained at any time.
- Explicit ordering constraints between data-flow problems are unnecessary; the only requirement is that dependences between problems cannot be cyclic.
- Implementations of data-flow problems are completely separated from each other and from the solver.

Implementation. To implement the demand-driven paradigm, FIAT relies on a set of *annotation managers*, one for each named interprocedural annotation. The distinction between an annotation and an annotation manager is that an annotation embodies a set of information, and the annotation manager embodies a method for computing an annotation. It is useful to separate these two notions since it is often possible to reuse an annotation representation for related problems. For instance FIAT uses the same annotation representation for MOD and REF variable sets.

When one demands by name an annotation on a node (or respectively, edge) in the call graph, the driver inspects the annotation table for the node (edge) for an annotation of the same name. If no such annotation already exists, the driver looks up an annotation manager by that name in a central registry and invokes the manager to compute the requested annotation on the node (edge). For interprocedural data-flow problems, the annotation manager invokes a data-flow solver (described in detail in section 5) to compute the requested annotation. To compute annotations that represent information other than the solution of interprocedural data-flow problems, an annotation manager is free to perform whatever actions are necessary. For example, an annotation manager used by the automatic data race detection system built upon FIAT (see Section 7) invokes a data dependence analyzer that uses interprocedural MOD information to determine a solution to this problem in the presence of procedure calls.

The annotation manager framework is also suitable for accommodating incremental data-flow analysis using a different data-flow solver. Incremental analysis could be used to partially compute solutions on the call graph, such as computing the solution to a forward interprocedural data-flow problem only for the demanded node and its ancestors. Furthermore, the system could incrementally update solutions on demand in response to editing changes in an interactive setting or during recompilation.

Ordering computation of data-flow problems. In addition to servicing annotation queries from tools using FIAT, the demand-driven organization also implicitly manages the ordering constraints in solving interprocedural problems. If an interprocedural data-flow problem requires the solution of some other problem, it merely demands the results. If they are not yet available, they are computed in response to the demand.

For example, the solution to the MOD problem requires ALIAS information since a variable is modified if any of its aliases is modified. Thus, the annotation manager computing MOD annotations demands ALIAS information. If ALIAS information is not already available, the analysis engine is invoked recursively to compute it.

This demand-driven organization ensures that any interprocedural results are available when they are needed without requiring an explicit representation of ordering among data-flow problems. Ordering information is implicitly represented by the code for computing interprocedural problems: a use of the solution to interprocedural problem *p1* in the code for computing interprocedural problem *p2* indicates that *p2* will be solved before computation of *p1* completes. The only restriction a set of interprocedural problems must satisfy for this demand-driven framework to function properly is that there may not be a cyclic dependence among the problems.

Maintaining separation of data-flow problems. The demand-driven organization and the use of a problem registry completely separate the implementations of individual data-flow problems from each other and from the analysis driver itself. The implementation of an annotation manager for a data-flow problem needs only to know which solutions to other data-flow problems it requires.

The separation of interprocedural problems from each other and from the analysis driver ensures that a configuration of FIAT for use with a particular tool includes only those functions related to the problems of interest to the tool. This property is particularly important because FIAT is used for a wide variety of applications (see Section 7). Different systems share some interprocedural problems, such as computation of scalar MOD and REF side effects, but other problems specific to compiling programs for distributed memory multiprocessors or automatically instrumenting shared-memory programs to detect data races are not included when building tools for any other purpose.

5 Parameterized Templates for Interprocedural Analysis

FIAT provides a framework for interprocedural data-flow analysis including a Kildall-style iterative solver [22]. To solve a new interprocedural analysis problem with FIAT, a programmer provides a local analysis module to collect the immediate effects of a procedure for the new data-flow problem, define an annotation to represent the problem's data-flow sets, instantiate a solver template for the the data-flow problem, and define an annotation manager to invoke the solver with the instantiated template. FIAT supports both flow-insensitive and flow-sensitive analysis.

Below we describe how a programmer specifies a new flow-insensitive data-flow problem in FIAT, how the data-flow solver applies this specification and extensions to support flow-sensitive analysis.

5.1 Flow-Insensitive Analysis

Data-flow analysis problem template. The programmer provides specifications to be used by the interprocedural data-flow solver to compute values of data-flow sets at nodes and edges in the call graph.

The functions provided to FIAT are simply the specifications for the Kildall data-flow analysis framework [22]:

- InitNode(n) and InitEdge (e) provide the initial annotations at node n and edge e, respectively. These functions collect information from ProcSummary or from the solutions to previous data-flow problems.
- A *meet function* $\bigwedge(s1, s2)$ for a node takes two sets and returns a conservative approximation of both.

- The *transfer function* $T_c(s)$ translates the elements in set s across call site c to the other endpoint of c, according to parameter passing at the call.[3] Similarly, $T_c^{-1}(s)$ maps in the opposite direction. Set s is met with the initial set at the edge returned by InitEdge.
- The *direction* represents whether information is propagated from a node to its descendants (*i.e.*, a forward problem) or from a node to its ancestors (a backward problem).
- $\top$ and $\bot$ sets are used to initialize the entry and exit nodes of the graph.

FIAT requires an additional function specification from the programmer, called FinalizeAnnotation, that may incorporate other data before installing the final solution to the data-flow problem. As an example, MOD analysis folds in modifications for aliases of modified variables.

The template is useful for two reasons. First, it succinctly identifies what a programmer must implement to solve a new interprocedural problem with FIAT. Second, the template greatly simplifies integration of new analysis problems into the system and enables functionality common to all data-flow problems to be implemented with shared code.

Iterative solver. FIAT provides a common iterative solver that is shared by all data-flow analysis problems. Abstractly, for forward data-flow problems, the solver calculates the solution to the following simultaneous equations[4]:

$$Set(n) = \bigwedge_{c=p \to n} T_c(Set(p)).$$

For backward problems the solver similarly calculates the result of the following equations:

$$Set(n) = \bigwedge_{c=n \to s} T_c^{-1}(Set(s)).$$

To compute the solution to the set of simultaneous equations representing a data-flow problem, the solver first initializes the data-flow set for each call graph node n to its initial value returned by InitNode:

$$Set(n) = InitNode(n),$$

and then iterates over the call graph applying the user-defined meet and transfer functions until the solution converges. For forward data-flow problems, the solver iterates over the call graph in reverse post order (in acyclic graphs, this means that each procedure is examined after all of its callers). Backward data-flow problems are processed similarly in post order.

For forward data-flow problems, the desired result is the data-flow set associated with each procedure node in the call graph. For backward problems, the data-flow set for each procedure node is translated to represent the side effects of a particular call site by projecting backwards across each incoming call site edge. Thus, the final solution for a backward problem at a call site is stored on the corresponding call site edge in the call graph.

---

[3] The transfer function is distinguished from its role in intraprocedural analysis because it maps information across an edge rather than within a node.

[4] The meet function actually computes the meet for a pair of sets at a time.

(1) $Set(entry_n) = Set(n)$

/* Collect information from the exit of called procedures */
(2)   for each return node r in $cfg(n)$
    let c be the corresponding call
    let q be the procedure invoked at the c
    $Set(r) = T_c^{-1}(Set(exit_q))$

/* Propagate within control flow graph */
for each node cn in $cfg(n)$
(3) $Set(cn) = Set(cn) \wedge \bigwedge_{p \in pred(cn)} Set(p)$

/* Project information to invoked nodes */
(4)   for each call node c in $cfg(n)$
    let q be the procedure invoked at c
    $Set(q) = Set(q) \wedge T_c(Set(c))$

Fig. 4. Iterative flow-sensitive solver

5.2 Flow-Sensitive Analysis

Flow-sensitive analysis requires modifications to the iterative solver. Further, local analysis places its immediate effects on a control flow graph representation of each procedure, which is also used during interprocedural propagation. Below we describe the only changes needed to the solver to support flow-sensitive analysis.

Iterative solver. The flow-sensitive solver iterates over both the call graph and the control flow graph. The solver begins by initializing sets at all nodes in both the call graph and the control flow graph to $\top$. For a forward problem, it then iterates over the nodes in the call graph until no more changes, performing the computation in Figure 4 for each procedure n. In this formulation $Set(n)$ for some node n representing a procedure contains the set on entry to the procedure. The set value on exit is available, if desired, at the exit node for the procedure.

For backward problems, propagation is similar, but the direction is reversed. Thus, at statement (1), we initialize the set for $exit_n$ rather than $entry_n$. At statement (2), the information at each call node c is initialized from $entry_q$. Statement (3) performs the meet of successors, not predecessors. Statement (4) projects information from the return node rather than the call node. The resulting set at a procedure node n is the value on exit from the procedure; the value on entry is available from the entry node.

An Example To illustrate how the flow-sensitive solver works, we compute the LIVE sets defined in Section 2.[5] The example program is shown in Figure 5. For

---

[5] At procedure nodes, the solution represents variables live on exit, similar to Callahan's definition [4].

the live problem, the meet function $\wedge$ is union, and the initial $\top$ set value is $\emptyset$. The following steps are required to converge at a solution.

	Initialize	Collect	Propagate	Project
Visit P	Live(b7) = Live(p) = $\emptyset$	Live(b2) = T_{b2}^{-1}(Live(b8)) = $\emptyset$ Live(b5) = T_{b5}^{-1}(Live(b8)) = $\emptyset$ Live(b6) = $\emptyset$	Live(b1) = Live(b0) = $\emptyset$ Live(b4) = Live(b3) = $\{y\}$	Live(q) = Live(q) $\wedge$ T_{b5}(Live(b6)) $\wedge$ T_{b2}(Live(b3)) = $\{b\}$
Visit Q	Live(b10) = Live(q) = $\{b\}$	/* no calls */	Live(b9) = Live(b8) = $\{a,b\}$	/* no calls */
Visit P	Live(b7) = Live(p) = $\emptyset$	Live(b2) = T_{b2}^{-1}(Live(b8)) = $\{x,y\}$ Live(b5) = T_{b5}^{-1}(Live(b8)) = $\{t,y\}$ Live(b6) = $\emptyset$	Live(b1) = Live(b0) = $\emptyset$ Live(b4) = Live(b3) = $\{y\}$	Live(q) = Live(q) $\wedge$ T_{b5}(Live(b6)) $\wedge$ T_{b5}(Live(b6)) $\wedge$ T_{b2}(Live(b3)) = $\{b\}$

Open Issues. General support for flow-sensitive analysis is difficult. Because of its potential for significant space requirements, algorithms for flow-sensitive analysis typically exploit specific aspects of their data-flow problem to reduce costs. Thus, our support for flow-sensitive analysis currently has two limitations. We outline them here and describe them in detail elsewhere [13]. After experience implementing a number of flow-sensitive data-flow problems, we will consider general solutions to these problems.

Unrealizable paths. In our example, we propagated information along paths in the graph that do not correspond to possible execution paths, or *realizable paths* [23]. Specifically, Set(b5) = $\{t,y\}$ is imprecise. It results from propagation of values along the following subpath in the graph: ..., $b4$, $b3$, $b10$, $b9$, $b8$, $b5$, ... The body of q is entered from the return at $b3$ and exits at the other call $b5$. This situation arises because flow-sensitive analysis propagates information into a procedure describing its *calling context* and information out of a procedure describing its *side effects*.

We plan to use procedure cloning (Section 6.1) to replicate procedures according to unique calling context information. With careful cloning we can avoid any loss of precision due to propagation along unrealizable paths.

Sparse program representations. The program representation used in flow-sensitive analysis contains the control flow graph for every procedure, annotated with initial information needed by the propagation phase. This program representation may be quite large, and it may be an inefficient representation for data-flow analysis. We are considering sparser program representations, but it appears that the most appropriate representation is highly dependent on the data-flow problem being solved.

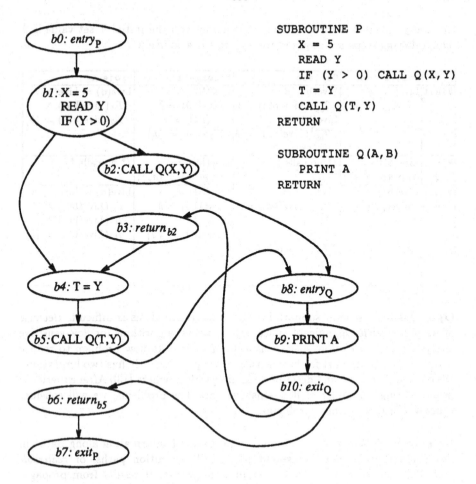

```
SUBROUTINE P
    X = 5
    READ Y
    IF (Y > 0) CALL Q(X, Y)
    T = Y
    CALL Q(T, Y)
RETURN

SUBROUTINE Q(A, B)
    PRINT A
RETURN
```

Fig. 5. Flow-sensitive LIVE problem example.

6 Interprocedural Transformations

This section discusses how a compiler may use FIAT to locate opportunities for profitable interprocedural transformations, as defined in Section 2. When performed in concert with interprocedural data-flow analysis, these transformations expose better information to analysis and enable moving code across procedure boundaries. FIAT *does not* manipulate source code; it supports interprocedural transformations with algorithms that examine annotations on the call graph to locate opportunities where interprocedural transformations are safe and profitable. A compiler may then use this information to perform the mechanical modifications to source code required to complete the transformation.

We present FIAT's existing prototype framework for one of these interprocedural transformations, *procedure cloning*. We then briefly discuss the requirements for frameworks to support other interprocedural transformations.

6.1 A Framework for Procedure Cloning

The design of the cloning framework is based on previous research on how to apply cloning to expose better data-flow information while avoiding the potential for exponential code growth [7]. Two key insights about cloning motivated the implementation:

Refines forward data-flow information. Cloning changes the structure of the call graph in a way that allows interprocedural analysis to proceed along distinct paths. For a forward data-flow problem cloning removes some of the points of confluence — those points where the analysis uses a meet function to approximate the facts that are true along two converging paths. Thus, we can use cloning to directly sharpen the results of data-flow analysis problems by replicating nodes with significantly different interprocedural information for different invocations. Our cloning algorithm may be used with any forward flow-insensitive interprocedural data-flow problems, such as constant propagation, alias analysis and type analysis. [6]

Goal-directed cloning. The above discussion suggests that we calculate solutions to the forward interprocedural problems and use these directly as the basis for cloning decisions. However, compilers cannot capitalize on every new data-flow fact that is exposed. For example, it would not be profitable to clone based on constant values of a variable that is not referenced in the procedure or its descendants. Other examples of desirable cloning filters are discussed elsewhere [7, 15]. We define a cloning strategy that filters the data-flow sets to target specific optimization opportunities as *goal-directed* [28]. FIAT's cloning framework supports goal-directed cloning by allowing the programmer to specify a filtering function to distinguish between data-flow facts that have an impact on code quality and those that do not, thus avoiding unnecessary code growth.

Programmer Specifications The cloning framework does not require specifications beyond the forward flow-insensitive data-flow problem to be used as the basis for cloning. The programmer may optionally specify a Filter function to perform goal-directed cloning. For an input data-flow set S at edge e, Filter(S, e) returns a set S' which eliminates insignificant data-flow facts from S. For example, to clone based on interprocedural constant propagation, one might specify the following filter:

---

[6] Note that the change in the graph may also indirectly sharpen solutions to backward data-flow problems. For example, changes in the results of alias analysis or constant propagation (both forward problems) can change the results of MOD analysis (a backward problem). However, it is unclear how to predict the impact a cloning decision will have on the solution to a backward data-flow problem.

```
        for each node n in topological order
            /* Partition filtered data-flow sets contributed by calls to n */
            for each call c_in invoking n
                tmpSet = Filter (Set(c_in))
                InsertPartition (c_in, tmpSet, Π(n))
            endfor

            /* Replicate n in call graph and incrementally update its data-flow set */
            for each partition π in Π(n) until threshold for partitions exceeded
                newNode = SplitNode(π)
                IncrementalUpdates(newNode, π)
            endfor
        endfor


    IncrementalUpdates(node, π)
        /* Node's set is meet of incoming calls in partition */
        nodeSet = ⋀_{c_in ∈ π} Set(c_in)
        attach nodeSet to node
        for each call c_out in n
            edgeSet = T_{c_out} (nodeSet)
            attach edgeSet to edge representing c_out
        endfor
```

Fig. 6. Cloning Algorithm.

$$Filter(\text{CONSTANTS}(e), e) = \{ \langle v, c \rangle | \langle v, c \rangle \in \text{CONSTANTS}(e) \land v \in \text{GREF}(\text{callee}(e)) \}.$$

S' only contains pairs associated with variables globally referenced by the procedure invoked at the edge.

Cloning Algorithm The algorithm for procedure cloning is given in Figure 6. The algorithm examines the filtered data-flow sets contributed by each incoming edge to a node, partitioning the edges into equivalence classes. Whenever the partitioning results in multiple equivalence classes, an opportunity for cloning exists. Following partitioning of the calls to a node, the algorithm replicates the node and its outgoing edges in the call graph, reassociates the incoming edges to invoke the appropriate cloned version, and incrementally updates the data-flow information at the node and its outgoing edges. The nodes are visited in topological order so that the cloning decision at a node can incorporate the effects of cloning all of its ancestors in the call graph.

For clarity of presentation, this algorithm assumes that the call graph contains no cycles (signifying recursion). Support for recursion is described elsewhere [7]. The algorithm relies on the following two functions:

- The function SplitNode(n) replicates node n in the call graph, replicates its outgoing edges, reassociates its incoming edges, and copies its annotations and other associated data.
- The function InsertPartition(e, S, Π) creates a new partition $\langle e, S \rangle$ for the collection Π if the data-flow set S does not already appear in the collection. If S is in the collection, it simply adds the edge e to a list representing the call sites to the procedure with the same value for their filtered data-flow set. These call sites will share the same cloned procedure body.

The incremental updates to data-flow sets rely on the transfer function T and the meet function $\bigwedge$, specified as part of the data-flow problem (see Section 5). The algorithm forms the meet of the sets contributed by the edges in the partition. The resulting set may not be identical to the set associated with the partition since some data-flow facts may have been eliminated by Filter, but the differences should not significantly affect optimization. Once the algorithm derives the annotation for a new node, it applies the transfer function T at each outgoing edge to map variable names across a call, and then incorporates initial data-flow information at the call graph edge. These incremental updates prepare the information for cloning analysis of descendant nodes in the call graph.

Open Issues Two remaining issues need to be considered for the cloning framework. The first deals with incrementally updating the solutions to problems other than the cloning problem. Since the cloning algorithm changes the graph structure, solutions to other forward and backward problems may indirectly become more precise, and the algorithm should also incrementally update these solutions. A similar issue arises when cloning is based on flow-sensitive data-flow problems. In this case, information resulting from cloning at a node must be propagated through emanating call chains to determine the effects for descendants.

Example We demonstrate the algorithm with an example, shown in Figure 7. The example program contains two calls to procedure P in MAIN, and two calls to procedure Q in P. The constants sets for the calls to P are as follows:

$$\text{CONSTANTS}(c1) = \{\langle I, 1 \rangle, \langle G, 20 \rangle\}. \quad \text{CONSTANTS}(c2) = \{\langle I, 3 \rangle, \langle G, 20 \rangle\}.$$

The algorithm begins by filtering these two sets. Since the variable G does not appear in P or its descendant Q, the algorithm eliminates these elements. Two partitions are created for P: $\{\langle I, 1 \rangle\}$ and $\{\langle I, 3 \rangle\}$. The algorithm replicates P in the call graph, associating the first full set (including the pair for G) with P and the second with P'. It calculates the sets for the four calls to Q, using the transfer function to map names across the call and to include the initial pair $\langle N, 10 \rangle$ at each call. Sets for the calls to Q are the follows.

$$\text{CONSTANTS}(c3) = \{\langle N, 10 \rangle, \langle INC, 1 \rangle, \langle G, 20 \rangle\}.$$
$$\text{CONSTANTS}(c4) = \{\langle N, 10 \rangle, \langle INC, 1 \rangle, \langle G, 20 \rangle\}.$$
$$\text{CONSTANTS}(c3') = \{\langle N, 10 \rangle, \langle INC, 3 \rangle, \langle G, 20 \rangle\}.$$
$$\text{CONSTANTS}(c4') = \{\langle N, 10 \rangle, \langle INC, 1 \rangle, \langle G, 20 \rangle\}.$$

```
PROGRAM MAIN            SUBROUTINE P (A,I)         SUBROUTINE Q (A,N,INC)
        COMMON G        c3: CALL Q (A,10,I)              ...
        G = 20          c4: CALL Q (A,10,MOD(I,2))
    c1: CALL P(A,1)
    c2: CALL P(A,3)
        PRINT *, G
```

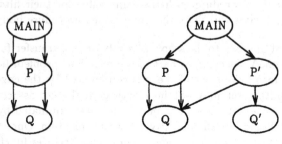

Fig. 7. Example for cloning algorithm.

The algorithm creates two partitions for Q and updates the sets, arriving at the final call graph shown in Figure 7.

Importance of Cloning Opportunities for cloning based on interprocedural constants arise often in scientific codes when using multi-purpose, utility or library code. Cloning often exposes constant loop bounds for parallel loops (and thereby enables the compiler to directly evaluate whether parallelization is worthwhile). Cloning also simplifies subscript expressions or control flow in a way that exposes parallelism. While our implementation has located a number of profitable cloning opportunities in the Perfect benchmark programs, it appears that benefits of cloning are increased for very large programs. As evidence of this point, cloning based on constants in the Convex Applications Compiler increased the number of constant values appearing in codes by more than 50% for 14 programs [26]. These programs were part of a suite of 29 programs with average size greater than 62,000 lines.

6.2 Other Interprocedural Transformations

Similar frameworks are necessary to support other interprocedural transformations such as inline substitution, loop embedding and loop extraction. FIAT could provide a framework to drive inline substitution. The inlining framework would walk the edges in the call graph, invoking a decision procedure at each edge to determine whether inlining is desirable. The framework would manipulate the call graph in response to inlining decisions and take care of incremental updates of the data-flow information. A programmer of the framework would need to provide the decision procedure, which would be permitted to examine information in the call graph.

Loop embedding and loop extraction require support similar to inlining. The system could determine whether embedding and extraction are safe [17]. For instances of safe embedding or extraction, a decision procedure could be invoked to determine if the techniques are desirable. The system would respond by marking the call sites as embedded or extracted, and in the case of embedding, include specifications about the loop index bounds for the embedded loop. The cloning algorithm could use these marks to make decisions on what callers may share the same optimized procedure body.

7 Applications of the System

The FIAT interprocedural analysis engine is being used to support tools that require solutions to a variety of interprocedural data-flow analysis problems. Below we describe the several experimental systems developed at Rice and Stanford that rely on FIAT's interprocedural analysis.

Interactive parallelization. The ParaScope Editor supports interactive restructuring of FORTRAN programs for execution on shared-memory parallel architectures [21]. In order to safely restructure a program to execute the iterations of a loop containing a procedure call in parallel, the tool requires knowledge of the side effects of the call. The editor uses *data dependence analysis* in conjunction with interprocedural analysis of scalar MOD and REF side effects to understand potential parallelism among loop iterations. For more precise analysis of procedure side effects to arrays, we are developing subsystems that will compute interprocedural MOD, REF, and KILL information for subportions of arrays (regular sections [6]) affected by a call and interprocedural symbolic analysis that will help eliminate dependences by deriving information about loop bounds and subscript expressions.

Data race detection. The ERASER system was developed to instrument shared-memory parallel FORTRAN programs to automatically detect data races at run time [25]. To reduce the number of variable references instrumented and the amount of additional storage required to support data race detection, ERASER uses the FIAT interprocedural analysis engine to solve three interprocedural problems: determining which formal parameters and global variables need data race instrumentation inside each procedure, which local variables in a procedure require auxiliary storage for use by the race detection run-time library, and which global variables require auxiliary storage.

For the three programs tested with ERASER thus far, using interprocedural analysis in combination with data dependence analysis reduced the dynamic overhead of instrumentation by 70–100% over a naive instrumentation strategy. Without interprocedural analysis, data dependence analysis alone provided only modest benefits reducing instrumentation overhead by less than 10%.

Compiling Fortran D. Fortran D is a version of Fortran augmented with data decompositions that specify how data is mapped onto the nodes of a parallel machine. The Fortran D compiler for distributed-memory machines uses data decompositions to partition a program so that a processor only performs computations for data stored locally; it also inserts communication for nonlocal data accessed by each processor. The compiler performs extensive program analysis as well as optimizations such as extracting messages out of loops in order to reduce communication cost [18].

The semantics of Fortran D dictate that a procedure inherits the data decompositions of its formal parameters and global variables from its callers. The compiler must thus propagate decompositions interprocedurally in order to determine how data is partitioned locally. Moreover, an interprocedural approach to communication optimization would enable communication to be extracted out of loops across procedure boundaries [15]. The current compiler implementation, based on FIAT, contains analysis of decompositions reaching a procedure, and interprocedural analysis of storage requirements for nonlocal data.

Static performance estimation. Parallelization and loop transformations are not always profitable if the amount of computation in a loop is insufficient to overcome the synchronization and other overhead of parallelization. Moreover, often when performing loop transformations, the system has a number of possible options that may have substantially different effects on performance. To assist the compiler in making optimization choices, the ParaScope system contains static performance estimation [20]. To make decisions about loops containing procedure calls, these performance estimates must be propagated interprocedurally.

Interprocedural optimization in SUIF. The above applications characterize uses of FIAT within ParaScope. Within the Stanford SUIF compiler, we are using FIAT in an experiment to measure the parallelism available in scientific codes exposed by interprocedural optimization. The analysis required is similar to those described above for interactive parallelization in ParaScope. However, our approach is distinct because we use precise analysis techniques and filtered procedure cloning to obtain the same quality of information as if the program were fully inlined while managing the costs of the analysis. The current system in the SUIF compiler contains MOD and REF analysis and interprocedural constant propagation; the cloning framework performs cloning based on constant propagation. We also have prototype implementations of interprocedural array privatization and symbolic analysis.

We plan to extend this analysis to support compiling to distributed-memory and distributed-shared-memory architectures. We will analyze reaching decompositions and perform communication optimization, similar to the techniques used by the Fortran D compiler. However, the SUIF compiler operates on Fortran 77, automatically partitioning data and computation, rather than relying on programmer specifications [1]. A purely automatic compiler requires much more precise analysis information. For example, reaching decompositions requires flow-sensitive analysis.

8   Summary and Future Plans

FIAT provides a framework for interprocedural analysis and transformation that facilitates incorporating interprocedural techniques into existing systems. Parameterized templates for data-flow analysis and procedure cloning and their underlying drivers enable rapid prototyping of new data-flow analysis techniques. System-independent abstractions make FIAT suitable for use in different systems with distinct intermediate representations of programs. Demand-driven analysis maintains a clean separation between data-flow problems, enabling different configurations of data-flow problems to be completely independent.

FIAT has proven useful as a vehicle for experimenting with interprocedural techniques. It has been incorporated into both the ParaScope programming tools and the "D system" programming tools under development at Rice and the SUIF compiler at Stanford without modification to the core system. In addition, new data-flow problems can be added without any modifications to the analysis engine. In a short period of time, a number of external users have developed configurations of the system for a variety of application domains. These different configurations share some data-flow problems, but typically also have problems unique to their domain.

We anticipate a number of extensions to this system. Our current efforts are focused on completing the flow-sensitive analysis support. We plan to use the system to solve a number of flow-sensitive data-flow problems and derive features of these problems that will ultimately lead to efficient, general support. We are also actively developing a better general-purpose interface for specifying local analysis as part of the FIAT system. In the future, we will fully incorporate frameworks for interprocedural transformations other than procedure cloning, particularly inline substitution.

Acknowledgements. The authors wish to thank Jennifer Anderson, Monica Lam, Brian Murphy and Chau-Wen Tseng for their insightful comments on this paper and John Hennessy, Ken Kennedy and Monica Lam for encouraging this work.

References

1. S. Amarasinghe, J. Anderson, M. Lam, and A. Lim. An overview of a compiler for scalable parallel machines. In *Sixth Annual Workshop on Languages and Compilers for Parallel Computing*, Aug. 1993.

2. W. Blume and R. Eigenmann. Performance analysis of parallelizing compilers on the Perfect Benchmarks programs. *IEEE Transactions on Parallel and Distributed Systems*, 3(6):643–656, Nov. 1992.

3. M. Burke and L. Torczon. Interprocedural optimization: Eliminating unnecessary recompilation. *ACM Transactions on Programming Languages and Systems*, to appear 1993.

4. D. Callahan. The program summary graph and flow-sensitive interprocedural data flow analysis. In *Proceedings of the SIGPLAN '88 Conference on Program Language Design and Implementation*, Atlanta, GA, June 1988.

5. D. Callahan, K. Cooper, K. Kennedy, and L. Torczon. Interprocedural constant propagation. In *Proceedings of the SIGPLAN '86 Symposium on Compiler Construction*, SIGPLAN Notices 21(7), pages 152–161. ACM, July 1986.

6. D. Callahan and K. Kennedy. Analysis of interprocedural side effects in a parallel programming environment. *Journal of Parallel and Distributed Computing*, 5:517–550, 1988.

7. K. Cooper, M. Hall, and K. Kennedy. A methodology for procedure cloning. *Computer Languages*, 19(2), Apr. 1993.

8. K. Cooper, M. W. Hall, R. T. Hood, K. Kennedy, K. S. McKinley, J. M. Mellor-Crummey, L. Torczon, and S. K. Warren. The ParaScope parallel programming environment. *Proceedings of the IEEE*, 81(2):244–263, Feb. 1993.

9. K. Cooper, M. W. Hall, and L. Torczon. An experiment with inline substitution. *Software—Practice and Experience*, 21(6):581–601, June 1991.

10. K. Cooper, K. Kennedy, and L. Torczon. The impact of interprocedural analysis and optimization in the R^n programming environment. *ACM Transactions on Programming Languages and Systems*, 8(4):491–523, Oct. 1986.

11. J. W. Davidson and A. M. Holler. A study of a C function inliner. *Software—Practice and Experience*, 18(8):775–790, Aug. 1988.

12. D. Grove. Interprocedural constant propagation: a study of jump function implementations. Master's thesis, Dept. of Computer Science, Rice University, Mar. 1993.

13. M. Hall. Comparing FIAT's support of flow-sensitive interprocedural data-flow analysis with existing techniques. Technical Note Available from First Author. To be published as a Stanford Dept. of Computer Science Technical Report.

14. M. W. Hall. *Managing Interprocedural Optimization*. PhD thesis, Dept. of Computer Science, Rice University, Apr. 1991.

15. M. W. Hall, S. Hiranandani, K. Kennedy, and C. Tseng. Interprocedural compilation of Fortran D for MIMD distributed-memory machines. In *Proceedings of Supercomputing '92*, Minneapolis, MN, Nov. 1992.

16. M. W. Hall and K. Kennedy. Efficient call graph analysis. *ACM Letters on Programming Languages and Systems*, 1(3), Sept. 1992.

17. M. W. Hall, K. Kennedy, and K. S. McKinley. Interprocedural transformations for parallel code generation. In *Proceedings of Supercomputing '91*, Albuquerque, NM, Nov. 1991.

18. S. Hiranandani, K. Kennedy, and C. Tseng. Compiling Fortran D for MIMD distributed-memory machines. *Communications of the ACM*, 35(8):66–80, Aug. 1992.

19. J.P. Banning. An efficient way to find the side effects of procedure calls and the aliases of variables. In *Proceedings of the Sixth Annual Symposium on Principles of Programming Languages*, pages 29–41. ACM, Jan. 1979.

20. K. Kennedy, N. McIntosh, and K. S. McKinley. Static performance estimation in a parallelizing compiler. Technical Report TR91-174, Dept. of Computer Science, Rice University, Dec. 1991.

21. K. Kennedy, K. S. McKinley, and C. Tseng. Analysis and transformation in an interactive parallel programming tool. *Concurrency: Practice & Experience*, to appear 1993.

22. G. Kildall. A unified approach to global program optimization. In *Conference Record of the Symposium on Principles of Programming Languages*, pages 194–206. ACM, Jan. 1973.

23. W. Landi and B. Ryder. A safe approximate algorithm for interprocedural pointer aliasing. In *SIGPLAN '92 Conference on Programming Language Design and Implementation*, SIGPLAN Notices 27(7), pages 235–248, July 1992.

24. S. McFarling. Procedure merging with instruction caches. In *SIGPLAN '91 Conference on Programming Language Design and Implementation*, SIGPLAN Notices 26(6), pages 71–79, June 1991.

25. J. M. Mellor-Crummey. Compile-time support for efficient data race detection in shared-memory parallel programs. In *Proc. ACM/ONR Workshop on Parallel and Distributed Debugging*, San Diego, CA, May 1993.

26. R. Metzger and S. Stroud. Interprocedural constant propagation: an empirical study. *ACM Letters on Programming Languages and Systems*, 1993. to appear.

27. E. Myers. A precise inter-procedural data flow algorithm. In *Conference Record of the Eighth Annual Symposium on Principles of Programming Languages*. ACM, Jan. 1981.

28. P. Briggs and K.D. Cooper and M.W. Hall and L. Torczon. Goal-directed interprocedural optimization. Technical Report TR90-148, Dept. of Computer Science, Rice University, Nov. 1990.

29. S. Richardson and M. Ganapathi. Interprocedural analysis versus procedure integration. *Information Processing Letters*, 32(3):137–142, Aug. 1989.

30. J. Singh and J. Hennessy. An empirical investigation of the effectiveness of and limitations of automatic parallelization. In *Proceedings of the International Symposium on Shared Memory Multiprocessors*, Tokyo, Japan, Apr. 1991.

31. S. Tjiang, M. E. Wolf, M. Lam, K. Pieper, and J. Hennessy. Integrating scalar optimization and parallelization. In U. Banerjee, D. Gelernter, A. Nicolau, and D. Padua, editors, *Languages and Compilers for Parallel Computing, Fourth International Workshop*, Santa Clara, CA, Aug. 1991. Springer-Verlag.

32. R. Triolet, F. Irigoin, and P. Feautrier. Direct parallelization of CALL statements. In *Proceedings of the SIGPLAN '86 Symposium on Compiler Construction*, Palo Alto, CA, June 1986.

33. Z. Li and P. Yew. Efficient interprocedural analysis for program restructuring for parallel programs. *ACM SIGPLAN Notices*, 23(9):85–99, 1988.

An Exact Method for Analysis of Value-based Array Data Dependences

William Pugh   David Wonnacott
pugh@cs.umd.edu   davew@cs.umd.edu

Dept. of Computer Science
Univ. of Maryland, College Park, MD 20742

Abstract. Standard array data dependence testing algorithms give information about the aliasing of array references. If statement 1 writes a[5], and statement 2 later reads a[5], standard techniques described this as a flow dependence, even if there was an intervening write. We call a dependence between two references to the same memory location a memory-based dependence. In contrast, if there are no intervening writes, the references touch the same value and we call the dependence a value-based dependence.

There has been a surge of recent work on value-based array data dependence analysis (also referred to as computation of array data-flow dependence information). In this paper, we describe a technique that is exact over programs without control flow (other than loops) and non-linear references. We compare our proposal with the technique proposed by Paul Feautrier, which is the other technique that is complete over the same domain as ours. We also compare our work with that of Tu and Padua, a representative approximate scheme for array privatization.

1 Introduction

There is a flow dependence from an array access $A(\mathcal{I})$ to an array access $B(\mathcal{I}')$ iff

- A is executed with iteration vector $\mathcal{I}$,
- B is executed with iteration vector $\mathcal{I}'$,
- $A(\mathcal{I})$ writes to the same location as is read by $B(\mathcal{I}')$,
- $A(\mathcal{I})$ is executed before $B(\mathcal{I}')$, and
- there is no write to the location read by $B(\mathcal{I}')$ between the execution of $A(\mathcal{I})$ and $B(\mathcal{I}')$.

However, most array data dependence algorithms ignore the last criterion (either explicitly or implicitly). While ignoring this criterion does not change the total order imposed by the dependences, it does cause flow dependences to become contaminated with output dependences (storage dependences). This can reduce the effectiveness of several optimizations: First, it can inhibit the use of techniques (such as privatization, renaming, and array expansion) that eliminate storage-related dependences. These techniques cannot be applied if they appear

to affect the flow dependences of a program. Second, it reduces the compiler's
ability to make effective use of caches or distributed memories. Flow dependences
represent the flow of information in the program being compiled; accurate information about this flow is critical for memory use optimizations.

Array flow dependences in which the value written at the source is actually
used at the sink of the dependence are referred to as *value-based* flow dependences
[PW92] or *data-flow dependences* [May92, MAL93]. Dependence tests that are
based on only the first four of the above criteria are said to find *memory-based*
dependences [PW92].

Data dependence testing is undecidable in general. Within the restricted domain described in Section 2, performing exact memory-based array dependence
testing is NP-complete [Pug92]. Paul Feautrier [Fea91] showed that performing
exact value-based dependence analysis of arrays within this restricted domain
is decidable, and gave an algorithm for doing so. Many other researchers have
also studied value-based array data dependence analysis, however no other work
is complete over the same domain as Feautrier's, with the exception of recent
work by Maslov [Mas94]. Some of these other methods handle larger domains
(such as complicated control flow) but are not complete within that domain
[Bra88, Rib90, GS90, Ros90, Li92, Fea91, MAL92, MAL93, DGS93].

We describe an extension of our previous work on dependence analysis [Pug92,
PW92]. This extension makes us complete over the same domain as Feautrier's
technique, and produces the same information (although using a different computational method and a different dependence abstraction). In this paper, we
review this extension and compare it with Feautrier technique.

Dror Maydan developed [May92, MAL93] a variant of Feautrier's techniques
that apply in a more restricted domain, but appears faster and to apply to most
real cases. Maydan's techniques integrate well with Feautrier's and in cases in
which Maydan's techniques do not apply, Feautrier's algorithms can be called.
We believe that when Maydan's methods apply, our methods will be fast as well.

We evaluate our methods on the examples evaluated by Feautrier [Fea91]
and find that our methods are 40-90 times faster than Feautrier's current implementation.

2 Dependence Analysis

For the methods we describe to apply, we must be able to determine which loops
and conditionals control the execution of each statement. This can be done in
a straightforward manner for code that uses only structured loops and if's for
control flow.

We can produce exact dependence information for any single structured procedure in which the expressions in the subscripts, loop bounds, and conditionals
are affine functions of the loop indices and loop-independent variables, and the
loop steps are known constants.

We start our dependence analysis by producing traditional dependence difference summaries. Dependence difference is equivalent to the more traditional

"dependence distance" when loops are normalized, as they are in all examples in this paper. The term "dependence distance" is not well defined for unnormalized loops – see [Pug93] for details.

Dependence difference summaries do not describe which iterations are involved in the dependence, and do not describe the effect of the values of symbolic constants. We therefore represent dependences with *dependence relations* [Pug91]. A dependence relation is a mapping from one iteration space to another, and is represented by a set of linear constraints on variables that represent the values of the loop indices at the source and sink of the dependence and the values of the symbolic constants (e.g., n). The notation we use in the constraints is adapted from [ZC91]:

$A, B, \ldots$	Refers to a specific array reference in a program
$\mathcal{I}, \mathcal{I}', \mathcal{I}'', \ldots$	An iteration vector that represents a specific set of values of the loop variables for a loop nest.
$[A]$	The set of iteration vectors for which A is executed
$A(\mathcal{I})$	The iteration of reference A when the loop variables have the values specified by $\mathcal{I}$
$A(\mathcal{I}) \overset{sub}{=} B(\mathcal{I}')$	The references A and B refer to the same array and the subscripts of $A(\mathcal{I})$ and $B(\mathcal{I}')$ are equal.
$A(\mathcal{I}) \ll B(\mathcal{I}')$	$A(\mathcal{I})$ is executed before $B(\mathcal{I}')$
$A(\mathcal{I}) \ll_D B(\mathcal{I}')$	The dependence difference from $A(\mathcal{I})$ to $B(\mathcal{I}')$ is described by the direction/difference vector D

The dependence relation below describes exactly the iterations and values of symbolic constants for which $A(\mathcal{I})$ and $B(\mathcal{I}')$ refer to the same element of the array, and $A(\mathcal{I})$ is executed before $B(\mathcal{I}')$ (i.e., it describes the memory-based dependence from A to B).

$$\{ \, \mathcal{I} \to \mathcal{I}' \mid \mathcal{I} \in [A] \wedge \mathcal{I}' \in [B] \wedge A(\mathcal{I}) \ll B(\mathcal{I}') \wedge A(\mathcal{I}) \overset{sub}{=} B(\mathcal{I}') \, \} \quad (1)$$

For example, the flow dependence from b(i) to b(j) in Example 1 is described by the direction vector (+), and the dependence relation:

$$\{ \, [i] \to [i', j'] \mid \underbrace{1 \le i \le n}_{\mathcal{I} \in [A]} \wedge \underbrace{1 \le j' < i' \le n}_{\mathcal{I}' \in [B]} \wedge \overbrace{i < i'}^{A(\mathcal{I}) \ll B(\mathcal{I}')} \wedge \underbrace{i = j'}_{A(\mathcal{I}) \overset{sub}{=} B(\mathcal{I}')} \, \}$$

This can be simplified to $\{ \, [i] \to [i', j'] \mid 1 \le i = j' < i' \le n \}$.

2.1 Value-based dependences

We can calculate value-based flow, output, and anti-dependences, but in this paper we are not concerned with the latter two. There is a value-based flow

```
1: for i := 1 to 2*n do
2:    a(i) := ...
1: for i := 1 to n do       3:    for j := 1 to n-1 do
2:    s := 0                 4:       a(2*j)   := ...
3:    for j := 1 to i-1 do   5:       a(2*j+1) := ...
4:       s := s + a(i,j)*b(j) 6:    endfor
5:    endfor                 7:    ... := a(i)
6:    b(i) := b(i) - s       8: endfor
7: endfor
```

| Example 1 | Example 2 |

dependence between an instance of a write $A(\mathcal{I})$ and an instance of a read $C(\mathcal{I}'')$ if and only if $C(\mathcal{I}'')$ reads the value that was written by $A(\mathcal{I})$. For this to occur, $A(\mathcal{I})$ and $C(\mathcal{I}'')$ must access the same element of the array, and that element must not be overwritten between $A(\mathcal{I})$ and $C(\mathcal{I}'')$. If the element is overwritten by $B(\mathcal{I}')$, we say $B(\mathcal{I}')$ kills the dependence from $A(\mathcal{I})$ to $C(\mathcal{I}'')$. Let B_1, B_2, ..., B_p be the array writes that might kill the dependence (note that A might be included in the list of B_q's). The value-based flow dependence from A to C is described by the relation:

$$
\{\, \mathcal{I} \rightarrow \mathcal{I}'' \mid \mathcal{I} \in [A] \wedge \mathcal{I}'' \in [C] \wedge A(\mathcal{I}) \ll C(\mathcal{I}'') \wedge A(\mathcal{I}) \stackrel{sub}{=} C(\mathcal{I}'')
$$
$$
\wedge\, \forall q, 1 \le q \le p, \neg \exists \mathcal{I}' \text{ s.t. } \mathcal{I}' \in [B_q] \tag{2}
$$
$$
\wedge\, A(\mathcal{I}) \ll B_q(\mathcal{I}') \ll C(\mathcal{I}'') \wedge B_q(\mathcal{I}') \stackrel{sub}{=} C(\mathcal{I}'') \,\}
$$

For example, consider the flow dependence from the write at line 2 to the read at line 7 in Example 2. We build the dependence relation by expanding the $\forall q, \ldots$ with a set of constraints for each B_q. The relation will have two "kill" terms (B_q's): the writes at lines 4 and 5 (there is no kill term for the write on line 2 because there is no self output dependence for this write). The unsimplified version of the relation is:

$$
\{\, [i] \rightarrow [i''] \mid \overbrace{1 \le i \le 2n}^{\mathcal{I} \in [A]} \wedge \overbrace{1 \le i'' \le 2n}^{\mathcal{I}'' \in [C]} \wedge \overbrace{i = i''}^{A(\mathcal{I}) \ll C(\mathcal{I}'')} \wedge \overbrace{i = i''}^{A(\mathcal{I}) \stackrel{sub}{=} C(\mathcal{I}'')}
$$
$$
\wedge \neg(\, \exists [i',j'] \text{ s.t. } (1 \le i' \le 2n \wedge 1 \le j' \le n-1) \wedge (i \le i' \wedge i' \le i'') \wedge (2j' = i'')\,)
$$
$$
\underbrace{\wedge \neg(\, \exists [i',j'] \text{ s.t. } (1 \le i' \le 2n \wedge 1 \le j' \le n-1) \wedge (i \le i' \wedge i' \le i'') \wedge (2j'+1 = i'')\,)\,}_{\forall q, 1 \le q \le p, \neg \exists \mathcal{I}' \text{ s.t. } \mathcal{I}' \in [B_q] \wedge A(\mathcal{I}) \ll B_q(\mathcal{I}') \ll C(\mathcal{I}'') \wedge B_q(\mathcal{I}') \stackrel{sub}{=} C(\mathcal{I}'')}\}
$$

By using techniques described in Section 3, we need 10 milliseconds on a Sun Sparc IPX to simplify this to:

$$
\{\, [i] \rightarrow [i''] \mid (1 = i = i'' \le n) \vee (1 \le i = i'' = 2n) \vee (1 \le i = i'' \le 2n \wedge n = 1)\,\}
$$

Thus, we have discovered that there is a dependence from the first write of Example 2 to the read only during the first iteration and last iteration (if $n = 1$, there are only 2 iterations).

2.2 Implementation details

Equation 2 is best thought of as a denotational description of how array kills are computed. There are a number of tricks we can use that will improve our efficiency while still computing the exact same results as if we had used Equation 2.

When computing value-based dependences, we use characterizations of the memory based dependences (such as the level that carries the dependence, or a direction/distance vector) that describes the dependence. The dependence between two variable accesses might need to be described by several such descriptions (for example, a dependence might be carried by several different levels). We treat each such description as a separate dependence, and use $A(\mathcal{I}) \xrightarrow{x} B(\mathcal{I}')$ to describe the dependence from $A(\mathcal{I})$ to $B(\mathcal{I}')$ that is characterized by x – the type of characterization does not matter.

To compute the value-based version of a flow dependence $A(\mathcal{I}) \xrightarrow{f} C(\mathcal{I}'')$, we need to consider all kills of the form $A(\mathcal{I}) \xrightarrow{o} B(\mathcal{I}') \xrightarrow{f'} C(\mathcal{I}'')$. For the dependence $B(\mathcal{I}') \xrightarrow{f'} C(\mathcal{I}'')$, we can ignore any dependences that we have already proven to not be value-based. We can perform a quick check based only on f, o and f' to see if we can prove that $A(\mathcal{I}) \xrightarrow{f} C(\mathcal{I}'') \cap A(\mathcal{I}) \xrightarrow{o} B(\mathcal{I}') \xrightarrow{f'} C(\mathcal{I}'') = \emptyset$. If so, we need not consider this kill combination. Otherwise, we can use o and f' to enforce the $\ll$ restrictions in the kill clause:

$$\{\, \mathcal{I} \to \mathcal{I}'' \mid \mathcal{I} \in [A] \wedge \mathcal{I}'' \in [C] \wedge A(\mathcal{I}) \ll_f C(\mathcal{I}'') \wedge A(\mathcal{I}) \stackrel{sub}{=} C(\mathcal{I}'')$$
$$\ldots \wedge \neg \exists \mathcal{I}' \text{ s.t. } \mathcal{I}' \in [B]$$
$$\wedge\, A(\mathcal{I}) \ll_o B(\mathcal{I}') \ll_{f'} C(\mathcal{I}'') \wedge B(\mathcal{I}') \stackrel{sub}{=} C(\mathcal{I}'') \,\}$$

While this seems to increase the number of clauses we need to consider, it actually saves us work. Equation 2 uses $\ll$ constraints, which are non-linear. Expanding these out to be linear would introduce a larger expansion than the one we get here by using the output dependences to the kill and the flow dependences from the kill.

Partial cover With respect to $A(\mathcal{I}) \xrightarrow{f} C(\mathcal{I}'')$, the dependence $B(\mathcal{I}') \xrightarrow{f'} C(\mathcal{I}'')$ is a partial cover iff there does not exist a dependence $B(\mathcal{I}') \xrightarrow{o'} A(\mathcal{I})$ such that

$$B(\mathcal{I}') \xrightarrow{f'} C(\mathcal{I}'') \cap B(\mathcal{I}') \xrightarrow{o'} A(\mathcal{I}) \xrightarrow{f} C(\mathcal{I}'') \neq \emptyset$$

We try to prove this based only by quick checks on f, o', and f'. If we can prove this, then if a memory location is touched by both $A(\mathcal{I}) \xrightarrow{f} C(\mathcal{I}'')$ and

$B(\mathcal{I}') \xrightarrow{f} C(\mathcal{I}'')$, then the write by $B(\mathcal{I}')$ comes after $A(\mathcal{I})$, and there can't be any flow of values from $A(\mathcal{I})$ to $C(\mathcal{I}'')$. In other words, we can ignore the dependence $A(\mathcal{I}) \xrightarrow{o} B(\mathcal{I}')$ in considering the effects of the kill. We can calculate the iterations $\mathcal{I}''$ of $[C]$ that might be involved in the dependence with the relation:

$$\mathcal{I}'' \in [C] \wedge \neg \exists \mathcal{I}' \text{ s.t. } \mathcal{I}' \in [B] \wedge B(\mathcal{I}') \ll_{f'} C(\mathcal{I}'') \wedge B(\mathcal{I}') \overset{sub}{=} C(\mathcal{I}'')$$

This has the effect of eliminating from $\mathcal{I}''$ any iterations that are supplied a value by B. Since the effects of this kill do not depend on $A(\mathcal{I})$, we can compute it just once and use this information for any dependence for which $B(\mathcal{I}') \xrightarrow{f'} C(\mathcal{I}'')$ is a partial cover.

Being somewhat more aggressive, we can sort the complete list of flow dependences to $C(\mathcal{I}'')$, so that the ones that are closest in time (according to the level that carries the dependence, the direction/distance vector, ...) are at the head of the list.

In computing each value-based dependence to $C(\mathcal{I}'')$, some dependences on this list will be legal to use as partial covers. Assume the first p are legal and the $p + 1^{st}$ is not (there may be others after the $p + 1^{st}$ that are legal, but we will ignore them). We can now compute the effects of the partial kills by the first p dependences on the list, and use that in computing the dependence. If we had previously computed the effects for the first q partial covers ($q < p$), we can simply extend that information by taking into account the $q + 1^{st}$ through the pth element of the list.

Of course, we may find that after considering the first r partial covers, the read is completely covered. In this case, any dependence that can use the first r partial covers has no value-based component.

Partial termination With respect to $A(\mathcal{I}) \xrightarrow{f} C(\mathcal{I}'')$, the dependence $A(\mathcal{I}) \xrightarrow{o} B(\mathcal{I}')$ is a partial terminator iff there does not exist a dependence $C(\mathcal{I}'') \xrightarrow{a} B(\mathcal{I}')$ such that

$$A(\mathcal{I}) \xrightarrow{o} B(\mathcal{I}') \cap A(\mathcal{I}) \xrightarrow{f} C(\mathcal{I}'') \xrightarrow{a} B(\mathcal{I}') \neq \emptyset$$

If we can prove this, then if a memory location is touched by both $A(\mathcal{I}) \xrightarrow{f} C(\mathcal{I}'')$ and $A(\mathcal{I}) \xrightarrow{o} B(\mathcal{I}')$, then the read by $C(\mathcal{I}'')$ comes after $B(\mathcal{I}')$, and there can't be any dependence from $A(\mathcal{I})$ to $C(\mathcal{I}'')$. In other words, we can ignore the dependence $B(\mathcal{I}') \xrightarrow{f'} C(\mathcal{I}'')$ in considering the effects of the kill, and the iterations $\mathcal{I}$ of A that might be involved in the dependence are:

$$\mathcal{I} \in [A] \wedge \neg \exists \mathcal{I}' \text{ s.t. } \mathcal{I}' \in [B] \wedge A(\mathcal{I}) \ll_o B(\mathcal{I}') \wedge A(\mathcal{I}) \overset{sub}{=} B(\mathcal{I}')$$

Putting it all together Now, when considering a kill of $A(\mathcal{I}) \xrightarrow{f} C(\mathcal{I}'')$, we get the appropriate information from the partial termination list for $A(\mathcal{I})$ and the partial coverage list for $C(\mathcal{I}'')$, and only need to directly consider the kills that we not handled as either a partial cover or as a partial terminator.

When considering kills, it is probably best consider all the dependences to a single read at a time, and to consider the flow dependencies in the order they appear on the partial cover list.

We describe this technique as partial cover and termination, since it is similar to the cover and termination tests described in [PW92], but records the effect of dependences that only partially cover or termination an array reference (just as Equation 2 is an extension of the kill test described in [PW92]).

3 Simplifying Formulas Containing Negation

When performing array kill analysis, we have to simplify formulas of the form:

$$\ldots \vee (C_0 \wedge \neg(\exists V_1 \text{ s.t. } C_1) \wedge \ldots \wedge \neg(\exists V_n \text{ s.t. } C_n)) \vee \ldots$$

Here, the C_i's are conjunctions of linear constraints, and the V_i's are (possibly empty) sets of variables. Techniques described in our previous papers ([Pug92, PW92]) allow us to eliminate existentially quantified variables, check for the feasibility of a conjunction of constraints, and perform other simplifications, but these techniques do not address negation. There are two problems involved in simplifying formulas containing negations:

- We must transform a formula into disjunctive normal form in order to verify the existence of solutions. A straightforward transformation of a formula containing negation into disjunctive normal form may lead to a huge explosion in the number of terms. We describe in Section 3.1 a method for replacing the formula with an equivalent form that, typically, will not suffer from as large an increase. By only evaluating the negation for one term at a time and reapplying the transformation in Section 3.1, additional savings may be obtained.
- If a negated term $\exists V_i$ s.t. C_i represents non-convex constraints (e.g., $\exists \alpha$ s.t. $x = 5\alpha$), we can not directly evaluate the negation. When standard Fourier-Motzkin variable elimination cannot eliminate an integer variable exactly, we can sometimes eliminate the variable exactly by introducing quasi-linear constraints (constraints containing floor and ceiling operators) [AI91]. For example, $(\exists \alpha \text{ s.t. } x = 5\alpha) \equiv \lceil x/5 \rceil \leq \lfloor x/5 \rfloor$. In these cases, negation is easy to apply (e.g., $\neg(\lceil x/5 \rceil \leq \lfloor x/5 \rfloor) \equiv (\lceil x/5 \rceil > \lfloor x/5 \rfloor)$).
  Although we can always eliminate one variable this way, we may not be able to eliminate multiple variables this way, since we may not be able to apply Fourier-Motzkin variable elimination to a set of constraints containing floor and ceiling operators. In these cases, we apply the technique given in Section 3.2, which is complete.

The complete set of steps we apply is described in Section 3.3, and some examples are given in Section 3.4.

3.1 Using Gist to Simplify Negations

The goal of the gist operator is to simplify a term B as much as possible, given than A is known to be true. In [PW92], we define gist B given A as a minimal subset of the constraints of B such that $(A \wedge (\text{gist } B \text{ given } A)) \equiv (A \wedge B)$. When performing negations, we rely on the fact that $(A \wedge \neg B) = (A \wedge \neg(\text{gist } B \text{ given } A))$ (see Step 1 of our algorithm in Section 3.3).

$$A \wedge \neg B \equiv A \wedge \neg(A \wedge B)$$
$$\equiv A \wedge \neg(A \wedge (\text{gist } B \text{ given } A))$$
$$\equiv A \wedge \neg(\text{gist } B \text{ given } A)$$

Since gist B given A will often have fewer constraints than B, the disjunctive normal form of $A \wedge \neg(\text{gist } B \text{ given } A)$ will often have fewer clauses than $A \wedge \neg B$.

3.2 Negating Non-Convex Constraints

To eliminate an integer variable x with Fourier-Motzkin variable elimination, we combine each upper and lower bound on x. In general, a lower bound $\alpha \leq ax$ and an upper bound $bx \leq \beta$ produce $\lceil \alpha/a \rceil \leq \lfloor \beta/b \rfloor$. If $a = 1$ or $b = 1$, then $\lceil \alpha/a \rceil \leq \lfloor \beta/b \rfloor$ is equivalent to $b\alpha \leq a\beta$, which is preferred as it does not introduce floor and ceiling operations.

Constraints involving floor and ceiling operations are called quasi-linear constraints [AI91]. When a set of constraints involves quasi-linear constraints, we cannot verify the existence of solutions, and our ability to eliminate redundant constraints is diminished. We normally avoid the introduction of quasi-linear constraints by simply avoiding the elimination of variables that would introduce them. Variables that we would like to eliminate but cannot because they would introduce quasi-linear constraints are called *wildcard* variables. When we need to verify the existence of solutions to sets of constraints, methods described in [Pug92] allow us to do so accurately in the presence of wildcard variables.

However, it is easier to negate sets of constraints containing quasilinear constraints than sets containing wildcards. We therefore use quasilinear constraints, when possible, to perform negation.

To eliminate a ceiling operation $\lceil \alpha/a \rceil$ we introduce a new wildcard variable c, add the constraints $ac - a < \alpha \leq ac$ and replace $\lceil \alpha/a \rceil$ with c. To eliminate a floor operation $\lfloor \beta/b \rfloor$ we introduce a new wildcard variable f, add the constraints $bf \leq \beta < bf + b$ and replace $\lfloor \beta/b \rfloor$ with f.

Quasi-linear Constraints are not Complete Unfortunately, using quasi-linear constraints is an incomplete method. Given a set of constraints involving ceiling and floor operators, we do not know of a general purpose method to eliminate an existentially quantified variable that appears inside a ceiling or floor operator. For example, consider

$$\exists x, y \text{ s.t. } 0 \leq x, y \leq 10 \wedge 4x + 7z \leq 3y \wedge 2y \leq 3x + z$$

After the elimination of y, this becomes

$$\exists x \text{ s.t. } 0 \le x \le 10 \wedge \lceil (4x + 7z)/3 \rceil \le \lfloor (3x + z)/2 \rfloor \wedge 4x + 7z \le 30 \wedge 0 \le 3x + z$$

Current methods for eliminating existential quantifiers cannot eliminate variables inside floor or ceiling functions.

Rather than introducing ceiling and floor operators, we can eliminate variables by using splintering [Pug92]. Splintering performs exact elimination by producing a set of problems, the union of which exactly describe the result of the quantifier elimination. The subproblems produced by splintering may contain wildcards (existentially quantified variables). In this case, the constraints in the final subproblems are of the form:

$$\{ \, \mathbf{x}, \mathbf{y} \mid \exists \alpha \text{ s.t. } \begin{bmatrix} \mathbf{x} \\ \mathbf{y} \end{bmatrix} = T \begin{bmatrix} \mathbf{x} \\ \alpha \end{bmatrix} + \begin{bmatrix} \mathbf{0} \\ \mathbf{c} \end{bmatrix} \wedge A \begin{bmatrix} \mathbf{x} \\ \alpha \end{bmatrix} \le \mathbf{b} \, \}$$

where T has the form:

$$\begin{bmatrix} I & 0 \\ S \end{bmatrix}$$

Here, $\mathbf{y}$ represent the variables that have been eliminated from the subproblem via substitution, $\mathbf{x}$ represent the variables that remain in the problem and α represent wildcard variables. Due to the way substitutions are performed, the mapping from $\mathbf{x}$ and α to $\mathbf{x}$ and $\mathbf{y}$ is 1-1, so the above equation is equivalent to the following: (where T^+ is the pseudoinverse [Str88] of T):

$$\{\mathbf{x}, \mathbf{y} \mid \exists \alpha \text{ s.t. } \begin{bmatrix} \mathbf{x} \\ \mathbf{y} - \mathbf{c} \end{bmatrix} \in \text{RowSpace}(T)$$

$$\wedge \begin{bmatrix} \mathbf{x} \\ \alpha \end{bmatrix} = T^+ \begin{bmatrix} \mathbf{x} \\ \mathbf{y} - \mathbf{c} \end{bmatrix} \wedge A T^+ \begin{bmatrix} \mathbf{x} \\ \mathbf{y} - \mathbf{c} \end{bmatrix} \le \mathbf{b} \, \}$$

Each wildcard now appears in only one equality constraint that enforces a modulo constraint (e.g., $\exists \beta$ s.t. $3\beta = x + 2y$). Such constraints can be easily negated (e.g., $\exists \beta$ s.t. $3\beta < x + 2y < 3\beta + 3$). Since we can negate each constraint in the subproblem, we can negate the entire subproblem.

It is unclear how often it will be necessary to resort to the handling of negation via splintering, or how expensive it will be to apply. However, we feel that it is important to have a complete method for handling negation.

3.3 Detailed algorithm

We convert such formulas to disjunctive normal form by repeatedly choosing a clause that contains a negated term, and applying the following steps:

1. We simplify each of the $\exists V_i$ s.t. C_i terms using the *gist* operation we defined in [PW92]. We replace each $\exists V_i$ s.t. C_i term with gist ($\exists V_i$ s.t. C_i) given C_0. This step is justified in Section 3.1. In doing this simplification, we use Fourier-Motzkin variable elimination to remove as many existentially quantified variables as is possible to do exactly.

   If we find that the simplified term contains a single inequality constraint, we immediately negate it and add it to C_0, discarding the C_i term. We repeatedly simplify terms until each negated term has been checked at least once since the last time C_0 changed.

   If a C_i simplifies to TRUE, we know that the entire clause is unsatisfiable.

2. Of the remaining negated terms, we pick a term that is likely to cause the least amount of combinatorial explosion when negated. A simple and effective estimate of the expansion factor is the number of inequality constraints needed to express the term (i.e., number of inequality constraints plus twice the number of equality constraints).

3. For the term we pick, we eliminate exactly *all* existentially quantified variables (see Section 3.2).

4. We then negate the term, producing a disjunction of constraints.

5. We remove any floor and ceiling operators from the constraints in the disjunction by introducing additional constraints and wildcards (see Section 3.2).

6. We now convert the entire clause into disjunctive normal form and simplify, producing a list of clauses that replace the original clause.

We repeat this process until there are no more clauses involving negation. This process may generate redundant clauses. If desired, we can eliminate many of them by testing for pairs of clauses C_i, C_j such that $C_i \Rightarrow C_j$ (in this case, C_i is redundant and can be removed).

3.4 Examples

In the following examples, we show examples of negation that would arise from direct use of Equation 2, ignoring the techniques described in Section 2.2. This is purely for illustrative purposes; the techniques described here for handling negation work with either a direct implementation of Equation 2, or the more sophisticated techniques described in Section 2.2.

The relation for Example 2 given in Section 2.1 contains negations. Figure 1 shows the results of each step (except #2) in our simplification of this relation. Step 2 involves selection of a term, and thus has no visible result in our table. After the initial simplification, each term can be represented as three inequalities, and thus we can choose either one (in the example, we choose the second). After the second application of step 1, each clause contains only one negated term, so there is no need to apply step 2.

When a group of assignments kills a dependence, but no single assignment from the group does so, we say the dependence is killed by a comb. Combs often involve a set of subscripts that differ only in the constant term. Figure 2

$$\begin{aligned}
&\{ [i] \rightarrow [i''] \mid 1 \leq i \leq 2n \wedge 1 \leq i'' \leq 2n \wedge i = i'' \wedge i = i'' \\
&\quad \wedge \neg (\exists [i', j'] \text{ s.t. } 1 \leq i' \leq 2n \wedge 1 \leq j' \leq n-1 \wedge i \leq i' \wedge i' \leq i'' \wedge 2j' = i'') \\
&\quad \wedge \neg (\exists [i', j'] \text{ s.t. } 1 \leq i' \leq 2n \wedge 1 \leq j' \leq n-1 \wedge i \leq i' \wedge i' \leq i'' \wedge 2j'+1 = i'') \}
\end{aligned}$$ — Unsimplified relation from Example 2

$$\begin{aligned}
&\{ [i] \rightarrow [i''] \mid 1 \leq i = i'' \leq 2n \wedge \neg (\exists \alpha \text{ s.t. } i = 2\alpha \wedge i+2 \leq 2n) \\
&\quad \wedge \neg (\exists \alpha \text{ s.t. } i = 2\alpha - 1 \wedge 3 \leq i) \}
\end{aligned}$$ — Simplify (1)

$$\{ [i] \rightarrow [i''] \mid \cdots \wedge \neg (\lceil (i+1)/2 \rceil \leq \lfloor (i+1)/2 \rfloor \wedge 3 \leq i) \}$$ — Introduce $\lfloor \ \rfloor, \lceil \ \rceil$ (3)

$$\{ [i] \rightarrow [i''] \mid \cdots \wedge (\lceil (i+1)/2 \rceil > \lfloor (i+1)/2 \rfloor \vee 3 > i) \}$$ — Apply negation (4)

$$\begin{aligned}
&\{ [i] \rightarrow [i''] \mid \cdots \wedge (3 > i \\
&\quad \vee \exists f, c \text{ s.t. } c > f \wedge 2f \leq i+1 < 2f+2 \wedge 2c-2 < i+1 \leq 2c) \}
\end{aligned}$$ — Introduce wildcards (5)

$$\begin{aligned}
&\{ [i] \rightarrow [i''] \mid 1 \leq i = i'' \leq 2n \wedge (\exists \beta \text{ s.t. } i = 2\beta) \wedge \neg (\exists \alpha \text{ s.t. } i = 2\alpha \wedge i+2 \leq 2n) \\
&\quad \vee 1 \leq i = i'' \leq 2n \wedge i \leq 2 \wedge \neg (\exists \alpha \text{ s.t. } i = 2\alpha \wedge i+2 \leq 2n) \}
\end{aligned}$$ — Convert to DNF and simplify (6)

$$\begin{aligned}
&\{ [i] \rightarrow [i''] \mid 1 \leq i = i'' \leq 2n \wedge (\exists \beta \text{ s.t. } i = 2\beta) \wedge \neg (i+2 \leq 2n) \\
&\quad \vee 1 \leq i = i'' \leq 2n \wedge i \leq 2 \wedge \neg (\lceil i/2 \rceil \leq \lfloor i/2 \rfloor \wedge i+2 \leq 2n) \}
\end{aligned}$$ — Simplify (1) and Introduce $\lfloor \ \rfloor, \lceil \ \rceil$ (3)

$$\begin{aligned}
&\{ [i] \rightarrow [i''] \mid 1 \leq i = i'' \leq 2n \wedge (\exists \beta \text{ s.t. } i = 2\beta) \wedge (i+2 > 2n) \\
&\quad \vee 1 \leq i = i'' \leq 2n \wedge i \leq 2 \wedge (\lceil i/2 \rceil > \lfloor i/2 \rfloor \vee i+2 > 2n) \}
\end{aligned}$$ — Apply negation (4)

$$\begin{aligned}
&\{ [i] \rightarrow [i''] \mid 1 \leq i = i'' \leq 2n \wedge (\exists \beta \text{ s.t. } i = 2\beta) \wedge (i+2 > 2n) \\
&\quad \vee 1 \leq i = i'' \leq 2n \wedge i \leq 2 \wedge (\exists f, c \text{ s.t. } c > f \wedge 2f \leq i < 2f+2 \wedge 2c-2 < i \leq 2c) \\
&\quad \vee 1 \leq i = i'' \leq 2n \wedge i \leq 2 \wedge i+2 > 2n \}
\end{aligned}$$ — Introduce wildcards (5) and convert to DNF (6)

$$\begin{aligned}
&\{ [i] \rightarrow [i''] \mid 1 \leq i = i'' = 2n \\
&\quad \vee 1 = i = i'' \leq 2n \\
&\quad \vee 1 \leq i = i'' \leq 2n \wedge n = 1 \}
\end{aligned}$$ — Simplify (6)

Fig. 1. Evaluating negations produced by Example 2

```
 1: for i := 1 to n do
 2:     x1(1) := ...
 3:     x1(2) := ...
    ...
15:     x1(14) := ...
16:     for j := 1,14 do
17:         if (abs(x1(j))>boxh)
18:             x1(j) := x1(j)-...
19:         endif
20:     endfor
21: endfor
```

$$\begin{aligned}
&\{ [i,j] \rightarrow [i'',j''] \mid \\
&\quad 1 \leq i < i'' \leq n \wedge 1 \leq j = j'' \leq 14 \\
&\quad \wedge \neg (\exists i' \text{ s.t. } i < i' = i'' \wedge j'' = 1) \\
&\quad \wedge \neg (\exists i' \text{ s.t. } i < i' = i'' \wedge j'' = 2) \\
&\quad \wedge \ldots \\
&\quad \wedge \neg (\exists i' \text{ s.t. } i < i' = i'' \wedge j'' = 14) \}
\end{aligned}$$

$$\begin{aligned}
&\{ [i,j] \rightarrow [i'',j''] \mid \\
&\quad 1 \leq i < i'' \leq n \wedge 1 \leq j = j'' \leq 14 \\
&\quad \wedge \neg (j \leq 1) \wedge \neg (j = 2) \wedge \ldots \wedge \neg (j \geq 14) \}
\end{aligned}$$

Dependence relation before and after step 1

Fig. 2. Example of dependence analysis in the presense of a comb kill

shows a comb used in the Perfect Club program MDG. This code demonstrates the advantages of the repeated simplification in step 1 of our technique.

To the right of the code is the dependence relation for the value-based flow dependence from the write of x1(j) on line 18 to the read of x1(j) on line 17. Our initial application of step 1 eliminates all of the existentially quantified variables. If we were to perform all of the negations at this time, we would produce twelve terms containing disjunctions, yielding 2^{12} clauses when we convert to disjunctive normal form. We would have to simplify all of these clauses to show that there is no value-based flow dependence.

We avoid this problem with our re-application of step 1: On our first pass, we negate $(j \leq 1)$ and $\neg (j \geq 14)$, producing the new $C_0 = 2 \leq j \leq 13$. Our second application of Step 1 reduces $\neg(j = 2)$ to $\neg(j \leq 2)$, and $\neg(j = 13)$ to $\neg(j \geq 13)$, allowing both of these terms to be negated without introducing disjunction. Thus, we never produce more than one clause, and perform fewer simplifications than we would perform without repeated use of step 1. Furthermore, a simplification may reduce the size of a term, speeding up future simplifications of that term.

3.5 Simplifying Arbitrary Presburger Formulas

The ability to negate conjunctions of linear constraints with wildcards or with quasilinear constraints gives us a complete method for simplifying Presburger formulas.

We propagate negations inwards, but not over quantifiers. We eliminate universal quantifiers by replacing formulas of the form $\forall x, P$ with formulas of the form $\neg \exists x$ s.t. $\neg P$. Given a quantified expression $\exists x$ s.t. P where P contains no embedded quantifiers, we convert P into disjunctive normal form, and then apply the methods of [Pug92] to eliminate the existential quantifier (possible leaving wildcards). When applying negation, we use the techniques of this section.

The best known upper bound on the performance of an algorithm for verifying Presburger formulas is $2^{2^{2^n}}$ [Opp78], and we have no reason to believe that this method be provide better worst-case performance. However, our method may be more efficient for many simple cases that arise in many applications.

4 Related Work

The method described by Feautrier [Fea88b, Fea91] was the first method for computing exact value-based dependence information over the restricted domain of programs with structured control flow and affine subscripts, guards and loop bounds. Dror Maydan and Monica Lam developed an alternative way of computing the same information as Feautrier does. This method is faster, but does not apply in some cases (in which case the falls back to Feautrier's method). Vadim Maslov [Mas94] has recently described a new framework for value-based dependence information that is exact over the same domain.

In previous work we described exact methods for computing memory-based dependences [Pug92] and methods for identifying some, but not all, dependences that were not value-based [PW92].

4.1 Feautrier's and Maydan's approach

Feautrier and Maydan compute a decision tree (called a *quast* or a *last write tree*(LWT)) to describe a dependence. This decision tree allows the computation of the source of any particular read. The internal nodes represent tests to be performed. The left branch corresponds to a false result, a right branch to a true result. The leaves are either a description of the statement and iteration that wrote the value read in the iteration of interest, or $\perp$, corresponding to a read of an uninitialized location. In the method described by Paul Feautrier and Dror Maydan, there are three basic steps to dependence analysis:

1. Computing the data-flow dependence from a single write to a single read, assuming there are no other writes.
2. Combining the dependences generated in step 1 from multiple writes to describe the data-flow dependences from many writes to a single read.
3. Check each leaf of the quast/LWT to verify that it is feasible. (Note: this check can be done on-the-fly while building the quast/LWT).

Parametric Integer Programming with the Omega test Paul Feautrier discusses parametric integer programming [Fea88a], which is the problem of finding the optimal/maximal solution to a set of linear constraints over integer variables. For example, $\max\{i \mid i \leq j \wedge i \leq k\} = $ if $j \leq k$ then j else k. Parametric integer programming is done with respect to finding the minimum or maximum lexical value for a vector of variables.

Parametric integer programming can be restated in a form of Presburger arithmetic that we can handle in the Omega test:

$$\max\{\mathcal{I} \mid P(\mathcal{I},\mathcal{I}'')\} \equiv P(\mathcal{I},\mathcal{I}'') \wedge \neg \exists \mathcal{I}' \text{ s.t. } \mathcal{I} \prec \mathcal{I}' \wedge P(\mathcal{I}',\mathcal{I}'')$$

Computing dependences from single writes to a read Paul Feautrier uses parametric integer programming to compute the value-based dependences from a single write to a read, ignoring all other writes. Dror Maydan and Monica Lam noted that in many common situations, faster techniques would suffice.

Computing dependences from many writes to a read When quasts or LWT's from multiple writes are combined to give a single description of which writes reach a read, the size of the quast/LWT can grow exponentially [Fea91, May92]. There is not yet enough experimental evidence to evaluate the growth of quast's/LWT's vs. the growth in the number of conjunctions produced by our methods. We suspect that the requirement that the quast/LWT be a decision tree will tend to make it grow faster. Whatever condition is tested as the root of the tree becomes part of the conditions of every leaf, even it is not relevant to some leaves.

Checking feasibility and handling negation The quasts or Last Write Trees constructed by combining quast's/LWT's may contain infeasible paths [Fea91, MAL93]. To enable compile-time transformations such as privatization, it is necessary to determine which of these paths are feasible. This cost is likely to be substantial, particularly since the number of leaves in a quast/LWT grows exponentially when multiple writes are considered.

Dror Maydan suggested that if we check the feasibility interior and leaf nodes, using a depth-first-search, we can avoid checking all nodes and leaves below any infeasible node found. No studies have yet been done to see what improvements could be obtained this way.

Determining which of the paths are feasible requires checking the feasibility of a problem such as:

$$P_1 \wedge P_2 \wedge \cdots \wedge P_n \wedge \neg N_1 \wedge \neg N_2 \wedge \cdots \wedge \neg N_m$$

where the P_i's are the conditions for the nodes where we take the true branch and the N_i's are the conditions for the nodes where we take the false branch. Each of these conditions is a conjunction of linear constraints, and may include non-convex constraints (e.g., constraints such as "i is even" specified using wildcards or quasi-linear constraints). Directly converting these expressions into disjunctive normal form would be infeasible for many real problems. The methods we describe in Section 3 should reduce this blow-up.

The methods described by [MAL93] can handle only special cases of negated non-convex constraints. Paul Feautrier uses quasi-linear constraints (constraints containing floor and ceiling operations) to handle negation. Unfortunately, this technique is not complete for all cases. In Section 3.2, we describe techniques that do not suffer this incompleteness.

It is our belief that the cost of checking the feasibility of all leaves of a quast/LWT is likely to be the major expense in an implementation of Feautrier's or Maydan's scheme.

A question of form   One advantage of the quasts/LWT's computed by Feautrier and by Maydan is that they are represented as a set of constraints over the read iteration and the symbolic variables, which can be easily tested at run-time, and by simple formulas that, given the values of the read iteration and symbolic variables, determine the write iteration.

If all constraints are affine, Equation 2 is guaranteed to produce a dependence relation such that, for any value of the read iteration of symbolic variables, there is exactly one write iteration that satisfies the constraints. However, we can make few guarantees about the form of the constraints in the dependence relation. For example, we might obtain a dependence relation of the form:

$$\{[i_w, i_r - 2i_w] \rightarrow [i_r] \mid 0 \le i_w \le m \wedge q \le i_r \le p \wedge i_r - 1 \le 2i_w \le i_r \wedge i_r \le n + 2i_w\}$$

In order to produce these properties of quasts/LWT's, we will need to recognize constraints that are equivalent to integer division (and perhaps integer remainder?). This would allow us to recognize the above dependence relation as:

$$\{[(i_r \div 2), i_r - 2(i_r \div 2)] \rightarrow [i_r] \mid 0 \le (i_r \div 2) \le m \wedge q \le i_r \le p \wedge i_r \% 2 \le n\}$$

It is currently an open question as to whether this extension will allow us to obtain these properties in all cases.

4.2 Maslov's approach

Vadim Maslov [Mas94] suggested that using just Equation 2 to compute value-based dependences would be inefficient. His observation was that it is wasteful to consider all possible killers for every possible dependence; instead, we can keep track of the upwards exposed iterations of a read, and utilize this information. Since the upwards exposed information can be calculated once per killer-read pair, as opposed to once per write-killer-read triple, this could lead to a substantial performance improvement. He also suggested reordering computations in a more lazy fashion, so as to avoid performing computations that might be rendered useless or irrelevant by later computations.

We have incorporated this idea into our system with the idea of partial covers (Section 2.2). We have extended it by also keeping track of the downwards exposed iterations of each write (using partial termination).

There are two other significant differences between this work and Maslov's. First, our method uses memory-based dependences to calculate the value-based dependences, while Maslov's does not require that memory-based dependences be calculated (which, in some cases, can save time). Second, Maslov uses a lexicographical maximum calculation instead of Equation 2.

It is our belief that any system using value-based dependence information will also need memory-based dependence information. Thus, we have not tried to avoid the cost of computing memory-based dependence information. However, our methods for computing value-based dependences work just fine if we start from a conservative approximation to the memory based dependences. If fact, if we start from the crude approximation that there is a dependence carried at every level between any two references to the same variable, our algorithm works in a fashion very similar to that of Maslov's, and Equation 2 and Maslov's lexicographical maximum performance almost identical computational steps. The main difference is that our use of partial terminators may save us some work.

In the case where we use better information about memory-based dependences, we may be able to save additional work. We may be able to handle more killers as partial covers and terminators and we may be able to avoid considering some killers at all.

Maslov utilizes our previous work on the Omega test [Pug92, PW92] and the techniques described here for handling negation (Section 3).

4.3 Tu's and Padua's Approach

We will briefly compare our scheme with that of Tu and Padua [TP92, PEH+93], as a representative example of other related work on array privatization [GS90, Ros90, Li92]. Their scheme handles control flow, while ours currently does not. We believe that a naive implementation of the methods described in their papers would be equivalent, in our scheme, to performing only those kills where the output dependence from the write to the kill or the flow dependence from the kill to the read was loop independent. Equivalently, we could perform the upward-exposed and downward-exposed calculations of Section 2.2. They [PEH+93] note that this is imprecise:

... a naive aggregation of $USE_b(L)$ may exaggerate the exposed use set....

They do not describe in [TP92, PEH+93] the algorithm used to perform the more sophisticated aggregation. It is our belief that the effect of the more sophisticated aggregation will be equivalent, in our scheme, to using only partial covers in computing kills.

The primary effects of these differences are that while they correctly determine whether or not a flow dependence is carried by a loop, they are approximate when determining the exact source of a dependence (i.e., which iteration of which write). Since their scheme is targeted at privatizing arrays, the information they determine is sufficient. For other purposes, such as analyzing communications [AL93] and scalar replacement, additional information is needed.

Another difference is that Tu's and Padua's method is based on determining which array elements are covered, while Feautrier's and our methods are based on determining which read iterations are covered. when all array references are linear, this does not make a difference. It could make a difference when non-linear subscripts occur, but it is unclear which would be advantageous.

Tu and Padua use an extension of regular sections [CK88] to represent used, defined and exposed array sections. Their intersection (and their difference?) operators are approximate. If exact calculations are desired, our algorithms for simplifying Presburger formulas may be useful.

5 Performance evaluation

In Table 1, we report Feautrier's performance evaluation of his techniques, and a performance evaluation of our techniques on the same problems. For our work, we list the times required to perform a standard, memory-based dependence analysis and to perform a value-based dependence analysis. Our times are on a SPARC IPX (a SPECint89 rating of 21.7), Feautrier's are on a SPARC ELC (a SPECint89 rating of 18.0). So that our results can be compared with Feautrier's, we analyze both array and scalar variables. We also report the time required to analyze just the array variables.

In analyzing memory based dependences as a pre-pass, we calculated conservative approximate memory-based dependences for scalar variables and for dependences with no common loops. Using approximate memory-based dependences still allows us to compute exact value-based dependences.

Our current implementation uses the partial covers described in Section 2.2; we do not currently use partial terminators. We found that using partial covers give a factor of 2-4+ improvement in analysis time, compared with use of Equation 2 alone. We also experimented with using Equation 2 with the complete cover and termination checks described in [PW92] (but not partial cover and termination). For a few programs, computing partial covers gave a nearly a factor of 2 improvement over doing only full cover and termination checks. But for most programs, they do not lead to a major improvement and in some cases even slows down the analysis. However, since partial covers and terminators reduce

Analyzing array variables only

From	Code	M	V	$M+V$	f77	D	$\frac{M+V}{D}$
[Fea91]	across	3	6	9	200	13	0.69
	burg	14	58	72	600	32	2.25
	relax	4	20	24	400	8	3.00
	gosser	5	52	58	700	16	3.63
	choles	4	7	12	600	12	1.00
	lanczos	29	78	107	1700	136	0.79
	jacobi	379	621	999	1600	255	3.92
[MAL93]	ocean (extract)	11	14	25	500	16	1.56
Perfect	olda (simplified)	51	338	389	3300	48	8.10
NASA	btrix	330	1036	1369	8600	771	1.78
NAS	cfft2d1	33	484	516	1500	52	9.92
Kernels	cholsky	86	156	242	2900	106	2.28
	emit	34	87	121	3700	129	0.94
	gmtry	25	70	95	3700	91	1.04
	vpenta	262	163	425	5700	1501	0.28

Analyzing array and scalar variables

From	Code	M	V	$M+V$	[Fea91]	D	$\frac{M+V}{D}$
[Fea91]	across	3	6	9	600	13	0.69
	burg	15	76	91	5600	46	1.98
	relax	4	19	24	1700	8	3.00
	gosser	6	56	62	2800	24	2.58
	choles	6	25	32	2600	32	1.00
	lanczos	28	91	119	12600	148	0.80
	jacobi	386	718	1104	81900	374	2.95
[MAL93]	ocean (extract)	10	15	25		16	1.56
Perfect	olda (simplified)	65	732	796		142	5.61
NASA	btrix	331	1175	1515		809	1.87
NAS	cfft2d1	37	540	577		103	5.60
Kernels	cholsky	84	162	246		107	2.30
	emit	37	144	181		181	1.00
	gmtry	34	146	180		161	1.12
	vpenta	253	220	473		1757	0.27

M - Memory-based dependence analysis time
V - Value-based flow dependence analysis time (needs M)
f77 - Time required to compile with f77 -c -O3
[Fea91] - Times reported by Feautrier
D - # of dependences for which value-based dependences are calculated

Table 1. Evaluation of times required to perform analysis

the number of situations in which we see worst-case "cubic number of terms" behaviour of Equation 2, we think they are a valuable idea.

Some of the dependence relations we calculate for olda and the NASA NAS kernels are conservative since they contain (non-loop) control flow and non-linear terms. We currently do not attempt to perform a kill using a non-linear dependence. However, a dependence might be linear unless carried by the outer loop (e.g., if the dependence involved a variable that was changing unpredictably in the outermost loop). We detect such cases and handle the linear components of the dependence.

The times reported for Feautrier's algorithm are from an implementation of his algorithm that has not been engineered for efficiency. While the PIP algorithm is implemented in C, the remainder of his algorithm is implemented in Lisp. Work is underway to recode Feautrier's algorithms more efficiently. Feautrier hopes that this will result in a significant speed-up.

Dror Maydan [MAL93] notes that his techniques require 100 milliseconds on a Decstation 3100 (a SPECint89 rating of 11.8) to evaluate the relax example and to calculate the dependence direction/distance vectors from the LWT's. The relax example does not require merging LWT's.

6 Implementation Status and Benchmark Availability

The techniques described here are being implemented in our extended version of Michael Wolfe's tiny tool [Wol91], which is available for anonymous ftp from ftp.cs.umd.edu:pub/omega. The programs analyzed in Table 1 come from a set of benchmark programs for comparing the performance and coverage of algorithms for analyzing value-based flow dependences between array references. Send email to omega@cs.umd.edu to receive a copy of the benchmarks and be added to the dataflow benchmarks mailing list.

7 Conclusion

The cost of performing exact value-based flow dependence analysis for arrays appears to be 2-7 times that required to do exact memory-based exact array dependence analysis using integer programming techniques [Pug92]. We believe that these methods are suitable for use in production compilers. However, we may wish to avoid applying them blindly. It may be cost effective to determine when it might be profitable to have exact value-based dependence information, and apply them only in those cases. Some methods for doing this are described in [PW93]. Also, the methods described here are more susceptible to bad worst-case performance than the methods described in [Pug92, PW92]. We might want to be able to detect when computing exact value-based dependence information is going to be very expensive, and use some approximation.

Neither Feautrier nor Maydan has does an analysis of which components of their algorithms are expensive. Therefore, we can only speculate on the reasons why our scheme appears 40-75 times faster than Feautrier's.

Use of the algorithm described by Maydan (which falls back to Feautrier's when the special cases handled by Maydan do not apply) is probably a reasonable way to determine the exact value-based dependence from a single write to a read. More work is needed to compare the two, but we do not expect more than an order of magnitude difference between our scheme and Maydan's.

The algorithm used by Feautrier and Maydan for merging quasts/LWT may be subject to problems with exponential growth in the number of leaves. Compared with our scheme, two factors might lead to a larger blow-up:

- We use the dependence direction/distance vectors for the flow *and* the output dependences to and from a kill to determine when a kill is feasible. This allows us to rule out more kills.
- Tests irrelevant to a particular dependence may increase the branching factor. For example, if there are three possible sources of a dependence (s_1, s_2 and s_3), the leaves for the dependence to s_3 will occur under both branches of a test that determines if the write by s_1 or s_2 is most recent.

The papers by Feautrier and Maydan have not addressed the issue of efficiently checking the feasibility of formulas containing negation. It is our belief that this is responsible for a substantial portion of the time required by Feautrier's algorithm. Some efficient scheme for testing the feasibility of a set of linear constraints is needed, such as [MHL91, Pug92]. In is unclear how effective PIP [Fea88a] is at checking feasibility (as opposed to parametric integer programming). In addition, some method like the one we describe here will be required to handle negation efficiently.

It is unclear if the exact information computed by our scheme and by Feautrier will ever be required, or if approximate information, computed by schemes such as [TP92, PEH+93], will suffice. For array privatization, approximate schemes may suffice but more advanced transformations [AL93, PW93] may require more exact information. We have pursued exact analysis methods because we want to determine exactly how expensive it will be to compute, and because we find that it gives us a better insight into the problem. If exact methods do not cost significantly more than approximate methods, then the justification for using approximate methods is weaker. If we find that exact methods are too expensive, we can decide to cut corners and know exactly what information we may be loosing.

The techniques we have described are impractical for real programs, since they do not handle control flow (other than loops) and procedure calls. We are currently exploring ways of extending our methods to deal with these cases. We expect that we will have to abandon our goal of being exact in all cases to deal with these features.

References

[AI91]   Corinne Ancourt and François Irigoin. Scanning polyhedra with do loops. In *Proc. of the Third ACM SIGPLAN Symposium on Principles and Practice of Parallel Programming*, pages 39–50, April 1991.

[AL93]   Saman P. Amarasinghe and Monica S. Lam. Communication optimization
           and code generation for distributed memory machines. In *ACM '93 Conf.
           on Programming Language Design and Implementation*, June 1993.

[Bra88]   Thomas Brandes. The importance of direct dependences for automatic par-
           allelism. In *Proc of 1988 International Conference on Supercomputing*, pages
           407–417, July 1988.

[CK88]   D. Callahan and K. Kennedy. Analysis of interprocedural side effects in
           a parallel programming environment. *Journal of Parallel and Distributed
           Computing*, 5:517–550, 1988.

[DGS93]   Evelyn Duesterwald, Rajiv Gupta, and Mary Lou Soffa. A practical data
           flow framework for array reference analysis and its use in optimizations.
           In *ACM '93 Conf. on Programming Language Design and Implementation*,
           June 1993.

[Fea88a]   P. Feautrier. Parametric integer programming. *Operationnelle/Operations
           Research*, 22(3):243–268, September 1988.

[Fea88b]   Paul Feautrier. Array expansion. In *ACM Int. Conf. on Supercomputing,
           St Malo*, pages 429–441, 1988.

[Fea91]   Paul Feautrier. Dataflow analysis of array and scalar references. *Interna-
           tional Journal of Parallel Programming*, 20(1), February 1991.

[GS90]   Thomas Gross and Peter Steenkiste. Structured dataflow analysis for arrays
           and its use in an optimizing compiler. *Software – Practice and Experience*,
           20:133–155, February 1990.

[Li92]   Zhiyuan Li. Array privatization for parallel execution of loops. In *Proc. of
           the 1992 International Conference on Supercomputing*, pages 313–322, July
           1992.

[MAL92]   Dror E. Maydan, Saman P. Amarasinghe, and Monica S. Lam. Data de-
           pendence and data-flow analysis of arrays. In *5th Workshop on Lan-
           guages and Compilers for Parallel Computing (Yale University tech. report
           YALEU/DCS/RR-915)*, pages 283–292, August 1992.

[MAL93]   Dror E. Maydan, Saman P. Amarasinghe, and Monica S. Lam. Array data-
           flow analysis and its use in array privatization. In *ACM '93 Conf. on Prin-
           ciples of Programming Languages*, January 1993.

[Mas94]   Vadim Maslov. Lazy array data-flow dependence analysis. In *ACM Confer-
           ence on Principles of Programming Languages*, January 1994.

[May92]   Dror Eliezer Maydan. *Accurate Analysis of Array References*. PhD thesis,
           Computer Systems Laboratory, Stanford U., September 1992.

[MHL91]   D. E. Maydan, J. L. Hennessy, and M. S. Lam. Efficient and exact data
           dependence analysis. In *ACM SIGPLAN'91 Conference on Programming
           Language Design and Implementation*, pages 1–14, June 1991.

[Opp78]   D. Oppen. A $2^{2^{2^{pn}}}$ upper bound on the complexity of presburger arithmetic.
           Journal of Computer and System Sciences, 16(3):323–332, July 1978.

[PEH⁺93]   David A. Padua, Rudolf Eigenmann, Jay Hoeflinger, Paul Petersen, Peng
           Tu, Stephen Weatherford, and Keith Faigin. Polaris: A new-generation par-
           allelizing compiler for mpps. CSRD Rpt. 1306, Dept. of Computer Science,
           University of Illinois at Urb ana-Champaign, June 1993.

[Pug91]   William Pugh. Uniform techniques for loop optimization. In *1991 Inter-
           national Conference on Supercomputing*, pages 341–352, Cologne, Germany,
           June 1991.

[Pug92]   William Pugh. The Omega test: a fast and practical integer programming
            algorithm for dependence analysis. *Communications of the ACM*, 8:102–114,
            August 1992.

[Pug93]   William Pugh. Definitions of dependence distance. *Letters on Programming
            Languages and Systems*, September 1993.

[PW92]   William Pugh and David Wonnacott. Going beyond integer programming
            with the Omega test to eliminate false data dependences. Technical Report
            CS-TR-2993, Dept. of Computer Science, University of Maryland, College
            Park, December 1992. An earlier version of this paper appeared at the
            SIGPLAN PLDI'92 conference.

[PW93]   William Pugh and David Wonnacott. Static analysis of upper and lower
            bounds on dependences and parallelism. Technical Report CS-TR-2994.2,
            Dept. of Computer Science, University of Maryland, College Park, June
            1993.

[Rib90]   Hudson Ribas. Obtaining dependence vectors for nested-loop computations.
            In *Proc of 1990 International Conference on Parallel Processing*, pages II–
            212 – II–219, August 1990.

[Ros90]   Carl Rosene. *Incremental Dependence Analysis*. PhD thesis, Dept. of Com-
            puter Science, Rice University, March 1990.

[Str88]   Gilbert Strang. *Linear Algebra and its Applications*. Harcourt Brace Jo-
            vanovich, Publishers, 1988.

[TP92]   Peng Tu and David Padua. Array privatization for shared and distributed
            memory machines. In *Proc. 2nd Workshop on Languages, Compilers,
            and Run-Time Environments for Distributed Memory Machines*, September
            1992. appeared in ACM SIGPLAN Notices January 1993.

[Wol91]   Michael Wolfe. The tiny loop restructuring research tool. In *Proc of 1991
            International Conference on Parallel Processing*, pages II–46 – II–53, 1991.

[ZC91]   Hans Zima and Barbara Chapman. *Supercompilers for Parallel and Vector
            Computers*. ACM Press, 1991.

Symbolic Analysis: A Basis for Parallelization, Optimization, and Scheduling of Programs *

Mohammad R. Haghighat and Constantine D. Polychronopoulos

Center for Supercomputing Research and Development
University of Illinois at Urbana-Champaign
Urbana, IL 61801-2932

Abstract. A symbolic analysis framework for parallelizing compilers is presented. Within this framework, various flow analysis problems are solved in a unified way. Symbolic analysis also serves as a basis for code generation optimizations and derivation of cost estimates. A loop scheduling strategy that utilizes timing information is also introduced.

1 Introduction

Empirical results indicate that existing parallelizing compilers cause insignificant improvements on the performance of many real application programs [5]. The speedups obtained by manual transformation of these applications [9] show the potential for significantly advancing parallelizing compiler technology. The poor performance of current restructuring compilers can be attributed to two causes: imprecise analysis and consequently inappropriate performance-wise transformations. The main problem of compile time analysis is the difficulty of collecting sufficient information in an efficient way to utilize the underlying architecture.

We have built a framework for Parafrase-2 [22] that supports a very precise compile time analysis of programs. Within this framework, symbolic analysis is used as an abstract interpretation technique to solve many of the program flow analysis problems in a unified way. Through symbolic analysis, the necessary information about a given program is gathered, and the relationships between program components are derived. These properties are used to answer questions about the dynamic behavior of the program. In particular, the program timing information can be used for selecting the right choice of transformations and directing scheduling and load balancing. Our preliminary results indicate that symbolic analysis supports compilation of very high precision, and is necessary for sophisticated parallelizing compilers and programming environments.

2 Symbolic Analysis

Symbolic analysis is a program analysis method in which values of program expressions are represented by symbolic expressions[6, 7]. The compiler tries to

---

* This work was supported in part by the National Science Foundation under Grant No. NSF-CCR-89-57310 and Texas Instruments.

understand what a program is doing by deriving the closed formulas for its computations in terms of program inputs. Using the concrete symbolic algebra kernel of Parafrase-2, our abstract interpretation method [16] derives the functional behavior of programs. This process eliminates the extraneous dependences introduced by the intermediate computations, and solves several flow analysis problems such as constant propagation, global forward substitution, and induction variable substitution. The collected information about the relationships between program expressions is a basis for a very precise symbolic dependence analysis scheme [15]. The compiler transforms the program into a more efficient one by suitable transformations based on the functional specification of the program. The original program is always an option if the compiler is not able to find a more efficient code.

The power of a parallelizing compiler critically depends on its ability to analyze program loops for extraction and exploitation of the available parallelism. Analysis of a loop involves solving the system of recurrence relations defined by the loop body. Parafrase-2 employs mathematical methods such as finite differences to solve the corresponding recurrences symbolically [16].

In the following sections we discuss a number of known optimization problems cast in the framework of symbolic analysis. The superiority of symbolic analysis approach over the traditional data flow analysis based on syntactical pattern matching will also be shown.

2.1 Interprocedural Symbolic Analysis

The symbolic analyzer of Parafrase-2 interprets programs in an abstract symbolic domain and discovers their concrete properties from their abstract characteristics. In the abstract interpretation method [8], for each operation in the concrete domain there is a corresponding operation in the abstract domain. Function and subroutine calls are not exceptions to the rule; they are modeled by their effect on the program variables. Subprograms are abstracted in closed form expressions which are the solutions to the system of recurrences defined by them. External side effects such as those of input/output statements are also taken into account. The derived information about actual parameters of subprograms can be used to further simplify or partially evaluate the subprograms. This specialization of subprograms may also be very beneficial in exploitation and enhancement of their available parallelism. In cases where there are several calls to a single subprogram, symbolic information about the formal parameters at call sites can be used to cluster the calls into various partitions with almost the same properties.

Figure 1 shows a toy Fortran code that we use to demonstrate the effect of an interprocedural symbolic analysis scheme of Parafrase-2. In this scheme, subprograms are summarized and modeled by the side effects of subprogram call on the parameters and global variables. The subroutine test contains a loop in which a function of the loop index variable is assigned to individual elements of an array. There is no output dependence due to the assignment to the array a. However, the call to the function swap has side effects on its first two parameters and prevents loop parallelization as it is in the original code. A more careful study of the body of the function swap indicates that this function returns the value of its first parameter, swaps its first two parameters, and updates them as functions of its third parameter. Figure 2 shows the automatic restructured code by Parafrase-2. The compiler has been able to express the value returned by the function swap in terms of the loop index variable i and the parameters m and n. The transformed print statement indicates that the compiler has also been successful in determining the net effect of the loop execution on the variables s and d, although the value of 2 * p, the number of iterations of the loop, is not known.

```
subroutine test (a, b, m, n, p)
real a (*), b (*)
integer d, p, s, swap
if (p .gt. 0) then
     s = m
     d = n
     do i = 1, 2 * p
          a (i) = b (swap (s, d, i))
     end do
     print*, s, d
end if
end

integer function swap (m, n, i)
k = m
m = n + 1
n = k + 2 * i
swap = k
return
end
```

Fig. 1. A toy Fortran program.

2.2 Generalized Induction Variables

Traditionally, induction variables of a loop have been defined as variables whose values at successive iterations of the loop form an arithmetic progression [2], and *induction variable substitution* has played a key role in the dependence analysis phase of parallelizing compilers [31]. In real applications, there are cases of variables, defined by recurrences, that do not necessarily form arithmetic progression, but for which there exist closed form solutions in terms of loop index variables. This class of variables are called *generalized induction variables* [9, 16, 32]. Programs ADM, MDG, MG3D, OCEAN, SPEC77, and TRFD from Perfect Benchmarks® are but some examples that contain such cases. Manual

```
SUBROUTINE test(a,b,m,n,p)
INTEGER m, n
REAL a(*)
REAL b(*)
INTEGER p
INTEGER i

IF (p .GT. 0) THEN
    CDOALL i = 1,2 * p
        a (i) = b (((m-n)*(-1)**(i-1)+(-i+i*i+m+n))/2)
    END DO
    PRINT *, m + p + 2 * p * p, n + 3 * p + 2 * p * p
END IF
END
```

Fig. 2. Transformation of the code of Fig. 1 by Parafrase-2.

transformation of a generalized induction variable in a loop that performs 40% of the computations of the whole OCEAN program results in a speedup of 8.1 on the Cedar multiprocessor [9]. Automatic handling of such cases is beyond the power of existing parallelizing compilers.

Figure 3 is a code segment extracted from the program TRFD of Perfect Benchmarks[R]. Elimination of the dependences introduced by the assignments to the variable mijkl requires sophisticated symbolic analysis and global forward substitution. To our knowledge, Parafrase-2 is the only existing parallelizing compiler capable of handling this case. The transformed code by Parafrase-2 is shown in Fig. 4. Program OCEAN in Perfect Benchmarks[R] contains cases even more complicated than this one; cases with conditional recurrences. Symbolic analysis is capable of handling those cases as well.

2.3 Symbolic Dependence Analysis

The effectiveness of parallelizing compilers and other parallel programming tools depend solely on the accuracy and effectiveness of their data dependence analysis techniques. Although powerful dependence analysis techniques have been employed in commercial and experimental systems, all these schemes fail in the presence of unknown symbolic terms. In our study on Perfect Benchmarks[R], summarized in Table 1, we found that close to 75% of loops in these programs had symbolic bounds. Also, a large percentage of array references in theses benchmarks contain symbolic terms other than the enclosing loop index variables. Parallelizing compilers handle some of these cases by applying classical optimization techniques such as constant propagation, induction variable substitution, and forward substitution. Nevertheless, standard dependence tests can not be applied in many of the unresolved cases, due to lack of information about the value of certain variables at compile time. Our proposed symbolic analysis

```
nrs = (num * (num + 1)) / 2
nij = (morb * (morb + 1)) / 2
mijkl = 0
mij = 0
mleft = nrs - nij
do mi = 1, morb
      do mj = 1, mi
            mij = mij + 1
            mijkl = mijkl + mi - mj + 1
            do mk = mi + 1, morb
                  do ml = 1, mk
                        mijkl = mijkl + 1
                        xijkl (mijkl) = xkl (ml)
                  end do
            end do
            mijkl = mijkl + mij + mleft
      end do
end do
end
```

Fig. 3. A code segment extracted from program TRFD.

```
DO mi = 1,morb
   DO mj = 1,mi
      DO mk = mi + 1,morb
         DO ml = 1,mk
            xijkl((mi * mi * num + mi * mi * num * num -
            mi * num - mi * num * num + 2 * mj * num +
            2 * mj * num * num - 2 * mk + 2 * mk * mk +
            4 * ml - 2 * num - 2 * num * num) / 4) = xkl(ml)
         END DO
      END DO
   END DO
END DO
END
```

Fig. 4. Transformation of the code segment of Fig. 3 by Parafrase-2.

framework supports a very accurate dependence analysis scheme in the presence of unknown symbolic terms [15].

The code segment shown in Fig. 3 is an example that requires symbolic dependence analysis. After elimination of the generalized induction variable mijkl, the subscript of array xijkl in Fig. 4 is a nonlinear function of the enclosing loop index variables, and contains an unknown symbolic term, num. Another unknown symbolic term, morb, also appears in the enclosing loop bounds. However,

Table 1. Loop bounds and array references in Perfect Benchmarks[B]

Program Name	% of Loops with Symbolic Bounds	% of Subscripts with Symbolic Terms
ADM	98	35
ARC2D	95	60
BDNA	69	47
DYFESM	85	26
FLO52	89	37
MDG	67	26
MG3D	100	89
OCEAN	93	45
QCD	67	18
SPEC77	24	38
TRACK	44	16
TRFD	72	41
Total	74	43

the compiler can use the following lemma, which is based on finite differences, to find a set of constraints sufficient to prove that the value of the subscript expression of the array xijkl is strictly increasing. Verification of these conditions at compile time indicates lack of dependences. If the compiler is not able to prove the validity of these conditions, they may be verified at run time to support a multi-version code.

Lemma 1. *Suppose that L is a nest of length n of normalized loops, indexed by $(i_1, i_2, \cdots, i_n)$, and characterized by the loop bounds:*

$$L_1 \leq i_1 \leq U_1,$$

$$L_2(i_1) \leq i_2 \leq U_2(i_1),$$

$$L_3(i_1, i_2) \leq i_3 \leq U_3(i_1, i_2),$$

$$\vdots$$

$$L_n(i_1, i_2, \cdots, i_{n-1}) \leq i_n \leq U_n(i_1, i_2, \cdots, i_{n-1}).$$

Given an expression $e = f(i_1, i_2, \cdots, i_n)$, let $\Delta^j e$ be defined as following $\forall j$, $1 \leq j \leq n$:

$$\Delta^j e = f(i_1, i_2, \cdots, i_{j-1}, i_j + 1, L_{j+1}(i_1, i_2, \cdots, i_j + 1), i_{j+2}, i_{j+3}, \cdots, i_n)$$

$$-f(i_1, i_2, \cdots, i_j, U_{j+1}(i_1, i_2, \cdots, i_j), i_{j+2}, i_{j+3}, \cdots, i_n).$$

The value of expression e is strictly $\begin{cases} \text{increasing if } \Delta^j e > 0 \\ \text{decreasing if } \Delta^j e < 0 \end{cases} \forall j, 1 \leq j \leq n.$

PROOF. *See [14].*

In the code segment of Fig. 4, let the value of the subscript expression of the array xijkl at the iteration (mi, mj, mk, ml) be denoted by $e(mi, mj, mk, ml)$. By applying Lemma 1, we get:

1. $\Delta^1 e = \left(num^2 + num + 2\right)/2,$
2. $\Delta^2 e = \left(mi^2 + mi - morb^2 + morb + num^2 + num\right)/2,$
3. $\Delta^3 e = 1,$
4. $\Delta^4 e = 1.$

$\Delta^3 e$ and $\Delta^4 e$ are trivially greater than zero. The compiler can also easily verify the fact that $\Delta^1 e > 0$, $\forall num \in \mathbb{N}$. For $\Delta^2 e$ to be greater than zero, it is sufficient to show that $\min_{mi} \Delta^2 e > 0$. This is equivalent to showing that $num^2 + num - morb^2 + morb + 2 > 0$. In the program TRFD, when the subprogram that contains the above code segment is called, the variable **morb** has the same value as **num**. Thus, the constraint for parallelization of the loops reduces to $num + 1 > 0$. But, this condition is always satisfied inside the loop body, since the loop will not be executed unless $num \geq 1$. Hence, the compiler concludes that the sequence of values that the expression e assumes in successive iterations of the loops of Fig. 4 is strictly increasing, and all the loops can run in parallel.

3 Program Optimization

Symbolic analysis can be used as a basis for a wide range of program optimizations such as strength reduction, restructuring of arithmetic computations, and elimination of redundant computations.

3.1 Generalized Strength Reduction

Strength reduction technique [3] can be generalized by considering computations in their entirety rather than their partial computations that appear in their functional definitions [16]. Using the information gathered by symbolic analysis, the compiler can basically perform the inverse of induction variable substitution in sequential loops. This scheme when applied selectively to a nest of sequential and parallel loops, reduces the operations in the sequential loops, while it does not prohibit the concurrent execution of parallel loops.

3.2 Restructuring of Arithmetic Computations

To evaluate an arithmetic expression under a set of algebraic laws, the compiler can generate code for any equivalent expression, obtained by successive applications of the algebraic laws [13]. An optimality criterion can be defined based on the cost of computations. In the general case, finding an optimal solution of code generation has been proven to be NP-Complete, however, for the cases where the DAG representation of expressions is a tree, efficient algorithms exist that find an optimal solution for machines that have a single instruction stream [1]. In many cases that the DAG representation of expressions is not a tree, symbolic values of expressions may be used to find an equivalent tree of the DAG, and thus generate the optimal code.

4 Program Performance Prediction

Optimizing compilers in general, and parallelizing compilers in particular, try to improve the performance of the programs by performing some kind of transformations. A transformation is an optimization if a set (possibly empty) of conditions is satisfied. These conditions are derived from comparison of cost functions of the original and the transformed code. The ideal cost function is the real execution time of the program, which in the case of an arbitrary program is not computable even if its data is given. Therefor, it is essential to find heuristics for the execution time of programs at various granularity level, i.e. program, subprogram, loop, basic block, statement, expression, and so on.

Symbolic analysis supports the capability of program performance prediction. It can derive closed form expressions for running time of many of programs in terms of their input data. In the cases of conditional branches, symbolic analysis may be able to find the branch probabilities, provided that the conditions are based on the structural properties of the data, such as *shape* and *size*. Symbolic analysis can even provide statistical information such as *minimum*, *maximum*, *average*, and *standard deviation* of the execution time of iterations of program loops. Such a metric for analysis of algorithms is proposed by Knuth [19] and used by Wegbreit [29, 30], Ramshaw [24], and Hickey and Cohen [18]. The metric for program performance should also take into account architectural issues such as type of memory accesses in computers with hierarchical memories.

The performance metric is useful for choosing the appropriate choice of transformations and scheduling strategies. In the case of dynamic scheduling, the compiler can use the generalized strength reduction scheme of Section 3 to instrument the code in such a way that each task of the program HTG [12] has its own metric computed in an efficient way. In the following sections it will be described how timing information can guide scheduling and how such information can be computed by compilers using symbolic techniques.

4.1 Loop Scheduling

The main issue in scheduling of parallel loops is the trade off between balancing the processors load and minimizing scheduling overhead. At one extreme, a strategy called *self scheduling* [27] schedules loop iterations one at a time, and thus achieves the best possible load balancing. However, self scheduling is not a good scheme if the overhead involved with each dispatch is comparable to the average execution time of the iterations. At the other extreme, another scheme called *chunk scheduling* [20] allocates a fixed number of iterations (a chunk) to each idle processor. This method reduces the scheduling overhead but may result in a poor performance when there is a considerable variation between execution time of loop iterations. This may be due to the structure of computations in each iteration, or could be the result of unpredictable characteristics of the computing system such as network latency or cache performance. Between these two schemes lie other approaches that attempt to compromise load balancing and overhead minimizing. *Guided self scheduling* [23], *factoring* [10, 11], and *trapezoidal self scheduling* [28] are examples of such schemes.

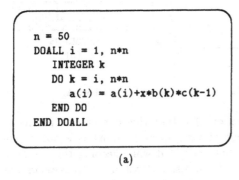

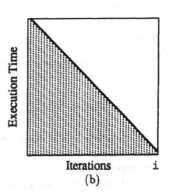

(a) (b)

Fig. 5. Parallel adjoint-convolution: (a) program, (b) parallel work.

All the above schemes can benefit the cost estimates provided by the symbolic analysis. We demonstrate this by modifying the chunk scheduling scheme to utilize the symbolic execution time information. We call this new scheme *balanced chunk scheduling* (or BCS). The performance of balanced chunk scheduling will be compared with that of chunk scheduling and self scheduling. The reported performance is the result of compiling and running our examples on a system developed by José Moreira at the University of Illinois [21].

It is the characteristics of loop iterations that make a scheduling scheme perform better than the other. In the case of coarse-grained iterations with variable execution times, self scheduling performs much better than chunk scheduling, while fine-grained iterations with constant execution time favor chunk scheduling. To compare the performance of balanced chunk scheduling against other schemes, we have selected two examples from [11] that cover a wide spectrum of characteristics. The benchmark program shown in Fig. 5 is an *adjoint-convolution*. The granularity of the parallel work is large, with a great deal of variance among the parallel iterations. On the other hand, the parallel loop of the Gauss-Jordan linear equation solver that is shown in Fig. 6 has a small granularity of parallel work, with a very small variance in iteration length.

Balanced Chunk Scheduling To schedule a loop with N iterations on P processors, chunk scheduling would roughly allocate N/P iterations to each processor. This may result in an unbalanced load if there is a large variance between execution time of the iterations. However, if the compiler has the cost estimate

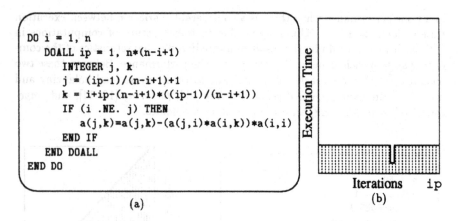

```
DO i = 1, n
   DOALL ip = 1, n*(n-i+1)
      INTEGER j, k
      j = (ip-1)/(n-i+1)+1
      k = i+ip-(n-i+1)*((ip-1)/(n-i+1))
      IF (i .NE. j) THEN
         a(j,k)=a(j,k)-(a(j,i)*a(i,k))*a(i,i)
      END IF
   END DOALL
END DO
```

(a)

(b)

Fig. 6. Parallel Gauss-Jordan: (a) program, (b) parallel work.

of an arbitrary iteration i, as a function of i, then the loop can be partioned into P chunks such that the amount of work in each chunk is equal or approximately equal. This results in a balanced load while keeping the overhead minimal. Note that assigning blocks of successive iterations to processors has other advantages such as increasing the chance of spatial locality and strength reduction. An example of such a partition is shown in Fig. 7 for a given work load and 4 processors.

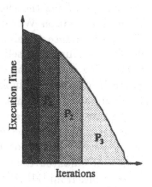

Fig. 7. A loop partition to chunks of equal work load.

When the number of processors and total number of iterations of a loop is known at compile time, an auto-scheduling compiler might be able to do the above scheduling statically, and thus avoids the run-time overhead. The adjoint-convolution program, discussed earlier, is such a case. The corresponding transformation for balanced chunk scheduling on 4 processors is shown in Fig. 8. In the transformed code, there are as many iterations of the parallel loop as the number of processors, i.e. 4 in this case. Furthermore, the work load of each processor is almost equal.

```
                                        ┌─────────────────────────────────────┐
                                        │ INTEGER iter (5), p                  │
                                        │ DATA iter /1,336,733,1251,2501/      │
┌─────────────────────────────────┐     │ DOALL p = 1, 4                      │
│ n = 50                          │     │    INTEGER i, k                      │
│ DOALL i = 1, n*n                │     │    DO i = iter(p), iter(p+1)-1       │
│    INTEGER k                    │ ⇨   │       DO k = i, 2500                 │
│    DO k = i, n*n                │     │          a(i)=a(i)+x*b(k)*c(k-1)     │
│       a(i)=a(i)+x*b(k)*c(k-1)   │     │       END DO                         │
│    END DO                       │     │    END DO                            │
│ END DOALL                       │     │ END DOALL                            │
└─────────────────────────────────┘     └─────────────────────────────────────┘
```

Fig. 8. A transformation that balances work load.

In more complicated cases, an auto-scheduling compiler can insert the appropriate code to do the loop partitioning at run time. For example consider the Gauss-Jordan program shown in Fig. 6. The total number of iterations of the parallel loop is not a constant, but rather it is equal to n*(n-i+1), where n is the problem size and i is the enclosing loop index variable. Hence, it is not possible to partition this parallel loop with the static scheme used in the previous example. However, the compiler can transform the Gauss-Jordan program to the one shown in Fig. 9. The shaded code segment partitions the parallel loop into chunks of equal work load. Note that strength reduction scheme discussed earlier has a direct application here. It has been used to efficiently partition the parallel loop.

For both the Gauss-Jordan and adjoint-convolution programs, the performance of balanced chunk scheduling is compared with self scheduling and chunk scheduling in Fig. 10. For the reasons discussed earlier, in the case of Gauss-Jordan program self scheduling has a poor performance. Similarly, chunk scheduling results in a poor speedup in the case of adjoint-convolution program. In both cases, however, the balanced chunk scheduling has an excellent performance. This indicates that symbolic cost estimates can be used to design robust scheduling strategies that perform very well on a wide range of cases. Sarkar has studied partitioning of parallel programs using cost estimates computed from the profile information [25, 26].

4.2 Derivation of Symbolic Cost Estimates

To illustrate how a compiler can automatically predict performance of programs, consider the example shown in Fig. 11. Suppose that the multiplication operations in this example are of floating point type. Let's see how the compiler can compute the total number of floating point multiplications in this example.

The total number of floating point multiplications performed by the unconditional assignment statement is equal to $\sum_{i=1}^{n} \sum_{j=1}^{i} \sum_{k=1}^{i} 1$, which is equal to $n(n + 1)(2n + 1)/6$. This computation may be carried on by the compiler capability of handling generalized induction variables. More precisely, the compiler

```
INTEGER iter (p+1)
np1 = n + 1
pp1 = p + 1
iter (1) = 1
work = n * n
DO i = 1, n

    load = work
    iter (pp1) = work + 1
    work = work - n
    start = 1
    procs = p
    DO ix = 2, p
        this = load / procs + 0.5
        procs = procs - 1
        load = load - this
        start = start + this
        iter (ix) = start
    END DO

    DOALL ix = 1, p
        INTEGER ip, j, k
        DO ip = iter (ix), iter (ix+1) - 1
            j = (ip - 1) / (np1 - i) + 1
            k = i + ip - (np1 - i) * ((ip - 1) / (np1 - i))
            IF (i .NE. j) THEN
                a (j,k)=a(j,k)-(a(j,i)*a(i,k))/a(i,i)
            END IF
        END DO
    END DOALL
END DO
```

Fig. 9. Dynamic partitioning of a parallel loop to chunks of equal work load.

can compute this function by assuming a variable , which has been initialized to zero, is incremented by one at the point where the unconditional multiplication is performed. The closed formula for the value of that variable, after execution of the entire loop nest, gives the total number of unconditional floating point multiplications.

Computing the total number of floating point multiplications performed by the conditional assignment statement requires more analysis. This corresponds to a *conditional induction variable* which can be computed precisely in this example. The convex polyhedron associated with the whole iteration space of the loops is shown in Fig. 12. The total number of points inside the convex poly-

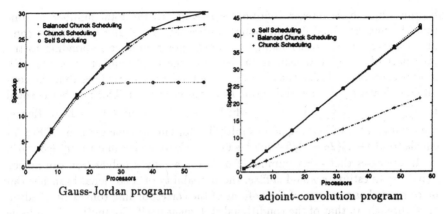

Gauss-Jordan program   adjoint-convolution program

Fig. 10. Performance of various scheduling schemes.

```
do i = 1, n
    do j = 1, i
        do k = 1, i
            x = x * a (i, j, k)
            if (i .le. j + k) then
                x = x * b (i, j, k)
            end if
        end do
    end do
end do
```

Fig. 11. A code segment with triangular loops and a conditional statement.

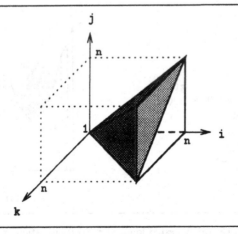

Fig. 12. The convex polyhedron associated with the *if* statement of the code of Fig. 11.

hedron which have integer coordinates is equal to the total number of time that the unconditional floating point multiplication is performed, and is computed above. On the other hand, the convex polyhedron corresponding to the *then* part of the *if* statement is shaded, and the total number of points with integer coordinates inside that equals to the total number of times that the conditional floating point multiplication has been performed. This number is equal to $\sum_{i=1}^{n}\left(\sum_{j=1}^{i}\sum_{k=1}^{j}1\right) + i - 1$, which is equal to $n(n^2 + 6n - 1)/6$. Hence, the total number of floating point multiplications in the code segment of Fig. 11 equals to $n(n+1)(2n+1)/6 + n(n^2 + 6n - 1)/6$, which is equal to $(n^3 + 3n^2)/2$.

In the cases that exact number of points in a convex polyhedron can not be found, or an estimate would suffice, the probability of conditional branches can be computed as the ratio of the volume of the corresponding convex polyhedron of the branch, to that of the conditional statement itself. Computing the volume of convex sets, in the general case, is proven to be an exponential problem in terms of the dimension of the convex set [4]. However, the convex polyhedra that we consider, have a nice property that makes computation of their volumes much easier. In the mathematical sense, these polyhedra are *cylinders*. An algebraic approach to the problem is discussed in the next section.

4.3 Computing Probabilities of Structural Conditions

In this section we discuss the problem of enumeration of points of a convex polyhedron in which a condition is satisfied. The frame of the convex polyhedron is defined by the bounds of a given loop nest, and the condition is a boolean function of the loop index variables. The problem of *zero trip loops* is one of the simplest instances of the above general problem.

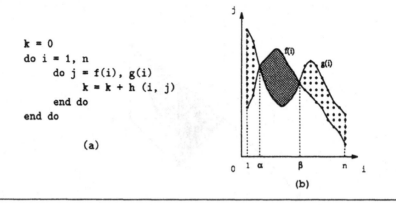

```
k = 0
do i = 1, n
      do j = f(i), g(i)
          k = k + h (i, j)
      end do
end do


        (a)
```

Fig. 13. (a) A nested loop, and (b) its iteration space.

Zero Trip Loops. Consider the program segment shown in Fig. 13(a). Given arbitrary arithmetic functions **f** and **g**, it is impossible for a compiler to compute the final value of **k** in a closed form as a function of **n**, even if **h** is a constant such as 1, and **f** and **g** are restricted to be polynomials. The reason is that we need to know the ranges of **i**, for which $g(i) \geq f(i)$. That means, we have to be able to solve $g(i) - f(i) \geq 0$. But, it is a well known fact in algebra that for any $n \geq 5$, there are polynomials over $\mathbf{Q}$ of degree n whose roots can not be expressed in terms of radicals of roots of polynomials of degrees ≤ 4.

The above problem, however, can be solved in many cases that happen in real applications. An equivalent problem in combinatorics is evaluation of nested sums with the possibility that the lower bounds of the sums might be greater than their upper bounds. A very simple example of this case is $\sum_{i=1}^{n} 1$. This sum is equal to n only if n is not negative, otherwise the sum is zero by definition. More generally, if $g(k) = \sum_{i=0}^{k} f_i$, $\forall k \geq 0$, then $\sum_{i=m}^{n} f_i = g(n) - g(m-1)$, $\forall n \geq m$. However, if $n < m$, then $\sum_{i=m}^{n} f_i = 0$, and $g(n) - g(m-1)$ will not necessarily be zero. In fact $g(n) - g(m-1) = -\sum_{i=n+1}^{m-1} f_i$ in case $n < m$.

Existing symbolic algebra packages do not handle such cases in a good way. For example, Maple$^{\circledR}$ evaluates $\sum_{i=1}^{n} \sum_{j=10}^{i} 1$ to be $n(n-17)/2$. For $n = 10$, $\sum_{i=1}^{n} \sum_{j=10}^{i} 1$ is mathematically defined to be equal to 1, while $10(10-17)/2 = -35$. Unfortunately, this is the way that the function $\sum$ is defined in Maple$^{\circledR}$. On the other hand, the current *SymbolicSum* package of Mathematica$^{\circledR}$ does not derive a closed form for this summation unless the value of n is given. And in the case that the value of n is given, the time spent to compute the summation is directly proportional to the value of n; it takes a long time for Mathematica$^{\circledR}$ to realize that $\sum_{i=1}^{m} \sum_{j=m}^{i} 1 = 1$ when m is relatively large.

In the following section, we will introduce an algebra for conditional values, that can be used to solve the above problems very efficiently.

4.4   Algebra of Conditional Values

Definition 2. The *truth value* function $\tau : \{\text{FALSE, TRUE}\} \rightarrow \{0,1\} \subset \mathbf{R}$ is defined as:

$$\tau(b) = \begin{cases} 1 \text{ if } b = \text{TRUE}, \\ 0 \text{ otherwise}. \end{cases}$$

A special case of τ function is quite useful in the cases where a compiler has to verify some constraints between program variables. Given the set of program variables, a compiler may need to verify an element of B, the set of boolean expressions defined on the program variables using the two binary operations $\wedge$ and $\vee$, and the unary operation complement '$\bar{}$', with the two binary constants TRUE and FALSE. Elements of B are formed by relational operations, or their complements, on the arithmetic expressions. Examples of such elements are: $x = 0$, $2x + 3y \leq z$, $(x \leq y) \vee (y \neq z)$, etc. These constraints can be reduced to inequalities of the general form $f > 0$. To smooth the process of program analysis, a special case of τ function is defined as following:

582

Definition 3. The *unit step* function $\mu : \mathbf{R} \to \{0,1\}$ is defined as:

$$\mu(x) = \tau(x > 0).$$

Figure 14 shows a diagrammatic representation of the functions τ and μ, and distinguishes their domains. Following relations are helpful in finding the truth value of boolean expressions involving relational operations.

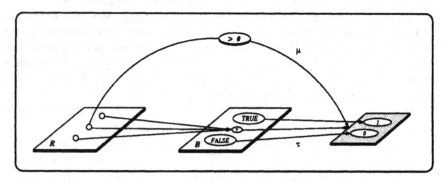

Fig. 14. The *truth value* and *unit step* functions.

Corollary 4. For any $x \in \mathbf{R}$, the following hold:

1. $\tau(x > 0) = \mu(x)$.
2. $\tau(x < 0) = \mu(-x)$.
3. $\tau(x = 0) = 1 - \mu(x) - \mu(-x)$.
4. $\tau(x \geq 0) = 1 - \mu(-x)$.
5. $\tau(x \leq 0) = 1 - \mu(x)$.
6. $\tau(x \neq 0) = \mu(x) + \mu(-x)$.

PROOF. Omitted due to space limitation.

The above algebra can be used to solve many instances of the zero trip problem.

Example 1. Suppose $s = \sum_{i=1}^{n} \sum_{j=3}^{i} \sum_{k=j}^{5} 1$. It can be shown [17] that the closed form of s is: $\mu(\min(n-2,3))\frac{-\min^3(n,5)+15\min^2(n,5)-38\min(n,5)+24}{2}+6\max(n-5,0)$.

Using the algebra of conditional values, a compiler can obtain the probability of conditional branches inside a loop nest if the conditions are functions of loop index variables. Given the code segment of Fig. 15, suppose that the compiler wants to compute the probability of the conditional branch, corresponding to the **then** part of the **if** statement in the whole iteration space of the code. That probability is equal to the ratio of number of times that the **then** part is taken to the total number of times that the **if** statement is executed. The latter is

```
do i = 1, 2 * n
    do j = 1, i
        if (i + j .le. 2 * n) then
            .
            .
            .
        else
            .
            .
            .
        end if
    end do
end do
```

Fig. 15. A loop nest with conditional statements.

equal to $\sum_{i=1}^{2n} \sum_{j=1}^{i} 1$, which equals to $2n^2 + n$ provided that $n > 0$. Algebra of conditional values can be used [17] to evaluate the total number of times that the **then** part is taken as $\sum_{i=1}^{2n} \sum_{j=1}^{i} \tau(i + j \leq 2n) = \mu(n) n^2$. Hence, the probability that the branch corresponding to the **then** part is taken is equal to $\mu(n) n^2 / (2n^2 + n)$, which can be simplified to $\mu(n) n / (2n + 1)$. In other words, if the loop is going to execute at all, then the probability of the execution of the **then** part of the **if** statement is equal to $n / (2n + 1)$.

5 Implementation

The interprocedural symbolic analysis framework, discussed in this paper, is implemented as the flow analysis scheme of Parafrase-2. Symbolic constant propagation, generalized induction expression recognition, symbolic global forward substitution, and detection of loop invariant computations are fully implemented. The transformation examples, presented in this paper, are all performed by the current version of Parafrase-2. The implementation of symbolic dependence analysis, generalized strength reduction, and symbolic timing analysis is underway. With the current capabilities of Parafrase-2, we were able to do the symbolic timing analysis of the program TRFD from Perfect Benchmarks®. It estimated the total number of floating point operations of TRFD to be 430.878M. The actual number of floating point operations of TRFD, obtained with the hardware performance monitor on a Cray X-MP, is 430.877M. The slight difference is the result of approximations in the cases of conditional branches that were not structural dependent, but rather data dependent.

6 Conclusion

Existing parallelizing compilers are unable to effectively detect and exploit the available parallelism in real programs mainly due to lack of accuracy in their analysis. Symbolic analysis provides a framework for a very precise analysis, parallelization, and optimization of programs. It can also supply information about the run time behavior of programs, such as estimates of execution time of each task of the programs. This information is critical for scheduling and load balancing schemes. Compilers can achieve such a precision and power by employing analytical techniques based on abstract interpretation, symbolic algebra, calculus of finite differences, number theory, theorem proving methods, convex analysis, and computational geometry.

References

1. A. V. Aho, R. Sethi, and J. D. Ullman. *Compilers : Principles, Techniques and Tools*. Addison Wesley, March 1986.
2. A. V. Aho and J. D. Ullman. *The Theory of Parsing, Translation, and Compiling*, volume II : Compiling. Prentice-Hall, 1973.
3. F. E. Allen, J. Cocke, and K. Kennedy. Reduction of operator strength. In S. S. Muchnick and N. D. Jones, editors, *Program Flow Analysis*, pages 79–101. Prentice-Hall, Englewood Cliffs, New Jersey, 1981.
4. I. Báráni and Z. Füredi. Computing the volume is difficult. In *18th Annual ACM Symposium on Theory of Computing*, pages 442–447, Berkeley, California, 1986.
5. W. Blume and R. Eigenmann. Performance analysis of parallelizing compilers on the perfect benchmarks programs. *IEEE Transactions on Parallel and Distributed Systems*, 3(6):643–656, November 1992.
6. T. E. Cheatham, JR., H. Holloway, G., and J. A. Townley. Symbolic evaluation and the analysis of programs. *IEEE Transactions on Software Engineering*, SE-5(4):402–417, July 1979.
7. L. A. Clarke and D. J. Richardson. Applications of symbolic evaluation. *Journal of Systems and Software*, 5(1):15–35, 1985.
8. P. Cousot and R. Cousot. Abstract interpretation: A unified lattice model for static analysis of programs by construction or approximation of fixpoints. In *Proceedings of the 4th Annual ACM Symposium on Principles of Programming Languages*, pages 238–252, Los Angeles, CA, January 1977.
9. R. Eigenmann, J. Hoeflinger, Z. Li, and D. Padua. Experience in the automatic parallelization of four perfect-benchmark programs. In *Languages and Compilers for Parallel Computing*, pages 65–82. Springer-Verlag, LNCS 589, August 7-9 1991.
10. L. E. Flynn and S. Flynn Hummel. Scheduling variable-length parallel subtasks. Technical Report RC15492, T.J. Watson Research Center, February 1990.
11. S. Flynn Hummel, E. Schonberg, and L. E. Flynn. Factoring: A method for scheduling parallel loops. *CACM*, 35(8):90–101, August 1992.
12. M. B. Girkar. *Functional Parallelism : Theoretical Foundations and Implementation*. PhD thesis, University of Illinois at Urbana-Champaign, December 1991.
13. T. Gonzalez and J. Ja'Ja'. Evaluation of arithmetic expressions with algebraic identities. *SIAM J. of Computing*, 11(4):633–662, November 82.

14. M. R. Haghighat. *Symbolic Analysis for High Performance Parallelizing Compilers*. PhD thesis, University of Illinois at Urbana-Champaign, May 1994. In preparation.

15. M. R. Haghighat and C. D. Polychronopoulos. Symbolic dependence analysis for high-performance parallelizing compilers. In A. Nicolau, Gelernter D., T. Gross, and Padua D., editors, *Advances in Languages and Compilers for Parallel Processing*, pages 310–330. The MIT Press, Cambridge, Massachusetts, 1991.

16. M. R. Haghighat and C. D. Polychronopoulos. Symbolic Program Analysis and Optimization for Parallelizing Compilers. *5th Annual Workshop on Languages and Compilers for Parallel Computing, New Haven, CT*, August 3-5 1992.

17. M. R. Haghighat and C. D. Polychronopoulos. Symbolic analysis: A basis for parallelization, optimization, and scheduling of programs. Technical Report 1314, CSRD, University of Illinois, August 1993.

18. T. Hickey and J. Cohen. Automating program analysis. *Journal of the Association for Computing Machinery*, 35(1):185–220, January 1988.

19. D. E. Knuth. *The Art of Computer Programming, Vol. 1 / Fundamental Algorithms*. Addison-Wesley, Reading, Mass., second edition, 1973.

20. C. Kruskal and A. Weiss. Allocating independent subtasks on parallel processors. *IEEE Transactions on Software Engineering*, SE-11(10), October 1985.

21. J. E. Moreira. *Auto-scheduling Compilers*. PhD thesis, University of Illinois at Urbana-Champaign, Urbana, Illinois, May 1994. In preparation.

22. C. D. Polychronopoulos, M. B. Girkar, M. R. Haghighat, C. L. Lee, B. P. Leung, and D. A. Schouten. Parafrase-2: An environment for parallelizing, partitioning, synchronizing and scheduling programs on multiprocessors. In *Proceedings of the 1989 ICPP*, St. Charles, IL, August 1989. Penn State.

23. C. D. Polychronopoulos and D. Kuck. Guided self-scheduling: A practical scheduling scheme for parallel computers. *IEEE Transactions on Computers*, C-36(12):1425–1439, December 1987.

24. L. H. Ramshaw. Formalizing the analysis of algorithms. Technical Report SL-79-5, Xerox Palo Alto Research Center, Palo Alto, CA, 1979.

25. V. Sarkar. Determining average program execution times and their variance. In *Proceedings of the ACM SIGPLAN '89 Conference on Programming Language Design and Implementation*, pages 298–312, Portland, Oregon, June 21-23 1989.

26. V. Sarkar. *Partitioning and Scheduling Parallel Programs for Multiprocessors*. The MIT Press, Cambridge, MA, 1989.

27. P. Tang and P. C. Yew. Processor self-scheduling for multiple-nested parallel loops. In *Proceedings of the 1986 ICPP*, August 1986.

28. T. H. Tzen and L. M. Ni. Dynamic loop scheduling for shared memory multiprocessors. In *Proceedings of the 1991 ICPP*, volume 2, August 1991.

29. B. Wegbreit. Mechanical program analysis. *Communications of the Association for Computing Machinery*, 18(9):528–539, September 1975.

30. B. Wegbreit. Verifying program performance. *Journal of the Association for Computing Machinery*, 23(4):691–699, October 1976.

31. M. J. Wolfe. Techniques for improving the inherent parallelism in programs. Technical Report 78-929, Department of Computer Science, July 1978.

32. M. J. Wolfe. Beyond induction variables. In *Proceedings of the ACM SIGPLAN '92 Conference on Programming Language Design and Implementation*, pages 162–174, San Francisco, California, June 17-19 1992.

Towards a Non-Intrusive Approach for Monitoring Distributed Computations through Perturbation Analysis[*]

Rajiv Gupta[1] and Madalene Spezialetti[2]

[1] University of Pittsburgh, Pittsburgh PA 15260, USA
[2] Lehigh University, Bethlehem, PA 18015, USA

Abstract. Programs representing distributed computations are often non-deterministic in nature and hence the execution of such programs is not only dependent upon the program input, but also on the timing of execution. Thus, an attempt to monitor the run-time behavior of a distributed program through code instrumentation can potentially alter the program's behavior. In this paper we develop static perturbation analysis techniques to identify the situations in which the run-time monitoring activities can be performed non-intrusively, that is, without affecting the outcomes of non-deterministic events.

1 Introduction

As distributed computing capabilities have become more widely available, the need for methodologies which aid in the monitoring of distributed computations has increased. The monitoring activity involves observing a program's behavior during execution. During program debugging, the goal of monitoring is to identify errors in the program which may be caused by inappropriate process synchronization. Examples of errors include the absence of mutual exclusion over critical sections and occurrences of deadlocks and infinite waits. Monitoring may also be carried out for detecting other forms of behavior which may not be caused by programming errors. For example, we may want to observe the fairness of a scheduling algorithm for identifying possibilities of starvation. Starvation may result if the processors in the system have different execution speeds and not because of an error in programming the scheduling algorithm.

The task of monitoring is typically relegated to a single dedicated process or a group of processes referred to as monitors. The processes belonging to the computation are then instrumented to communicate the relevant information to the monitor. The approach based upon instrumentation is intrusive, that is, it can alter the behavior of the program. Consider the example of a server that is processing requests from several processes. The order in which the requests

---

[*] This work is supported in part by the National Science Foundation through a Presidential Young Investigator Award CCR-9157371 to the University of Pittsburgh and NSF Grant CCR-9212020 to Lehigh University.

arrive may influence the order in which they are serviced. A delay introduced in a requester, due to instrumentation, can cause its request to be delayed and therefore alter the order in which the requests arrive at the server. Even if the order in which the requests arrive is not altered, a delay can influence the order in which the requests are processed. Consider a server which non-deterministically selects a request for processing from among the multiple requests that may be pending. A delay in one of the requesters can alter the pool of pending requests at the server and therefore alter the outcome of the non-deterministic selection process. Thus, we would like to develop techniques in which instrumentation does not alter the program behavior, that is, instrumentation is non-intrusive.

One approach to limit the affect of instrumentation code is to provide dedicated hardware for performing the monitoring tasks. Although, the cost of providing such support may be acceptable in the development of certain time-critical systems, this cost may be too high for non-real time systems. Furthermore, a large number of existing distributed systems will not be able to benefit from this approach. Thus, we would like to develop an approach which can function preferably without any hardware support or with minimal hardware support.

In this paper we develop an approach which is useful for the non-intrusive monitoring of non-real time distributed applications. We introduce the notion of non-intrusion under which the perturbation caused by a delay introduced due to code instrumentation is considered to be non-intrusive only if it is not expected to alter the outcome of a non-deterministic event. We develop perturbation analysis techniques to determine whether a perturbation at a specific program point is expected to be non-intrusive to the outcomes of future non-deterministic events. The algorithm for perturbation analysis is based upon static analysis of the program which computes the influence of a perturbation at a specific program point on non-deterministic events under all possible program executions. Thus, no hardware support is needed to carry out non-intrusive monitoring activities at the identified points. We also introduce the notion of conditional non-intrusion which considers the affects of perturbations on non-deterministic events for a subset of program executions. In particular, we consider only those executions under which a specified program statement is executed. As the execution of the program proceeds, using the results of such analysis, we can identify additional program points at which non-intrusive monitoring can be carried out. Hardware support is required to detect the execution of a statement and interrupt a process at appropriate monitoring points.

In section 2, we discuss previous work on the monitoring of distributed computations. In section 3, we define the notion of non-intrusion in context of deterministic and non-deterministic synchronous communication primitives. Sections 4 presents the perturbation analysis algorithm. In section 5 the analysis of multiple perturbations is considered and in section 6 we discuss conditional non-intrusion. We conclude with a brief discussion of some extensions to this work in section 7.

2   Related Work

Recently there has been a significant amount of interest in studying the tasks of monitoring and debugging of parallel programs through static and dynamic techniques. A common dynamic approach to analyzing distributed computations is to allow the user to specify activity of interest in the form of predicates, or event definitions [2] [21] [23] [25]. A monitoring system automatically collects data pertaining to the activity specified in the definitions, and the events are evaluated utilizing this data. When an event occurrence is recognized it is reported to the user. Various methodologies have been developed by which one can obtain a consistent view of the system state that is required for event evaluation [4] [5] [13] [15] [22] [26]. Event detection coupled with breakpointing provides an effective means for debugging distributed programs [9] [12] [19] [27]. The breakpointing can be performed during replay of a program's execution [7] [16] from an execution history or it can actually be attempted during the execution of the program [4]. In the context of shared-memory programs the research to date has primarily focussed on the detection of data races through run-time tracing and analysis of memory references [6].

Static analysis techniques for analyzing parallel programs has also been a subject of recent interest [3] [8] [18] [24]. The information collected using static analysis is typically a conservative estimate. Thus, static analysis by itself is not sufficient for reasoning about the behavior of the program. However, it is a valuable tool since it allows us identify portions of a program where potential for the occurrence of user specified events exists. Thus, run-time monitoring is only required for certain portions of the program as opposed to exhaustive monitoring of the entire program. This approach has been used to reduce the run-time monitoring overhead in [24]. Significant amount of research has been carried out for reducing the overhead associated with monitoring and debugging activities [1] [11] [27].

The task of monitoring is inherently intrusive since the program must be instrumented to collect the information relevant for inferring the program behavior. Very little research has focussed on non-intrusive monitoring of parallel programs. To our knowledge the only work that addresses the issue of intrusion is that of Malony et al [17] [20]. However, their work is primarily useful for analyzing the affect of program instrumentation on execution speed-ups of deterministic scientific applications.

3   A Notion of Non-Intrusion

We consider perturbations of program execution caused by execution time delays introduced due to the instrumentation of a distributed program. In general, any form of execution delay can be considered to be intrusive since it affects the timing behavior of the program. However, if we are interested only in certain aspects of a program's behavior it is usually possible to tolerate some limited form of intrusion. For example, for a non-real time application we may want to observe the execution of the program; however, we may not be interested in the precise timing of various activities. A restricted form of intrusion may be acceptable in this situation. A perturbation that does not alter the execution of the distributed computation is acceptable. In particular, we consider a perturbation to be non-intrusive if it can only delay the participants of a non-deterministic event in such a way that the order in which they arrive at the event is the same and hence the outcome of the non-deterministic event is unaltered. If none of the participants is delayed, we also consider the delay to be non-intrusive. A more precise definition of intrusion is given later in this section.

We assume that the distributed programming language supports synchronous communication primitives including both deterministic and non-deterministic communication primitives. We believe that these primitives are sufficient for modeling constructs found in various languages. For example, a select with guarded receives in CSP can be modeled using these primitives. The descriptions of the communication primitives follow.

Definition 1. During a *deterministic synchronous communication* $SD(P_2) \leftrightarrow SD(P_1)$, the blocking communication primitive $SD(P_2)$ in process P_1 communicates with a blocking communication primitive $SD(P_1)$ in process P_2. After both processes have arrived at their respective communication points they are allowed to proceed.

Definition 2. During a *non-deterministic synchronous communication* $SN(P_2) \rightarrow \Box SN(P_1)$ the blocking communication primitive $SN(P_2)$, in process P_1, communicates with a non-deterministic communication primitive $\Box SN(P_1)$, in process P_2. If process P_1 is waiting at $SN(P_2)$ when process P_2 arrives at $\Box SN(P_1)$ then the two process communicate and proceed. On the other hand if process P_2 arrives at $\Box SN(P_1)$ before process P_1 arrives at $SN(P_2)$ then process P_2 proceeds without communicating with P_1.

We consider a non-deterministic event to be unaffected if either both participants are delayed identically due to the presence of synchronous communication operations or none of the participants are delayed due to the absence of synchronous communication interactions. Consider the example in Fig. 1a. The perturbation delay introduced in process P will not delay the activities of processes P_1 and P_2 and therefore will not affect the outcome of the non-deterministic interaction between P_1 and P_2. The situation shown in Fig. 1b illustrates the case in which the synchronous interactions between P and P_1 followed by P_1 and P_2 cause both P_1 and P_2 to be delayed identically. Thus, the outcome of the non-deterministic interaction between P_1 and P_2 is unchanged. If the expected outcome of the non-deterministic event is known at compile-time, we consider the perturbation to be non-intrusive if it can only increase the likelihood of the expected outcome. In Fig. 1c the delay introduced in process P causes a delay in process P_1 but no delay in process P_2. If process P_2 was already expected to arrive at the communication earlier than process P_1, the likelihood of the expected outcome of the non-deterministic interaction between P_1 and P_2 can only increase. Thus, the perturbation is considered to be non-intrusive. On the other hand, if process P_1 was expected to arrive earlier than process P_2 the perturbation is considered to be intrusive. The above notion of non-intrusion is summarized below.

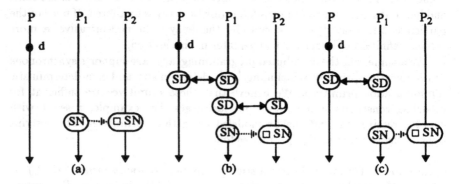

Fig. 1. Non-intrusive Perturbations

Definition 3. A perturbation, d, introduced in process P of a parallel program is considered to be *non-intrusive* with respect to the execution of a $SN(P_2) \rightarrow \square SN(P_1)$ if:

1. following the perturbation there is no direct or indirect deterministic synchronous communication between process P and processes P_1 and P_2 and thus $SN(P_2)$ and $\square SN(P_1)$ are unaffected (see Fig. 1a); or

2. following the perturbation there is a direct synchronous communication between processes P_1 and P_2 causing $SN(P_2)$ and $\square SN(P_1)$ to be affected identically (see Fig. 1b); or

3. $SN(P_2)$ is expected to execute after $\square SN(P_1)$. Following d and prior to $SN(P_2)$ there is a direct/indirect deterministic synchronous communication from P to P_1. However, following d and prior to $\square SN(P_1)$ there is no direct/indirect deterministic synchronous communication from P to P_2. Thus, the perturbation can delay the execution of $SN(P_2)$ but cannot delay $\square SN(P_1)$ (see Fig. 1c); or

4. $SN(P_2)$ is expected to execute before $\square SN(P_1)$. Following d and prior to $SN(P_2)$ there is no direct/indirect deterministic synchronous communication from P to P_1. However, following d and prior to $\square SN(P_1)$ there is a direct/indirect deterministic synchronous communication from P to P_2. Thus, the perturbation cannot delay the execution of $SN(P_2)$ but it can delay $\square SN(P_1)$ (see Fig. 1c).

4 Perturbation Analysis

In this section we develop static analysis techniques that enable us to determine whether or not the introduction of a perturbation at a given program point is non-intrusive to a non-deterministic event. The analysis will be performed on a flow graph containing two types of nodes: computational nodes and communication nodes. There are also two types of edges: interprocess bidirectional edges corresponding to deterministic synchronous communications and intraprocess control flow edges. Each process has its own start and stop node. Given a node n, $Succ(n)$ is the set of immediate intraprocess successors of n, $Pred(n)$ is the set of immediate intraprocess predecessors of n, and $Adj(n)$ is the set of nodes immediately adjacent to n which are connected to n by bidirectional interprocess deterministic synchronous communication edges.

Two kinds of information is computed using static analysis of the program. The first type of static information, the *indirect* information, simply captures the direct and indirect communication interactions among the processes. The set $IND(n)$ for a statement node n contains the names of processes that could have interacted directly or indirectly with the process containing n, along any execution path ending at n. The *indirect* information is computed simultaneously for all nodes by forward propagation of process names with which potential interactions exist along any path. Bidirectional propagation occurs across interprocess edges representing synchronous deterministic communications. The data flow equations given below define the computation of IND sets. The set $IND(n)$ is computed by unioning the set $IND_{intra}(n)$, which is computed from the IND_{intra} sets of predecessors of n, with the set $IND_{inter}(n)$, which is computed by unioning IND sets of nodes adjacent to n. This information is useful in identifying the situations shown in Fig. 1a and 1c since it will enable us to determine whether prior to the execution of SN or $\Box SN$ a process will synchronously communicate with the process containing the perturbation.

$$\boxed{\text{Indirect Information}}$$

Initialization :

$$\forall n, IND(n) = \phi$$

Computation :

$$IND(n) = IND_{intra}(n) \bigcup IND_{inter}(n)$$

$$IND_{intra}(n) = \bigcup_{p \in Pred(n)} IND(p)$$

$$IND_{inter}(n) = (\bigcup_{SD \in Adj(n)} IND_{intra}(SD) - \{P : n \in P\}) \bigcup \{P : Adj(n) in P\}$$

The second type of static information, the *direct* information, captures process pairs that have directly interacted through a synchronous deterministic communication. The set $DIR(n)$ for a statement node n contains processor pairs that are guaranteed to interact directly along all paths following the execution of n. The *direct* information is computed simultaneously for all nodes by backward propagation of processor pairs among which interactions exist along all paths. The data flow equations given below define the computation of DIR sets. The set of processes in the computation is denoted by $\mathcal{P}$. This information is useful for identifying the situation shown in Fig. 1b since it provides information on process pairs that are involved in direct synchronous communication.

Direct Information

Initialization :

$$DIR(stop) = \phi$$

$$DIR(n) = \{(P_i, P_j) : (P_i, P_j) \subseteq \mathcal{P}\}$$

Computation :

$$DIR(n) = DIR_{intra}(n) \bigcup DIR_{inter}(n)$$

$$DIR_{intra}(n) = \bigcap_{s \in Succ(SD)} DIR(s)$$

$$DIR_{inter}(n) = \bigcap_{SD \in Adj(n)} DIR_{intra}(SD) \bigcup \{(P_i, P_j) : n \in P_i, Adj(n) \text{ in } P_j\}$$

In order to analyze the influence of a specific perturbation on a given non-deterministic event, we need to disregard certain communications from consideration. For example, when identifying situation of the type in Fig. 1a, we may be interested in IND sets that disregard the communications that occur prior to the perturbation. Similarly during the detection of situation shown in Fig. 1b we may be interested in DIR sets that disregard the interactions among processes following the non-deterministic event being considered. For this purpose we employ the algorithm $OrderSDs(node)$ which orders the SD nodes in a process with respect to a specific statement $node$. The data flow equations given below propagate SD nodes in a process along paths. If the statement $node$ is encountered by a SD node, we append $node$ to SD and propagate $SD.node$. The presence or absence of SD and $SD.node$ in the set $Paths(stop)$ indicates the ordering between SD and $node$.

OrderSDs(node)

Initialization :

$$\forall SD, Paths(SD) = \{SD\}$$

$$\forall n \neq SD, Paths(n) = \phi$$

Computation :

$$Paths(n) = Paths(n) \bigcup_{p \in Pred(n)} \{f_n(x) : x \in Paths(p)\}$$

$$f_{node}(v) = SD.node, \quad v \in \{SD, SD.node\}$$
$$f_{SD}(v) = SD, \quad v \in \{SD, SD.node\}$$
$$f_n(v) = v$$

The algorithm *NonIntrusive* summarizes the use of static information to determine whether a perturbation d in process P is intrusive to the execution of $SN(P_j) \to \Box SN(P_i)$. We first eliminate the synchronous communications in P that are guaranteed to execute prior to d and then compute IND information. Using the IND information we initialize variables $InflSN$ and $Infl\Box SN$ which indicate whether or not the perturbation can influence the execution timing of SN and $\Box SN$ respectively. If neither SN or $\Box SN$ can be affected by d we can say that d is non-intrusive. If exactly one of SN or $\Box SN$ can be affected by d, then based upon the ordering of the execution of SN and $\Box SN$ we can determine whether d is non-intrusive. Finally if both SN and $\Box SN$ can be affected by d we carry out DIR analysis to determine whether both would be delayed identically or not. Before DIR analysis is performed we eliminate all synchronous communications that are executed after the execution of SN and $\Box SN$ nodes.

Algorithm NonIntrusive ($d \in P$, $SN(P_j) \to \Box SN(P_i)$) {
     – Eliminate SDs before d: if for every execution which executes
     – both d and SD at least once, d is guaranteed to be the
     – last of the two to be executed then eliminate SD.
     OrderSDs (d)
     $\forall\, SD.d \in$ Paths(stop) $\wedge$ $SD \notin$ Paths(stop), eliminate SD
     Compute IND sets
     $InflSN = (P \in IND(SN) \vee (P = P_i \wedge SN$ is reachable from $d))$
     $Infl\Box SN = (P \in IND(\Box SN) \vee (P = P_j \wedge \Box SN$ is reachable from $d))$
     if $\overline{InflSN} \wedge \overline{Infl\Box SN}$ **then**
             d is non-intrusive
     elseif $InflSN \wedge \overline{Infl\Box SN}$ **then**
         if SN executes after $\Box SN$ **then** d is non-intrusive
     elseif $\overline{InflSN} \wedge Infl\Box SN$ **then**
         if SN executes before $\Box SN$ **then** d is non-intrusive
     elseif $InflSN \wedge Infl\Box SN$ **then**
         – Eliminate SDs after $SN/\Box SN$: if $\exists$ an execution which
         – executes both $SN/\Box SN$ and SD at least once and SD is
         – the last of the two to be executed then eliminate SD.
         OrderSDs (SN)
         $\forall\, SD \in$ Paths(stop), eliminate SD
         OrderSDs ($\Box SN$)
         $\forall\, SD \in$ Paths(stop), eliminate SD
         Compute DIR sets
         if $(P_i, P_j) \in DIR(d)$ **then** d is non-intrusive
     else d is intrusive

}

To illustrate the preceding analysis algorithms we consider the program flow graph shown in Fig. 2. To distinguish between the various SD nodes we have added a unique subscript to the nodes. There are three perturbation points, d_1, d_2, and d_3, in this example. Let us first consider d_1. The sets $IND(SN)$ and $IND(\Box SN)$ both contain P_3; thus we require DIR analysis for d_1. The set $DIR(d_1)$ contains (P_1, P_2) due to the synchronizations $SD_5 \leftrightarrow SD_6$ and $SD_7 \leftrightarrow SD_8$ between P_1 to P_3. Thus, d_1 is non-intrusive to the execution of $SN \to \Box SN$. Now let us consider perturbation d_2. The sets $IND(SN)$ and $IND(\Box SN)$ do not contain P_3. Thus, d_2 is non-intrusive to the execution of $SN \to \Box SN$. Finally, for perturbation d_3 we find that P_2 is not in $IND(SN)$ while d_3 and $\Box SN$ both belong to P_2 and $\Box SN$ is reachable from d_3. Thus, in general d_3 is intrusive to the execution of $SN \to \Box SN$. However, if we can determine that SN executes before $\Box SN$ then d_3 is also non-intrusive to $SN \to \Box SN$ since d_3 can delay the execution of $\Box SN$ but not that of SN. In order to ensure that SN executes before $\Box SN$ we must ascertain that path from SD_7 to SN is shorter than the path from SD_8 to $\Box SN$ and also that the path from SD_5 to SN is shorter than the path from SD_6 to $\Box SN$.

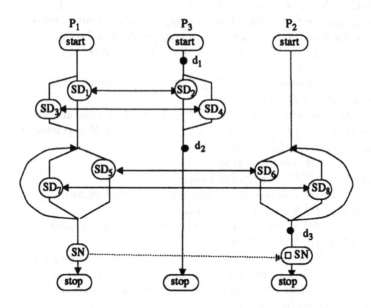

Fig. 2. An Example of Perturbation Analysis

5 Multiple Perturbations and Non-Deterministic Events

The perturbation analysis algorithm presented in the preceding section computes the IND and DIR information following the removal of synchronous communications prior to the perturbation and following the non-deterministic communication of interest. Thus, IND and DIR information must be recomputed for each perturbation and each non-deterministic communication respectively. There are two approaches that can be used to reduce the overhead of analysis. The first approach is to precompute the IND and DIR information without eliminating any synchronous communication. The IND and DIR information for a specific perturbation and non-deterministic event can be obtained by eliminating the appropriate synchronous communications and incrementally modifying the precomputed IND and DIR sets. The overhead of incremental modification is likely to be less then a complete recomputation since the removal of synchronous communications may affect a small portion of the program.

The second approach is to analyze the affects of multiple perturbations on multiple non-deterministic communications simultaneously. Thus, we can eliminate the synchronous communications prior all perturbations and following all non-deterministic communications of interest. Next we compute the IND and DIR information once from the resulting program graph. This integrated approach can be expected to terminate faster than the independent approach which considers each perturbation and each non-deterministic communication separately. By integrating the analysis for multiple perturbations we introduce imprecision in the IND information and by integrating the analysis of multiple non-deterministic communications we introduce imprecision in the DIR information. If any one of the perturbations is found to be intrusive to the execution of any one of the non-deterministic communications, the integrated approach must assume that the collection of perturbations is intrusive to the execution of the collection of non-deterministic communications. Thus, if we wish to determine whether a specific perturbation among the group is non-intrusive to a specific non-deterministic communication, we will not be able to answer this question based upon integrated analysis.

Integrated Analysis (D: perturbations; E: events) {
    $\forall d \in D$, Eliminate SDs before d
    Compute IND sets
    $\forall SN \rightarrow \Box SN \in E$
        Eliminate SDs after SN; Eliminate SDs after $\Box SN$
    Compute DIR sets
    if $\exists$ perturbation $d \in D$ and $SN \rightarrow \Box SN \in E$ such that
        d is intrusive to $SN \rightarrow \Box SN$ according to Algorithm NonIntrusive
    then consider all perturbations in D to be intrusive to all events in E
}

Consider the example shown in Fig. 3. For the situation shown in Fig. 3a, independent analysis yields the result that perturbations d_1 and d_2 are both intrusive to the non-deterministic communication between P_1 and P_2. During integrated analysis we find that the application of algorithm *NonIntrusive* yields the result that d_1 is non-intrusive (since the synchronous communication is removed prior to the computation of IND information) while d_2 is intrusive.

Thus, we must assume that both d_1 and d_2 are intrusive. Now consider the integrated analysis of the example shown in Fig. 3b. The analysis indicates that both perturbations in P, that is d_3 and d_4, are intrusive to the non-deterministic communication between P_1 and P_2. This is because in this case the algorithm *NonIntrusive* indicates that d_3 is intrusive and therefore we must assume that d_4 is also intrusive. The independent analysis on the other hand yields that d_4 is non-intrusive. Finally consider the situation shown in Fig. 3c. Here according to algorithm *NonIntrusive* the perturbation d is intrusive to the execution of E_1 and E_2 since the synchronous communication edge is removed during the computation of DIR sets. However, if independent analysis were to be carried out we would determine that d is intrusive to E_1 but not E_2.

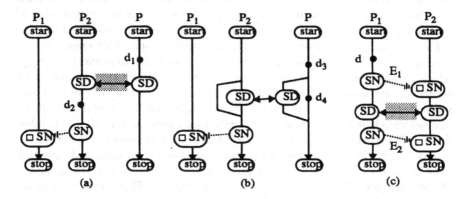

Fig. 3. Independent Analysis versus Integrated Analysis

6   Conditional Non-Intrusion

The analysis in the preceding sections identifies program points at which non-intrusive monitoring can be performed under all program executions, that is, monitoring at these points is guaranteed to be non-intrusive. However, there may be other program points at which monitoring may be potentially non-intrusive. In other words, for a restricted set of executions we can identify additional program points at which non-intrusive monitoring can be performed. Consider the example flow graph shown in Fig. 4a. Two possible executions of the program fragment are shown in Fig. 4b and 4c. In the case of the first execution, the perturbation introduced in process P_1 is not intrusive to the execution of the non-deterministic event. However, in the case of the second execution, the perturbation is intrusive. Thus, we can see that by knowing the path taken during a specific program execution we can identify additional points at which non-intrusive monitoring can be carried out. Once P_2 has taken the branch we can determine whether the perturbation will be non-intrusive. Thus, if P_1 hasn't already executed past the desired perturbation point, we can interrupt the execution of P_1.

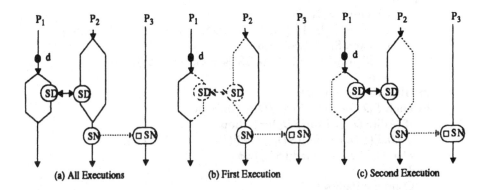

Fig. 4. Conditional Non-Intrusion

In the remainder of the section we describe the analysis required to determine whether certain perturbations would be non-intrusive for a subset of program executions in which a particular synchronous deterministic communication is executed. The first step in this process is to identify the set of SD nodes, $GSDs$, that are guaranteed to be executed. The postdominator relationships are exploited to compute this information. From this information we compute sets $Gadj(n)$ which contain only those subset of nodes from $Adj(n)$ that are guaranteed to interact with n. Also from the set $GSDs$ we compute the set of SD nodes, $NGSDs$, that are guaranteed not to be executed. Reachability information local to processes is used to compute $NGSDs$. Using this information we compute sets $Padj(n)$ which contain only those subset of nodes from $Adj(n)$ that can potentially interact with n. The details of the above analysis are summarized in algorithm *Guaranteed*.

Once having computed $Gadj$ and $Padj$ sets we carry out the IND and DIR analysis as follows. The computation of IND sets will be carried out using $Padj$ sets as opposed to Adj sets. This is because $Padj$ sets exclude the nodes from Adj which cannot be executed in the current execution and hence need not be considered. The modification of DIR analysis is more complex. First we propagate process pairs that are guaranteed to execute using the union operator and $Gadj$ sets resulting the computation of DIR^g sets. Next we propagate the process pairs that may execute using the intersection operator using $Padj$ sets. The union of information collected during the two phases provides us with the DIR information for the current subset of executions.

Algorithm Guaranteed (SD) {
    – SD is guaranteed to be executed
    — Compute Gadj sets:
    GSDs = {SD}
    repeat
        OldGSDs = GSDs
        GSDs = GSDs $\bigcup$ { SD': SD' postdominates a SD $\in$ GSDs }
        foreach SD $\in$ GSDs **do**
            if |Adj(SD)|=1 **then** GSDs = GSDs $\bigcup$ Adj(SD)
        end
    until OldGSDs = GSDs
    foreach $SD_1 \leftrightarrow SD_2$, $SD_1, SD_2 \in$ GSDs **do**
      if $|\text{Adj}(SD_1)|=|\text{Adj}(SD_2)|=1$ **then**
        Gadj(SD_1) = Adj(SD_1); Gadj(SD_2) = Adj(SD_2)
      else Gadj(SD_1)=Gadj(SD_2)=ϕ
    end
    — Compute Padj sets:
    NGSDs = ϕ
    foreach SD $\notin$ GSDs **do**
      if $\exists$ SD' $\in$ GSDs such that
        SD' is not reachable from SD and vice versa
      then NGSDs = NGSDs $\bigcup$ {SD}
    end
    NGSDs = NGSDs $\bigcup$ {SD: SD is control sibling of SD' $\in$ NGSDs}
    foreach SD **do**
      if SD $\in$ NGSDs **then** Padj(SD) = ϕ
      else Padj(SD) = Adj(SD) - NGSDs
    end
}

Indirect Information

Initialization :

$$\forall n, IND(n) = \phi$$

Computation :

$$IND(n) = IND_{intra}(n) \bigcup IND_{inter}(n)$$

$$IND_{intra}(n) = \bigcup_{p \in Pred(n)} IND(p)$$

$$IND_{inter}(n) = (\bigcup_{SD \in Padj(n)} IND_{intra}(SD) - \{P : n \in P\}) \bigcup \{P : Padj(n) in P\}$$

$$\boxed{\text{Direct Information}}$$

Initialization :

$$\forall n, DIR^g(n) = \phi$$

Computation :

$$DIR^g(n) = DIR^g_{intra}(n) \bigcup DIR^g_{inter}(n)$$

$$DIR^g_{intra}(n) = \bigcup_{s \in Succ(SD)} DIR^g(s)$$

$$DIR^g_{inter}(n) = \bigcup_{SD \in Gadj(n)} DIR^g_{intra}(SD) \bigcup \{(P_i, P_j) : n \in P_i, Gadj(n) in P_j\}$$

Initialization :

$$DIR(stop) = \phi$$

$$DIR(n) = \{(P_i, P_j) : (P_i, P_j) \subseteq \mathcal{P}\}$$

Computation :

$$DIR(n) = DIR_{intra}(n) \bigcup DIR_{inter}(n)$$

$$DIR_{intra}(n) = \bigcap_{s \in Succ(SD)} DIR(s) \bigcup DIR^g(n)$$

$$DIR_{inter}(n) = \bigcap_{SD \in Padj(n)} DIR_{intra}(SD) \bigcup \{(P_i, P_j) : n \in P_i, Padj(n) \text{ in } P_j\}$$

In order to take advantage of techniques described in this section we require hardware support. The hardware should be capable of non-intrusively observing the current point of execution of each process and interrupting the execution of a process at the desired point. Each processor, P_i, in the system can be provided with an associated monitoring processor, MP_i. The monitoring processor, MP_i, should be capable of observing the program counter, PC_i, of processor P_i to determine the current execution point of the process executing on P_i. In addition, MP_i should be able to set an interrupt register, IR_i, in P_i to indicate the next point in execution at which the process executing on P_i is to be interrupted. The monitoring processor should be capable of setting and clearing the interrupt register directly, without intruding on the execution of P_i. The information from static analysis should be available to all monitoring processors. Furthermore, the monitoring processors should be able to communicate with each other in order to coordinate their monitoring activities. The communication medium used by the monitoring processors and the executing processors should not be shared.

7 Concluding Remarks

In this paper we introduced a notion of non-intrusion for the monitoring of non-deterministic distributed programs. This notion of non-intrusion is useful for observing the types of program behavior that characterize the patterns of interaction among various processes as opposed to the precise timings of various activities. We also presented perturbation analysis techniques based upon static analysis that allow us to determine whether a perturbation at a specific program point is non-intrusive.

Although asynchronous forms of communication were not considered in this paper, we have developed extensions to our analysis techniques which enable us to take advantage of asynchronous communication [10]. In addition, we have also devised strategies for non-intrusively observing behaviors of scheduling algorithms for non-real time systems. Our current research is focusing on the development of perturbation analysis techniques for real-time applications. Actual values of monitoring delays can be introduced and their effect on the execution timing of various tasks can be studied. If monitoring delays can be absorbed by delays already present in the schedule, we can consider the monitoring activity to be non-intrusive. The advantage of this approach is that we can use the compiler to select appropriate points for monitoring activity before actually executing the program.

References

1. Aral, Z., Gertner, I., Schaffer, G.: Efficient debugging primitives for multiprocessors. Proc. Third International Conference on Architectural Support for Programming Languages and Operating Systems. (1989) 87–95
2. Bates, P.C., Wileden, J.C.: High-Level debugging of distributed systems: the behavioral abstraction approach. J. Systems and Software. **3(4)** (1983) 225–264
3. Callahan, D., Subhlok, J.: Static analysis of low-level synchronization. Proc. ACM Workshop on Parallel and Distributed Debugging. (1989) 100–111
4. Cooper, R., Marzullo, K.: Consistent detection of global predicates. Proc. ACM-ONR Workshop on Parallel and Distributed Debugging. (1991) 140–150
5. Chandy, K.M., Lamport, L.: Distributed snapshots: determining global states of distributed systems. ACM Transactions on Computer Systems. **3** (1985) 63–75
6. Dinning, A., Schonberg, E.: An empirical comparison of monitoring algorithms for access anomaly detection. Proc. Second ACM SIGPLAN Symposium on Principles and Practice of Parallel Programming. (1990) 1–10
7. Duesterwald, E., Gupta, R., Soffa, M.L.: Distributed slicing and partial re-execution for distributed programs. Fifth Workshop on Languages and Compilers for Parallel Computing. (1992) 329–337
8. Duesterwald, E., Soffa, M.L.: Static concurrency analysis in the presence of procedures using a data-flow framework. Proc. ACM Symposium on Testing, Analysis and Verification. (1991) 36–48.
9. Fowler, J., Zwaenepoal, W.: Causal Distributed Breakpoints. Proc. Tenth International Conference on Distributed Computing Systems. (1990) 134–141.

10. Gupta, R., Spezialetti, M.: Perturbation analysis: a static analysis approach for the non-intrusive monitoring of parallel programs. Technical Report, University of Pittsburgh. (1993)

11. Gupta, R., Spezialetti, M.: Loop monotonic computations: an approach for the efficient run-time detection of races. Proc. SIGSOFT Symposium on Testing, Analysis, and Verification. (1991) 98–111

12. Joyce, J., Lomow, G., Slind, K., Ungar, B.: Monitoring distributed systems. ACM Transactions on Computer Systems. 5(2) (1987) 121–150

13. Haban, D., Weigel, W.: Global events and global breakpoints in distributed systems. Proc. 21st Hawaii International Conference on Distributed Computing Systems (1988)

14. Hoare, C.A.R.: Communicating sequential processes. Communications of the ACM. 21(8) (1978) 666–677

15. Lamport, L.: Time, clocks and the ordering of events in distributed systems. Communications of the ACM. 21(7) (1978) 558–565

16. LeBlanc, T., Mellor-Crummey, J.M.: Debugging parallel programs with instant replay. IEEE Transactions on Computers. (1987) 471–481

17. Malony, A., Reed, D.: Models for performance perturbation analysis. Proc. ACM/ONR Workshop on Parallel and Distributed Debugging. (1991) 15–25

18. Masticola, S.P., Ryder, B.G.: Non-concurrency analysis. Proc. 4th ACM SIGPLAN Symposium on Principles and Practices of Parallel Programming. (1993) 129–138

19. Miller, B., Choi, J.D.: Breakpoints and halting in distributed systems. Proc. 8th International Conference on Distributed Computing Systems. (1988) 141–150

20. Sarukkai, S.R., Malony, A.: Perturbation analysis of high level instrumentation for SPMD programs. Proc. 4th ACM SIGPLAN Symposium on Principles and Practices of Parallel Programming. (1993) 44–53

21. Spezialetti, M., Kearns, J.P.: A general approach to recognizing event occurrences in distributed computations. Proc. 8th International Conference on Distributed Computing Systems. (1988) 300–307

22. Spezialetti, M., Kearns, J.P.: Simultaneous regions: a framework for the consistent monitoring of distributed systems. Proc. 9th International Conference on Distributed Computing Systems. (1989) 61–68

23. Spezialetti, M., Kearns, J.P.: A general methodology for the system state characterization of event recognitions. Proc. 9th Symposium on Reliable Distributed Systems. (1990) 175–184

24. Spezialetti, M., Gupta, R.: Exploiting program semantics for the efficient detection of global events. Technical Report - University of Pittsburgh. (1992)

25. Tsai, J.P, Fang, K.F., Chen, H.: A noninvasive architecture to monitor real-time distributed systems. IEEE Computer. 23(3) (1990) 11–23

26. Mattern, F.: Virtual time and global states of distributed systems. M. Cosnard, editor, Parallel and Distributed Algorithms. (1989) 215-226

27. Netzer, R., Miller, B.: Optimal tracing and replay for debugging message-passing parallel programs. Proc. Supercomputing. (1992) 502–511

Efficient Computation of Precedence Information in Parallel Programs

Dirk Grunwald   Harini Srinivasan[*]

Department of Computer Science,
Campus Box 430, University of Colorado,
Boulder, CO 80309-0430
(Email:{grunwald,harini}@cs.colorado.edu)

Abstract. For any two statements in a parallel program, S_i and S_j, S_i is said to *precede* S_j if the execution of S_j implies that S_i must have already executed across all possible execution orders. There are many uses for precedence information for parallel programs, including program debugging and program optimization. The problem of finding exact precedence information is Co-NP-Hard [5]. Existing approaches to compute a conservative approximation to the precedence information at compile time are very expensive. In this paper, we present a more efficient algorithm to compute precedence that exploits known properties of sequential and parallel programs. In sequential programs, the precedence relation is the same as the *dominance* relation. We use this, and other information, to develop a more efficient algorithm.

1 Introduction

A parallel program is composed of a set of statements $S_1 \ldots S_n$. Programs may contain loops, and there may be multiple instances $S_i^1 \ldots S_i^m$ of an individual statement S_i when a program executes. Analysis of shared memory parallel programs requires information about the order in which statements and statement instances are executed. Compilers can use information concerning *all possible* program executions when optimizing explicitly parallel programs. Since the compiler can only analyze the static representation of the program, it must concern itself with all possible statement execution orders. This paper shows an efficient algorithm for computing relations between statements in the program that apply for all program executions. Previous work has shown an $O(n^3)$ method for this problem; while our method is also $O(n^3)$ in the worse case, the complexity will be closer to $O(n^2)$ for actual programs.

The *precedence* and *concurrency* relations are important tools when analyzing parallel programs. Statement S_i is said to *precede* S_j if the execution of S_j implies that S_i must have already executed across all possible execution orders. Likewise, statement S_i is said to be *concurrent* with S_j if we can not show that S_i precedes S_j or that S_j precedes S_i. This information is useful in predicting if there is a

---

[*] This work supported in part by an IBM Graduate Fellowship

data race in the program because of parallel reads and writes to a memory location [2, 6, 7, 8, 12]. We have also used this information to compute data flow information in parallel programs [10].

1.1 Example Programs

We describe two short explicitly parallel programs that demonstrate the complexity of the precedence computation and the uses for this information. The computation of the *precedence* relation is usually straightforward for explicitly parallel (cobegin/coend) programs without additional synchronization. These programs exhibit *DAG parallelism*, providing a simple partial order of program events. Programs containing additional synchronization, particularly those containing synchronization in loops or conditional statements, greatly increase the problem complexity. Callahan et al [5] have shown that computing the 'exact' precedence information is Co-NP-Hard for parallel programs with Parallel Cases and post/wait synchronization. In general, it may be intractable to compute this information, because synchronization patterns may rely on input expressions.

Consider the program in figure 1. The executions of statements S_6 and S_{14} can be unordered: if P evaluates to true then, the event ev2 is posted before S_6. Hence, S_{14} may execute before S_6. On the other hand, if P is false and Q is true, S_6 must execute before S_{14}. In the former case, the value of variable T in S_{14} is 0 or 1 and in the latter, the value is 1.

Despite the presence of the Post and Wait statements, the execution of S_6 and S_{14} can occur in any order and there is no precedence relation between them; they are concurrent statements, implying there is a potential race in the program. This example shows that the presence of a post/wait synchronization between two statements need not imply that the execution of the statements are ordered.

We must compute a *conservative approximation* to the desired precedence information. For example, a compiler may use precedence information to perform certain optimizations; the compiler must rely on information that is valid for *all possible* program executions. We assume it is more conservative to omit a correct precedence relation than to accidently include an incorrect relation. This assumption is plausible for compilers *and* parallel program debuggers. For example, a compiler could perform an optimization such as common subexpression elimination if it could determine a precedence relation between statements; if it introduces false precedence relations, this optimization may be incorrect. Likewise, omitting precedence relations would indicate potential data races to a parallel debugger; including incorrect precedence relations may cause a debugger to ignore potential data races.

We are interested in using the precedence information for compiler optimization of explicitly parallel programs, although these optimizations are not the topic of this paper. The program in figure 2 illustrates the use of sequence counters to synchronize two loops that are in different branches of a parallel.-sections construct. The sequence counters S1 and S2 are initialized to zero. The

```
(1)     T = 0; Z = 26              (1)     Sequence S1, S2
(1)     Parallel Sections          (1)     j = 2; k = 0; l = 0
(2)         Section A              (1)     Parallel Sections
(3)             Wait(ev1)          (2)     Section A
(3)             X = X + Y          (3)         loop
(4)             if (P) then        (4)             k = k + 1
(5)                 Post(ev2)      (4)             m = (k * 4)**j
(6)             end if             (4)             advance(S1,k)
(6) S₈          T = 1              (5)             A(k) = m + k
(6)             Post(ev2)          (5)             await(S2,k)
(7)         Section B              (6)         end loop
(8)             if (R) then
(9)                 Y = 15         (7)     Section B
(9)                 Post(ev1)      (8)         loop
            else                   (9)             l = l + 1
(10)                Y = Z + 12     (10)            await(S1,l)
(10)                Post(ev1)      (10)            n = (k * 4)**j
(11)            end if             (10)            B(l) = n + 1
(12)            if (Q) then        (10)            advance(S2,l)
(13)                Wait(ev2)      (11)        end loop
(14)            end if             (12)     End Parallel Sections
(14) S₁₄        S = T
(15)    End Parallel Sections
```

Fig. 1. Example illustrating that precedence computation is complicated

Fig. 2. Example Illustrating Synchronization and Loops

execution of the await statement in Section B can not complete unless S1 has been incremented by the advance statement in Section A. Similar semantics hold for the advance and await statements acting on S2. The iterations of the loops in Section A and Section B (loop-A and loop-B respectively) execute in an interleaved fashion due to this synchronization pattern, resulting in a *synchronization cycle*. In other words, the increment of variable k in iteration i of loop-A must execute before the increment of variable l in iteration i of loop-B. In addition, the increment of l in iteration i of loop-B must execute before the increment of k in iteration $i+1$ of loop-A. Hence, k is an induction variable not just in loop-A, but also in loop-B.

We see that information concerning the synchronization cycle, indicates that the expression assigned to variables m and n in the two loops is common to both loops and we can eliminate one of the expression evaluations by computing the value of the expression in loop-A and communicating the value to the thread executing loop-B. In the absence of the advance and await statements corresponding to S2, k is no longer an induction variable in loop-B and it is not possible to apply the common subexpression elimination optimization to this program.

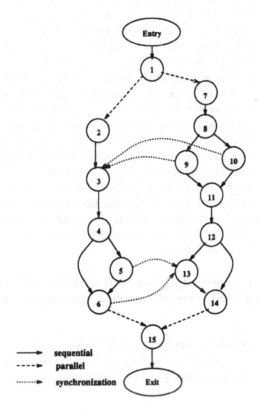

Fig. 3. Parallel Flow Graph

1.2 Parallel Constructs

We consider the parallel_sections construct from Parallel Computing Forum FORTRAN [13]. The parallel_sections construct is similar to cobegin/coend [3] and parallel cases [11] and specifies parallelism between identified sections of code. The different sections of a parallel_sections construct must be data independent, except when an appropriate synchronization mechanism is used. We consider *event synchronization* where a Post statement posts an event variable, *i.e.*, sets it to be true. A Wait statement waits for the event variable to be set to true. Execution of the Wait is suspended until the event variable has been posted. As in [5], we do not consider Clear statements in this work. Ignoring Clear statements yields a conservative approximation of the precedence information. We can accommodate synchronization within or between loops by using *sequence counters*. The synchronization semantics of *sequence counters* is the same as Post/Wait with Clear statements or Post/Wait with event arrays. Though not all synchronization patterns with Post/Wait and event arrays or Clears can be handled by sequence counters, we believe the latter should handle most synchronization patterns between and within loops.

We represent these parallel programs using the *Parallel Flow Graph* (PFG) where nodes in the graph represent extended basic blocks, *i.e.*, with at most one Wait statement at the beginning of the basic block and at most one Post statement at the end of the basic block. The edges represent sequential flow of control, parallel flow of control or synchronization. A synchronization edge appears between every Post and Wait operating on the same event variable. Formally, a PFG is a tuple, $\langle Entry, Exit, N, E \rangle$ where N is the set of nodes, E is the set of edges and *Entry* and *Exit* are the unique entry and exit points in the parallel program. The Control Flow Subgraph (CFSG) of the PFG is $\langle Entry, Exit, N, E_c \rangle$ where E_c is the set of control flow edges (parallel and sequential) in the PFG. Figure 3 shows the Parallel Flow Graph for the example program in figure 1. We use the Parallel Flow Graph to analyze the parallel program for precedence information. Formally, we define the precedence information for any node n in the PFG, *Preserved(n)*, as follows:

Definition 1. $m \in Preserved(n)$ if and only if for all parallel executions of the parallel program, if n and m are both executed, m is completed before n is begun [2].

The rest of the paper is organized as follows: Section 2 describes prior work. Section 3 describes our algorithm to compute precedence information in parallel programs. In §4, we extend this algorithm to programs with loops. We summarize our work in §5.

2   Related Work

Callahan and Subhlok [5] have presented a data flow framework to compute a conservative approximation to the actual precedence relation. They also show that computing the exact *Preserved* sets information is a CO-NP Hard problem. Their data flow framework is based on a flow graph of the parallel program that represents both control flow and synchronization in the program, much like the PFG. The iterative algorithm to compute the approximate precedence information (called the *SCPreserved* sets) is an $O(N^3)$ algorithm.

---

[2] We say a Wait node has started execution if the code following the Wait statement has started executing.

The data flow equations in [5] are partitioned into sets concerning control flow edges and synchronization edges. The *SCPreserved* set for a pair of nodes i and k is defined as the set of nodes j such that if both j and k are executed then execution of j is completed before execution of i is begun. The data flow equations are $O(n^2)$, but the equation must be solved for every pair of nodes in the PFG, giving an $O(n^3)$ algorithm. We compute similar information using a more efficient method.

In [6], this technique was extended to programs containing loops with known loop bounds. Essentially, the loops are "unrolled" during the data flow computation; we view this as a severe restriction on the applicability of the method for compiler analysis and optimization. The loop analysis in [6] extended the work of [9], where synchronization edges in the PFG were augmented with loop distance vectors. Emrath *et al* later refined their technique using a combination of static and trace analysis [8].

There are a wealth of other references in related work that does not directly apply to this problem. For example, numerous researchers have considered the analysis of explicitly parallel Ada programs or attempted to reconstruct program event ordering from *post mortem* execution traces.

Our work is most similar to the work by Callahan *et al* and the earlier work by Emrath *et al*. Our work also bears resemblance to [4], because we also use the dominance relation to compute the precedence information. However, Bristow *et al* did not consider programs with nested parallel constructs or synchronizations in loops.

3 Precedence Information In the Absence of Loops

In this section, we show how to efficiently compute precedence information using the *dominance relation*. The explicitly parallel program is modeled using the Parallel Flow Graph. For each node n, we define:

$Pred_s(n)$: the set of predecessors nodes connected by sequential control flow edges.

$Pred_p(n)$: the set of predecessor nodes connected by *parallel edges* (i.e., statements immediately following a parallel_section).

$Pred_{sy}(n)$: the set of predecessor nodes connected by synchronization edges. Thus, if node n contains a Wait statement, nodes in $Pred_{sy}(n)$ contain Post statements.

We use the dominance relation from sequential control flow edges and the semantics of parallel and synchronization edges to account for precedence relations between nodes. The closure of this information determines the precedence relation between all nodes. Since our algorithm is not an iterative one, it reduces the complexity of computing precedence information.

3.1 Definitions and theorems

A node n **dominates** node m (n <u>dom</u> m) in the Control Flow Subgraph of the PFG if n appears on all paths from *Entry* to m [1]. If n <u>dom</u> m, then if n and m both execute then, n must execute before m. Hence, the $Dom(n)$ is a subset of the nodes in the precedence set of n. A node m **post dominates** node n (n <u>pdom</u> m) in the Control Flow Subgraph (CFSG) of the PFG if m appears on all paths from n to *Exit*. Nodes i and j in the PFG are *Coexecutable* [5] if they are in different out-going branches (i.e., tasks) of the corresponding cobegin node or there is a path of control flow edges from $n \xrightarrow{+} m$ or $m \xrightarrow{+} n$. For example, nodes 9 and 10 in Figure 3 are *not* coexecutable, while nodes (2) and (7) are. This predicate is used in our algorithm to handle conditional Posts and Waits.

Theorem 2. *If a* Wait *node* w *has the associated* Post *nodes* $P = \{p_1, p_2, \ldots p_n\}$, *and there is no pair of coexecutable nodes in* P, *then if* $p_i \in P$ *and* w *both execute, then* p_i *must complete before* w *executes.*

Proof: By definition, nodes p_i and p_j are not *Coexecutable* iff they are in the same branch of some parallel_sections construct *and* there is no path in the PFG from p_i to p_j or p_j to p_i. Hence, for all executions of the program, only one of p_i or p_j may execute.

If there are no coexecutable Post nodes, only one of the nodes, $p_i \in P$ will execute. Execution of the Wait statement in w can not complete unless the corresponding event variable has been posted; thus, the execution of p_i must precede the execution of w. $\square$

Theorem 3. *If a wait node* w *has the corresponding post nodes* $P = \{p_1, p_2, \ldots p_i\}$ *and there exists a node* q *in the control flow subgraph that dominates all nodes in* P *then* q *must precede* w *in execution order.*

Proof: We consider two cases here:

q is one of the posting nodes:

If n dominates m in the CFSG of the PFG then n must precede m during all executions of the parallel program because a node m in the PFG can not proceed with execution unless control is transferred to m.

Since q dominates all nodes in P in the CFSG, it must execute before all nodes in $P - \{q\}$. Hence, the event variable (that is common to all the Posts in this case) is first posted in node q. The execution of the Wait statement in w can start either before q or after. Suppose the Wait statement in w starts executing and if q has not completed execution, *i.e.*, the event has not been posted then, w suspends execution *i.e.* 'waits' until the event is posted. By definition of an extended basic block, since the Post statement is the last statement in a basic block, execution of q must precede that of w. Suppose q has posted the event even before w started execution, then again q precedes w in execution order. In both cases, it is possible that nodes in $P - \{q\}$ would execute before w, but at compile time we will not be able to assert which of these nodes must execute before w.

q is not a posting node: Since q dominates all the nodes in P, the execution of q must precede the execution of all the nodes in P. Since the wait node w can not proceed unless the corresponding event variable has been posted, it can not start executing unless at least one of the posting nodes has completed execution. Transitively, the execution of q must precede the execution of w. $\square$.

3.2   Precedence between nodes in the Parallel Flow Graph

Our algorithm to compute a conservative approximation to the precedence information between nodes in the PFG follows a systematic approach of combining known information about precedence given by the definitions and theorems we have stated:

1. **Sequential Control Flow**: For each sequential section of code in the parallel program, the dominance relation can be used to compute precedence within that section. The information is complete for nodes that are connected by sequential control flow edges. We actually update the precedence information at each node in the PFG with its dominators in the Control Flow Subgraph.

2. **Parallel Control Flow**: At parallel branch points, *i.e.*, *cobegin* nodes, all successors must always execute. This is required by the semantics of parallel control flow. Hence, we update the precedence information at such successors to include the corresponding *cobegin* node. Similarly, the execution of a *coend* node can begin only if all its predecessors have completed execution, allowing us to update the precedence information of a *coend* node to include all its control flow predecessors.

3. **Synchronization**: To handle synchronization edges, we consider certain synchronization patterns for which we can statically predict precedence very easily. For all other synchronization patterns, we would assume *no precedence* relation between the Post and the corresponding Wait. Such a conservative answer would be *safe* for all the applications of precedence information that we have come across so far.

   - If there is exactly one Post statement corresponding to a Wait statement, the posting node must precede the waiting node.
   - If there are multiple Posts for a Wait node and if the different Posts execute concurrently, *i.e.*, are in different tasks, then we can not guarantee execution order between any of the Posts and the Wait.
   - If there multiple posting nodes for a Wait node, we apply Theorem 2 and Theorem 3 to introduce new precedence information.

4. **Propagating Precedence Information**: In order to propagate the precedence information computed locally at each node with respect to its control flow or synchronization predecessors or dominators, we traverse the PFG in topological order. The topological sort order preserves the property that every node is visited only after all its predecessors have been visited (this does

not include back edges, but it doesn't affect the precedence computation). While visiting each node, the precedence information at that node is updated with the precedence information of the nodes that have been computed to precede it by steps 1, 2 and 3.

At sequential and synchronization merge points, the precedence information is updated with the intersection of the precedence information at the predecessor nodes. Note that since we traverse the graph in topological order, this is not an iterative algorithm. In fact, steps 1, 2 and 3 help make this an elimination algorithm as opposed to an iterative algorithm as in [5].

We use the above approach to compute *Prec*, our approximation to the precedence information. We have not proved that *Prec* is identical to the *SCPreserved* set of [5], however it is identical for all the examples we have considered.

3.3   Example

Figure 4 shows the dominator tree for the Control Flow Subgraph of the PFG in figure 3. In step 1 of the above algorithm, the dominators of a node n are in the set of nodes that must precede n, $Prec(n)$. For node (9) in the figure, $Prec(9)$ after this step is $\{Entry,1,7,8\}$. After step (2), node (1) $\in Prec(2)$ and $Prec(7)$ and nodes (6) and (14) $\in Prec(15)$. In step 3 of the above algorithm, nodes (9) and (10) are in $Prec(3)$ since they are in the same thread and are not coexecutable; nodes (5) and (6) *are not* in $Prec(13)$ since (5) and (6) are coexecutable. Finally, in step 4 of the algorithm, the precedence information computed in steps 1,2 and 3 are propagated to the other nodes in the PFG. The final precedence information for this example is given in figure 5.

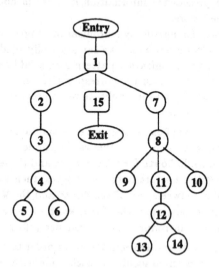

Fig. 4. Dominator Tree for CFSG of PFG in Figure 3

n	Prec(n)
Entry	
1	Entry
2	Entry,1
3	Entry,1,2,7,8,9,10
4	Entry,1,2,3,7,8,9,10
5	Entry,1,2,3,4,7,8,9,10
6	Entry,1,2,3,4,7,8,9,10
7	Entry,1
8	Entry,1,7
9	Entry,1,7,8
10	Entry,1,7,8
11	Entry,1,7,8
12	Entry,1,7,8,11
13	Entry,1,7,8,11,12
14	Entry,1,7,8,11,12
15	Entry,1,2,3,4,6,7,8,9,10,11,12,14

Fig. 5. Precedence information for the example

3.4 Correctness and Complexity

The algorithm to compute precedence information is given in figure 6. In this figure, $Prec(n)$ gives the set of nodes that must precede n in execution order. The function Topsort($\mathcal{N}$) is the set of nodes in $\mathcal{N}$ in topological order.

In the rest of this section, we give the proof of correctness of the algorithm and also analyze the complexity of this algorithm. In showing correctness, we prove that the nodes in $Prec(n)$ must in fact execute before n for all parallel executions of the parallel program, i.e., $Prec(n)$ is a subset of $Preserved(n)$ (definition 1). The proof proceeds by induction on the topsort number, Tpn, of the node in the Parallel Flow Graph.

Theorem 4. $Prec(n) \subseteq Preserved(n)$.

Proof: The proof proceeds by induction on $Tpn(n)$.

Base case: When $Tpn(n) = 0$. Since *Entry* is the unique start node in the PFG, $n = Entry$. By definition, $Preserved(n) = \emptyset$. Since $Pred(Entry) = \emptyset$ and $Dom(Entry) = \emptyset$, $Prec(n) = \emptyset$.

Induction Hypothesis: Suppose $Preserved(n) \subseteq Prec(n)$ for all nodes n such that $Tpn(n) < t$.

Induction Step: Suppose $Tpn(n) = t$. We want to show that $Prec(n) \subseteq Preserved(n)$. Suppose $m \in Prec(n)$. There are many different cases:

1. $m \in Dom(n)$: Since a node can not execute until control is transferred to it, by definition of dominance on the CFSG, m must execute before n for all executions of the parallel program. Hence, $m \in Preserved(n)$.

A_1 **for** $n \in \mathcal{N}$ **do** $Prec(n) = Prec(n) \cup Dom(n)$ **end for**

A_2 **for** $n \in \mathcal{N} \mid n$ **a parallel merge node do**
$\qquad Prec(n) = Prec(n) \cup Pred(p)$
$\quad$ **end for**

A_3 **for** $n \in \mathcal{N} \mid n$ **a parallel fork node do**
$\qquad Prec(p) = Prec(p) \cup Succ(n)$
$\quad$ **end for**

A_4 **for** $n \in \mathcal{N} \mid n$ **is a Wait node do**
$\qquad$ **if** $|Pred_{sy}(n)| = 1$ **then**
A_5 $\qquad\qquad Prec(n) = Prec(n) \cup Pred_{sy}(n)$
$\qquad$ **else**
A_6 $\qquad\qquad$ **if** $\exists p, q \in Pred_{sy}(n) \mid Coexecutable(p, q)$ **then**
$\qquad\qquad\qquad$ **if** $\exists p \in Pred_{sy}(n) \mid \forall q \in Pred_{sy}(n)$
$\qquad\qquad\qquad\qquad$ **and** $p \underline{\text{dom}}\ q$ **then**
$\qquad\qquad\qquad\qquad\qquad Prec(n) = Prec(n) \cup \{p\}$
$\qquad\qquad\qquad$ **end if**
$\qquad\qquad$ **else**
$\qquad\qquad\qquad Prec(n) = Prec(n) \cup Pred_{sy}(n)$
$\qquad\qquad$ **end if**
$\qquad$ **end if**
$\quad$ **end for**

/* **Propagate precedence information**
$\quad$ **in topological order** */
A_7 **for** $n \in$ **Topsort**$(\mathcal{N})$ **do**
$\qquad T = Prec(n)$
$\qquad$ **for** $p \in Prec(n)$ **do**
$\qquad\qquad T = T \cup Prec(p)$
$\qquad$ **end for**
$\qquad$ **if** $n \in$ **Seq merge nodes then**
$\qquad\qquad T = T \cup \bigcap_{p \in Pred_s(n)} Prec(p)$
$\qquad$ **end if**
$\qquad$ **if** $n \in$ **Wait node then**
$\qquad\qquad T = T \cup \bigcap_{p \in Pred_{sy}(n)} Prec(p)$
$\qquad$ **end if**
$\qquad Prec(n) = T$
$\quad$ **end for**

Fig. 6. Algorithm 1: Computation of precedence information

2. *m is a parallel fork node and n ∈ Succ(m)*: Since parallel control flow edges always execute, by definition of *Preserved(n)*, $m \in Preserved(n)$.

3. *n is a parallel join node and m ∈ Pred(n)*: Again, since parallel control flow edges always execute, $m \in Preserved(n)$.

4. *n is a Wait node and has exactly one synchronization predecessor = m*: By semantics of Post and Wait statements, the execution of the Wait will not succeed until the event variable has been posted by the Post statement. Hence $m \in Preserved(n)$.

5. *n is a Wait node, $m \in Pred_{sy}(n)$ and $\forall p, q \in Pred_{sy}(n)$ Theorem 2 is satisfied*: Since $\forall p, q \in Pred_{sy}(n)$, p and q are not in different branches of a parallel_sections construct and there is no path in the PFG between them (*i.e., Coexecutable(p,q) is true*), the Posts must execute conditionally implying only one of them execute at run time. For different parallel executions for a given input data set to the program, only one of the Posts always executes. Therefore, by definition of *Preserved(n)*, it must contain all the posting nodes.

6. *n is a Wait node, m is a corresponding Post node and the Post nodes satisfy theorem 3*: The proof of this case is direct from theorem 3.

7. *n is a sequential merge node and $m \in Prec(p), \forall p \in Pred_s(n)$*: Algorithm 1 computes *Prec(n)* as the intersection of $Prec(p), p \in Pred_s(n)$. Since for all parallel executions, at least one of the sequential control flow predecessors must execute before n, by definition of *Preserved*, we know that the nodes common to the *Preserved* sets of all the sequential predecessors must execute before n. Hence,

$$\bigcap_{p \in Pred_s(n)} Preserved(p) \subseteq Preserved(n). \tag{1}$$

It is possible that some of the predecessors p of node n are earlier than n in topological order and the rest are later than n in topological order. Let *Forw(n)* be the set of nodes whose $Tpn < Tpn(n)$. Let *Back(n)* be the set $Pred_s(n) - Forw(n)$.

By inductive hypothesis,

$$Prec(p) \subseteq Preserved(p) \forall p \in Forw(n). \tag{2}$$

Hence, from equations (1) and (2),

$$\bigcap_{p \in Forw(n)} Prec(p) \subseteq \bigcap_{p \in Forw(n)} Preserved(p)$$

Clearly, for all $p \in Back(n)$, p is not yet visited in step 4 of the algorithm in §3.2. Any node $q \in Prec(p)$ comes from steps 1, 2 or 3 of this algorithm. In all these steps, we have proved in the earlier cases of this proof that $Prec(p) \subseteq Preserved(p)$.

Hence,

$$\bigcap_{p \in Back(n)} Prec(p) \subseteq \bigcap_{p \in Back(n)} Preserved(p)$$

Therefore, $Prec(n) \subseteq Preserved(n)$.

8. *n is a* Wait *node*: The proof of this case is similar to the previous case since we know that the Wait statement in *n* succeeds if even one of the Posts succeeds.

9. $m \in Prec(p)$ *and* $p \in Prec(n)$: This occurs when propagating the *Prec* information in topological order. Since $p \in Prec(n)$, either p must appear before n in topological order or $p \in Prec(n)$ because of steps 1, 2 or 3 of algorithm in §3.2. In the former case, we know by inductive hypothesis that $p \in Prec(n)$ implies $p \in Preserved(n)$. Similarly, $m \in Preserved(p)$. In the latter case, the argument in the previous steps of this proof asserts that $p \in Preserved(n)$ and $m \in Preserved(p)$. In both cases, by transitivity, $m \in Preserved(n)$.

□.

Steps A_1, A_2 and A_3 in Figure 6 are $O(n)$ where n is the number of nodes in the PFG. The loop marked A_4 is executed w times, where w is the number of wait nodes in the program. In that loop, we either perform a constant amount of work (A_5) or $\max_p{}^2$ iterations of another loop (A_6), where $\max_p$ is the maximum number of post nodes for any event variable. Usually, $w \ll n$ and $\max_p \ll n$; in many programs, $\max_p$ is one. The remaining loop, A_7, is executed for each node in the PFG, and propagates the precedence information using the topsort order. This has $O(n^2)$ complexity in the worst case.

The limiting case is step A_4; in the extreme, this could have $O(n^3)$ complexity. In practice, it has $O(w\max_p{}^2)$ complexity, where w and $\max_p$ are very small. By comparison, the other algorithms we have examined have $O(n^3)$ complexity even in the absence of synchronization operations.

4 Precedence information in the presence of loops

The presence of loops in the parallel program can complicate the computation of precedence information as mentioned in section 1 with figure 2 as the illustrating example. For this example, the precedence algorithm described in section 3 (that ignores loop back edges) will compute (4) to be in $Prec(10)$ and (10) to be in $Prec(5)$. As mentioned in section 1, we would like to infer the following precedence information:

Every i-th instance of (4) is in *Prec* of every i-th instance of (10) and furthermore, every i-th instance of (10) is in *Prec* set of every (i+1)-th instance of (4).

Our approach to compute such precedence relation between instances of nodes in the PFG is to use additional information such as *synchronization distance* and distance information on loop back edges. The distance information on loop back edges is 1 for each loop [3] and since we use sequence counters, the distance information on synchronization edges representing sequence synchronization is 0.

---

[3] We will have a vector of distances to handle nested loops.

Once we have this information along with the *static* precedence information between nodes in the PFG (computed using the algorithm in section 3), we can
easily derive the precedence information between instances of different nodes in
the PFG.

We are working on the detailed algorithm and will present the complete
algorithm in a later paper. We also believe that this approach can be extended
to handle event arrays and parallel loops.

5 Conclusions

The intent of this work is to compute synchronization precedence information
suitable for compiler analysis of explicitly parallel programs.

We have shown an algorithm to efficiently compute precedence information
for explicitly parallel programs. Previous algorithms had $O(n^3)$ complexity. Although our algorithm also has an $O(n^3)$ worst case complexity, it exhibits $O(n^2)$
complexity for practical programs because it directly examines synchronization
operators. In a later paper, we will extend this method to programs with loops,
using the notion of dependence vectors.

We have implemented this algorithm in the SETL programming language,
and used it to compute precedence information for example programs. We have
also implemented the dataflow framework presented in [5], and compared the
results of the two algorithms. For all examples we have considered, they produce
identical precedence information.

References

1. A. V. Aho, R. Sethi, and J. D. Ullman. *Compilers: Principles, Techniques, and Tools*. Addison-Wesley, Reading, MA, 1986.
2. Vasanth Balasundaram and Ken Kennedy. Compile-time detection of race condi-
   tions in a parallel program. In *Proc. 3rd International Conference on Supercomputing*, pages 175–185, June 1989.
3. Per Brinch Hansen. *Operating Systems Principles*, pages 57–59. Automatic Computation. Prentice-Hall, 1973.
4. G. Bristow, C. Drey, B. Edwards, and W. Riddle. Anomaly detection in concurrent programs. In *Fourth Intl. Conf. on Software Eng.*, pages 265–273, 1979.
5. D. Callahan and J. Subhlok. Static Analysis of low-level synchronisation. In *Proc.
   of the ACM SIGPLAN and SIGOPS Workshop on Parallel and Distributed Debugging* [14], pages 100–111.
6. David Callahan, Ken Kennedy, and Jaspal Subhlok. Analysis of event synchronisation in a parallel programming tool. In *Second ACM SIGPLAN Symposium
   on Principles and Practice of Parallel Programming* [15], pages 21–30.
7. Anne Dinning and Edith Schonberg. An empirical comparison of monitoring algorithms for access anomaly detection. In *Second ACM SIGPLAN Symposium on
   Principles and Practice of Parallel Programming* [15], pages 1–10.
8. Perry Emrath, Sanjoy Ghosh, and David A. Padua. Event synchronisation analysis
   for debugging parallel programs. In *Proc. Supercomputing 89*, pages 580–588, Reno,
   NV, November 1989. IEEE Computer Society Press.

9. Perry Emrath and David Padua. Automatic detection of nondeterminacy in parallel programs. In PDD88 [14], pages 89–99.

10. Dirk Grunwald and Harini Srinivasan. Data flow equations for explicitly parallel programs. In *Conf. Record 4th ACM Symp. Principles and Practices of Parallel Programming*, San Diego, California, May 1993.

11. IBM Corporation, Kingston, NY. *Parallel FORTRAN Language and Library Reference*, 1988.

12. Robert Netzer. *Race Condition Detection for Debugging of Shared-Memory Parallel Programs*. PhD thesis, University of Wisconsin - Madison, 1991.

13. Parallel Computing Forum. PCF Parallel FORTRAN Extensions. *FORTRAN Forum*, 10(3), September 1991. (special issue).

14. *Proc. of the ACM SIGPLAN and SIGOPS Workshop on Parallel and Distributed Debugging*, Madison, WA, May 1988.

15. *Second ACM SIGPLAN Symposium on Principles and Practice of Parallel Programming*, Seattle, Washington, March 1990. ACM Press.

Trace Size vs Parallelism in Trace-and-Replay Debugging of Shared-Memory Programs

Robert H. B. Netzer
rn@cs.brown.edu

Dept. of Computer Science
Brown University
Box 1910
Providence, RI 02912

Abstract

Execution replay is a debugging strategy where a program is run repeatedly on an input that manifests bugs. Replaying nondeterministic parallel programs requires special tools; otherwise, successive runs (on the same input) can differ, making bugs impossible to track. These tools must trace an execution so it can be replayed. We present improvements over our past work on an *adaptive* tracing strategy for shared-memory programs. Our past approach makes run-time tracing decisions by detecting and tracing exactly the non-transitive dynamic data dependences among the execution's shared data. Tracing the non-transitive dependences provides sufficient information for a replay. In this paper we show that tracing exactly these dependences is not necessary. Instead, we present two algorithms that introduce and trace *artificial* dependences among some events that are actually independent. If no data dependence exists between two memory references during execution, we are free to artificially force them to execute in a specific order during replay. Artificial dependences reduce trace size, but introduce additional event orderings that have the potential of reducing the replay's parallelism. We present one algorithm that always adds dependences guaranteed not to be on the critical path (which do not slow replay). Another algorithm adds as many dependences as possible, slowing replay but reducing trace size further. Experiments show that we can improve the already high trace reduction of our past technique by up to two more orders of magnitude, without slowing replay. Our new techniques usually trace only 0.00025–0.2% of the shared-memory references, a 3–6 order of magnitude reduction over past approaches that trace every access.

This research was partly supported by ONR Contract N00014-91-J-4052 (ARPA Order 8225) and NSF grant CCR-9309311.

1. Introduction

Cyclic debugging is a powerful strategy. If an execution can be reproduced over and over, enough information can eventually be collected to understand its bugs. However, because shared-memory parallel programs can be nondeterministic, cyclic debugging requires special tools — bugs cannot always be reproduced by a simple re-execution. By tracing the order in which each process references shared memory relative to others, the execution can be replayed by forcing exactly the same dependences to occur during a re-execution. This tracing problem can be viewed as recording enough information to construct a graph that represents the execution's dynamic shared-data dependences. Our past work shows that only the dependences that comprise the graph's transitive reduction need be traced (since it shows the dependences of the original graph), and that we can trace only these dependences with a type of on-the-fly race detection[6]. Our experiments showed that only $0.01 - 2\%$ of the shared-memory references often need be traced. Although this approach traces the minimal information required to exactly reproduce the dependences, *exact* reproduction is unnecessary. If there is no dependence between two references during execution, we are free to decide at run-time that an *artificial* dependence between them should be introduced during replay. Since the events are actually independent, the order in which they execute does not matter, so the artificial dependence does not affect the replay's correctness. The advantage of an artificial dependence is that, if carefully placed, it can reduce the size of the graph's transitive reduction and thus the number of references that are traced. In this paper we explore how artificial dependences can be added by an adaptive tracing strategy to further reduce the size of the trace required for replay. We present an algorithm that achieves up to two orders of magnitude additional trace reduction over our past work, resulting in a $3 - 6$ order of magnitude reduction over past techniques that trace every reference.

Our original adaptive tracing algorithm works by tracking how the dynamic data dependence graph develops during execution. The algorithm uses on-the-fly race detection to identify and trace the non-transitive edges in the graph; transitive edges are not part of the transitive reduction and can be ignored. At each shared-memory reference b, all events a that recently accessed the same location are looked up from a table and checked to see whether the dependences from them are transitive. This determination is made by incrementally maintaining a representation of the graph on-line. If a path from a to b already exists in the graph, the dependence is transitive and can be ignored. Otherwise, if no path currently exists, the dependence is traced and an edge is added to the graph to reflect the new dependence.

Our main results in this paper are two modifications to this algorithm that add edges representing artificial instead of actual dependences. An artificial dependence is a dependence that the algorithm records as existing, but it is between references that are actually independent. Artificial dependences might result in fewer non-transitive edges, reducing the number of dependences traced. The drawback is that they introduce orderings that may not have originally occurred, possibly forcing some events to wait during replay for events they did not originally wait for during execution. These orderings can slow replay by reducing the amount of parallelism achievable. Our two algorithms consider this trace-size *vs* replay-parallelism trade-off. Our first algorithm always guarantees that dependences are added that do not slow replay; our second algorithm attempts to add as many as possible, regardless of the replay slowdown. We also prove that adding artificial dependences to obtain a minimal trace is an NP-hard problem; these two algorithms are heuristics.

Our first algorithm adds artificial dependences that are guaranteed to never be on the critical path, and thus will not slow replay. When a non-transitive dependence from a to b is detected, our modified algorithm adds an edge from the current event executing in a's process to b (instead of from a to b). This edge is artificial because its tail is not connected to a but is further down in a's process. However, since the tail is placed at the currently executing event in a's process, the dependence will not introduce event orderings not already present in the execution. As a result of the edge, some future dependences that the original algorithm would normally trace are rendered redundant and thus not traced. An advantage of this algorithm is that it requires less space than our original algorithm and traces much less. Experiments show that it usually traces only $0.00025 - 0.2\%$ of the shared-memory references.

Our second result is a further modification that attempts to add as many artificial dependences as possible, whether or not they are on the critical path. This algorithm shows how much the trace size can be reduced if we are willing to tradeoff replay speed. When a non-transitive dependence from a to b is located, instead of immediately adding and tracing an artificial dependence, the algorithm delays the trace as long as possible, adding an artificial dependence to b from as far down in a's process as possible. At some point a dependence will exist from b's process back to a's, below which this artificial dependence cannot be placed (otherwise, a cycle would be introduced into the graph). When such a return dependence is finally found, the artificial dependence is finally added. This approach forces as many events in a's process as possible to be ordered before b. Experiments show that trace size is reduced modestly over our first algorithm (up to an additional 10%). These results suggest that our first algorithm performs well, reducing traces substantially without slowing replay.

In Section 2 we discuss past trace-and-replay work and illustrate how adding artificial dependences can reduce trace size. Section 3 outlines our model, used in Section 4 to formally define the tracing problem. Section 5 overviews our past adaptive tracing algorithm that exactly reproduces the dependences, and Sections 6 and 7 present two new algorithms that instead trace artificial dependences. In Section 8 we present experimental results. This work is part of our larger effort of developing adaptive tracing strategies[7, 5, 10, 6].

2. Related Work and Motivation

Replaying an execution of a shared-memory parallel program requires information about how its processes interacted during that execution. All past solutions either trace every shared-memory access or assume the program is race free. Our earlier work avoids tracing every reference, but traces more than absolutely necessary since it attempts to exactly reproduce the execution's data dependences. Below we outline how these past schemes work and illustrate that trace size can be reduced by adding artificial dependences.

Past replay schemes trace the *order* in which processes interact[4, 1]. Each process records the order in which operations are performed on shared objects (Leblanc and Mellor-Crummey's *Instant Replay*)[4], or the order in which synchronization operations are performed (Carver and Tai's SYN-sequence trace)[9]. Another approach is to trace the *data* read from every shared-memory location[8], but too much is traced to be practical (Pan and Linton[8] report a trace of 1 megabyte/sec per process on a VAX 11/780). Even though no values are traced, tracing only the order is sufficient to replay from the execution's start. By forcing a re-execution to access shared objects in the same order, the original data will be recomputed. To be efficient, these schemes trace at a coarse level by assuming the program contains a correct mechanism for coordinating coarse-grain operations on shared objects, and instruments this mechanism to record the order in which these operations are performed. This assumption is reasonable if all interprocess communication is through structured primitives (e.g., message-passing libraries) that encapsulate all manipulation of shared data structures, or if the program is race-free. However, when debugging, this assumption is tenuous and in the worst case these techniques fail. In this case, to be correct the approach of tracing process interactions reduces to tracing the relative order of individual shared-memory references, and the resulting overhead could be prohibitive.

Although tracing every shared-memory reference is sufficient for replay, it is not necessary; only a subset of the accesses actually need be traced. Figure 1 shows an example program execution containing two processes (the variables "Q" and "head" are shared). The first process inserts data into a shared queue and increments the head pointer. After these operations are finished, the second process reads the head pointer and queue (if there were synchronization between the two processes, it would be treated as additional shared-memory references). Figure 1a shows a graph representing the dynamic shared-data dependences exhibited by this execution (a shared-data dependence exists between references a and b iff a accesses a shared location that b later accesses, and a or b modifies the location). A trace of every process interaction would generate one trace record for each dependence, indicating the order in which the variables are accessed. From this trace a re-execution can be forced to exhibit exactly the same data dependences, and indeed *reproducing* these dependences is necessary for correct replay.

However, *tracing* every dependence is unnecessary to record enough information to reproduce the dependences. In an earlier paper we presented a technique that traces only what is necessary to exactly reproduce the dependences. Figure 1b shows the dependences' transitive reduction, which is all that is necessary. The transitive reduction of a directed graph is a (unique) graph with all edges otherwise

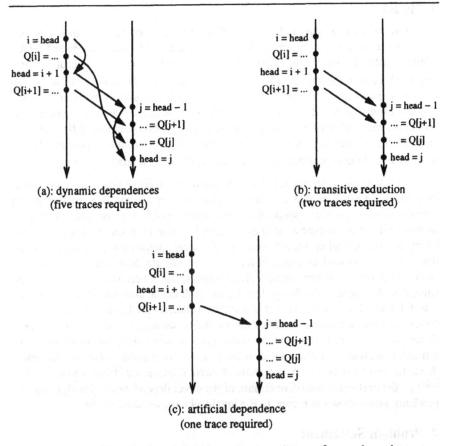

(a): dynamic dependences
(five traces required)

(b): transitive reduction
(two traces required)

(c): artificial dependence
(one trace required)

Figure 1. (a) dynamic shared-data dependences and trace of every dependence, (b) transitive reduction and minimal trace that exactly preserves the dependences, (c) transitive reduction after adding artificial dependence.

connected by a path omitted. However, as discussed earlier, the dependences need not be *exactly* reproduced. Artificial dependences can be introduced between independent events without affecting correctness. Figure 1c shows an artificial dependence that renders the two dependences in the transitive reduction redundant — only the artificial dependence then need be traced. By forcing this artificial dependence during replay, the other two (actual) dependences will be preserved by transitivity. In general, carefully placing artificial dependences can reduce the number of references requiring tracing. The drawback is that they introduce orderings that may not have originally occurred, slowing replay by reducing the amount of parallelism achievable. However, if "Q[i+1]=..." happened to have executed before "j=head-1" during execution anyway, the artificial dependence will not slow replay.

3. Model

Our model is a notation for representing program executions. A *program execution* is a triple, $P = \langle E, \xrightarrow{T}, \xrightarrow{D} \rangle$, where E is a finite set of *events* and $\xrightarrow{T}$ and $\xrightarrow{D}$ are relations defined over E. To reason about replay, we always view executions at a low level as a collection of individual shared-memory references[1]. We define an *event* to represent the execution of a read or write to a shared location, and we say that two events *conflict* if they both access the same location that at least one writes. We do not view references that comprise synchronization operations differently, but view all shared memory references uniformly. We also assume a fixed number of processes exist during execution, and denote the ith event in process p as $e_{p,i}$.

The *temporal ordering* relation, $\xrightarrow{T}$, shows the relative order in which events execute: $a \xrightarrow{T} b$ means that a executes before b. We assume that the underlying memory system provides sequential consistency, which ensures that all shared-memory references appear as if they execute in some total order. Since we view events as the individual shared-memory references, sequential consistency means that $\xrightarrow{T}$ can be viewed as a total order. The *shared-data dependence* relation, $\xrightarrow{D}$, shows when one event can causally affect another, either because of a direct or transitive data dependence involving shared data. A direct shared-data dependence from a to b (denoted $a \xrightarrow{DD} b$) exists if a accesses a shared variable that b later accesses (where at least one access modifies the variable); we also say that a direct dependence exists if a precedes b in the same process, since data can in general flow through non-shared variables local to the process. A transitive shared-data dependence ($a \xrightarrow{D} b$) exists if there is a chain of direct dependences from a to b; $\xrightarrow{D} = (\xrightarrow{DD})^+$, the irreflexive transitive closure of the direct dependences. The dynamic dependence graph shown in Figure 1a is a graphical representation of $\xrightarrow{D}$.

4. Problem Statement

Section 2 illustrated that tracing each shared-data dependence provides sufficient information for replay but is not necessary. In this section we formally define what is sufficient for correct replay, and prove that tracing only what is necessary is an NP-hard problem. In later sections we present heuristic algorithms that trace only a fraction of the dependences.

To support trace and replay, enough information must be traced during the initial execution to ensure that a replay on the same input is always identical. We consider a replay identical if it exhibits the execution's shared-data dependences (although it may exhibit other dependences as well). As discussed in Section 2, by forcing replay to exhibit the same shared-data dependences as the initial execution,

---

[1]In past work we called such a low-level view a *single-access* view, denoted as $P = \langle E, \xrightarrow{Ts}, \xrightarrow{Ds} \rangle$. In this paper we omit the "S" subscripts for brevity, but always implicitly assume a single-access view.

the same execution will result[2]. Although we could exactly reproduce the dependences, it is sufficient for correct replay to ensure that any dependence between two events during execution is preserved during replay[3].

Definition 1

Given two program executions, $P = \langle E, \xrightarrow{I}, \xrightarrow{D} \rangle$ and $P' = \langle E', \xrightarrow{I'}, \xrightarrow{D'} \rangle$, P' is a *sufficient replay* of P iff

(1) $E' = E$, and
(2) for all $a, b \in E$, $a \xrightarrow{D} b \Rightarrow a \xrightarrow{D'} b$.

The dependences used for the sufficient replay, $\xrightarrow{D'}$, are allowed to force an ordering among memory references between which no dependence existed during execution. These cases (where $a \xrightarrow{D'} b$ but $a \xrightarrow{D} \not\!\!\to b$) are exactly the artificial dependences.

Our goal is to trace enough information about the execution for a sufficient replay. In past work, we proved that tracing the dependences that make up the transitive reduction of $\xrightarrow{D}$ was necessary and sufficient for exactly reproducing the dependences[6]. In this paper, we only want to trace just enough to obtain a sufficient replay, by possibly tracing some artificial dependences in place of actual dependences, if they result in smaller traces. However, computing where to add artificial dependences to obtain a minimal trace is an NP-hard problem.

Theorem 1

Given a program execution, $P = \langle E, \xrightarrow{I}, \xrightarrow{D} \rangle$, it is NP-hard to compute the relation $\xrightarrow{D'}$ such that

(1) $\xrightarrow{D'}$ has the minimal number of inter-process dependences, and
(2) for all $a, b \in E$, $a \xrightarrow{D} b \Rightarrow a \xrightarrow{D'} b$ (i.e., $\xrightarrow{D'}$ can be used for a sufficient replay of P).

We will present two heuristic algorithms that add artificial dependences to attempt to cover as many actual dependences as possible, thereby reducing the total number of dependences that must be traced.

5. Original Tracing Algorithm

In this section we briefly outline our original tracing algorithm[6]. This algorithm dynamically locates and traces exactly the shared-memory references that comprise the non-transitive dependences (dependences in the transitive reduction of

---

[2] All replay schemes also require interactions with the external environment to be reproduced, and we do not discuss this issue here.

[3] For debugging, replays that do not preserve the dependences but still cause the same events to execute may be useful (e.g., if we replay an execution that contains only writes to shared memory, it may not matter in what order we re-execute those writes). Investigating such replays is left to future work.

$\overset{D}{\rightarrow}$, such as the inter-process edges in Figure 1b)[4]. In the next two sections we present two modifications of this algorithm that locate the same (actual) dependences, but then add and trace artificial dependences.

Figure 2 outlines a simplified version of our algorithm which is based on a previous on-the-fly data race detection algorithm[2] suitably modified to locate non-transitive dependences. Although the full algorithm contains features to keep time and space overhead low[6], Figure 2 shows the essence of the algorithm. The algorithm works by dynamically maintaining a graph (like the ones in Figure 1) that tracks the shared-data dependences which occur during execution. At each shared-memory reference, e, the algorithm first identifies the most recent event in each process on which e is data dependent (i.e., events x such that $x \overset{D}{\rightarrow} e$). The graph is then checked to determine if any of these dependences represent a transitive edge. A transitive dependence edge can be ignored; a non-transitive dependence is traced (and the graph is updated to reflect the new edge).

To identify the events on which a reference is data dependent, we maintain an *access history*[2] for each shared variable S. An access history is a list of events, one per process, that most recently accessed S. Events are identified by <process #, serial #> pairs, and each process maintains a local counter with which it assigns serial numbers to its events. The access history consists of the *writer*, showing the last event that wrote S, and the *readSet*, showing the last event in each process that read S. Because only the last read event in each process is remembered, the history requires $O(p)$ space (where p is the number of processes). In addition, readers on which the writer or other readers are data dependent also need not be remembered (since they can never form non-transitive dependences).

```
 1: /* Check for non-transitive dependences to e */
 2: lookup S's readSet, readTs, writer, and writeTs;
 3: for all events, h, in readSet and writer
 4:     if h conflicts with e and h is unordered with e
 5:         trace that a non-transitive dependence exists between h and e;
 6:         /* update this process' timestamp to indicate the new edge from h to e */
 7:         update ts by a component-wise max with readTs if h is a read or
 8:             writeTs if h is a write;
 9: /* Update access history */
10: remove from S's access history all events ordered before e (those with a path to e);
11: add e to the access history;
```

Figure 2. Original algorithm, invoked after each event e that accesses shared variable S

---

[4]In past work we called such references *frontier races*[6].

To dynamically track the dependence graph, each process maintains a *vector timestamp*, a vector (of length p) of event serial numbers. Timestamps are a standard way of dynamically tracking causality by encoding the current state of the dependence graph[3]. The timestamp for a process q has an entry for every other process, and the ith entry contains the serial number of the latest event in process i from which a path to q currently exists. The timestamp can be viewed as a frontier (or cut) that divides the execution in half; all events above the frontier have paths to q, and all events below do not. Timestamps allow a constant-time determination of whether a dependence is transitive. If process q is about to perform an event e, and a dependence exists from an event x in process i (i.e., $x \xrightarrow{D} e$), then that dependence is transitive if x's serial number is less than or equal to the ith entry of e's timestamp.

The algorithm performs these checks after every event e that accesses a shared variable S to determine if any events in S's access history form non-transitive dependences with e. An event h forms a non-transitive dependence if (1) h conflicts with e, and (2) h is *unordered* with e: no path from h to e in the dependence graph yet exists (determined by checking the process' timestamp as described above). In this case, an edge from h to e has been found (because they data conflict), and no path previously connected them (because they are unordered), so the new edge is non-transitive and is thus traced. The process' timestamp (ts) is then updated to indicate the new edge from h to e, reflecting that all paths to h are now also paths to e. This update requires knowing h's timestamp when h executed. So this information is available when e is finally reached, in the access history we store the *writer*'s timestamp ($writeTs$), and a single timestamp for the *readSet* (denoted *readTs*). To add the edge, we compute the component-wise maximum with these timestamps (line 7). After the algorithm finishes, the timestamp shows a frontier above which are all events with a shared-data dependence to e.

6. Adding Dependences without Increasing the Critical Path

We next present a modification (shown in Figure 3) to our original algorithm that adds artificial dependences to reduce trace size, but ensures they are never on the critical path (and will thus not slow replay), and uses less space than our original algorithm. When a non-transitive dependence is detected from h to e, instead of updating the timestamps to indicate an edge from h to e, we add an artificial dependence from the event *currently* executing in h's process to e. For example, Figure 4a shows two non-transitive dependences detected by the original algorithm. After detecting the first dependence (from "head=i+1" to "j=head-1"), the original algorithm updates timestamps to reflect that an edge exists between these two events. Thus, when the second dependence is detected, it is recognized as non-transitive (and traced). Figure 4b shows the artificial dependence our modified algorithm adds instead, formed by moving the tail of the actual dependence down to P1's currently executing event (the one executing while the dependence involving "j=head-1" is being detected). This edge is added by updating P2's timestamp from P1's current timestamp, instead of from the timestamp P1 had when "head=i+1" executed.

```
1:  /* Check for non-transitive dependences to e */
2:  lookup S's readSet and writer;
3:  for all events, h, in readSet and writer
4:      if h conflicts with e and h is unordered with e
5:          trace an artificial dependence from h's currently executing event to e;
6:          /* update this process' timestamp to indicate an artificial edge */
7:          /* from the current event in h's process to e (instead of from h to e) */
8:          update ts by a component-wise max with the current ts of h's process;
9:  /* Update access history */
10: remove from S's access history all events ordered before e (those with a path to e);
11: add e to the access history;
```

Figure 3. Modified tracing algorithm, invoked after each event e that accesses shared variable S. The artificial dependences added do not increase the critical path.

Creating this artificial dependence has several advantages. First, some events below "head=i+1" in P1 are no longer unordered with events below "j=head-1" in P2. Thus, when the second dependence is detected (from "Q[i+1]=..." to "...=Q[j+1]") it is recognized as a transitive edge and is *not* traced — the artificial edge rendered it redundant. The experimental results discussed in Section 8 show that many dependences can be rendered redundant, substantially reducing what needs to be traced. Second, because the artificial edge is drawn from the current execution point in P1, it introduces no orderings not already present in the execution (and therefore does not increase the critical path). Thus, assuming that replay exhibits the same relative timing among events, the artificial dependence will not force any event during replay to wait for an event it did not originally wait for during execution. Finally, because the timestamps are updated from the current timestamps of other processes, timestamps of the events in the access history (*readTs* and *writeTs* in Figure 2) need not be stored. That is, the location of the tail of an artificial dependence is determined by which event is currently executing in another process, instead of which event had executed in the past (the one that caused the dependence). This reduced space requirement is desirable since the space overhead of storing *readTs* and *writeTs* is a drawback of our original algorithm.

7. Adding Dependences on the Critical Path

We now present an idea for a second modification to our original algorithm. This idea is to add artificial dependences as above, but push the tail of each artificial dependence down as far as possible (instead of drawing it from the currently executing event in another process). This modification itself is not necessarily intended to be practical, so we omit discussing its implementation details. It allows us to see how much additional trace reduction can be obtained if we are willing to introduce artificial dependences that would slow replay. By comparing its performance to our

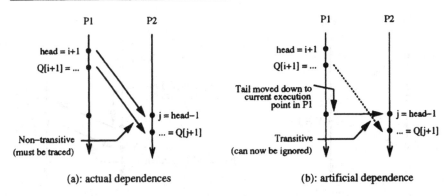

(a): actual dependences   (b): artificial dependence

Figure 4. **(a) actual dependence edges added by original algorithm,
(b) artificial dependence edge added by modified algorithm, created by moving
the actual edge's tail down, rendering the other edge redundant**

first modification, we can assess how good the first modification is. In the next section we show that the two approaches perform about the same; the first modification finds most of the opportunities for trace reduction.

As shown in Figure 5, we can extend the earlier approach by pushing the tail of an artificial dependence down in P1 as far as possible. Because the resulting graph must remain acyclic, the edge's tail can only be pushed down to just above the point at which a dependence exists from P2 back to P1 (a "blocking" dependence). Because the tail of each edge is pushed further down in P1 than in the first modification, more event orderings are introduced. More dependences that would otherwise be non-transitive become transitive, so fewer things are traced. However, the orderings force events during replay to wait for events not waited for during the original execution, reducing the amount of parallelism during replay. The next section shows that this modification performs only marginally better than our first modification. Thus, in practice, replay need not be slowed to achieve small traces.

8. Performance Measurements

To test the effectiveness of our tracing algorithms, we analyzed executions of shared-memory parallel programs on the Sequent Symmetry multiprocessor. To compare our original algorithm with the two modifications, we simulated them from a complete address trace of each execution, instead of running them on-line (otherwise, the programs' nondeterminacy would cause multiple runs to differ). Three pro-

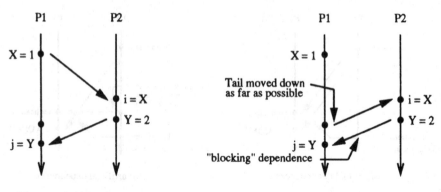

(a): actual dependences   (b): artificial dependence

**Figure 5. (a) actual dependence edges added by original algorithm,
(b) artificial dependence edge created by moving the actual edge's tail down
as far as possible, up to a blocking dependence.**

grams are from Stanford's Splash suite; others are from colleagues[5]. Each was run on small inputs using two processors. Table 1 shows the total number of shared-memory references (which is the number of trace records previous schemes emit) and the fraction of those references our original algorithm traced. Usually only $0.02 - 2\%$ of the references were traced, already a substantial reduction over techniques which trace every reference. In half of the programs, our two modifications reduced the trace by an additional $1 - 2$ orders of magnitude, resulting in traces of only $0.00025 - 0.2\%$ of the references. In one program (*mtxmult*) the reduction was three orders of magnitude. These programs shared data in a regular way, and adding artificial dependences caused most of the dependences to become redundant. Interestingly, our second modification did not substantially improve these reductions; pushing the tail of each artificial dependences down as far as possible did not introduce enough additional orderings to significantly reduce trace size. These results suggest that our first modification is effective, achieving substantial trace reductions with artificial dependences that will not slow replay.

The large reductions achieved by our original algorithm are caused by the small number of shared writes in the programs, making most dependences transitive. Because good program performance on shared-memory machines requires limiting the amount of data sharing (programs that frequently share data run slowly), we expect these results to be typical. The dramatic additional reductions achieved by our modified algorithms were caused by variable access patterns like those shown in Fig-

---

[5]Not all Splash codes were run because insufficient disk space was available to store the exhaustive address traces. This limitation illustrates the need for adaptive tracing strategies.

Program	# of references	# of traces		
		Orig. algorithm	Artificial dependences not on critical path	Artificial dependences on critical path
barnes	175671	461 (0.26%)	171 (0.097%)	155 (0.088%)
gauss	162023	20806 (13%)	197 (0.12%)	150 (0.093%)
gcd	478675	3764 (0.8%)	1728 (0.36%)	1575 (0.33%)
join	35672	61 (0.2%)	36 (0.10%)	35 (0.098%)
locus	1932827	11257 (0.6%)	1282 (0.066%)	1203 (0.062%)
mp3d	127041	625 (0.5%)	87 (0.068%)	87 (0.068%)
mtxmult	400209	2453 (0.6%)	1 (0.00025%)	1 (0.00025%)
pnet	104298	2570 (2.5%)	2519 (2.4%)	2504 (2.4%)
ptycho	112372	102 (0.09%)	5 (0.0045%)	5 (0.0045%)
quicksort	11040	22 (0.2%)	22 (0.2%)	22 (0.2%)
shpath	3760213	8973 (0.2%)	8072 (0.2%)	6940 (0.2%)
sort	14846	3 (0.02%)	1 (0.0067%)	1 (0.0067%)

Table 1. Comparison of original and modified algorithms

ure 1. For example, in *mtxmult* (a simple matrix multiply), the program first initializes (with a single process) two arrays with random values, then forks off a second process. The two processes then read rows and columns of the arrays, performing the multiply. Many of the data dependences between the initialization and the multiply (which only reads the two initialized arrays) are "parallel", like the non-transitive dependences illustrated in Figure 1b. Thus, because they were non-transitive, they were traced by the original algorithm. However, when artificial dependences are added, the single dependence added just after the fork point renders all of these "parallel" dependences transitive — only one artificial dependence was traced, from the last event of the initialization phase (in process 1) to the first event of the multiply (in process 2). Half of the programs exhibited this type of data sharing, allowing our modified algorithms to achieve significant trace reductions. It is not completely clear why our second modification did not yield further reductions of significance. Enough blocking dependences (as illustrated in Figure 5) usually occurred to prevent the tail of each artificial dependence to be moved down very far, meaning that not very many additional orderings were being introduced (and thus not very many additional dependences were being rendered redundant).

Although we did not measure run-time overheads, we expect our algorithm to perform well. As discussed in more detail in another paper[6], a dependence need be checked only when the access is in a *different* process than the previous conflicting access to the same shared variable. This information can be stored as one additional entry to the access history. In 10 of the programs, only 2 – 20% of the references required such checks. In addition, one of the most time consuming parts of the check is the timestamp update after detecting a non-transitive dependence. Since these case are rare (as Table 1 shows), the common case is a simple check of the access history, which is on the order of a dozen assembly language instructions.

Table 1 reflects two-processor executions. The same relative improvements were achieved by our modifications on four- and 16-processor runs as well. As reported in our other paper[6], the trace reductions tend to reduce as the number of processors is increased. It is unclear whether this trend is an artifact of fixing the input size while increasing the number of processes. More experience is necessary to assess our algorithm's performance on large-scale programs. In any case, the relative cost of writing traces to disk is becoming so expensive that adaptive tracing should be an effective way of coping with the I/O bottleneck.

9. Conclusion

We have shown that an adaptive strategy can reduce the tracing overhead of trace-and-replay debugging by $3 - 6$ orders of magnitude over past techniques. Our first modification performs strictly better than our original algorithm, producing traces up to two orders of magnitude smaller and requiring less space. With such reduced traces, new tools that enter the realm of practicality should be feasible.

Future work includes more sophisticated algorithms for adding artificial dependences. Our modification uses a simple approach to guarantee that artificial dependences are not on the critical path. Better approaches might track the critical path on-line, possibly adding dependences that increase the critical path by at most a specified amount, allowing the user to specify the acceptable parallelism/trace-size tradeoff. Finally, real implementations are required to fully assess the tradeoffs.

Acknowledgements

We thank Ashim Garg and Shieu-Hong Lin for looking at the artificial dependence problem as part of a graduate seminar project. They initially proved the NP-hardness result (with a different reduction) and developed the initial ideas for adding as many artificial dependences as possible.

References

[1]   Richard H. Carver and Kuo-Chung Tai, "Reproducible Testing of Concurrent Programs Based on Shared Variables," *6th Intl. Conf. on Distributed Computing Systems*, pp. 428-432 Boston, MA, (May 1986).

[2]   Anne Dinning and Edith Schonberg, "An Empirical Comparison of Monitoring Algorithms for Access Anomaly Detection," *2nd ACM Symposium on Principles and Practice of Parallel Programming*, pp. 1-10 Seattle, WA, (March 1990).

[3]   C. J. Fidge, "Partial Orders for Parallel Debugging," *SIGPLAN/SIGOPS Workshop on Parallel and Distributed Debugging*, pp. 183-194 Madison, WI, (May 1988). Also appears in *SIGPLAN Notices* **24**(1) (January 1989).

[4]   Thomas J. LeBlanc and John M. Mellor-Crummey, "Debugging Parallel Programs with Instant Replay," *IEEE Trans. on Computers* **C-36**(4) pp. 471-482 (April 1987).

[5]   Robert H.B. Netzer and Barton P. Miller, "Optimal Tracing and Replay for Debugging Message-Passing Parallel Programs," *Supercomputing '92*, pp. 502-511 Minneapolis, MN, (November 1992).

[6]   Robert H.B. Netzer, "Optimal Tracing and Replay for Debugging Shared-Memory Parallel Programs," *ACM/ONR Workshop on Parallel and Distributed Debugging*, pp. 1-11 San Diego, CA, (May 1993).

[7]   Robert H.B. Netzer and Jian Xu, "Adaptive Message Logging for Incremental Replay of Message-Passing Programs," *To appear in IEEE Parallel and Distributed Technology*, (1994). Also appears in Supercomputing '93

[8]   Douglas Z. Pan and Mark A. Linton, "Supporting Reverse Execution of Parallel Programs," *SIGPLAN/SIGOPS Workshop on Parallel and Distributed Debugging*, pp. 124-129 Madison, WI, (May 1988). Also appears in *SIGPLAN Notices* **24**(1) (January 1989).

[9]   K. C. Tai, Richard H. Carver, and Evelyn E. Obaid, "Debugging Concurrent Ada Programs by Deterministic Execution," *IEEE Trans. on Software Engineering* **17**(1) pp. 45-63 (January 1991).

[10]   Jian Xu and Robert H.B. Netzer, "Adaptive Independent Checkpointing for Reducing Rollback Propagation," *IEEE Symp. on Parallel and Distributed Processing*, Dallas, TX, (Dec 1993).

Appendix. Proof of Theorem

Theorem 1

The minimal artificial dependence problem is NP-hard.

Proof. We use a reduction from the independent set problem, known to be NP-complete: given an undirected graph, $G = (V, E)$, does G have an independent set with k or more vertices? An independent set is a subset V' of the vertices such that no two edges in V' are connected by an edge in E. Given a graph, G, we reduce the problem of determining whether it has an independent set with k or more vertices to the problem of determining whether artificial dependences can be added to a program execution, P, so that it requires tracing K or fewer (non-transitive) dependences (where P and K are defined below).

From the graph G we construct P as follows. For every $v \in V$, P contains a two-process gadget, $gad(v)$, and two edges between $gad(a)$ and $gad(b)$ iff an edge exists between a and b in G (illustrated in Figure 6). The gadget for a node a is designed so that in isolation (with no edges to another gadget), an artificial dependence can be added from $a1$ to $a2$ that reduces the transitive reduction by one edge. The edges connecting two gadgets are designed so that such an artificial dependence can be added only to one of the gadgets (a cycle results if edges are added to both).

We claim G has an independent set of k or more vertices iff artificial dependences can be added to reduce P's transitive reduction k or more edges. To show the if part, assume that P can be augmented with artificial dependences that reduce its transitive reduction by k or more edges. Because of P's construction, the only opportunity for reducing the number of edges in its transitive reduction is by augmenting with an artificial edge from $a1$ to $a2$ in the gadget for some node a. Artificial edges between any other nodes in the gadget (or between nodes in different gadgets) will not reduce the transitive reduction's size. However, two gadgets, $gad(a)$ and $gad(b)$, cannot both have their size reduced iff a and b are connected in G. Thus, if there is some way to reduce the size of P by k or more, the k or more gadgets to which artificial dependences are added cannot be connected, and thus correspond to an independent set of size k or more. To show the only if part, assume that an independent set exists of size k or more. Since no two nodes in this set are connected, each of their corresponding gadgets can be augmented with an artificial dependence that reduces their transitive reduction by one edge. Since k or more such nodes exist, P's transitive reduction can be reduced by k or more. QED

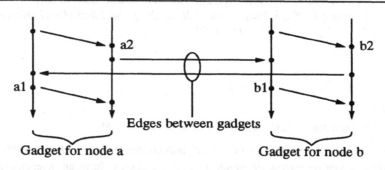

Edges between gadgets

Gadget for node a   Gadget for node b

Figure 6. Gadgets for two nodes, a and b, and connecting edges (that exist iff a and b are connected in G)

Parallel Program Graphs and their Classification

Vivek Sarkar   Barbara Simons

IBM Santa Teresa Laboratory, 555 Bailey Avenue, San Jose, CA 95141
({vivek_sarkar,simons}@vnet.ibm.com)

Abstract. We categorize and compare different representations of program dependence graphs, including the Control Flow Graph (CFG) which is a sequential representation lacking data dependences, the Program Dependence Graph (PDG) which is a parallel representation of a sequential program and is comprised of control and data dependences, and more generally, the Parallel Program Graph (PPG) which is a parallel representation of sequential and (inherently) parallel programs and is comprised of parallel control flow edges and synchronization edges. PPGs are classified according to their graphical structure and properties related to deadlock detection and serializability.

1   Introduction

The importance of optimizing compilers has increased dramatically with the development of multiprocessor computers. Writing correct and efficient parallel code is quite difficult at best; writing such software and making it portable currently is almost impossible. Intermediate forms are required both for optimization and portability. A natural intermediate form is the graph that represents the instructions of the program and the dependences that exist between them. This is the role played by the Parallel Program Graph (PPG). The Control Flow Graph (CFG), in turn, is required once portions of the PPG have been mapped onto individual processors. PPGs are a generalization of Program Dependence Graphs (PDGs), which have been shown to be useful for solving a variety of problems, including optimization [15], vectorization [7], code generation for VLIW machines [19], merging versions of programs [22], and automatic detection and management of parallelism [3, 33, 32]. PPGs are useful for determining the semantic equivalence of parallel programs [35, 10, 34], and also have applications to automatic code generation [25].

In section 2, we define PPGs as a more general intermediate representation of parallel programs than PDGs. PPGs contain *control* edges that represent parallel flow of control, and *synchronization* edges that impose ordering constraints on execution instances of PPG nodes. *MGOTO* nodes are used to create new threads of parallel control. Section 3 contains a few examples of PPGs to provide some intuition on how PPGs can be built in a compiler and how they execute at run-time. Section 4 characterizes PPGs based on the nature of their control edges and synchronization edges, and summarizes the classifications of PPGs according to the results reported in sections 5 and 6.

Unlike PDGs which can only represent the parallelism in a sequential program, PPGs can represent the parallelism in inherently parallel programs. Two important issues that are specific to PPGs are *deadlock* and *serializability*. A PPG's execution may deadlock if its synchronization edges are incorrectly specified i.e. if there is an execution sequence of PPG nodes containing a cycle. This is also one reason why PPGs are more general than PDGs. In section 5, we characterize the complexity of deadlock detection for different classes of PPGs. Serialization is the process of transforming a PPG into a semantically equivalent sequential CFG with neither node duplication nor creation of Boolean guards. It has already been shown that there exist PPGs that are not serializable [14, 38], which is another reason why PPGs are more general than PDGs. In section 6, we further study the serialization problem by characterizing the serializability of different classes of PPGs.

Finally, section 7 discusses related work, and section 8 contains the conclusions of this paper and an outline of possible directions for future work.

2 Definition of PPGs

2.1 Control Flow Graphs (CFGs)

We begin with the definition of a *control flow graph* as presented in [31, 11, 33]. It differs from the usual definition [1, 15] by the inclusion of a set of labels for edges and a mapping of node types. The label set $\{T, F, U\}$ is used to distinguish between conditional execution (labels T and F) and unconditional execution (label U).

Definition 1. A *control flow graph* $CFG = (N, E_{cf}, TYPE)$ is a rooted directed multigraph in which every node is reachable from the root. It consists of:

- N, a set of nodes. A CFG node represents an arbitrary sequential computation e.g. a basic block, a statement or an operation.
- $E_{cf} \subseteq N \times N \times \{T, F, U\}$, a set of *labelled* control flow edges.
- $TYPE$, a node type mapping. $TYPE(n)$ identifies the type of node n as one of the following values: $START, STOP, PREDICATE, COMPUTE$.

We assume that CFG contains two distinguished nodes of type $START$ and $STOP$ respectively, and that for any node N in CFG, there exist directed paths from $START$ to N and from N to $STOP$.

Each node in a CFG has at most two outgoing edges. A node with exactly two outgoing edges represents a conditional branch (predicate); in that case, the node has $TYPE = PREDICATE$ and we assume that the outgoing edges are distinguished by "T" *(true)* and "F" *(false)* labels[1]. If a node has $TYPE = COMPUTE$ then it has exactly one outgoing edge with label "U" *(unconditional)*.

□

---

[1] The restriction to at most two outgoing edges is made to simplify the discussion. All the results presented in this paper are applicable to control flow graphs with arbitrary out-degree e.g. when representing a computed GOTO statement in Fortran, or a switch statement in C. Note that CFG imposes no restriction on the in-degree of a node.

A *CFG* is a standard sequential representation of a program with no parallel constructs. A *CFG* is also the target for code generation from parallel to sequential code.

2.2 Program Dependence Graphs (PDGs)

The *Program Dependence Graph* (PDG) [15] is a standard representation of control and data dependences derived from a sequential program and its CFG. Like CFG nodes, a PDG node represents an arbitrary sequential computation e.g. a basic block, a statement, or an operation. An edge in a PDG represents a *control dependence* or a *data dependence*. PDGs reveal the inherent parallelism in a program written in a sequential programming language by removing artificial sequencing constraints from the program text.

Definition 2. A *Program Dependence Graph* $PDG = (N, E_{cd}, E_{dd}, TYPE)$ is a rooted directed multigraph in which every node is reachable from the root. It consists of [15]:

- N, a set of nodes.
- $E_{cd} \subseteq N \times N \times \{T, F, U\}$, a set of labelled *control dependence* edges.
  Edge $(a, b, L) \in E_{cd}$ identifies a control dependence from node a to node b with label L. This means that a must have $TYPE = PREDICATE$ or $TYPE = REGION$. If $TYPE = PREDICATE$ and if a's predicate value is evaluated to be L, then it causes an execution instance of b to be created. If $TYPE = REGION$, then an execution instance of b is always created [15, 33].
- $E_{dd} \subseteq N \times N \times Contexts$, a set of *data dependence* edges.
  Edge $(a, b, C) \in E_{dd}$ identifies a data dependence from node a to node b with context C. The context C identifies the pairs of execution instances of nodes a and b that must be synchronized. *Direction vectors* [40] and *distance vectors* [26] are common approaches to representing contexts of data dependences; the *gist* [30] and the *last-write tree* [27] are newer representations for data dependence contexts that provide more information. Context information can identify a data dependence as being *loop-independent* or *loop-carried* [4]. In the absence of any other information, the context of a data dependence edge in a PDG must at least be *plausible* [8] i.e. the execution instances participating in the data dependences must be consistent with the sequential ordering represented by the CFG from which the PDG is derived.
- *TYPE*, a node type mapping. $TYPE(n)$ identifies the type of node n as one of the following values: *START, PREDICATE, COMPUTE, REGION*.
  The *START* node and *PREDICATE* node types in a PDG are like the corresponding node types in a CFG. The *COMPUTE* node type is slightly different because it has no outgoing control edges in a PDG. By contrast, every node type except *STOP* is required to have at least one outgoing edge in a CFG. A node with $TYPE = REGION$ serves as a summary node for a

set of control dependence successors in a PDG. Region nodes are also useful for *factoring* sets of control dependence successors [15, 12].

□

2.3 Parallel Program Graphs (PPGs)

The *Parallel Program Graph* (PPG) is a general intermediate representation of parallel programs that includes PDGs and CFGs. Analogous to control dependence and data dependence edges in PDGs, PPGs contain *control* edges that represent parallel flow of control and *synchronization* edges that impose ordering constraints on execution instances of PPG nodes. PPGs also contain *MGOTO* nodes that are a generalization of *REGION* nodes in PDGs. What distinguishes PPGs from PDGs is the complete freedom in connecting PPG nodes with control and synchronization edges to span the full spectrum of sequential and parallel programs. Control edges in PPGs can be used to model program constructs that cannot be modelled by control dependence edges in PDGs e.g. PPGs can represent *non-serializable* parallel programs [37, 36, 34]. Synchronization edges in PPGs can be used to model program constructs that cannot be modelled with data dependence edges in PDGs e.g. a PPG may enforce a synchronization with distance vector (-1), from the "next" iteration of a loop to the "previous" iteration, as in (say) Haskell array constructors [24] or I-structures [5], while such data dependences are prohibited in PDGs because they are not plausible with reference to the sequential program from which the PDG was derived.

Definition 3. A *Parallel Program Graph* $PPG = (N, E_{cont}, E_{sync}, TYPE)$ is a rooted directed multigraph in which every node is reachable from the root using only *control* edges. It consists of [34]:

1. N, a set of nodes.
2. $E_{cont} \subseteq N \times N \times \{T, F, U\}$, a set of labelled *control* edges. Edge $(a, b, L) \in E_{cont}$ identifies a control edge from node a to node b with label L.
3. $E_{sync} \subseteq N \times N \times SynchronizationConditions$, a set of *synchronization* edges. Edge $(a, b, f) \in E_{sync}$ defines a synchronization from node a to node b with synchronization condition f.
4. $TYPE$, a node type mapping. $TYPE(n)$ identifies the type of node n as one of the following values: *START, PREDICATE, COMPUTE, MGOTO*.
   The *START* node and *PREDICATE* node types in a PPG are just like the corresponding node types in a CFG or a PDG. The *COMPUTE* node type is more general because a PPG compute node may either have an outgoing control edge as in a CFG or may have no outgoing control edges as in a PDG. A node with $TYPE = MGOTO$ is used as a construct for creating parallel threads of computation: a new thread is created for each successor of an *MGOTO* node. *MGOTO* nodes in PPGs are a generalization of *REGION* nodes in PDGs.

We distinguish between a PPG node and an *execution instance* of a PPG node (i.e., a dynamic instantiation of that node). Given an execution instance I_a of PPG node a, its *execution history*, $H(I_a)$, is defined as the sequence of PPG node and label values that caused execution instance I_a to occur. A PPG's execution begins with a single execution instance (I_{start}) of the *start* node, with $H(I_{start}) = <>$ (an empty sequence).

A *control* edge in E_{cont} is a triple of the form (a, b, L), which defines a transfer of control from node a to node b for branch label (or branch condition) L. The semantics of *control* edges is as follows. If $TYPE(a) = PREDICATE$, then consider an execution instance I_a of node a that evaluates node a's branch label to be L: if there exists an edge $(a, b, L) \in E_{cont}$, execution instance I_a creates a new execution instance I_b of node b (there can be at most one such successor node) and then terminates itself. The execution history of each I_b is simply $H(I_b) = H(I_a) \circ < a, L >$ (where $\circ$ is the sequence concatenation operator). If $TYPE(a) = MGOTO$, then let the set of outgoing control edges from node a with branch label L (which must be $= U$) be $\{(a, b_1, L), \ldots, (a, b_k, L)\}$. After completion, execution instance I_a creates a new execution instance (I_{b_i}) of each target node b_i and then terminates itself. The execution history of each I_{b_i} is simply $H(I_{b_i}) = H(I_a) \circ < a, L >$.

A *synchronization* edge in E_{sync} is a triple of the form (a, b, f), which defines a PPG edge from node a to node b with synchronization condition f. $f(H_1, H_2)$ is a computable Boolean function on execution histories. Given two execution instances I_a and I_b of nodes a and b, $f(H(I_a), H(I_b))$ returns *true* if and only if execution instance I_a must complete execution before execution instance I_b can be started. For theoretical reasons, it is useful to think of synchronization condition f as an arbitrary computable Boolean function; however, in practice, we will only be interested in simple definitions of f that can be stored in at most $O(|N|)$ space. Note that the synchronization condition depends only on execution histories, and not on any program data values. Also, due to the presence of synchronization edges, it is possible to construct PPGs that may deadlock. □

A PPG node represents an arbitrary sequential computation. The control edges of a PPG specify how execution instances of PPG nodes are created (unravelled), and the synchronization edges of a PPG specify how execution instances need to be synchronized. A formal definition of the execution semantics of *mgoto* edges and *synchronization* edges is given in [34].

We would like to have a definition for synchronization edges that corresponds to the notion of *loop-independent* data dependence edges in sequential programs [40]. If nodes a and x are in a loop in a sequential program and have a loop-independent data dependence between them, then whenever x is executed in an iteration of the loop, an instance of a also must be executed prior to x *in that same loop iteration*. However, if in some iteration of the loop x is not executed, say because of some conditional branch, then we don't care whether or not a is executed. This is the notion we are trying to capture with our definition of *control-independent*, below. First we need a couple of other definitions.

Consider an execution instance I_x of PPG node x with execution history $H(I_x) = < u_1, L_1, \ldots, u_i, \ldots, u_j, \ldots, u_k, L_k >$, $u_k = x$ (as defined in [34]). We define $nodeprefix(H(I_x), a)$ (the $nodeprefix$ of execution history $H(I_x)$ with respect to the PPG node a) as follows. If there is no occurrence of node a in $H(I_x)$, then $nodeprefix(H(I_x), a) = \perp$. If $a \neq x$, $nodeprefix(H(I_x), a) = < u_1, L_1, \ldots, u_i, L_i >, u_i = a, u_j \neq a, i < j \leq k$; if $a = x$, then $nodeprefix(H(I_x), a) = H(I_x) = < u_1, L_1, \ldots, u_i, \ldots, u_j, \ldots, u_k, L_k >$.

A *control path* in a PPG is a path that consists of only control edges. A node a is a *control ancestor* of node x if there exists an acyclic control path from *START* to x such that a is on that path.

A synchronization edge (x, y, f) is *control-independent* if a necessary (but not necessarily sufficient) condition for $f(H(I_a), H(I_b)) = true$ is that $nodeprefix(H(I_x), a) = nodeprefix(H(I_y), a)$ for all nodes a that are control ancestors of both x and y.

3 Examples of PPGs

In this section, we give a few examples of PPGs to provide some intuition on how PPGs can be built in a compiler and how they execute at run-time.

Figure 1 is an example of a PPG obtained from a thread-based parallel programming model that uses create and terminate operations. This PPG contains only control edges; it has no synchronization edges. The create operation in statement S2 is modeled by an *MGOTO* node with two successors: node S6, which is the target of the create operation, and node S3, which is the continuation of the parent thread. The terminate operation in statement S5 is modeled by making node S4 a leaf node i.e. a node with no outgoing control edges.

Figure 2 is another example of a PPG that contains only control edges and is obtained from a thread-based parallel programming model. This is an example of "unstructured" parallelism because of the goto S4 statements which cause node S4 to be executed twice when predicate S1 evaluates to true. The PPG in Figure 2 is also an example of a non-serializable PPG. Because node S4 can be executed twice, it is not possible to generate an equivalent sequential CFG for this PPG without duplicating code or inserting Boolean guards. With code duplication, this PPG can be made serializable by splitting node S4 into two copies, one for parent node S2 and one for parent node S3.

Figure 3 is an example of a PPG that represents a parallel sections construct [29], which is similar to the cobegin-coend construct [20]. This PPG contains both control edges and synchronization edges. The start of a parallel sections construct is modelled by an *MGOTO* node with three successors: node S1, which is the start of the first parallel section, node S2, which is the start of the second parallel section, and node S5, which is the continuation of the parent thread. The goto S0 statement at the bottom of the code fragment is simply modelled by a control edge that branches back to node S0.

PARALLEL THREADS EXAMPLE

S1: ...

S2: create S6

S3: ...

S4: ...

S5: terminate

S6: ...

....

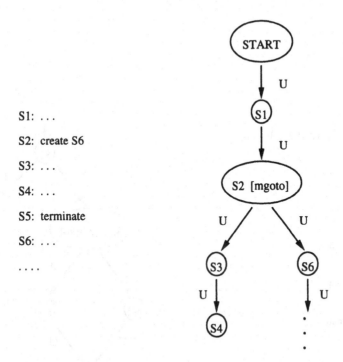

Fig. 1. Example of PPG with only control edges

The semantics of parallel sections requires a synchronization at the end sections statement. This is modelled by inserting a synchronization edge from node S2 to node S5 and another synchronization edge from node S4 to node S5. The synchronization condition f for the two synchronization edges is defined in Figure 3 as a simple function on the execution histories of execution instances I.S2, I.S4, I.S5 of nodes S2, S4, S5 respectively. For example, the synchronization condition for the edge from S2 to S5 is defined to be true if and only if $H(I.S2) = concat(H(I.S5), < S1, U >)$; this condition identifies the synchronization edge as being control-independent. In practice, a control-independent synchronization is implemented by simple semaphore operations without needing to examine the execution histories at run-time [18].

As an optimization, one may observe that the three-way branching at the $MGOTO$ node (S0) in Figure 3 can be replaced by two-way branching without any loss of parallelism. This is because node S5 has to wait for nodes S2 and S4 to complete before it can start execution. A more efficient PPG for this example can be obtained by deleting the control edge from node S0 to node S5, and then replacing the synchronization edge from node S2 to node S5

EXAMPLE OF UNSTRUCTURED PARALLELISM

S1: if ( ) mgoto S2, S3

S5: ...

. . . .

terminate

S2: ...
    goto S4

S3: ...
    goto S4

S4: ...
    terminate

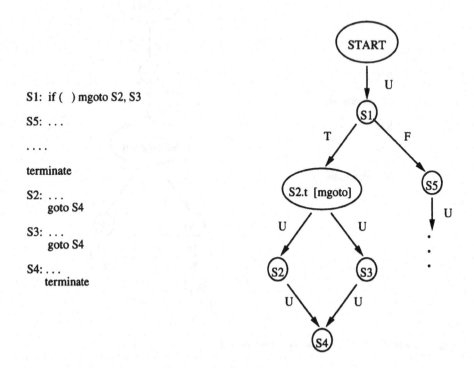

Fig. 2. Example of unstructured PPG with only control edges

by a control edge. This transformed PPG would contain the same amount of ideal parallelism as the original PPG but would create two threads instead of three, and would perform one synchronization instead of two, for a given instantiation of the parallel sections construct[2]. This idea is an extension of the *control sequencing* transformation used in the PTRAN system to replace a data synchronization by sequential control [13, 33].

Further, if the granularity of work being performed in the parallel sections is too little to justify creation of parallel threads, the PPG in Figure 3 can be transformed into a sequential CFG, which is a PPG with no *MGOTO* nodes and no synchronization edges (this transformation is possible because the PPG in Figure 3 is serializable). Therefore, we see that PPG framework can can support a wide range of parallelism from ideal parallelism to useful parallelism to no

---

[2] Note that if both synchronization edges coming into S5 were replaced by control edges, the resulting PPG would perform node S5 twice for a given instantiation of the parallel sections construct, which is incorrect.

EXAMPLE OF PARALLEL SECTIONS (COBEGIN–COEND)

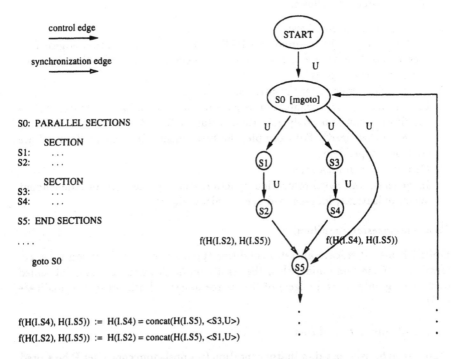

Fig. 3. Example of structured PPG with control and synchronization edges

parallelism. As future work, it would be interesting to extend existing algorithms for selecting useful parallelism from PDGs (e.g. [32]) to operate more generally on PPGs.

4 Classification of PPGs

4.1 Classification criteria

In this subsection, we characterize PPGs based on the nature of their control edges and synchronization edges.

Control edges. The control edges of PPGs can be *acyclic*, or they can have loops, which in turn can be *reducible* or *irreducible*. For reducibility, we extend the definition used for CFGs so that it is applicable to PPGs as well: a PPG is reducible if each strongly connected region of its control edges has a single entry node [2, 21, 1]; otherwise, a PPG is said to be irreducible. This classification of a PPG's control edges as acyclic/reducible/arbitrary is interesting because of the characterizations that can then be made. Note that each class is properly contained within the next, with irreducible PPGs being the most general case.

Synchronization edges. PPGs can also be classified by the nature of their synchronization edges as follows:

1. No synchronization edges:
   A CFG is a simple example of a PPG with no synchronization edges. Figures 1 and 2 in section 3 are some more examples of PPGs that have no synchronization edges.

2. control-independent synchronizations:
   In this case, all synchronization edges are assumed to have synchronization conditions that cause only execution instances from the same loop iteration to be synchronized[3]. For example, the two synchronizations in Figure 3 are control-independent.

3. General synchronizations:
   In general, the synchronization function can include control-independent synchronizations, loop-carried synchronizations, etc.

Predicate-ancestor condition.

Definition 4. Predicate-ancestor condition (pred-anc cond): If two control edges terminate in the same node, then the least common control ancestor (obtained by following only control edges) of the source nodes of both edges is a predicate node.

No-post-dominator condition.

Definition 5. No-post-dominator condition (no-post-dom cond): let P be a predicate and S a control descendant of P, then S does not post-dominate P if there is some path from P to a leaf node that excludes S. The no-post-dominator condition assumes that for every descendant S of predicate P, S does not post-dominate P.

4.2   Characterization of PPGs based on the Deadlock Detection Problem

Table 1 classifies PPGs according to how easy or hard it is to detect if a PPG in a given class can deadlock. A detailed discussion of these results is presented in section 5.

4.3   Characterization of PPGs based on Serializability

One of the primary distinctions between a CFG and a PDG or PPG is that the CFG is already serialized, while neither the PDG or the PPG is serialized. Table 2 classifies PPGs according to how easy or hard it is to detect if a PPG in a given class is serializable. A detailed discussion of these results is presented in Section 6. Note that serializability is a stronger condition than deadlock detection because a serializable program is guaranteed never to deadlock.

---

[3] We assume START and STOP are part of a dummy loop with one iteration.

Control edges	Sync. edges	Characterization
Arbitrary	None	PPGs in this class will never deadlock, because they have no synchronization edges (Lemma 6).
Acyclic	Acyclic (in conjunction with control edges)	PPGs in this class will never deadlock, because it is not possible for a cyclic wait to occur at run-time (Lemma 7).
Reducible	Control-independent, no synchronization back-edges	PPGs in this class will never deadlock (Lemma 8).
Acyclic, satisfies pred-anc and no-post-dominator conditions	control-independent	This is a special case of PPGs with acyclic control edges. There are known polynomial-time algorithms that can determine whether such a PPG is serializable. If it is serializable, then it is guaranteed to not deadlock.
Acyclic	control-independent	The problem of determining an assignment of truth values to the predicates that causes the PPG to deadlock is shown to be NP-hard. It is easy to specify an exponential-time algorithm for solving the problem by enumerating all possible assignments of truth values to predicates.
Arbitrary	Arbitrary	The problem of detecting deadlock in arbitrary PPGs is a very hard problem. We conjecture that it is undecidable in general.

Table 1. Characterization of deadlock detection problem for PPGs

5 Deadlock detection

The introduction of synchronization edges makes deadlock possible. Deadlock occurs if there is a cyclic wait, so that every node in the cycle is waiting for one of the other nodes in the cycle to proceed. Formally, we say that a PPG *deadlocks* if there is an execution instance (dynamic instantiation) v_i of a node v, that instance is never executed (scheduled), no other new execution instances are created, and no other node is executed. We refer to v as a *deadlocking node* and v_i as a *deadlocking instance*; there might be multiple deadlocking nodes and instances. Note that our definition of deadlock implies that there is no infinite loop. The motivation for this definition is to distinguish between deadlock and non-termination.

Given a synchronization edge (u, v, f) and an execution instance v_i of v, we say that (u, v, f) is *irrelevant* for v_i if for all execution instances u_j of u that are created, $f(H(I_{u_j}), H(i_{v_i})) = false$, and for all u_j such that $f(H(I_{u_j}), H(i_{v_i})) = true$, no execution instance of u_j can ever be created. (u, v, f) is *relevant* for v_i if it is not irrelevant for v_i.

Control edges	Sync. edges	Characterisation
Reducible, satisfy pred-anc and no-post-dominator conditions	control-independent	Section 6 outlines known algorithms for determining whether or not a PPG in this class is serialisable (without node duplication or creation of Boolean guards).
Do not satisfy pred-anc condition	None	It is known that PPGs that do not satisfy the pred-anc condition are not serialisable (without node duplication or creation of Boolean guards).

Table 2. Characterisation of serializability detection of PPGs

Lemma 6. *A PPG with no synchronization edges will never deadlock.*

Proof: Follows from the definitions of control edges and deadlock. □

A PPG G is *acyclic* if it is acyclic when both the control and the synchronization edges are considered.

Lemma 7. *Let $G = (N, E)$ be an acyclic PPG. Then G never deadlocks.*

Proof: The proof is by induction on the size of N. If $|N| = 1$, then G consists of only $START$ and will never deadlock. Suppose for induction that the lemma holds for all PPGs with k or fewer nodes, and consider $G = (N, E)$, with $|N| = k + 1$. Suppose $v \in N$ is a deadlocking node with deadlocking instance v_i. By lemma 6 there must be a synchronization edge (u, v, f) that is relevant for v_i and that is causing v_i to deadlock. Since G is acyclic, $u \neq v$. By the definition of deadlock, v_i is created but not executed. Suppose v_i is the only instance of v that is created. If u or some predecessor of u is a deadlocking node, then we get a contradiction to the induction assumption by considering the subgraph of G that contains all nodes except for v. So either there are no instances of u created, or all instances u_j of u that are created are executed. Since (u, v, f) is relevant, either f will evaluate to *false* or (u_j, v_i, f) is not a deadlocking edge for all created u_j.

If multiple instances of v are created, then since there are no synchronization edges between any pair of instances of v, the instances are all independent. Consequently, the above argument holds for any deadlocking instance of v. □

A *cycle* is a path of directed synchronization and/or control edges such that the first and last nodes on the path are identical. Given cycle C, node $a \in C$ is an *entry point* of C if there exists some path π of all control edges from the root to a such that π contains no other nodes from C. A cycle is *single-entry* if it contains only one entry point; otherwise, it is *multiple-entry*.

Synchronization edge (v, u, f) or control edge (v, u) is a *back-edge* if u is a control ancestor of v. Note that the definition of back-edge can include self-loops, i.e. a synchronization edge (v, v, f).

Lemma 8. *Let $G = (N, E)$ be a PPG which contains only control-independent synchronization edges. Suppose also that there are no synchronization back-edges and that all cycles are single-entry. Let $G' = (N', E')$ be the PPG that is obtained from G by deleting all back-edges in G (i.e. $N' = N$ and $E' \subseteq E$). Then for all $a, x \in N$, if a is a control ancestor of x in G, then a is a control ancestor of x in G'.*

Proof: The proof is an induction on the number of back-edges removed from G. Initially, suppose that G has only a single back-edge (u, v), a is a control ancestor of x in G, but a is no longer a control ancestor of x when G' is created from G by removing (u, v). By the definition of control ancestor, there exists some acyclic control path π_x in G from $START$ to x that contains a. Because a is not a control ancestor of x in G', we must have $(u, v) \in \pi_x$. By the definition of a PPG and back-edges, there must be an acyclic control path π_v from $START$ to v such that $u \notin \pi_v$.

Case 1: $a \in \pi_v$. Since π_x contains a subpath from v to x, $a \in \pi_v$ implies that there is a control path from a to x that does not contain (u, v). Consequently, a remains a control ancestor of x after the removal of (u, v), a contradiction.

Case 2: $a \notin \pi_v$. Because (u, v) is a back-edge, v is a control ancestor of u, and consequently v is the entry point of some cycle containing (u, v). Because $a \notin \pi_v$, there must be a node on π_x that is another entry point to that cycle. Consequently, (u, v) belongs to a multiple-entry cycle, a contradiction.

If G has k back-edges, we instead consider $\tilde{G}$, which is constructed from G by removing back-edges such that the set of control ancestors of each node remains unchanged, and the removal of any additional back-edge would cause some node to loose a control ancestor. We then apply the above argument to $\tilde{G}$. $\square$

Lemma 9. *Let $G = (N, E)$ be a PPG, and assume that all cycles in G are single-entry, all synchronization edges are control-independent, and none is a back-edge. Then G will not deadlock.*

Proof: Let $\tilde{G}$ be the graph that it obtained from G by removing all back-edges from G. By lemma 8 every node in N has the same set of control ancestors in G and in $\tilde{G}$. Since all back-edges are control edges, G and $\tilde{G}$ have the same synchronization edges. By lemma 7 $\tilde{G}$ never deadlocks.

Assume for contradiction G deadlocks, and let $v \in N$ be a deadlocking node in G with deadlocking instance v_i such that no predecessor of v in $\tilde{G}$ is a deadlocking node in G. By lemma 6 there exists a synchronization edge (u, v, f) that is relevant for v_i and which is causing v_i to deadlock. If v is not part of a cycle in G, then the arguments of lemma 7 hold. If v is part of a cycle, then since u is a predecessor of v in $\tilde{G}$, no instance u_j of u that is created deadlocks. Consequently, since (u, v, f) is relevant, there must be some instance u_j of u such that $f(H(I_{u_j}), H(I_{v_i})) = true$, but u_j is not created. It follows from the definition of control-independent synchronization edges that $nodeprefix(H(I_{u_j}), a) = nodeprefix(H(I_{v_i}), a)$ for all nodes a that are control ancestors of both u_j and v_i. Therefore, if v_i is created, so is u_j, and consequently v_i cannot deadlock. □

Theorem 10. *If all cycles are single-entry, the presence of a synchronization edge that is a potential back-edge or is not a control-independent edge is necessary for deadlock to occur.*

Proof: Follows from lemma 11. □

Let C be an multiple-entry cycle with entry points $x_1, x_2, \ldots, x_k$. We define C_{x_i} to be the single-entry cycle that is obtained by deleting all edges $(y, x_j), j \neq i$, such that $y \notin C$. We say that C_{x_i} is a *single-entry cycle with entry point* x_i. Edge (v, x_i) is a *potential* back-edge if (v, x_i) is a back-edge of C_{x_i}. A back-edge is also a potential back-edge.

We conjecture that lemma 11 and theorem 12 hold, but we have not yet formalized the proof.

Lemma 11. *[Conjecture]. Suppose G contains multiple-entry cycles. If all synchronization edges are control-independent and none is a potential back-edge, then G cannot deadlock.*

Theorem 12. *[Conjecture]. The presence of a synchronization edge that is a potential back-edge or is not a control-independent edge is necessary for deadlock to occur.*

We now show that determining if there exists an execution sequence that deadlocks in a PPG with acyclic control edges is NP-hard. The transformation is from *3-SAT* [17]: Given a Boolean expression $E = (a1_i \vee a1_j \vee a1_k) \wedge (a2_i \vee a2_j \vee a2_k) \wedge \ldots \wedge (am_i \vee am_j \vee am_k)$, with each clause $c_p = (ap_i \vee ap_j \vee ap_k)$ containing 3 literals, $1 \leq p \leq m$. Assume all the literals that occur in E are either positive or negative forms of variables $a_1, a_2, \ldots, a_n$. Is there a truth assignment to the variables (predicates) such that E evaluates to *true*?

Theorem 13. *Determining if there exists an execution sequence that contains a deadlocking cycle is NP-hard for a PPG with an acyclic control dependence graph.*

Proof: To prove that the problem is NP-hard, let E be an instance of *3-SAT* with n variables, $a_1, a_2, \ldots, a_n$, and m clauses, $c_1, c_2, \ldots, c_m$. We assume that there is some occurrence of both the *true* and *false* literals of every variable in E, since otherwise we could just set the truth assignment of the variable equal to the value that makes all of its literals true, and eliminate all clauses containing that literal.

We construct a PPG G with a *START* node, n (variable) predicate nodes, $2n + 1$ *MGOTO* nodes, and m (clause) *COMPUTE* nodes. We first describe the control edges of G. *START* has an *MGOTO* node as its only child. That *MGOTO* node has the n predicate nodes as its children. Each predicate node corresponds to one of the variables that occur in E. If A_i is the predicate node corresponding to the variable a_i, then the *true* branch of A_i has an *MGOTO* node as its child, and the *false* branch of A_i has a second *MGOTO* node as its child. Let c_r be a clause in E with corresponding *COMPUTE* node C_r in G, and suppose that $C_r = (a_i \vee \bar{a}_j \vee a_k)$. Then there are control edges from the *MGOTO* children of the *true* edges of A_i and A_k and from the *false* edge of A_j to C_r. In general, if a_i occurs in c_j in its *true* (*false*) form, then there is an edge from the *MGOTO* descendant of the *true* (*false*) branch of A_i to C_j in G.

The synchronization edges are directed from C_i to C_{i+1} for $1 \leq i < m$, and from C_m to C_1. The synchronization condition, f, for the synchronization edges is *ALL* i.e. all instances of the source node must complete execution before any instance of the destination node can start execution. For each *COMPUTE* node, the *wait* operations for all incoming synchronization edges must be completed before the *signal* operation for any outgoing synchronization edges can be performed. So a *COMPUTE* node will send its synchronization signal to its neighbor only after having received a similar signal from its other neighbor.

If all *COMPUTE* nodes have at least one instantiation, then the execution sequence for G will deadlock. If one of the *COMPUTE* nodes C_i is not executed at all, then no instance of C_{i+1} needs to wait for synchronization messages from C_i, and so the instances of C_{i+1} will complete execution and send their synchronization messages to instances of C_{i+2}, which will then send messages to instances of C_{i+3}, and so on.

If there is a truth assignment to the variables of E so that E is satisfied, then for that truth assignment each *COMPUTE* node will be executed at least once, and deadlock will occur. Conversely, if G deadlocks, then we can obtain a truth assignment to the variables of E such that E is satisfied. $\square$

For each clause node there are three node disjoint paths from the *MGOTO* child of *START* to that clause node. Therefore, the PPG used in the above reduction does not satisfy the pred-anc cond[4]. The effect of the pred-anc cond is that in a PPG with acyclic control edges, a node is executed only zero or one times. In section 3, Figures 1 and 3 are examples of PPGs that satisfy the anc-prec cond, while Figure 2 is an example of a PPG that does not satisfy the anc-prec cond. As we show in section 6, the pred-anc cond is a necessary, but not sufficient, condition for a PPG to be serializable without node duplication or the introduction of guard variables. Furthermore, if the predicate-ancestor and no-post-dominator conditions hold, then determining whether or not a PPG can be serialized without node duplication can be done in polynomial time.

An obvious question is: if the pred-anc cond holds, can deadlock detection also be done in polynomial time? One observation is that if the PPG is found to be serializable, then we can assert that it will not deadlock. So, the reduced question is: if the pred-anc condition holds and the PPG is known to be non-serializable, can deadlock detection also be done in polynomial time? Since we don't have the answer to that question, a possibly easier but related question is the following: Given a set of PPG nodes, none of which is a control ancestor of the other, and assuming that the pred-anc cond holds, can we determine in

---

[4] But it satisfies the no post-dominance rule.

polynomial time if there exists an execution sequence such that all the nodes in the set are executed? We are also unable to answer this question, but we can give a necessary and sufficient characterization for the existence of an execution sequence in which all the nodes in the set are executed. This characterization implies a fast algorithm for detecting "bogus" edges in an acyclic PPG that satisfies the pred-anc cond.

Lemma 14. *Let G be an acyclic PPG and assume that the pred-anc cond holds. Let S be a set of nodes in G such that none is a control ancestor of the other. Then there exists an execution sequence of G in which all the nodes in S are executed if and only if there is a rooted spanning tree T (not necessarily spanning all the nodes of G) consisting of only control edges of G such that all nodes in T with multiple out-edges are MGOTO nodes and all nodes in S are leaves in T.*

Proof: If such a T exists, then since the root of T is reachable from $START$ and since all out-edges of an $MGOTO$ nodes are always taken, then there exists an execution sequence for which all the nodes of S are executed. Conversely, suppose that there exists an execution sequence such that all the nodes of S are executed. Let G' consist of only the nodes and edges in G that are executed in that execution sequence. Because the pred-anc cond implies that every node is executed zero or one time, if two nodes $X, Y \in S$ have a predicate least common control ancestor P_1 in G', then since P_1 is executed at most once, at most one of X and Y will be executed whenever P_1 is executed. If X and Y have two predicate least common ancestors, P_1 and P_2, then there must be two node disjoint paths to each of X and Y, one containing P_1 and the other containing P_2. Therefore, by the pred-anc cond, the least common ancestor of P_1 and P_2 must be a predicate P_3, and at most one of P_1 and P_2, and consequently X and Y, will be executed whenever P_3 is executed. It follows from induction that the least common control ancestor in G' of any pair of nodes in S must be an $MGOTO$ node. A similar argument shows that any pair of these $MGOTO$ either lie in a path in G' or have another $MGOTO$ node as their least common ancestor. Finally, the configuration of the $MGOTO$ nodes and the nodes in S must be a tree, since otherwise some $MGOTO$ node would violate the pred-anc cond. □

Definition 15. A synchronization edge (a, b, f) is said to be "*bogus*" if there is no execution sequence of the PPG in which it is executed i.e. there are no possible instantiations I_a and I_b of nodes a and b that satisfy $f(H(I_a), H(I_b)) = true$ and that can be obtained from the same execution of the PPG.

Corollary 16. *If an acyclic PPG satisfies the pred-anc cond, then all bogus synchronization edges can be detected in $O(|E_{sync}| \times |E_{cont}|)$ time, where $|E_{sync}|$ is the number of synchronization edges and $|E_{cont}|$ is the number of control edges in G.*

Proof: Lemma 14 implies that a synchronization edge (u, v, f) is bogus if and only if there is no $MGOTO$ node which is the least common ancestor of both

u and v in G. Consequently, a simple backtracking search from each endpoint of the synchronization edge being tested is sufficient to determine if the two endpoints have an $MGOTO$ least common ancestor. □

6 Serializability of PPGs

After a PPG has been used to optimize and possibly parallelize code, the optimized code frequently must be mapped into sequential target code for the individual processor(s). An equivalent problem can arise when trying automatically to merge different versions of a program which have been updated in parallel by several people [22, 23].

Serialization customarily involves transforming the PPG to a CFG, from which the sequential code is then derived. Whenever possible, the CFG is constructed without duplicating nodes or inserting Boolean guard variables. Node duplication is undesirable because of potential space requirements which can create cache and page faults, and the introduction of guard variables is undesirable because of the additional time and space needed to store and test such variables.

6.1 The model

In this section, we analyze a restricted model of a PPG, as defined in [16, 38, 37]. We allow only the $MGOTO$ node to have multiple control in-edges. This is not a restriction on the model, since if a $PREDICATE$ or $COMPUTE$ node a has multiple control in-edges, we can always direct the in-edges into a new $MGOTO$ node f, which is then made the (unique) parent of a. We also assume that all $COMPUTE$ nodes are leaves in the control subgraph of the PPG, and that all predicates have precisely two out-going control edges, one labelled $true$ and the other labelled $false$.

Finally, we assume that pred-anc condition holds. This is indeed a restriction, since if the pred-anc cond does not hold, then any CFG constructed from a PPG that violates the pred-anc cond provably requires node duplication, as is illustrated in figure 4. In the example of figure 4 the least common ancestor of two paths terminating at $s3$ is $MGOTO$ node $f1$. Therefore, there is an execution sequence in which $s3$ is executed twice, and any sequential representation will have two copies of $s3$.

Since a CFG has no parallelism, construction of a CFG from a PPG involves the elimination of $MGOTO$ nodes and the merging of the subgraphs of their children. For the remainder of this section, we assume as input a PPG that satisfies the pred-anc cond and the node restrictions discussed above.

Even if the pred-anc cond is satisfied, there are PPGs for which node duplication or guard variable insertion is unavoidable [37].

The Control Dependence Graph (CDG) is the subgraph of the PPG that represents only the control dependences (or control edges). The CDG encapsulates the difficulty of translating the PPG into a CFG. The result presented in

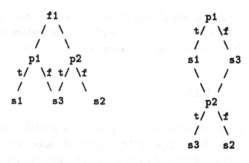

Fig. 4. A PPG subgraph and equivalent sequential CFG subgraph with duplication

this section also assumes that the CDG satisfies the no post-dominator condition defined in section 4.

In order to determine when a PPG can be serialized, we need some notion of equivalence between a CDG and a CFG. One approached, taken by Ball and Horwitz [6], is to say that a CFG G' is a *corresponding* CFG of CDG G if and only if the CDG that is constructed from G' is isomorphic to G, with the isomorphism respecting node and edge labels. We have chosen a definition that does not depend on isomorphism [37, 36].

Given two graphs G and G', where G is an acyclic CDG and G' is a CFG, we say that G' is *semantically equivalent* to G if:

1. All *PREDICATE* and *COMPUTE* nodes in G' are copies of nodes in G, and every *PREDICATE* or *COMPUTE* node in G has at least one copy in G'.
2. For every truth assignment to the predicates, the *PREDICATE* and *COMPUTE* nodes that are executed in G' are copies of exactly those *PREDICATE* and *COMPUTE* nodes executed in G. If *PREDICATE* or *COMPUTE* node a is executed $c(a)$ times in G under some truth assignment, then the number of times a copy of a is executed in G' is equal to $c(a)$[5].

Because a CDG G has no post-dominance, one can prove that the following condition must hold in any CFG G' that corresponds to an acyclic CDG G that satisfies the pred-anc cond [36].

3. Suppose a and b are *PREDICATE* or *COMPUTE* nodes in G. Then if a precedes b in G, then no copy of b precedes a copy of a in G'.

The definition of semantic equivalence is extended to cyclic graphs with reducible loops by first applying it to the acyclic graphs in which the loops are replaced by "supernodes" and then applying the definition recursively to the acyclic subgraphs within corresponding supernodes.

---

[5] If the PPG satisfies the pred-anc cond, then $c(a) \le 1$.

6.2 Algorithms for constructing a CFG from a PDG

There are two algorithms for constructing a CFG from a PDG, each of which uses a somewhat different model for the PDG. Both assume that all loops in the PDG are reducible and that the no-post-dominator condition holds; both have a running time of $O(ne)$, where n is the number of nodes and e is the number of edges in the PDG. The complexity involves the analysis of the control dependences.

Constructing a CFG and reconstituting a CDG. The algorithm presented in [6] determines orderings that must exist in any CFG G' that "corresponds" to the CDG G^6. If the algorithm fails to construct a CFG G', or if it constructs a CFG that does not correspond to G, i.e. for which there is not a CDG that is isomorphic to G, then the algorithm fails. Although the algorithm does not explicitly deal with data dependences, it can be modified to do so.

The difficulty with the above approach is that when the algorithm fails, it does not provide any information as to why it fails.

Algorithm Sequentialize. Algorithm Sequentialize [37, 36] is based on analysis that states that a CFG G' can be constructed from a PDG G without node duplication if and only if there is no "forbidden subgraph". The intuition behind the forbidden subgraph is that duplication is not required if and only if there is no set of "forced" execution sequences which would create a cycle in the acyclic portion of the graph. A forbidden subgraph implies the existence of such a cycle. A cycle can also exist if data dependences contradict an ordering implied by the control dependences. When duplication is required, the algorithm can be used as the basis of a heuristic that duplicates subgraphs or adds guard variables.

7 Related Work

The idea of extending PDGs to PPGs was introduced by Ferrante and Mace in [14], extended by Simons, Alpern, and Ferrante in [38], and further extended by Sarkar in [34]. The definition of PPGs used in this paper is similar to the definition from [34]; the only difference is that the definition in [34] used *mgoto edges* instead of *mgoto nodes*. The PPG definition used in [14, 38] imposed several restrictions: a) the PPGs could not contain loop-carried data dependences (synchronizations), b) only reducible loops were considered, c) PPGs had to satisfy the no-post-dominator rule, and d) PPGs had to satisfy the pred-anc rule. The PPGs defined in this paper have none of these restrictions. Restrictions a) and b) limit their PPGs from being able to represent all PDGs that can be derived from sequential programs; restriction a) is a serious limitation in practice, given the important role played by loop-carried data dependences in representing loop parallelism [40]. Restriction c) limits their PPGs from being

---

[6] The model presented in [6] differs somewhat from that of [37, 36]. However, the models are essentially equivalent.

able to represent CFGs. Restriction d) limits their PPGs from representing thread-based parallel programs in their full generality e.g. the PPG from Figure 2 cannot be expressed in their PPG model because it is possible for node S4 to be executed twice.

The Hierarchical Task Graph (HTG) proposed by Girkar and Polychronopoulos [18] is another variant of the PPG, applicable only to structured programs that can be represented by the hierarchy defined in the HTG.

One of the central issues in defining PDGs and PPGs is in defining their parallel execution semantics. The semantics of PDGs has been examined in past work by Selke, by Cartwright and Felleisen, and by Sarkar. In [35], Selke presented an operational semantics for PDGs based on graph rewriting. In [10], Cartwright and Felleisen presented a denotational semantics for PDGs, and showed how it could be used to generate an equivalent functional, dataflow program. Both those approaches assumed a restricted programming language (the language W), and presented a value-oriented semantics for PDGs. The value-oriented nature of the semantics made it inconvenient to model store-oriented operations that are found in real programming languages, like an update of an array element or of a pointer-dereferenced location. Also, the control structures in the language W were restricted to if-then-else and while-do; the semantics did not cover programs with arbitrary control flow. In contrast, the semantics defined by Sarkar [34] is applicable to PDGs with arbitrary (unstructured) control flow and arbitrary data read and write accesses, and more generally to PPGs as defined in this paper.

The serialization problem has been addressed in some prior work. Generating a CFG from the CDG's of well-structured programs is reported in [22, 23]; such CDG's are trees and do not require any duplication. The IBM PTRAN system [3, 9, 33] generates CFGs from the CDGs of unstructured (i.e. not necessarily trees) FORTRAN programs. The work presented in [14, 16] uses assumptions about the structure of CFG's derived from sequential programs, thereby limiting its applicability. The results presented in [16] consider the general problem in an informal manner by determining the order restrictions that had to hold for region node children of a region node.

8   Conclusions and Future Work

In this paper, we have presented definitions and classifications of Parallel Program Graphs (PPGs), a general parallel program representation that also encompasses PDGs and CFGs. We believe that the PPG has the right level of semantic information to match the programmer's way of thinking about parallel programs, and that it also provides a suitable execution model for efficient implementation on real architectures. The algorithms presented for deadlock detection and serialization for special classes of PPGs can be used to relieve the programmer from performing those tasks manually. The characterization results can be viewed as also identifying PPGs that are easier for programmers to work with e.g. PPGs for which deadlock detection and/or serializability are hard to perform are quite likely to be PPGs that are hard for programmers to understand and that lead to programming errors.

We see several possible directions for future work based on the results presented in this paper:

— *Extend sequential program analysis techniques to the PPG*
All program analysis techniques currently used in compilers (e.g., constant propagation, induction variable analysis, computation of Static Single Assignment form, etc.) operate on a sequential control flow graph representation of the program. There has been some recent work in the area of program analysis in the presence of structured parallel language constructs [28, 39]. However, just as the control flow graph is the representation of choice (due to its simplicity and generality) for analyzing sequential programs, it would be desirable to use the PPG representation as a simple and general representation for parallel programs.
In particular, we are interested in extending to PPGs the notions of dominators and control dependence that have been defined for CFGs. These extensions should provide us with a way of automatically transforming a given PPG into a form that satisfies the no-post-dominator condition, so that assuming the no-post-dominator condition will not restrict the applicability of the results obtained from that assumption.

— *Investigate the complexity of deadlock detection for acyclic PPGs that satisfy the pred-anc and no-post-dominator conditions*
In section 5, we showed that the problem of detecting deadlock in PPGs with acyclic control edges is NP-hard. Moreover, for PPGs with acyclic control edges that satisfy the pred-anc and no-post-dominator conditions, section 6 provides a polynomial-time algorithm for determining whether or not the PPG is serializable. We have observed that serializable PPGs cannot deadlock. Therefore, the remaining open issue is: what is the complexity of deadlock detection for PPGs that satisfy the pred-anc and no-post-dominator conditions but are non-serializable? We are interested in resolving this open issue by either obtaining a polynomial-time deadlock detection algorithm for such PPGs or by proving that the problem is NP-hard.

— *Develop a transformation framework for PPGs*
Current parallelizing compilers optimize programs for parallel architectures by performing transformations on perfect loop nest, on CFGs, and on PPGs. It would be interesting to extend existing algorithms and design new algorithms in a transformation framework for PPGs. In this paper, we discussed serialization and the elimination of bogus edges, which can also be viewed as transformations on PPGs. In the future, we would like to perform other transformations to match the performance characteristics and code generation requirements of different parallel architectures.

— *Develop a common compilation and execution environment for different parallel programming languages*
The PPG can be used as the basis for a common compilation and execution environment for parallel programs written in different languages.

The scheduling system defined in [34] can be developed into a PPG-based interpreter, debugger, or runtime system for parallel programs, that provides feedback to the user about the parallel program's execution (e.g. parallelism profiles, detection of read-write or write-write hazards, detection of deadlock, etc.). Currently, such programming tools are being developed separately for different languages, with different (ad hoc) assumptions being made about their parallel execution semantics. The PPG representation could be useful in leading to a common environment for different parallel programming languages.

- *Study the limitations of the PPG representation*

Though we showed in this paper how PPGs are more general than PDGs and CFGs, we are aware that there are certain parallelism constructs that do not map directly to PPGs. Examples of such constructs include general post-wait synchronizations in which the synchronization condition depends on data values (not just on execution histories) and single-program-multiple-data (SPMD) execution in which the number of times a region of code is executed can depend on a run-time parameter such as the number of processors. It would be interesting to see how such constructs can be represented by PPGs without losing too much semantic information. We conjecture that parallel programming constructs that are hard to represent by PPGs are also hard for programmers to understand. A study of the limitations of PPGs will shed more light on this conjecture.

References

1. A.V. Aho, R. Sethi, and J.D. Ullman. *Compilers: Principles, Techniques, and Tools*. Addison-Wesley, 1986.
2. F. E. Allen. Control flow analysis. *ACM SIGPLAN Notices*, 19(6):13–24, 1970.
3. Frances Allen, Michael Burke, Philippe Charles, Ron Cytron, and Jeanne Ferrante. An Overview of the PTRAN Analysis System for Multiprocessing. *Proceedings of the ACM 1987 International Conference on Supercomputing*, 1987. Also published in The Journal of Parallel and Distributed Computing, Oct., 1988, 5(5) pages 617-640.
4. Randy Allen and Ken Kennedy. Automatic Translation of FORTRAN Programs to Vector Form. *ACM Transactions on Programming Languages and Systems*, 9(4):491–592, October 1987.
5. Arvind, M.L. Dertouzos, R.S. Nikhil, and G.M. Papadopoulos. Project Dataflow: A parallel computing system based on the Monsoon architecture and the Id programming language. Technical report, MIT Lab for Computer Science, March 1988. Computation Structures Group Memo 285.
6. Thomas Ball and Susan Horwitz. Constructing Control Flow from Data Dependence. Technical report, University of Wisconsin-Madison, 1992. TR No. 1091.
7. William Baxter and J. R. Bauer, III. The Program Dependence Graph in Vectorization. *Sixteenth ACM Principles of Programming Languages Symposium*, pages 1 – 11., January 11-13 1989. Austin, Texas.
8. Michael Burke and Ron Cytron. Interprocedural Dependence Analysis and Parallelization. *Proceedings of the Sigplan '86 Symposium on Compiler Construction*, 21(7):162–175, July 1986.

9. Michael Burke, Ron Cytron, Jeanne Ferrante, and Wilson Hsieh. Automatic Generation of Nested, Fork-Join Parallelism. *Journal of Supercomputing*, 2(3):71–88, July 1989.

10. Robert Cartwright and Mathias Felleisen. The Semantics of Program Dependence. *SIGPLAN '89 Conference on Programming Language Design and Implementation*, pages 13–27, June 1989.

11. Ron Cytron, Jeanne Ferrante, and Vivek Sarkar. Experiences Using Control Dependence in PTRAN. *Proceedings of the Second Workshop on Languages and Compilers for Parallel Computing*, August 1989. In Languages and Compilers for Parallel Computing, edited by D. Gelernter, A. Nicolau, and D. Padua, MIT Press, 1990 (pages 186-212).

12. Ron Cytron, Jeanne Ferrante, and Vivek Sarkar. Compact Representations for Control Dependence. *Proceedings of the ACM SIGPLAN '90 Conference on Programming Language Design and Implementation, White Plains, New York*, pages 337–351, June 1990.

13. Ron Cytron, Michael Hind, and Wilson Hsieh. Automatic Generation of DAG Parallelism. *Proceedings of the ACM SIGPLAN '89 Conference on Programming Language Design and Implementation, Portland, Oregon*, 24(7):54–68, June 1989.

14. J. Ferrante and M. E. Mace. On Linearizing Parallel Code. *Conf. Rec. Twelfth ACM Symp. on Principles of Programming Languages*, pages 179–189, January 1985.

15. J. Ferrante, K. Ottenstein, and J. Warren. The Program Dependence Graph and its Use in Optimization. *ACM Transactions on Programming Languages and Systems*, 9(3):319–349, July 1987.

16. Jeanne Ferrante, Mary Mace, and Barbara Simons. Generating Sequential Code From Parallel Code. *Proceedings of the ACM 1988 International Conference on Supercomputing*, pages 582–592, July 1988.

17. Michael R. Garey and David S. Johnson. *Computers and Intractibility: A Guide to the Theory of NP-Completeness.* W.H. Freeman and Company, 1979.

18. Miland Girkar and Constantine Polychronopoulos. The HTG: An Intermediate Representation for Programs Based on Control and Data Dependences. Technical report, Center for Supercomputing Res. and Dev.-University of Illinois, May 1991. CSRD Rpt. No.1046.

19. Rajiv Gupta and Mary Lou Soffa. Region Scheduling. *Proc. of the Second International Conferenece on Supercomputing*, 3:141–148, May 1987.

20. P. Brinch Hansen. The programming language Concurrent Pascal. *IEEE Transactions on Software engineering*, SE-1(2):199–206, June 1975.

21. Matthew S. Hecht. *Flow Analysis of Computer Programs.* Elsevier North-Holland, Inc., 1977.

22. Susan Horwitz, Jan Prins, and Thomas Reps. Integrating Non-Interfering Versions of Programs. *Conf. Rec. Fifteenth ACM Symposium on Principles of Programming Languages*, pages 133–145, January 1987.

23. Susan Horwitz, Jan Prins, and Thomas Reps. On the Adequacy of Program Dependence Graphs for Representing Programs. *Conf. Rec. Fifteenth ACM Symposium on Principles of Programming Languages*, pages 146–157, January 1987.

24. Paul Hudak and Philip Wadler et al. Report on the Functional Programming Language Haskell. Technical report, Yale University, 1988. Research Report YALEU/DCS/RR-666.

Printing: Weihert-Druck GmbH, Darmstadt
Binding: Buchbinderei Schäffer, Grünstadt

Lecture Notes in Computer Science

For information about Vols. 1–690
please contact your bookseller or Springer-Verlag

Vol. 691: M. Ajmone Marsan (Ed.), Application and Theory of Petri Nets 1993. Proceedings, 1993. IX, 591 pages. 1993.

Vol. 692: D. Abel, B.C. Ooi (Eds.), Advances in Spatial Databases. Proceedings, 1993. XIII, 529 pages. 1993.

Vol. 693: P. E. Lauer (Ed.), Functional Programming, Concurrency, Simulation and Automated Reasoning. Proceedings, 1991/1992. XI, 398 pages. 1993.

Vol. 694: A. Bode, M. Reeve, G. Wolf (Eds.), PARLE '93. Parallel Architectures and Languages Europe. Proceedings, 1993. XVII, 770 pages. 1993.

Vol. 695: E. P. Klement, W. Slany (Eds.), Fuzzy Logic in Artificial Intelligence. Proceedings, 1993. VIII, 192 pages. 1993. (Subseries LNAI).

Vol. 696: M. Worboys, A. F. Grundy (Eds.), Advances in Databases. Proceedings, 1993. X, 276 pages. 1993.

Vol. 697: C. Courcoubetis (Ed.), Computer Aided Verification. Proceedings, 1993. IX, 504 pages. 1993.

Vol. 698: A. Voronkov (Ed.), Logic Programming and Automated Reasoning. Proceedings, 1993. XIII, 386 pages. 1993. (Subseries LNAI).

Vol. 699: G. W. Mineau, B. Moulin, J. F. Sowa (Eds.), Conceptual Graphs for Knowledge Representation. Proceedings, 1993. IX, 451 pages. 1993. (Subseries LNAI).

Vol. 700: A. Lingas, R. Karlsson, S. Carlsson (Eds.), Automata, Languages and Programming. Proceedings, 1993. XII, 697 pages. 1993.

Vol. 701: P. Atzeni (Ed.), LOGIDATA+: Deductive Databases with Complex Objects. VIII, 273 pages. 1993.

Vol. 702: E. Börger, G. Jäger, H. Kleine Büning, S. Martini, M. M. Richter (Eds.), Computer Science Logic. Proceedings, 1992. VIII, 439 pages. 1993.

Vol. 703: M. de Berg, Ray Shooting, Depth Orders and Hidden Surface Removal. X, 201 pages. 1993.

Vol. 704: F. N. Paulisch, The Design of an Extendible Graph Editor. XV, 184 pages. 1993.

Vol. 705: H. Grünbacher, R. W. Hartenstein (Eds.), Field-Programmable Gate Arrays. Proceedings, 1992. VIII, 218 pages. 1993.

Vol. 706: H. D. Rombach, V. R. Basili, R. W. Selby (Eds.), Experimental Software Engineering Issues. Proceedings, 1992. XVIII, 261 pages. 1993.

Vol. 707: O. M. Nierstrasz (Ed.), ECOOP '93 – Object-Oriented Programming. Proceedings, 1993. XI, 531 pages. 1993.

Vol. 708: C. Laugier (Ed.), Geometric Reasoning for Perception and Action. Proceedings, 1991. VIII, 281 pages. 1993.

Vol. 709: F. Dehne, J.-R. Sack, N. Santoro, S. Whitesides (Eds.), Algorithms and Data Structures. Proceedings, 1993. XII, 634 pages. 1993.

Vol. 710: Z. Ésik (Ed.), Fundamentals of Computation Theory. Proceedings, 1993. IX, 471 pages. 1993.

Vol. 711: A. M. Borzyszkowski, S. Sokołowski (Eds.), Mathematical Foundations of Computer Science 1993. Proceedings, 1993. XIII, 782 pages. 1993.

Vol. 712: P. V. Rangan (Ed.), Network and Operating System Support for Digital Audio and Video. Proceedings, 1992. X, 416 pages. 1993.

Vol. 713: G. Gottlob, A. Leitsch, D. Mundici (Eds.), Computational Logic and Proof Theory. Proceedings, 1993. XI, 348 pages. 1993.

Vol. 714: M. Bruynooghe, J. Penjam (Eds.), Programming Language Implementation and Logic Programming. Proceedings, 1993. XI, 421 pages. 1993.

Vol. 715: E. Best (Ed.), CONCUR'93. Proceedings, 1993. IX, 541 pages. 1993.

Vol. 716: A. U. Frank, I. Campari (Eds.), Spatial Information Theory. Proceedings, 1993. XI, 478 pages. 1993.

Vol. 717: I. Sommerville, M. Paul (Eds.), Software Engineering – ESEC '93. Proceedings, 1993. XII, 516 pages. 1993.

Vol. 718: J. Seberry, Y. Zheng (Eds.), Advances in Cryptology – AUSCRYPT '92. Proceedings, 1992. XIII, 543 pages. 1993.

Vol. 719: D. Chetverikov, W.G. Kropatsch (Eds.), Computer Analysis of Images and Patterns. Proceedings, 1993. XVI, 857 pages. 1993.

Vol. 720: V.Mařík, J. Lažanský, R.R.Wagner (Eds.), Database and Expert Systems Applications. Proceedings, 1993. XV, 768 pages. 1993.

Vol. 721: J. Fitch (Ed.), Design and Implementation of Symbolic Computation Systems. Proceedings, 1992. VIII, 215 pages. 1993.

Vol. 722: A. Miola (Ed.), Design and Implementation of Symbolic Computation Systems. Proceedings, 1993. XII, 384 pages. 1993.

Vol. 723: N. Aussenac, G. Boy, B. Gaines, M. Linster, J.-G. Ganascia, Y. Kodratoff (Eds.), Knowledge Acquisition for Knowledge-Based Systems. Proceedings, 1993. XIII, 446 pages. 1993. (Subseries LNAI).

Vol. 724: P. Cousot, M. Falaschi, G. Filè, A. Rauzy (Eds.), Static Analysis. Proceedings, 1993. IX, 283 pages. 1993.

Vol. 725: A. Schiper (Ed.), Distributed Algorithms. Proceedings, 1993. VIII, 325 pages. 1993.

Vol. 726: T. Lengauer (Ed.), Algorithms – ESA '93. Proceedings, 1993. IX, 419 pages. 1993

Vol. 727: M. Filgueiras, L. Damas (Eds.), Progress in Artificial Intelligence. Proceedings, 1993. X, 362 pages. 1993. (Subseries LNAI).

Vol. 728: P. Torasso (Ed.), Advances in Artificial Intelligence. Proceedings, 1993. XI, 336 pages. 1993. (Subseries LNAI).

Vol. 729: L. Donatiello, R. Nelson (Eds.), Performance Evaluation of Computer and Communication Systems. Proceedings, 1993. VIII, 675 pages. 1993.

Vol. 730: D. B. Lomet (Ed.), Foundations of Data Organization and Algorithms. Proceedings, 1993. XII, 412 pages. 1993.

Vol. 731: A. Schill (Ed.), DCE – The OSF Distributed Computing Environment. Proceedings, 1993. VIII, 285 pages. 1993.

Vol. 732: A. Bode, M. Dal Cin (Eds.), Parallel Computer Architectures. IX, 311 pages. 1993.

Vol. 733: Th. Grechenig, M. Tscheligi (Eds.), Human Computer Interaction. Proceedings, 1993. XIV, 450 pages. 1993.

Vol. 734: J. Volkert (Ed.), Parallel Computation. Proceedings, 1993. VIII, 248 pages. 1993.

Vol. 735: D. Bjørner, M. Broy, I. V. Pottosin (Eds.), Formal Methods in Programming and Their Applications. Proceedings, 1993. IX, 434 pages. 1993.

Vol. 736: R. L. Grossman, A. Nerode, A. P. Ravn, H. Rischel (Eds.), Hybrid Systems. VIII, 474 pages. 1993.

Vol. 737: J. Calmet, J. A. Campbell (Eds.), Artificial Intelligence and Symbolic Mathematical Computing. Proceedings, 1992. VIII, 305 pages. 1993.

Vol. 738: M. Weber, M. Simons, Ch. Lafontaine, The Generic Development Language Deva. XI, 246 pages. 1993.

Vol. 739: H. Imai, R. L. Rivest, T. Matsumoto (Eds.), Advances in Cryptology – ASIACRYPT '91. X, 499 pages. 1993.

Vol. 740: E. F. Brickell (Ed.), Advances in Cryptology – CRYPTO '92. Proceedings, 1992. X, 593 pages. 1993.

Vol. 741: B. Preneel, R. Govaerts, J. Vandewalle (Eds.), Computer Security and Industrial Cryptography. Proceedings, 1991. VIII, 275 pages. 1993.

Vol. 742: S. Nishio, A. Yonezawa (Eds.), Object Technologies for Advanced Software. Proceedings, 1993. X, 543 pages. 1993.

Vol. 743: S. Doshita, K. Furukawa, K. P. Jantke, T. Nishida (Eds.), Algorithmic Learning Theory. Proceedings, 1992. X, 260 pages. 1993. (Subseries LNAI)

Vol. 744: K. P. Jantke, T. Yokomori, S. Kobayashi, E. Tomita (Eds.), Algorithmic Learning Theory. Proceedings, 1993. XI, 423 pages. 1993. (Subseries LNAI)

Vol. 745: V. Roberto (Ed.), Intelligent Perceptual Systems. VIII, 378 pages. 1993. (Subseries LNAI)

Vol. 746: A. S. Tanguiane, Artificial Perception and Music Recognition. XV, 210 pages. 1993. (Subseries LNAI).

Vol. 747: M. Clarke, R. Kruse, S. Moral (Eds.), Symbolic and Quantitative Approaches to Reasoning and Uncertainty. Proceedings, 1993. X, 390 pages. 1993.

Vol. 748: R. H. Halstead Jr., T. Ito (Eds.), Parallel Symbolic Computing: Languages, Systems, and Applications. Proceedings, 1992. X, 419 pages. 1993.

Vol. 749: P. A. Fritzson (Ed.), Automated and Algorithmic Debugging. Proceedings, 1993. VIII, 369 pages. 1993.

Vol. 750: J. L. Díaz-Herrera (Ed.), Software Engineering Education. Proceedings, 1994. XII, 601 pages. 1994.

Vol. 751: B. Jähne, Spatio-Temporal Image Processing. XII, 208 pages. 1993.

Vol. 752: T. W. Finin, C. K. Nicholas, Y. Yesha (Eds.), Information and Knowledge Management. Proceedings, 1992. VII, 142 pages. 1993.

Vol. 753: L. J. Bass, J. Gornostaev, C. Unger (Eds.), Human-Computer Interaction. Proceedings, 1993. X, 388 pages. 1993.

Vol. 754: H. D. Pfeiffer, T. E. Nagle (Eds.), Conceptual Structures: Theory and Implementation. Proceedings, 1992. IX, 327 pages. 1993. (Subseries LNAI).

Vol. 755: B. Möller, H. Partsch, S. Schuman (Eds.), Formal Program Development. Proceedings. VII, 371 pages. 1993.

Vol. 756: J. Pieprzyk, B. Sadeghiyan, Design of Hashing Algorithms. XV, 194 pages. 1993.

Vol. 757: U. Banerjee, D. Gelernter, A. Nicolau, D. Padua (Eds.), Languages and Compilers for Parallel Computing. Proceedings, 1992. X, 576 pages. 1993.

Vol. 758: M. Teillaud, Towards Dynamic Randomized Algorithms in Computational Geometry. IX, 157 pages. 1993.

Vol. 759: N. R. Adam, B. K. Bhargava (Eds.), Advanced Database Systems. XV, 451 pages. 1993.

Vol. 760: S. Ceri, K. Tanaka, S. Tsur (Eds.), Deductive and Object-Oriented Databases. Proceedings, 1993. XII, 488 pages. 1993.

Vol. 761: R. K. Shyamasundar (Ed.), Foundations of Software Technology and Theoretical Computer Science. Proceedings, 1993. XIV, 456 pages. 1993.

Vol. 762: K. W. Ng, P. Raghavan, N. V. Balasubramanian, F. Y. L. Chin (Eds.), Algorithms and Computation. Proceedings, 1993. XIII, 542 pages. 1993.

Vol. 763: F. Pichler, R. Moreno Díaz (Eds.), Computer Aided Systems Theory – EUROCAST '93. Proceedings, 1993. IX, 451 pages. 1994.

Vol. 764: G. Wagner, Vivid Logic. XII, 148 pages. 1994. (Subseries LNAI).

Vol. 765: T. Helleseth (Ed.), Advances in Cryptology – EUROCRYPT '93. Proceedings, 1993. X, 467 pages. 1994.

Vol. 766: P. R. Van Loocke, The Dynamics of Concepts. XI, 340 pages. 1994. (Subseries LNAI).

Vol. 767: M. Gogolla, An Extended Entity-Relationship Model. X, 136 pages. 1994.

Vol. 768: U. Banerjee, D. Gelernter, A. Nicolau, D. Padua (Eds.), Languages and Compilers for Parallel Computing. Proceedings, 1993. XI, 655 pages. 1994.